Dedicated to

Prabha and Ram Kumar Agarwala
my parents

Preface

Liberalization and privatization have brought about changes in the business environment, resulting in heightened competition and growth of the services sector. Changes in political, economic, social, technological, and employment environments over the past decade have caused organizations to confront several unique challenges to survive and to excel. The most unique challenge for organizations comes with respect to the management of human resources to ensure the availability of sufficient number and quality of human resources at all times for the successful achievement of organizational objectives.

The competitive advantage of a firm is no longer defined by the traditional factors of success, such as management of natural resources, technology, and economies of scale. Instead, a firm's success today is defined by how well it manages its human resources, or how well it incorporates human resource management into its business strategy.

While firms compete intensely to attract, retain, and motivate skilled and talented professionals, professionals expect and demand more from firms—more job satisfaction, better quality of work life, and greater recognition, rewards, and compensation—and prefer mutuality and shared destiny over job security.

Strategic human resource management is, therefore, critical to a firm's success in the contemporary business environment.

About the Book

Strategic Human Resource Management explores the strategic role of human resources in organizational performance, human resource environment in organizations, human resource evaluation, measuring employee performance, mentoring, and career management. Among the important topics it discusses are human resources as strategic assets; management of human resources from an investment perspective; integration of human resource strategy and business strategy; human resource planning, training and development; and strategic management of performance, rewards, careers, work–life balance, mentoring, and diversity in human resources.

Each chapter begins with learning objectives and ends with a summary of the discussion. Every chapter contains

- a list of key words along with explanations that refresh and deepen the student's understanding of terms used;
- a case study of a leading firm's practice of strategic human resource management that explores the concepts discussed;
- concept review questions that test the student's understanding of those concepts; and
- critical thinking exercises and field and classroom assignments that develop teamwork skills and train the student to apply concepts to solve practical problems.

Management students will find this book useful for its coverage of the fundamental concepts of strategic human resource management.

Human resource managers will also find the book helpful for decision-making and establishing business strategy—HR strategy linkage.

Coverage and Structure

This book has twelve chapters.

Chapter 1 introduces the concept of strategic human resource management, explains it, differentiates it from traditional HRM, and discusses the significance of viewing it as an investment and a source of sustainable competitive advantage for firms. The human resource environment, that forms the context of the concept and of its applications, is described in Chapter 2. It explains the significance of global business trends and their implications on human resource management and discusses the multiple activities that a human resource manager needs to perform in the contemporary firm.

Among these activities are human resource evaluation—a human resource manager needs to evaluate the organization's human resources and human resource practices to be able to manage them effectively. Chapter 3 discusses the importance of human resource evaluation and its different approaches, provides an overview of human resource evaluation, and describes and analyses the range of measures used to evaluate human resource performance. Chapter 4 introduces the concept of human resource planning and explains its linkage with business strategy, analyses the different strategies adopted by organizations for managing human resource surplus and shortage, and provides insight into the interaction between human resource planning and outsourcing.

Acquisition of human resources, therefore, becomes the focus of the book at this stage. Chapter 5 provides an overview of the methods of recruitment and selection, explores the importance of human resource acquisition in the contemporary business environment, explains the strategic alignment between business strategy and the recruitment and selection efforts of an organization, and provides insight into the new approaches to recruitment and selection. Once an organization has acquired the human resources it requires, it needs to train and develop them. Chapter 6 defines the terms 'training' and 'development', explores the significance of employee training and development in the contemporary business environment, explains the linkage between business strategy and training, provides an overview of the methods of training and development, and discusses the role of technology in changing the ways in which training is imparted in organizations.

After an organization's employees have begun delivering business results, their performance needs to be evaluated, managed, and rewarded. Chapter 7 explains the term 'performance management' and its evaluative and developmental objectives, describes the steps in the design and implementation of a performance management system, explains the characteristics of an effective performance management system, provides an overview of the important performance appraisal methods, and analyses the strategic linkage of performance management with the stages of the organizational life cycle. Chapter 8 explains the objectives, components, and determinants of financial and non-financial compensation and rewards, the role of equity perception in the design of a compensation and rewards strategy, analyses the significance of a total compensation and rewards strategy, and explores the linkage between compensation and rewards strategy and business strategy.

An employee works and performs to advance his career; because one's life and lifestyle depends largely on one's career success, one needs help to advance in one's career and to balance work and personal lives. Chapter 9 defines the terms 'career', 'career planning', 'career development', and 'career management' and explores the dimensions of each term, describes career planning practices and career development interventions appropriate for each stage of a career, explores the individual and organizational perspectives of career management, and explains the importance of adopting a strategic approach to career management. Chapter 10 attempts an understanding of the term 'mentoring', of the career and psychosocial functions of mentoring relationships, and of the components essential to the design and implementation of a successful formal mentoring programme in an organization, discusses the importance of mentoring in an increasingly diverse workforce, and explores the strategic human resource management aspects of mentoring relationships. Chapter 11 explores work–life issues and explains the ideas of 'work–family conflict', 'work–life balance', and 'work–life integration', identifies the main types of formal work–life initiatives and details the benefits of each, and explains the importance of a family-friendly workplace and the value of a strategic approach to work–life integration.

At this stage, the book considers the aspects of managing human resources in the context of international business; one effect of globalization is that more organizations conduct business beyond national boundaries. Chapter 12 explores the dimensions of international human resource management and its differences from domestic human resource management, analyses the importance of managing cultural differences for the success of international business operations, discusses three approaches—ethnocentric, polycentric, and geocentric—to managing and staffing subsidiaries of multinational organizations, and attempts an understanding of international HR practices.

Acknowledgements

Many people have made this book possible. I would like to acknowledge all those who contributed, directly or indirectly, to the successful completion of this book.

First and foremost, I wish to express sincere thanks to Prof. Abad Ahmad, who has always expressed confidence in me and continues to encourage me in my academic pursuits.

I express deep gratitude to Prof. Deepak Pental, whose vision and words provided inspiration and enthusiasm for my endeavour towards academic excellence.

I also extend grateful thanks to Prof. O.P. Chopra and Prof. A.S. Narag, who always encouraged me to keep myself focussed on work and to determinedly pursue my goals. I would also like to acknowledge Prof. K. Mamkoottam, who gave generously of his time and insight and helped organize my thoughts and the contents of this book.

I am extremely indebted to Prof. Udai Pareek and Prof. T.V. Rao for their readiness to extend guidance and provide material whenever I requested. I also acknowledge Prof. C.P. Thakur, Prof. S. Ramnarayan, and Prof. Sunil Maheshwari for supporting me in my pursuit in various ways.

Thanks are also due to Prof. J.K. Mitra, Dr V.K. Seth, Prof. Vivek Suneja, Prof. Anup Singh, Dr Madhu Vij, and Dr Anupama Vohra for extending helpful comments whenever requested.

I gratefully acknowledge all those who permitted me to use their material/case study for inclusion in the book.

Thanks are also due to the entire team of OUP who provided me constant motivation for writing this book and patiently and diligently helped shape this book. I especially acknowledge the reviewers who read the manuscript and gave valuable feedback.

Special thanks are due to Ms Chitra and Ms Rashmi for typing the manuscript.

The Faculty of Management Studies, University of Delhi deserves a special mention for providing infrastructure and support. I specially thank the members of the staff of the Computer Centre at the Faculty of Management Studies, University of Delhi, those of the Library at the Faculty of Management Studies, University of Delhi, and those of the Ratan Tata Library, Delhi School of Economics for extending cooperation during the period.

I acknowledge the students at the Faculty of Management Studies because of whom I am.

I am grateful to all my family members who encouraged my writing this book and enquired patiently after its progress.

I don't have enough words to thank my parents whose contribution to shaping the book cannot be measured. They taught me to be sincere, stay grounded, believe in myself, and to work hard and with honesty and devotion. This book is for them.

Thanks are also due to all my friends who stood by me at all times. Vanita, Vasundhara, Bharati, Soumi, and Sandeep deserve special mention.

Last, but not the least, I thank the Almighty for giving me opportunities.

TANUJA AGARWALA

Contents

Preface   *v*

Acknowledgements   *viii*

CHAPTER 1

Strategic Human Resource Management: An Introduction   **1**

    Role of Human Resources in Strategy   2

    Evolution of SHRM   13

    Strategic Fit: A Conceptual Framework   18

    Distinctive Human Resource Practices   27

    Theoretical Perspectives on SHRM   29

    SHRM Approaches: The Indian Context   33

    Alternative HR Strategies   36

CHAPTER 2

Human Resource Environment   **50**

    Human Resource Environment: A Brief Overview   51

    HRM in Knowledge Economy   80

    Case Study

        Organizational Redesign at Bharat Petroleum Corporation Limited:

        The Challenge of Privatization   111

CHAPTER 3

Human Resource Evaluation   **121**

    HRM Evaluation: A Background   122

    Human Resource Evaluation: Definition and Overview   123

    HRM and Firm Performance   126

    Rationale for HR Evaluation   132

    Measures of HRM Performance   133

    Approaches to HR Evaluation   144

    Case Study

        Measurement of Human Resource Management at Eastman Kodak   173

CHAPTER 4

Human Resource Planning   **180**

HRP: An Overview   181
Business Strategy and HRP   182
Significance of HRP in a Changing Environment   186
Perspectives of HRP   191
Objectives of HRP   193
Job Analysis   195
Job Analysis and SHRM   206
HRP Horizons   212
HRP Process   214
Special Challenge: HRP and Outsourcing   242
Case Study
   Human Resource Issues in Private Participation in Infrastructure—
   A Case Study of Orissa Power Reforms   250

CHAPTER 5

Acquiring Human Resources   **260**

Human Resource Acquisition: An Overview   261
External Influences on Staffing   265
Internal Influences on Staffing   267
Recruitment Sources: Internal versus External   268
Methods of Recruitment   269
New Approaches to Recruitment   280
Outsourcing the Recruitment Function   286
Methods of Employee Selection   287
New Approaches to Executive Selection   295
Staffing Process: Recruiting and Selecting Employees   302
Evaluation of Staffing Process   314
Selection Outcomes   316
Strategic Recruitment and Selection   317
Hiring for a Diverse Workforce   323
Alternatives to Hiring Permanent Employees   327
Hiring Considerations in BPO Firms   334
Case Study
   Hiring for Excellence at Cisco Systems   346

CHAPTER 6

Training and Development of Human Resources 355

The Need for Training and Development 356
Training and Development: Basic Concepts 357
Purposes of Training and Development 361
Significance of Training and Development 364
HRM Approaches to Training and Development 368
Linkage between Business Strategy and Training 369
The Process of Training and Development 373
Special Forms of Training and Development 397
New Developments in Training and Development 408
Case Study
McDonald's 426

CHAPTER 7

Performance Management and Development Systems 433

Performance Management 434
Developing Performance Management Systems 443
Problems in Performance Management 464
Effective Performance Management Systems 467
Developments in Performance Management 469
Technology and Performance Management 492
Strategic Linkage of Performance Management 496
Case Study
Performance Appraisal at Amber Limited 504

CHAPTER 8

Compensation and Rewards Management 510

Compensation and Rewards 511
Compensation and Rewards—Determinants 525
Compensation and Rewards—Approaches 530
Pay-for-Performance Approaches 531
Equity in Reward Decisions 535
Compensation and Rewards—New Developments 538
Trends in Top-level Executive Compensation 543
Business Strategy and Compensation 547

Total Compensation and Rewards Strategy 560

Case Study

Rewards System of a University 569

CHAPTER 9

Managing Careers 574

Careers—Contemporary Notions 575
Career Planning, Development, and Management 577
Career Stages 581
Career Planning 584
Career Development 590
Career Management Systems 598
Design and Implementation of Career Management Systems 607
Organizational Career Management: A Typology 612
Career Management for Specific HR Issues: HRD Approach 617
Career Management: An SHRM Approach 613
Case Study
Career Development at Dataware Services and Systems 632

CHAPTER 10

Mentor Relationships 636

The Concept of Mentoring 637
Perspectives of Mentoring 644
Outcomes of Mentoring Programmes 656
Design and Implementation of Formal Mentoring Programmes 666
Barriers to Mentoring 679
Mentoring Relationship: A Strategic HRM Approach 681
Special Issues in Mentoring 686
Case Study
Mentoring at Coca-Cola Foods 701

CHAPTER 11

Work–Life Integration 708

Changing Notions of the Work–Family Relationship 709
Work–Life Issues 710
Work–Life Balance 723

Family-friendly Workplace   733
Work–Family Culture   735
HRD Approaches to Work–Life Integration   738
Development of Work–Life Initiatives   742
Towards a Strategic Approach to Work–Life Integration   745
Case Study
  Narmada Bank International   756

CHAPTER 12

International Human Resource Management   **761**

Types of International Organizations   762
International Human Resource Management   764
External Environment and IHRM   767
IHRM Practices   769
Case Study
  Natural Pharmaceuticals Ltd   793

Index   797

1

Strategic Human Resource Management: An Introduction

OBJECTIVES

After studying this chapter, you will be able to:

- explain the meaning of strategic human resource management (SHRM) and differentiate it from traditional human resource management (HRM)

- discuss the significance of viewing human resources as 'investment' and a source of sustainable competitive advantage for organizations

- acquire an overview of the conceptual framework of SHRM

- explain the linkage between HR strategy and business strategy

- understand different theoretical approaches to SHRM

- appreciate the Indian approach to the concept of HRM and its linkage with organizational goals

INTRODUCTION

Since the 1990s, there has been an increased focus on the strategic role of human resource management (HRM). The strategic approach to HRM refers to the relationship between human resource (HR) practices and the strategic objectives, that is, the long-term goals of the organization. With the increasing recognition of the potential of human resources in providing competitive advantage, organizations have begun to consider employees as valuable 'assets' or 'investments'. This view has become more significant in today's knowledge economy that depends on the skill and knowledge of the workforce. From being a routine, administrative, and reactive function, the HR function today has evolved to being proactive and strategic.

The past decade has seen HR researchers and practitioners directing their attention to important questions. For instance, what is HR strategy? What factors determine whether an organization adopts a strategic approach to HRM? Is there a relationship between the characteristics of the organization and the adoption of a particular strategic human resource management (SHRM) approach? Does an organization achieve competitive advantage by linking HR strategy with business strategy?

The present chapter explores SHRM, a particular approach to the management of human resources that views people as assets. The criteria for understanding the contribution of human resources to the competitive advantage of the organization are reviewed. The factors that affect the degree to which an organization is 'investment oriented' in its management of human resources are also discussed. The chapter also presents the conceptual framework explaining the 'strategic fit' between business strategy and HR strategy and highlights the theoretical perspectives on SHRM. Finally, the chapter addresses the Indian applications to understanding the management of human resources.

ROLE OF HUMAN RESOURCES IN STRATEGY

Human resources refer to the people who work in an organization. The term seeks to communicate the belief that the employees of an organization are not just people, but valuable resources that help an organization to achieve its objectives. People are central to organizations. The financial capital, technology, or processes of the organization, by themselves, cannot accomplish organizational goals. These resources depend on human resources for their effective and efficient utilization. At the same time, human resources also need to be managed. Figure 1.1 depicts the centrality of human resources for the achievement of organizational goals.

Human resource management (HRM) is concerned with a holistic approach towards the management of people working in an organization, who contribute to the achievement of organizational objectives. Human resource management ensures the most effective and efficient use of human talent for accomplishing the goals of an organization. In order to successfully utilize and manage the human resource of an organization to achieve organizational objectives, each organization needs to develop a well-defined HR strategy. Chandler (1962) defined 'strategy' as the 'determination of the long term goals and objectives of an organization, and the allocation of resources necessary for carrying out these goals'.

Like strategy, HR strategy is concerned with two key elements (Richardson and Thompson, 1999):

1. Determining the strategic objectives (What goals is the strategy supposed to achieve? For example, the goals may be high productivity, reduced accidents, etc.).

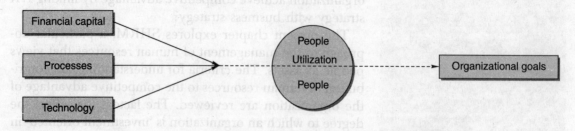

Figure 1.1:   Centrality of Human Resources for Organizational Goal Achievement

2. Developing a plan of action (How will the human resources be organized and allocated to accomplish the objectives of the organization?).

Human resource strategy, therefore, involves the planned and effective use of human resources by an organization to help it to gain or maintain an edge over its competitors. This definition indicates the central role that the people of the organization play in the organizational pursuit of a competitive advantage. An organization is said to achieve *competitive advantage* when it is able to gain and maintain an edge over its competitors by differentiating its products or services from those of its competitors, thereby increasing its market share. The centrality of people is most evident in knowledge-based organizations, such as software and information services, where the difference between success and failure depends on the skills and knowledge of its workforce rather than on the level of technology.

Strategic Human Resource Management: Definition and Components

Given the increasingly significant role of human resources in an organization, HRM has become strategic in nature. Strategic human resource management (SHRM) is concerned with the relationship between HRM and strategic management in an organization. Strategic human resource management is an approach which relates to decisions about the nature of employment relationship, recruitment, training, development, performance management, reward, and employee relations. Wright and McMahan (1992) defined SHRM as 'the pattern of planned human resource deployment and activities intended to enable the firm to achieve its goals'. This definition implies the following four components of SHRM (Figure 1.2):

1. It focuses on an organization's *human resources* (people) as the primary source of competitive advantage of the organization.
2. The *activities* highlight the HR programmes, policies, and practices as the means through which the people of the organization can be deployed to gain competitive advantage.
3. The *pattern* and *plan* imply that there is a fit between HR strategy and the organization's business strategy (*vertical fit*) and between all of the HR activities (*horizontal fit*).
4. The people, practices, and planned pattern are all purposeful, that is, directed towards the achievement of the goals of the organization.

On the whole, SHRM is concerned with people issues and practices that affect or are affected by the strategic plan of the organization. The critical issues facing an organization in the contemporary environment are mainly human issues, such as ensuring the availability of people, retaining, motivating, and developing these resources. To stay ahead of its competitors, an organization will continuously look for ways to gain an edge over others. Today, an organization competes less on products or markets, and more on people.

In the 21st century, there is increasing recognition among management thinkers and practitioners of the potential of human capital resources in providing competitive advantage. Two organizations using the same technology may show different levels of performance. What leads to this difference? The quality of human resources and their contribution to the organization determine the performance, and therefore, the success of the organization.

An organization uses a combination of several resources—tangible and intangible—in the pursuit of its objectives. These resources can be grouped into three basic types:

(a) physical capital resources—the plant, equipment, and finances
(b) organizational capital resources—the organization's structure planning, HR systems, history, and organizational culture

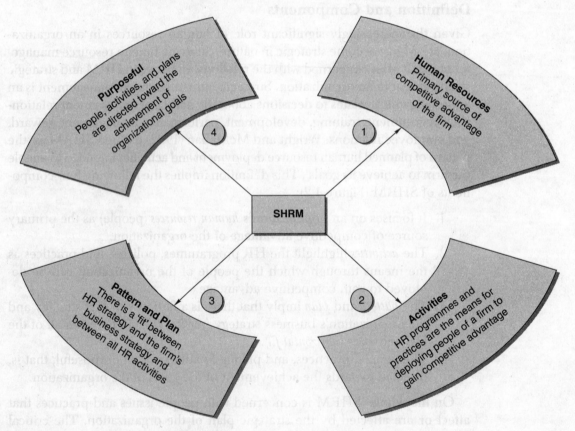

Figure 1.2: Four Components of SHRM

(c) human capital resources—the skills, knowledge, judgement, and intelligence of the organization's employees

An organization may have huge capital and the most advanced machinery, but if it does not have capable, motivated, and high performing employees, the organization is not likely to demonstrate sustained levels of high performance. Since all physical and capital resources depend on people for their efficient use, maintenance, and management, the quality of the *people* of an organization is important in attaining competitive advantage.

Human Resources as Assets

Of all the resources available to an organization, human resources are considered the most important for attaining the objectives of the organization. Hence, employees are now variously referred to as human capital, human assets, or human resources.

Human Capital

The term *capital* refers to wealth, money, or property. Capital is used to generate more wealth for an organization. When employees are referred to as human capital, it is implied that they are the resources that generate more 'wealth'. *Human capital* refers to the collective skills and knowledge of the total workforce of an organization that hold economic value for the organization. It enhances the productivity and profitability of the organization. In order to ensure that human capital generates more wealth as well as leads to value creation, it is important that human capital is utilized and managed efficiently and effectively. When the value of people is enhanced, it enhances the value of the organization. For example, when an organization provides opportunities for development and an environment conducive to performance, it will result in higher levels of retention. This aspect is explored in more detail in a later chapter of the book.

Today, it is possible for any organization to buy machinery and equipment comparable to that available in leading global organizations. Therefore, machinery or finance, and access to these resources, are no longer the factors that differentiate between organizational success or failure. Rather, it is the ability to use these tangible resources (money, machinery, etc.) that serves as the distinguishing factor. An organization that holds on to and builds on the skills, competencies, and knowledge of its workforce can bounce back into business rather quickly, even if it loses all of its equipment. However, an organization that loses its workforce but holds on to its tangible assets has little hope of recovering.

The emphasis on human resources has become all the more important as there is a marked movement towards a knowledge-based economy and organizations. The *knowledge economy* refers to those jobs, organizations, and industries in which the skills, knowledge, and capabilities of people, rather than the capabilities of machines, technology, etc., determine the competitive advantage.

Along with physical and capital resources, the human capital constitutes the decisive capability of an organization since it prepares the organization to adapt in future. The use of new and improved technology and lowering of overhead costs are the obvious methods of attaining competitive advantage that can be used by an organization. The quality of human capital of an organization and its efficient management can also contribute to higher levels of productivity and lower costs. In fact, human capital helps the organization attain sustained competitive advantage in a manner that is neither too obvious, nor accessible, to all organizations.

This truism has come to be recognized by many organizations over the last two decades. Human resources are viewed as the most important asset of an organization—an asset that creates value for the organization.

An *asset* is something that is owned and has an exchange value. Today, human resources are considered as assets of an organization. In the traditional sense, however, human resources can 'walk' and are not owned by the organization, unlike physical assets. Human assets may walk over to other organizations, taking with them their accumulated knowledge, skills, and experience.

The value of people as human assets is the sum of an individual's knowledge, experience, skills, and competencies that are matched with the individual's job. The value of people is dynamic, not static. It grows with time as the individual gains experience, and as organizations invest in the training and development of people. However, under certain conditions, the value of human assets can also depreciate. Some of these conditions are as follows:

- placing an individual in a job that does not fit with the individual's skills, competencies, etc.
- an individual performing below his/her potential owing to reduced motivation and satisfaction

Thus, the manner in which human resources are managed determines their value as assets. Human assets, unlike physical and capital assets, cannot be duplicated, and therefore, become the competitive advantage of an organization. This quality of 'non-duplication' of human assets has gained greater significance in the knowledge economy, where organizations rely more on conceptual and knowledge-based skills rather than manual skills. The information technology (IT) revolution has brought about a situation in which knowledge workers are replacing blue-collar workers. In such a scenario, an organization needs to invest more in human assets in order to gain a competitive

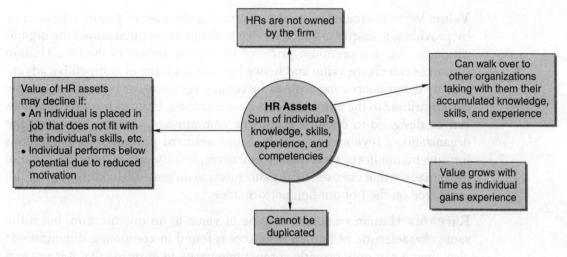

Figure 1.3:   Main Features of Human Resource Assets

advantage over other organizations. Figure 1.3 provides an overview of the main features of human resource assets.

The VRIO Framework

The recognition of the potential of the human assets of organizations in providing competitive advantage has prompted scholars to apply the resource-based view (RBV) proposed by Barney (1991) to understand the role of human resources in organizations. According to the RBV, human resources contribute to a sustained competitive advantage for an organization when they are valuable, non-tradable, non-imitable, and non-sustainable.

Popularly referred to as the VRIO framework, the resource-based view of an organization determines the value of human resources for the organization on the basis of four criteria—*value, rareness, imitability,* and *organization* (VRIO). People can become a source of sustained competitive advantage for an organization if these four criteria are met. The VRIO framework is presented in Figure 1.4.

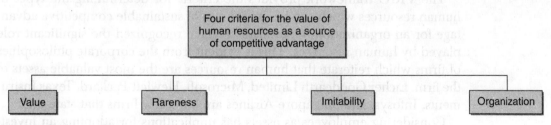

Figure 1.4:   The VRIO Framework

Value Value is created either by decreasing the cost of product/service, or by providing a unique product/service to the customer that allows the organization to charge a premium price, or by a combination of the two. Human resources can create value and hence become a source of competitive advantage by either decreasing costs or increasing revenues, or both. Thus, people can contribute to the efficiency of the organization. Human resource practices can be designed to enhance employee commitment, thereby impacting the organization's revenues positively. Empowerment programmes, continuous improvement efforts, total quality initiatives, quality circles, etc., are some of the initiatives that are used by organizations to increase the contribution of the employee on the bottom-line performance.

Rareness Human resources may be of value to an organization, but if the same characteristic of human resources is found in competing organizations also, then it can only provide competitive parity in ensuring that it is not at a competitive disadvantage. To attain competitive advantage through people, it is important to develop and exploit rare characteristics of the human resources of the organization.

Thus, an organization should try to ensure that it has an edge over competing organizations in terms of the skills, knowledge, and abilities of its people. This can be achieved by hiring and training the best available talent.

Imitability People provide competitive advantage to an organization when HR characteristics cannot be easily imitated by competitors. An organization's unique history or culture is difficult to imitate and can be used to get high levels of performance and commitment from the employees.

Organization Finally, for people to provide competitive advantage to an organization, it is important for the organization to have its systems and practices in place that allow HR characteristics to be exploited fully. Teamwork is a way to ensure an organized workforce—one that can be deployed to work on new assignments at short notice. In this context, HR activities need to be viewed as integrated activities rather than viewing them in isolation. This is discussed later in the chapter.

The VRIO framework provides the criteria for determining the types of human resources which can be the sources of sustainable competitive advantage for an organization. Organizations have recognized the significant role played by human resources. This is evident from the corporate philosophies of firms which reiterate that human resources are the most valuable assets of the firm. Eicher Goodearth Limited, Microsoft, Hewlett-Packard, Texas Instruments, Infosys, and Singapore Airlines are but a few firms that state this.

Considering employees as assets has implications for adopting an investment perspective on human resources. It is important to take this perspective on human assets since other physical assets, such as technology, facilities, etc., can be easily imitated by competitors.

The Investment Perspective of Human Resources

Traditionally, human resources have been viewed as a 'cost to the organization'. The other resources, such as capital, technology, material, etc., are treated as investments. Keeping with the 'cost' view of human resources, an organization accounted for all HR-related budget, such as salaries, employee training, etc., as expenses in the balance sheet that resulted in no returns for the organization. Recent times, however, have seen a change in the cost view of human resources.

In order to remain competitive an organization needs to invest in its human resources. Organizations have begun to consider employees as valuable investments. This view is especially significant because of the emergence of the knowledge economy, which needs highly skilled knowledge workers.

The knowledge economy 'encompasses all jobs, companies, and industries in which the knowledge and skills of people, rather than the capabilities of machines and technologies, determine competitive advantage' (Lengnick-Hall and Lengnick-Hall 2003). Thus, knowledge, and not goods, services, or technology, is important for all economic activities. Human skills and knowledge are crucial to everything that is produced, including goods and services. From retail sales to computers to biotechnology, jobs are becoming more knowledge intensive in their demands on workers and organizations. Though the service sector is obviously more knowledge intensive in character, the manufacturing sector is also becoming more dependent on knowledge and human capabilities, as computers pervade all facets of work. Agricultural and industrial jobs are increasingly becoming knowledge based. For example, some of the agricultural equipments are now computer controlled and their operation requires specific knowledge. Further, skill requirements change over time in all industries, companies, and jobs. Therefore, investment in human resources is important to attain competitive advantage. In the knowledge economy, the winners will be those organizations that constantly reach out to knowledge that can lead to the development of new products and services, and develop the skills, capabilities, and competencies of its employees to keep pace with the changes in technology, processes, etc.

The physical and capital assets of an organization are acquired and subsequently managed by treating them as investments. The strategic objectives of the organization determine the optimal type and quality of physical and capital assets needed. An analysis of the cost and benefit, extent of risk involved, and the potential returns on expenditure on these assets is also undertaken. When human resources are viewed from an investment perspective, an organization goes on to determine how best to invest in its people. Therefore, just as an organization determines the expenditure allocation for physical and capital assets, it also considers the expenditure allocation for human assets to meet its long-term performance goals. For example, if an organization plans to expand its operations, it needs to consider the kind of training and development to extend to its current employees as well as the number and types of new recruitments that will be required. Rapidly growing organizations, such as those in the IT sector (e.g., Wipro, Infosys, TCS, etc.) often state the number of people they are likely to hire in the next two years based on their business growth projections.

In taking a decision related to expenditure on a new training programme, an organization needs to consider not only the cost of training (with respect to the training material cost, trainers' fees, etc.) but also the related costs such as time spent away from work by the employees during training (time lost on the job). At the same time, the potential benefits of training should be considered. These include improved job performance, enhanced commitment to the organization, and increase in employee motivation. The cost of training should be weighted against the benefits. The training also needs to be assessed in relation to the associated risks such as enhanced employability of employees that makes them more desirable to competitors.

Risks Involved in Investing in Human Assets

Investment in human assets is not without risks, and is a source of dilemma for organizations. When an organization does not invest in its employees, it is regarded as less attractive by prospective employees. The organization also finds it more difficult to retain current employees who see no opportunities for growth and advancement. Frequent employee turnover weakens the competitive position of an organization by diverting the attention of the organization to the recruitment and hiring of new employees. On the other hand, an organization that invests in its employees also faces the likelihood of losing them to its competitors. Trained employees are more sought after, especially by competitors. Competitors are often willing to pay more to these employees because they save employee training costs. Thus, there is a risk involved in human asset investment. Organizations need to develop an appropriate and integrated approach to HRM to ensure that employees stay long enough with the organization and contribute to an acceptable return on investment (ROI) relative to the skills and knowledge they have acquired.

In certain types of organizations, employee mobility may not be alarming because the skills needed are not rare or valuable. For example, the transferability of these skills may not matter much in the fast food industry. An organization needs to be concerned about both employee mobility and skill mobility. Stevens (1994) defined *skill mobility* as the ease with which employees with a particular skill set can move from one employer to another with little loss in pay or responsibility. Employees who have a particular skill set that is valuable to the organization, but still easily transferable to its competitors, can be the target of competing organizations. Therefore, investment in this set of employees has a high degree of associated risk. For example, employees with an IT skill set can easily move from one organization to another, where the cost of switching jobs is quite low. This has compelled IT firms to frequently adjust and improve their employment packages and design HR strategies to stay ahead of their rivals.

Factors Determining the Investment Orientation of an Organization

Not all organizations view human assets from an investment perspective. Mello (2003) identified five major factors that affect how investment oriented a company is in its management of human resources:

1. management values
2. attitude towards risk
3. nature of skills needed by employees
4. 'utilitarian' or 'bottom-line' perspective
5. availability of outsourcing

Management values The extent to which management values its people is a critical factor that determines an organization's willingness to invest in human assets. The values of the senior management play an important role in decision making in regard to the investment in human assets. An organization is more likely to be investment oriented if it considers its people as central to its mission, and if the organization's mission statement emphasizes the role of human assets in achieving organizational goals. For example, an organization which values its employees will engage in extensive communication programmes when significant events such as mergers are planned. The manner in which the employees are treated post-merger is also a reflection on the values an organization holds for its employees.

Attitude towards risks An important aspect of investment is that it is accompanied by risks as well as returns. As a general rule, investments with higher risks generally result in greater potential return, while those with lower risks are expected to have a more modest return (e.g., investment in bonds versus investment in stocks and shares). Investment in human assets is considered more risky for an organization than investment in physical assets. An organization with a risk-aversive management philosophy is less likely to invest heavily in people. Other organizations willing to take higher levels of risk will invest more in employees. They will, alongside, develop strategies to minimize the potential risks of losing their investments. For example, they can institute employment contracts, offer stock ownership programmes as incentives for employees, and also offer further developmental opportunities, such as study leave, etc. Thus, an organization can gain employee 'ownership' through these strategies, reducing the possibility of employee turn over, or losing their investment in human assets.

Nature of skills The nature of skills needed by the employees of an organization also determines the extent to which investment in human assets is risky and the willingness of the organization to invest in its employees. When an organization requires the employees to develop and utilize specialized skills that may not be applicable or transferable to other organizations, the investment in people is less risky. However, when an organization needs employees who have skills that are highly marketable and who can move from one employer to another, then investment in human assets involves more risk. The high-risk employee investment requires an organization to develop a strong retention strategy, since the trained employees are sought after by organizations that do not invest in employee training. For instance, Infosys was the first Indian company to start an employee stock option plan to retain employees. The company now offers variable compensation packages as well as cutting-edge training programmes. HCL Technologies and Patni computers, are among the innumerable companies that have developed retention strategies when the problem of employee turnover turned acute.

Utilitarian/bottomline perspective Investment orientation of an organization is also determined by the utilitarian, that is, bottom-line perspective. Organizations which adopt the utilitarian perspective evaluate all investments through a cost-benefit analysis. In cost-benefit analysis, the costs of any investment are compared with its benefits to determine whether that investment is profitable. The utilitarian approach quantifies all costs and benefits. For example, in delivering a training programme, it will consider not only the direct cost of delivering a training programme, but also costs such as employee time spent away from work, unfinished job duties during the training period, and so on. The problem with cost-benefit analysis with reference to investment in people arises because many benefits of HR programmes and policies are difficult to quantify. For example, in a firm that provides internet services, it is difficult to assess objectively the measures of effective service and to determine how much service may be necessary to prevent customers from switching loyalties to other service providers.

Availability of outsourcing A final factor that determines an organization readiness to invest in employees is the availability of outsourcing. The organization can determine whether employee investment can produce a sustainable competitive advantage over time. When specialists are available outside the organization, who may be more efficient than internal employee resources, the internal human investment is likely to be limited. Further, an organization will invest in human resources to such an extent that it results in the greatest potential return as compared with the investments in market and product development, physical facilities, or technology. When investment in human assets is not expected to give higher returns, it is unlikely for an organization to invest in the employees at the cost of other resources. For example, in the fast food industry, there is high turnover of workers, and the skill set they require is easily developed, requires minimal experience, and does not require high levels of investment in training. Employers in the fast food industry, therefore, invest little in their employees and tend to invest more in competitive advertising, physical expansion, etc.

Just as human resources have come to be perceived as valuable assets over time, the HR function has also transformed from being a routine administrative function to a strategic one. The next section briefly discusses this transformation.

EVOLUTION OF SHRM

The HR function has evolved over time. The history of the function pre-dates Taylor's theory of scientific management and Fayol's administrative theory. However, it was only during the 1930s and 1940s that the function grew in significance, largely due to the war-time imperatives. At this time, the HR functions matured and focused largely on labour relations and staffing. In India, the Tata Iron and Steel Company (TISCO) was one of the first organizations to set up a personnel department in the year 1947. Figure 1.5 presents the evolution of the HR function.

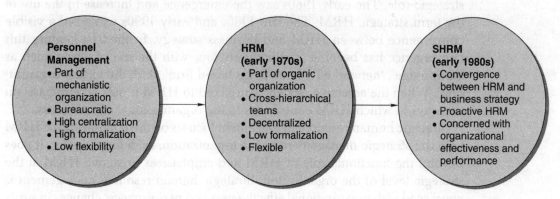

Figure 1.5: Evolution of the HR Function

From Personnel Management to HRM

The early 1970s witnessed the emergence of the term HRM as a replacement for personnel management. The change in terminology also suggests a change in the objectives and boundaries of the function. The main objective of HRM is to ensure the achievement of organizational goals through people. The HRM function emphasizes the following two aspects:

- the importance of gaining the commitment of the people to the goals of the organization
- the need for a strategic fit between business strategy and HR strategy

Personnel management and HRM differ from each other on several counts. One major difference being that while personnel management is part of the more mechanistic form of organization, HRM is aligned with the organic design of the organization. Thus, personnel management is more bureaucratic with high levels of centralization and formalization and lower levels of flexibility. Human resource management, on the other hand, is decentralized, flexible (with low levels of formalization), and has cross-functional and cross-hierarchical teams. Another difference between personnel management and HRM that has been pointed out is the *strategic nature of HRM.* Personnel management is not viewed as involved in the strategic areas of business. Despite these differences, it is often believed that HRM is just a more modern term for personnel management. Hence, HRM may be seen as an *approach* rather than as an alternative to the traditional personnel management.

From HRM to SHRM: Shift in Focus

The dynamic and competitive business environment resulting from globalization has led management to bring a new focus on how human resources should be organized and managed. The HR function now has to develop a more strategic role. The early 1980s saw the emergence and increase in the use of the term strategic HRM. The late 1980s and early 1990s witnessed a visible convergence between HRM and business strategy. In the 21st century this convergence has become startlingly obvious with the use of terms, such as 'knowledge', 'networked', 'knowledge-based firm', and 'the virtual organization'. When the adjective *strategic* is prefixed to HRM it puts an emphasis on the ways in which HRM contributes to the organizational effectiveness.

Strategic human resource management focuses on the relationship of HRM with the strategic management of the organization, as defined earlier. It goes beyond the functional role of HRM and emphasizes proactive HRM at the strategic level of the organization. Strategic human resource management is concerned with organizational effectiveness and performance, changes in structure and culture, matching resources to the present and future requirements of the organization, capability development, employment relationship, and change management. Since corporate plans are implemented through people and because human resources provide competitive advantage to the organization, it is important to integrate HR considerations with the development of the strategic corporate/business plans.

Hendry and Pettigrew (1986) put forward four meanings of SHRM:

1. the use of planning in human resource management
2. an integrated approach to the design and implementation of HR systems
3. matching HRM policies and activities with the business strategy of the organization
4. viewing people as a strategic resource for the achievement of competitive advantage

Fombrun, Tichy, and Devana were the first to formulate the concept of strategic HRM in 1984. These researchers emphasized a strategic fit between HRM and corporate strategy. The concept of 'fit' is discussed later in the chapter.

Objectives of SHRM

The major objectives of SHRM are as follows:

- To ensure the availability of a skilled, committed, and highly motivated workforce in the organization to achieve sustained competitive advantage.
- To provide direction to the organization so that both the business needs of the organization and the individual and collective needs of its workforce are met. This is achieved by developing and implementing HR practices that are strategically aligned.

The extent of application of SHRM within organizations, as well as the form and content of SHRM, vary from one organization to another. Strategic human resource management is practiced in only those organizations that have a clearly articulated corporate or business strategy. Organizations that lack a corporate plan cannot have SHRM. Rather, in such organizations, HR personnel carry out the traditional administrative and service roles and are not concerned with strategic business issues.

Difference between SHRM and Traditional HRM

Strategic human resource management and the traditional HR function differ from each other in several ways. The major points of differences between the two are highlighted in Table 1.1.

Table 1.1:   Traditional HRM versus SHRM

	Traditional HRM	**SHRM**
Responsibility for HR programmes	Staff personnel in the HR department	Line managers, who are responsible for people as HR managers
Focus of activities	Employee relations—ensuring employee motivation and productivity, compliance with laws	Partnerships with internal (employees) and external (customers, stakeholders, public interest groups) groups
Role of HR	Reactive and transactional	Proactive and transformational, change leader
Initiative for change	Slow, piecemeal, and fragmented, not integrated with larger issues	Fast, flexible, and systemic, change initiatives implemented in concert with other HR systems
Time horizon	Short-term	Consider various time frames as necessary (short, medium, or long-term)
Control	Bureaucratic control through rules, procedures, and policies	Organic control through flexibility, as few restrictions on employee behaviour as possible
Job design	Focus on scientific management principles—division of labour, independence, and specialization	Broad job design, flexibility, teams and groups, and cross-training
Important investments	Capital, products, technology, and finance	People and their knowledge, skills, and abilities
Accountability	Cost centre	Investment centre

Adapted from: Mello 2003

Difference between SHRM and HR Strategies

The terms *strategic human resource management* and *human resource strategies* are often used interchangeably, however some distinction can be made between the two. In a general sense, the difference between SHRM and HR strategies is similar to that between strategic management and corporate business strategies. Both SHRM and strategic management describe an approach adopted by the management and focus on the long-term issues and provide direction to the organization. Human resource strategies and business strategies, are outcomes of this approach which focus on the organizational view concerning key issues and specific functions, or activities.

Table 1.2:   Difference between SHRM and HR Strategies

SHRM	HR Strategies
▪ A general approach to strategic management of human resources ▪ Aligned with the organizational intention about its future direction ▪ Focus on long-term people issue ▪ Defines the areas in which specific HR strategies need to be developed ▪ Focus on macro concerns such as structure, culture ▪ Strategic HRM decisions are built into the strategic business plan	▪ Outcome (manifestation) of the general SHRM approach ▪ Focus on specific organizational intentions about what needs to be done ▪ Focus on specific issues that facilitate the achievement of corporate strategy ▪ Human resource strategy decisions are derived from SHRM

Adapted from: Armstrong 2000

Strategic human resource management deals with macro concerns such as quality, commitment, performance, culture, and management development. It defines the areas in which specific HR strategies need to be developed. Human resource strategies, on the other hand, are concerned with ensuring the availability of an efficient workforce, training, rewards, good employee relations, etc. Human resource strategies are more specific and facilitate the successful achievement of the corporate objectives and goals. The major differences between SHRM and HR strategies are presented in Table 1.2.

Link between HR Strategy and Business Strategy

Central to the concept of SHRM is the idea of *strategic fit*. In order to ensure that HR strategies facilitate the achievement of business strategies, a strategic integration between the two is necessary. A key factor that influences the linkage between business strategy and HR strategy is the organization's quest to attain competitive advantage. An organization may pursue several different strategies to achieve its goals.

Three types of business strategies that may be adopted by an organization are *cost leadership, differentiation,* and *focus*. This classification of business strategies was advanced by Porter (1985), and has been extensively used in SHRM literature. According to Porter, an organization may adopt any one of the three business strategies in order to compete successfully in a particular market, and gain and sustain superior performance as well as an advantage over its competitors. The three business strategies and their characteristics are presented in Table 1.3.

Table 1.3: Porter's (1985) Classification of Business Strategies

Type of Business Strategy	Characteristics	Examples
Cost leadership	▪ The firm increases its efficiency, cuts costs so that products or services may be priced lower than the industry average ▪ Assumes that a small change in price will significantly affect customer demand ▪ Assumes that customers show greater price sensitivity than brand loyalty—this is because the products/services of each firm are non-distinguishable	Retailers such as Vishal Mega Mart
Differentiation	▪ The firm distinguishes its products/services from its competitors or at least attempts to make consumers perceive that there are differences ▪ The firm charges a premium for its products/services because it offers its customers something that is unique, extraordinary, or innovative ▪ The firm seeks to develop brand loyalty	Nike, Sony
Focus	▪ The firm recognizes that different segments of the market have different needs and attempts to satisfy one particular group ▪ The firm can charge a premium for its services since the market has overlooked these market segments	Clothes manufacturers that cater to petite women, restaurants that target only families

Adapted from: Mello 2003

Each of the business strategies presented in Table 1.3 requires different types of HR strategies or strategic approaches to managing people. That is, there should be a congruence or 'fit' between the organization's business and HR strategies. The 'fit' perspective provides a conceptual framework for SHRM and is discussed next.

STRATEGIC FIT: A CONCEPTUAL FRAMEWORK

Organizations are often confronted with a dilemma—should they adopt business strategies that fit the available competencies and capabilities in the firm, or should they first decide their business strategy, and then stretch and modify their competencies and capabilities to fit the business strategy? The strategic fit proposes that if an organization seeks to maximize its competitive advantage, it must match its internal resources and skills (organizational competencies) with the opportunities available in the external environment. When an organization attempts to implement new strategies with outmoded or inappro-priate HR strategies, it can face problems. Strategic human resource management is largely about integration.

Guest (1989) emphasized that it is important to ensure that HRM is fully integrated into strategic planning. In 1997, Guest identified the following five types of fit (Figure 1.6):

1. fit as strategic interaction (best fit approach)—HR practices linkage with the external context
2. fit as contingency—HR approaches to ensure that internal practices of the organization respond to external factors such as the nature of the market, skill availability, etc.
3. fit as an ideal set of practices (best practice approach)—there are 'best practices' which all firms can adopt
4. fit as gestalt—emphasizes the importance of finding an appropriate combination of practices
5. fit as 'bundles' (the configuration approach)—suggests a search for distinct configuration or bundles of HR practices that complement each other, in order to determine which 'bundle' is likely to be most effective

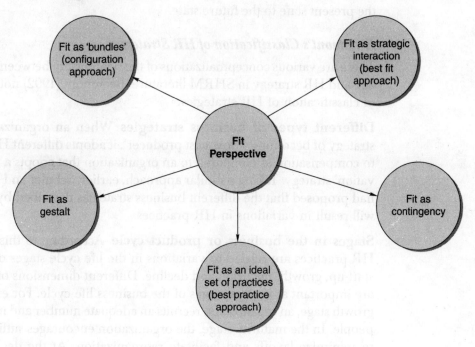

Figure 1.6:   Types of 'Fit' between HR and Business Strategy

Three of the above five types of fit provide the following possible approaches to SHRM:

- the best fit approach
- the HR bundles or configuration approach
- the best practice approach

Best Fit Approach

The focus of the best fit approach is on the linkage of HR strategies with business strategies. This linkage is also referred to as *external fit* or *vertical integration*. Differences in business orientations or strategies of organizations give rise to the need for different types of people as well as diverse approaches towards investment in human capital.

Best fit also means that HR strategies should match the stages of development of the firm, namely start-up, maturity, decline or degeneration, and regeneration or transformation. Business strategies, and therefore HR strategies, will differ between a greenfield firm and one that is in the transformation stage. Whenever an organization embarks upon a change or a transformational programme as part of its business strategy, appropriate change strategies need to be developed. Human resource strategies, supportive of business initiatives, should be developed to manage the organizational transition from the present state to the future state.

Beaumont's Classification of HR Strategies

There are various conceptualizations of the relationship between business strategy and HR strategy in SHRM literature. Beaumont (1992) noted three bases of classification of HR strategies:

Different types of business strategies When an organization selects a strategy of becoming a 'low-cost producer', it adopts different HR approaches to compensation as compared to an organization that adopts a 'product innovation' strategy. Taking a similar approach, earlier, Schuler and Jackson (1987) had proposed that the different business strategies described by Porter (1985) will result in variations in HR practices.

Stages in the business or product cycle According to this classification, HR practices are related to variations in the life cycle stages of a business—start-up, growth, maturity, and decline. Different dimensions of HR practices are important at various stages of the business life cycle. For example, in the growth stage, an organization recruits an adequate number and mix of qualified people. In the maturity stage, the organization encourages sufficient turnover to minimize layoffs and facilitate reorganization. At the decline stage, the

Table 1.4:   HR Practices Corresponding to the Stages of an Organization's Life Cycle

Life Cycle Stages	HR Practices
Start-up	<ul><li>Flexible patterns of work</li><li>Recruitment of highly motivated and committed employees</li><li>Competitive pay</li><li>Little formality</li><li>No unions</li></ul>
Growth	<ul><li>More sophisticated recruitment and selection</li><li>Training and development</li><li>Performance management processes</li><li>Reward systems</li><li>Focus on high commitment</li><li>Developing stable employee relations</li></ul>
Maturity	<ul><li>Attention to the control of labour costs</li><li>Focus on increasing productivity</li><li>Strained employee relations</li><li>Control compensation</li></ul>
Decline	<ul><li>Emphasis on rationalization of workforce and downsizing</li><li>Abandoning some longstanding practices to cut costs</li><li>Trade unions have a marginalized role</li><li>Retraining and career consulting services</li></ul>

Adapted from: Armstrong 2000

organization plans and implements workforce reductions and reallocation. The HR practices corresponding to the four stages of an organization's life cycle are provided in Table 1.4.

Types and numbers of products Fombrun et al. (1984) suggested that the strategy aimed at achieving variations in product focus (the numbers and types of products), results in structural modifications and influences HR strategy. For example, an organization with a single product strategy having a functional structure is likely to be subjective in its selection criteria and appraisals, and rewards are rather unsystematic and allocated in a paternalistic manner. On the other hand, an organization that follows a strategy of growth by acquisition (holding company) of unrelated businesses, with separate self-contained businesses, has different criteria of selection that vary from business to business. Performance appraisals and rewards are impersonal and are based on the return on investment and profitability. Development is cross-functional but not cross-business.

Schuler and Jackson's HR Strategy Classification

The types of business strategy and the adoption of complementary HR strategies is the most popular approach to HR strategy classification. Porter emphasized the fit point of view by stating that all the activities of an organization must be tailored to fit its business strategy. Schuler and Jackson focused on Porter's classification of the three generic business strategies, i.e., *cost leadership*, *differentiation*, and *focus*. They argued that HR practices should be designed to reinforce the behavioural implications of these generic strategies. Based on the role requirements, each competitive strategy is defined in terms of a matching HRM strategy, as shown in Table 1.5.

Table 1.5:   Linking Business Strategy and HR Strategy

Business Strategy	HR Strategy
Cost Leadership ■ Suitable for repetitive and predictable behaviour ■ Concerned with short-term focus and quantities (volumes) ■ Result-oriented	**Utilization HR Strategy** ■ HR strategy focussed on short-term performance measures, that is, results or outcomes ■ Efficiency is the norm, job assignments are specialized, explicit job descriptions ■ Hierarchical pay, few incentives ■ Narrow career paths, limited training ■ Limited employment security ■ Cost-cutting may involve incentives for employees to leave the firm ■ Limited participation
Differentiation ■ Long-term focus ■ Creative job behaviour ■ Moderate concern for quality and quantity	**Facilitation HR Strategy** ■ Broad career paths ■ Extensive training ■ Equal and fair pay, many incentives for creativity ■ Long-term performance measures ■ External recruitment and hiring of people who bring in new ideas ■ High employee participation ■ Some employment security
Focus ■ High concern for quality ■ Moderate concern for quantity ■ Long/medium-term focus	**Accumulation HR Strategy** ■ Equal and fair pay with many incentives ■ Hiring employees belonging to the target market ■ Broad career paths with extensive training ■ High employee participation ■ Some employee security

Source: O'Riordon 2005

Miles and Snow's Classification of Organizational Strategy

Miles and Snow (1984) suggested that HRM practices should be tailored to the demands of the business strategy. They identified four types of organizational strategies on the basis of the dominant culture of the organization. These are *defenders, prospectors, analysers,* and *reactors.* The first three strategies pursue consistent business strategies. The reactors do not have consistency in their strategies. The type of HR practices that are likely to be adopted by an organization with the three consistent strategies are presented in Table 1.6.

Other Frameworks Linking Business Strategy with HR Strategy

Two other frameworks linking business strategy with HR strategy that have received a great deal of attention in the literature on the subject are presented in Table 1.7.

Table 1.6: Dominant Culture of Organization and HR Strategy

Dominant Culture of the Organization (Business Strategy)	HR Strategy
Defenders ▪ Find change threatening ▪ Favour strategies which encourage continuity and security	▪ Bureaucratic approach ▪ Planned and regularly maintained policies to provide for lean HR ▪ Build human resources ▪ Likely to emphasize training programmes and internal promotion
Prospectors ▪ Thrive on change ▪ Favour strategies of product and/or market development	▪ Creative and flexible management style ▪ Have high quality human resources ▪ Emphasize redeployment and flexibility of HR ▪ Little opportunity for long-term HR planning ▪ Acquire human resources ▪ Likely to emphasize recruitment, selection, and performance-based compensation
Analysers ▪ Seek to match new ventures with the present business set-up ▪ These firms are followers—the ventures are not new to the market, only new to the firm	▪ Low levels of monitoring and coordination ▪ 'Buy' as well as 'make' key human resources ▪ Emphasize HR planning

Source: O'Riordon 2005 and Khatri 2000

Table 1.7: Frameworks Linking Business and HR Strategy

Scholars	Frameworks
Golden and Ramanujam (1985)	Proposed the following four types of linkages between HRM and strategic planning process: 1. **Administrative Linkage**: HR department adopts the traditional personnel role, provides routine operational support, and handles paperwork. Functional managers see HR function as relatively unimportant. 2. **One Way Linkage**: There is a sequential relationship between strategic planning and the HR function. The HR function reacts to and designs HR programmes to support the strategic objectives of the firm. 3. **Two Way Linkage**: There is a reciprocal, interdependent relationship between strategic planning and HR function. Business plans affect and are affected by HR activities. HR function is seen as important. 4. **Integrative Linkage**: There is a dynamic interaction, formal as well as informal, between HR function and strategic linkage. The senior HR executive is a strategic business partner with other senior executives of the firm.
Schuler (1992)	Proposed the 5-P model that links the strategic business needs with strategic HRM activities. The 5Ps are: *HR philosophy, HR policies, HR programmes, HR practices,* and *HR processes*. Strategic human resource management begins with the identification of strategic business needs. It is seen as consisting of all those activities that formulate and implement the strategic business needs. These activities have an influence on the behaviour of people. If SHRM helps meet business needs, then it is important to assess the impact of business on HRM activities including the 5Ps.

Source: Khatri 2000

Drawbacks of the Best Fit Approach

The *best fit* approach implies that an organization's performance will improve when HR practices reinforce the organization's competitive position. The best fit approach and its proposition that HR practices should be driven by the competitive strategy of the organization have been criticized on a number of grounds. First, the approach is seen as failing to align employee interests with those of the organization. Secondly, the criticism of the model relates to viewing the competitive strategy in the form of a typology. The competitive strategy is multidimensional and subject to important variations across industries. Hence, devising HR strategies based on a typology of competitive strategy that may not be appropriate in a particular context can be misleading. Thirdly, and related to the second criticism, the approach is viewed as lacking attention to the dynamic scenario.

It is suggested that the model needs to go beyond a fit between HR and competitive strategies, to simultaneously incorporate flexibility in the range of skills and behaviours that may be important for coping with the changing and dynamic competitive scenarios of the future, such as technological advances or changes in customer expectations. This criticism leads to the notion of internal coherence of HR practices around a desirable theme, that is, bundling.

The 'HR Bundles' Approach

Bundling refers to the development and implementation of several HR practices together so that they are interrelated and internally consistent. Each HR practice complements and reinforces the other. MacDuffie (1995) referred to 'bundling' as the use of 'complementarities', while Delery and Doty (1996) called it the adoption of a 'configurational mode'. In general terms, the bundles approach is also termed as *internal fit* or *horizontal integration.* The purpose of bundling is to bring about coherence between HR practices. Coherence exists when a mutually reinforcing set of HR practices is developed to contribute to the strategic objectives of the organization, so that these practices ensure the matching of resources to the needs of the organization, and bring about improvement in performance and quality. Coherence is achieved when the firm has an overriding driving force or strategic imperative. For example, the driving force for a firm may be quality, or high performance, or it could be the development of competencies. This driving force leads to various HR practices that are designed to operate in concert with each other to achieve this imperative. If high performance is the driving force, recruitment standards can be specified, development needs identified, and the required standards of behaviour and performance specified.

MacDuffie conducted research in flexible production manufacturing plants in the United States, and on the basis of his findings pointed out that flexible production techniques need to be supported by bundles of high commitment human resource practices such as performance-contingent pay, employment security, etc. The research also indicated that plants which use flexible production systems that bundle HR practices into a system outperform plants which use more traditional mass production systems in both productivity and quality. Based on the research work in 43 automobile plants in the US, Pil and MacDuffie (1996) established that when a high-involvement HR practice that is complementary to other HR practices, is introduced in a firm, the new practice produces an improvement in performance. At the same time, the other complementary HR practices also lead to incremental improve-ment in performance.

Integration between HR practices is more likely to take place if HR personnel and line managers share their values on how HR policies should be implemented. Integration is also about ensuring that when any innovation in a particular HR practice is planned, its implications on other aspects of HR policies and practices are understood in order to work out how the innovation can support these practices.

However, there are problems associated with the achievement of internal fit also. These problems arise when, for example, senior managers call for changes in a particular HR practice as a quick fix, and the changes are isolated from complementary HR practices. Problems can also arise when performance-related pay is introduced without the existence of a related performance management system or when there is difficulty in determining which 'bundles' are likely to be most appropriate in a situation.

In general, however, both the internal and external fit models propose that HR strategy becomes more effective when it is designed to fit the contingencies within the specific context of the organization.

The Best Practice Approach

Contrary to the internal and external contingency perspectives, is the view that organizations should adopt the *best practice* irrespective of the context. According to this view, superior management practices are readily identifiable and are transferable across organizations. An organization, therefore, should identify any organization with a reputation for excellence in some function, and copy its practices in order to perform well. That is, all organizations can attain performance improvements if they identify and implement the best practice or benchmark. However, the notion of best practice is not new. It was an important theme in personnel management literature in the 1970s. Pfeffer's (1994) list of sixteen practices has been the most significant influence on the definitions of best practice. Subsequently, Pfeffer summarized this list down to seven, viz.:

1. employment security
2. selective hiring
3. teamworking
4. high pay contingent on company performance
5. extensive training
6. reduction of status differences
7. information sharing

Drawbacks of the Best Practice Approach

Most definitions of best practice draw from four functions of personnel psychology, that is, selection, training, appraisal, and pay. Aspects of best practices are widely acknowledged by researchers and practitioners. For example, not many scholars advocate a trait-based performance appraisal over appraisals that are behaviour or outcome based. Beyond this, however, agreements are relatively few. For instance, the list of desirable best practices varies significantly in literature. Moreover, advocates of the approach do not answer *what* goals are being served by best practices, nor do they specify *whose* goals are being served.

An important point of disagreement with the best practice approach relates to the fact that many successful organizations refuse to adopt these practices. Hence, the assumption that perhaps, competition will drive out firms that do not adopt the best practices, leading to the failure of these firms, does not hold ground.

There is, thus, a counterpoint to the best practice approach that argues that the notion of a single set of best practices may be overstated. This view adopts the premise that distinctive HR practices lead to the competitiveness of a particular firm.

DISTINCTIVE HUMAN RESOURCE PRACTICES

In virtually every industry, there are firms that follow very distinctive HR practices. Cappelli and Crocker-Hefter (1999) suggested that these HR practices help to create unique competencies that differentiate a firm's products and services. An essential function of strategic management is to bring about product differentiation. This differentiation leads to competitiveness of the firm.

Hamel and Prahalad (1993, 1994) argued that competitive advantage of a firm, over the long run, results from building the 'core competencies' in the firm that are superior to those of its rivals. According to these management thinkers, the chief executive officers (CEOs) of multidivisional and international firms need to identify the underlying clusters of expertise in their companies that cut across all the strategic business units. The distinctive human resource practices shape the core competencies that determine how firms compete with each other. This notion of a fit between business strategy and HR practices has already been discussed. What is unique in this approach is the view that HR practices are the drivers that lead to core competencies, and, in turn, to business strategies.

Cappelli and Crocker-Hefter (1999) examined pairs of successful organizations competing in the same industry. For instance, Sears and Nordstrom in the retailing industry, Boston Consulting Group (BCG) and McKinsey & Company in strategic consulting, and Harvard Business School and Wharton School, among business schools. Each organization in the pair had very different HR practices. The distinctive competencies and competitive advantages of each organization were identified. In most organizations, the competencies were clearly associated with particular employee groups, for example, customer service, marketing, etc. The HR practices of the relevant employee group were also described. The paired comparisons revealed clear patterns in the relationship between business strategies and HR practices. For example, organizations that move rapidly to seize new opportunities to get the first mover advantage, or to quickly respond to changing customer preferences, compete by being flexible. These firms do not develop employee competencies from within since it does not pay to do so. Examples of such organizations include BCG, and Pepsi, which rely on the 'outside' market to take in new competencies. Such organizations are called *prospectors* (Figure 1.7). On the other hand, organizations that compete through their dominance in an established/stable market rely on capabilities that are specific to the organization and are developed internally. McKinsey & Company and Coca-Cola are examples of firms belonging to this category. These firms are called *defenders* (Figure 1.7).

According to Cappelli et al., flexible organizations like Pepsi exist in part because they have competitors with established markets, such as Coca-Cola, that do not, or perhaps cannot, respond quickly to new opportunities. Organizations like McKinsey & Company succeed because they have competitors such as BCG that cannot match the depth of competencies and long-term investments that the former has established. It has been suggested that it is difficult for firms to change strategies, from a flexible business strategy/outside development to established markets/inside selection and vice versa. When a firm invests in a particular approach, it creates a reputation for the firm that, in turn, makes it difficult for the firm to change strategies. Hindustan Lever Limited (HLL) is an example of such firms. General Electric (GE) is one of the firms that did make this transition in its business strategy (from established market to flexibility) and HR strategy (from the inside approach to the outside approach). However, it took GE a decade to make this transition. While start-up firms can make the transition in their HR strategy from the outside approach to the inside approach more readily, it is much more difficult for mature organizations to change their HR strategy. Some of IBM's recent problems may be seen within this context, that is, the inability of IBM to respond to the changing market due, in part, to the lack of new talent.

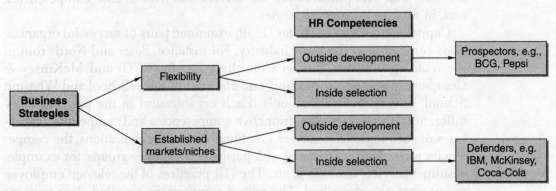

Figure 1.7:   Business Strategies and HR Competencies

Since HR practices are so difficult to change and transfer, it explains the basic premise underlying the notion that the core competencies should drive the business strategy of the firm and not vice versa. According to Cappelli and Crocker-Hefter, it is easier for firms to find a new business strategy to go with the existing HR practices and competencies, than to develop new HR practices and competencies to match new business strategies. This is especially true for firms that rely on 'inside' competencies (firms that develop employee competencies from within). However, firms that secure skills from the outside market (rely on outside market to get new competencies) have HR strategies that can be reproduced by other firms. That is, these competencies are available to everyone in the open market. To obtain competitive advantage in this case, a firm needs to be better at spotting talent in the open market than its competitors, who may also be trying to secure the same competencies. For example, BCG achieves competitive advantage because it is able to hire new consultants at salaries somewhat lower than those of its leading competitors.

Literature on the approaches to SHRM has multiplied rapidly, so much so that it is now possible to identify the emergent SHRM perspectives. The following section discusses the different perspectives on SHRM that have evolved over time.

THEORETICAL PERSPECTIVES ON SHRM

Swiercz (2002) identified four perspectives on SHRM, namely, fit, functional, economic, and typological perspectives. This classification is proposed to organize a range of related yet distinct views on SHRM (Figure 1.8). A brief discussion of each of these perspectives follows.

The Fit Perspective

In a literal sense, the term fit means 'congruity'. In HR literature, Dyer was the first to discuss the idea of 'fit' in 1983. Baird and Meshoulam (1988), took it further and argued that HRM practices should be integrated with the strategic planning process of the organization. They also distinguished between the two types of fit—internal and external. These have already been discussed in the previous section. The primary proposition of Baird and Meshoulam (1988) was that an organization's performance can be enhanced if it adopts HRM practices that complement other HR practices (internal fit), as well as the strategic objectives of the organization (external fit). Empirical investigations of the proposed benefits of the internal fit perspective are limited. However, the proposed benefits of the external fit perspective have been examined by a number of scholars. They have reported that HRM practices varied systematically with the type of manufacturing system, firm environment, etc. Studies also indicate a significant relationship between the adoption of high-performance

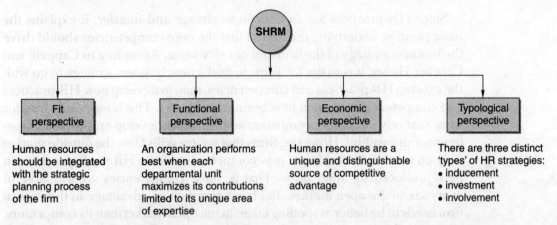

Figure 1.8:   Theoretical Perspective on SHRM

HR practices and organization performance indicators. The fit perspective, therefore, proposes HR as a critical success variable that must be integrated into all phases of organizational planning. Moreover, even the best laid strategic plans cannot be implemented without taking into account the HR practices.

Functional Perspective

Strategic human resource management literature classified as 'functional' has two characteristics.

1. Human resource is seen as a staff function and, therefore, as advisory and subordinate to the core line functions. This is in accordance with the classical organization design theory.
2. The sub-functional strategies, such as the compensation and recruitment strategies, are equated with the overall HR strategy.

This perspective relies on the principle that an organization performs best when each departmental unit maximizes its contributions, limited to its unique area of expertise. It further accepts that organizations should be structured around differences in rank or grade, resulting in the creation of staff func-tional specialists. General managers at the top have the responsibility of giving direction to the firm, functional managers with independent expertise (HR functional staff specialists) are in the middle, and subordinates who carry out supervisors' directives are at the bottom. Schuler and Jackson's (1987) frame-work is representative of this perspective. Strategic HRM, according to this perspective, is defined as a carefully planned effort by functional HR managers to shape subordinate behaviour so as to make it consistent with the desires of top management as expressed in the strategic plan. This approach repre-sents the traditional definitions of HR wherein HR was proposed to be a staff activity.

The second characteristic of the functional perspective treats functional sub-strategies as equivalent with the overall concept of strategic HR. These sub-strategies include recruitment, compensation, human resource information systems, career development, training, job analysis, and international HRM. According to this perspective, the difference between strategic staffing and conventional staffing is that strategic staffing helps the organization to procure long-term human assets, while conventional staffing fulfils the immediate operational objectives. Similarly, strategic compensation aligns compensation practices with the critical contingencies facing the firm. Any HR practice, therefore, becomes a strategy when it is carefully selected to complement the pressing concerns faced by the management.

Economic Perspective

This perspective views human resources as a unique and distinguishable source of competitive advantage. Barney's resource-based VRIO framework, discussed earlier, takes an economic perspective on SHRM. Wright and McMahan (1992) extended Barney's view and argued that human resources can be a source of sustained competitive advantage when four basic requirements are met—human resources must add value to the firm's production processes, skills sought by the firm must be rare, human capital must not be easily imitable, and human resources must not be subject to replacement by technological advances or other substitutes.

Typological Perspective

Typologies help in developing systematic comprehensive theories for the study of new innovations in managerial thought. Dyer and Holder (1988) identified three 'ideal' HR strategic types based on their observations of HR practices in several firms in the US. They intended their typology to specify the content of HR strategic decisions and also to highlight the underlying philosophical considerations that are the major determinants of strategy. The three distinct types of HR strategies identified by them were as follows:

Inducement strategy It is used by firms to support a business environment that is highly competitive with respect to price and/or quantity. In this strategy, the decision making power is highly centralized, with supervisors accepting only a moderate amount of employee initiative, while discouraging innovation and spontaneity. Human resource strategies focus on cost, expecting high performance in a minimally staffed organization. Loyalty and commitment are rewarded by the organization to discourage high employee turnover.

Investment strategy It is most likely to be found in firms where the business strategy is based on differentiation, such as quality, features, or service, rather than price. The organization is characterized by a tall structure, power is centralized, and the technology is modern and adaptable. The HR strategy encourages creativity, initiative, and high performance standards. Formal rules and procedures are minimal. The organization is comfortably staffed, jobs are broadly defined, and continuous employee development is encouraged. Compensation is a balance of fixed and variable components. The Compensation programmes encourage and reward creativity and initiative.

Involvement strategy It is found in firms with a business strategy based on innovation and flexibility when they are confronted with a market that is characterized by a highly competitive price and/or quality. This strategy is also found in firms that use innovation to continuously provide differentiated products or services, and also respond fast as there is a change in markets or when their competitors catch up. Involvement firms are usually smaller, but if the size of these firms is large, they employ decentralized units with flat structures. The HR strategy seeks to provide autonomy and challenge to the employees to motivate them for high and meaningful performance. The firm expects high levels of commitment from its employees. Decision-making is pushed down to the lowest levels and performance is rewarded by compensation that links personal outcomes to the organizational performance.

There is empirical evidence that suggests a causal relationship between the SHRM orientation, business strategy, and financial performance of an organization. The typological perspective has generated a lot of enthusiasm. A primary reason for this is that the perspective is directly linked to the resource-based view of the firm by the assumption that the unique bundles of HR practices distinguish firms from each other, and are also a source of sustainable competitive advantage for some organizations. The typologies, in fact, provide a tool to capture the 'bundle' of HR practices that are associated with particular business strategies. By extension, then, it also agrees with the 'fit' perspective, for it agrees with the assumption that improved performance will result when there is a congruency between the organization's overall competitive strategy and its strategic HR orientation.

The linkage between HR strategies and business strategies are complex and multi-faceted. The questions being raised pertain to the manner in which HR strategies relate to business strategies, and what the organization expects to accomplish through the design of new HR strategies. However, all approaches to SHRM agree on one point, that is, particular HR strategies should (or will) vary with the type of business strategy. Also, there is no one best approach to SHRM. One particular combination of HR strategy cannot be applied to all situations. Theorists who follow a typological perspective have emphasized that a particular business strategy can have a single or a range of HR strategies appropriate to that business strategy. Thus, a cost reduction strategy will have different implications for HR strategy than an innovation strategy.

SHRM APPROACHES: THE INDIAN CONTEXT

As is evident, conceptual and theoretical developments in the management of human resources have largely been limited to the contributions made by Western scholars. However, the concept and practice of HRM, as also the linkage of HRM with the overall goals of the organization, are not entirely new to India. Three major approaches to understanding the 'people' function developed in India are presented in Figure 1.9.

The Integrated Systems Model

As proposed by Rao (1986), this model has development at its core, which suggests that the development of motivated, dynamic, and committed employees is a means to achieve better organizational performance. This perspective views HRM as a process, and not merely as a set of practices, mechanisms, or techniques. Human resource practices such as performance appraisal, training, rewards, etc. are used to initiate, facilitate, and promote this process in a continuous way. These subsystems are designed to work together in an integrated system. Although some of these practices may exist in isolation in an organization that does not have a long-term plan, these mechanisms lack the synergistic benefits of integrated systems. Thus, the viewpoint agrees with the internal fit or horizontal integration approach to SHRM discussed earlier. It is also close to the resource-based view which suggests a bundling of HR practices or subsystems.

On the basis of years of work in the field of Human Resource Development (HRD), Pareek and Rao (1992) developed a *systems framework* that is useful for an in-depth understanding of HRD/HRM. The component systems of HRD, according to them, are the career system (manpower planning, recruitment, retention, continuous potential appraisal and career planning, and development activities), work-planning system (helping individuals understand organizational needs, plan, and improve their work), development system (training, counselling, and other development mechanisms), self-renewal system (team building, survey feedback, research), and culture system

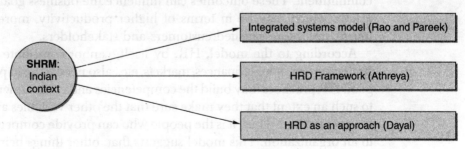

Figure 1.9: Approaches to SHRM: The Indian Context

(a climate that sets norms, values, and culture, and ensures a high level of motivation for employees). It is not necessary for a firm to use all the systems at the same time.

An organization can facilitate the process of development by allocating resources for the purpose and by exemplifying an HRD philosophy that values human beings and promotes their development. The model also emphasizes a linkage between the HRD subsystems and corporate plans of the organization. Thus, the framework also incorporates the external fit perspective. The basic themes underlying these subsystems are as follows:

- human resources are the most important assets of the organization
- a healthy climate is essential for the development of human resources
- employee commitment is enhanced with the opportunity to discover and actualize one's potential in one's work
- human resource development practices can be monitored so as to make them beneficial to both the individual and the organization

A periodic evaluation of the functioning of these systems or practices helps in re-engineering and realigning HRD to the organization's business needs. Rao proposed a model to explain the linkages between HRD instruments (put in operation they become practices), processes, outcomes, and organizational effectiveness. In this model, the HRD instruments include various tools, that is, subsystems such as performance appraisal, training, compensation, etc. The HR practices, if effectively used, can create a conducive HRD culture and learning processes. Human resource development processes are inter-mediate variables and affect the HRD outcomes. They are less easily observ-able and are softer dimensions that indicate the effectiveness of HR practices. Human resource development process variables include role clarity, com-munication, and the practice of HRD values such as openness, collaboration, trust, autonomy, confrontation, etc. Such HRD culture and processes can result in more observable and quantifiable outcomes.

The HR outcomes may include a higher level of employee competence and better utilization of human resources through higher motivation and commitment. These outcomes can influence the business goals of the organi-zation, which may be in terms of higher productivity, more profits, better image, and more satisfied customers and stakeholders.

According to the model, HR, by itself, cannot contribute to profits. The strategies, technology, finances, markets, etc., also need to be in place. However, good HR practices may build the competencies and commitment of employees to such an extent that they make sure that the other variables are taken care of to a great extent. Thus, it is the people who can provide competitive advantage to an organization. This model suggests that, other things being the same, an organization that has a better HRD climate and processes, and competent and committed employees, is likely to do better than an organization that scores low on these counts. Also, various HR practices/subsystems contribute to the organizational effectiveness through HRD climate and HR outcomes.

The HRD Framework

According to Athreya (1988), the ultimate aim of HRD is full participation of the individual in his/her job and life. The starting point for moving towards fuller employee participation is the reaffirmation of the HR philosophy. The HR philosophy has an underlying belief in the employees' potential for growth. A positive HRD climate is important to make the organization more receptive to the introduction of relevant additional systems, and to make the existing systems more effective. In order to sustain HRD on a long-term basis, it is important to support the improved climate through the introduction of a comprehensive HR system. An integrated HRD system has many potential benefits, such as moving from alienation to participation, enhancing individual effectiveness, improving organizational climate and organizational effectiveness. The very concept of a system implies that one may intervene at any point of the system, but it will logically lead through the other subsystems towards the total system. The point of entry depends on the needs of the organization.

HRD as an Approach

This perspective has been put forward by Dayal (1993), who advocates that HRD is an approach, and not a function. This perspective highlights that the underlying belief of all HR programmes of an organization is individual growth and development, which lead to improved organizational performance. Dayal propounds that HR programmes are need-based, and may vary significantly in their approach and emphasis in the following ways:

- *Emphasis on philosophy*: When an organization articulates its beliefs about people and operationalizes them in personnel systems and managerial practices in the organization, it views HRD as a way of life, and not as a programme.
- *Emphasis on programmes*: Human resource initiatives by an organization are integrated with the problem areas identified by the organization.
- *Emphasis on leader behaviour*: In some situations, leader behaviour is regarded as the central feature of HR initiatives. Transformational leaders create an environment in which employees can improve their capabilities and achieve an impressive growth.

Growth of individuals without that of the organization is not sustainable. Hence, HR initiatives should aim at the development of the system as a whole.

The Indian Approach vis-à-vis the Western Approach

It is apparent from the above discussion that the Indian HRM frameworks suggest that HR practices should be aligned with the business plans of the organization and with each other, and that HR approaches should be adapted to the specific business strategies followed by the organization. The main distinguishing feature of the Indian approach is that it is anchored in *values*. However, both the Indian and the Western perspectives agree on the point that HR programmes should contribute towards both individual development and organizational effectiveness. Moreover, there needs to be a judicious blend between concern for the organization and that for the people. Other points of similarity between these perspectives are as follows:

- People are an important resource of the organization.
- Human resource systems and practices are strategically integrated. Changes in business strategy necessitate corresponding changes in HR strategy.
- Human resource systems lead to high employee commitment, cost effectiveness, low turnover, as also enhanced organizational effectiveness and profitability.
- There is a reciprocal interaction between HR practices and content, on one hand, and the climate of the organization, on the other. A supportive culture characterized by dominant values is proposed as essential for the successful implementation of HR practices in such a manner that both the individual and organizational objectives are achieved.

Over the last decade, the importance of HRM has increased, and it has become closely associated with business strategies. Thus, SHRM can be defined as a particular approach to the management of the employment relationship with a distinctive set of HR practices designed to produce specific individual and organizational outcomes—to secure the greater commitment of employees and promote synergy in order to increase organizational effectiveness. Since SHRM is an approach to manage the employment relationship, it follows that in seeking to gain competitive advantage, alternative strategies to the management of the workforce can be adopted by organizations. This has been discussed in the following section.

ALTERNATIVE HR STRATEGIES

Following are some examples of the business–HR linkage and the alternative HR strategies adopted by firms in different industries.

Contract Companies in the Manufacturing Sector,

The use of contract workers has increased significantly at the production sites in the electric and auto industries since the 1990s. The purpose is to reduce personnel costs by transforming employee costs into a variable cost. Nowadays, contract workers provide services that are indispensable for manufacturing goods at many production sites. Accordingly, there has been a spurt of contract firms since the 1990s. Contract firms have managed to increase their client base through 'price competition' and their ability to supply the needed personnel speedily to client firms. Client firms also expect the contract firms to handle more skilled and technically challenging operations, and also to provide onsite operation management. Therefore, it has become essential for contract firms to encourage long-term commitment from contract workers, raise the skill levels of contract workers, and train the onsite production managers by devising training programmes and compensation systems.

It has become important for contract companies to practice strategic management so that they can utilize their resources most effectively. It is also important for contract companies to establish HRM practices that suit their business strategies if they are to generate high profits.

Business Strategies of Contract Firms

Fujimoto and Kimura classified the business strategies of contract firms on the basis of two criteria:

- Workers' skill levels: Whether the firm focuses on operations that require highly technical skills to add value to its services (development type), or on those operations that do not require highly advanced skills (acquisition type).
- Assigning onsite managers and improving operation management: Whether operation management is administered by the contract company (contractor-managed type) or the client company (client-managed type).

A firm that attaches importance to high skill levels, that is, *development type* of firms, will have an HRD system for its contract workers that will be characterized by training programmes emphasizing skill development, skill-based wage systems, promotion and pay-raise schemes, and encouragement to workers for long-term commitment. In contrast, a firm that has an *acquisition type* of policy on workers' skills will not feel the need to invest in an HRD system, or in other measures such as promotion/pay increase schemes. Such a firm cannot differentiate itself by the quality of human resources since it does not emphasize highly advanced skills. Instead, it adds value to its services by offering low contract fees.

Contractor-managed firms generate more value by providing operation management as well, even if they do not handle high-skill operations. These firms also add value to their services by raising their productivity levels. *Client-managed firms* find it easier to reduce personnel costs and offer services at lower levels since they do not have to assign personnel for administering operation management.

Based on the two criteria just discussed, four possible business strategies of contract firms were identified. These are shown in Table 1.8.

Each of the above four types of business strategies that can be followed by contract firms, will require appropriate and matching HR strategies. Some of these have been discussed below:

Development/contractor-managed type These firms add value by handling high-skill contract work and improving their operation management. The HRM practices of these firms include careful screening during selection to increase retention, providing candidates a realistic job preview, selection-board screenings for long-term commitment among candidates, skill-based evaluations, wage increases based on skill evaluations, offer of regular employment contracts to employees, and job rotations to expand the skill range of workers.

Acquisition/client-managed type These firms stay competitive through the speedy supply of contract workers and by handling contract operations that can be executed at the current skill level in a wide range of industries. The HRM practices include maintaining a human resource database of workers wishing to work as contract workers, but these firms have no evaluation and

Table 1.8: Types of Business Strategies of Contract Firms

	Workers' Skill Level	
Operation Management Policy	**Require highly technical skills** (*development type*)	**Do not require highly advanced skills** (*acquisition type*)
Administered by contract company, assigns onsite managers, in addition to operating production lines (*contractor-managed type*)	Development/ contractor-managed type	Acquisition/ contractor-managed type
Administered by client company. Contract firm operates only the production lines and relegates production management to the client company (*client-managed type*)	Development/ client-managed type	Acquisition/ client-managed type

Source: Fujimoto and Kimura

no system for rewarding the skill development of the contract workers. They are not active in providing training for their workers.

Restructuring and SHRM in Healthcare Organizations

The healthcare industry is in a growth mode and there is a high level of focus on healthcare costs. As part of the strategy, the hospital industry is likely to engage in downsizing and restructuring. Restructuring and downsizing have largely been associated with job loss and other psychological consequences. More recently, there have been attempts to understand the effectiveness of restructuring as an organizational tool for increasing profits, reducing costs, and increasing shareholder returns on investments.

Wooten and Decker (1996) proposed a strategic HRM model for downsizing/restructuring based on best-case practices. This model has three major components, that is, *pre-structuring, restructuring,* and *post-restructuring activities.* Wooten and Decker suggested that if hospitals and healthcare organi-zations are engaged in strategies involving these three components, they can adopt the practices that are known to be successful during restructuring.

According to the strategic HRM model proposed, the following steps should be adopted by hospitals that plan to restructure:

1. Environmental scan prior to developing and restructuring activities given the turbulent nature of the hospital industry. The scan should involve collecting, categorizing, and interpreting environmental information related to competitors and regulatory agencies, and a SWOT (strengths, weaknesses, opportunities, and threats) analysis.

2. The environmental scan will result in defining the business strategy—cost leadership, differentiation, or focus.

3. Pre-structuring should involve clarifying the core issues and the mission related to the strategy. The specific HR issues to be considered at this stage are:
   - Deciding the organizational design (hospitals generally use hybrid forms of structure due to the unique environmental conditions).
   - Conducting human resource audit (examining the knowledge, skills, and abilities of the employees and workforce utilization).
   - Conducting risk analysis.
   - Examining the existing culture and articulating what aspects of the culture and sub-culture need to be changed. The culture should support the proposed new mission and the strategy of the firm.
   - Deciding on reward systems and linking them to the business strategy (these reinforce the culture of the organization).
   - Deciding on support systems to assist employees, for instance, outplacement services for dismissed employees.

- Training communicators within the firm to systematically disseminate information about the restructuring to employees and to answer their queries and concerns.

4. Restructuring involves communicating decisions and implementing policies. At this stage, the following issues are important:
   - Communication from the top leadership about the plans for the restructuring, and the need to communicate a sense of justice. Reduction of workforce, job sharing, and voluntary separation incentives occur at this time.
   - Providing support and transition services after the downsizing. These range from hiring outplacement firms and establishing in-house career centres to involvement in community-based employment services. The transition services affect the commitment of the employees remaining with the organization.
   - Re-assignment of responsibility.
   - The need to alter the manner in which employees are recruited and retained.

5. The post-restructuring stage involves helping the organization evolve and adapt, rebuild trust, and clarify rewards. Several issues need to be addressed at this stage. These include the following:
   - Reinforcing the new mission, culture, and values of the restructured healthcare organization by redefining beliefs, structures, and practices. Since change is usually accompanied by disenchantment and disorientation, it is important to provide assistance to the employees in the form of workshops, stress management, and a general awareness of the stages of change.
   - Human resource activities directed towards survivors and other employees who may subsequently leave. Realistic future expectations should be generated among this group. To foster commitment and career growth, career development opportunities should be provided.
   - Recruitment and selection should support the new culture.
   - Rewards should support mission-related performance.

The above model reinforces the view that business strategy changes need to be accompanied by concomitant SHRM initiatives to ensure the success of the business strategy.

Competition-related HRM Changes in the Retail Banking Industry

Since the mid-1990s, the retail banking divisions of commercial banks are under pressure to change the way they do business. Banks are faced with an extremely competitive environment as well as threats from non-banking institutions. Information technology has changed the way people interact with their banks. In the 1970s and 1980s, the manufacturing industry had difficulty in switching over from the established methods of managing people when faced with increased competition. Manufacturing firms were seen as having failed to adopt HR strategies that could have produced higher quality products and made these organizations more flexible and cost-effective. In the 1990s, the retail banking sector was confronted with similar challenges. The intensely competitive environment has resulted in changes in HRM practices in retail banks. It is important for firms to manage people in ways that are consistent with their organizational strategy.

At the corporate level, retail banks are typically owned by a holding company that has its own strategic agenda. Sometimes, the retail banks may be strong and have independent lines of business. The strategy of the holding company must be understood along with the role of the retail bank in carrying out that strategy. In addition to its contribution to broader corporate aims, a retail bank may also have its own competitive strategy.

Focus or Niche Strategy

The consumer financial services industry is characterized by mergers and the likelihood of merger activity shapes much of the thinking of top manage-ment in most banks. New technologies for delivering financial services continue to be developed rapidly. The environment is increasingly dynamic and non-banking competitors are increasingly attracting investment funds and other products (such as alternatives for auto and home equity financing). This environment has encouraged retail banks to move to sales-oriented practices in order to compete successfully.

Larry Hunter (1995) from the Wharton School, University of Pennsylvania, concluded that retail banks mostly used the 'focus' strategy in terms of Porter's classification of business strategy. While all banks claim to be cutting costs (cost advantage strategy), none of the banks follow the goal of being the lowest cost provider. Moreover, true differentiation is nearly impossible to achieve in consumer-oriented financial services. The features can easily be imitated by competitors and there are very few barriers to the introduction of new products. Therefore, most banks follow the *focus* and *niche strategies*; the typical initiatives are as follows:

- being a 'one-stop' financial service provider
- aggressive selling to new customers
- aggressive cross-selling of new products to existing customers
- establishing a presence in chosen geographical markets

- establishing alternative channels of delivery of financial services
- developing a reputation for providing the highest quality service

Each strategy has implications for human resource imperatives. For example, the strategy focusing on gaining market share by selling a broader range of financial services to young professionals, will result in success for retail banks when the corresponding HRM strategies include incentive pay and performance appraisal systems that reward these kind of sales, specific training programmes aimed at these goals, the hiring and promotion of staff based on their ability to make such sales, and job designs that encourage customer contact.

Thus, it is evident from this discussion that strategic decisions should be backed by appropriate HRM practices for an organization to succeed.

Summary

All physical and capital resources depend on people for their efficient utilization, maintenance, and management. Hence, there is an increasing recognition among management thinkers of the importance of human resources in providing competitive advantage to organizations. As a result, employees are now referred to as human capital or human assets. Instead of viewing human resources as a cost to the organization', firms have begun to consider employees as 'investments'. Since business objectives are achieved through people, it is important to integrate HRM with the business strategy of the organization.

In this chapter, we discussed the meaning of SHRM and the evolution of HR function over time into a strategically focused one. According to the resource-based view (RBV) of the firm, human resources become a source of sustained competitive advantage for a firm when the four criteria of value, rareness, non-imitability, and organization are met. Factors that determine how investment oriented a firm is in its management of human resources were highlighted. Three conceptual approaches to SHRM, that is, the 'best practice', 'best fit', and 'HR bundles' approach, were examined to understand the concept of 'fit' between business strategy and HR strategy. The premise that distinctive HR practices are the drivers that lead to core competencies, firm competitiveness and, in turn, business strategies, was also discussed. Four theoretical perspectives of SHRM, viz. fit, functional, economic, and typological perspective, were presented and the relationship between business strategy and HR strategy was examined. The chapter discussed three bases of classification of HR strategies, that is, stages of business life-cycle, type of business strategy, and types and numbers of products. The Indian perspective on SHRM was also presented. The chapter ends with a few examples of the business-HR strategy linkage from the manufacturing, hospital, and retail banking industries.

Keywords

Administrative Theory is a classical organization theory proposed by Henri Fayol. The focus of this approach was on the most efficient way of structuring organizations. This approach attributed managerial success to certain principles of management.

Asset is something that is owned by the firm and that has an exchange value.

Best Practices are superior management practices that are readily identifiable and transferable across organizations irrespective of the context. All firms will attain performance improvements only if they identify and implement 'best practice' or 'benchmark'.

Change Management refers to specific efforts undertaken by a firm to steer a planned change in a specified direction with the help of a change agent.

Competitive Advantage is a situation where an organization is able to differentiate its products or services from those of its competitors to increase its market share and gains, and maintains an edge over its competitors.

Distinctive HR Practices refer to unique HR practices that help to create unique competencies that differentiate the products and services. This differentiation leads to competitiveness of the firm.

Employee Stock Option Plans (ESOP) give employees the right to purchase a fixed number of shares of the company stock at a specified, usually lower, price for a limited period of time. ESOPs are used by firms as an incentive for executives and as a retention tool.

External Fit is a theory that proposes that differences in business orientations or strategies of organizations call for different types of people as well as different HR strategies. This is also called vertical integration.

Greenfield Firms are high performing firms that are started from scratch at a new site.

HR Strategy refers to the planned and effective use of human resources by an organization to facilitate the successful achievement of the corporate strategy. It is concerned with ensuring that the organization has the required people, training, rewards, and good employee relations.

Human Capital is a term used to refer to the collective skills and knowledge of the total workforce of an organization that have an economic value to the organization and enhance its productivity and profitability.

Human Resource Management (HRM) is an overall approach towards the management of people working in the organization for accomplishing the goals of the organization.

Human Resources is a term used to refer to the people who work in an organization. These are the resources on which other resources depend for their effective and efficient utilization.

Internal Fit refers to the development and implementation of several HR practices together so that they are interrelated and internally consistent with each HR practice, complementing and reinforcing the other. This is also known as 'horizontal integration' or 'bundling'.

Knowledge Economy refers to all jobs, companies, and industries in which the knowledge and skills of people, rather than the capabilities of machines and technologies, determine competitive advantage.

Resource-Based View (RBV) is a view that holds that human resources contribute to sustained competitive advantage for a firm when they are valuable, non-tradable, non-imitable, and non-substitutable. This view is popularly called the VRIO framework

Scientific Management is an early approach to management and organizational behaviour proposed by F.W. Taylor. The approach focused on the role of employees as individuals and emphasized the importance of designing jobs as efficiently as possible.

Skill Mobility refers to the ease with which employees with a particular skill set can move from one employer to another with little loss in pay or responsibility.

Strategic Fit is a theory that proposes that if an organization seeks to maximize competitive advantage, it must match its internal resources and skills (organizational competencies) with the opportunities available in the external environment.

Strategic Human Resource Management (SHRM) is the relationship between HRM and strategic management in a firm. It is the pattern of planned human resource deployment and activities intended to enable the firm to achieve its goals.

Strategy refers to the determination of the long-term goals and objectives of an organization, and the allocation of resources necessary for carrying out these goals.

The Mission Statement of a company is a brief statement that represents 'why' the organization exists. It is a statement of the purpose of the firm.

Concept Review Questions

1. Define strategic human resource management (SHRM). What are the main points of difference between SHRM and human resource strategies?

2. Are people always an organization's most valuable asset? Why or why not? Discuss with reference to the growth of knowledge-based organizations. Give examples.

3. Should organizations view human resources from an investment perspective? Discuss the factors that determine the extent to which an organization is investment oriented in its management of human resources.

4. Compare and contrast the best fit and best practice approaches to the management of human resources.

5. Describe the Indian perspective on SHRM. How is it different from the Western view of SHRM?

6. Identify and discuss the different bases for classifying HR strategies. How can HR strategies help an organization to create competitive advantage?

Critical Thinking Questions

1. 'Strategic human resource management is largely about integration or strategic fit between HR strategy and business strategy'. Do you agree? Differentiate between external fit and internal fit. Give examples of organizations you know of, that have achieved a fit between business strategy and HR strategy. Describe and evaluate the type of fit that exists in each of these organizations.

2. Read the section on Barney's resource-based view (RBV). According to the VRIO framework, which type of human resources can be a source of competitive advantage for a firm? How can the application of VRIO transform HR function from being a 'cost' into a strategic function that contributes to the performance of an organization?

3. Describe the business strategy classification proposed by Porter. Which types of HR practices are likely to be adopted by organizations for each of the three generic business strategies proposed in this classification? Give examples of a few firms you know of that practice each of the three business strategies. Also, examine the corresponding HR strategies for each firm. Compare the HR strategies of the firms and explain how they depend on the characteristics of the business strategy of the firm.

4. According to one viewpoint, it is easier for a firm to find a new business strategy to go with the existing HR practices and competencies, than to develop new HR practices and competencies to match with the new business strategies. Do you agree? Explain the rationale behind this viewpoint. Cite examples of organizations that have relied on distinctive HR practices to attain competitive advantage.

Simulation and Role Play

1. Mr Apte has recently been deputed from a large public sector manufacturing firm to head the HR department of a national airline. He does not have prior experience in the airline industry. However, he has extensive experience as an HR person and has high levels of functional expertise. He has proved himself by successfully aligning HRM with the strategic objectives of the organization in his parent firm. The national airline has lost its monopoly with the entry of private players in the airline industry. As the head of HR, Mr Apte feels that the national airline has failed to align its strategy around its distinctive competencies. Mr Apte has resolved to bring up this issue in a meeting with the top management and highlight the need to build business strategy around the distinctive competencies of the firm.

   Six students should volunteer for the role-play, each playing the role of a member of the top management team. One student plays the role of Mr Apte. The other five play the following roles respectively: Head of Marketing, Head of Business Strategy, Head of Finance, Head of Operations, and the CEO. As Mr Apte, the student should convince the members of the team about the importance of designing the business strategy around the distinctive competencies of the firm. Further, he should emphasize that instead of attempting to imitate the strategy of its competitors, the airline should focus on its distinctive competencies. The other team members should raise questions about the suggestion and discuss its pros and cons. All the members should keep the contemporary scenario of the airline industry in mind. The role-play should end with a draft preparation that identifies the distinctive competencies of the airline and suggests the business strategy that would be most appropriate. Alternatively, the members may suggest what business strategy (according to Porter's classification) the airline should adopt and why. They should also suggest the HR strategy that will match the suggested business strategy.

2. Assume that you are an external consultant hired by a firm that is planning a restructuring exercise. After an extensive study of the firm, you discover that it continues to be traditional in its approach to managing human resources. You have taken an appointment with the Vice President (HR) of the firm to discuss your findings and to suggest changes. Structure your discussion around the following aspects:

   - the need to view human resources as an asset and a source of competitive advantage
   - the need to move towards a strategic perspective of HR function
   - major HR issues during and after the restructuring
   - changes in the HR strategy of the firm

Classroom Projects

1. The purpose of this activity is to discuss the direction of business–HR strategy linkage. Half the students in the class should take Position 1 and the other half should take Position 2 with respect to the notion of fit between business strategy and HR practices:

   Position 1: 'The competitive strategy of the firm should determine the HR strategy'

   Position 2: 'Distinctive HR practices of the firm determine the core competencies that determine the competitive strategy of the firm'

   Each student should individually develop and write his/her ideas in support of the position taken. The students of the class can be divided into two groups according to the position they take. The members of each group should share their individual ideas and develop arguments in support of their chosen position. After allowing 15 minutes time for group discussion, each group should present its arguments. Each group can have a presentation time of 10 minutes. An open discussion with the class should highlight the pros and cons of each position. The students should also be encouraged to cite examples of successful firms that have relied on either of the above positions to support their arguments.

2. This exercise needs some out-of-class preparation. As the first part of the project, students are asked to read the description of traditional HR versus strategic HR presented in the chapter. Each student should choose an organization and collect information about the HR function and strategy of this organization. The organizations should belong to one of the following industries: FMCG, pharmaceutical, airlines, hospitality, or software. The information should relate to the various aspects on which traditional HR differs from strategic HR. To obtain this information, the student can use Internet resources as well as available company documents. The students should prepare and submit this report to the class instructor prior to the class.

For the second part of the project, the students should be divided into small groups based on their chosen industry. Each group should consist of the students who choose the same industry. Each group member should identify and discuss the nature of the HR function and practices followed by the organization he/she selects within the particular industry. They should also compare the organizations within the industry and discuss the similarities and differences, and the causes for the same. Class presentations should follow discussions on the importance of SHRM, transformation of HR function from a traditional to a strategic function, significance of linking business strategy and HR strategy, and intra-industry and inter-industry differences with respect to HR strategy.

3. Form groups of four to five members and discuss the significance of human resources for achieving competitive advantage with respect to the manufacturing as well as the service sector. Also, discuss whether human resources are a cost or an investment for an organization. Report your discussion to the class.

4. Apply the resource-based view (RBV) model to your institute/University. In groups of four, determine the value of the institute's human resources in terms of Barney's four criteria for achieving competitive advantage. Compare your institute/University with a competitor on these criteria. Develop an HR strategy to best deploy and utilize the human resources of the institute. Prepare a report for class discussion.

Field Projects

1. For this project, the instructor should divide the class into groups of five each. Each group should visit two organizations, both of which should be at the same stage of development in the business life cycle, that is, start-up, growth, maturity, or decline. The group members should conduct interviews with HR managers as well as a few senior line managers of the organizations to obtain information about the business strategies and HR strategies of these organizations. Each group should prepare a report for class presentation as well as a written report for submission to the instructor. The groups should make presentations in the class highlighting the development stage of the organizations they visit, their business strategy, and the nature of the HR strategy of these organizations. When all groups have made their presentations, the instructor should engage the class in a discussion about the need to match the HR strategies with the stage of development of the organization. The discussion should

also focus on how and why HR strategies of organizations at different stages of business life cycle differ from each other.

2. Visit a retail bank that has been through a merger or acquisition. Interview one or two senior managers of the bank in order to obtain information about the business strategies of the two banks, prior to as well as after the merger/acquisition. Use Porter's classification of business strategy to determine the strategy of the banks. Also interview the HR managers of the banks to understand the HR strategy of each of these organizations before the merger or acquisition. Obtain information on the changes in HR practices after the merger/acquisition. Based on the information, answer the following questions:

- What type of business strategy was followed by each bank prior to merger/acquisition?
- Was there a change in the business strategy of these banks after the merger/acquisition?
- What HR strategies were followed by each bank prior to the merger/acquisition?

- Did the HR strategies change post merger/acquisition?
- What were the main HR aspects related to the mergers and acquisitions that were faced by these banks? How were these issues handled?
- Were the HR practices and strategy congruent with the business strategy in the newly formed entity as a result of the merger/acquisition?

You may also interview four to five line managers to obtain their perception of and satisfaction with the merger/acquisition. Find out what human resource practices were used and obtain their evaluations on what was helpful or harmful. Also obtain their appraisal about the success or failure of the merger/acquisition. On the basis of the above information present a critical appraisal of the role of HR strategy in the success or failure of business decisions such as mergers and acquisitions. Prepare a written report for classroom submission.

References

Armstrong, M. 2000, *Strategic Human Resource Management: A Guide to Action*, Kogan Page, London, pp. 44–5, 69.

Athreya, M.B. 1988, 'Integrated HRD System-Intervention Strategies', in T.V. Rao, K.K. Verma, Anil K. Khandelwal, and E. Abraham S.J. (eds), *Alternative Approaches and Strategies of HRD*, Rawat Publications, Jaipur, p. 378.

Baird, L. and I. Meshoulam 1988, 'Managing Two Fits of Strategic Human Resource Management', *Academy of Management Review*, vol. 13, pp. 116–28.

Barney, J. 1991, 'Firm Resources and Sustained Competitive Advantage', *Journal of Management*, vol. 17, pp. 99–120.

Beaumont, P.B. 1992, 'The US Human Resource Management Literature', in G. Salaman et al. (eds), *Human Resource Strategies*, Sage, London.

Cappelli, P. and A. Crocker-Hefter 1999, 'Distinctive Human Resources Are Firms' Core Competencies', in R.S. Schuler and S.E. Jackson (eds), *Strategic Human Resource Management*, Blackwell Business, UK, pp. 191–206.

Chandler, A.D. 1962, *Strategy and Structure*, MIT Press, Boston, Massachusetts.

Dayal, Ishwar 1993, 'Planning HRD Initiatives', *Designing HRD Systems*, Concept Publishing Co., New Delhi, pp. 9–28.

Delery, J.E. and H.D. Doty 1996, 'Modes of Theorizing in Strategic Human Resource Management: Tests of Universality, Contingency and Configurational Performance Predictions', *International Journal of Human Resource Management*, vol. 6, pp. 656–70.

Dyer, L. 1985, 'Strategic Human Resource Management and Planning', in K. Rowland and G. Ferris (eds), *Research in Personnel and Human Resources Management*, JAI Press, Greenwich, Connecticut, pp. 1–30.

Fombrun, C.J., N.M. Tichy, and M.A. Devanna 1984, *Strategic Human Resource Management*, Wiley, New York.

Fujimoto, M. and T. Kimura, 'Business Strategy and Human Resource Management at Contract Companies in the Manufacturing Sector', http://www.jil.go.jp/english/documents/JLR06_fujimoto.pdf, pp. 104–22, accessed on 23 November 2005.

Golden, K. and V. Ramanujam 1985, 'Between a Dream and a Nightmare: on the Integration of the Human Resource Management and Strategic Planning Process', *Human Resource Management*, vol. 24, pp. 429–52.

Greer, C.R. 2002, *Strategic Human Resource Management: A General Managerial Approach*, 2nd edition, Pearson Education, Singapore.

Guest, D.E. 1989, 'Personnel and HRM: Can you tell the Difference?', *Personnel Management*, January, pp. 48–51.

Guest, D.E. 1997, 'Human Resource Management and Performance: A Review of the Research Agenda', *The International Journal of Human Resource Management*, vol. 8, no. 3, pp. 263–76.

Hamel, G. and C. Prahalad 1993, 'Strategy as Stretch and Leverage', *Harvard Business Review*, vol. 71, no. 2, pp. 75–84.

Hamel, G. and C. Prahalad 1994, *Competing for the Future*, Harvard Business School Press, Boston.

Hendry, C. and A. Pettigrew 1986, 'The Practice of Strategic Human Resource Management', *Personnel Review*, vol. 15, pp. 2–8.

Hunter, L.W. 1995, 'How will Competition Change Human Resource Management in Retail Banking? A Strategic Perspective', *The Wharton Financial Institutions Centre*, Working Paper Series, February, p. 26, http://fic.wharton.upenn.edu/fic/papers/95/9504.pdf, accessed on 23 November 2005.

Khan, S.A. 1998, 'Transformation of Human Resource Management: Dimensions in the Twenty-First Century', *Management & Change*, vol. 2, no. 1, pp. 105–17.

Khatri, N. 2000, 'Managing Human Resource for Competitive Advantage: A Study of Companies in Singapore', *International Journal of Human Resource Management*, vol. 11, no. 2, pp. 336–65.

Lengnick-Hall, M.L. and C.A. Lengnick-Hall 2003, *Human Resource Management in the Knowledge Economy*, Berrett-Koehler Publishers Inc., San Francisco.

Lundy, O. 1994, 'From Personnel Management to Strategic Human Resource Management', *The International Journal of Human Resource Management*, vol. 5, no. 3, September, pp. 687–720.

MacDuffie, J.P. 1995, 'Human Resource Bundles and Manufacturing Performance', *Industrial Relations Review*, vol. 48, no. 2, pp. 191–221.

Mello, J.A. 2003, *Strategic Human Resource Management*, Thomson Asia Pte Ltd, Singapore.

Miles, R.E. and C.C. Snow 1984, 'Designing Strategic Human Resources Systems', *Organizational Dynamics*, vol. 13, no. 1, pp. 36–52.

O'Riordon, F., 'The Context of HRM', http://dubmail.gcd.ie/student/faculties/graduatebus/FionaORiordon/SHRM/Strategy1.ppt, accessed on 23 November 2005.

Pareek, U. and T.V. Rao 1992, *Designing and Managing Human Resource Systems*, 2nd edition, New Delhi, Oxford & IBH Publishing Co.

Pfeffer, J. 1994, *Competitive Advantage Through People*, Harvard Business School Press, Boston.

Pfeffer, J. 1998, *The Human Equation: Building Profits by Putting People First*, Harvard Business School Press, Boston.

Pil, F.K. and J.P. MacDuffies 1996, 'The Adoption of High-Involvement Work Practices', *Industrial Relations*, vol. 35, no. 3, pp. 423–55.

Porter, M. 1985, *Competitive Advantage: Creating and Sustaining Superior Performance*, Free Press, New York.

Rao, T.V. 1986, 'Integrated Human Resource Development System', in T.V. Rao and D.F. Pereira (eds), *Recent Experiences in Human Resource Development*, Oxford and IBH Publishing Co., New Delhi, pp. 3–19, 70–7.

Richardson, R. and M. Thompson 1999, 'The Impact of People Management Practices on Business Performance: A Literature Review', *Institute of Personnel and Development*, London.

Schuler, R. and S. Jackson 1987, 'Linking Competitive Strategies and Human Resource Management Practices', *Academy of Management Executive*, vol. 1, no. 3, pp. 207–19.

Schuler, R.S. 1992, 'Strategic Human Resource Management: Linking the People with Strategic Needs of the Business', *Organizational Dynamics*, Summer, pp. 18–31.

Schuler, R.S., P.J. Dowling, and H. De Cieri 1993, 'An Integrative Framework of Strategic International Human Resource Management', *The International Journal of Human Resource Management*, vol. 4, no. 4, pp. 717–64.

Stevens, M. 1994, 'A Theoretical Model of on-the-job Training with Imperfect Competition', *Oxford Economic Papers*, 46, Oxford University Press, pp. 537–62.

Swiercz, P.M. 2002, Research Update, 'Strategic HRM', *Human Resource Planning*, pp. 53–9.

Wooten, K.C. and P.J. Decker 1996, 'A Strategic Human Resource Management Model for Restructuring in Healthcare Organizations', *Hospital Topics*, vol. 74, no. 1, Winter, p. 10, Database: Academic Search Elite.

Wright, P. and G. McMahan 1992, 'Theoretical Perspectives for Strategic Human Resource Management', *Journal of Management*, vol. 18, pp. 295–320.

Wright, P.M. 1998, 'Introduction: Strategic Human Resource Management Research in the 21st Century', *Human Resource Management Review*, vol. 8, no. 3, pp. 187–91.

2 Human Resource Environment

After studying this chapter, you will be able to:

- understand the significance of global business trends and their implications for human resource management

- discuss the human resource management challenges resulting from the changing nature of workforce and of employment relationship

- acquire an overview of the demographic and societal trends that affect human resource management

- understand the significance of human resource management in the knowledge economy

- discuss the multiple roles that a human resource management professional must perform in contemporary organizations

- explain the trend towards outsourcing of human resource management activities

- describe the impact of technology on human resource management

- appreciate the role of human resource management in managing organizational change

INTRODUCTION

Several factors in the business environment (increased competition, corporate downsizing, and rapid technological advances) and the social environment (changing values regarding work/non-work–life balance and changing workforce demographics) have brought about a new employment relationship. These changes have had major implications for the management of the workforce within organizations. The transformation of the economy from a primarily manufacturing economy to a primarily service economy has increased the importance of knowledge in job performance. As people become the most valuable asset of a firm, there has emerged a new class of highly-skilled knowledge workers. High demand for knowledge workers coupled with their limited availability in the workforce has created a 'war for talent' among organizations. With firms competing for skilled workers, employee mobility has increased. Therefore, organizations have to develop new strategies to attract, retain, motivate, and develop employees. Human resource management challenges have become more significant with an increase in the number of knowledge workers, inter-firm competition, changes in technology, and societal and business trends.

The present chapter discusses significant environmental trends and the unique challenges confronted by the HR function and professionals as a result of these trends. It examines the increasingly important role of HRM in the knowledge economy and in managing knowledge workers. Within the context of the impact of the knowledge economy, the chapter examines the changing role of HRM professionals, such as that of 'strategic business partner', and 'HR–Line Manager partnership'. It is emphasized that in contemporary organizations, the HRM manager has multiple roles to play. It also provides an insight into the trend towards outsourcing of HRM activities. The impact of technology on the way HRM managers work and the manner in which the HRM function is structured has also been reviewed. The chapter ends with a discussion on the role of HRM in managing organizational change as well as in developing a change-ready organizational culture.

HUMAN RESOURCE ENVIRONMENT: A BRIEF OVERVIEW

From the industrial era or the machine age to the information age—the evolution of the business environment has been phenomenally fast. In the industrial era, the focus was on manufacturing goods in a plant. The manufacturing process was organized around the concept of assembly-line production. This resulted in job specialization in factories. The blue-collar worker performed his or her part of the job without any idea of how it related to the end product. There was a separation of 'planning' and 'doing'. The worker was hired to 'do' and not to 'think and plan'. The white-collar workers were rewarded for loyalty.

The end of the twentieth century heralded the era of the post-industrial economy, that is, the emergence and evolution of the service economy. This era of the service economy came to be called the 'age of information and knowledge'. Rather than producing goods, the service firms produce 'ideas'. Organizations in the 'services era', such as software, financial services, and biotechnology firms, depend on 'intellectual capital'. People create 'intellectual capital' and are therefore the most valuable asset of a firm.

The shift from a manufacturing economy to a services economy, from production of goods to production of ideas, and from the machine age to the information age has been accompanied by many transformations. The environment within which firms conduct business today is very different and much more complex and dynamic when compared to the environment 15 years ago. Firms no longer compete or operate nationally only. Organizations are no longer governed by the business, legal and political environment of their own nations only. As the world becomes one global playing field, the environmental changes in countries other than the home country of a firm affect business decisions and the performance of firms. Several societal and global phenomena have challenged the management of human resources. Changes in the economic, business, social, and cultural environments have brought about a transformation in the HR function and the roles and responsibilities of HR professionals.

Some of the significant environmental trends and changes faced by HR managers that pose major challenges are (see Figure 2.1) as follows:

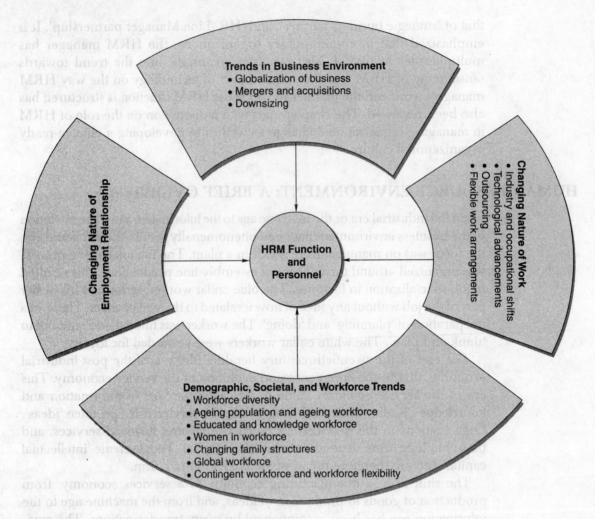

Figure 2.1:   Environmental Trends Affecting HRM

- trends in the business environment
- the changing nature of work
- demographic, societal and workforce trends
- the changing nature of the employment relationship

The next section discusses each of these trends in detail. A brief overview is presented in Table 2.1.

Trends in Business Environment

Several changes in the business environment have been taking place during the past two decades. These include globalization of business, mergers and acquisitions, and downsizing. Each of these business trends has set forth unique HRM challenges.

Globalization of Business

A major environmental change that has taken place in the last 15 years is the globalization of business. The world has become a global village, and business has become global in character. Organizations are venturing beyond national boundaries in the pursuit of business opportunities. Goods and services are produced and marketed around the world. Production and marketing are no longer constrained by national boundaries. Toyota Motor Corporation makes cars in USA and India, McDonald's sells hamburgers in India and China, and Marks & Spencer Group PLC sells products in India. Every other product sold by Wal-Mart Stores Inc. (Wal-Mart) is made in India. Some of the world's largest manufacturers in many industries are based in India and export to the US, the European Union, and other parts of the world. This is the time when buildings are conceptualized in the US, designed in India, and built in China. Very recently, Ford Motor Company (Ford) announced its plans to invest $1 billion in products and plants in the Asia-Pacific region in the next few years to maintain its presence in fast-growing markets.

Domestic firms are competing with foreign companies the world over. Global competition has resulted in a high level of cost consciousness on the part of companies. A number of companies from the US, Japan, and other countries have set up their manufacturing plants in countries that provide them labour cost advantage. Outsourcing has made India a manufacturing hub, especially for the automobile sector, with cheap labour providing one of the competitive advantages. Government policy reforms and growth against an appreciating rupee have also facilitated this trend. Large numbers of manufacturing assembly jobs that require low skills have moved from the US and western Europe to developing countries like China, Thailand, Malaysia, and India. This is primarily because wages are much lower in developing countries. While the labour cost in other developing countries is about 30–35% of sales, it is only about 8–9% in India. This effects a lower total average cost of production. Business process outsourcing (BPO) firms are also part of the cost advantage strategy of firms. At the same time, Indian firms are also investing abroad. India's manufacturing and services companies invested $10 billion overseas in 2004. The top 15 Indian IT, software and related service companies have invested mostly in developed countries. Like the IT and automobile industries, domestic hospital chains from India, such as Apollo Hospitals Group, Fortis Healthcare, and Max Healthcare Institute Private Limited, also have ambitious expansion plans in markets as far away as the US, UK, Mauritius, and south-east Asia.

A major impetus to the globalization of business was provided by changes in economic policies. For India, June 1991 marked the beginning of economic liberalization. Lowering of customs duties, more liberal foreign exchange regulations, and fewer restrictions on foreign trade have all integrated India into the world economy. Therefore, today India is affected by exogenous developments more than it was in the past. Indian business is also thinking global, and needs to be more vigilant about the global economy.

As Indian companies move aggressively to capture overseas markets, they have been forced to raise product standards in order to meet world-class quality. There is benchmarking, a requirement for health checks, drive towards productivity improvements, a policy framework that encourages flexibility in labour markets, and trade policy. These clearly indicate the impact of the global economy on Indian business. Today, multinational corporations (MNCs), those that maintain significant operations in two or more countries, have become a norm rather than an exception. Multinational corporations require employees who can adapt to different cultures, customs, social practices, values, economic and political systems, and management approaches, and who can work with other employees from differing backgrounds. This has caused new challenges for HR managers. The HRM function of a company must develop systems that will help individuals from different cultural backgrounds to work together. Human resource managers must ensure that employees with the requisite knowledge, skills, abilities, and cultural adaptability are available so that they may be successful in global assignments.

The globalization of business also requires firms to comply with the legislation of the country they wish to conduct business in. For instance, the apparel production industry of India has been affected by the norms imposed by global retailers. Global retailers outsourcing from India impose non-tariff barriers in the form of security and social audit norms. For example, Wal-Mart, a leading retailer, imposes stiff conditions which cost a lot in implementation. Global buyers are quick to cancel contracts if they find that compliance norms have been violated. Since compliance is too expensive for small apparel production firms, many, in Mumbai, the hub of small apparel production firms, have gone out of business. They are either switching over to apparel trading or venturing into new businesses. Another example is that of Indian pharmaceutical majors who have postponed their plans to acquire German generic pharmaceutical companies because of the new German Healthcare Bill. The Bill, effective 2006, mandates all pharmaceutical companies selling generic products in Germany to price them 30% lower than patented products, and cap prices for two years. Companies not meeting this mandate will need to cut prices on generic products. Cutting prices will lower the valuations of German generic companies, and so, Indian companies who were scouting for acquisitions of companies in Germany have had to shelve their plans for the moment. Thus, globalization of business brings with it several HR challenges. These include issues such as managing a global workforce, focus on cost to enhance a firm's competitiveness, and ensuring legal compliance while conducting business abroad.

Mergers and Acquisitions

A major consequence of globalization has been a spate of mergers and acquisitions (M&A). As geographical boundaries break down for business, this is one way firms ensure their presence in different parts of the world. The trend was started by IBM when it bought Daksh (a BPO firm, now IBM Daksh) and HR services leader Adecco took over Bangalore-based HR services company PeopleOne. Teva Pharmaceutical Industries Limited (Teva), the world's largest generic drugs maker, made its first investment in India in 2003 when it acquired Regent Drugs Limited from JK Drugs and Pharmaceuticals Limited. Since then Teva has also entered into alliances with other Indian firms to source raw materials. Three global companies at the top of their respective sectors have been on an acquisition spree in India. Merrill Lynch and Company, Incorporated, the financial services powerhouse, bought Hemendra Kothari to form a joint venture, DSP Merrill Lynch Limited. Oracle Corporation (Oracle) acquired a 41% stake in i-flex solutions in 2005. Axis Computers, a subsidiary of the US-based knowledge process outsourcing (KPO) firm Axis Group, and Noida-based call centre IT&T merged to create a Rs 400 million integrated IT services company.

Foreign investment is no longer something that flows only from a developed country to a developing one. Indian companies are on an expansion drive. Indian business houses, like the Tata Group, and firms like Ranbaxy Laboratories Limited (Ranbaxy), Wipro Limited (Wipro), Sun Pharmaceutical Industries Limited, Crompton Greaves Limited, Asian Paints, and Cognizant Technology Solutions, have struck merger and acquisition deals worldwide to become global players. The Aditya Birla Group, along with an overseas joint venture partner, bought Canada's St. Anne-Nackawic Pulp Company Limited for $100 million, one of the biggest acquisitions in Canada by an Indian company. Many of these firms belong to industries that are witnessing tough worldwide competition. Hence, gaining scale is important for them and one way they achieve this is through acquisitions. Acquisitions by Indian companies have now become strategic in nature, by which they have been able to take leadership positions in Asia.

Though most of India's investment overseas has been dominated by the manufacturing sector, huge investments have been made by the IT sector as well. There are more than 400 Indian firms in Britain alone, many of which are in the IT sector. In 2005, BPO firms were on a buying spree, with Tata Consultancy Services Limited (TCS) leading the way on the acquisition front.

The acquisition deals are likely to help boost the revenues of TCS in transaction processing and call centre services from $45 million in 2005 to more than $200 million in 2007.

Mergers and acquisitions can create certain problems for an organization. One of the problems associated with M&As is the retrenchment of staff that becomes surplus due to rationalization of operations. Managers look at retrenchment as an opportunity to cut cost and increase profit. For example, in the financial services sector, M&A activity between 1996 and 2006 caused an aggregate employment decline. This industry has traditionally been associated with stable and even lifetime employment. Due to M&A, sector experts predicted a loss of more than 300,000 jobs in the banking sector between 1999 and 2002. When negotiations for M&A are on, employees of the concerned firms are subject to several rumours that cause insecurity about the future. Longtime loyal employees learn suddenly that their jobs are on the line. This results in lower morale and productivity. Employees may respond by looking for alternative jobs and voluntarily leaving the firm, or there may be instances of organizational conflict as each individual tries to protect his/her own job. Thus, HRM is faced with several challenges before, during, and after the M&A decision.

Downsizing

Downsizing is the elimination of jobs in a planned manner. These include early retirement and voluntary retirement schemes (VRS). For example, when Gillette India Limited (Gillette) announced its merger with Procter and Gamble India early in 2006, the firm started a restructuring exercise. The new cost-efficient structure and processes are likely to make some employees redundant. Gillette has planned a VRS package for redundant staff. Downsizing is part of the larger goal of a firm to balance its staff to be able to meet changing needs. A more appropriate term would be 'rightsizing', or matching employee needs to organizational requirements.

Even though there is a shortage of skilled labour, firms are going in for layoffs. The percentage of the skilled unemployed has gone up. Earlier, the rule followed by organizations was to hire in good times and fire in bad times. This rule is no longer true for most of the world's organizations. The past decade has seen many firms in most industrialized nations making significant cuts in their overall staff. These include IBM, AT&T, and more recently Ford. Ford, faced with a deepening financial crisis, has announced that it will cut 25,000–30,000 jobs from plant payrolls by 2012. The German-US auto giant DaimlerChrysler also plans to axe up to 6,000 general and administrative jobs by 2008 in order to cut annual costs by 1.5 billion euros. General Motors Corporation (GM) announced in November 2004 that it would cut 30,000 manufacturing jobs. West Virginia, the former Weirton Steel Corp, and since

December 2005 part of Mittal Steel Co., had 13,000 employees in 1986. It had just 1,300 workers left on the job in January 2006. Indian firms too have gone in for a planned reduction of workforce. The Steel Authority of India Limited (SAIL) offered VRS to its employees.

Historically, layoffs have affected manufacturing firms, and line workers in particular. Recently, however, white-collar and managerial employees have also faced layoffs. Vanguard Info Solutions, provider of IT and BPO services with headquarters in US, has undertaken what may be the first rightsizing case in the BPO sector, a sector that is plagued by high employee turnover. Vanguard closed down one of its functions in its Gurgaon operations and asked a number of employees to resign.

Firms downsize to increase profit, to increase flexibility so that it responds to change better, and because more efficient processes need fewer employees, but mainly to increase profit. Technological advances have resulted in higher productivity. Therefore, fewer people can do more work. Maruti Udyog Limited had cut its workforce from 5,000 to 4,000 by 2004 even as production soared. Many firms find it necessary to reduce workforce due to a decline or crisis in the firm, for example, reduced demand for products/services. Ford's intention to slash many jobs and shut down 14 manufacturing sites is directed to cut costs and stem losses in market share. Organizational restructuring has resulted in firms that are less hierarchical, and therefore require fewer employees.

Human resource managers play a very important role during organizational downsizing. A major HR challenge resulting from downsizing is to manage the organizational relationship with the survivors. Downsizing is often accompanied with low morale and commitment among survivors—employees who stay with the firm. This is because employees become anxious about job security when they see their colleagues leaving. Human resource managers need to re-establish morale and motivation following the layoff. To manage issues related to morale, firms are making efforts to retrain employees for new positions when their jobs are eliminated. Outplacement efforts have increased. Firms may provide outplacement services for employees who lose their jobs, or help them with relocation, or provide them personal and family counselling. Companies are using the services of HR consultancy firms to help 'place' executives 'in need of attrition'. While responsible companies in the West have followed 'career transition services', the trend is now picking up with Indian firms and arms of MNCs. In India, the trigger for outplacement has been mergers and acquisitions, rather than recessions, as in the West. Following the merger of two leading fast moving consumer goods (FMCG) companies in early 2006, the merged entity approached an HR consultancy firm for outplacing more than 35% of its existing manpower. Human resource consultancy firms are helping organizations with outplacement or 'career transition management' of their executives. Transitioning employees are helped by consultancy firms to find an alternative job, 'to successfully plan, practically implement, and effectively conclude the job change process'. They are also helped with insights on career fits and counselled on coping with change to make the transition less traumatic. Outplacements, therefore, are used to manage the reputation of the firm as a quality employer.

Table 2.1: Environmental Trends and Human Resource Challenges

S. No.	Environmental Trends	Human Resource Challenges
1.	**Business environment**	
	Globalization and increased competition	▪ Managing a global workforce ▪ Ensuring availability of employees who have the skills for global assignments ▪ Focussing increasingly on employee productivity to ensure competitiveness ▪ Ensuring legal compliance when conducting business abroad
	Mergers and acquisitions	▪ Managing employee insecurity during mergers ▪ Ensuring continued employee productivity ▪ Developing HR initiatives to manage employee morale
	Downsizing	▪ Managing organizational relationship with survivors (employees who stay with the firm) ▪ Managing morale and commitment of survivors ▪ Providing outplacement services or relocation for employees who lose jobs ▪ Providing personal and family counselling to employees who lose their jobs
2.	**Changing nature of work**	
	Industry and occupational shifts	▪ Managing workforce with flexible working patterns ▪ Focussing on competencies during hiring process ▪ Designing incentive-based compensation ▪ Developing proactive employee development programmes
	Technological advancements	▪ Managing a virtual workforce ▪ Managing employee alienation ▪ Developing training modules and conducting programmes to provide employees with required skills ▪ Retraining current employees to manage obsolescence ▪ Providing work–life balance initiatives
	Outsourcing	▪ Managing employee concerns about losing jobs due to outsourcing ▪ Managing employee morale and productivity

Contd

Table 2.1 Contd

S. No.	Environmental Trends	Human Resource Challenges
	Flexible work arrangements	▪ Managing the loss of organizational control over work ▪ Developing programmes for motivating the flexible workforce ▪ Developing ways of ensuring commitment of the flexible workforce to the firm
3.	**Demographic, societal, and workforce trends**	
	Workforce Diversity	
	Workforce composition	▪ Devising customized HR strategies for hiring, retaining, and motivating employees belonging to different generations ▪ Developing lifestyle-driven perks for the new generation employees ▪ Developing work–life balance programmes
	Workforce availability	▪ Ensuring the availability of skilled talent to fulfill organizational needs
	Ageing population and workforce	▪ Finding replacements for retirees ▪ Managing the demand–supply gap for qualified managerial talent due to a large retiring workforce ▪ Developing mentoring programmes to ensure the skills of experienced managers are passed on to new managers ▪ Obsolescence training and retraining of older employees ▪ Managing retirement policies ▪ Conducting programmes to retain experienced employees
	Workforce of educated knowledge workers	▪ Ensuring the continued supply of trained manpower ▪ Training new hires ▪ Partnering with universities and developing academic initiatives to meet projected shortage of skilled manpower ▪ Training employees in computer skills, communication skills, and customer handling skills ▪ Emphasizing re-training and development activities
	Women in workforce	▪ Strategising to attract and retain educated and skilled women workers ▪ Conducting programmes for women who opt for career breaks ▪ Providing facilities such as crèches, flexible working hours, etc.
	Changing family structures	▪ Developing work–life balance programmes

Contd

Table 2.1 Contd

S.No.	Environmental Trends	Human Resource Challenges
	Global workforce	▪ Developing diversity training programmes ▪ Developing HR initiatives directed to workforce diversity ▪ Identifying and training expatriate managers for overseas assignments ▪ Developing equitable pay plans for individuals working in different countries
	Contingent workforce/ workforce flexibility	▪ Developing systems to motivate the temporary workforce and elicit commitment from them ▪ Helping the temporary employees to quickly adapt to the organization to reach their full potential
4.	**Changing nature of employment relationship**	▪ Offering challenging jobs to employees ▪ Managing rewards for enhancing employee performance ▪ Providing opportunities for enhancing skills through training, development, and educational programmes ▪ Developing programmes for employee commitment ▪ Understanding value differences across different employee groups and customizing HR programmes

Changing Nature of Work

Traditionally, the signing of a contract of employment between an individual and a firm suggested that the employee had a job to do. But the way jobs were done was not given importance. Though the contract of employment still exists, it is accompanied with a contract of performance. With the advent of a 'performance culture' in an increasingly competitive global business environment, there is an expectation of performance from individuals, teams, as well as businesses. This has resulted in practices such as performance-related pay, profit-related pay, objective setting, and the intangible of employee commitment. Some of the work-related trends and concomitant HR challenges are discussed here.

Industry and Occupational Shifts

Globally, there has been a shift in the predominance of industry, from manufacturing to services. Industrialization was characterized by mass production, specialized jobs, and structured and formal workplaces. Blue-collar workers performed routine repetitive jobs. Since World War II, there has been a shift from manufacturing jobs to service jobs. This is true of India also with India being the first major developing economy to become services-led, with services outpacing manufacturing and agriculture. Services played a supporting role to production of goods in the decade between 1981 and 1990. Annual industrial growth during 1981–1990 was 6.8% and annual services growth was 5.8%. However, during 1991–2000, the order got reversed; services grew by 7.8% annually against 5.8% for industry (manufacturing). At the end of 2004, India's services-to-GDP (gross domestic product) ratio stood at 51%, which is similar to that of other Asian countries like Pakistan (53%), Sri Lanka (54%), and Bangladesh (51%). The services-to-GDP ratio for high-income countries stood at 71% in the same year. Of late, large overseas investments have been made by the Indian IT sector.

More jobs are being created in the services sector than in the manufacturing sector. Employment in the services sector touched one million at the end of 2004, which is by no means large if compared with a total workforce of 400 million. However, it is projected that the services sector in India will have an employment growth of around 20% per year, which means that jobs will double by 2008 (over 2004), and quadruple in eight years by 2012, to a total of 16 million. Employment in software/BPO is projected to rise from 0.8 million in 2004 to 3.2 million in 2012, according to a NASSCOM-McKinsey report. Further growth is expected in the services sector. The growth in services is fuelled not only by software, but also by high-skill outsourcing in legal services, engineering services, film animation, biotechnology, etc. The present rapid growth of the services sector and its demand for engineers has resulted in a shortage of engineers in the manufacturing sector. Larsen & Toubro Limited (L&T), a heavy industries and infrastructure giant, is finding it difficult to fulfill its demand for engineers since most engineering graduates go to work in the IT sector. According to an estimate, about 3,000 engineers graduate annually from the Indian Institutes of Technology in India, and about 2,400 of these opt for jobs in IT and BPO. Only 5% work in infrastructure.

Manufacturing jobs have decreased. According to the Statistical Outline of India 2001–2002, employment in the manufacturing sector as a percentage of the total employment in the organized sector in India stood at approximately 28% in 1999, while for the services sector it was 58%. A major factor has been 'rising productivity'. While production has been rising in companies, the number of workers has been steadily declining. Use of high-productivity technology and adoption of new organizational techniques, such as just-in-time management, have contributed to increased productivity. Tata Motors Limited produced 129,400 vehicles with 35,000 workers in 1994, but 311,500 vehicles with 21,400 workers in 2004. Similarly, Bajaj Auto Limited (Bajaj) produced 1 million vehicles in the mid-1990s with 24,000 workers while in 2004 it produced 2.4 million vehicles with just 10,500 workers. At Bajaj, production rose from 1.21 million units in 2001 to 1.52 million in 2004, and exports rose by 16%. The workforce reduced from 21,273 in 1997 to 13,819 in 2001 and to 11,531 in 2004. Productivity per worker more than doubled. Output per employee in 1997 was 67.7 vehicles in 1997, which rose to 87.8 in 2001 and was further up in 2004 at 131.5. The story has been repeated at other firms like Maruti.

The manufacturing industry in India, which earlier used protectionist barriers, today welcomes competition. The industry is becoming globally competitive as highly-skilled brain power, which initially boosted the services sector, is spilling into manufacturing through research and development (R&D). Industries like pharmaceuticals and automobiles are using R&D as a key input to develop indigenous technology. Moreover, many newly competitive Indian export-led manufacturing sectors (like auto ancillaries) are also becoming knowledge- and skill-intensive, with new innovations resulting in quality improvement and cost reduction. Indian manufacturing is becoming world class, which is likely to lead to a higher growth rate in the manufacturing sector. In 2004-2005, the manufacturing sector in India grew at 8.9%; it is expected to grow further. Many Indian firms have become lean and thin due to competitive pressure, but the main reason that the manufacturing sector is becoming competitive is the brain power. Manufacturing has also become knowledge-intensive. Thus, even if India becomes a manufacturing-led economy again, there will be continued demand for knowledge workers from both services and manufacturing.

The proportion of manufacturing jobs to total jobs is highest in Japan, at about 20%. In 2001, employment in the manufacturing sector (as a percentage of total employment) was 30% in Japan and 17% in China. The corresponding figures for the US in the year 2002 were 22%. In contrast, services made up about 75% of the total workforce in the US in 2002. Employment in services sector for Japan was 39% in 2001 and 13% for China. Job growth in services is rising. According to the World Investment Report of 2004, total employment in the ITeS sector in India has grown from 106,500 in 2001-2002 to 245500 in 2003–2004. Manpower Inc's Global Employment Outlook Survey during the second quarter of 2005, which takes into account employers' intentions to increase or decrease the number of employees in their workforce, revealed that all seven sectors that were part of the survey had positive hiring intentions during the first quarter of 2006. The most optimistic picture was for the finance, insurance, and retail industries with a net employment outlook (NEO) of 32% for the first quarter of 2006 as against 43% for the fourth quarter of 2005, followed by the services industry (30% for the first quarter of 2006 as against 45% for the fourth quarter of 2005). The NEO is the percentage of employers anticipating increase in total employment minus the percentage of employers expecting decrease in employment. The NEO for the manufacturing sector was 25% for the first quarter of 2006 against 38% for the fourth quarter of 2005.

The changing pattern of industrial employment affects the pattern of different occupational groups. Thus, while there is an overall growth in employment, manual and skilled jobs are decreasing in the knowledge economy. The growth in demand for labour is expected to be concentrated among the higher-skilled occupations, and in particular among professional, managerial, scientific, and technical occupations. The occupational shift, or growth of the service sector, has implications for work arrangements also. The service sector has different requirements from those of the manufacturing sector, especially in a 24-hour work scenario. Occupations, particularly in the service sector, are more likely to offer flexible terms of employment to professional employees, as well as flexible working patterns. The shift from the manufacturing era to the knowledge era has been accompanied by a shift from the 'labour model' to the 'talent model'. The labour model was prevalent in the manufacturing era. However, 'talent' is important for knowledge-based firms today. The adherents of the labour model hired for skills, whereas talent model adherents hire for competencies. Competencies represent a blend of skills, intelligence, attitudes, and behaviour. Human resource strategies are very important for the 'talent model'. Talent would prefer salaries to be linked with performance, incentive-based compensation, and proactive employee development programmes.

Technological Advancements

Technological advancements and the use of computers have permanently altered the way organizations and people work. Twenty years ago no one had heard of, leave alone seen, a cellular phone or a laptop. E-mail, the internet, and computer networks were unheard of. Computer networks have made it possible to store and retrieve vast amounts of data. The use of computers ranges from simple recordkeeping to controlling complex processes. The advanced power of networks and greater bandwidth has also influenced the world of work. The ability to connect to the head office by cell phones or wireless laptops has changed the way business is conducted. Use of the internet to conduct business has resulted in growth of e-business and *virtual organizations*. Virtual organizations are those firms that are connected via computer-mediated relationships. The traditional hierarchical organizations of the past held all assets internally. On the other hand, virtual organizations are increasingly organized as networks, focussing on their core competencies and outsourcing peripheral work to other firms that enables them to expand their scope and adaptability in a dynamic environment. These virtual firms are able to simultaneously increase efficiency, flexibility, and responsiveness. A new generation of *virtual workers* has emerged. A virtual workforce, which operates on-site with clients rather than on-site in the office, is a common reality.

Earlier, the workplace and working hours were clearly specified. This is no longer true for the contemporary workforce. The internet economy, with its 24/7 culture, has put a lot of pressure on people. Many take work home. They log on to their email and the internet at home at night and work for another 2–3 hours. Technology has thus caused work to invade life and ensured that one is always working. Though people always worked long hours, technology has blurred the boundary between work and home and put more work pressure on people. Mobile phones, instant messengers, e-mail, and video conferencing ensure that work is always a click away. People worry that if they do not put in more hours they may not have a job or they may lose out on career growth. Organizations are also asking employees to put in longer hours. The competitive business environment has increased competitive pressures on employees. It is important that firms take initiatives to reduce this compulsion to carry work home.

The intrusion of technology into life has taken another jump with the global distribution of work—services are carried out offshore. Distribution of employees worldwide, as in BPO firms, means that it is no longer possible to walk to the next cabin or floor to get an update on the progress of some project. Globalization of support services, or back-end work, means that both customers and vendors have to adjust to working in each other's time zones. Technology has drastically changed the scope of working hours. A global client base and delivery schedule in different time zones has brought about longer working hours. Long working hours have become integral to the global IT industry. Many employees of global firms are 'on call' 24 hours a day to teleconfer with colleagues in a different time-zone. Whether it is work that is done offshore, near shore, or even outsourced in the same city, there is a flattening or levelling of work hours. Since different people from different locations work on the same project in different time zones, there is a great levelling of work hours. Globalization and outsourcing of services has resulted in most executives working harder than they ever did.

Initiatives by firms towards providing a less stressful environment help employees balance work–life demands and must be offered to enhance employee creativity. To provide an outlet for employees who work very hard in a stressful environment, HR managers in BPO firms are creating a fun-filled environment at work by organizing various social events, like cricket competitions, cultural programmes by employees, etc. Managing a remote workforce presents a number of challenges. One of the challenges is to maintain connectivity among workers. Virtual workforces have become common, and organizations must provide employees with opportunities to be together physically. These opportunities let employees share the corporate culture and reinforce their relationships with others.

The use of advanced technology has also resulted in more jobs that require high skills; more knowledge workers are required. Hence, there is a need for training programmes to provide employees with skills so that they can move into technical and/or service-oriented jobs. Technology has made many existing skills obsolete by creating a need for new skills. This has made it important for firms to re-train their current employees. Technology training has become an important part of all formal training. Firms also need to ensure the supply of tech-savvy people in future. For this, firms need to interact with educational institutions. Two large firms that have developed ties with educational institutes are IBM and Infosys Technologies Limited (Infosys). Thus, technology and its use in the workplace have an impact on the management of human resources.

Outsourcing

Outsourcing is hiring someone outside the company to perform tasks that could be done internally. For example, firms hire advertising firms to handle product promotions, law firms to handle legal issues, and specialized testing agencies to screen potential employees. Outsourcing has resulted from firms' efforts to focus their activities on their core competencies to lower overhead costs, increase organizational flexibility, and access others' expertise. It is a response to increased competition. Several HR concerns emerge with regard to outsourcing. A major one is that employees are likely to lose their jobs when the work is outsourced. This results in lower morale and productivity in the firm. The HR personnel must respond to these challenges by developing appropriate initiatives.

Flexible Work Arrangements

Conventionally, employment is viewed in terms of full-time work. But, full-time employment has seen steady decline over the past few years. A range of optional forms of working has emerged. Part-time work is seen as a way of increasing flexibility in the workforce. More temporary employees are being hired. Firms in seasonal businesses, such as retail stores, prefer temporary employees so that it is possible for them to employ more people when required without increasing their fixed employee cost. Temporary work and flexible work hours provide employees with greater control over their personal lives. This coincides with changing social values. For the older generation nearing retirement, work was a means of sustenance and loyalty to the employer was primary. On the other hand, the younger generation is more materialistic, and looks for a career, rather than just a job. They are more likely to change jobs if their jobs do not satisfy their career aspirations.

India has seen significant growth in the number of temporaries. Insurance, telecom, IT, and ITeS companies currently employ over 50,000 of them. Teamlease, a temping firm providing temporaries to firms, has over 10,000 on its rolls. This growth in the number of workers seeking temporary jobs has been driven by the services sector. However, globally, it is the traditional or light industrial sectors that account for 65–70% of temporaries. Labour laws stand in the way of growth in temping in the manufacturing sector in

India. A modification in labour laws to make them more contemporary will extend the benefits of flexi-staffing to manufacturing companies as well.

Permanent employees are also being offered greater flexibility in their work hours. Organizations are moving away from the typical 9-to-5 eight-hour day to flexible working hours. This trend is more visible in firms with a large population of knowledge workers, such as the software industry. Flexi time is a non-traditional work arrangement in which work hours are flexible. The individual puts in 8 hours but can choose his/her starting and ending times. For example, a mother can go to pick up her child from school at 3 p.m. IBM has had a long tradition of flexible working hours. Under this arrangement, an employee at IBM organizes work according to requirements and can, for instance, arrive at work at 11 in the morning.

Another form of work that has emerged as a result of technological advancements is 'teleworking' or 'distance working'. Teleworking involves work that is completed by an individual away from the employer's premises, such as home-based teleworking. Such employees are said to be telecommuting. In addition to this individualized form of teleworking, another category has emerged, that is, the collective form of teleworking. Collective teleworking involves work completed on non-domestic premises and managed by the employer or third party. This includes call centres. As employees telecommute, work from home, and have flexible work hours, the distinction between work time and family/leisure time is no longer clear. The line between work and non-work time has blurred. More workers complain of personal conflicts and stress.

Though the number of individuals who telecommute is small, this form of employment does provide the employee with flexibility in work. The employer also benefits from reduced office accommodation costs and an increase in productivity. As more women enter the workforce, firms are increasingly offering the option of telecommuting to women employees who may otherwise leave the job due to personal reasons such as relocating after marriage.

Demographic, Societal, and Workforce Trends

The labour market has undergone a transformation in recent years. These have an impact on the labour supply of an organization in terms of its size, as well as its characteristics like gender, age, etc. Changes in the composition of employee age, education, gender, and background throw up significant HR challenges (such as workforce diversity and gender issues at workplace) since these bring about a change in the nature of workforce. The nature of jobs on offer also affects attitudes toward education which, in turn, influence the type of labour supply. For example, a large increase in the demand for management graduates led to MBA courses being much sought after. This has certainly affected the number of people wanting to join the armed forces. The motive for work is also important: is it money to make a living that people seek from work or a meaningful career? Motives are often influenced by social context. A single 25-year-old without any dependents would have different aspirations than a 40-something married employee with children and aged parents to care for. The demographic and workforce trends are discussed below.

Workforce Diversity

The demographic mix in the workplace has become highly diverse. The term 'workforce diversity' refers to the varied personal characteristics that make the workforce heterogeneous, such as gender, race, age, lifestyles, culture, etc. The various aspects of workforce diversity are presented below.

Workforce composition   The 21st century is unique since it is the first time that the workforce is composed of three generations:

- Baby Boomers—Born between 1946 and 1964
- Generation X (Baby Bust or Gen Xers)—Born between 1965 and 1979
- Generation Y (Net Generation, or Millennium generation or Gen Y)— Born in or after 1980

Each generation grew up in a specific context that helped them develop a particular frame of reference. Baby Boomers grew up in an era that experienced the breakdown of the manufacturing economy. They witnessed restructuring, reengineering, and layoffs of white-collar workers. When Gen Xers entered the workforce, the manufacturing model had completely broken down. Each generation also views employment differently. The older generation looked for job security, while the younger generation seeks career enrichment. This shift has also resulted in a shift in the employer–employee relationship, discussed later in this chapter. Just as consumers have become more important, 'employees' have also assumed greater 'power' vis-à-vis the employer. They no longer stay with a firm until retirement. They are open to changing jobs.

The attitude of the young workforce is different from their older counterparts. Younger employees want to be recognized for their contributions. If they believe that they are not valued by their employer, they are likely to change jobs. The older generation, on the other hand, emphasize loyalty to their employer, a value that developed because it did not have the range of employment options available to the contemporary generation. Gen X and Gen Y employees also want their work to be meaningful. They work for a company as long as they feel they are growing, learning, and contributing. The younger generations value their lifestyles, and also seek work–life balance. They are also not ashamed to ask 'What is in it for me?' Many young workers have come to expect various perks and privileges as enticements to work. A lot of these perks are lifestyle-driven, such as childcare services, children's education, services that provide people to run errands like paying bills, picking up dry-cleaning, etc. These perks have come to play an important role in the retention of the best talent.

Another trend is that employees no longer work only to earn money or a living. Salaries, perquisites, and the work environment are not the only factors that motivate employees today. They are equally motivated by the work challenge, their relative position in the organizational hierarchy, and the company's work ethic and culture. They are looking for a fulfilling and satisfying life. They give equal importance to personal lives and look for balancing work and family life. This shift in priorities affects the way in which HR personnel must motivate and manage employees. Since each generation has different attitudes towards work and employment, it is important for HR managers to understand the expectations and aspirations of employees from all generations. Human resource managers must customize strategies for hiring, retaining, and motivating employees belonging to different generations. Thus, HRM has become more complex today.

Workforce availability Demographic trends have an impact on labour supply. A declining birth rate and an increasingly greying population have led to a shortage of skilled labour. Some of the demographic trends are presented in Table 2.2. As is evident from the table, the total fertility rate (births per woman) has declined between the time period 1970–1975 and 2000–2005 for all countries. The percentage of the population below 15 years of age is projected to decline between 2003 and 2015 for most countries, while the percentage above 65 years is projected to increase.

Table 2.2: Demographic Trends

Countries	Total Fertility Rate (Births per Woman)		Population under Age 15 (% of total population)		Population over Age 65 (% of total)		Education Index*
	1970–75	2000–2005	2003	2015	2003	2015	2003
USA	2.0	2.0	21.1	19.7	10.7	14.1	0.97
Japan	2.1	1.3	14.2	13.3	16.0	26.0	0.94
UK	2.0	1.7	18.4	16.4	13.8	18.1	0.99
China	4.9	1.7	22.7	18.5	5.9	9.6	0.84
India	5.4	3.1	32.9	28.0	4.1	6.2	0.61

Source: Human Development Report 2005

* The education index, according to the United Nations Development Programme, measures a country's relative achievement in both adult literacy and combined primary, secondary, and tertiary gross enrolment. First, an index for adult literacy and one for combined gross enrolment are calculated. Then these two indices are combined to create the education index, with two-thirds weight given to adult literacy and one-third weight to combined gross enrolment.

These trends suggest that most countries will experience a decline in the working population in the long term. However, India will have a higher fertility rate compared to other countries and a higher percentage of the population below 15. This means that India is expected to have the largest and the most productive workforce in the world by the year 2030. In 2005, 70% of the population in India was less than 36 years old and the country was home to 20% of the world's population under the age of 24. In 2030, a high percentage of the population in most countries including China will be graying. At that time, India will have one of the most youthful populations, with 38% of the population in the working age group. According to an article in *Businessworld* (9 January 2006), in 2030, India will have about 544 million people aged between 20 and 44 and at the peak of their working careers.

Between 2030 and 2040, India will close in on the peak of her 'demographic dividend', when there is neither too much of an ageing population, nor too much of a child population, but a high supply of labour. The demographic dividend (bonus) stems from a combination of two things: a fall in the birth rate and an increase in the working age population. As the birth rate declines, the growth rate of the working age population rises sharply above that of the overall population growth rate. As the work participation rate, or the share of workers in the total population, rises, the per capita income also rises. (The per capita income is the product of output per worker, and the share of workers in the total population, or the economy's gross output, divided by the total population.) Today, for India, being the second-most populated nation in the world is proving to be an advantage. For instance, the high rate of growth in the BPO sector in the last two years left no choice for companies but to grow. Wipro Spectramind Services Private Limited (Wipro Spectramind, now known as Wipro BPO) had 2,000 employees in 2002; 4,000 in 2003; and 9,500 in early 2004. Convergys, EXL Service India Private Limited, and 24/7 Customer also experienced similar rapid growth. This trend was made possible by the demographic advantage that India has. East Asia saw the benefits of such a demographic dividend in the 1990s. According to economists, the East Asian economic miracle of the 1990s was largely due to the structure of the population pyramid. With the decline in birth rate, the share of people who do not work and depend on incomes of those in the workforce (dependency ratio) falls. However, this demographic bonus is temporary, because when the working population enters old age and ceases to work, the bonus disappears, especially when the birth rate falls rapidly. China's working population will start its decline in 2016, and in 2050, almost 23% of China's population will be over 65, compared to India's 15%.

According to a report on the global demographic projections for supply and distribution of workforce, prepared by Boston Consulting Group (BCG), India will be part of a group of emerging markets that shall have a surplus working population by 2020, and will account for the biggest chunk of surplus labour in the world by 2020. China, the only other country that has as big a population, is expected to suffer a deficit of about 10 million workers. In contrast, India will have a surplus of about 47 million workers. Other countries expected to have a surplus workforce include Mexico, Brazil, Egypt, Turkey, Iraq, Pakistan, Malaysia, and Bangladesh. However, it is possible to squander the potential demographic dividend. There is no guarantee that an individual will find work just by entering the workforce. It is, therefore, important to create jobs. Labour productivity is expected to go up in the networked economy and global integration. This will compensate for some of the negative effects of unemployment on per capita income.

Shortage of Skilled Talent

Even though there is an increase in the working population in India, the total number of job seekers has also risen. Based on the statistics available from employment exchanges, the total number of registered job seekers (both men and women) increased in 2003 over that of 2002. Registered job seekers are not necessarily the unemployed, since those seeking employment include those who are employed and looking for a job change. There has also been a rise in the number of the skilled unemployed in all countries. Figures from the International Labour Organization (ILO) suggest that the number of the skilled unemployed rose the most in the US (78.6%) between 2000 and 2002. The corresponding increase in the UK was 14.67%, 29.8% in Japan, and 2.94% in India. The data also suggested a gender divide among the skilled jobless—more women were unemployed than men. This indicates that there is a huge potential waiting to be tapped.

The world economy in the 1990s was robust. Demand for skilled workers was higher than the supply. By 2001, most developed countries faced economic recession and layoffs. Supply of skilled workers went up. Today, however, there are not only fewer workers, but also fewer workers having the skills that are required. There is a shortage of skilled talent in India too, and it is predicted to intensify during the period between 2004 and 2014. The IT sector foresees a shortfall of nearly 500,000 people by 2010. McKinsey estimates that India will need 73 million factory workers in 2015, one-and-a-half times as much as in 2006. There will be 500,000 retail jobs available, direct and indirect, in 2006. By 2010, airlines will require 2,000 pilots more than there are today. There will be a shortage of 500,000 knowledge workers by 2010. Although half the 1.2 billion population is under 25 and there are 40 million unemployed (*Times of India*, New Delhi, 29 January 2006), very few can be employed; although 3.6 million graduate from college every year, only 0.9 million of these graduates are employable. There are not enough skilled people to fill all the positions available; this is because of the poor education index (see

Table 2.2). If the index continues to be poor, India will continue to be short of skilled workers, and will not be able to capitalize on her demographic dividend. It is a challenge for HR managers to ensure the availability of skilled talent to fulfill the needs of the firm. Many firms are adopting innovative and proactive measures to tackle skill deficit and to create the skills they require. For example, ICICI has tie-ups with 27 educational institutes to get 100,000 trained people by 2011–2013.The bank provides the institutes with banking curricula, test material, multimedia packages, and trainers.

Ageing Population and Ageing Workforce

The world's population is ageing and the number of those older than 65 has increased (see Table 2.2), because of a rise in life expectancy and of improvement in healthcare. There are more elderly, and therefore more dependent on the working population, especially working women. Human resource personnel need to innovate ways (elder care benefits, flexible working hours) to help employees care for their elderly dependents. The data also indicated more elderly job seekers (both male and female) than before. This is probably because more elderly people need to support themselves.

In Germany, Japan, and the US, the workforce has greyed. Most Baby Boomers, who constitute a high percentage of the workforce, are near retirement age. This has raised the number of older workers in the workforce. The increase in ageing workforce has affected the retirement policies of organizations. In theory, the idea of retirement is to ensure that successive generations get sufficient opportunities to join the workforce. The retirement age is linked, roughly, to life expectancy. The age demographics of a country are expected to mirror the retirement age. The retirement age ought to have increased, as life expectancy has increased and the birth rate has declined, but it has stayed largely the same. Many countries are experiencing a rapid decline in the working population as there are fewer young people than jobs vacated by retirees. This is especially true of France, Germany, Spain, and Italy. In the US and Japan also, the workforce of the 'right' age is steadily decreasing. Some countries are now recognizing the HR issues resulting from ageing employees. In 1994, USA scrapped the earlier retirement age of 70 years for university faculty. Australia and New Zealand have also scrapped the mandatory retirement. In India, however, all central government employees retire at 60. Organizations worldwide, including in India, follow different retirement policies—one policy for employees and one for board members. A higher retirement age is fixed for board members. While the retirement age for most employees in many Indian firms is 58–60, for board members it is 70. This is true for most US and Japanese firms also. General Motors Corporation, one of the largest employers in the world, has fixed 65 years as the retirement age for its employees and 70 years for its board members. Board members at

Microsoft Corporation (Microsoft) retire at 75 and at The Walt Disney Company at 72. Many organizations prefer that older and experienced managers run businesses because they want to use these employees' talent and prevent competitors from tapping it. When many employees of a firm retire simultaneously, they take away their valuable expertise. Also, they have to be replaced. However, fewer Gen Xers are available to fill the shoes of the retiring employees. This creates a demand–supply gap. This is because the proportion of Gen Xers is much lower. Hence, when Baby Boomers retire, there will not be enough Gen Xers to replace them. This shortage will encompass most industries. Healthcare, engineering, and IT are examples of types of industries that will face the impact. When employees belonging to the older generation retire, Gen Xers will enter the middle and upper management ranks. Gen Y will enter the lower management levels, resulting in a younger and less experienced workforce. As the numbers of younger staff decline as a proportion of the whole workforce, the importance of retaining advanced and more experienced employees increases.

Such demographic changes and the resulting imbalance in the age distribution of the workforce mean that demand for managerial talent will outstrip supply. Human resource managers must strategize to meet this shortfall. The search for high-quality people has shaken up most organizations. Larsen and Toubro (L&T), India's largest construction and engineering conglomerate, when faced with fast-approaching retirement at senior and top levels, drew up a succession plan that identified the next level of leaders for all positions where current incumbents are reaching retirement age. This plan reaches up to the board, a number of whose members shall retire by 2008. The succession plan will involve internal and lateral movement of employees within L&T.

Older employees have special knowledge and relational skills based on experience and can be an asset for the firm. Younger employees usually have an original outlook, knowledge, and energy. These can be beneficial to senior people. Thus, age diversity encourages the transfer of knowledge and experience between generations. Setting up mentoring programmes where older employees serve as mentors for younger employees helps the firm in ensuring that skills are passed on to new managers. Nestle, for instance, retains retiring salespeople to coach the sales force of its distributors and stockists. Hindustan Lever Limited's 'Project Dronacharya' also follows a similar model. Firms employing older employees have to evolve suitable medical and social support schemes. Older employees pose some unique problems. For example, older employees may not have the skills required when the nature of jobs change due to technological advancements. Organizations need to undertake obsolescence training and retraining of older employees. Exhibit 2.1 presents case examples of HR initiatives for ageing employees in two firms.

Exhibit 2.1

Managing the Challenge of Ageing Workforce: Case Examples

Siemens AS, established in 1898, is one of Norway's leading electro-mechanical companies. It is a subsidiary of the German concern Siemens AG. The company employs about 3,000 people at 26 sites throughout the country, of which one-third are engineers or engineering scientists. Men make up 84% of the workforce. The company became concerned about its ageing workforce towards the end of the 1980s. There was hardly any internal mobility and employees faced stagnation. The company was looking for more mobility and development of employees, especially among managerial staff. In 1987, it implemented a new career system called 'Constructive Management Mobility' or CMM. Under the CMM system, professionals did not need to take administrative responsibility to advance. The CMM system was a training programme that was established following advice from organizational psychologists and employee input. Leaders in the age group of 55-64 enrolled in the programme that consisted of three two-day meetings over a period of eight months. There was a combination of plenary sessions, group work, and individual work. Between the first and second meeting, a four-hour dialogue with an organizational psychologist took place that focussed on individual interests, options, and resources. Between the second and third meetings there was an exchange with the Director of Personnel on other job opportunities in the company. Each programme had 12 to 15 participants who belonged to one of four small groups, called coaching groups, throughout the process. The members of each group are recruited from different divisions of the company. One year after the CMM programme, two-thirds of the participants experienced a major change—they had new tasks or new jobs. Some moved to another division of the company. About 10% found jobs outside the company. Only 3% took early retirement. Participants reported that they took more responsibility for their own development, increased their competence, and became more open to change.

Deutsche Bank AG is a leading international financial services provider with headquarters in Germany. The bank developed a 'global diversity strategy' and set up a team to support its implementation to ensure that its employees could work successfully anywhere in the world. The global diversity strategy anticipates the type of employees the organization will need to grow in the manner planned. It encourages cooperation between employees who differ in, for example, age, gender, culture, etc. The bank believes that the diversity approach fosters an inclusive work environment, in which all employees contribute their full potential, and in which teams of people from different backgrounds work to maximize performance. Part of the global diversity strategy is to promote cooperation between generations in teams and projects. Deutsche Bank AG also participates in a European initiative to improve working conditions for the elderly. The ageing workforce and an anticipated lack of experience among the younger generation in the future raise the intrinsic value of older staff, making 'age management' essential. In Germany early retirement used to be a practice. But early retirement is not only costly in financial terms, but also in terms of the loss of experience needed to strengthen the bank's planned continuity and growth. Deutsche Bank AG talks about an 'advanced or experienced professional', not 'an older employee'. The reason is that an age label is discriminatory. Moreover, the value of a particular employee lies in their knowledge and

Contd

Exhibit 2.1 Contd

experience, usually related to age. It is not sufficient to focus only on the sustained productivity and work satisfaction of experienced professionals. The bank wants a culture where advanced and more experienced employees are appreciated, and where all ages work together and learn from each other. Some of the age diversity initiatives of Deutsche Bank AG are:

- Employability Initiatives—These provide employees the opportunity to take the initiative to improve their own employability. They can ask for the training that they feel they need, such as skills training or a language course.
- Experience Sharing Model—Project teams use the personal knowledge and experience of an older employee. The advanced professional mentors the younger employees.
- Intergenerational Team Model—This promotes the cooperation between young and experienced employees within one project team. Both generations learn from each other by taking turns at being teacher and learner.
- Knowhow Tandem Model—Knowhow tandems are typically of two employees, one young and one experienced, working together. Both teach and learn, with the emphasis on the younger learning from the experienced.
- X% Job—An activity specific to the ageing workforce, this is about building up knowledge and experience in fields outside of one's function within a defined time frame.
- Special Training—Special training to older employees to handle needs such as healthcare, and a balance between private life and work.

The key results of the approach are a more efficient and motivated workforce, the preservation and transfer of knowledge, and a culture of learning spreading throughout the company enabling inter-generational and life-long learning.

Adapted from: http://www.emcc.eurofound.eu.int/content/source/eu0409a.html, accessed on 23 January 2006, and http://ww.emcc.eurofound.eu.int/content/source/eu04014a.html, accessed on 22 January 2006

An Educated Knowledge Workforce

The 1970s brought in the age of information. Technological advancements transformed society from a manufacturing society to a service society. More jobs were created in low-skilled services (fast food, call centres) and in high-skilled knowledge and technical work. Knowledge workers are those individuals (engineers, software programmers, technologists) who perform jobs that need the acquisition and application of information.

With the growth of the knowledge economy, employers have become more demanding and look for a more educated workforce to add value to their work. The adult literacy rate has improved globally. In China 86.5% of women and 95.1% of men who are 15 or older are literate; in India 47.8% of women and 73.4% of men are literate, according to the 2005 Human Development Report. However, despite the increase in the population of the educated workforce, there are skill deficiencies in the workplace. A recent NASSCOM-McKinsey report stated that India will need a 2.3 million strong IT and BPO workforce by 2010 if it seeks to maintain the market share it commanded in 2005. The software and BPO industries are expected to generate over 1.6 million additional direct jobs and another 5 million indirect or induced jobs between 2004 and 2009, for which there will be a shortfall of 500,000 qualified employees by 2010. IBM estimates that approximately 250,000 IT students graduate every year; the demand is for over 400,000. In December 2005, only 25% of technical graduates and 10–15% of general college graduates were suitable for employment in the offshore IT and BPO industries, respectively.

The retail, aviation, hospitality, and automobile industries are faced with a severe resource crunch at senior management positions. The retail sector is expected to grow at 15.6% and is likely to create over 2 million direct jobs by 2010. Its biggest challenge is the lack of a skilled and trained workforce, particularly in middle and senior management.

Clearly, there is no shortage of workforce in India, but that of a trained workforce. Raman Roy of Wipro Spectramind admitted that hiring had become tougher with many firms trying to tap into an increasingly limited talent pool. Customers demand higher quality and better value. It is therefore important for HR to train new hires extensively. Firms are partnering with colleges and universities to educate students better so that there is a pool of fresh skilled graduates to hire from. IBM invested Rs 66 million during 2004-2005 for its university programmes and academic initiatives to reach out to over 75,000 students across 300 institutes. Oracle and Microsoft also have such initiatives.

In addition to increased demand for high-skilled jobs, there is also a demand for more skills within jobs. The skills required for an average worker have increased, resulting in a gap between skills required and the skills on offer. Employees at all levels need computer, communication, and customer handling skills. Therefore, HR has to emphasize training, re-training, and development activities. As there is a more educated workforce, the knowledge worker has become more demanding. Higher education has led them to demand greater autonomy at work along with what they expect from employment (social status, career, and self-esteem).

Developing countries such as India and China are also faced with the problem of skill-based immigration. Developed countries have large ageing populations, and require workers from countries with growing economies. This means that growing economies will become a source of trained manpower for the developed world. A look at the premier engineering colleges of India, the IITs, confirm this trend. Forty per cent of IIT graduates move abroad every year.

Women in Workforce

More women are entering the workforce today than they did earlier. In the US, women professionals and technical workers comprise 55% of the total workforce. The figure for the UK was 45% and for Japan 46%. This high level of female participation in the labour market is due to several reasons, such as later marriage, increased return to work after childbirth, higher education among women, and increased availability of part-time work.

Labour market data show that a sharp gender divide has developed in the working-age group since 1998. Women applicants in all age groups increased during 1998–2002. The number of men between 20 and 40 seeking jobs decreased, while in the other age groups it increased. Among women, higher the age group, higher was the percentage increase in job applicants. Women constitute 24% of the software industry workforce. The National Association of Software and Service Companies (NASSCOM) expects this figure to go up to 35% by 2007. However, the overall percentage of women employees as part of the total employee strength of companies is still very small. At the Kinetic Group of Companies (Kinetic), women comprise just 7.5% of the total employees. At LG India (LG), women make up only 5.6% of the workforce. However, there is a larger corresponding percentage of women in the HR divisions of these firms: 50% at Kinetic and 20% at LG. According to a Confederation of Indian Industry (CII) study of 149 companies in India, although 16% of junior managers were women, only 4% of senior managers and 1% of CEOs were women. About 14% of companies had policies excluding women from manufacturing, production, shop floor, sales, marketing, and top positions.

Many women professionals are mothers; losing them would mean losing many skilled employees. This has challenged HR to develop strategies to attract and retain educated and skilled women workers. It is also important to develop initiatives to ensure that women return to work after childbirth, since the maximum attrition among women employees happens at this stage. The extent to which firms are able to attract and retain women employees is likely to be influenced by the firms' ability to provide family-friendly practices and facilities such as crèches, training for returners and career breakers (women who return to jobs after a gap due to factors such as taking care of young children). Sony, P&G, IBM, and H-P are some of the firms with family-friendly practices.

Changing Family Structures

There has been a change in the family composition—the number of nuclear families has increased. There is also an emerging pattern of late marriages, single working women, and dual-career couples. It is important for firms to recognize these changes to family structures since it implies changing characteristics of the workforce and the domestic circumstances of the employees. There is no single pattern on which HR practices can be based. Human resource managers must understand what the people living in these situations think about work and what they want from it. Several working women may forgo promotions or career moves due to family reasons; women employees coming from a nuclear family are likely to take a break from work when they have children.

With more dual-career families, couples find it difficult to have the time to fulfill diverse commitments—home, spouse, children, friends, and ageing parents. Often there is no one to take care of children or old parents. Thus, many employees are seeking a balance between personal life and work. Because of changes in the forms of family (dual-career couples, nuclear families), companies consider it necessary to provide employees with family-friendly options, such as part-time work and day care. Some of the most progressive companies, such as IBM and Hewlett-Packard (HP), promote flexibility. throughout their organizations. Arthur Andersen has a flexible work programme that allows new parents to lighten their workloads for up to three years. Firms that fail to help employees achieve work–life balance are likely to find it difficult to attract and retain a motivated workforce. Balancing work and family is an issue affecting the management of HR. Work–life balance programmes help firms increase productivity, reduce absenteeism, and retain valued workers.

Global Workforce

Globalizing businesses have globalized staffing that bring with it cultural diversity in the workforce. Managers are moving across borders to work for subsidiaries of parent firms. This has led to a breed of 'global managers'. India's premier consumer goods company, Hindustan Lever Limited (HLL), shook off half a century of heritage by appointing an expatriate as its CEO. A number of subsidiaries of MNCs and Indian companies in sectors as diverse as IT, aviation, banking, consumer goods and durables are hiring expatriates for top jobs. At the same time, Indian managers are finding big opportunities overseas. There is a global talent pool. Increasingly, leading Indian firms, such as Wipro, Indian Hotels Company Limited, Ranbaxy, the Aditya Birla Group, and L&T, are expanding overseas and transforming themselves into global corporations. Having worked in protected markets for long, these firms do not quite have the exposure or the large talent pool to execute their global agenda and therefore need a CEO who has experience in managing global operations. Globalization has resulted in several countries experiencing a society that embraces people from different countries. Thus, multiculturalism is an issue related to diversity. In India, there are cultural differences across regions and states. Today, there is greater movement of people across the country.

As the workforce increasingly becomes multicultural, firms need to embrace the diversity of their employees and offer opportunities for everyone to learn each other's backgrounds. Firms have to accept and recognize that people come to organizations with different values, needs, and expectations. Workforce diversity requires HR managers to recognize and respond to individual differences to retain and motivate employees. Firms must develop diversity training programmes to help employees overcome their biases in their interaction with people from different backgrounds. As organizations become more diverse, they have been developing workforce diversity programmes. Examples are Motorola and The Coca–Cola Company.

Several HR issues have emerged, such as identifying expatriate managers who work overseas, designing expatriate training programmes to enhance managers' understanding of foreign cultures, and adjusting compensation plans to ensure that pay levels are equitable for individuals working in different countries with different costs of living.

Contingent Workforce and Workforce Flexibility

DeCenzo and Robbins (2005) defined the term 'contingent workforce' as 'the part-time, temporary, and contract staffing used by organizations to fulfill staffing needs or perform work not done by core employees'. Core employees are a firm's full-time permanent employees. Having too many permanent full-time employees limits the ability of organizations to react and adjust to a changing environment. For example, when there is a sudden economic downturn resulting in decreased revenues, the firm may have to reduce staff. The process of reducing workforce by laying off permanent full-time employees is extremely complex and painful. One way firms have discovered to reduce employee costs and increase their flexibility is by converting many jobs into temporary or part-time work. This has resulted in the growth of a contingent workforce. Firms that rely on a contingent workforce have more flexibility, since these workers can be easily added or taken off. Temporary workers can be found in secretarial, accounting, computer programming, marketing, and even senior management positions. Executives in senior management positions who are in their 40s are looking to develop new competencies and to confront new challenges These executives prefer to take a break from regular employment and opt to be an interim manager or 'executive temp'. There are firms, especially in the software sector, who are hiring even temporary CEOs. A CEO may be hired for a specific project of six months. These senior executives find these short-term contractual jobs challenging since they have specific deadlines that allow them to show results.

A contingent workforce raises several issues for HR management. Contingent workers may not feel the same loyalty and commitment to the firm as permanent workers. Human resource managers have to develop systems to motivate both groups. Temporary employees also need to be helped to adapt quickly to the organization to realise their full potential.

Changing Nature of Employment Relationship

Changes in the economic and social environments within which firms operate have brought about fundamental changes in the nature of the employment relationship in the twenty-first century. Increasing globalization and competitive markets led employers to resort to headcount management to gain flexibility, remain competitive, and ensure survival, as discussed earlier. Corporate downsizing across all industries and hierarchical levels led to a breakdown of the traditional employer–employee relationship that was characterized by mutual loyalty and lifelong employment. A new employment relationship has emerged today. The new relationship has shifted away from the long-term relationship involving loyalty to an economic contract between the employer and employee.

The nature of employment relationship has important implications for HR practices. Therefore, it is important for HR managers to understand these changes. Today, the employer offers the employee a challenging job, individual reward for performance, and opportunities to learn valuable skills, but less job security. The employee pays back the employer through job performance but does not promise a strong commitment to the organization. Different employee groups require and value different things in an employment relationship. For examples, those at different career and life stages, employees from different countries, cultures, and backgrounds, core employees and peripheral employees, will have different priorities and values.

There is a reciprocal relationship between a firm's business environment and its social environment that affects the nature of the employment relationship. For example, with more women in the workforce, and especially in BPO jobs, the issue of the security of women employees has assumed importance. This has resulted in a move toward developing safety norms in call centres for women who have to work in shifts.

One important contributor to the new employment relationship is the employer's responsibility to provide training, education, and skill development opportunities and the employees' responsibility to take advantage of those opportunities to develop and utilize their skills. The new relationship is also characterized by a desire for flexibility by both employer and employee. Organizations faced with increasing competition and rapid technological changes seek greater flexibility, which may be reflected in the number of contractual or part-time employees. Employees desire flexibility to be able to address work and non-work needs and interests.

The new employment relationship has made employee commitment more important and central, because employers want to be assured that empowered employees use their autonomy and discretion to further the interest of the organization. A highly-skilled employee lacking commitment will be of little value to the organization. Today, employers need new and different approaches to developing and maintaining employee commitment.

Tsui and Wu (2005) report that organizational performance is best when organizations adopt a 'mutual investment' employment relationship. The goal of a mutual investment approach is to obtain higher commitment from employees. The approach induces employees to make significant contributions. The employees are expected to contribute to their organization overall instead of focussing only on performing their own jobs. The firm on its part focusses on developing a long-term relationship with its employees, through practices such as extensive training, profit-sharing, and promotion from within. This relationship recognizes and meets the needs of both employer and employee. It also acknowledges that employee satisfaction goes beyond payment of wages and includes social as well as economic needs. Hence, mutuality leads to a psychological contract or commitment.

In the traditional employment relationship, job security, career advancement within the firm, and pay increases were used to build employee commitment. Several characteristics of the new employment relationship are linked to employee commitment, such as two-way communication, participative decision-making, respectful and fair treatment, intrinsically rewarding work, accommodating employees' desires for work–life balance, and providing employees meaningful and challenging work. These approaches for generating employee commitment require sustained effort on the part of HR managers. Human resource managers will be challenged to consider the mutual investment employment relationship as a competitive tool and design HR practices to realize competitive advantages.

The successful management of the new employment relationship will require HR professionals to take on new roles, such as strategic partner, change agent, and employee champion. The new employment relationship has increased the importance of managers' soft skills. The HR managers also will face the challenge of developing technical and interpersonal skills. The changing role of the HR function and the HR professional is discussed next. The specific focus is on the emerging role of HR in managing the knowledge worker.

HRM IN KNOWLEDGE ECONOMY

It is believed that in the present era, the competitive advantage of organizations is linked to knowledge. There is a lot of emphasis upon knowledge work, knowledge workers, and the nature of knowledge within organizations. Therefore, there is an increased focus on management of the knowledge resource in organizations. The interest in the relationship between knowledge management and HRM has increased. Thinking about HRM invariably brings to mind terms such as hiring, firing, promotions, and training. This is, at best, a bureaucratic perspective that views HRM as a set of discrete practices organized around a set of specific functions. Although this narrow HRM perspective worked well for organizations during the industrial era, it appears too limited in the knowledge economy. If the HRM function has to add value, it must respond to changes brought about by the shift from a traditional economy to a knowledge-based economy.

In the twenty-first century, the HRM function has a key role to play in shaping the competitive position of the organization. To compete effectively in the knowledge economy, a firm must have what Ulrich calls 'organizational capabilities'. Organizational capabilities are a necessary but not sufficient condition for organizational success. Human resource management plays an important role in creating, developing, and managing the organizational capabilities that are necessary for competing successfully in the knowledge economy. Human resource managers have to create effective teams within a diverse workforce; tap talent throughout the organization by recruiting, retaining, and developing people at all levels; build and integrate cultures as mergers and acquisitions become common; and develop employee commitment toward organizational vision. Human resource management is confronted with major challenges in the knowledge economy (see Exhibit 2.2).

Exhibit 2.2

Challenges Facing HRM in the Knowledge Economy

The challenges facing HRM in the knowledge economy are

- Attracting and retaining knowledge workers, who are the intellectual capital of the firm
- Obtaining commitment from workers in the context of a changed employer–employee contract
- Ensuring the availability, development, and utilization of human capital to enhance its value
- Motivating knowledge workers
- Ensuring maximum utilization of temporary or contingent employees

- Encouraging employees to commit to continuous learning
- Facilitating sharing of knowledge within organizations
- Facilitating work–life balance
- Rewarding knowledge acquisition and knowledge sharing
- Enhancing cross-functional teamwork and team identification
- Creating a flexible human resource management team that sets and supports the agenda for change
- Co-ordinating between organizational functions

Adapted from: Lengnick-Hall and Lengnick-Hall 2003

Thus, HRM is no longer simply focussed on 'managing people' or confined to traditional HR functions such as recruitment, training and development, and performance management, etc. Rather, HRM is now responsible for managing the capabilities within the organization. Hindustan Lever Limited places a lot of emphasis on continuous training of employees, both internal and external, to develop employee capabilities and help them realize their potential. The firm also has knowledge management workshops that strongly support capability building in the areas of knowledge creation and knowledge sharing. At HLL, development and sharing of knowledge is incorporated as one of the key competencies to be monitored and developed. Though the traditional HRM functions continue to be performed, HRM has had to adapt to new roles to address the new challenges of the knowledge economy. The new roles release HRM from the traditional functional constraints and allow it to contribute to organizational success and performance. In order to respond to the demands of the knowledge economy, a revitalization of HRM function is required that necessitates major changes in the key roles of the HR manager.

Lengnick-Hall and Lengnick-Hall identified four HR roles that help create organizational capabilities for managing the HRM challenges of the knowledge economy: human capital steward, knowledge facilitator, relationship builder, and rapid deployment specialist (see Figure 2.2). The *Human Capital Steward* recognizes the value of intellectual capital and ensures the availability, conservation, and retention of the collective knowledge, skills, and abilities (KSAs) within a firm so that it grows in value. The HR specialist creates an environment that develops competencies and commitment among employees, builds a reservoir of talent among employees, and makes the best people want to

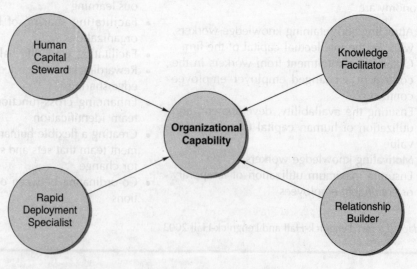

Figure 2.2:   Four HRM Roles in the Knowledge Economy

stay. The *Knowledge Facilitator* facilitates management of knowledge and learning and development and creates an environment conducive to the sharing and dissemination of knowledge between employees and departments throughout the organization and also among customers and suppliers. The *Relationship Builder* develops partnerships and networks among employees within and across functions in the organization. The *Rapid Deployment Specialist* develops the capability of the firm to respond quickly to a turbulent environment by ensuring rapid deployment of human capital to achieve specific strategic goals. The HR manager may train, develop potential, and plan succession to achieve this goal.

The knowledge economy demands that HRM should develop and deploy human capital and manage knowledge to develop the core competencies of the firm that distinguish it from its competitors. The emphasis needs to be on long-term strategic planning. It also needs to be translated into short-term strategic plans that will help determine HR demands; HR needs to be continuously renewed and developed. Human resource management should develop new relationships that emphasize the shared responsibility among managers, employees, customers, and suppliers of the firm. There is also a need for constant learning and the new role of HRM should place emphasis on openness to change and readiness to adapt within the firm.

HRM: A Changing Function

Environmental changes had put pressure on the HRM function to justify its existence. Though the HRM function and personnel continue to be in a transitional phase, dramatic changes have taken place in the past two decades. High uncertainty in the environment has been a major reason for the increasing influence of the HR function on business strategy over the years. Human resource management is placed at the centre of business strategy today. Two major changes that have occurred in HR function are in the roles associated with HRM and the partnership of HR managers and line managers (see Figure 2.3).

Roles Associated with Management of HR

The HR function today is seen as composed of two roles: an *administrative* role and a high-level *strategic* role. In its *administrative* role, the HR function performs the traditional administrative tasks associated with the day-to-day management of people within organizations. Though the administrative part of the HR function is one aspect of contemporary HR, it is clearly insufficient for the diverse challenges faced by HR, such as motivation of a highly skilled workforce or linking HRM to the needs and aspirations of the workforce. The HR function also has the critically important strategic role of supporting line management in achieving organizational goals. The *strategic* role of the HR

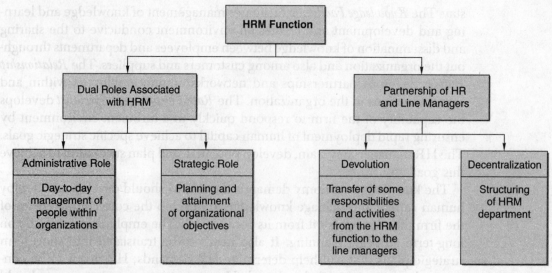

Figure 2.3: Changes in HRM Function

function has increased in importance since the 1990s. The strategic focus of HRM is concerned with the planning and attainment of organizational objectives. Key business plans are considered in the light of their HR implications. In the traditional model of HR personnel as business partners, HR was called only to implement business decisions. In the new model, HR professionals are there during the decision-making process and the development of the implementation plan. Thus, today the HR manager is a strategic business partner with clearly defined responsibilities and accountabilities. Human resource managers need to understand business goals and make their arguments in terms of these goals, rather than push people issues for their own sake. This transformation is reflected in the change in designations and the hierarchical position of HR personnel. Firms have HR personnel at the corporate level as part of the strategic planning team. The designations range from director (HR) and vice president (HR) to executive head (HR). Thus, as observed earlier, HRM is an expanded function and both the administrative and the strategic roles are necessary and must exist together.

Partnership of HR and Line Managers

Human resource activities are no longer seen to be the sole responsibility of HR managers. In the knowledge economy, line managers play an important role in the formation as well as implementation of HR practices. As HRM work expands, responsibility for HR is increasingly shared among HR managers and line managers. For example, without the participation of line managers, an employee involvement programme cannot succeed in a firm. Similarly, though firms spend huge amounts on employee training and development, the best developments take place on-the-job through coaching by a senior and more experienced manager. There is both devolution and decentralization of the HR function. *Devolution* involves transferring some of the responsibilities and activities from the HR personnel function to the line managers. The belief is that reduction in overheads and de-layering can be achieved by pushing more responsibility to line managers. However, though some activities like recruitment and selection are being devolved to the line, some other areas such as salaries and fringe benefits are not released. Devolution sometimes produces a decentralizing effect, or, on the other hand, it may be a response to business decentralization. *Decentralization* refers to how the HR department is structured. When the firm is organized around strategic business units, each business unit has its own HR staff. These HR personnel report to the head of the business unit rather than to the head of the central HR department at corporate headquarters. Line managers must play a strategic role in formulating HR strategies. People concerns and task issues have to be integrated, and not seen as separate domains. Line managers and HR managers must jointly own all aspects of the business. Therefore, there are many HR skills that line managers must have. Thus, line managers are taking over HRM roles. By corollary, the roles of HR managers are changing rapidly. Human resource managers have moved from being 'deliverers of services' to 'deliverers of HR competencies'. Given the complexities of organizational life, it is important for HR managers to keep growing. One way to achieve this is for HR people to coach line managers to develop HR competencies. When this happens, a useful partnership develops between line managers and HR managers.

In the twenty-first century, the roles of the HR professional go even beyond the dual administrative and strategic business partner roles and include the roles of champion of change, advocate of employee issues, administrative expert, operational role, partner in strategy execution, and service provider. These roles are described in Table 2.3.

Table 2.3:   Multiple Roles of the HR Manager in the Twenty-first Century

S. No.	Roles of HR Managers	Description
1.	Administrative Expert	Once only an administrator, the HR manager has assumed a new role, that of an administrative expert. In making this role transition, HR personnel need to improve the efficiency of their own function as well as that of the entire organization. Various HR processes, such as screening resumes, in-house surveys, etc. can be performed faster, better, and cheaper. The HR manager must also find ways of improving processes throughout the firm to make them more

Contd

Table 2.3 Contd

S. No.	Roles of HR Managers	Description
		efficient, such as a system that allows departments to share administrative services and avoid duplication. The new HR manager must identify the processes that can be improved, improve the quality of HR work, and lower costs. One way of doing this is by leveraging technology.
2.	**Operational Role**	In their operational role, HR managers work in cooperation with operational (line) managers to identify and implement HR practices needed in the firm. However, in this role, HR managers may not be involved in strategic decision-making in the organization. This role includes the traditional activities of the HR function and also goes beyond these since it involves coordinating HR activities with actions of line managers in the organization.
3.	**Employee Champion**	As the old employment contract gives way to the new contract, employee relationship with the organization becomes transactional. They give their time to the firm but are not emotionally attached. In their employee champion role, HR managers must ■ ensure full employee commitment and contribution to the organization ■ train line managers about the importance of high employee morale and how to achieve it ■ be the 'voice' for employee concerns and advocate their rights
4.	**Partner in Business Strategy**	In the new 'knowledge-based' economy, companies face the double challenge of the need for more highly-trained employees and that of meeting a shortage of qualified workers. It is important for HR managers to become strategic HR planners. In their strategic role, HR managers must ■ focus on the strategic implications of HR issues. For example, HR managers must understand how a shortage of skilled manpower will affect the ability of the organization to achieve its plans, and develop plans for addressing these shortages over time ■ help in running the business as a member of the senior management team by contributing to strategy, setting goals, choosing ways to accomplish the goals, and measuring results ■ conduct an organizational audit to identify areas of improvement or change and to facilitate implementation of strategy. HR initiatives need to have a business/bottom-line rationale The activities that form part of the strategic HR role include ■ developing activities that contribute to superior organizational performance, and therefore, the strategic success of the firm

Contd

Table 2.3 Contd

S. No.	Roles of HR Managers	Description
		<ul><li>participating in organizational strategic planning rather than merely implementing strategic decisions</li><li>participating in discussions with top management on decisions relating to mergers and acquisitions. Human resource managers focus on various human resource issues associated with these business decisions such as combining organizational cultures, lay-offs, and pay parity</li><li>modifying and changing organizational structure and the division of work in the firm to complement and facilitate the achievement of strategic plans</li><li>demonstrating that HR activities contribute to the financial results and therefore the performance of the firm</li><li>defining, setting, tracking, and measuring specific and measurable goals, and holding HR accountable for results</li></ul>
5.	**Change Agent**	The pace of change has increased manifold and business success depends on the firm's ability to respond to the pace of change. In their role of change agent, HR professionals have the responsibility<ul><li>to build the organization's capacity to accept and capitalize on change. For example, HR must ensure that a change effort focused on implementing new technology gets delivered in time</li><li>to make sure that vision statements get translated into specific behaviours by helping employees understand what behaviour is required to realize the vision of the organization</li><li>to facilitate culture change in the organization</li></ul>
6.	**Customer Orientation**	There is an increase in the 'customer responsiveness' and 'service orientation' in the HR function. A service/customer orientation has brought about important changes in the way HR professionals think about their roles in the organization. Human resource professionals are encouraged to determine the needs of internal customers, develop strategies to satisfy those needs, and evaluate the extent to which internal customers' needs are satisfied. From the perspective of the HR function, internal customers include employees, line managers, and staff. Embracing the customer orientation perspective of the HR function shifts the focus of HR from practices and activities to outcomes. For example, instead of focussing on performance appraisal formats and processes, the focus of the HR function will shift to determining how performance appraisal can be used to add to organizational capabilities

Adapted from: Mathis and Jackson 2003; Mello 2003

For the firm to be successful, Wilhelm (1990) suggested that the HRM professional should

- help line managers understand and manage planned change,
- help design compensation systems and differential reward systems,
- help design and implement skill-development processes for employees at all levels, and
- help ensure that sufficient core human capabilities critical to the firm's long-term success are always available.

Since firms are faced with unique challenges, HR professionals also require new and unique HR competencies to be successful in the new knowledge economy. Ulrich et al identified the future HR competencies that are expected to be most important. These are knowledge of the business, delivery of HR practices, and managing change.

It is evident that virtually every business issue has HR implications. But that is not enough. The HR personnel need to demonstrate that the HR function adds value and provides the firm a high return on investment. The HR personnel must measure what they do. They need to measure productivity, culture change, and performance quality. Measurement and evaluation of HR activities will be discussed in the next chapter. A development related to cost competitiveness is outsourcing of HR activities.

HR Outsourcing

In the twenty-first century, there has been a change in how the HR function is being structured in order to help firms compete. A new trend has emerged in the HR function. Just as firms are outsourcing some of their 'non-core' processes as part of a movement towards cost saving, some HR activities are also being outsourced. Greer (2002) defined *outsourcing* as the permanent contracting out of activities that were previously performed in-house. Organizational surveys, reward programmes, headhunting, testing, and employee selection are some of the HR activities that are outsourced. Outsourcing of HR activities made its appearance in the late 1980s in firms that were reorganizing for cost-cutting due to recession. The trend has gained momentum globally, as also in India. Human resource activities are outsourced to

- reduce overheads, gain value for money, and establish the HR function as an independent profit centre. However, if the reason for outsourcing is to reduce cost, the view that HR activities are a cost rather than an investment, and therefore should be eliminated, is supported. The movement from being a cost centre to a profit centre is the first step towards HR outsourcing. When the HR function becomes a profit centre, it assumes the role of a service provider, but for a 'fee'. The line managers are the 'customers' of HR and the employees are the 'consumers'. The idea that HRM could function as a business, both internally and externally, has gained credence. Training departments of several firms function as independent profit centres. These departments organize training programmes for the employees of the organization and also sell courses to other organizations in order to utilize spare capacity.

- focus on certain skills and competencies and outsource the others. Many skills and competencies are needed to perform HRM activities. Therefore, it may be better to concentrate on developing some of these skills and competencies and contract out the others. For example, a firm may outsource selection testing services, and focus on issues such as performance appraisal. Similarly, certain specialized HR skills that are rarely needed may also be outsourced. For instance, if a firm wishes to undertake a major job evaluation exercise for the first time in ten years, it is more cost-effective to outsource the initial work. The in-house HR people may not have the skills for the activity. Moreover, recruiting job evaluation experts may also not be a good idea since they would not have any work after the exercise is over.
- react better to external environmental factors, such as the labour market situation, which also affect the outsourcing decision. When labour supply is high, any recruitment effort may generate large number of applicants. This will require much processing. Therefore, it would be prudent for the firm to use the services of a recruitment consultancy.
- participate in economic reshaping. One rationale for outsourcing is economic reshaping. In-house activities are moving out to independent suppliers. The same thing is happening in HRM.

Outsourcing of HR activities is a form of virtual HR that is becoming very prevalent in organizations. Lepak and Snell (1998) defined *virtual HR* as a network-based structure built on partnerships and typically mediated by information technologies to help the organization acquire, develop, and deploy intellectual capital. Several factors have contributed to an increased reliance on outsourcing, partnerships, and other forms of network-based structural arrangements in HR. In general, emergence of virtual HR may be attributed to the increasing demands being placed on the HR department as organizations continue to strive to attain competitive advantage. Specifically, HR departments are expected to be strategic, flexible, efficient, and customer-oriented.

The need for HR to be a 'strategic business partner' has already been emphasized earlier in the chapter. As part of the strategic role, the HR function also needs to bring flexibility to its programmes, practices, and services. Strategic fit in HR suggests that HR must be able to adapt to change, and must work with senior management in organizational change management. The HR function is also expected to consider cost containment as a priority.

Human resource managers have to prioritize where they can most efficiently utilize their time, talents, and resources and where they can cut costs. Cost restrictions also bring increased accountability to HR. Finally, the HR function is expected to continue to be a service provider to managers and employees. The responsibility for maintaining employee relations will continue to be the foundation of HR.

Achievement of these multiple objectives is a tall order for HR managers, and one that has contributed to the growth of virtual HR, just like the simultaneous need for increasing efficiency, flexibility, and responsiveness of firms in a dynamic environment contributed to the emergence of virtual organizations. Virtual HR may be seen as a parallel transformation to the growth of virtual organizations. Executives in the HR function are challenged to rethink ways of organizing it to make it more flexible, while at the same time, providing the complete range of HR services. In order to meet their strategic objectives, many HR functions are becoming more virtual in nature. The HR function is increasingly relying on external sources to perform some, if not all, of the HR activities of an organization.

The use of external sources or outsourcing helps meet several objectives. Though HR outsourcing and other forms of virtual arrangements have a number of benefits, there are potential downsides also. The benefits and pitfalls of HR outsourcing are presented in Table 2.4.

It has been of considerable research and practical interest to determine which components of a firm's HR 'architecture' should be managed internally and which should be outsourced. A number of options have been advanced about which HR activities may be outsourced. However, two dimensions, that is, value and uniqueness, have been stated to serve as the criteria for determining which HR activities should or should not be externalized. These two dimensions are discussed below.

Value of HR activities

Any resource of the firm, such as, skill, knowledge, or task, is said to have value when it helps a firm enact strategies that result in enhanced efficiency and effectiveness (Barney 1991). Thus, the value of an HR activity depends on the extent to which the activity helps a firm achieve a competitive advantage or develop core competencies. Those HR activities that are not valuable, that is, the activities that do not contribute to the core competencies of the firm, are the ones that are outsourced. Activities that are valuable are retained internally. The value of HR activities is defined as 'the strategic benefits derived from a particular HR activity relative to costs associated with its deployment'. Benefits may refer to the extent to which an HR activity contributes to the customers' perception of the effectiveness of the HR function. As the benefit to the customer increases, the value of HR activities increases as well. For

Table 2.4: Benefits and Pitfalls of HR Outsourcing

Benefits	Pitfalls
■ Outsourcing helps to meet the demands of efficiency and strategic support. It can help an organization reduce costs by externalizing routine, administrative tasks that do not directly contribute to the competitive success of the firm. The HR department can focus only on those activities that create value. ■ Outsourcing allows managers to allocate resources on just-in-time basis. Certain HR services are needed infrequently or for only a short time. A firm may turn to external specialists to provide these HR services when needed instead of investing resources to establish and maintain in-house capability. ■ Certain specialized HR services that the organization cannot perform internally may be provided by external vendors who perform these services better and more efficiently.	■ Outsourcing decisions are too often driven by cost considerations rather than broader strategic considerations. The focus of managers in purchasing skills or services from an outside source tends to have a short-term focus that may sometimes backfire. When outsourcing is not managed well or is poorly monitored, the cost of outsourcing actually increases. ■ When specific HR functions are externalized there is a significant possibility that the firm loses operating control over these functions. ■ When there is continued reliance on external sources by a firm, the HR function's ability to execute activities critical to competitiveness may actually be eroded. Thus, if outsourcing is pushed too far or poorly managed, the HR function may actually decrease its ability to support the firm's strategic objectives and also limit its flexibility.

Adapted from: Lepak and Snell 1998

example, though extensive internal training may facilitate the creation of a highly talented workforce, it requires much time and money. These costs may diminish the value resulting from training. The extent to which different HRM activities, such as performance appraisal, recruitment, training, and compensation are valuable varies from one organization to another as they depend on the strategic context of each firm.

Uniqueness of HR activities

Uniqueness refers to rarity or scarcity in the external market. For example, Pepsi's fast track career growth orientation programme for new recruits is well known and is considered unique. It is more efficient for firms to internalize those HR activities that are idiosyncratic to the firm. For HR activities that are unique, relying upon an external arrangement may lead to higher cost for the firm since these activities may not be readily available in the open market. By contrast, those HR activities that are generic or standardized across firms may not justify the costs of their internal deployment. Externalization may be appropriate for these HR activities since external vendors may provide these services more efficiently.

These two dimensions, that is, value and uniqueness, may be seen as existing on two different continuums. Human resource activities may range from those that are directly instrumental in achieving organizational objectives (high value) to those that are primarily administrative in nature (low value). They may also range from those that are routine (low uniqueness) to those that are idiosyncratic to the firm (high uniqueness). By combining these two dimensions of value and uniqueness, it is possible to understand how virtual HR can be structured to achieve the four objectives of enhanced efficiency, flexibility, strategic focus, and customer responsiveness. Particular combinations of value and uniqueness determine the different types of HR activities within a firm. Whether a firm will outsource an activity or deploy it internally will depend on the type of HR activity. Table 2.5 presents the types of HR activities, whether they are internally or externally deployed, and the rationale for the decision of outsourcing.

Table 2.5: Types of HR Activities and Decisions about Internal/External Deployment

Location on the Two Dimensions of Value and Uniqueness	Type of HR Activities	Internal Deployment versus External Deployment or Outsourcing	Rationale and Benefits
High value, high uniqueness	Core HR activities	Internal deployment	▪ May not be available in the external market ▪ Firms have a strategic interest to retain and internally deploy these valuable activities ▪ Helps the firm achieve competitive advantage
High value, low uniqueness	Traditional HR activities	Outsourced to external vendors	▪ Generic activities are spread throughout industry, and are fairly standardized ▪ Though valuable, their development and use do not require significant internal investments by the firm ▪ By retaining external vendors for these standardized HR activities, the firm significantly saves on developmental expenditure ▪ The firm gets instant access to a wide variety of capabilities of external specialists

Contd

Table 2.5 Contd

Location on the Two Dimensions of Value and Uniqueness	Type of HR Activities	Internal Deployment versus External Deployment or Outsourcing	Rationale and Benefits
Low value, low uniqueness	Peripheral HR activities	Outsourced to external vendors	■ Generic activities, but with low value, such as routine, administrative tasks (e.g., payroll, benefits, or pension administration) ■ Do not require any firm-specific customization. These are codified in industry standards ■ Contributes little, if at all, to the competitiveness of the firm ■ Outsourcing reduces overhead costs by accessing capabilities of external specialists who can perform these activities more efficiently
Low value, high uniqueness	Idiosyncratic HR activities	Ongoing partnerships between the firm and external consultants	■ Though unique, these HR activities are not directly instrumental in creating value ■ Limited or infrequent strategic value, such as personnel research by industrial psychologists for customizing reports to help strategic decisions of the firm ■ Partnerships help the firm meet its unique requirements without drawing resources from other functions ■ Partnership allows the firm to capitalize on an external party's specialized knowledge without incurring the costs of internal deployment ■ Compared to short-term contractual arrangements, ongoing partnerships allow the firm and the external party to work together over time to co-design and execute HR activities that meet the unique needs of the firm

Adapted from: Lepak and Snell 1998

There is, however, no one way of classifying HR activities as core, traditional, peripheral, or idiosyncratic. Each organization and its managers must determine which activities will be classified into which quadrant. There is no general rule about classification of HR activities. The following general principles hold true in understanding the classification of HR activities into one of the four types of HR activities:

- An activity that is core in one firm may be peripheral in another firm. For example, recruitment and selection may be core in some firms, while compensation and benefits may be peripheral, and compensation may be traditional. In other firms, compensation and performance appraisal may be core activities.
- A firm may decide to outsource an entire HR sub-function, that is, internally handle all activities related to a particular HR activity, such as staffing. At the same time, the firm may outsource all the aspects related to compensation, and partner with external vendors to develop and conduct training programmes.
- Some firms may handle only some aspects of a particular HR sub-function internally while outsourcing other aspects. For example, within the compensation sub-function, a firm may maintain control over final compensation decisions, but may outsource payroll administration and the benefits programme. The firm may simultaneously partner with external consultants for conducting wage surveys and job evaluations.

Thus, there is no ideal prescription for outsourcing or retaining HR activities. Each organization needs to decide for itself on the basis of the value and uniqueness of a particular HR activity. One factor of HR outsourcing is the use of information technology (IT). The next section discusses the increasing significance of technology in organizations, the impact of technology on the HRM function, and its usefulness in virtual organizations.

Technology and HRM

Technology has had a huge impact on our lives. Cellular telephones and wireless technology have changed our lives. Technology has also revolutionized the world of work. Today, virtually all office and professional workers use technology, whether by virtue of the telephone, fax, computer, internet, or e-mail. Technological advancements at the workplace require people to learn to use technology. A firm is likely to be more efficient and productive as the interaction between people and technology increases. This relationship enhances the value of the human capital of the firm. It is important for firms to invest in technology and human capital simultaneously to improve productivity. Many firms introduce technology to the workplace without training workers adequately. This is a mistake. For example, when the activities of nationalized banks were computerized without training employees to use computers, bottlenecks developed, decreasing productivity and making employees feel insecure. Whenever new technology such as a new computer system or a software upgrade is adopted by a firm, it is important that employees are trained and given access to a help desk to deal with questions that may arise. Firms should adopt technology only if it makes the business more productive and the workers more efficient.

Technology has also changed the way HR managers work and the manner in which the HRM function is structured (see an example in Exhibit 2.3). The new HR function must identify the processes that can be improved and take actions to improve the quality of HR work and lower costs. One way of doing this is by leveraging technology. Technology has changed the manner in which administrative functions of HR are performed. In most contemporary firms HR functions are available electronically or on the internet or an intranet. This form of availability may be called e-HR. For example, vacancies may be posted and applications and self-appraisal forms may be submitted on the intranet or the internet. E-HR has improved the administrative efficiency and responsiveness of HR to employees. It started with the automation of basic HR transactions, but the impact of technology on HR goes far beyond automating clerical activities. For example, an intranet helps internal communication, and enables the conduction of online employee satisfaction surveys. Some of the changes that result in HR due to technological trends are described below.

- Use of data warehouses enables fast and cheap access to accurate real-time HR information. Access and the ability to analyze, assess, interpret, and share information effectively are key to a competitive edge.
- Instant and remote access to data, information, and knowledge enable working from anywhere and at any time. This improves employee efficiency and effectiveness.
- Use of analytics and decision trees help managers analyse options and make better decisions.

The use of technology by the HR function has resulted in the need for fewer staff. However, they add more value to their organizations. The HR department of ICICI Bank is an example. It serves 26,000 employees and interviews 100,000 job applicants annually but employs 95 people only. If it were not for technology, the department would have been thrown out of gear by logistics, or probably required many more people. By automating most processes and integrating them into a central HR management system, the HR department can run not only with fewer people but also more efficiently. At the organizational level, the use of technology for HR delivery results in

Exhibit 2.3

Worldwide Implementation of @HP Employee Portal in a Subsidiary of Hewlett-Packard

Human resource portals are complex IT applications that place information and application forms online so that all employees can access them. These portals reduce employees' reliance on HR personnel. The Web has permitted HRM to implement HR processes where business-to-employee (B2E) solutions are possible. When more administrative tasks are available on HR portals, HR professionals have more time for strategic HR activities. There are many tools that HR portals offer, such as employee communications (who is who, what's new, FAQs), pension schemes, benefit enquiries, etc. Administrative activities such as the updating of an employee's personal data (such as change of address), are the responsibility of employees themselves. Through HR portals, managers are able to generate reports (headcount, salary listings), examine employee activities (transfers, promotions, retirements), and manage their own activities (travel arrangements, expense management).

Although the technical installation of an HR portal has several benefits, the associated human challenges should not be overlooked during the implementation phase. Users must become accustomed to establishing a new kind of relationship with HR personnel and accept interacting with a computer rather than with a person. These challenges of IT acceptance and organizational change management can be very daunting, especially if not managed effectively. Introduction of an HR portal, which replaces personal face-to-face interactions with computer-based information, may make some employees uncomfortable.

The Italian subsidiary of Hewlett-Packard (HP)

introduced the @HP Employee Portal in January 2000. The primary purpose was to simplify the relationship between the HR function and internal clients (the employees of HP served by the function). The @HP Employee Portal was designed to increase the ease and speed of access to internal communications and corporate information in an attempt to increase management effectiveness and the production capacity of HP employees. Employees can interact directly with the company. Information on the @HP Employee Portal is standardized and global. Local concerns are addressed by using multilingual formats. HP introduced the portal to reduce HR and IT operating costs while simultaneously maintaining high-quality and up-to-date services and content. Ultimately, HP's aim was to increase integration among diverse businesses and to benefit from cost reduction, increased efficiency, and overall HR effectiveness. Before the @HP Employee Portal was introduced, the HR function provided basic administrative services. The portal was built to have HR add value in its typical functions, such as recruiting, compensation and benefits, training, etc. The declared objective was to create an HR department that would become a strategic partner in managing company change and professional growth for all employees. The @HP Employee Portal would improve HP's HR effectiveness and increase employee satisfaction with the HR department. The interface of the portal is divided into four folders (as on March 2001): home, life/work, organization, and my@HP. Each folder contains specific information and enables the completion of transactions (see Table 2.6). Thus, the portal is interactive.

Contd

Exhibit 2.3 Contd

Table 2.6: The @HP Employee Portal Folders

Home	Life/Work	Organization	My@ Portal
• General corporate news • Popular links to HR, finance, etc. • The current status of the portal • Contact information of HP colleagues (e-mail addresses, telephone numbers)	This section is password protected. It contains personal employee data and transactions (change banking information, register for a training programme, job posting, candidacy, etc.) This is where employees can interact directly with HP	Contains information from various divisions of HP and the domestic branch intranet. Business news and press releases are also posted	This is the most personalized section and is password protected. Each employee can create his/her own portal, adding those functions they use most, as well as other information that is specific to their jobs. This contains various corporate applications and is in constant evolution. Some of the the applications are • internal communications: HP corporate guidelines and procedures • personnel database: performance evaluation, salary planning • employee self service: personal data, training and salary history, staffing candidacy • e-learning courses and registration, online classes • e-procurement: travel reservations, net meetings, electronic reporting, press release archive, corporate strategy information, best practices

Adapted from: Ruta 2005

several benefits: swift and simultaneous communication with a large number of employees, faster turnaround times, and a support tool for employees that lets them seek and receive information that is accurate and available round the clock. By taking away routine functions, technology allows HR personnel to focus on issues that require human intervention. Today, e-HR is a key element in the transformation of the HR department into a strategic business partner. Now firms are implementing and leveraging their HR systems at all stages of the employee life-cycle, from recruitment to compensation and rewards to managing exits. PepsiCo India (Pepsi), for example, has a global human resource management system (HRMS) portal. All employees can log on to the portal to manage their profiles, and set development goals for the future. At Infosys, appraisals are done online. Companies like Infosys are utilizing the vast amount of data generated through their automated systems to understand patterns like workforce utilization levels and to track employee attrition rates, the people they are losing, and the places they are losing them.

Technological changes bring about uncertainty in today's business environment. Virtual HR outsourcing may be viewed as a special case of organizations' attempts to cope with uncertainty. Virtual organizations have altered the organizational structure by collaborating with specialists external to the organization. The growth of HR consultants and HR service firms has provided structural alternatives for a firm's HR function that were not available earlier. Now, the HR function of a firm can establish partnerships with specialists outside the firm. As the HR function becomes differentiated externally, it is important for HR departments to innovate for coordinating dispersed activities. Traditionally firms have relied upon managers, task committees, etc. to coordinate various specialized sub-units or activities. Now, IT provides HR with a much more powerful mechanism to coordinate externalized HR relationships. Snell, Pedigo, and Krawiec (1995) suggested that IT affects integration and coordination within HR in its operational aspects, its relational aspects, and its transformational role (see Figure 2.4).

Operational Aspects of HR

Information technology can help streamline HR operations, reduce much of its administrative burden, reduce cost, improve productivity by automating routine tasks and practices, and enable firms connect with external vendors when HR activities are outsourced.

Relational Aspects of HR

Information technology increases the timeliness and service levels with employees and managers as well as external partners. By making HR functions available online, and providing employees and managers with remote

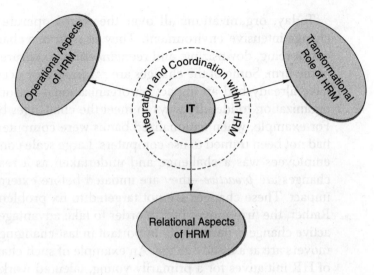

Figure 2.4: Three Ways in which IT affects HRM

access to HR databases and information, it is possible to enable employees perform HR activities themselves. This reduces response time and improves service levels.

Transformational Role of HR

Information technology plays a major role in supporting virtual teams and network organizations by enabling people to share information and communicate across geographical boundaries. It has thus eliminated barriers of time and space.

Thus, IT has emerged as an invaluable tool for coordinating and integrating widely dispersed HR activities that also extend beyond the boundaries of the firm. The HR function and the HR professional must assume leadership to bring about the transformation of the firm in this extraordinary shift of the economy from the industrial era to the knowledge era. The HR function has to be an agent of change and adaptation. The next section discusses the role that HRM has in managing major organizational changes.

HRM and Change

Change is inevitable in all walks of life. The pace and scope of change has increased substantially. Globalization and technology have been two major forces that have brought about change in organizations as well as in HRM. Strategic organizational decisions such as mergers, acquisitions, technological advancement, organizational restructuring, redeployment, etc. have become a way of life and are accompanied by change.

Today, organizations all over the world operate in a hyper-turbulent change-intensive environment. They use various change processes, such as outsourcing, downsizing, and reengineering, to ensure the continued success of the firm. Some of the changes are *reactive*—they occur when various forces have already had an impact on organizational performance. This leads the organization to identify ways to meet the challenges brought by the change. For example, when nationalized banks were computerized, bank employees had not been trained to use computers. Large scale computer training of bank employees was a challenge and undertaken as a reactive measure. Other changes are *proactive*—they are initiated before external forces have had an impact. These changes are not targeted to fix problems in the organization. Rather, the firm moves first in order to take advantage of opportunities. Proactive change is particularly important in fast-changing industries where slow movers are at a disadvantage. An example of such change is the introduction of HR initiatives for a primarily young, talented workforce at NIIT Limited (NIIT). These initiatives helped NIIT attract and retain talent that was in short supply. It is important for firms to develop their capability for managing change and transformation to attain a sustainable competitive advantage.

According to Webster's Dictionary, a transformation is 'a change in the shape, structure, nature of something'. Organizational transformation may involve changes in the structure, culture, and processes of the organization. It may be limited to a change in the way in which particular parts of the organization function. On the other hand, change may be aimed at making an impact on the whole organization. Change may also be incremental, transactional, or transformational. *Incremental change* takes place bit by bit, that is, one step at a time. *Transactional change* merely alters the way in which an organization does business and in which people interact with one another daily. It is effective only when the firm wants more of what already exists. An example is that of an organization that reinforces an already participatory culture. *Transformational change* brings about a discontinuous improvement in the capabilities of the firm. It may include introduction of new technology, decentralization, and change in culture, norms or values of the organization. In managing transformational change, it is important to develop strategies for managing the transition from where the organization is to where it wants to be.

According to Armstrong, strategies for organizational transformation are concerned with the planning, development, and implementation of programmes that will ensure that the organization responds strategically to new demands, and that it continues to function effectively in the dynamic environment in which it operates. To manage organizational transformation, a manager needs to

- define the future state, or where the organization wants to be;
- diagnose the present state, or where the organization is today;

- define the new processes, systems, procedures etc. that need to be developed to move from the present state to the future state; and
- strategize a plan for transformation.

Employees should be involved in the process. The manager should communicate what is happening, and how it will affect them. Communication ensures the commitment of employees to the change.

Role of HR in Managing Organizational Change and Transformation

Change management depends on the acceptance, participation, and commitment of all employees in the change process. All managers, including HR managers, have an important role in facilitating the process of change. Management of change in an organization requires that managers develop a future vision; communicate the vision to employees; set clear expectations of performance; and develop organizational capabilities by reorganizing people and reallocating assets.

It is important that the HR function is a partner in an exercise to transform an organization. The HR manager has to be a change agent and a strategic business partner. A major strategic role of a successful HR manager is to develop and implement strategies to change and transform the organization (see Exhibit 2.4). Human resource managers can contribute to managing organizational transformation in their role as change agents by

- analysing and diagnosing the present state of the organization;
- communicating business needs and objectives to employees to ensure that employees welcome change;
- highlighting the people issues or implications that will affect the success of the organizational transformation strategy, such as lowered employee morale due to job insecurity during organizational restructuring;
- planning and implementing the important aspects of the transformation process, such as training, reward, communication, and other HR practices;
- hiring, developing, and retaining people who can deal with change;
- anticipating people problems, such as downsizing humanely and with minimum disruption to people's lives;
- managing employee resistance to change as well as the concerns of employees resulting from proposed changes;
- encouraging organization-wide participation in managing change efforts; and
- creating and supporting a culture that can assist the organization to survive in an uncertain and rapidly changing environment.

Exhibit 2.4

Mergers—Role of the HRM Function in Managing Organizational Change

There has been a marked increase in merger activity since the mid-1990s. Mergers take place to increase shareholder value, dominate or penetrate new markets, develop new products and services, and defend the organization against a takeover. The rationale for the merger affects how the merger is managed. The reason for the merger affects whether the organization's strategy includes a reduction in headcount, relocation, or other such HR issues which have a direct impact on employees. The critical issue seems to be not so much whether there are job losses but how these processes are carried out. When senior managers of the acquired company lose their jobs following a merger, employees may feel uncertain and vulnerable. Open and honest communication is very important in maintaining employee commitment.

Mergers and acquisitions set off waves of change within the concerned firms. Mergers need to be managed. Unless managed, business performance can go down due to employee uncertainty. The role of the HR manager is very crucial during mergers. Mergers have three phases: the run-up or pre-merger phase; the immediate transition (the first 100 days or 6 months); and the integration, or the long-term coming together of the two merging entities.

The run-up period should be used to carry out an effective HR assessment and develop an understanding of the likely challenges and pressure points. It is essential to explain to employees the business reasons for the merger, and also to understand the differences in cultures of the two firms, as well as their ways of working. Employees should be allowed to grieve the losses brought about by the merger as well as celebrate the opportunities. The pace of change is extremely fierce during the transition phase. Anxiety is highest at this time, since the first job losses are announced then. The rumour mills are most active and employees are uncertain about their positions and jobs. Pay and working conditions can become major issues and must be dealt with early in the transition period. Typically, most firms abandon all communication during this time and cause employees much uncertainty. It is important to manage the integration as a critical project alongside business. Some companies focus on people issues right from the start. These firms have specialists for handling the merger process. However, even when handled professionally, mergers can backfire. For example, this happens when the people whose jobs are made redundant and who receive generous pay-offs, go straight to a rival company, taking their expertise and competitor knowledge with them.

Communication is extremely important throughout the process, particularly during the pre-merger phase. HR must work alongside or as part of management teams ensuring that formal communication is effective and that communication is both bottom-up and top-down. Gaining emotional and intellectual buy-in from employees is also very important. Employees should be told why the merger is happening, its rationale, whether it is a merger or a takeover, etc. Rumours should be managed to prevent their disruptive effect. Typically, mergers are both mechanical/structural and psychological/cultural. All the aspects of a merger need managing. The fear of the unknown is a major contributor to employee uncertainty during mergers. The HR function should address this uncertainty. It should consider the psychological impact on employees of these changes and answer employee concerns. Though there is no rule about which issue should be addressed first, it is important to communicate the broad structure of the merger process, along with the HR and management

Contd

Exhibit 2.4 Contd

actions performed at each stage, to reassure employees.

Contributions of HR during Merger:

1. Involvement in planning, transition, and integration teams during the merger process
2. Identifying HR issues such as comparing terms and conditions of employment and salary scales in the two firms, incentive and bonus schemes, understanding organizational structure, identifying likely levels of redundancies, and identifying which job descriptions will need to be changed
3. Carrying out effective HR integration on remuneration, benefits, terms and conditions, culture and management style, employee relations, etc.
4. Ensuring that line managers have the necessary skills (personal, strategic management, change management, and cultural) they need to manage the merger
5. Helping line managers to communicate effectively during the transition phase
6. Managing individuals with dignity. For example, handling of key changes for individuals such as job changes, relocations, or exits determines how employees view the new organization
7. Developing and implementing HR initiatives to retain key employees. This may be done by using financial incentives or even by just letting them know that they are valued and by utilizing their talent in significant ways
8. Keeping the top management in touch with the bottom by building a bottom-up feedback mechanism so that senior managers understand people's perceptions as well as expectations
9. Helping employees to clarify their roles, that is, where they fit in the organization and how to be successful in the new firm

Reconstructed from: Holbeche 2002

Two major reasons why change or planned strategy of the firm may not achieve its goal are a lack of commitment on the part of employees and the way in which the organizational culture operates.

Introduction of change is accompanied with resistance and, hence, lack of commitment to change. Human resource managers have a major role to play in overcoming employee resistance to change. Organizational change seems threatening to employees when the change is imposed top-down. For example, when there is a decision to acquire another company or to sell off part of the organization, employees feel that they have no control over what is likely to happen. This is when employees may perceive change negatively and resist it. Most change programmes in an organization—whether mergers or acquisitions—are introduced to increase its business benefits. But if the change affects employees negatively, for example, if a merger leads to job insecurity among employees, then change can actually lead to a downturn in profits, at least in the immediate future. This was evident in the recent merger of operations between two airlines (Jet Airways and Sahara Airlines Limited). Sahara pilots went on mass sick leave on 12 February 2006 disrupting flight schedules across the country. They alleged that management had not been transparent about the merger plan and its implications on the career of senior professionals. Many senior pilots grudged that they were getting a raw deal following the merger, which they believe will result in many of them losing out on their seniority. They also apprehend lower pay after the merger.

The HR functions of the merging companies may manage and overcome employee resistance by

- helping employees understand the need for change by sharing information about the business strategy;
- involving people in the change process, for example, in gathering data and solving problems; and
- helping people to benefit from change, for example, through new development opportunities and re-aligned reward systems.

Communication plays a major role in managing change and employee resistance. Communication can be used to manage relationships, build trust and commitment, and create buy-in to new ways of operating. Human resource personnel play a major role in managing communication within the organization. According to Devine (1999), formal communication during organizational change should aim to

- inform—about the organizational/personal implications of change;
- clarify—the reason for change, the strategy and benefits;
- provide direction—about the emerging vision, values, and desired behaviour;
- focus—on immediate work priorities and actions, together with medium-term goals; and
- reassure—that the organization will treat them with respect and dignity.

Role of HRM in Managing Culture Change

As mentioned in the last section, one of the reasons that an organizational change programme may fail to achieve its objectives is the culture of the firm. The biggest challenge for strategic HRM is to build the type of culture that will facilitate the objectives of the organization (see Figure 2.5 for the role of HRM in culture change). This culture is one that is characterized by a positive work climate, adaptable work practices, and flexible, skilled, and committed people. Change in organizational culture may be a part of the transformation programme. Management of organizational culture focusses on developing shared values and gaining commitment to them. These values encompass the behaviour that the management believes is appropriate and important to the functioning of the organization. For example, the approach to culture management adopted by HP is based on a statement of values called 'The HP Way'. This value focusses on 'belief in people, confidence, and respect

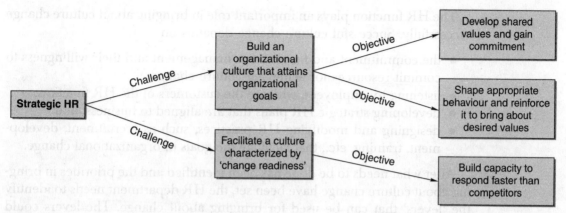

Figure 2.5:   Role of HRM in Culture Change

for people'. The two critical issues of 'managing organizational performance through business planning' and 'the HP way' are related and determine the success and performance of HP. Employees experience the culture as very open, supportive, and with a team ethic. Thus, managing culture in HP may focus on strategies that translate these values into action. However, not all firms have such a deeply embedded culture. These organizations therefore do not focus on development of shared values directly. Rather, these focus on shaping and reinforcing appropriate behaviour to bring about the desired values. It follows that strategies for culture management should first analyse which behaviours are appropriate. Organizational processes such as performance management that will encourage the development of those behaviours should be introduced. For example, if it is important that employees function as effective team members, then team performance management processes should be introduced and behaviour contributing to good team work should be rewarded by financial or non-financial means. Culture management involves changing the culture in specific ways (culture change) or reinforcing the existing culture of an organization (culture reinforcement).

Culture change strategies are concerned with how the culture of an organization can be transformed from the present state to a future desired state. Culture change strategy involves an analysis of the present culture and the extent to which it facilitates organizational goal achievement, the identification of areas where change is desirable, the specification of the nature and objectives of change, and the development and implementation of plans for change.

Culture reinforcement strategies are also based on an analysis of the existing culture and the way in which it supports the achievement of organizational goals. To the extent that culture is seen as supportive of organizational goals, initiatives are developed and implemented to ensure the continued maintenance of the desirable feature of the culture.

The HR function plays an important role in bringing about culture change successfully. Successful culture change depends on

- the commitment and focus of top management and their willingness to commit resources for achieving culture change;
- listening to employees, who are the customers of the HR function;
- developing strategic HR plans that are aligned to business; and
- designing and modifying HR practices, such as recruitment, development, training, etc., that facilitate the goals of organizational change.

After what needs to be done has been identified and the priorities in bringing about culture change have been set, the HR department needs to identify the 'levers' that can be used for bringing about change. The levers could include

- performance—performance-linked pay, performance management processes, leadership training;
- commitment—participation and involvement programmes, the development of a climate of trust and openness;
- customer service—customer care programmes;
- teamwork—team building, team rewards, team performance management; and
- training—attitude training, managing resistance to change.

Firms that are successful in a change-intensive environment have developed cultures that are 'change-ready', that is, 'they have the capacity to respond faster than their competitors' (Kossek and Block 2000). Employees of these organizations accept and embrace change, and passionately and relentlessly participate in bringing about the desired change. Wal-Mart is an example of a change-conscious organization. According to its founder Sam Walton, his company was able to successfully vanquish the competition because it was better at making changes. Intel Corporation, Microsoft, and HP are other companies that appreciate the need to institutionalize receptivity to change. An important impact of a change-intensive environment is the increasing importance of intellectual capital when compared to physical capital. Developing and managing human intellect and skills is an important concern for managers in successful firms. The role of the HR function, therefore, has increased in significance in the dynamic environment. The HR function has the responsibility to facilitate a culture characterized by 'change readiness'. The challenge to create an adaptive organizational culture has resulted because the ability to adapt to external change is considered the single most important organizational capability for the future.

Summary

The shift from the machine age to the information age has been accompanied by several changes in the economic, business, and socio-cultural environments. Changes such as globalization, increased competition, industry and occupational shifts, technological advancements, global and diverse workforce, flexible work arrangements, contractual employment, etc. all have uniquely challenged HRM in the twenty-first century. The chapter discussed the environmental trends that have brought about a transformation in the HR function and the roles of HR professionals. The challenges facing HRM in the knowledge economy were highlighted. It was emphasized that HRM has had to adopt new roles to address the challenges of the knowledge economy. The chapter discussed the multiple roles of HR managers in the twenty-first century and emphasized that the responsibility for HRM is shared jointly between HR managers and line managers.

The trend towards HR outsourcing, reasons for outsourcing of HR activities, benefits and pitfalls of HR outsourcing, as well as the criteria for determining which HR activities should or should not be outsourced, were examined. The impact that technological advancements have had on the way HR function is structured and the way HR managers work was also discussed. Finally, the significance of HRM in managing organizational change and transformations was highlighted. The chapter ended by suggesting that the HR function has an important role in facilitating an organizational culture characterized by change-readiness.

Keywords

Collective Teleworking is the act of work completed on non-domestic premises and managed by the employer or third party. This includes call centres.

Contingent Workforce are part-time, temporary, and contract workers who fulfill staffing needs of organizations or perform work not done by core employees.

Core Employees are the full-time permanent employees of a firm.

Demographic Dividend refers to a condition in which there is neither too much of an ageing population nor too much of a child population; rather, there is a high supply of labour, that is, the working age population.

Devolution of the HRM Function is the transference of some of the personnel activities and responsibilities from the HRM function to the line managers.

Downsizing is the elimination of jobs in a planned manner through practices such as early retirement, voluntary retirement schemes (VRS), sabbaticals for continuing education, etc.

Individualized Teleworking, also called 'distance working' or 'telecommuting', is the act of work done by an individual away from the employer's premises.

Knowledge Workers are individuals who perform jobs that are designed around the acquisition and application of information (such as engineers, software programmers, technologists, etc.)

Organizational Capabilities are necessary but not sufficient conditions for organizational success.

Outsourcing is the permanent contracting of organizations' activities that were previously performed in-house to focus on the core competencies of the firm, lower overhead costs, increase organizational flexibility, and access others' expertise.

Value of HR Activity is the strategic benefit derived from a particular HR activity relative to costs associated with its deployment; it depends on the extent to which the activity helps the firm achieve a competitive advantage or develop core competencies.

Virtual HR is the outsourcing of HR activities by organizations to cope with business uncertainties.

Virtual Organizations are firms that are connected via computer-mediated relationships. These firms are organized as networks that focus on their core competencies and outsource peripheral work to other firms. Outsourcing enables them to expand their scope and adaptability in a dynamic environment.

Virtual Workforce is the workforce that operates on-site with clients rather than on-site in the office.

Workforce Diversity refers to heterogeneity of the workforce, such as differences in gender, race, age, lifestyles, culture, etc.

Concept Review Questions

1. Identify the major trends in the business environment and explain how these trends have influenced HRM practices.

2. What are the most important demographic, societal, and workforce trends affecting HRM today?

3. What factors have led to a growth in the contingent workforce? What unique challenges does the management of contingent workforce pose for HRM? Give examples from industry.

4. Why is it important for the HR manager to be a strategic business partner? What other roles are HR managers expected to play in the knowledge economy?

5. Describe the impact of technology on the world of work. Has technology changed HRM? If it has, in what way?

6. What is 'virtual HR'? What are the benefits and pitfalls of HR outsourcing? What are the criteria that firms can use for determining which HR activities should or should not be outsourced?

7. Why is it important to manage organizational change? In what specific ways can HR managers contribute to managing organizational change and transformation? Do you agree with the premise that HRM has an important role to play in influencing or changing organizational culture? Support your answer with examples.

Critical Thinking Questions

1. Discuss the factors that have led to changes in the nature of employment relationship in the contemporary business environment. Identify the major differences between the traditional employer-employee relationship and the new employer–employee relationship. What strategies can be used by HR managers for generating employee commitment to the firm in the new employment relationship? Give examples of organizations you know of that are using some of these strategies.

2. Examine the causes and problems of mergers among firms. What role do HR managers have in managing mergers? Name two organizations that have merged with another firm in the recent past. Discuss the reasons for the merger. What HR challenges did these firms confront as a result of mergers? Were these firms successful in managing these challenges? Do you think there were better ways of approaching these issues? Describe them.

Simulation and Role Play

1. Mr Diwakar, the general manager (HR) of a leading automobile organization, is of the firm opinion that the HR function should use technology in its operations. He is convinced that technology will help the function become more efficient as well as add value to the

organization. Despite his requests on several occasions earlier, the executive director (plant operations) and the vice president (finance) have remained unmoved. This is the new financial year and each department is making projections for fund allocations. Mr Diwakar has once again submitted the budget for the HR department incorporating investment on technology in his projected budget. He has been summoned by Mr Kapahi, executive director (plant), and Mr Dadoo, vice president (finance). Mr Diwakar is determined to get the sanction for 'technology in HRM'.

Three students volunteer for the role play, each student taking on the role of the three major characters in the above situation. Mr Diwakar should persuade Mr Kapahi and Mr Dadoo of the rationale for introduction of technology in HR operations. Mr Dadoo and Mr Kapahi should question the investment in technology. The players debate the pros and cons. The role play should end with Mr Dadoo and Mr Kapahi getting persuaded by Mr Diwakar's rationale. The three should also draw up a rough strategy for the introduction

of technology in HR activities.

The role play should be followed by a class discussion on the impact of technology on HRM and the importance of this transformation.

2. Assume you are the general manager (HR) of a reputed multinational heavy engineering firm with operations in several countries. A number of senior and experienced employees of this firm are nearing retirement. Though there is a pool of young and talented employees, the firm is likely to experience a shortage of employees ready to assume leadership roles after the retirement of senior employees. The near retirees provide a lot of value addition to the firm. In addition, the success of the firm is largely due to the respect and reputation that the senior employees of the firm enjoy in the industry globally. As general manager (HR),

- persuade the top management of the importance of age diversity in attaining competitive advantage, and

- suggest age diversity initiatives and activities that may be adopted by the firm.

Classroom Projects

1. The purpose of this activity is to debate the motion 'Introduction of workforce diversity (cultural, age, gender, etc.) is sound business strategy and a source of competitive advantage for the firm'.

Steps

- All students sitting on the left side of the room will propose the motion; those sitting on the right side will oppose the motion.

- Divide the class into groups of five or six students and divide each group into sub-groups. Have both sides in each sub-group develop arguments in support of their positions. Allow 15 minutes for group discussion.

- Have both sides in each sub-group develop a master list of arguments supporting their

positions. Representatives of each subgroup meet each other and compare their arguments to develop the master list. Thus there will be two master lists, one proposing the motion and the other opposing it.

- The sub-group representatives will form the debate teams.

- The debate will be conducted according to the following procedure.

  – **Round 1**: Each team presents its arguments. Give 10 minutes to each team. All debaters should participate. The proposing team goes first.

  – **Round 2**: Each team gets 5 minutes to rebut the arguments of the other side and reconstruct and re-emphasize its own arguments, as needed. The rebuttal should directly address the arguments of the opposite side. The purpose of the rebuttal is to question and cast doubt on the arguments of the opposite team. The opposing team goes first. (Note: Each team should be careful about giving only their position in Round 1, and not to rebut until Round 2).

– **Round 3**: The other students are given 10 minutes to cross-examine members of each team. The students are also encouraged to cite examples of successful firms that have relied on either of the above positions to support their arguments. The class ends with a vote on which position they hold.

2. The objective of this exercise is to help the students understand the potential influence of trends in the external environment on HR practices of the firm.

Steps

• Divide the class into groups of four or five.

• Introduce the exercise to the class by clarifying the objective of the exercise. Explain to the students that external environmental changes and trends, such as economic and business environment changes, demographic trends, etc. result in significant HR challenges for the organizations. Give them an example of how an ageing of a firm's workforce raises issues such as obsolescence, retirement age, etc.

• Each group is asked to list the major trends

or changes that have taken place in the economic, business, demographic, sociocultural, and employment environment since the early 1990s.

• Each group is asked to list some ideas for each trend it identifies about the major human resource issues faced by organizations because of these changes and the impact of these trends on major HRM practices such as recruitment, selection, manpower planning, training, performance appraisal, compensations, employee relations etc.

• Each group prepares and presents a report followed by a general discussion.

• Students may be provided a guide sheet as follows (optional).

S. No.	Environmental Trends	Major HR issues faced by firms and impact on HRM practices
1.	Ageing workforce	
2.	Shift from manufacturing to service economy	
3.	Increasing women workforce	
4.	Globalization	
5.	Increasing workforce diversity	
6.	Mergers and acquisitions	

Adapted from: Nkomo, Fottler, and McAfee 1992

Field Projects

1. Divide the class into groups of five each. Have each group select one industry (BPO/ITeS, FMCG, travel and tourism, aviation, retail, automobile, etc.) and visit two organizations in the industry it chooses. Group members are to interview HR and top managers to find out

• which HR activities have been outsourced by these firms;

• why these activities have been outsourced;

• when these firms began to outsource;

• which HR activities have not been outsourced and why;

• which activities are likely to be outsourced in the near future;

• the benefits that the firm has reaped by outsourcing; and

- the employee strength of the HR department.

  Each group prepares a report that it presents to the class and writes a report that it submits to the instructor. Each presentation in the class highlights the trends in HR outsourcing and the rationale for those trends. When all the groups have made their presentations, engage the entire class in a discussion about the importance of HR outsourcing in the current business environment, and the pros and cons of HR outsourcing. The discussion should also focus on industry differences in HR outsourcing trends.

2. The objective of this field project is to help students appreciate the importance of HRM when dealing with knowledge workers and women workers.

Steps

- Divide the class into groups of four or five.
- Half the groups are to identify a firm that has a high percentage of knowledge workers. The other groups are asked to identify a firm that has a high percentage of women workers. To identify the firms, students are encouraged to rely on secondary sources, such as newspapers, business magazines, the internet, etc.
- Each group visits the firm it chooses. Students interview one or two HR and top/senior managers to find out:

- the percentage of knowledge workers/women employees in the workforce;
- the major HR issues (attrition, retention, motivation, etc.) faced by the organization in managing these categories of employees;
- the HR practices introduced by firms to manage these HR issues; and
- the benefits that these firms have achieved or hope to achieve as a result of these practices.

- Each group also interviews a few employees to obtain their perception of HR practices, their satisfaction with HR practices, and their expectations of the HRM function.
- Each group prepares a written report for submission to the instructor as well as a report for class presentation.
- The groups make presentations in the class highlighting the unique needs of the selected employee group(s) and the unique challenges they pose for HRM.
- After the presentations, lead a discussion in the class focussing on the increasingly important role of HRM in managing knowledge workers and women employees. Encourage the students to deliberate on the shift in emphasis of the HR activity from 'labour management' to 'talent management'. The role of HRM in the knowledge economy is emphasized.

=============================== **Case Study**[1] ===============================

Organizational Redesign at Bharat Petroleum Corporation Limited: The Challenge of Privatization

During his annual inspection visit to one of the refineries during mid-2001, Mr S. Behuria, the Chairman of Bharat Petroleum Corporation Limited (BPCL), wondered if the corporation would

[1] The case was written by Ashok Som, Associate Professor of Management at ESSEC Business School. It is intended to be used as a basis for class discussion rather than to illustrate either effective or ineffective handling of a business situation. © 2004, A. Som, ESSEC Business School, France. Distributed by The European Case Clearing House, England and USA. http://www.ecch.com. Case used with permission of the author.

survive impending privatization or if its ownership would change. How could he motivate employees to be ready for upcoming competition in 2002 when state-owned enterprises in India would be privatized? Would workers deal with the momentum of the proposed organizational redesign process or would everything crumble with full deregulation of the petroleum industry?

Background History of the Company

Bharat Petroleum Corporation Limited (BPCL), a government-owned company incorporated under the Companies Act, 1956, is in the business of refining, storing, marketing and distributing of petroleum products. The paid-up capital of BPCL is Rs 300 million[1], of which the Government of India (GOI) holds 66.2%. The balance (33.8%) of the equity is held by foreign institutional investors, financial institutions, employees, and other investors.

The history of BPCL dates back to 1975 when the GOI, pursuant to an agreement, acquired Burmah-Shell Refineries Limited (BSR). The Burmah-Shell Oil Storage and Distributing Company of India Ltd (BSM), a foreign company established in England in 1928, was in the business of distribution and marketing of petroleum products in India. Burmah-Shell Refineries Limited was renamed Bharat Refineries Limited (BRL) in 1976 and to BPCL in 1977. Burmah-Shell Refineries Limited was incorporated in 1952 as a company under the Companies Act in 1913 in Bombay. Between 1991 and 1994, the GOI had disinvested part of its holdings to financial institutions and BPCL employees. As a result, the equity holding of the GOI was reduced to 66.2%. The GOI planned to fully divest its share by the end of 2002.

Crisis

Bharat Petroleum Corporation Limited operates in the retail, lubricant, liquid petroleum (LPG) and aviation fuel sectors. With the ongoing liberalization process in India, sectors like LPG and lubricants have been deregulated. Bharat Petroleum Corporation Limited owns one refinery in Mumbai, which has a capacity of 7–8 million tons, and it sells about 16 to 18 million tons of crude per year. As the market is controlled in the retail business, there is a national pool of oil, controlled by the Oil Coordination Cell (OCC), which distributes crude to the three main oil retailers in India. There is one private firm in the industry, Reliance Petroleum, which cannot openly compete in the market, but which has its own refinery. The output generated from its refinery is bought and distributed by one or more of the three state owned enterprises (SOEs), i.e., BPCL, Hindustan Petroleum (HPCL), and Indian Oil Limited (IOL), all three of which had enjoyed a monopoly under the administered pricing mechanism (APM) of the GOI. With full deregulation of the industry proposed in 2002, the market structure will change and there will be open competition in the industry. One of BPCL's senior managers reflected, 'In the lubricants sector BPCL had a market share of 12–16%. In 1999, when the lubricants market was deregulated, BPCL's market share came down to 4%. There is worry about what will entail when the entire sector is deregulated.'

Retention of market share would be a serious threat with the entry of new local (private) and global players in this sector in the country. Bharat Petroleum Corporation Limited ought to redesign itself and shift from a SOE mindset operating under a regulated market to an lean, agile, competitive, and customer-oriented player to compete for market share.

Industry Environment and Market Structure

The business environment saw many changes after the initial phase of deregulation. India's petroleum retail sector (Table 2.7) is currently dominated by SOEs, and private domestic firms such as Reliance and Essar Oil have been barred from tapping the market directly. This market structure faces impending change. With new private investment, both BPCL and HPCL will be well positioned to attract

---

[1] All figures and data are at the time the case was written, that is before 2002.

Table 2.7:   Key Players in the Oil Industry in India[1]

Company	Ownership	Refining Capacity (barrels per day, bpd)	Market Share
Indian Oil Corporation (IOC)	84% state-owned	620,000 bpd	55%
BPCL	66% state-owned*	180,000 bpd	20%
HPCL	51% state-owned*	295,000 bpd	20%
Indo Burmah Petroleum (IBP)	Controlling 33% stake held by IOC	–	5%
Reliance Industries	Privately owned	540,000 bpd	Presently barred from access to the marketing/retail sector
Essar Oil	Privately owned	210,000 bpd refinery due to be commissioned in 2004	

* Controlling 25% stakes due to be sold off (source: www.indiainfoline.com).

[1] All figures and data are at the time the case was written, that is, before 2002.

investment and increase their market share at the expense of IOC, the leader. Naturally the concern remains that the strategic sale of HPCL will simply be palmed off to SOEs, as in the case of Burmah Petroleum.

India's demand for petroleum products is expected to increase after liberalization, and is therefore attracting the attention of multinational oil companies and other private Indian players. Domestic private firms are trying to complete the construction of their refineries to exploit future prospects. This is bound to increase competition in this lucrative sector. This will mean a significant loss in the market share of the SOEs. Deregulation would also bring other changes, such as the determination of product prices by import parity prices. Margins set by competitive pressures will be more volatile and highly uncertain. Dealers and distributors may shift their allegiance and consequently, the existing firms may lose retail sites and LPG warehouses. Firms may react by offering

minimal facilities in their highway segment of retail outlets to keep costs low and reduce lead times.

Trained and experienced manpower in the industry will be lured away by the new entrants. Non-fuel offerings such as convenience stores and ATMs are likely to be threshold activities, especially in metros and urban markets. One of BPCL's managers summed up, 'The increasing demand for hydrocarbons in India is a tremendous opportunity. The major concern is the possible and inevitable loss of market share due to an increase in the number of players in the market place. The greatest challenge will be to retain our customers and remain profitable.'

Redesign Strategy

A BPCL manager reflected on strategy, 'Our broad strategy is to win in the deregulated environment, focus on customer service, and improve our profitability. In order to beat the competition, a very strong customer focus is needed in the whole organization. It is necessary to understand and respond quickly to customers' needs and expectations. The speed at which the staff responds in the market will determine the success of the corporation. The measure of success in the competitive scenario will be customer loyalty. The whole organization has to align itself to meet customer requirements and to acquire new competencies and skills.'

In the refinery sector, which is still regulated, BPCL has a capacity of 7-8 million tons, whereas it sells about 16 to 18 million tons of crude per year. To address this gap, BPCL acquired Kochi Refineries, which has a capacity of about 8 million tons and is looking to expand opportunities in the refinery business. Following the international model, opportunities into related and unrelated diverse fields in the non-fuel sector are experimented.

Bharat Petroleum Corporation Limited hired the internationally renowned consultancy firm McKinsey to formulate a strategy for retailing effectively and for opening convenience and grocery stores. The deregulation of the industry forced top management to realize that BPCL had to focus on its customers and make decisions faster. That would be possible only by de-layering the hierarchical organization and by empowering its staff. Two senior managers pointed out, 'Most employees do not understand the nature of the business, what we are doing. Our core competence is not refining crude oil but selling products. This is where the market will be after deregulation. The aim of redesign was to be ready for change. This meant changing ourselves to be tuned to the external changes. Our national competitors are Reliance and MRPL (a joint venture by the Birla Group of Companies) and foreign competitors will be Castrol, TotalElfFina, BP, and ExxonMobil, as was witnessed with the deregulation of the lubricants sector.'

Organizational redesign started in 1998 with the help of consultancy firm Arthur D. Little and its group of consultants. They formed a project group with over 30 people drawn from different functions and regions with a general manager as their leader. It was called Project CUSECS, meaning

customer service and cutomer satisfaction. Their main thrust areas were better customer service, profitability, creation of strategic business units (SBUs), and division of the organization into regional units.

The redesign of BPCL saw the change of the organization structure from a functional to a divisional enterprise with six SBUs spread over four geographical regions (north, south, east, and west). Before the redesign at the corporate level, the structure was functionally oriented, consisting of the functions of sales and distribution, information systems (IS), marketing, and HRM. In this structure, although the depots reported to the divisional manager, there was very little coordination at the field level amongst the sales officers and the operational officers. One of the senior managers summed it up, 'The functional structure made it difficult for senior managers to focus on developing and implementing strategies for particular business such as lubricants and LPG. It created a bottleneck between the process of strategy formulation and its implementation'. The redesigned structure had six SBUs: (1) refinery; (2) retail; (3) industrial/commercial; (4) lubricants; (5) LPG; and (6) aviation. The HRM function (both human resource services and human resource development) played a critical role in the redesign process. As one of the members of the board of directors pointed out, 'BPCL has undergone a very interesting HRD-powered transformation process ... it was orchestrated by Mr. Arun Maira and his team from Arthur D. Little. Instead of providing BPCL with a package of vision, strategy, structure, process ... he asked the management to carry through a very broad visioning exercise. Some 2500 managers participated. It resulted not only in a clear corporate vision, identification of shareholders, and statement of core values, but visions were collectively evolved by each function, department, branch, and section. This envisioning and agenda setting was facilitated by trained individuals, many of them volunteers from functions other than HRM.'

The main theme of the vision is 'Business partner first, business partner last.' The themes vary for each SBU. For the lubricants SBU, it is 'Survive today, to be there in the future'; for the retail SBU it is 'People above oil. We care for you, we exist because of you.'

The necessity and the competencies required for the redesign were summed up by a senior manager, 'Competition is with both national and multinational companies. The key to compete is to deliver quality products at a cheaper price, cut costs, and keep costs in control. There should be a concern for financials by all stakeholders with a profit building motive and sustaining the bottom line. The required functional competency is in selling and distributing products. Customers, both internal and external, should be satisfied. The challenge is to manage this situation with effective leadership at all levels.'

The redesigned organization has four elements: (1) corporate centre; (2) SBUs; (3) support services; and (4) lateral thinking mechanisms. The corporate centre has four directors (marketing, finance, refineries, and personnel). The marketing director and his team of eight members are responsible for leading and coordinating the brand building and brand management functions of the SBUs. The finance director and his team of six members are responsible for leading and coordinating the strategy development effort at the corporate level. The directors facilitate the SBUs in developing and integrating their respective strategies across the businesses. They also assist top management in optimally allocating resources while managing the business portfolio.

The support services are HRM, finance, IS, and engineering and projects (marketing). Executives in each embedded unit report to the head of that SBU. For example, the embedded HRM function in the LPG SBU reports to the head of the LPG SBU. Dedicated teams called shared services perform the support tasks that have enterprise-wide or region-wide implications and that are not business-specific. This is done to bring down the operating costs of these services by pooling some of the activities outside the business.

Before the redesign, the organization was 'totally hierarchical', according to some executives. Today, it is mostly participatory and team-based

with absolute delegation of authority. An example of this is the new performance management system; it is open. Most personnel understand the role they have to play. One of the managers pointed out, 'The attitude shift has taken place in a span of three years only'. Bharat Petroleum Corporation Limited recruited generalists and trained them to be specialists. Most senior managers at BPCL are generalists; only a few are specialists. One of the managers pointed out, 'Due to the historical recruitment structure, the personnel are generalists while we need bright specialists like MBA graduates. If we cannot look into this, there would be a wide gap as 70% of our recruits are not as good as our competitors; they are average. The profile, experience and expertise for the job are not there.'

One of the vehicles used for facilitating the change process has been communication. Plenty of communication workshops have been conducted, in which staff from various locations, irrespective of their positions in the organization, have participated. This has brought about much better understanding and commitment to the change process.

Human Resource Management at BPCL: 'It is a great place to work'

The HRM function has been classified along with the other support services like finance and information systems. The support services are organized into three types of structures: (1) embedded support services; (2) shared support services; and (3) corporate services. Before the redesign, the regional HR manager was responsible for all the functions in the region, and all the personnel in the region reported to the regional manager. The regional manager had a very formal relationship with the corporate HRM department. Now, each SBU has HRM personnel known as 'Embedded HRM' who assist the SBU in HRM issues like transfers, organizational learning, performance appraisal, and discipline. The embedded HRM departments

- administer the performance management system;
- plan the workforce;

- design functional training programmes and deliver them;
- anchor organizational learning;
- transfer workers within business units; and
- manage discipline.

The shared services entail support tasks that have enterprise-wide and region-wide implications. They are not confined to being business-specific and are transactional in nature. All SBUs and entities share teams performing these tasks. Pooling some of the activities together outside the businesses leads to economies of scale. The HRM services team in each region is headed by the head of regional services, who is supported by the HR manager (employee relations), responsible for recruitment of non-management staff.

The role of the HRM function is to provide support to the main business. The HRM function should provide information and support proactively. It should know the business the company is in. It should not concentrate only on HRM practices, but also implement those practices in helping the business.

Recruitment Process

Recruitment at BPCL takes place mostly at the entry level. The company believes in building its human potential rather than buying it from the market. Until now it was seen as a lifetime job, and people worked their way up to management. The redesign entailed strengthening the field force to boost marketing and customer focus. The consultants advised a 50% increase in the sales force and frontline staff, but without any additional recruitment. The sales force was increased by redeploying management staff from the back office and retraining them. After the initiation of the redesign process, there has been a hiring freeze. Recruitment is done only for specialized and new jobs. Competency mapping will be introduced.

Selection within the organization is done by matching the job profile and appraisal. Scope for promotion is limited at BPCL. The average age at BPCL is 35–40. A promotion can be expected only

after three years. There is a system of job-rotation. To occupy a responsible position, an executive needs to have work experience in at least three departments. One of the managers reflected, 'There is no clear cut policy on promotion'.

Retraining and Redeployment

Retraining and redeployment play a very important role after the redesign process. It is a part of the business strategy to redeploy and transfer personnel. The excess workforce is trained and redeployed. But the decision to redeploy is not taken ad hoc. Retraining and redeployment is discussed first with the personnel and then carried out. This is a big challenge, as employees do not want to be redeployed. One of the senior managers pointed out, 'After the implementation of an ERP system in the areas of dispatch, logistics, project, and HRM, there is a surplus in the workforce. We were trying to find new opportunities and to train the excess workforce to absorb them where they can build new competencies'.

Performance Management System

The extensive team-based structures proposed by Arthur D. Little were pilot-tested with six retail projects. Visionary leadership and planning (VLP) workshops were held to clarify shared visions, document the current situation, and devise concrete plans for bridging the gap between vision and reality. During the redesign process, the consultants understood that the new organization needed new competencies and a new mindset to make the redesign successful. The functional perspective needed to be changed into a team-based, collaborative, cross-functional mindset. It was a difficult task. Employees were invited to participate in learning experiences through the foundations of learning (FOL) programme, which was designed to develop their abilities to work in high-performing cross-functional teams. One example of the many observations is: 'In one of the questions, before the new performance management system (PMS), there were four options in the performance appraisal system on the question of the dependability of the subordinate:

(1) generally dependable; (2) dependable; (3) mostly dependable; and (4) trustworthy. Supervisors who did not know the difference between these terms could hamper the career of a bright subordinate as the terms are ambiguous and can be represented in different ways.' One of the managers reflected, 'One of the critical elements in the success of a redesign of an organization is the reward process. The only reward for good performance we have today is promotion. As the number of vacancies is always limited, all eligible staff in a job group cannot be promoted. Rewarding good performers/teams is a solution to achieve performance. A task force is looking into a reward structure that has a combination of monetary and non-monetary reward.'

Rightsizing/retaining BPCL is a public enterprise; there is no scope of rightsizing. Hence, efforts are made to retrain and redeploy personnel from departments that have a surplus of workforce. A current example is in the refinery after the implementation of ERP. One of the managers pointed out, 'Voluntary retirement schemes (VRS) should come in immediately. We should have a policy like that of Indian Oil Company, where employees have a choice to opt for VRS. Interviews are held for the employees who opt for VRS scheme. These interviews form the basis for deciding whether VRS should be given or not. IOC does not give VRS to an employee if he/she wants to quit, and just let him/her quit. This will bring some scope for new recruitment of professionals within the company.'

Changes in performance Bharat Petroleum Corporation Limited decided to measure performance in both financial and customer satisfaction terms. Financial performance was measured by return on capital employed (ROCE), return on investment (ROI), and internal rate of return (IRR). Customer satisfaction was measured by market share and customer loyalty index. The index was constructed on the basis of periodic customer surveys. The capabilities of key business (corporate and business strategies, IS plan, brand strategy, and HRM strategy) were gauged by the quality of their outputs. For example, the retail SBU measures its performance by assessing return on capital employed, customer loyalty index, cycle time of retail engineering projects, security of sites, and morale of staff.

A series of activities were taken by consultants to implement the redesign mechanism and link it to performance. The performance of retail sites was monitored closely. Dramatic improvements were seen in the resolution (and prevention) of customer complaints, as well as the reduction of open items (accounts receivable). Productivity and operating efficiency increased; the increase was felt throughout the units. Both managerial and non-managerial personnel understood the need of the hour after going through an intense communication process and felt the need to do their best to save their company from imminent competition.

The redesign process, the reinforcement of HRM strategies, and the communication exercises together reduced absenteeism, improved morale, and heightened employees' co-operation with management. Employees felt that they had to put in their best to fight the challenge. This saw the beginning of innovations in product, process, systems, and management at all levels.

Constraints

Some nationalistic and protectionist ministers have opposed the planned sell-off because the government will be relinquishing much of its influence over the pricing of fuels, a particularly sensitive issue that has precipitated unrest and caused criticism of past governments, and because they feel that the companies will not be sold at a fair price. The process of privatization has so far raised only Rs 50 billion (US $1 billion), against a governmental target of Rs 120 billion (US $ 2.4 billion).

Future Outlook and Implications

Along with Reliance and Essar Oil, foreign operators such as Shell, BP, ExxonMobil, and Petronas are expected to bid for controlling stakes. Private investment will then enable investment in marketing and retail infrastructure, which should lead to improved service levels, if not lower prices. The surge in the companies' share prices reflects investor confidence that the biggest hurdles have now been navigated and should help the Indian government to get its privatization agenda back on track after several months of uncertainty.

Questions

1. What changes have occurred in the business environment after liberalization and after the deregulation of the LPG and lubricant sectors?

2. What were the major HR challenges confronted by BPCL after liberalization?

3. What changes were introduced by BPCL in HRM as part of the redesign strategy? How did these changes benefit BPCL? According to the case study, what are the elements critical to the success of a redesign strategy?

4. What steps can be adopted by BPCL to achieve its long-term vision and to beat the competition resulting from deregulation? Give evidence from the case.

5. Critically evaluate the role of HRM in transforming BPCL from being a state-owned enterprise in a regulated market to a competitive, customer-oriented firm.

6. To what extent do you think the HR function plays a critical role in supporting organizational changes?

7. Given the future outlook of the petroleum sector, what role can the HRM function play in ensuring that BPCL continues to remain competitive?

References

Aldisert, L.M. 2002, *Valuing People: How Human Capital can be Your Strongest Asset*, Dearborn Trade Publishing: A Kaplan Professional Company, USA.

Armstrong, M. 2000, *Strategic Human Resource Management: A Guide to Action*, 2nd Edition, Kogan Page, London.

Bohlander, G., S. Snell, and A. Sherman 2002, *Managing Human Resources*, Thomson South Western, Singapore.

DeCenzo, D.A. and S.P. Robbins 2005, *Fundamentals of Human Resource Management*, 8th edition, John Wiley & Sons Inc. Student Edition, Singapore.

Devine, M. 1999, *A Mergers Checklist*, Roffey Park Management Institute.

Greer, C.R. 2002, *Strategic Human Resource Management: A General Managerial Approach*, 2nd edition, Pearson Education, Singapore.

Hall, L. and D. Torrington 1998, *The Human Resource Function: The Dynamics of Change and Development*, Financial Time, Pitman Publishing, London.

Holbeche, L. 2002, *Aligning Human Resources and Business Strategy*, Butterworth Heinemann, Oxford, pp. 394–422.

Kossek, E.E. and R.N. Block 2000, *Managing Human Resources in the 21st Century: From Core Concepts to Strategic Choice*, South Western College Pub, Thomson Learning, USA.

Lengnick-Hall, M.L. and C.A. Lengnick-Hall 2003, *Human Resource Management in the Knowledge Economy: New Challenges, New Roles, New Capabilities*, Berrett-Koehler Publishers, Inc., San Francisco, pp. 36–43.

Lepak, D.P. and S.A. Snell 1998, 'Virtual HR: Strategic Human Resource Management in the 21st Century', *Human Resource Management Review*, 8 (3), pp. 215–34.

Mathis, R.L. and J.H. Jackson 2003, *Human Resource Management*, 10th Edition, Thomson South Western, Singapore, pp. 15–21.

Mello, J.A. 2003, *Strategic Human Resource Management*, Thomson Asia Pte Ltd, Singapore, pp. 112–16.

Nkomo, S.M., M.D. Fottler, and R.B. McAfee 1992, *Applications in Human Resource Management. Cases, Exercises, and Skill Builders*, 2nd edition, PWS-KENT Publishing Company, Boston.

Reilly, P. 2001, *Flexibility at Work: Balancing the Interests of Employer and Employee*, Gower Publishing Ltd., England.

Roehling, M.V., M.A. Cavanaugh, L.M. Moynihan, and W.R. Boswell 2000, 'The Nature of the New Employment Relationship: A Content Analysis of the Practitioner and Academic Literatures', *Human Resource Management*, vol. 39, no. 4, pp. 305–20.

Ruta, C.D. 2005, 'The Application of Change Management Theory to HR Portal Implementation in Subsidiaries of Multinational Corporation', *Human Resource Management*, vol. 44, no. 1, pp. 35–53.

S.A. Snell, P.R. Pedigo, and G. Krawiec 1995, 'Managing the Impact of Information Technology on Human Resource Management', in G.R. Ferris, S.D. Rosen, and D.T. Barnum (eds), *Handbook of Human Resource Management*, Blackwell Publishers, Oxford, pp. 159–74.

Tsui, A.S. and J.B. Wu 2005, 'The New Employment Relationship versus the Mutual Investment Approach: Implications for Human Resource Management', *Human Resource Management*, 44 (2), pp. 115–21.

Wilhelm, W.R. 1990, 'Revitalizing the Human Resource Management Function in a Mature, Large Corporation', *Human Resource Management*, 29 (2), pp. 129–44.

Notes

Aiyar, S.S.A., 'Return of Manufacturing', *The Economic Times*, New Delhi, 22 December 2004, p. 10.

Aiyar, S.S.A., 'The Crowd Swells in Our Back-Office', *The Economic Times*, New Delhi, 15 September 2004, p. 10.

Anand, M., 'India in 2030', *Businessworld*, 9 January 2006, pp. 54–5.

Arun, T.K., 'People Power: Gain Sans Pain', *The Economic Times*, New Delhi, 19 December 2005, pp. 1, 17.

Biswas, S., 'Knowledge Services Sector to Generate $200-b Economy by '20', *The Economic Times*, New Delhi, 12 April 2005, p. 16.

Chaudhuri, A.R. and K. Muthukumar, 'The World's Ageing, and It's an Old Hand at Work All Around You', *The Economic Times*, New Delhi, 15 June 2004, p. 9.

Economic Survey 2004–2005, Government of India, Ministry of Finance, Economic Division.

Gloet, M. and B. Martin 2005, 'Knowledge Management and HRM as a Means to Develop Leadership and Management Capabilities to Support Sustainability', Kmap2005.vuw.ac.nz/papers/knowledge%20Mgmt%20&%20hrm.pdf, accessed on 3 February 2006.

http://www.emcc.eurofound.eu.int/content/source/eu0409a.html, accessed on 23 January 2006.

http://www.emcc.eurofound.eu.int/content/source/eu04014a.html, accessed on 22 January 2006.

Human Development Report 2005: International Cooperation at Crossroads (2005) United Nations Development Programme, Oxford University Press, India.

Jha, M.S., 'Headhunters Now Plot Soft Exit for Misfits', *The Economic Times*, New Delhi, 19 January 2006, p. 10.

Mehta, P.S., 'Banking Mergers and Workers', *The Economic Times*, New Delhi, 20 May 2005, p. 16.

Sachdeva, S.D. and N. Raaj, 'Hiring Headache for Corporates: Firms, Colleges Tie Up to Tackle Skill Deficit', *The Sunday Times of India*, 29 January 2006, p. 1.

Shah, K., 'The Dream Nightmare', *The Economic Times*, New Delhi, 10 June 2006, p. 7.

Sinha, V., 'More Educated Women Are Jobless', *The Economic Times*, New Delhi, 24 November 2004, p. 5.

Sinha, V., 'There are More Out on the Streets Looking for Jobs', *The Economic Times*, New Delhi, 25 October 2004, p. 14.

Statistical Outline of India 2001-2002 (2001), 8th Edition, TATA Services Ltd, Department of Economics and Statistics, Mumbai.

Subramanyam, R., 'IT, ITeS Cos Find Themselves in a Spot as Talent Pool Shrinks', *The Economic Times*, New Delhi, 29 September 2004, p. 8.

The Economic Times, 10 February 2006, 'The Man Machines', in Corporate Dossier.

The Economic Times, 15 June 2005, 'Employers in India Upbeat about Hirings in Q2: Survey', New Delhi, p. 4.

Yearbook of Labour Statistics 2003, 62nd Edition, International Labour Office, Geneva.

3

Human Resource Evaluation

After studying this chapter, you will be able to:

- appreciate the importance of human resource evaluation
- acquire an overview of human resource evaluation
- describe the range of measures used to evaluate human resource performance
- discuss different approaches to human resource evaluation
- explain the usefulness of the Balanced Scorecard for determining the impact of human resource management on firm performance
- discuss benchmarking as an approach to evaluating human resource performance

INTRODUCTION

The human resource management (HRM) function has struggled for years to justify its existence and value. From being viewed as a staff function and a cost centre, the HRM function has evolved to being viewed as a line function and a profit centre. The function is today seen as playing an important role in organizational performance and success. As has been emphasized in earlier chapters, today HRM is a strategic business partner. However, it is no longer sufficient to emphasize that a firm's human resources and HRM strategies are important for accomplishing the strategic goals of the firm. The HRM function needs to be proactive and developmental in approach. It also needs to be accountable, demonstrate its contribution to organizational performance, contribute to the goal of business, and deliver value to its stakeholders—employees, customers, investors, and the organization itself—just like other functions such as marketing, finance, etc. A number of interrelated trends, such as high competition and the transformation of the employment contract, have contributed to an enhanced interest in measuring the tangible benefits resulting from HR activities. Therefore, firms have developed a range of HR measures.

This chapter begins with an overview of HR evaluation. It reviews the rationale for the increasing significance and focus on evaluation of HR programmes and of the HR function. The chapter provides an insight into the difficulties involved in the measurement of HR programmes. The range of measures that may be used to evaluate HR performance, as well as the range of approaches to HR measurement, is also examined. The chapter ends with contemporary approaches for assessing the value of the HR function and its strategic alignment, such as balanced scorecard, HR scorecard, benchmarking, and business excellence model.

HRM EVALUATION: A BACKGROUND

The performance of the HRM function, until recently, did not attract any attention or concern. The main mission of HRM was seen to be to 'improve morale', 'help employees', and 'perform routine administration'. Therefore, the HRM function was not evaluated. Even when it was, the evaluation was vague and subjective. For example, the quantum of HRD budget was seen as indicative of the significance of the HRM function. This perpetuated the attitude in the organization as well as in the HR department that the HRM function was not very important for the business results of the organization. This attitude has changed in the recent past. Jeffrey Pfeffer (1995), professor at the Stanford Graduate School of Business, argued that the 'basis for competitive success has changed'. Human resources are viewed as the 'most important asset' of an organization—an asset that creates value for the firm and helps the firm attain as well as sustain competitive advantage.

As mentioned already, until recently evaluation of HR programmes or of the HR function was not a priority for most organizations. Intense business competition has increased the need for all organizational functions, such as finance, management information systems (MIS), marketing, etc. to demonstrate how they contribute to higher business performance. The HR function is also required to quantify and measure its impact on business performance. Traditionally, the HR manager could be abstract and talk about the importance of HR practices in terms of employee morale, commitment, and turnover. This is not enough today. The HR strategies of a firm can no longer be simply 'best in class'. They must, rather, add value. 'Adding value' typically refers to increasing the gap between revenue and costs, usually by reducing costs. It is not obvious how the HR function or HR programmes add value. Nevertheless, firms are recognizing the increasingly important need to demonstrate efficient utilization of resources. Restructuring, downsizing, modifying HR practices, and technological innovations are all means for reducing costs within HRM. Some firms *believe* that HRM contributes significantly to a firm's profitability without collecting evidence to support this belief. However, organizations are beginning to focus on assessing the tangible benefits that result from HR activities. Thus, questions such as the following are posed and expected to be answered:

- What is the cost per hire?
- How many man-days of training have been imparted to employees?
- How many new recruits have been retained at the end of one year?

- Has training led to improved capabilities and performance?
- Have improved employee capabilities and performance resulted in higher organizational profits?

To be accepted as a strategic business partner, the HRM function should be evaluated to demonstrate its value in quantitative terms. It must replace ideas with results and perceptions with assessments and back up its claims with evidence. Today, human resource measurement and evaluation is receiving considerable attention from academics and practitioners alike. Before discussing the perspectives of HR evaluation, it is important to understand the meaning of HR evaluation.

HUMAN RESOURCE EVALUATION: DEFINITION AND OVERVIEW

'To evaluate' means 'to determine the value of'. Human resource evaluation refers to determining the value of HR for achieving organizational goals. Bratton defined HRM evaluation as 'the procedures and processes that measure, evaluate and communicate the value added of human resource management practices to the organization'.

There are several benefits of HR evaluation. These include

- the promotion of change by identifying strengths and weaknesses;
- an assessment of the performance of the HR function;
- a demonstration of the bottomline contribution of the HR function through, for example, reduced turnover; and
- a demonstration of the function's role in the achievement of organizational goals.

While recognizing the importance of HR evaluation, it is also essential to answer questions such as the following:

- What should be evaluated—the overall HR effectiveness or only the effectiveness of the HR function?
- What should be evaluated—HR activities and practices, or the impact of HR policies on the organization and employees?
- What should be evaluated—HR practices, the HR department, or HR professionals?
- What should be the level of analysis in HRM evaluation within the organizational structure?
- What criteria should be used to assess the effectiveness of the HR function/ department?

Greer (2001) states that answers to the above questions help one gain a complete overview of HR evaluation. Let us consider each of the questions raised above (see Figure 3.1).

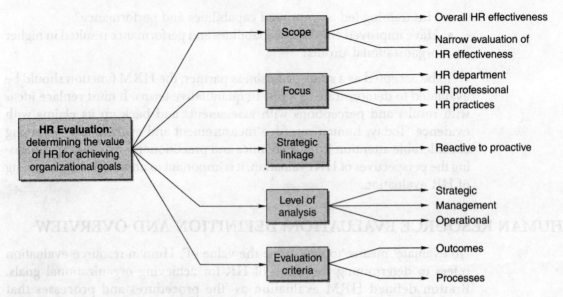

Figure 3.1: An Overview of HR Evaluation

Scope of evaluation Evaluation of HR may be directed towards overall HR effectiveness or towards the effectiveness of the HR function. Measures of overall HR effectiveness include turnover, workers' compensation claims, employee satisfaction, etc. A narrower evaluation of the HRM function, on the other hand, includes measures related to the efficiency in administering an HR programme, such as benefits and recruiting applicants. Overall HR outcomes and effectiveness are influenced by the performance of the line managers of the firm. In a narrower evaluation, measures of HR are affected only by the performance of the HR staff or personnel. Such an evaluation may be misleading and suggest that HRM is the sole responsibility of the HR department and personnel. This is, however, far from the truth. All line managers and departments affect the quality of HRM. Most HRM activities are shared between HR personnel and line managers. Hence, evaluation of HR function is not a simple issue.

The scope of evaluation also incorporates a *time perspective*, that is, the time it takes for an HR practice to have an impact on performance. Depending on the nature of the programme, the time lag between implementation of a programme and its impact on performance can vary. Moreover, the impact of an HR programme may remain stable or increase or decrease over time.

Focus The decision related to HRM evaluation needs to be clear about *who* or *what* is being evaluated. Is the HRM department being evaluated, or the HR personnel, or HR practices? It is imperative that the scope of evaluation includes all three. This aspect is dealt with in greater detail later in this chapter in the section on HR audit.

Strategic linkage Chapter 1 discussed how the HRM function changed from having a reactive approach to having a proactive approach. This change is accompanied with a change in the focus of HRM evaluation. There has been a shift to a focus on the impact of HRM practices on the organization and on the employees (proactive) from a focus on how well a problem has been solved (reactive). In the past, evaluations focussed on criteria such as the number of self-appraisal forms filled or the turnover rate. Now, evaluations focus on finding out whether appraisals result in training need identification, whether the firm is losing high performers, etc.

Level of analysis Another important aspect of HRM evaluation relates to the level of analysis. Human resource management may be evaluated at three levels: (1) strategic; (2) management; and (3) operational. At the strategic level, the objective of HRM evaluation is to determine the consistency between HR policies and company strategy. At the management level, the focus of HRM evaluation is on control, for example, cost effectiveness of a benefit programme. At the operational level, it is the quality of HR services and programmes that are in focus, for example, satisfaction with the services of the HR department relates to the operational level of HRM evaluation.

Evaluation criteria The determination of criteria for evaluating the effectiveness of the HR function is another significant issue. The responsiveness of the department; how proactive they are; and the quality of their training and development activities may be the criteria that the HR function is judged on. An important issue related to evaluation concerns whether the evaluation criteria will involve outcomes or processes. *Outcomes* are the end results or products of work. *Processes* are the behaviours or the activities performed to reach the outcomes. Productivity ratios of the workforce of a firm, turnover rate, etc. are examples of outcome criteria. However, outcome criteria may be contaminated by factors external to the HR activity being evaluated. For example, high turnover rates may be due to high demand for a particular skill rather than due to a firm's HR policy. Similarly, process criteria may pose several difficulties in defining HR evaluation objectives. Specifying the right behaviour in the attainment of a goal refers to process criteria for evaluation. When the 'right behaviour' becomes an evaluation criterion, the emphasis on the attainment of outcomes is likely to be reduced. Therefore, evaluation criteria should take into account the objectives for which evaluation data is being obtained. Either outcome evaluation criteria or process evaluation criteria may be used for determining HR effectiveness depending on the evaluation objectives.

In the past two decades, the HRM function has become a strategic partner in the achievement of business goals of the firm. The resource-based model of SHRM, discussed in Chapter 1, emphasized the importance of using human capital to attain competitive advantage and sustain it. The human capital of a firm contributes to its bottomline. While most firms believe that their people are their most valuable asset, they have found it difficult to understand how the HRM function translates this vision into reality or how HR practices add value to a firm and contribute to its competitive advantage. Organizations require HR professionals to demonstrate the impact of HR on firm performance. In the sections that follow we will briefly review the literature on the linkage between a firm's HR practices and its performance and also discuss the rationale for measuring the contribution of HR to the achievement of the strategic goals of the firm.

HRM AND FIRM PERFORMANCE

The question that the HRM function and personnel are frequently required to address today is, 'Do HRM practices make a difference to business results?' Human resource management practices usually reflect a strategy of managing people as assets. Thus, expenditure on HRM practices is viewed as investment in HR that will ultimately result in economic returns (value added) to the firm. Even though there is some evidence suggesting the potentially significant contribution of HR investment to a firm's performance, not all firms approach HRM from an investment perspective. These firms believe that an investment perspective is only one way of managing HR to enhance performance. The investment perspective was discussed in Chapter 1. Some firms adopt another approach for managing HR to enhance business performance—they manage HR as an expense or cost that must be contained or reduced.

Firms do not uniformly adopt the investment perspective of managing HR because their workforce is typically of two types: core workforce and peripheral workforce.

The core workforce consists of the full time employees of a firm who are paid a regular salary or wage. They also receive fringe benefits, training and development opportunities, opportunity for promotions, and participate in decision-making activities of the firm. The peripheral workforce consists of temporary, part time, contractual, and outsourced employees. They get paid a fixed wage or a project-based fee. They are only partially, if at all, covered by fringe benefits.

The core workforce is typically managed as an asset or investment. The peripheral workforce is managed as an expense to be reduced. This explains the duality in the relationship between HRM and business performance. Expenditures made by a firm on account of the core workforce should be treated as investments that must result in increase in the value added to the business by this segment of employees. Expenditures on peripheral employees should be treated as an expense that must be reduced by the business. This also adds value to the business. Both the perspectives suggest maximizing the return, or value, over cost. That is, they should result in higher profit margins (revenue – cost = profit margin).

The relationship between HRM and business performance rests on logic— better deployment and utilization of HRM practices should result in better firm performance. This relationship was assumed with little evidence available to support the assumption. It was in the 1980s that serious efforts were directed towards testing the linkage between HRM and a firm's performance. However, the conclusions from these studies were equivocal and no definite answers emerged. The 1990s witnessed extended assessment of the impact of HR practices on financial performance. Studies were carried out to link the impact of HR practices to specific firm outcomes, such as turnover, productivity, etc. (see Table 3.1)

Table 3.1: Summary of Research on Linkage between HRM and Firm Performance

Decade	Researcher	Linkage between HRM and Firm Performance
1980s		
1.	Nkomo (1987)	Investment in HRM planning process did not correlate with business performance
2.	Lewin et al. (1988–1989)	No relationship
3.	Ulrich et al. (1984)	Some correlation between specific HR practices and business results obtained. But no overall indicators of how HR practices affect business performance.
1990s		
4.	Yeung et al. (1993)	Alignment of HR practices and strategy had an impact on business performance.
5.	Delaney (1996)	Relationship observed between progressive HRM practices and firm performance in manufacturing.
6.	Ichniowski et al. (1994)	Relationship observed between innovative HRM practices and organizational productivity.
7.	Arthur (1994)	HRM commitment systems had higher productivity and lower turnover than those with control HR systems.
8.	MacDuffie (1995)	Integrated HRM practices correlated with higher productivity and quality in automotive plants.

Contd

Table 3.1 Contd

Decade	Researcher	Linkage between HRM and Firm Performance
9.	Ostroff (1995)	The index of HRM quality was related to four financial measures: market/book value (market value of the firm based on stock price divided by firm's assets, which represents 'value added' by management); productivity (dollar value sales divided by number of employees); market value (stock price multiplied by outstanding shares); and sales. All four financial measures increased significantly with the quality of HR practices.
10.	Huselid (1995)	An increase of one standard deviation in the high-performance work practices of a firm reduced turnover, increased productivity, and increased sales, market value, and profits.

Source: Ulrich 1997

It is not a simple task to demonstrate a direct linkage between HRM and a firm's performance. The linkage is mediated by HR performance measures, such as improved employee satisfaction, higher organizational capabilities, etc. The model proposed by Rao (Chapter 1) also emphasized that HR practices result in positive HR outcomes, such as a proactive culture, employee commitment, and competence. The HR outcomes, in turn, influence the business goals of the organization (see Figure 3.2a).

Bratton also demonstrated that HRM strategy, policies, practices, and systems directly influence the performance measures of the HRM function and employees at both the individual level and the team level. Examples of

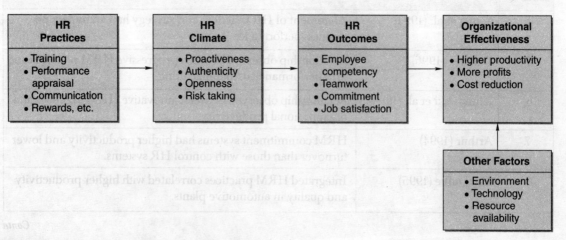

Figure 3.2(a): Linkage between HRM and Firm Performance

Source: Rao 1990

performance measures at the individual level are absenteeism, resignations, commitment, etc. At the team level, the examples are group dynamics, processes, and performance. Individual employee and team measures, in turn, affect organizational performance (see Figure 3.2b). A number of organizational performance measures may be used including productivity ratios, product and service quality, and return on investment (ROI).

Many financial variables used as measures of organizational performance are profit-related indices. These measures may relate to the operating performance or the financial performance of the firm. Profits, market share, and ROI are measures of the financial performance of the firm. Labour productivity, product or service quality, and perceptual measures of goal attainment are measures of operating performance. Labour productivity is defined as the quantity or volume of the major product or service that the organization provides and is expressed as a rate (productivity per worker or per unit of time). For example, the measure of sales per employee is a measure of productivity. Quality refers to the attributes of the primary service or product provided by the firm. For example, improvements in quality may be measured in terms of reduction of the number of complaints of unit defects. In addition to the use of 'hard' financial data to measure organizational outcomes, perceptual measures are also used to quantify performance. Perceived workplace economic performance may be measured by asking managers to compare their own organizations in a particular area (for example, productivity) relative to other organizations in the same industry, using a subjective scale ranging from 'a lot above average' to 'a lot below average'. The organizational performance measures are most directly influenced by employee/HR performance measures.

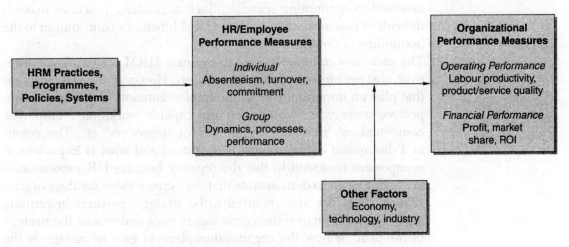

Figure 3.2(b):   Model of Linkage between HRM and Firm Performance

Source: Bratton and Gold 2003

However, the linkage between HRM and a firm's performance is complicated because the measures of employee performance and of HRM performance are only one set of variables that impact a firm's performance. Other variables such as the economy, technology, industry, etc. also affect a firm's performance. For example, the revenues of an export firm may rise or fall steeply because the currency of the firm's country of operations has risen or fallen.

While HRM professionals have no doubt about the strategic value of the HRM function, line managers are often sceptical of the role of HRM in the firm's performance. This scepticism arises largely because it is difficult to determine and measure the degree to which different HRM practices impact bottomline performance (see Figure 3.3). Measurement is central to the linkage between HRM and a firm's performance. However, selecting and using appropriate measures is difficult because (1) the measures of an organization's financial performance that are assumed to be objective and accurate may actually be inaccurate and misleading; (2) there may be a difference between the parameters that are measured and the parameters that are important; (3) the relationship between HRM activities and a firm's performance is often difficult to establish; and (4) business performance may be affected by causes external to the firm. These reasons are explored in detail below.

1. Variables may be measured inaccurately. For example, income statements of a firm are considered objective and accurate measures of an organization's financial performance. However, these may sometimes be based on measures that are inaccurate and misleading, as in the cases of WorldCom, Inc. and Enron, only two of a spate of companies involved in accounting scandals. Such accounting practices make it difficult to measure accurately the HRM function's contribution to the bottomline of the firm.

2. The measures commonly used to evaluate HRM are employee turnover, cost per hire, employee attitudes, etc. However, the HR attributes that play an important role in the implementation of the firm's competitive strategy are 'committed and capable workforce', 'employee competencies', 'training programmes for employees', etc. This results in a disconnect between what is measured and what is important. It is important to attend to this discrepancy because HR professionals are under strain to demonstrate that they create value for their organizations. They are also required to be strategic partners in running the business. Human resource managers must understand the strategy of the firm, or how the organization plans to gain advantage in the market place, and the implication of business strategy for human resources.

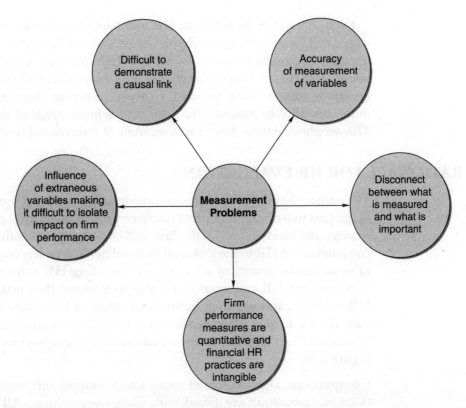

Figure 3.3:   Measurement Problems in Determining HR–Firm Performance Relationship

3. The measures of business success are quantitative and financial: return on investment (ROI), profit/earnings (P/E) ratio, etc. Human resource management practices, on the other hand, are intangible and largely subjective. Therefore, the relationship between HRM practices and firm performance frequently appears indirect and is difficult to prove. This is the reason that the belief about the critical significance of HRM remains largely at the 'hunch' level or is considered 'an act of faith'. Nonetheless, several studies of HRM and business performance have demonstrated that certain HRM practices contribute positively to market value, rate of return on capital employed, revenue per employee, productivity, etc. (see Table 3.1). These HRM practices include selection, workplace teams, performance-contingent pay, etc.

4. It is difficult to measure accurately the impact of HR practices on a firm's financial performance because of the impact of extraneous variables. For example, exchange rates affect a firm's financial performance and make it difficult to assess the extent to which performance has been influenced by HR practices.

Even if accurate measures of HR and firm performance were available, it would still be a challenge to demonstrate a causal link between the two. The question frequently raised is: Do certain HRM practices lead firms to perform better, or do firms that perform better adopt certain HRM practices? There is no simple answer to this question. However, it is clear that there is an increase in the pressure to measure the costs and achievements of the HR function. This emphasis can be traced to a number of interrelated trends.

RATIONALE FOR HR EVALUATION

The earlier chapters have discussed the transformation of the HRM function in the past two decades. Human resource professionals must contribute to the strategic decision-making of the firm and communicate to other managers the contribution of HR to the financial bottomline. Today, it is important for firms to measure the results of all activities, including HR activities. Hence, it is important for HR managers to be able to evaluate the costs and benefits of HR strategies and practices in financial terms. A few major trends that have contributed to the increased interest in HR evaluation are competition, benchmarking, and the transformation of the employment contract (see Figure 3.4).

Competition Due to technological advancements and economic liberalization, organizations are faced with high competition. All organizational functions are under pressure to justify their use of resources. As a result, organizations focus on cutting costs. This search for cost efficiency in all activities of the organization also extends to staff functions, such as HRM. International competition has challenged companies to ensure an efficient utilization of investment in intellectual capital or human capital. Competition has made it imperative for HRM personnel to demonstrate, with data, that HRM activities add value and significantly enhance competitive advantage.

Benchmarking There is a trend toward benchmarking that has also affected the HRM function. In human resource management, benchmarking 'entails a comparison of a given organization's costs (in this instance) or performance to those of its competitors or to other organizations in general'. Clear and specific indicators are essential to enable such comparisons. Some common indicators used in HR benchmarking include staffing ratios, number of HR professionals per hundred employees, the cost to fill a vacancy, the time to fill a vacancy, etc. Benchmarking is discussed in greater detail in the latter part of the chapter.

The transformation of the employment contract This has increased the interest in HR measurement. The concept of 'job for life' is no longer valid. The workforce consists of a large number of contingent employees. In such a

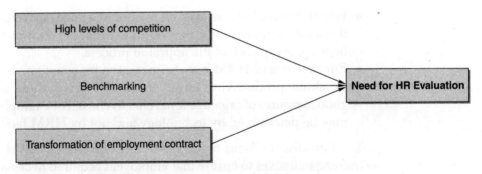

Figure 3.4:   Trends Creating Need for HR Evaluation

scenario, the very existence of the HRM function that performs activities such as career development, salary determination, succession planning, training, etc. gets questioned. The HRM function must demonstrate its business contribution to justify its existence.

There is often only a loose relationship between what is important and what is easily measurable. This is true of all aspects of an organization and, therefore, for the HRM function also. There is a general consensus on the importance of intangibles (such as human capital) for business performance. However, the measurement of intangibles poses a challenge for several reasons. Before we consider that, let us develop an understanding of the measures that can be used to demonstrate HRM performance.

MEASURES OF HRM PERFORMANCE

The performance of the HRM function is measured on the basis of the extent to which it 'creates value' for the firm. 'Value creation' refers to contributing in a measurable way to achieving the strategic goals of the organization. The HRM function creates value through HR activities that result in employee behaviour and competencies needed to achieve the strategic goals of the company. A key factor of organizational success is the effectiveness of the management of a firm's human resources. Therefore, it is important to develop measures of HRM effectiveness that can be related to a company's financial success. There are several views about the measurement of HRM effectiveness.

- Measures of organizational effectiveness can serve as measures of HRM effectiveness as the two are not distinct. However, this approach overlooks the fact that external forces such as vagaries of market forces or economic policies may adversely affect organizational performance, as discussed earlier, HRM practices may still continue to be effective.

- Effectiveness of HRM may be measured against specific goals, such as the implementation of a new appraisal scheme. However, such a goal neglects the quality of the appraisal process.
- Effectiveness of HRM may be measured by quantitative measures such as labour productivity, turnover, etc. However, these are not always good measures of organizational effectiveness. For example, productivity may be determined by technology and not by HRM factors alone.

Traditionally, the focus of the HRM function was on HRM activities such as training initiatives to ensure that employees acquired necessary skills; compensation and incentives that offered rewards to employees and teams for good performance; staffing to ensure that the firm had the right people in the right job, etc. A number of measures have been traditionally used to demonstrate HRM performance. The majority of these measures focussed on the *efficiency* with which the HRM function performed tasks (for example, the time taken to address employee grievances) or on the cost of the support functions (for example, expenditure on training per employee, cost per hire, etc.). Moreover, the HRM function was evaluated on those factors for which the actual responsibility rested with the operating managers. For example, employee retention, employee motivation, etc. are influenced more by the actions of the operating manager rather than by HRM practices.

These early measures of HRM performance were consistent with the role that the HRM function performed in organizations. The HR function was seen in a 'servant role' and was expected to work for operating managers. In this role, HR personnel and the function were useful as long as they provided services to customers but stayed 'out of the way' of running the business. This explains the emphasis of the early measures of HR productivity on indicators such as meeting requests on time and with lower cost.

In the past decade, HRM has moved towards emphasizing the implementation of strategy. There has also been a shift in the focus of HRM from activities to outcomes. Traditional activity measures of success of the HRM function need to be replaced with the outcome measures of HR activities. The role of HRM has also evolved over time. Today, the HRM function is viewed as having an important role in helping operating managers build organizational capability for successfully accomplishing business strategies. The role of HR has moved away from *working for* operating managers to *working with* them and helping them work. In the new role, the traditional HR measures are inappropriate and irrelevant. Since HR professionals are now expected to provide solutions, measures such as cost per hire or efficiency are clearly insufficient to understand the success of HR performance. The evolution of the role of HRM and the corresponding measures of evaluating HRM performance are given in Table 3.2.

Table 3.2:   Evolving Role of HRM and its Measurement

Dimensions of HRM Function	Traditional HRM	Progressive HRM	Truly Advanced HRM
HRM mission	To provide requested HR services	To shape the success of business	To lead the creation, preservation, and utilization of human and intellectual capital
HRM role	Viewed as 'servants', expected to do what the manager asks them to do	Viewed as 'partner' in defining business strategies to achieve competitive advantage	Viewed as primary source of competitive advantage, and essential for success
HR professionals	Inexpensive employees, kept away from business decisions	Part of strategic decision-making; expected to contribute to the decisions; considered an asset for the firm	Very well respected in the firm; decide when and where meetings to decide business direction will take place
Criteria for HR evaluation	Measures based on administrative activities, e.g., speed of response to customer requests, hiring graduates on time, number of benefit claims processed, cost per new hire, etc.	Measures emphasize HR's impact on business strategy and involve measuring HR's contribution to defining the strategic direction of business, focus is on quality (not quantity) of HR contribution	Measures emphasize ability of HR to grow, retain, and access intellectual capital, as well as knowledge of current and future employees of the organization (turnover rates, number of positions needed to be filled externally due to lack of internal talent, form supporting information)

Adapted from: Wintermantel and Mattimore 1997

It is important to develop appropriate measures for evaluating the effectiveness of HRM so that it may demonstrate its strategic value to an organization; establish its status as a strategic business partner; and substantially contribute to business success (see Exhibit 3.1 for an example). The objectives of HRM should be tangible so that they can be translated into measures of HR success. The measures used to evaluate HRM performance should be consistent with the mission of the HR function. The HRM function must define its mission (why do we exist?); identify tangible objectives that can be translated into measures of their success (what should we do?); and determine strategies for achieving the objectives (how will we do it?). The measure used to evaluate the HRM function should determine whether it was able to

Deloitte—HR can be Strategic

The following is a commissioned study conducted by Forrester (Consulting, Data, and Custom Consumer Research) on behalf of Deloitte:

Human resource management (HRM) executives have emphasized for years that HRM is strategic. However, there are a few difficult questions. What is strategic HRM? How is it measured? The answers to such questions have been largely subjective and qualitative. Many firms know intuitively that good human capital management practices lead to improved shareholder value. Yet, they struggle to identify and quantify the effect of these practices on the strategic initiatives of the firm. Deloitte developed the Human Capital Management Value Map (HCMVM) to demonstrate how the firm delivers value through people and HRM. By extending its Enterprise Value Map (EVM) into the HCMVM, Deloitte clearly demonstrated the strategic value that HRM brings to an organization.

The EVM is a highly structured method for a company to examine the components that drive shareholder value and identify potential improvement initiatives. This map helps the firm focus on what it is doing and why. The purposes of EVM are (1) to help companies change what they do and (2) to help them improve what they do (improve execution). According to the EVM, there are four main value drivers for increasing shareholder value:

1. *Revenue Growth* A function of how much product or service a firm can sell and at what price.
2. *Operating Margin* Revenue growth must be achieved profitably.
3. *Asset Efficiency* This has three major components: property, plant, and equipment.

4. *Expectations* These include company strengths and external factors and are concerned with management and execution capabilities that are required to ensure strong future performance.

The HCMVM is a matrix. Along one axis are four value drivers of (1) revenue growth; (2) operating margin; (3) asset efficiency; and (4) expectations. Along the other axis are seven human capital dimensions: (1) strategic HR alignment; (2) learning and development; (3) performance management and improvement; (4) workforce planning, talent management, acquisition, and deployment; (5) organizational capability; (6) change leadership and transformation; and (7) HR services and administration. The current HCMVM has more than 400 possible initiatives along these seven dimensions that can be used for business improvement. No firm can have all of them nor can all apply to each firm. The power of the value map lies in its ability to visually identify those key initiatives that will have the most effect on improving one or more of the four value drivers.

The HCMVM demonstrates the contributions of human capital initiatives toward shareholder value and helps executives prioritize and align their HR investments with their company's overall strategic objectives. It is an effective tool for companies that seek to leverage their human capital better for strategic advantage. Once an organization creates its value map, it has a powerful tool for focussing, prioritizing, and communicating improvement initiatives that will lead to increased shareholder value.

Adapted from: http://www.forrester.com, accessed on 20 February 2006, used with permission accomplish its objectives. For example, the HR function of a firm may have the mission 'Corner the market on the best software design talent'. Its objectives might include identifying at least three exceptional candidates for each available software design position. Another objective may be ensuring that the skills of the newly hired software designers are appropriate for implementing business strategies. The measures appropriate for these HR objectives might include the number of qualified candidates available/interviewed for each software design position, and the appropriateness of the skills of the newly hired managers (measured by the manager's satisfaction with skills). Measures such as cost per hire would be irrelevant here since they are inconsistent with the mission of the HRM function.

Most measures of HR focus on the *expenditure of resources* because it is most easily tracked in accounting and financial reporting systems. However, there are certain problems inherent in financial and accounting measures of HR performance (see Exhibit 3.2).

Exhibit 3.2

Are traditional financial and accounting indicators appropriate measures of HR performance?

Traditionally, financial indicators such as return on investment (ROI), earnings per share (EPS), net profit, etc. are used as measures of firm performance. At the functional or departmental level, the accepted measures of performance are controlled by budget.

Measures related to accounting and financial indicators have limitations when extended to the HR function. Yet, it often ends up using an organization's financial and accounting indicators for measurement of HR performance in spite of their limitations. The reasons that traditional financial and accounting indicators may not be appropriate measures of performance of human resources are discussed below.

1. The accounting, that is, measurement system in use today evolved during the time when tangible capital (physical capital, financial capital, etc.) was seen as the main source of competitive advantage. Today, however, there is a greater emphasis on knowledge and intangible assets. Hence,

conventional accounting systems do not appear appropriate. This is because the conventional accounting systems treat expenditures as expenses rather than investments in assets. Therefore, financial and accounting statements of firms tend to show all activities related to people, such as, recruitment, training, etc., as costs only. Thus, employees are seen as liabilities. Tangible assets such as machinery or building are treated differently and the revenues (income) they generate are taken into account. Investments in buildings or machinery, that is, the tangibles, depreciate over their useful lives. For example, a manager may invest Rs 1 million on machinery and the same amount in people. The investment on machinery depreciates over time, and earnings are gradually reduced over a 20–30 year period. On the other hand, the investment in people is viewed as an expense in its entirety during that year. Therefore, earnings

Contd

Exhibit 3.2 Contd

get reduced by Rs 1 million, the entire amount, in one year. If a manager's pay is tied to a year's earning, the manager would naturally prefer investing in tangible assets rather than intangible assets. This pressure to reduce expenses leads to poor decisions vis-à-vis human capital, such as employee layoffs, cancellation of training programmes, etc. These decisions are directed toward short-term cost savings.

It is imperative to move away from the accounting perspective that treats the HRM function as a cost centre and sees minimization of cost as a primary measure of success.

2. Traditional financial measures such as ROI, EPS, etc. lead to a short-term orientation on the part of the firm with respect to the management of human assets. Companies strive for profitability in the short-term even at the cost of long-term profitability. Training may be neglected due to this short-term perspective since training results in benefits over a long time. Human capital generates more value in the long run. However, because of a short-term perspective, companies often invest in physical capital instead of human capital.

3. Traditional accounting data provide only an aggregate financial reflection of the real business processes. It does not provide any feedback for corrective action. For example, a financial statement that shows a department to be under budget does not indicate what went wrong or right.

4. There is a time horizon implicit in most measurement systems. Most financial and accounting systems focus on resource consumption over a short time. One year is considered long-term. In measurement-driven organizations, HR managers need to demonstrate results and performance in less than a year. However, most HR practices take longer to demonstrate their impact. For example, culture-building is a long process that takes several years. When managers or firms make long-term investments in building culture, the costs of these efforts are quickly visible, but not the returns. Therefore, many organizations refrain from investing in long-term HR efforts. Training is the first casualty when budgets are tight.

The problems inherent in traditional financial and accounting measures for the management of human resources necessitate the development of HRM indicators that avoid these problems. Therefore, instead of profits, cash flow per employee (CFPE) appears to be a better measure of a firm's success. It measures the average contribution of an employee to the financial success of a firm and lessens the dependence of the measurement system on accounting principles. Shareholder value orientation is a long-term profitability measure, but it does not explicitly reflect employee's performance. The cash flow measure directs the attention of the management to the human resources of the firm. Managers prefer to measure shareholder value on the basis of capital invested in the business. Therefore, the cash flow per employee needs to be divided by the capital invested per employee.

(Cash flow/number of employees)/(total investment/number of employees) = (cash flow/capital invested)

When cash flow per capital invested is divided into the employee-related terms cash flow per employee and total investment per employee, it shows the average contribution that an employee has to make in relation to the money invested by shareholders. For example, installation of an additional facility in an industry may require an investment of Rs 8,000,000. If the cost of capital is 10% per annum, each employee must generate an average of Rs 800,000 per year.

Source: Buhner 1997; Becker, Huselid, and Ulrich 2001

Therefore, measures emphasise the cost of operating HR function, staffing ratio (number of HR personnel per 100 employees), and so on. These measures also track changes over time toward greater efficiency. However, these measures have several inherent problems (see Table 3.3a):

- Staffing ratios and measures of resources expended do not indicate how wisely or effectively the resources are being used. For example, one firm may have one person in their training department for every 60 employees. Another firm may have one HR person for every 75 employees in a department that performs several other functions along with training. Does this mean that the first firm has too many trainers? The answer depends on what the strategic approach of each firm is, and the extent to which training is a source of competitive advantage.

- It is also possible to misinterpret ratios. When a firm makes a shift from permanent employees to contractual hiring, the firm may appear to be more efficient. However, this may not always be actually true. To pursue the goal of 'efficiency', spending fewer resources and having fewer people becomes an end in itself. Efficiency is defined 'in terms of the resources used to produce a product or service'. Since anything divided by zero is infinity, one way to make HR appear more efficient would be to shrink the denominator (the number of employees or the value of resources consumed). However, consuming fewer resources by itself does not always suggest efficiency. This is because such measures do not take into account how these resources are being used. To determine the efficiency of the HR function, the focus must be not only on seeing what it costs or how many people it employs, but also what it does.

Other HR measures focus on the *level of activity* or *effort*. The number of people hired, number of people trained, etc. are the kinds of indicators used in this system. When the level of activity is taken as an indicator of HR performance, it does not reflect whether the activity is being performed effectively or whether organizational needs are being met. It is not enough to state the number of employees hired or the price at which they are hired. Rather, it is important to hire people who will likely work for the firm for a long while. Similarly, it is not enough to state the number of employees who were trained, but also that the employees trained were retained and resulted in improved organizational performance.

Some organizations have started focussing on employee attitudes, staff turnover, and employee satisfaction with HR services. Information about attitudes and satisfaction are obtained through surveys and interviews. Although obtaining information from the clients of HR is clearly advantageous, such responses may be susceptible to varying biases. Firms may obtain useful measures related to employee affect and perceptions of work environment. Yet,

Table 3.3(a):   HR Measures—Examples and Problems

HR Measures	Examples	Problems
Efficiency	Cost-per-hire, time-to-fill, training costs, time taken to process grievances	Do not reflect talent value, fixation on cost reduction can reject more expensive decision options that are of better value
Employee turnover	Percentage of employees leaving the firm	More directly influenced by line managers, only indirectly influenced by HR managers
Staffing ratios	Ratio of HR staff per 100 employees	Do not indicate how efficiently resources have been used
Expenditure of resources	Cost of HR function	Using fewer resources does not always suggest efficiency in utilization
Level of activity/effort	Benchmarks, number of people hired, number of people trained	Does not indicate effective HR performance, no way to know if organization's needs are being met
Employee attitudes	Satisfaction survey scores	Influenced more by line managers, responses obtained from employees are subject to bias
Indicators of Effectiveness of HR Practices		
HR planning	Extent to which the organization must hire in the open labour market, speed of filling up positions internally by qualified candidates	Influenced by whether line managers prepare subordinates for higher responsibilities
Staffing	Cost per hire, number of resumes received	Influenced by factors outside the HR function
Training	Annual cost of training	May not be related to need for training and hence performance improvement

Adapted from: Pfeffer 1997

these measures do not have much to do with the HR function, since employee attitudes and satisfaction are influenced more by line managers as compared to HR managers or the HR function. The HR function designs the HR practices but it is the line managers who implement them. Providing useful performance feedback to employees is largely up to peers or supervisors, not the HR manager. Other measures such as employee turnover are also only indirectly influenced by the HR function. This is a pitfall in most measures of HR effectiveness. As HR is a staff function, it has very little direct effect on many of the HR measures. Also see Table 3.3(b) for a summary of HR measures related to HR practices, HR professionals, and the HR function.

As what one measures is what one gets, it is important to develop appropriate measures of HR effectiveness, efficiency, and value. Measures driven by HR are no longer sufficient. The HR driven measures are of value only to HR professionals. It is necessary to develop business-driven HR measures (how HR can impact business success). The new HR measures are different from those traditionally used (see Table 3.4).

The range of available HR measures may be classified into three main clusters: internal operational measures, internal strategic measures, and external strategic measures (see Figure 3.5).

Table 3.3(b):   Summary of HR Practice Measures

Contd

HR Practice	Possible Measures	HR Practice	Possible Measures
Staffing	■ Acceptance per offer ratio ■ Number of applicants contacted compared with those reporting for job interview ■ Time to fill a job ■ Cost of filling a job ■ Percentage of internally filled jobs ■ Performance of hired applicants ■ Ratio of backup talent (number of prepared backups in place for top jobs)	Performance appraisal	■ Percent of employees receiving performance appraisal ■ Average merit increase granted by performance classification ■ Extent to which measurement systems are seen as credible
Training and development	■ Cost per trainee hour ■ Percentage of employees involved in training ■ Number of courses taught by subject ■ Payroll expense per employee ■ Time for new programme design ■ Number of training days and programmes held per year	Safety and health	■ Lost work days ■ Cost of injuries ■ Incidence of injuries ■ Trends in workforce illness
		HR professionals	■ HR competencies
Performance appraisal	■ Acceptance of appraisal process by employees	HR function	■ Ratio of total employees to HR professionals (measure of productivity) ■ Ratio of rupees spent on HR function to total sales ■ Administrative costs (efficiency of HR function) ■ Performance against the annual HR department budget

Contd

Source: Ulrich 1997

Table 3.4: Differences Between Traditional HR Measures and New HR Measures

Traditional HR Measures	New HR measures
HR-driven	Business-driven
Activity oriented (what the HR function does and how much it does of it)	Impact-oriented (how much the function improves business results)
Backward-looking (what has happened)	Forward-looking (diagnose processes and people capabilities to predict the future success of the firm)
Focus on individual HR practices (the performance of staffing practices, training and development practices, etc.)	Focus on entire HR system taking into account the synergy of all HR practices

Adapted from: Yeung and Berman 1997

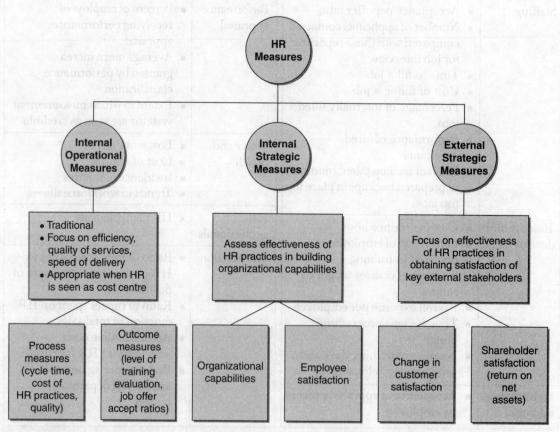

Figure 3.5: Three Clusters of HR Measures

Internal operational measures These measure the effectiveness of the design and implementation of the HR practices of a firm. Internal operational measures are the traditional HR measures for which the HR function and personnel are and have been held accountable. These measures focus on the efficiency and quality of HR services, the speed of delivering HR practices, and the quality of management of the overall HR function. Typical operational measures for HR practices may be divided into two types—*process measures* and *outcome measures*. Examples of process measures are cycle time, quality, and cost of HR practices. Levels of training evaluation, business impact of training, and job offer acceptance ratios are examples of outcome measures. Operational measures for HR function include the HR ratio (number of HR personnel to employee population), HR expenses as a percentage of operating expenses, the results of employee satisfaction surveys, etc. Operational measures are appropriate when the HR function is seen as a cost centre. However, today when the HR function has become more aligned with business strategy, these traditional measures are not viewed as adequate or sufficient to assess the performance of HR in its new and expanded role.

Internal strategic measures This category of HR measures assesses the effectiveness of HR practices in building organizational capabilities and enhancing employee satisfaction. Examples of organizational capabilities may include leadership effectiveness, competencies of employees, performance based culture, etc. To measure and track employee satisfaction, firms may develop an employee satisfaction index and peg the bonuses of its managers to the employee satisfaction levels. Motorola has developed an index called the individual dignity entitlement to measure the degree to which employee needs and expectations are met through HR practices.

Human resource managers design and develop HR practices such as performance appraisal, reward systems, promotion process, etc. However, the effectiveness of HR practices depends on their implementation by line managers. Therefore, line managers should be held accountable for internal strategic measures, for example, at Hewlett-Packard Development Company, (HP), the line managers are responsible for people management.

External strategic measures This category of measures focusses on the effectiveness of HR practices in obtaining satisfaction of key external stakeholders (customers and shareholders). Human resource practices are used to enhance satisfaction of customers and shareholders. To do so, organizations use various HR practices to build employees' understanding of the needs of customers. The key HR performance measure is the extent of change in customer satisfaction as a result of HR practices. Measures linking HR practices with shareholder satisfaction include return on net assets (RONA), ROI, etc.

To decide which HR measures add business value, HR professionals must understand how HR contributes to business success. A framework is required to develop specific HR measures. The steps in the design and development of HR measures are discussed in Table 3.5.

The stress on all HRM activities to 'add value' has led to an explosion of HRM measurement approaches. In the following section we will discuss various approaches for measuring the value of HRM activities.

APPROACHES TO HR EVALUATION

The productivity and efficiency of any function can be measured by some combination of cost, time, quantity, or quality indices. The HRM function must develop measurement approaches that will help it demonstrate its contribution to the firm's performance and ensure its place as a strategic partner. The goal of all HRM measurement approaches is to focus on activities and decisions related to human resources and thus enhance organizational success. The key objective of any approach to HRM measurement is to demonstrate the relationship between HRM and organizational outcomes and to use this understanding to improve the quality of HR decisions.

We now briefly discuss some general approaches to HR evaluation (see Table 3.6).

Table 3.5:   Steps in Design and Development of HR Measures

Steps	Measures
Determine the critical success factors of the firm	▪ Important business trends that impact the firm ▪ Factors in current and future business environment that will determine firm's success or failure ▪ The critical stakeholders ▪ Resources that are scarce but important for the success of the firm
Understand how HR can add value to the critical success factors	▪ Ways in which HR creates sustainable competitive advantage for the firm—organizational capabilities (customer service, innovation, etc.); intellectual capital; committed and competent employees; or loyal customers? ▪ What constitutes the highest value-added/unique contribution of HR in the firm?
Design the appropriate HR measures to be aligned with the framework	▪ Develop HR measures that reinforce and accomplish the intended contribution of HR ▪ Measures that are easy to implement should be adopted only if they are useful ▪ A 'weak' measure on the right issue is better than a 'strong' measure on the wrong issue

Adapted from: Yeung and Berman 1997

Table 3.6:   General Approaches to HR Evaluation

	Approaches to HR Evaluation		
	Stakeholder/Audit Approach	**Utility/Analytical Approach**	**Business Consulting Approach**
Focus	To determine the satisfaction of key users with HR services	Cost benefit analysis, and determining financial utility of HR services	HR functions as a strategic business unit and helps customers achieve maximum value from HR products and services
Criteria of HR Effectiveness	Employee satisfaction surveys; Perceived effectiveness of HR; Absenteeism rate; Cost of HR as a percentage of sales; Average number of days taken to hire an employee	*Asset method:* Value of employees (cost of training/total number of employees) *Expense model:* Economic effects of employee behaviour like absenteeism, turnover, etc. *Economic profitability:* Employees' contribution to the firm's performance (reward programme that improves productivity) *Cost benefit ratio:* Comparing benefits of HR practice to cost of delivery (ROI)	▪ HR viewed as profit centre ▪ *Quantitative measures:* decrease in turnover translated in financial terms to determine money value of training benefits ▪ *Qualitative measures:* changes in employee satisfaction index

Adapted from: Greer 2001

Stakeholder Approach

It focusses on determining the satisfaction of key users with the services provided by the HR function. This is perhaps the most important indicator of HRM effectiveness. According to this perspective, HR will be considered successful if the stakeholders (employees, customers, unions, suppliers, shareholders, etc.) report satisfaction with the HR function and its various practices. Typically, data for satisfaction with HR and for its perceived effectiveness is obtained through surveys or interviews. This approach is closely aligned with service orientation. Different stakeholders look for different goals. For example, shareholders want ROI; employees want a satisfying work environment; and customers want good service. Therefore, the measures or criteria

Exhibit 3.3

Xerox Focusses on Customer Satisfaction

Xerox Corporation (Xerox) attempts to quantify customer satisfaction. The company conducts an annual survey of about 500,000 customers regarding product and service satisfaction. The survey uses a five-point scale ranging from 5 (high) to 1 (low). It was found that providing excellent service (score of 5) was significantly more likely to lead to repeat business than just giving good service (score of 4). Xerox aims to create customers who are so delighted with the service they have received that they will tell others and convert those who are sceptical about Xerox. At the same time, Xerox intends to avoid making customers unhappy because they will speak about a poorly delivered service. It is believed that the real 'cost of quality' is more dramatically linked to the lost opportunities caused by an unhappy customer spreading bad publicity about the firm than to the loss of that customer alone. According to Xerox, the key to customer satisfaction involves ensuring employee satisfaction.

Source: Holbeche 2002

of effectiveness used include the degree of employee satisfaction measured through employee satisfaction surveys (ESS); cost effectiveness in delivery of HR practices; cost of HR as a percentage of sales; average number of days to hire an employee; absenteeism rates, etc. The stakeholder approach is also referred to as the audit approach. Several firms use the stakeholder approach for evaluating HR. For example, Xerox India Limited conducts an ESS every year involving all its employees (see how Xerox focusses on quantifying customer satisfaction at Exhibit 3.3). The results of the ESS are analysed to identify areas of improvement, and teams are organized to develop action plans to improve performance in these areas and to implement these plans before the next ESS. The ESS becomes a monitoring index, since the impact of the action taken can be seen in the next poll. Standard Chartered Bank has begun to include employee survey results in their report to external stakeholders. Hewlett-Packard India, Wipro Limited, American Express, and 3M India Limited are some other companies that monitor ESS results. Maruti Udyog Limited tracks customer satisfaction meticulously to enhance product and service quality.

Utility or Analytical Approach

The utility approach translates quantitative measures of HR effectiveness into financial indices. This approach is also called HR financial valuation since it involves a cost benefit analysis and determines the financial utility of HR services. However, valuation of HR services poses a major problem because the HRM function has not quantified its activities in financial terms (how HR helps in improving profits, reducing costs, or adding financial value). Expressing evaluation of HR in economic terms, nevertheless, is important because other function managers understand HR's contribution easily and because organizations' human resources are a source of competitive advantage. There are several optional utility approaches that may be used by a firm to quantify the value from HR activities. These are the asset method, the expense model, economic profitability, and cost benefit ratio.

Asset method This treats employees as assets. The firm's investment in each employee (asset) is measured by the costs incurred on that employee, such as the cost of training. Thus, the value of employees is determined in a way similar to that of capital resources. The value of an employee is determined by dividing the cost of training by the total number of employees.

Expense model This treats employees as an expense. It determines the economic effects of employee behaviour, such as absenteeism, job performance, turnover, etc. New HR initiatives are assessed by the extent to which they 'favourably influence controllable costs'. Controllable costs are, for example, voluntary turnover. A new HR initiative may be seen as effective if it reduces voluntary turnover.

Economic profitability It measures the employees' contribution to the firm's profitability. For example, a compensation plan that rewards employees for increasing the firm's profits improves profitability more than a plan that pays a fixed salary to employees.

Cost benefit ratio This compares the benefits of an HR activity to its cost. This is similar to calculating ROI. It helps justify a new HR programme.

Although the utility approach provides an effective measure of HR activities, it is difficult to apply to several HR applications since it requires much resources and effort. Certain HR practices such as succession planning or career planning have strategic impact but are difficult to measure in quantitative terms.

Business Consulting Approach

This approach requires the HRM function to act as a business consultant and help formulate important policies in the organization. Thus, an effective HR is one that functions as a strategic business unit (SBU). It focusses on helping customers achieve maximum value from HR products and services. Human resource activities and practices are seen as services and products rather than just policies. For example, benefits resulting from HRM programmes, such as decrease in turnover or improved performance, can be translated to financial terms by determining the money value of these benefits. According to this approach, the effectiveness of the HR function can be measured as a profit centre. It is quite possible, though, to evaluate HR function as a cost centre. Different quantitative and qualitative measures can be used to measure a firm's

HR effectiveness. However, excessive dependence on quantitative measures of HR evaluation may not be useful. Qualitative measures such as changes in the employee satisfaction index can also be good indicators of the effectiveness of HR.

These approaches are not mutually exclusive; some of the effectiveness measures may fit more than one category. Some other general evaluation approaches have also been applied to HR practices in recent years. These include the balanced scorecard, HR scorecard, benchmarking, and business excellence model (see Table 3.7).

Table 3.7: Contemporary Approaches to HR Evaluation

Approaches	Features
Balanced Scorecard	▪ Diagnostic tool that ensures that companies utilize the right processes and people to improve the performance of both customers and the business. ▪ Measures the satisfaction of investors, customers, and employees—the three key stakeholders—because that is the key to business success. ▪ Helps measure overall business performance. ▪ Ensures that the results of each activity will be aligned towards the achievement of an organization's strategic goals.
HR Scorecard	▪ Assesses the value of the HR function. ▪ Measures the contribution of HR to the financial success of the firm. ▪ HR audit is conducted; it assesses the maturity of HR systems, HR competencies, culture, business linkage, and assigns a score to each of these.
Benchmarking	▪ An approach to monitoring and evaluating HR performance. ▪ Compares selected performance indicators from different organizations, typically in the same industry, or with comparable organizations that are considered 'best in class'. ▪ Helps an organization know how well its HR practices compare with the 'best' HR practices in other, more successful, organizations.
Business Excellence Model (BEM)	▪ Assists organizations in achieving excellence through continuous improvements in the management and deployment of processes. ▪ Covers all the areas for business success and serves as a blueprint for total organizational performance. ▪ Anchored in quality management. ▪ Focus of BEM questionnaire is on 'generic' design, and not on the specific strategic goals of the organization. ▪ Less useful than the Balanced Scorecard as an organization-specific management tool. ▪ Used as a diagnostic tool by organizations.

Balanced Scorecard

The Balanced Scorecard first appeared in the results of a multi-company research study conducted in the US in 1990. The study was a reaction to the growing dissatisfaction with traditional financial measures as the main measure of corporate performance. It identified the need to develop a system based on an understanding of actual performance measured against key strategic goals. This came to be called the Balanced Scorecard. It was popularized by Kaplan and Norton in 1992. It is based on the stakeholder approach and defines what it takes for a company to succeed. Every business has multiple stakeholders. The business must interact with all stakeholders to function smoothly. According to the Balanced Scorecard, if a business is to be considered successful, it must satisfy the requirements of three stakeholders—investors, customers, and employees (see Figure 3.6). The investors want financial performance, measured by economic profitability, market value, and cash flow. The customers, who use the products or services of the firm, want quality and service, measured by market share, customer commitment, customer retention, etc. The employees of a firm want a good working environment, measured by employee and organizational actions.

The scorecard expresses the company strategy as a set of measurable goals. The goals take into account all the three stakeholders mentioned above. The scorecard helps the managers to focus on the actions required to achieve these goals, and thus it helps the organization in achieving the strategic goals. The Balanced Scorecard results in a clearly defined statement of vision and

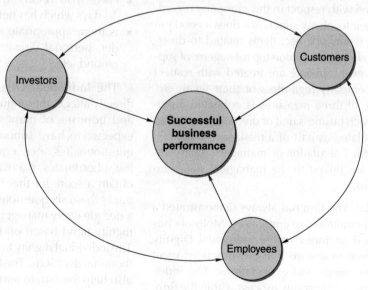

Figure 3.6:   The Three Stakeholders in Balanced Scorecard

strategy; a set of measurable goals with clearly specified and agreed targets; and a set of priority initiatives linked to the goals and targets.

Generally, however, the information from the Balanced Scorecard does not directly lend itself to cross-industry comparisons or other activities such as benchmarking. The balanced scorecard is being used by a number of firms to measure overall business performance. Prominent among these firms are AT&T, Sears, Eastman Kodak, and American Express. See Exhibit 3.4 for some examples of the application of the Balanced Scorecard.

Exhibit 3.4

Examples of Use of Balanced Scorecard by Some Firms

AT&T: The firm began the Balanced Scorecard approach in 1994. It tracks three indices: economic value added (EVA), customer value added (CVA); and people value added (PVA). The EVA is tracked by measuring financial results such as cash flow, profitability, etc. The CVA is tracked by internal and external surveys. The PVA is tracked by a survey that measures employee perception of leadership and diversity processes within their business. Some of the items included in the survey on leadership are: morale in my group is generally high; people are treated with respect in this company regardless of their level; my supervisor does a good job building teamwork, etc. Items related to diversity include: in my opinion top management supports diversity, people are treated with respect in this company regardless of their level, etc. Data on all three measures is collected annually for each business unit or division. The scores are calculated as part of a manager's Balanced Scorecard. Calculation of managers' salary increases are linked to the managers' Balanced Scorecard.

Motorola: The firm has always demonstrated a strong commitment to employees. Motorola has developed an index called Individual Dignity Entitlement to ensure that HR practices meet employee needs and expectations. The index helps monitor the equity process within the firm.

The index has six questions for determining the extent to which employees are being treated fairly:

- Do you have a meaningful job that contributes to the success of Motorola?
- Do you have the on-the-job behaviour and knowledge base to be successful?
- Is training available to upgrade your skills continuously?
- Do you have a career plan that is exciting, achievable, and being acted on?
- Have you received feedback in the last 30 days which has helped your performance?
- Is there appropriate sensitivity to your gender, personal circumstances, cultural background, etc.?

The Individual Dignity Entitlement index directly affects the annual performance review and bonuses of managers. Each manager is expected to have subordinates complete these questionnaires once a quarter. The scores of all the subordinates of a manager are calculated to obtain a score for that manager. The company tracks these six questions. The intent is that over a decade every manager will have an individual dignity trend based on the score on the index. The individual dignity trend may be used for promotional decisions. The tracking of the trend can also help the firm to ensure that its practices are

Contd

Exhibit 3.3 Contd

adding value through a more committed and competent workforce.

Sears: The company works on the premise that being a 'Compelling place to work', 'Compelling place to shop', and 'Compelling place to invest' are three critical success factors that will ensure and sustain the success of the firm in the long run. The logic of this premise is: by creating a 'compelling place to work', the behaviour of employees will change, which will, in turn, create a 'compelling place to shop'. This will result in more satisfied customers who will be more likely to visit Sears again. Thus Sears will be able to retain its clientele. When loyal customers return to shop, Sears will improve its productivity and financial results which will attract and also retain shareholders. Hence, Sears can become a 'compelling place to invest'. To implement this model, Sears understands that all senior managers must be evaluated on their performance on all the three critical success factors, not just on financial success. Sears undertook an extensive study to assess whether the model was in fact working. In 1995 a Sears taskforce collected data from 800 stores. Statistical tools were used to assess the relationship between the three critical success factors. The results show that for every 5% improvement in employee's behaviours (compelling place to work), customer retention was increased by 1.3% (compelling place to shop), and profit by 0.4% (compelling place to invest).

Sears translates 'soft' business issues (people) into 'hard' business issues (financial results). It also proposes that people are the drivers of business success. The firm has developed a measure called Total Performance Index. The bonuses of all managers are tied to this index; 25% of the index is based on a manager's success at making Sears a compelling place to work; 25% on making it a compelling place to shop; and 50% on making it a compelling place to invest. In this way managers at Sears are encouraged to focus on not only the financial outcomes, but also on the processes that contribute to such outcomes.

General Electric (GE): Though GE does not use the term 'Balanced Scorecard', the 2 ×2 matrix it uses actually helps the firm keep a balanced scorecard. The matrix consists of two dimensions of managerial behaviour—performance and values. Performance refers to the degree to which the manager accomplishes financial objectives. Values refer to the ways in which the manager behaves. Both the dimensions, performance and values, may be high or low. Combining the two dimensions in a 2×2 matrix produces four cells: cell 1(low performance/low values), cell 4 (high performance/high values), cell 2 (low performance/high values), and cell 3 (high performance/low values). Cell 1 and Cell 4 are easy to deal with. Cell 3 and Cell 2 pose a challenge. Managers in Cell 3 (high performance/low value) get rewarded because they meet their targets even though they did not use the GE values. However, to ensure the continuance of GE values, the firm does not tolerate managers who do not practice them and so managers in Cell 3 are replaced. Managers in Cell 2 (low performance/ high values) would be given a second chance to learn to meet the goals.

General Electric developed the GE Leadership Effectiveness Survey (LES) to measure the extent to which GE managers practise the GE values. The GE-LES describes 8 GE values in behavioural terms. The LES has 48 behaviourally anchored questions about the 8 GE values. Data is collected about each manager through the 360 degree feedback method, that is, from subordinates, peers, clients, and supervisors. The data from LES is used to track and monitor the process of value adherence by managers.

Source: Ulrich 1997; Yeung and Berman 1997

The Balanced Scorecard approach assumes that all the stakeholders are interrelated (see Figure 3.6). Employee attitudes and behaviour influence customer satisfaction and retention which in turn influence the satisfaction of shareholders and the investments made in the firm. Shareholder satisfaction influences employee satisfaction through stock options, bonuses, or the investments made in employee growth and development. A breakdown in even one of the components leads to a drop in performance.

Of the three stakeholders, employees are the most difficult to measure. Employee measures in the Balanced Scorecard include measures of productivity, people, and processes. Employee success is tracked through these three measures (see Figure 3.7). These measures, thus, document the outcome of HR practices.

Productivity Productivity measures generally involve output divided by input. Output may be any indicator of what the organization is trying to achieve, for example, revenue, profits, etc. Input measures are time, labour, capital, or any other resource used in producing goods and services. As part of the Balanced Scorecard, productivity measures generally rely on some indicators of output per employee. For example, revenue per employee is an example of overall productivity measure; productivity may be measured by dividing the total revenue by the total number of employees.

Productivity measures are simple, understandable, and comparable across firms within an industry. Hence, productivity indices are useful measures of employees on the Balanced Scorecard. However, these measures also have a disadvantage. The productivity measures may not be true indicators of employee competence. For example, manufacturing firms with high technology investment may have higher output per employee. But these firms may not necessarily have more capable or committed employees.

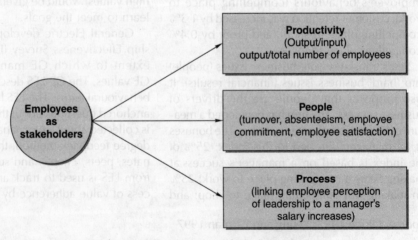

Figure 3.7: Balanced Scorecard—Measures of Employee Success

Productivity measures vary by industry since some industries are more labour-intensive than others. Apart from broad productivity measures, specific industry productivity measures may also be used as part of the Balanced Scorecard. For example, in the financial services industry, productivity may be measured in terms of transactions per employee. In an automobile industry, productivity may be measured in cars produced per employee.

People To measure people as part of the Balanced Scorecard, assessment may focus on what people do, how they feel, and what they know. These measures relate the response of employees to the practices of the firm.

The most common measures of what people do or how they behave are turnover, absenteeism, and grievances. Attitude of employees is reflected in their behaviour. Turnover or retention may be used to indicate employee commitment. It is a common idea that when employees are dissatisfied with business, they may show their dissatisfaction by leaving the organization. Similarly, absenteeism may also indicate employee attitude. Most organizations use a morale or attitude survey to track how employees feel about various aspects of their work. The employee survey data is useful for the Balanced Scorecard when the data is longitudinal and results in action.

Another measure of people relates to identifying what people know, or their knowledge and competencies. One way this can be identified is by determining how many people below the top 100 jobs are qualified to move into these jobs immediately. Over time, this measure may show, for example, that there is a change from about 3:1 (three back-ups for each of the 100 jobs) to 1:1 (one back-up for each of the 100 jobs). This measure is an indicator of employee back-up or the bench strength within a firm.

Processes This aspect of the Balanced Scorecard is more concerned with systems and dynamics within a firm rather than with people. For example, an organization can use surveys to track employee perception of the leadership processes within the firm, as is done by AT&T. This data is collected on an annual basis for each business unit. The scores are used as part of a manager's Balanced Scorecard and are considered while calculating salary increases.

Balanced Scorecards have not evolved recently. Managers have always been accountable to investors, customers, and employees. However, the use of Balanced Scorecards emphasizes that the employee dimension must be measured accurately. Tracking productivity, people, and process measures helps ascertain the impact of HR on the business performance of the firm. The usefulness of the Balanced Scorecard framework derives from the simple conceptual and diagnostic tool that it provides to ensure that companies utilise the right processes and people to further customer and business performance.

HR Scorecard Approach

Another approach often used by managers to assess the value of the HR function is the HR Scorecard approach. The HR Scorecard measures the effectiveness and efficiency of the HR function in producing those employee behaviours that are important for a firm to achieve its strategic goals. The HR Scorecard is a system of measurement. The Scorecard shows the 'metrics' that the firm uses to measure HR activities as well as the employee behaviours resulting from these activities. The HR Scorecard manages HR as a strategic asset and also measures the contribution of HR to the financial success of the firm. Thus, the Scorecard highlights the causal link between HR activities, employee behaviours, and the resulting organizational outcomes and performance. The Balanced Scorecard discussed earlier incorporates measures that describe the actual value creation process rather than focussing on the financial results only. The HR Scorecard approach strengthens one aspect of the Balanced Scorecard, that is, how best to integrate the role of HR into an organization's measurement of business performance.

To create an HR Scorecard, the manager must

1. know the company strategy;
2. understand the causal links between HR activities, employee behaviours, organizational outcomes, and the organization's performance; and
3. have the metrics to measure HR activities, emergent employee behaviours, the strategically relevant organizational outcomes, and the performance of the organization.

Steps in Creating an HR Scorecard

The HR Scorecard approach can be used to create a strategically result-oriented HR system. There are seven steps towards creating such a system (see a synopsis at Table 3.8).

Defining the business strategy Building a results-oriented HR system starts by defining the company's strategic plans. For example, 'to become a global leader' may be the strategic plan of a firm. Senior HR managers provide important planning input at this stage by way of their insights about the human resources in their own company and in those of the competition. Towards the end of this stage, broad strategic plans get translated into specific strategic goals.

Outlining the company's value chain A business needs to perform strategic activities to achieve its strategic goals. For example, to become a global leader, a firm in the FMCG sector must develop new and unique products. Each such activity requires certain employee behaviours. The FMCG firm requires employees who have the expertise to develop new products.

Table 3.8:   HR Scorecard Approach—Creating a Strategically Result-oriented HR system

Steps in Using the HR Scorecard	Example of an FMCG firm
1. Define business strategy	▪ To be a global leader
2. Outline the value chain of the company	▪ Develop new and unique products, which requires certain employee behaviours and also requires employees who have the expertise to develop new products
3. Identify strategic organizational outcomes	▪ Development of new products
4. Identify required workforce competencies and behaviour	▪ Creativity and proactivity, working to find novel solutions
5. Identify relevant HR systems and practices	▪ Training to enhance workforce creativity and innovation
6. Design HR Scorecard measurement	▪ Has morale gone up or down as a result of HR practices?
7. Periodically evaluate the measurement system	▪ Does the HR practice have desired impact on employee competencies?

Adapted from: Dessler 2005

Identify the strategic organizational outcomes In order to achieve strategic goals, every company must produce critical, strategically relevant outcomes. The development of new products is one such strategic outcome for the FMCG company mentioned above. Hence, an organization at this stage identifies and specifies the strategically relevant organizational outcomes.

Identify the required workforce competencies and behaviours At this stage the managers should attempt to identify those employee competencies and behaviours that must be exhibited by the employees in order for the organization to produce strategically relevant organizational outcomes and, hence achieve its strategic goals. The employees of the FMCG company must be willing to work proactively to find novel solutions.

Identify relevant HR systems and policies Once the required employee competencies and behaviours have been identified, the manager can focus on identifying the HR activities that will help to produce these employee competencies and behaviours. For example, the HR activities to develop these competencies may include special training programmes. However, the manager has to be specific about the kind of training programme required.

Design the HR scorecard measurement This stage seeks to determine how to measure organizational outcomes, employee competencies, and specific

HR activities. Thus, specific measures need to be developed. This requires considerable thought. For example, how will morale be measured? The measures help quantify HR activities, employee behaviours, and organizational outcomes, and thereby assess HR performance unambiguously and quantitatively. For example, it can be shown whether employee morale has gone up or down and by how much. This also helps the HR professional demonstrate how the HR activities of the firm affect employee behaviour, customer satisfaction, and thus, the financial performance of the firm. The HR Scorecard is crucial to this measurement process.

Periodically evaluate the measurement system The HR manager should evaluate measures and links periodically to make sure they are still valid. There is no certainty that the various measures in HR scorecard will always stay the same. It is also possible that a particular HR activity is not having the desired impact on employee competencies and behaviours.

Another HR Scorecard to measure the maturity level of HR in an organization was developed in India by Rao (1999). The model is based on the following assumptions:

- Competent and motivated employees are needed to provide quality products and services to enhance customer satisfaction.
- The commitment and competencies of employees can be developed through HR practices. An organization with high HRM maturity has well-developed HR practices. The maturity of HRM can be measured through an HRD audit.
- The human resource competencies of HR and line managers play an important role in the implementation of HR practices and systems to enhance the linkage between employee satisfaction, competency building, and customer satisfaction.
- The HRD culture created through HR practices and systems and by HR professionals plays a crucial role in building sustainable competencies in the organization.
- The HR practices, systems, competencies, and culture must be aligned with the business goals of the organization. This alignment is ensured through linkages with customer satisfaction and employee motivation.

HR Audit

An HR audit is conducted to obtain a score on the HR scorecard. It involves assessing each of the above factors (HR systems maturity, HR competencies, culture, and business linkage) and assigning a score to each factor (see Figure 3.8).

An HR audit is concerned with the assessment of the HR function. It is a comprehensive evaluation of HR strategies, practices, skills, and systems in

Name of the Organization				
HR Practices Maturity	HR Competencies of HR and Line managers	HRD Culture	HR and Business Linkage	Overall Grade/ Rating
A	A	B	C	AABC

Figure 3.8: Sample HR Audit Format

Source: Rao 1999

the context of the business goals of the organization. The future needs of the firm are determined on the basis of an assessment of the present HR activities and the competencies of HR personnel. There should be an alignment between the HR function and the business goals of the firm to ensure that the HR function contributes to organizational goal achievement. Moreover, the skills of the HR personnel should be aligned with HR goals. An HR audit assesses and ensures these alignments. The HR audit process comprises four steps.

1. Determine the scope of the audit. Will the audit focus on the entire HR function or on a specific HR practice?
2. How will the audit be conducted? Information on ratios and measures of turnover, absenteeism, etc. is important at this step.
3. Collect data using interviews, questionnaire survey, observations, etc.
4. Analyse the data, and take corrective action, if required.

An HR audit yields a report that typically provides a summary of the strengths and weaknesses of the HRM function. It also describes the deficiencies of the function and provides suggestions for corrective action to address these deficiencies. An HR audit can help to improve the efficiency of the HR function. However, it is *not* counted as one of the most valid approaches to measuring the HRM contribution to the organization's bottom-line performance.

An overview of the questions that are asked as part of an HR audit is presented in Exhibit 3.5. Several purposes are served when firms undertake an audit of HR function, practices, and professionals. The reasons firms undertake HR audits are highlighted in Exhibit 3.6.

Three types of audits may be carried out on HR: the HR practices, HR professional, and the HR department or function (see Figure 3.9).

HR practices An audit of HR services involves an assessment of the various services offered by the HR department (see Figure 3.10). These services include, for example, staffing, training and development, appraisal, rewards,

---

Exhibit 3.5

Questions Addressed in HR Audit

- What are the short-term and long-term business plans of the firm? Where does the company want to be ten years from now or one year from now?
- What types of core competencies will be required by the firm to achieve its goals?
- What skills will be required by employees at different levels and in different functions to ensure organizational goal achievement?
- What is the current skill base or the available competencies of the employees in the company?

- What HR practices and systems are available within the firm to help the organization build its competency base for the immediate future as well as in the long term?
- How effective are the current HR practices in developing people and competencies?
- How effective is the existing skill base of HR professionals?
- Are the structure of the HR department, the number of HR personnel, and the HR budget appropriate?

Adapted from: Rao 1999

Exhibit 3.6

Why do Firms Undertake HR Audits?

Firms undertake HR audits to

- make HR practices and activities relevant to the business goals of the firm. Changes in business environment, organizational restructuring, introduction of new technology should be accompanied by changes in HR function to ensure that the HR function is aligned with business goals and strategies;
- take stock of the present status and to use the HR audit information for moving in a new direction;
- measure and understand dissatisfaction with

some current HR practices (for example, HR audit may be conducted to obtain feedback about the current performance appraisal system based on which the firm may identify what aspects of the system need to be changed or improved upon);
- track the performance of the HR function on a regular basis and align the audit score with the managers' salary increases; and
- track the competencies of HR professionals with a view to identify gaps and bridge these gaps through training.

Adapted from: Rao 1999

---

etc. Four types of assessment are made for each of these services: activity, customer value, cost/benefit, and research.

The beginning of the audit on HR practices describes what services are offered. This is referred to as an activity audit. An *activity audit* answers questions

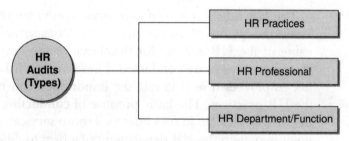

Figure 3.9: Types of HR Audits

such as: Do the HR practices focus on the more operational (day-to-day) issues or on strategic (long-term) issues? What are the responsibilities of the HR managers and the line managers for the different aspects of HR services? What resources are being used to accomplish HR work? Sometimes, activity assessment may point out that some work related to employees lies outside the HR department, though, in fact, it should have been within the HR department. For example, the communications department of a firm was part of the public relations department of the firm. An activity analysis found that effective communication included activities such as sharing information with employees, building employee commitment, announcements of compensation programmes, etc. that were intricately linked with HR processes. Hence, as a result of activity analysis, the communication department of this firm was merged into the HR department.

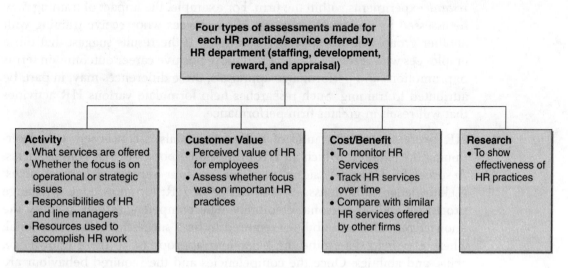

Figure 3.10: Summary of Auditing Process of HR Practices

Adapted from: Ulrich 1997

The HR function is seen as a service provider and the users of the service assess the quality of service provided. *Customer value* refers to the perceived value of the HR activity for the users, or the employees. Human resource customer surveys are conducted. These surveys list all HR practices and then ask employees (users) to rate the importance and/or effectiveness of each of the HR practices. The basic premise of conducting a customer survey is that the user of services knows how well those services are delivered. This assessment may help the HR department of a firm to determine whether company efforts were directed towards HR activities that were important. This information is then used by the firm to prioritise its efforts towards important activities.

However, obtaining information from the users of HR services about how well the services are delivered poses its own challenges. For one, the users of HR services may know what they want but they may not know what is important for the success of the firm. For example, employees may want flexible benefit programmes, but they may not understand the financial impact of these benefit programmes.

A *cost benefit analysis* of each HR service can be carried out using certain formulae. Cost benefit analysis of HR services help monitor HR services, track them over time, and compare them to similar HR services being offered by other firms. These cost benefit measures are conceptually referred to as 'utility' analyses since they define the utility or value of an HR practice. It is possible through these measures to translate HR practices into financial results.

The effectiveness of HR practices can be demonstrated by conducting *research* experiments within the firm. For example, the impact of training may be assessed by comparing a group of employees who receive training with another group who do not receive training. If the results suggest that those employees who received training had more positive career outcomes in terms of promotions and performance appraisals, these differences may, in part, be attributed to training. Such researches help formulate various HR activities that will result in greater firm performance.

HR professionals An audit of HR professionals is concerned with determining the extent to which an HR professional possesses HR competencies. A successful HR professional must possess four clusters of competencies: (1) knowledge of business; (2) knowledge of HR; (3) knowledge of change processes; and (4) personal credibility. The competencies help identify the knowledge, skills, and abilities required to be a successful HR professional. These also help determine the behaviour appropriate to these knowledge, skills, and abilities. Once the competencies and the required behaviour are identified, data is collected about the extent to which an HR professional demonstrates the identified competencies. Data may be collected through self-assessment where the HR professional rates himself/herself or by conducting a survey of the employees of the firm. The collected data must then be summarized to provide feedback to the HR professionals. The feedback is designed to help HR professionals improve their competencies. Data may be summarized for a single HR professional or they may be combined and summed into an HR competence audit of the overall HR function. An action plan can be created based on the data to improve the competencies of an HR professional or of the entire HR function. Auditing HR professionals should be an ongoing continuous activity rather than a single event.

Human resource department or function As mentioned above, the competency of the HR function may be determined by summing the individual competencies of HR professionals. It is also possible to audit the HR department by obtaining ratios that indicate the HR function's performance or effectiveness (for example, the ratio of HR professionals to total employees; the ratio of the HR budget to total sales; operating within HR budget).

As is evident, HR audits provide important information about HR effectiveness and help determine the quality of HR within a firm. An HR audit helps in calculating the scores for the HR Scorecard. The Scorecard presents a numerical grading to reflect the level of maturity of HR practices, HR personnel, and the HR function in the firm.

Benchmarking

Organizations can strive for competitive advantage and to improve performance by benchmarking standards of excellence from other firms in the area of HR just like in finance, marketing, research and development, etc. Though first used in the US quality movement, benchmarking has gained popularity in the last decade as an approach to monitoring and evaluating HR performance. The term *benchmarking* denotes a comparison of selected performance indicators of an organization with those from different organizations, typically in the same industry, or with comparable organizations that are considered 'best in class'. Xerox is generally credited with the origination of benchmarking. It used this approach to reduce its manufacturing cost. Benchmarking helps an organization know how well its HR practices compare with the 'best' HR practices in other, more successful, organizations. Thus, it involves a comparison of the aspects of one organization's practices with those of other organizations. Products, services, and practices must be measured against those of competitors or of market leaders on an ongoing basis to study how they are better at certain activities. Sometimes, comparisons may be made with firms from a different industry. It is thus a form of auditing.

A successful benchmarking exercise requires careful selection and manipulation of comparison measures. For example, a performance indicator for the marketing function may be 'marketing expenditure per marketing employee'. When applied to HR, benchmarking involves the collection of information about specific HR practices from a large number of respondents from several firms. Benchmarking HR practices serves a number of purposes (see Figure 3.11):

1. It enables a firm to determine how it is delivering HR services. By looking at how other organizations are accomplishing various tasks and responsibilities, a firm can audit itself. The self-audit will help the firm identify areas in which its activities are within or outside a given norm.

2. It helps a firm to learn from the successes and mistakes of other organizations.

3. It serves as a tool that can be used by the firm for creating motivation to change. By learning what successful firms are doing by way of HR activities, line managers and HR managers can build a strong case for allocating resources to HR activities in similar ways.

4. It also helps set direction and priorities for an HR manager. Rather than fall into the trap of trying to do everything well within limited resources, benchmarking helps HR managers to focus on critical HR activities.

5. It enables a company to see how its competencies in HR practices compare with those of its competitors. It also helps assess improvement in HR competencies over time.

Benchmarking is likely to be beneficial for an organization; therefore, HR indicators that contribute relatively more to the overall performance of the firm must be identified. Some examples of HR indicators for benchmarking are presented in Exhibit 3.7.

These indicators help a firm not only to evaluate its own HR practices in relation to its operational and strategic goals, but also to compare the effectiveness of HR practices between companies, divisions, or business units. Organizations can use internal client (employee) feedback about existing HR practices and prioritise the critical success factors within the HR function based on this feedback. Critical success factors are those that make a difference to the success or failure of an organization. Appropriate indicators for benchmarking are selected on the basis of these critical success factors.

Figure 3.11: Purposes of Benchmarking HR Practices

Exhibit 3.7

Performance Indicators for HR Benchmarking

HR Function
- Ratio of HR managers to line managers
- Structure of HR function (decentralized/centralized/divisionalized)
- Number of HR professionals per employee

HR Practices
- Retention rates for key worker groups
- Percentage of new recruits who are still with the organization after six months
- Percentage of salary bill spent on training
- Organizational climate index (degree of employee commitment)
- Customer satisfaction index
- Total revenue per employee
- The ratio of the total cost of employment to total expenditure
- The ratio of the number of training days to the number of employees
- The ratio of the total training budget to the total employment expenditure
- The ratio of total compensation cost to total revenue

Competencies of HR Personnel
- Knowledge of business (extent to which HR professional understands the financial, strategic, and technological capabilities of the organization)
- Quality of service (extent to which HR manager provides high quality HR services such as training and development)
- Management of change (extent to which HR professional increases the firm's capability for change through creativity, problem solving, etc.)

Adapted from: Hiltrop and Despres 1994; Holbeche 2002

The process of benchmarking consists of the following phases when used for HRM evaluation (see Figure 3.12):

1. The identification of the HR practices that the organization wishes to benchmark. Does it wish to benchmark compensation or training or HR performance measures such as turnover and absenteeism? The factor chosen for benchmarking should be critical to the organization's success and overall effectiveness.

2. The identification of the people who will be part of the team involved in the benchmarking exercise. A team is required because of the range of activities important for conducting benchmarking evaluation.

3. Identification of the internal units/departments/divisions, competitors in the same industry, and other firms against whom the firm wishes to benchmark. These are called the 'benchmarking partners'. The chosen partners should be willing to participate in the exercise by sharing information, and should have the so-called best practices.

4. Collection of data from each of the benchmarking partners.

5. Analysis and interpretation of the data.

6. Preparation of a written report of the major findings from the benchmarking exercise based on the analysis.

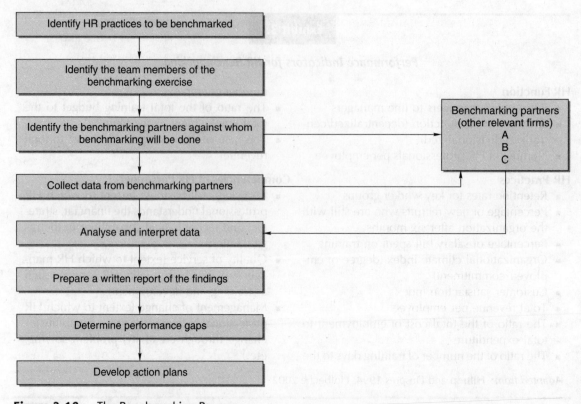

Figure 3.12:   The Benchmarking Process

Adapted from: Bratton and Gold 2003

7. Determination of performance gaps between the way things are in the organization and the desired or 'best practice'. The best practice for a particular organization depends on the business strategy of the firm.
8. Development of action plans to address the performance gaps and to implement the best practices in the areas in which the gap has been identified. This will help improve HR strategy and practice.

Benchmarking can be used to find out exactly what is meant by 'added value' in different contexts, and the role of HR in adding that value. For benchmarking to help a firm create a long-term source of competitive advantage, the information derived from benchmarking will need to be rare, difficult to imitate, and valued by the internal and external customers of the firm. However, if a firm readily shares such information with other firms, it probably means that it does not have much strategic value for the firm. Here it would be interesting to consider the case of HP, one of the most widely benchmarked companies in the world. The HR practices of HP have also been widely reported in the business press and many academic books and articles. Why should HP share this information that will certainly become available to competitors? This may be due to two reasons: first, just knowing what a firm does is of no great help unless information about how the firm generated the solution is available, as well as the context in which it was implemented; and secondly, HP relies a lot on leveraging employee competencies and talents in new and different solutions. Thus, HP is continuously improving its intellectual capital. Hence, by the time a firm replicates what it learned during the benchmarking process, HP is likely to have already created new competencies to allow it to adapt to new situations. HP is an example of learning with great speed and hence it comes out the winner.

Though benchmarking brings certain advantages, it also has some limitations. Benchmarking gets bad press when organizations copy 'best practices' from other organizations. When firms use benchmarking solely for the purpose of emulating best practices rather than for improving performance, advantages may be short-lived and also expensive. Moreover, mere implementation of a particular HR practice may not result in benefits. The most important information during benchmarking does not come from the actual data, but rather from the qualitative information on how and why the outcomes were achieved. There are, of course, those sceptics who believe that it is not appropriate to measure the effectiveness of HRM. According to them, HRM is concerned with attitudes like satisfaction, commitment, etc. and hence it is sufficient to measure HRM in humanistic terms alone.

Nevertheless, a well-conceived and well-designed benchmarking programme helps a firm to initiate focussed programmes that move the firm from its current position. The most commonly used form of HR benchmarking involves salary surveys. One of the reasons for not going beyond benchmarking compensation is the difficulty of finding standard and acceptable performance indicators as are available in financial management, such as ROI. The lack of benchmarking is also because of the reluctance of firms to divulge sensitive information about their HR practices related to employee retention, employee costs, etc.

Benchmarking HR practices has an important implication for the strategic role of HRM—it provides the organization a basis for concentrating attention and efforts on the highest value-adding HR activities that are more likely to be practiced by successful companies. Benchmarking allows HR professionals to commit limited resources to the most critical HR activities instead of trying to do everything well and please everyone.

Business Excellence Model

The roots of the concept of 'business excellence' can be traced to the publication of the book *In Search of Excellence* by Peters and Waterman. Developments in management science such as total quality management (TQM), business process reengineering (BPR), benchmarking, etc. focussed only on specific aspects of business (such as quality, processes, or systems). They did not encompass overall organizational performance. This gap was filled by the Business Excellence Model (BEM) developed by the European Foundation for Quality Management (EFQM). The Model is designed 'to assist organizations achieve excellence through continuous improvements in the management and deployment of processes to encourage a wider use of best practice activities'. The model covers all the areas of business success and serves as a blueprint for total organizational performance. Another broadbased business excellence model is the Malcolm Baldrige National Quality (MBNQ) Award that was introduced in the US for those firms that excelled in quality management and quality achievement.

The BEM is anchored in the idea of quality management. The model has been most widely adopted by the manufacturing industry. However, the EFQM states that the BEM applies equally across a wide range of industries, from service sector firms to public sector bodies. The BEM uses seven criteria to evaluate performance:

1. Result orientation
2. Customer focus
3. Leadership and constancy of purpose
4. Management by processes and facts
5. People development and involvement
6. Partnership development
7. Public responsibility

The model assesses the quality of the performance of the organizational processes relative to previous years and to competitors or benchmark organizations. Relative performance is assessed in the areas of *enabling activities* and *observed results*. The five enabling criteria are (1) leadership; (2) people; (3) policy and strategy; (4) partnerships and resources; and (5) processes. The four results criteria are (1) performance; (2) customers; (3) people; and (4) society. The current performance of the firm is evaluated against these nine criteria (five enablers and four results) on the basis of a questionnaire consisting of 32 standard statements. Scores are obtained on the basis of answers to these questions. Scoring treats all organizations alike and no adjustments are made for size or industry. The scoring system allows an organization to benchmark its score against those of other firms or against its own scores from previous years. Areas of poor or low performance against previous years or competitors can be identified based on scoring comparisons. Thus, opportunities of improvement are identified against poor performance relative to standard criteria. The model does not provide information on how low scores can be improved. However, it is believed that an organization can improve its systems by introducing quality management systems.

The Tata Group has evolved the Tata Business Excellence Model (TBEM). The TBEM framework features the Malcolm Baldrige Core Values (see Figure 3.13). The objective of the TBEM is to ensure that all Tata Group companies achieve well-defined levels of business excellence. Only those Tata Group companies that qualify based on the TBEM excellence criteria are permitted to use the Tata brand name. Tata Main Hospital adopted the model in 1995. The basic framework and features of the TBEM model are presented in Exhibit 3.8.

The Malcolm Baldrige criteria incorporate 11 key values and concepts woven into the seven Baldrige categories. These core values and concepts are integrated into the principles and practices of the highest-performing organizations. They are critical to how successful a firm is in developing its approach to quality and performance improvement.

The BEM focusses on generic processes such as new product development, training, etc. Though improvements in these generic processes are useful in themselves, they may not necessarily be relevant to an organization's strategic goals and priorities. To enable benchmark comparisons, the focus of the BEM questionnaire is on 'generic' design, and not on the specific strategic goals of the organization. This makes the BEM less useful than the Balanced

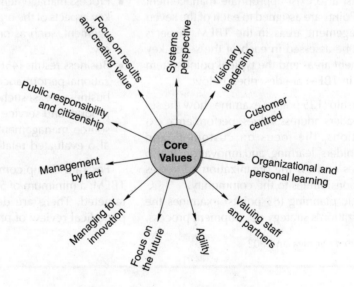

Figure 3.13:   Malcolm Baldrige Core Values

Adapted from: http://www.communityactionpartnership.com/about/about_partnership/ award_for_excellence/Baldrige_Core_Values.pdf, accessed on 1 May 2006

Exhibit 3.8

Tata Business Excellence Model (TBEM)

The basic framework and features of the TBEM are

- delivering continuously improving value to customers;
- improvement of overall effectiveness of the organization; and
- organizational and personal learning.

The framework of the model comprises a set of core values derived from the Malcolm Baldrige Award. There are eleven core values. These core values form the foundation of the model and are drivers of organizational excellence. The core values demonstrate the management's commitment to the stakeholders of the organization.

The model also elaborates the seven key management areas where action is required in specific and measurable terms. The organization has to exhibit a strong sense of result orientation. There must also exist appropriate management systems. Points are assigned to each of the seven key management areas in the TBEM. Aspects that must be assessed in each of the seven key management areas and the typical point system followed in TBEM are described below.

- Leadership (125 points) examines how the senior leaders address values, performance expectations, the focus on customers and stakeholders, learning, and innovation. It also focusses on how the organization addresses its responsibilities to the community.
- Strategic planning (85 points) examines the organization's strategy development process,

or how it develops strategic objectives, action plans, and related human resource plans; how it deploys plans; and how it tracks performance.

- Customer and market focus (85 points) examines how the organization determines requirements, expectations, and preferences of customers, and builds customer relationships.
- Information and analysis (85 points) examines the performance measurement system of the firm and how it analyses performance data and information.
- Human resources (85 points) examines how the organization helps employees develop and utilize their full potential in keeping with the organizational objectives, and how the organization builds and maintains an environment conducive to performance excellence and personal growth.
- Process management (85 points) examines the key aspects of the organization's process management, such as product and service delivery.
- Business results (450 points) examine organizational performance and improvement in key business areas, such as customer satisfaction, product and service performance, human resource management results. Performance is also evaluated relative to competitors.

For Tata Group companies that are using the TBEM, a minimum of 500 points in four years is targeted. There are detailed assessments and periodical review of progress toward the target.

Adapted from: Srinivasan 2002

Scorecard as a basis of an organization-specific management tool, unless the organization's specific strategic goals are aligned (coincidentally) with the generic strategic goals included in the standard BEM design.

In the Balanced Scorecard, on the other hand, the firm is required to explain its own strategic plans for improvement. Therefore, the budgets, strategic plans, incentives and rewards, etc. can all be meaningfully linked. This ensures that the results of each activity that forms part of the linkage will be aligned towards the achievement of an organization's strategic goals.

Most organizations use the BEM as a diagnostic tool and seek alternative systems to link the findings from BEM to strategy and business planning. The Balanced Scorecard may be used in conjunction with the BEM to obtain an effective system for strategic management.

Summary

Intense business competition has made it imperative for all organizational functions to demonstrate their contribution to the organization's performance. The HR function is also required to quantify and measure its impact on organizational performance, just like other functions. Therefore, organizations are focussing on determining the tangible benefits resulting from HR activities.

The chapter explained the meaning of HR evaluation and presented an insight into the linkage between the HR function and the firm's performance. The measurement problems relating to this linkage were also discussed. The major trends that have led to an increase in the interest in HR evaluation were identified. It briefly traced the evolution of HR measurement. The range of HR performance measures, such as cost-per-hire, staffing ratios, employee attitude, etc. that are used by firms was outlined. The chapter also discussed the three clusters of HR performance measures (internal operational measures, internal strategic measures, and external strategic measures). Three general approaches to HR evaluation—stakeholder approach, utility approach, and business consulting approach—were examined. The chapter ended with a discussion of Balanced Scorecard, HR Scorecard, Benchmarking, and Business Excellence Model and their implications for determining the contribution and value of HR in overall organizational performance.

Keywords

Adding Value refers to increasing the gap between revenue and cost, usually by reducing cost.

Balanced Scorecard tracks business success through the measures of productivity, people, and processes as a business is considered successful only when it satisfies the requirements of investors, customers, and employees.

Benchmarking denotes a comparison of a given organization's costs or performance to those of its competitors, typically in the same industry, or with comparable organizations that are considered 'best in class'.

Business Consulting Approach sees HR activities and practices as services and products rather than just policies. An effective HR is one that functions as a strategic business unit (SBU) and focusses on helping customers achieve maximum value from HR products and services.

Cash Flow Per Employee is a measure of the average contribution of each employee to the financial success of a firm.

Core Workforce are the full time employees of a firm who are paid a regular salary or wage. They also receive fringe benefits, training and development opportunities, opportunity for promotions, and participate in decision making.

Earnings Per Share (EPS) is the income earned on each share of a company's outstanding common stock. It indicates what the earnings are for each common share held. EPS is calculated by dividing a company's net profit by the number of outstanding shares.

External Strategic Measures are HR measures that focus on the effectiveness of HR practices in satisfying key external stakeholders, or customers and shareholders.

HR Audit assesses the HR function. An HR audit may be carried out on HR practices, HR professionals, and the HR department or function.

HR Evaluation is the determination of the value of HR in achieving organizational goals.

HR Scorecard measures the effectiveness and efficiency of the HR function in producing those employee behaviours that are important for a firm to achieve its strategic goals. The Scorecard highlights the causal link between HR activities, employee behaviour, and the resulting organizational outcomes and performance.

Internal Operational Measures are the traditional HR measures that focus on the effectiveness of the design and implementation of HR practices of a firm.

Internal Strategic Measures are HR measures that assess the effectiveness of HR practices in building organizational capabilities and enhancing employee satisfaction.

Net Profit is the income of a company after all expenses have been deducted from the total revenue. It is also called 'net income' or 'profit after taxes'.

Peripheral Workforce are the temporary, part time, contractual, and outsourced employees who get paid a fixed wage or a project-based cost, and are only partially, if at all, covered by fringe benefits.

Return on Investment (ROI) shows the earnings achieved by the investment made in the business. It is measured as net profit divided by investments.

Stakeholder Approach is a perspective according to which HR is considered successful if all stakeholders (employees, customers, unions, suppliers, shareholders, etc.) report satisfaction with various HR practices and the HR function.

Utility Approach translates quantitative measures of HR effectiveness into financial indices. It involves cost benefit analysis and determines the financial utility of HR services.

Value Creation is the measurable contribution towards achieving the strategic goals of the organization.

Concept Review Questions

1. What is HR Evaluation? What factors have made HR evaluation a priority in most organizations?
2. Discuss the challenges confronted in the measurement of HRM.
3. What are the major differences between traditional HR measures and new HR measures?
4. Identify and discuss the three categories of HR measures.
5. Compare and contrast the 'analytical' and 'business consulting' approaches to HR Evaluation.
6. Define the term 'benchmarking'. What purposes are served by benchmarking of HR practices?
7. Discuss the main propositions of the Business Excellence Model. In what ways is the Business Excellence Model different from Balanced Scorecard?

Critical Thinking Questions

1. According to a famous maxim, 'You can't manage what you can't measure'. How valid is this maxim when applied to HRM? What measures can be used to evaluate HR? Can the

measurement of HRM's contribution to business goals be truly objective?

2. Examine the Balanced Scorecard approach for measuring a firm's performance. Identify and discuss the 'employee measures' included in a Balanced Scorecard. Why is it difficult to measure employees? Give example of an organization you know of that has adopted the Balanced Scorecard approach. How does this organization ensure that its HR practices and processes 'add value'?

3. If you had to choose, which approach to HR measurement would you prefer? Defend your choice.

Simulation and Role Play [1]

Situation

Robin Ray is the newly appointed hotel manager of a famous resort located in Goa called Sea Star. Ray has received a mandate to ensure that the resort remains a destination of choice for foreign tourists. He has also been directed to reduce the operating cost of the resort without harming the strategic goals of Sea Star. Ray recently participated in an executive development workshop on accountability in human resource management. He put this item on the agenda for the management meeting scheduled for the following month. He has also attached data regarding the indices of HRM effectiveness of the major hotels in the region. The indices of HRM effectiveness culled from 20 hotels are presented in Table 3.9.

Table 3.9: Indices of HRM effectiveness of 20 major hotels in the region

Indices	Score on HRM Effectiveness (number of hotels = 20) Score of 1 = very low; Score of 6 = very high
Customer satisfaction	4.50
Employee commitment	2.10
Employee satisfaction	3.90
Absenteeism	4.20
Turnover	5.10
Overall productivity	3.80

[1] *Adapted from*: Bratton and Gold 2003

Sea Star employs 1,100 during the peak season. The HR department hires and trains employees, administers salary and benefits, and maintains trade union relations. There were six managers including Ray in the monthly management meeting. When Ray spoke about the accountability of HRM, the members responded as follows.

Sanath (assistant general manager) HR should be outsourced if the HR function cannot do its job better and more cheaply.

Rohit (front desk manager) Does HR follow best practices? How does HR help the resort reduce operating expenses? How does our HR compare with the main competitors'?

Natasha (food services manager) I appreciate the work done by HR. Training conducted by the HR department has resulted in an increase in sales and revenue.

Akshay (HR manager) It is good to evaluate the contribution of the HR to the hotel's bottomline but it is too difficult and time-consuming.

Nakul Sarin (corporate vice president, HR) I think Ray, here, has a point.

- Six students should volunteer for this role play exercise, each assuming the role of one of the managers present in the management meeting of Hotel Sea Star.

- Each volunteer should support the viewpoint of the manager whose role the student volunteer has assumed in this simulation. There should be a discussion on the different views expressed. All members should contribute to the discussion.

- After listening to the managers' arguments, the student playing the role of corporate vice president (HR) must persuade the HR manager about the merits of measuring the HR contribution and of demonstrating its value. He should also suggest some of the things the HR manager should do to demonstrate the value added by the HRM department. The arguments should persuade all present.

- The group should then discuss the pros and cons of various HR evaluation approaches, such as Balanced Scorecard, HR Scorecard, Benchmarking, and Business Excellence Model, in measuring the contribution of HRM to the hotel's performance. Every volunteer should provide arguments to support his/her viewpoint.

- The role play should end with the members reaching a consensus on making HR accountable, and the HR evaluation approach to be adopted by the hotel and why.

- After the role play is over, the facilitator should open the discussion to the rest of the class and seek their reactions on the role play, as well as the views expressed.

- The facilitator should summarize the discussion at the end.

Classroom Projects [1]

1. Form groups of four or five students each. Ask each group to take a position, for or against, the topic 'HRM impacts a firm's performance and it is possible to measure the impact'. Ask the members of each group to develop arguments in support of their chosen position. Allow 15 minutes for a group discussion and have each group present its arguments after that. Give 10 minutes to each group for the presentation. Conduct an open discussion with the class. The discussion should draw arguments from the approaches to HR evaluation presented in the chapter. The class may also be encouraged to debate the pros and cons of extending financial indicators to the measurement of HR.

2. The purpose of this classroom exercise is to provide an experience to the students of developing an HR Scorecard. This exercise requires some out-of-class preparation time. The students should be asked to read and understand the HR Scorecard approach to measuring HR contribution. The students are to form groups of four or five and develop an HR Scorecard for their educational institution. Each group should address every step used in developing the HR Scorecard as discussed in this chapter. The linkages between the strategy of the college, employee behaviours, college outcomes, and performance must be brought out. The measures that will be used for each of the factors must be specified. Each group is to prepare a written report. Each group should be asked to present its HR scorecard to the class. After all groups have shared their scorecards, a discussion should be held to identify similarities and differences and the reasons for them.

[1] *Adapted from*: Dessler 2005

Field Projects

1. Students are to visit two organizations in two industries in groups of three. Each group must collect information about whether and how the organization measures the performance of its HR function, HR practices, and HR personnel. The HR managers are to be interviewed for information on the evaluation measures used by these organizations and on how HR evaluation

indices are tracked over time. Based on the information collected, a written report is to be prepared that answers the following questions.

- Are the two firms using different measures of HR effectiveness?
- Are there any HR measures that are common to both the firms?
- Do these firms track HR indices over time? If yes, have these indices improved over time?
- Is the improvement in HR indices part of the strategic objectives of these firms? How?
- How do these firms link HR measures with business performance?
- How does the HR department improve the market position of the firm?

The report should present a critical appraisal of HR evaluation within these firms with respect to the above issues. Which of the three clusters of HR measures presented in the chapter is used most often?

2. The purpose of this project is to help students gain a better understanding of the HR audit

process and/or the benchmarking process. Students are to form groups of three or four each. Then, they proceed further as follows.

- Review business magazine articles and/or surf the internet to identify firms that conduct HR benchmarking exercises or HR audits.
- Approach the HR department of one of the firms and obtain an approval to gather information from the firm for the purpose of an academic assignment.
- Design a series of questions to learn the auditing or benchmarking process. Conduct interviews in the firm. Gather information from the firm concerning each of the steps in benchmarking as well as the HR audit. For example, describe the scope of the audit, identify what to benchmark, and so on.
- Analyse the results of your interviews. Prepare a written report for presentation to the class.
- Draw conclusions about the HR auditing or the benchmarking process and about the HR function of the firm.

=========== **Case Study** [1] ===========

Measurement of Human Resource Management at Eastman Kodak

Company Background

The history of Eastman Kodak Company dates back to 1 January 1881, when a partnership was formed between Eastman and Strong. The Eastman-Strong partnership led to the formation of a new firm in 1884, with 14 shareowners, called Eastman Dry Plate and Film Company. The company invented the Kodak camera in 1888 and laid the foundation for making photography available to everyone. The Kodak camera, pre-loaded with enough film for 100 exposures, could be carried and held in the hand easily. It was priced at US$25. After exposure, the camera had to be returned to Rochester where the film was developed, prints were made, and new film

was inserted, for US$10. A successive concern, the Eastman Company, was formed in 1889. The company has been called Eastman Kodak Company since 1892, when Eastman Kodak Company of New York was organized. The present firm, Eastman Kodak Company of New Jersey, was formed under the laws of that state.

Eastman built his business on four basic principles:

1. mass production at low cost;
2. international distribution;
3. extensive advertising; and
4. a focus on the customer.

[1] *Adapted from*: Yeung, A.K. and B. Berman 1997, 'Adding Value through Human Resources: Reorienting Human Resource Measurement to Drive Business Performance', *Human Resource Management*, vol. 36, no. 3, pp. 321–35, © John Wiley & Sons, Inc., reprinted with permission of John Wiley & Sons, Inc.

He saw all four as being closely related. Mass production could not be justified without wide distribution. Distribution, in turn, needed the support of strong advertising. From the beginning, he imbued the company with the conviction that fulfilling customer needs and desires was the only road to corporate success.

To his basic principles of business, he added these policies:

- Foster growth and development through continuing research
- Treat employees in a fair, self-respecting way
- Reinvest profit to build and extend the business

Eastman Kodak's history is one of progress in developing these basic principles and policies. Since its early years, the company has been devoted to providing photographic tools to the greatest number of people at the lowest possible price. The rapid growth of business made large-scale production a necessity. In 1896, the 100,000th Kodak camera was manufactured. The pocket Kodak camera used to cost US$5 then. Eastman wished to make a camera that would be available for US$1. The result was the introduction of the Brownie camera in 1900. By 1900, distribution outlets had been established in France, Germany, Italy, and other European countries.

Today, Eastman Kodak has manufacturing operations in North and South America, Europe, and Asia and its products are available in virtually every country across the globe. It is the world's foremost imaging innovator, providing leading products and services to the photographic, graphic communications, and healthcare markets. According to the market research firm IDC, Eastman Kodak retained its no. 1 position in the US market in digital still cameras in 2005. Worldwide, the company was at the no. 2 position. The company was also

- no. 1 worldwide in snapshot printers, competing against specialized printer companies;
- no. 1 in retail photo kiosks, with nearly 75,000 installed worldwide; and

- no. 1 in online services with the Kodak EasyShare Gallery, which today has more than 30 million registered members.

With sales of US$14.3 billion in 2005, the company is committed to a digitally oriented growth strategy focussed on helping people use meaningful images and information better in their life and work. The firm has an obsessive focus on the customer. It emphasizes innovation, ease of use of product, customer satisfaction, wide distribution, system solutions, and excellent value compared to competitors. The company has seen continuous growth in earnings per share from a low point in 2003. It maintains a solid financial position with its earnings per share in 2006 expected to be US$3, and revenues in 2006 expected to be US$16 billion.

The Three Stakeholders of Eastman Kodak

Eastman Kodak has traditionally been a technology-driven company. The firm has capitalized on its brand name, focussed on customer satisfaction through technical innovation, and sought to achieve shareholder satisfaction through customer satisfaction. The implicit assumptions were that employee satisfaction could be achieved when the company was financially successful; employee satisfaction was the result, not a driver, of business success; and shareholder satisfaction was the result of customer satisfaction (see Figure 3.14a).

The performance of Eastman Kodak as measured by the share price declined from 1990 to 1993. During this period employee satisfaction levels also declined drastically. In the third quarter of 1990, approximately 50% of employees were satisfied;

Figure 3.14(a): Traditional Paradigm of Employee Satisfaction at Eastman Kodak

but in the third quarter of 1993, less than 30% of employees were satisfied.

When George Fisher became CEO at Eastman Kodak in 1993, he decided to restore employee satisfaction as the driver for business success. Fisher said, 'We will never achieve total customer satisfaction without a much higher level of employee satisfaction....My fundamental responsibility is to make sure this is a strong company and that the employees who exist in this company have a great place to work'. Under Fisher's leadership, the company embarked on a transformation process. Fisher instituted a new paradigm that used employee satisfaction to drive customer satisfaction and then shareholder satisfaction (see Figure 3.14b).

Along with other ongoing initiatives of Eastman Kodak, the new paradigm appears to be working. The employee satisfaction increased by about 80%

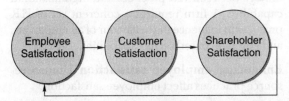

Figure 3.14(b):   The New Paradigm of Employee Satisfaction at Eastman Kodak

between 1993 and 1995. The market value also increased by approximately 90% during the same period. It would be naïve, however, to claim that the increase in Eastman Kodak's market value is completely attributable to the increase in employee satisfaction. Nevertheless, the Eastman Kodak story is powerful in two ways: (1) It illustrates how Fisher re-thought the relationship among employees, customers, and shareholders to drive business success; and (2) It provides some empirical support of how such a paradigm shift can make a difference in business performance. Eastman Kodak is an example of how companies use people to drive their business performance. The balanced scorecard provides a business framework. This framework highlights what is required for a company to succeed by meeting the expectations of employees, customers, and shareholders.

HR Practices and Business Strategy

Eastman Kodak attempts to align HR practices with business strategy. The strategic HR framework at Eastman Kodak involves three components—business strategy, organizational capabilities, and human resource practices. The company formulates plans for each component based on some pertinent questions (see Table 3.10).

Table 3.10:   The Three Components of the Strategic HR Framework at Eastman Kodak

S.No.	Components of Strategic HR Framework	Pertinent Questions
1.	Business strategy	■ What is the business strategy of our firm? ■ How do we win in the marketplace based on customer satisfaction, competition, government regulations, supplier situations, etc.?
2.	Organizational capabilities	■ What critical organizational capabilities does the firm need to develop to implement the business strategy? These capabilities might include competitive shared mindset, speed to market, innovation, etc.
3.	Human resource practices	■ How should HR practices be designed and delivered to build these organizational capabilities? ■ Are our managers and employees competent and motivated to the fullest extent in the development of these capabilities?

The strategic HR framework aims to leverage and/or align HR practices to build critical organizational capabilities that enable Eastman Kodak to win in the marketplace. To enhance the impact of HR practices on business, Eastman Kodak has connected its strategic HR framework to its business framework.

Integrating Strategic HR Framework and Business Framework

The strategic HR framework has three components (business strategy, organizational capabilities, and HR practices); so does the business framework (shareholder satisfaction, customer satisfaction, and employee satisfaction). These six components are inter-related along two chains of linkage (see Figures 3.15a and b).

Figure 3.15(a):   HR Practices as Key Drivers

Figure 3.15(b):   Organizational Capabilities as Key Drivers

1. Human resource practices are key drivers in building organizational capability, enhancing employee satisfaction, and shaping customer satisfaction. In turn, both organizational capabilities and employee satisfaction impact customer satisfaction.

2. Organizational capabilities are the key drivers for implementing business strategy, impacting customer satisfaction, and eventually, contributing to shareholder satisfaction. In addition, both business strategy and customer satisfaction, if properly managed, increase shareholder satisfaction.

According to the Eastman Kodak framework, there are three ways in which HR contributes to business success:

Building organizational capability There is a linkage between HR practices and organizational capability. A firm requires a coherent set of HR practices to influence the behaviour of all employees and compete based on its capabilities.

Enhancing employee satisfaction Human resource practices affect employee satisfaction.

Shaping customer satisfaction Human resource practices are leveraged to drive customer satisfaction.

The integration of its strategic HR framework and its business framework helps Eastman Kodak align its HR planning process with its business planning process. The business framework (balanced scorecard) highlights what the firm needs to focus on to succeed. The strategic HR framework provides specific tools to determine how it can leverage its HR practices and organizational capabilities to succeed. The model also shows the high value-added contribution of HR practices within Eastman Kodak.

HR Measures that Drive Business Performance

Based on its HR-business integrative framework, Eastman Kodak has developed three clusters of HR measures:

1. Internal operational measures (how well do we design HR practices and deliver them?)

2. Internal strategic measures (how effectively do our HR practices build the desired organizational capabilities and enhance employee satisfaction?)

3. External strategic measures (how well do our HR practices enhance the satisfaction of customers and shareholders?)

The firm identifies three critical organizational capabilities—leadership effectiveness, workforce competencies, and performance-based culture—and develops specific HR measures (internal strategic measures) to track progress in these capabilities. Eastman Kodak uses 360 degree assessment to measure leadership competency and also tracks leadership diversity on the basis of race, gender, and nationality of its managers. Workforce competencies are measured by three aspects of the development process:

- the percentage of employees with clearly laid down development plans to develop required competencies;
- the number of hours devoted to development; and
- the results of developmental programmes as measured on four levels (reactions, learning, behaviour, and results).

The firm assesses its culture of performance by (1) tracking of aligned performance commitments, and (2) employee surveys that focus on management accountability for performance, clarity of performance expectations, adequacy of performance feedback, and rewards for achieving goals.

Eastman Kodak experiments with several HR programmes that drive customer and shareholder satisfaction (external strategic measures). One of the HR programmes at Eastman Kodak is called 'Champions for Customer Success'. This is a customer-oriented programme that (1) creates a learning situation that connects manufacturing employees directly with customers and (2) shares best practices and expertise with customers in areas in which they need help (such as reducing paper waste, establishing self-managed teams, etc.) to build their capabilities in those areas. By achieving these two

goals, the HR function intends to drive customer satisfaction and commitment to Eastman Kodak products. The programme also serves to build employee understanding of customers' needs. The simple measures necessary for this programme include incremental sales and earnings as a result of establishing these customer relationships and change in customer satisfaction and commitment.

Another HR effort at Eastman Kodak directed towards enhancing customer satisfaction involves leveraging the executive education process. Eastman Kodak invites senior executives of companies that are major customers to attend and share an executive education experience with Eastman Kodak executives. This helps Eastman Kodak create a shared mindset with key customers and enables it to meet customer needs more effectively. The performance measure is the degree of change in customer satisfaction and commitment as a result of the shared executive education experience.

Also, a number of processes have been changed at Eastman Kodak to create a greater connection between HR practices and shareholder satisfaction. For example, traditionally there was a programme called 'wage dividend'. This programme was essentially an annual bonus payment that, over time, became a pure entitlement for employees. The employees could expect 7–8% of their base pay as a bonus at the end of every year. Eastman Kodak changed the programme; now the wage dividend is a function of shareholder satisfaction as measured by return on net assets (RONA). This was supported by a communication process driven by the HR function to help employees understand the measure and how it translates to their particular operation within the company. In this way they could understand what they could do to influence their wage dividend. The HR measure for this programme is the change in employee mindset from entitlement to contribution. The purpose is to use the bonus system to drive shareholder value.

Eastman Kodak has used a strategic investment approach to plan and evaluate incentive compensation plans. The firm has taken a similar approach to evaluating the effectiveness of various wellness programme initiatives. Data is collected from both participants and non-participants in the wellness programmes on a variety of healthcare experiences.

Based on this data, Eastman Kodak has assessed the financial return it is realizing from these wellness programmes.

Questions

1. Based on the principles of Balanced Scorecard, illustrate how Eastman Kodak refocussed its HR practices and used people to drive business performance.

2. Given the Balanced Scorecard framework, how can the HR function add value to business success? Give evidence from the case.

3. On the basis of the integrative framework of Eastman Kodak, discuss how HR practices affect and contribute to the key result areas of business.

4. Examine the combination of HR measures that can be used to enhance the satisfaction of employees, customers, and shareholders. What are the most effective HR measures that can demonstrate the value added of the HR function?

5. Is the Balanced Scorecard approach the most effective approach for linking HR with business performance? Based on the information provided in the chapter, suggest some other approach(es) that Eastman Kodak may adopt to ensure that HR contributes to its business performance.

References

Andersen, H., G. Lawrie, and M. Shulver 2000, *The Balanced Scorecard vs the EFQM Business Excellence Model*, 2GC Working Paper, pp. 1–14.

Becker, B.E., M.A. Huselid, and D. Ulrich 2001, *The HR Scorecard: Linking People, Strategy, and Performance*, Harvard Business School Press, Boston.

Bratton, J. and J. Gold 2003, *Human Resource Management: Theory and Practice*, 3rd edition, Palgrave Macmillan.

Buhner, R. 1997, 'Increasing Shareholder Value Through Human Asset Management', *Long Range Planning*, vol. 30, no. 5, pp. 710–17.

Dessler, G. 2005, *Human Resource Management*, 10th edition, Prentice Hall of India Pvt. Ltd., New Delhi, pp. 87–91.

Greer, C.R. 2002, *Strategic Human Resource Management: A General Managerial Approach*, 2nd edition, Pearson Education, Singapore.

Guest, D.E. and R. Peccei, 1994, 'The Nature and Causes of Effective Human Resource Management', *British Journal of Industrial Relations*, vol. 32, no. 2, pp. 219–42.

Hiltrop, J.M. and C. Despres 1994, 'Benchmarking the Performance of Human Resource Management', *Long Range Planning*, vol. 27, no. 6, pp. 43–57.

Holbeche, L. 2002, *Aligning Human Resources and Business Strategy*, Butterworth Heinemann, Oxford, pp. 51–83.

Kossek, E.E. and R.N. Block 2000, *Managing Human Resources in the 21st Century: From Core Concepts to Strategic Choice*, South Western College Pub, Thomson Learning, USA.

Pfeffer, J. 1995, 'People, Capability and Competitive Success', *Management Development Review*, vol. 8, no. 5, pp. 6–10.

Pfeffer, J. 1997, 'Pitfalls on the Road to Measurement: The Dangerous Liasion of Human Resources with the Ideas of Accounting and Finance', *Human Resource Management*, vol. 36, no. 3, pp. 357–65.

Rao, T.V. 1999, *HRD Audit: Evaluating the Human Resource Function for Business Improvement*, Response Books, New Delhi.

Rao, T.V. 1990, *The HRD Missionary*, Oxford University Press and India Book House, New Delhi.

Symons, C., T. Pohlmann, N. Lambert, and O. Ester 2005, 'The Human Capital Management Value Map: Deloitte Demonstrates that HR can be Strategic', http://www.forrester.com/Research/Document/Excerpt/0,7211,36456,00.html, accessed on 20 February 2005.

Ulrich, D. 1997, 'Measuring Human Resources: An Overview of Practice and a Prescription for Results', *Human Resource Management*, vol. 36, no. 3, pp. 303–20.

Wintermantel, R.E. and K.L. Mattimore 1997, 'In the Changing World of Human Resources: Matching Measures to Mission', *Human Resource Management*, vol. 36, no. 3, pp. 337–42.

Yeung, A.K. and B. Berman 1997, 'Adding Value through Human Resources: Reorienting Human Resource Measurement to Drive Business Performance', *Human Resource Management*, vol. 36, no. 3, pp. 321–35.

Notes

http://i.i.com.com/cnwk.1d/html/itpForr051103645600.pdf, accessed on 20 February 2006.

http://uob-community.ballarat.edu.au/~coconnor/bratton%20%20chapter%2013%20slides.ppt, accessed on 28 April 2006.

http://www.communityactionpartnership.com/about/about_partnership/award_for_excellence/Baldrige_Core_Values.pdf, accessed on 1 May 2006.

http://www.forrester.com, accessed on 20 February 2006.

http://www.kodak.com

Srinivasan 2002, http://www.blonnet.com/2002/09/14/stories/2002091400020900.htm, accessed on 4 May 2006.

4 Human Resource Planning

OBJECTIVES

After studying this chapter, you will be able to:

- explain the relationship between business strategy and human resource planning
- understand the significance of human resource planning in a changing context
- appreciate the objectives of human resource planning
- understand the meaning and strategic importance of job analysis
- describe the need for a competency based approach to job analysis
- discuss human resource demand and supply forecasting techniques
- appreciate various strategies followed by organizations for managing human resource surplus and shortage
- gain insight into the interaction between human resource planning and outsourcing

INTRODUCTION

The twenty-first century is unique in the pace at which change occurs. The business environment of organizations is more complex and dynamic when compared to the environment 15 years ago. This is the age of contradictions—economic growth as well as recession, shortage of skilled workforce as well as increase in the percentage of skilled unemployed, massive layoffs as well as large-scale recruitments. A question emerges: is 'planning' meaningful in this age of discontinuous change? Is it feasible or even possible for organizations to develop future business plans and forecast human resource requirements? When the meaning of 'job' itself has undergone transformation and when the world of work has altered beyond what could be imagined just a decade earlier, is it possible to describe jobs precisely? Although Mintzberg (1994) commented that 'the most successful strategies are visions, not plans', planning remains critical. However, it is more challenging now.

Chapter 2 discussed various business and demographic changes, changes in the nature of jobs, and the transformation of the employment contract. All these changes have implications for human resource management and employment levels. As there is a limited pool of skilled workers, firms compete for them; this competition poses a challenge for HRM. Human resource planning (HRP) assumes importance in this scenario. Strategic business plans need to be translated into HR plans. It is important for organizations to know whether their business plans are realistic in HR terms. If they are not realistic, organizations must develop strategies to ensure the availability of the required workers. The changing nature and meaning of jobs has also caused a change in the way jobs are viewed. Job analysis and HRP are major components of the HR strategy. All other HR activities flow from the HRP process.

The present chapter begins with a discussion of the relationship between business plans and HR plans. An insight into the increasing significance of HRP in a dynamic business environment is presented. The macro and micro perspectives of HRP and their objectives are highlighted. The chapter goes on to provide a complete overview of job analysis, the basis of all HR activities. The chapter explores the strategic importance of job analysis and its significance in the changing world of work. It discusses the competency-based approach to job analysis. The HRP process is outlined and the range of techniques available to managers for forecasting HR demand and supply is presented. A discussion of the range of action plans available to a firm to manage human resource surplus and shortages is presented. The chapter ends with exploring the role of HRP in a firm considering outsourcing of processes.

HRP: AN OVERVIEW

Human resource planning is 'the process of analysing and identifying the need for and availability of human resources so that the organization can meet its objectives'. It helps determine the HR requirements of firms and develop strategies for meeting those requirements so that the organization achieves its objectives. It seeks answers to questions such as:

- What are the implications of proposed strategic plans with respect to human resources?
- What are the implications of proposed strategic plans for staffing, training and development, and management succession?
- How will a projected shortfall in the supply of skilled employees impact various HR practices of the firm?
- What are the implications for attracting, retaining, motivating, and rewarding workers with skills that are in short supply?

Human resource planning is not carried out in a vacuum. Organizational goals and objectives provide the context for HRP. The HRP process examines the implications of business strategies and goals on human requirements—the number and type of people required; the training they will require; and whether the organization will have to employ additional employees. Hence, HRP is a proactive process. It anticipates changes in industry, marketplace, economy, society, and technology to ensure that the organization is well prepared to meet these changes when they occur.

Earlier, HRP used to be a reactive process. Business needs defined HR needs. Strategic business decisions were taken in isolation without appreciating

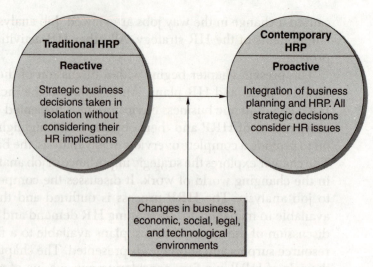

Figure 4.1:   The Transition from Reactive HRP to Proactive HRP

the HR implications of those decisions. For example, a firm that decided to acquire a rival because it made good economic sense would have thought about integrating the workforces of the two firms and deploying human resources in the new firm only after the business decision had been made. Today, however, changes in business, economic, and social environments have led to an integration of business planning with HRP and also to a long-term, proactive perspective of HRP (see Figure 4.1). In the contemporary business environment, human resources are part of the strategic planning process. Human resource issues are considered at every stage of strategic plans (mergers, acquisitions, expansions, etc.) from planning to implementation. Human resource planning is essentially the means to the end of building more competitive organizations. The next section discusses the interaction between business strategy and HRP.

BUSINESS STRATEGY AND HRP

The word 'strategy' has been defined earlier in this book as the 'determination of the long-term goals and objectives of an organization, and the allocation of resources necessary for carrying out these goals'. An organization achieves its goals and objectives through its employees or human resources. As emphasized earlier in this book, a firm having a lot of capital and the most advanced machinery may not demonstrate sustained levels of high performance or achieve its objectives if it does not have capable, motivated, and high-performing employees. Hence, an organization must ensure that it has the appropriate number of workers with the required skills so that it may achieve its goals. If it does not, it must determine a way to ensure the availability of the workers it needs.

The quality of HR and their contribution to the organization is of strategic importance for bringing about competitive advantage for the firm. For example, a public sector bank defined its business strategy as 'improving corporate image through improved customer service'. Service improvement depends on the quality of employees and their skills. An initial diagnosis revealed that the employees of the bank lacked basic interpersonal and communication skills. A series of training programmes was designed and implemented to bridge this skill gap. Armed with the required skills, the employees helped the bank achieve its business objective of 'improved customer service'. Therefore, it is important for strategic business plans to include planning for human resources, and for HR plans to support business plans.

It is clear that HRP does not take place in isolation. It is guided by organizational goals and objectives. Different business strategies result in different HR issues, since strategic plans have HR implications (see Figure 4.2). Business strategy directly affects HR strategies and activities. Chapter 1 discussed several classifications of business strategies. It was emphasized that each business strategy presented requires different types of HR strategies or strategic approaches to managing people. Figure 1.1 in Chapter 1 presented HR strategies corresponding with each of the business strategies (cost leadership and differentiation) suggested by Porter (1985). This chapter goes a step further and shows how HR planning activities are related to the business strategy of the firm (see Table 4.1a).

Table 4.1(a): Relationship between Business Strategy of a Firm and HRP

Business Strategy Focus (Classification by Porter)	HR Strategy	HRP Activities
Cost leadership ■ Cost control ■ Stable business environment ■ Efficiency and quality	■ Job and employee specializations ■ Employee efficiency ■ Long HR planning horizon	■ Internal promotions ■ Emphasis on training ■ Hiring and training for specific capabilities
Differentiation ■ Long-term focus ■ Growth ■ Creative job behaviour ■ Decentralization	■ Shorter HR planning horizon ■ Hire the HR capabilities required ■ Flexible jobs and employees	■ External staffing ■ Hire and train for broad competencies

Adapted from: Mathis and Jackson 2004

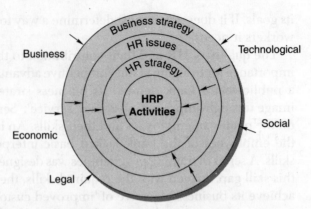

Figure 4.2: HRP in Context

Cost Leadership Strategy

The cost leadership strategy may be appropriate in a relatively stable environment. A firm with this strategy approaches competition on the basis of cost leadership, or low price and high quality product or service. This strategy requires the firm to develop specialized skills in its employees. The HRP horizon is longer; hence it may be difficult to develop specific skills necessary for a new market quickly.

Differentiation Strategy

The differentiation strategy is more appropriate in a dynamic environment characterized by rapid change. This strategy continuously looks for new markets and products. A firm with this strategy is responsive to market changes and hence the HRP horizon also has a shorter time frame to respond. The firm may use external sources, such as acquisition of another company with specialized employees, to staff itself.

Miles and Snow (1984) also adopted a position similar to Porter's, and suggested that HRM practices should be tailored to the demands of business strategy. On the basis of the dominant culture of the organization, they identified four types of organizational strategy: (1) defender, (2) prospector, (3) analyser, and (4) reactor. To demonstrate the relationship between business strategy and HRP, let us analyse the defender, prospector, and analyser strategies. The defender strategy, followed by firms in a stable environment, is to compete on the basis of low price. Firms that follow this strategy build their human resources to meet their specialized needs, like firms that follow the cost leadership strategy. The prospector strategy, followed by firms in an unstable, rapidly changing environment (such as the computer software industry), is to launch new products and venture into new markets. Firms that follow this strategy 'buy' their human resources rather than 'grow' them internally (see Table 4.1b).

Table 4.1(b):   Relationship between Business Strategy of a Firm and HRP

Business Strategy (Classification by Miles and Snow)	HR Strategy	HRP
Defender ■ Finds change threatening ■ Favours strategies which encourage continuity and security	■ Bureaucratic approach ■ Planned and regularly maintained policies to provide for lean HR	■ Build human resources ■ Likely to emphasize training programmes and internal promotion
Prospector ■ Thrives on change ■ Favours strategies of product and/or market development	■ Creative and flexible management style ■ Have high quality human resources ■ Emphasize redeployment and flexibility of HR ■ Little opportunity for long-term HR planning	■ Acquire human resources ■ Likely to emphasize recruitment, selection, and performance-based compensation
Analyser ■ Seeks to match new ventures with the present business set-up ■ Launches ventures new to the firm but not new to the market	■ Emphasize HR planning	■ 'Buy' as well as 'make' key human resources

Adapted from: Mathis and Jackson 1997

These business strategies are not mutually exclusive. A firm may follow a combination of business strategies. It is important for a firm to adapt to the changing economic and business environment irrespective of the strategy it chooses. This aspect is very important in HRP since the economic and business environment affects employment levels. When the economy is booming there are more jobs, and firms hire either on a permanent basis or on a contractual basis; however, when there is an economic downturn, many organizations lay off employees.

The external environmental forces affect the strategic plans of a firm and hence the corresponding HR plans. Strategic planning is the process of determining organizational objectives and the actions needed to achieve those objectives. Strategic business plans involve analysing all aspects of business, such as finance, marketing, human resources, etc. in order to assess organizational readiness to meet the stated objectives. Human resource planning takes place within the context of strategic business planning. It involves forecasting the future human resource needs of an organization and planning to meet them. A major objective of HRP is to facilitate an organization's effectiveness. Therefore, HRP must be integrated with the organization's short-term and long-term business objectives and plans.

Without strategic plans, the firm may face problems such as surplus or deficit of employees. Both strategic plans and HR plans need to be monitored and updated continuously in today's dynamic business environment. Economic and business changes make HRP more difficult and at the same time more critical. Let us now understand why HRP has gained significance in the contemporary business environment.

SIGNIFICANCE OF HRP IN A CHANGING ENVIRONMENT

The increase in the attention directed to HRP may be attributed to several factors. The most significant of these factors are environmental forces such as globalization, new technology, economic conditions, and a changing workforce. The external environment within which firms operate has undergone

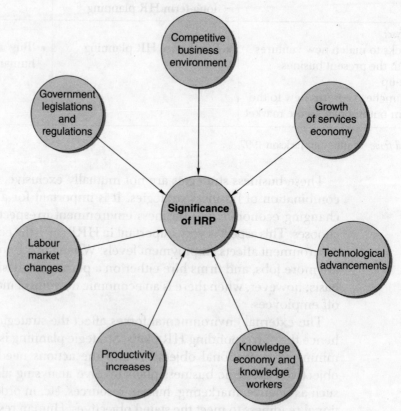

Figure 4.3: Factors that have Enhanced the Significance of HRP

tremendous transformation in the past two decades. Increased competition, mergers and acquisitions, corporate downsizing, and rapid technological advances characterize the business environment. Chapter 2 discussed several business, industry, and demographic trends. These trends have important implications for demand as well as supply of skills in the workforce. Several HR issues and challenges emerge as firms compete with each other to ensure the availability of skilled talent to fulfil organizational needs in a changed environment. These trends create complexity and uncertainty for firms. Organizations seek to reduce uncertainty since it can potentially interfere with the performance of the firm. Formal HRP is one strategy used by firms to shield themselves from environmental uncertainty. We may briefly recapitulate the changes in the business environment that raise HRP issues: competitive business environment; shift from manufacturing economy to service economy; technological advancements; knowledge economy and knowledge worker; productivity increases; labour market changes; and government legislation and regulations (see Figure 4.3).

Competitive Business Environment

Globalization of the economy has increased the competitive pressure on both revenues and costs. Many Indian firms have become lean to manage costs. Manufacturing firms have reduced the employment levels. The competitive environment causes competition between firms for ensuring that each has employees with the right kind of skills at the right time. Poaching has become a reality leading to high employee mobility. As the concept of lifetime employment becomes obsolete, HRP gains in significance. Organizations faced with increasing competition and rapid technological changes also seek greater flexibility. This may be reflected in more contractual or part-time employees. Employees, on their part, also desire flexibility to be able to address work and non-work needs and interests.

Manufacturing Economy to Service Economy

As the economy becomes largely service-led, more jobs are being created in the service sector than in the manufacturing sector. The number of jobs in the manufacturing sector has gone down and is shrinking further while total employment in the service sector has gone up. The present rapid growth of the service sector has resulted in a shortage of engineers available to work in the manufacturing sector. Larsen & Toubro (L&T), a heavy industries and infrastructure giant, is finding it difficult to fulfill its demand for engineers since most engineering graduates are attracted towards the IT sector. This is also true of the chemical industry, which is facing a serious shortage of young and talented engineers. The chemical industry is losing its skilled workforce to the service industry. The changing pattern of industrial employment affects the pattern of the different occupational groups. The occupational shift from the manufacturing sector to the knowledge sector has resulted in increased focus on competencies. Earlier, industry hired for certain skills; now the emphasis is on competencies and talent. There is a shift in the type of worker that is in demand.

Technological Advancements

Advancement in technology has resulted in changes in the nature of current jobs and in the creation of new jobs. These changes render certain skills redundant and cause a shortage of certain other skills. Through creating a need for new sets of skills, technology often makes existing skills obsolete. This has made it important for firms to retrain their current employees. Technology training has become an important part of all formal training. Firms also need to ensure the supply of 'tech-savvy' people in future. For this, they need to interact with educational institutions. Some of the firms that have developed ties with educational institutions are IBM, Infosys, Microsoft, and Oracle. Technology and its use in the workplace has an impact on the management of human resources.

Knowledge Economy and Knowledge Workers

Several industrial sectors, including manufacturing, are becoming knowledge- and skill-intensive, with new innovations resulting in quality improvements and cost reductions. For example, Indian export-oriented manufacturing sectors (like auto ancillaries) have become knowledge intensive. The numbers of jobs in manual and skilled categories are going down in the knowledge economy. The growth in demand for labour is expected to be concentrated among the higher-skilled occupations, and in particular among professional, managerial, scientific, and technical occupations. There is a shift in requirement towards knowledge workers. These highly skilled employees are in short supply. It is proving costly for firms to acquire and retain this group of employees. This has also created concern for their full utilization, as also for ensuring that employees are assigned jobs appropriate to their competencies. Skill shortages of some kinds may be a major barrier to progress for industries as well as nations. India is predicted to face a huge shortage of skilled workers in the next decade in almost all growing sectors—retail, airlines, IT, telecom, banking, and BPO. To meet the HR demand of India's growing economy, national planners must pay greater attention to educational policy, set up new educational institutions to develop skills that are in short supply, and tap the latent potential by formulating policies to encourage youth toward higher education. It is important to forecast the skills that will be required to ensure their availability. Otherwise, even the best business plans may fail.

In addition to the increased demand for high-skilled jobs, there is also a demand for more skills within jobs. The skills required of an average worker have increased resulting in a gap between skills required and skills available. All employees increasingly need computer literacy, communication skills, and customer handling skills. Thus, HR has to emphasize training, retraining, and development activities to provide employees with the required skills so that they can move into more technical and/or service-oriented jobs. Even if India becomes a manufacturing-led economy again, demand for knowledge workers will continue from both service and manufacturing sectors. This has important implications for national planners and educational policy-makers.

Productivity Increases

Competition has contributed to 'rising productivity'. Labour productivity in Indian industries has increased steadily since the mid-nineties and the number of workers has been declining steadily. The average annual productivity of an industrial worker measured in terms of value of output per worker has grown by an annual compound rate of 10% between 1996–97 and 2002–03. Use of high-productivity technology has also contributed to increased productivity. As labour productivity goes up in the networked economy, fewer people are required to do the same amount of work. Thus, the growth rate of employment will be lower than that of output. In the services sector also, there is a rise in labour productivity, mainly because of concentration in sub-sectors like ITeS and IT that are dependent on skilled labour. This has led to a slow growth of jobs in the services sector also. In Silicon Valley, changes in technology and business strategy have led companies to create more value with fewer workers. While demand, sales, and profits are rising quickly, job growth continues to stagnate. This is partly due to outsourcing of work to lower-cost regions such as India and China, and partly due to a big leap in productivity. Cisco Systems had annual sales of US$680,000 per employee in 2005 (mid-year) compared to US$480,000 in 2001. Value added per employee rose to 3.7% in 2004.

Labour Market Changes

The transformation of the labour market in recent years is another factor that has implications for HRP. A labour market is a geographical region where the supply and demand of labour interact. It has an impact on the labour supply of an organization in terms of its size, as well as its characteristics like gender, age, etc. Demographic trends also affect labour supply. The declining birth rate and an increasingly greying population has led to the shortage of skilled labour in most countries. India has a high percentage of the under-15 population and is expected to have a high supply of labour between 2030 and 2040; she will then have the biggest chunk of surplus labour in the world. There is an increase in the working population in India. Though labour supply is high, there are not enough adequately skilled or trained workers. Firms are competing for a limited talent pool. At present, only 25% of technical graduates and 10–15% of general college graduates in India are suitable for employment in the offshore IT and BPO industries, respectively. Clearly, there is no shortage of raw workforce in the country. Yet, despite the increasing educated population as well as workforce, there are still some skill deficiencies in the workplace. It is important to increase the supply of trained workforce.

Government Legislations and Regulations

Government policies and regulations relating to employment influence HRP. Affirmative action requires firms to hire women, members of minority groups, and disabled people. The reservation of jobs and of seats in educational institutions limits both supply and demand. The decision of the Government of India to reserve 27% of seats in undergraduate medicine courses in central universities seems to have made many students consider journalism, engineering, or even humanities over medicine. With just about 27,000 seats in the 244 undergraduate medical colleges in the country, and approximately 200,000 aspirants, it comes as no surprise that students who would have liked to study medicine are applying for other courses. With reservations going up to 49.5% (when the 27% reservation of OBCs gets implemented), there will be only 13,500 unreserved seats. In this way legislation regarding reservation is likely to affect the choice of careers in society, and also affect the supply of workforce to certain sectors.

Legislation relating to contract labour also has implications for workforce flexibility and therefore on a firm's ability to respond to market changes. For instance, the Indian government is considering amendments to labour norms for increasing working hours, allowing hiring of seasonal workers, and making contract labour rules flexible. It is proposed to amend the Factories Act 1948 to increase working hours from 48 hours per week to 60 hours per week and daily work hours from 9 to 12, so that overtime limit could be extended. In order to meet the seasonal demands of export-oriented industries, such as textiles, it has been proposed to amend the Industrial Disputes Act 1947 to allow employment of seasonal workforce. However, the amendment would be conditional so that there should not be any reduction in the existing labour force, and temporary employees shall not exceed a certain percentage of the permanent workforce. It has been considered to amend the Contract Labour (Regulation and Abolition) Act 1970 to bring rules for specific non-core activities in tune with modern outsourcing practices. The Prime Minister, Dr Manmohan Singh, stated at the 40th Indian Labour Conference that more flexible and transparent labour laws are expected to contribute to increased employment.

It is evident that HRP has become more complex and difficult in a grossly altered environmental context. At the same time, it has become more important than ever as firms seek competitive advantage through superior service, quality, and lower costs. The human resource plans of a firm should be relevant to the human resource issues resulting from a dynamically changing environment.

PERSPECTIVES OF HRP

From the above discussion, it is evident that human resource issues arising from new environmental trends are firm-specific as well as national or global. Human resource planning may be viewed from two perspectives: a macro perspective and a micro perspective. The perspectives of HRP are presented in Figure 4.4.

Macro HRP

Macro HRP refers to assessing and forecasting the demand for and availability of skills at the national or global level. It takes into consideration the industrial and economic growth of the country, industry shifts, and the changing nature of jobs. Macro HRP seeks to predict the kinds of skills that will be required by industry in the future and compare these with what is or will be available in the country. For instance, the IT industry has achieved high sales growth (between 30% and 36%) and profit growth (around 35%) in fiscal 2006. Most IT firms have predicted even higher growth in fiscal 2007. If the present growth rates continue, the big four IT firms (Infosys, Wipro, Satyam, and TCS), could add over one million to their head count. However, there is a fear of workforce shortage because of a lack of availability of skilled manpower and of a high attrition rate.

Similarly, India needs 8,000–10,000 fashion designers a year. About 400 companies contact the National Institute of Design (NID) at Ahmedabad every year to hire graduates in diverse disciplines. Only 128 students graduated from NID in 2005; this suggests a shortage of fashion designers. More design schools need to be set up in the country to bridge this demand-supply gap.

If a gap between skills required and skills available is anticipated, macro HRP seeks to bridge the gap through professional and technical courses in colleges and universities. As firms compete globally and skill-transfer across industries becomes increasingly common, macro level HRP assumes great significance. In this scenario, policy-makers have the responsibility for ensuring that educational institutions are geared to the present and future demands of industry. Educational programmes that focus on training the potential workforce in skills that will be required by different industries or sectors of a country in future need to be established. For example, the realization came with the IT revolution that there were not enough IT professionals in the country to meet the growing demand for them. Educational programmes such as BIT (Bachelor in IT), courses in software programming, etc. were started to serve the need for IT professionals.

Macro HRP requires close interaction between the government, industry, and the educational policy of the country. To ensure that India's working population is able to meet the rapidly changing needs of industry, the Government of India proposes to set up the Workers' Technical University. The aim of this university will be to ensure that the 400 million strong workers' population—of whom about 98% is in the unorganized sector—is able to upgrade its skills continually. The university will ensure that workers continually upgrade their skills, thereby helping industry remain globally competitive. China, Japan, the US, and Mexico have such universities.

The Government of India is planning to set up a National Centre of Governance that will train bureaucrats in public administration, management, public relations, and customer relations. This is in response to the growing recognition that new types of leaders and leadership must emerge who can be both managers and decision-makers. There is a realization that civil servants lack managerial skills.

In the steel sector too, there is an anticipation of a huge demand-supply gap. The Indian steel sector will require an additional workforce of 136,000 to achieve the anticipated production of 68 million tons by 2011–12. Both skilled and semi-skilled workers will be required. In order to meet the growing human resource requirement of the industry, the Ministry of Steel is planning to bring all existing steel research and training institutes under an umbrella organization, and also to raise its funding for research and development activities in the steel sector.

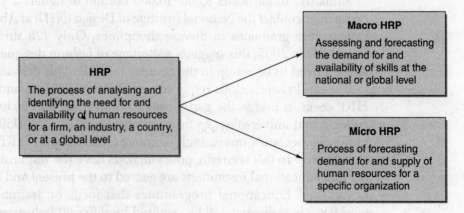

HRP
The process of analysing and identifying the need for and availability of human resources for a firm, an industry, a country, or at a global level

Macro HRP
Assessing and forecasting the demand for and availability of skills at the national or global level

Micro HRP
Process of forecasting demand for and supply of human resources for a specific organization

Figure 4.4: Perspectives of HRP

Micro HRP

When the term 'HRP' is used to refer to a firm's strategy to optimize its human resources, the perspective referred to is a micro perspective. Micro HRP is the process of forecasting demand for and supply of human resources for a specific organization. When an IT firm raises wages to counter attrition or when it shortlists students in their second year of college for future employment, it is engaging in HRP from a micro perspective. These students do their summer internships with the company and are ready to join the workforce immediately after graduating. To manage its projected demand-supply gap, Genpact, a business and technology services firm, has launched an associate trainee programme with Hyderabad's Osmania University. Under this initiative, students are allowed to work while studying for a bachelor's degree in commerce at Osmania University. At the end of the three-year programme, students are offered full-time employment with the company. Industry is increasingly looking upon educational institutions to meet their HR demand.

OBJECTIVES OF HRP

Human resource planning serves important purposes for a firm's strategic human resource management. Mello (2003) outlined five major objectives of HRP:

1. to prevent overstaffing and understaffing;
2. to ensure employee availability;
3. to ensure that the organization is responsive to the environment;
4. to provide direction to all HR activities; and
5. to build line and staff partnership.

Preventing overstaffing and understaffing A firm that employs more workers than it needs (overstaffing) is inefficient. This is because its fixed cost of employee compensation shoots up. Moreover, in a manufacturing firm, it may result in surplus production and lead to a high level of inventory as the firm may not be able to market the entire stock. Having fewer employees than required (understaffing) also results in organizational loss. The loss stems largely from the inability of the firm to meet or satisfy customer demand for its products and/or services. Consequently, both existing and future customers may turn to competitors. Human resource planning helps to ensure efficiency and timely response to customers' needs and obviates the need to dismiss employees suddenly.

Ensuring employee availability It would be a fallacy on the part of organizations to assume that skilled workers will be freely available in the labour market when needed. Human resource planning ensures that the organization has the right number of employees with the right skills in the right places at the right times. It is important for firms to anticipate the kinds of employees they need in terms of skills, competencies, and other characteristics. Recruiting efforts of the firm must ensure that personnel are hired, trained, and readied to deliver on the job when required.

Ensuring that the organization is responsive to the environment changes The changes anticipated in the external environment form an important input for HR planning. For example, the economy may grow or stagnate; competition may increase or decrease; government regulations may change; there may be changes in technology as well as in workplace composition. Human resource planning helps a firm respond to these changes in time.

Providing direction to all HR activities Human resource planning ensures that all other HR activities, such as selection, training, performance appraisal, and rewards, function as an integrated system. For example, HRP may suggest that certain employees need to be trained in a particular area. The training goals should be incorporated into the performance measurement of these employees, and these factors should also be used in reward decisions.

Building line and staff partnership Though HRP is usually initiated by HR managers, it requires cooperation of all managers. A departmental head is in the best position to know the HR requirements of the department. Hence, communication between line and staff managers is important for the success of the HRP effort. The objectives of HRP, both macro and micro, are presented in Table 4.2.

Table 4.2: Objectives of HRP

Objectives of HRP	
Macro HRP	**Micro HRP**
<ul><li>To forecast economic and business environment</li><li>To estimate future demand of numbers and types of skills by various industries</li><li>To ensure effective labour supply to different industries through activities such as interacting with educational institutions</li><li>To ensure more effective utilization of HR</li><li>To make labour supply projections for the future</li></ul>	<ul><li>To prevent overstaffing and understaffing</li><li>To ensure employee availability</li><li>To ensure that the firm is responsive to the environment</li><li>To provide direction to all HR activities</li><li>To build line and staff partnerships</li></ul>

Adapted from: Mello 2003

Irrespective of its scope—macro or micro—HRP is grounded in the recognition that an adequately qualified workforce may not always be available. This recognition makes it important for firms to identify how to attract, develop, and retain a qualified workforce, and ensure optimum performance from them. Micro HRP is the focus of this chapter. Decisions about people-related needs of an organization essentially require two types of information: a description of the job/work to be performed, the skills needed, and the training required for different types of jobs; and a description of the strategic plans, business strategy, and the future direction of the business.

Once these two types of information are obtained, it is possible for the firm to forecast the numbers and skills mix of the people required to perform its jobs and accomplish its strategic plans. A firm needs to take stock of the nature of the jobs available to be able to forecast its HR requirements. It needs to ask the following questions.

- What are the plans and objectives of the firm?
- What are the types of jobs that will be required to achieve organizational objectives?
- What are the duties and responsibilities associated with each job?
- What are the types of employees that will be required to perform these duties successfully? How many will be required?

Therefore, job analysis is an essential prerequisite of HRP. Before the HRP process is set rolling, it is important for the firm to perform a job analysis and lay down clear job descriptions and job specifications. We will now discuss job analysis and its components before examining the HRP process in detail.

JOB ANALYSIS

Examine the following scenario of a FMCG firm. This firm witnessed a 75% turnover of sales professionals in the last 2 years. (A number of factors, both external to the firm, such as better alternative opportunities, as well as internal forces, such as poor working conditions, can lead to high employee turnover). An analysis of the resignations in this firm suggested that sales professionals stayed with the firm for an average of 7–8 months. High turnover was resulting in loss of productivity and revenue for the firm. An investigation was undertaken to understand the cause(s) of such high turnover. Those who had resigned were contacted to find out why they quit. Responses indicated that the main reason for their exit was a discrepancy between what they were 'hired' to do and what they were actually 'required' to do. Since the skills required of them were different from what they possessed, these sales professionals felt frustrated. At the same time, the training budget of the firm had also skyrocketed. When senior managers of the firm were asked what made it difficult to match job requirements with actual employee skills, they had no answer. It turned out that the organization had never bothered to find out what the 'job' was about and what skills will be appropriate for an employee to be successful in this job. In other words, the job analysis process had not been undertaken.

Before we go on to discuss the importance of job analysis and its strategic significance in HRM, we must familiarize ourselves with its terminology (see Exhibit 4.1). We must also distinguish between terms such as 'job', 'position', 'job family', 'task', 'job design', etc. The terms 'job' and 'position' are often used interchangeably. However, the two terms differ in their emphases. A 'job' refers to a group of positions that have similar duties, tasks, and responsibilities. A 'position', on the other hand, is the set of duties and responsibilities performed by one person. Thus, if a firm has a hundred employees, there are a hundred positions. However, the number of jobs may be fewer. For example, in a college that has 50 lecturers, there are 50 positions (one for each lecturer) but just one job (lecturer). A 'job family' is a group of two or more jobs that have similar duties or characteristics. Lecturers, readers, and professors may together be seen as a job family. The characteristics these three jobs share in common include teaching, research, and supervising students.

Job analysis is a systematic process by which management gathers and analyses information related to the tasks, duties, and responsibilities of the jobs with in the organization. A 'task' is a separate, distinct, and identifiable

---

Exhibit 4.1

Terminology Commonly Used in Job Analysis Literature

Job A group of positions that have similar duties, tasks, and responsibilities.

Position It is a set of duties and responsibilities performed by one person.

Job family A group of two or more jobs that have similar duties or characteristics

Task A separate, distinct, and identifiable work activity.

Duty Several tasks that are performed by an individual.

Responsibilities Obligations to perform certain tasks and duties.

Job Analysis A systematic process by which management gathers and analyses information related to the tasks, duties, and responsibilities of the jobs with in the organization.

Job Design Process to ensure that individuals have meaningful work and one that fits in effectively with other jobs.

Job Description A written summary of the content and the context of the job, outlining the tasks, duties, and responsibilities of a job, as well as performance standards of each job.

Job Specification A written statement of the knowledge, skills, and abilities (KSA) and other characteristics (human requirements) that are necessary for performing the job effectively and satisfactorily.

---

work activity. For example, in an interview, the interviewer 'asks questions'. This is a task. A 'duty' is composed of several tasks that are performed by an individual. One of the duties of an HR manager is to 'interview applicants'. Both tasks and duties describe work activities. Therefore, it is not always easy or even necessary to distinguish the two. 'Responsibilities' refer to obligations to perform certain tasks and duties.

At this point, it may be useful to clarify the differences between 'job design' and 'job analysis'. The main objective of job design is to ensure that individuals have meaningful work and one that fits in effectively with other jobs. Job design is concerned with enlarging, enriching, simplifying, or otherwise changing jobs in such a way that each worker's job fits in with other jobs in the firm. It is about integrating the needs of the individuals performing the jobs with the productivity needs of the organization.

Job analysis, on the other hand, focusses on gathering data about each job with respect to what an individual does on that job. The information obtained is useful in the design or redesign of jobs. However, the primary purpose of job analysis is to determine what is done on a job and what skills and other human qualities are required to perform the job 'as it has been designed'. It, thus, has a much narrower focus than job design.

Information Obtained from Job Analysis

The information obtained in job analysis provides answers to three main questions about the job:

- What is to be done? How is it to be done? (the content of the job)
- Under what conditions is the job to be done? (the context in which jobs are performed)
- What skills, knowledge, competencies, and attitudes are required to perform the job? (the human requirements of the job)

Typically, the types or nature of information gathered through job analysis include the following (see Figure 4.5).

Job content Job content includes the following aspects:

Duties and responsibilities The list includes the actual activities, and how, why, and when each activity is performed

Job demands Human behaviours like sensing, deciding, etc. and other job demands like frequent tours out of the city.

Machines, tools, and equipment Information about the tools and machines used in performing the job, and services rendered such as counselling.

Performance standards Acceptable levels of performance on each aspect of the job. This information may be used for appraising employees.

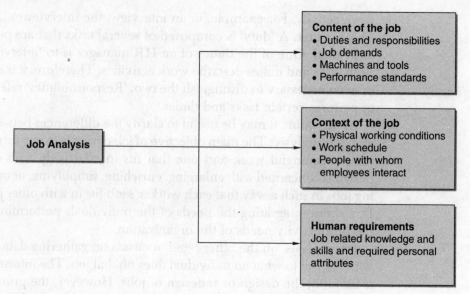

Content of the job
- Duties and responsibilities
- Job demands
- Machines and tools
- Performance standards

Context of the job
- Physical working conditions
- Work schedule
- People with whom employees interact

Human requirements
Job related knowledge and skills and required personal attributes

Job Analysis

Figure 4.5: Types of Information Obtained through Job Analysis

Adapted from: Dessler 2005

Job context The physical, organizational, and social context in which the job is performed, the work conditions, and work schedule. For example, a worker in an assembly line may be working in a humid atmosphere and may not be interacting with other workers.

Human requirements Job analysis provides information regarding job-related knowledge, skills, education, experience, and personal attributes such as personality, interests, etc.

Components of Job Analysis

A job analysis provides information that result in a job description, job specification, and job evaluation (see Figure 4.6). A *job description* provides a written summary of content and the context of the job. It outlines the tasks, duties, and responsibilities of a job. It also helps define performance standards of each job. Performance standards clearly indicate what the job seeks to accomplish and the acceptable or satisfactory performance standard. For a customer relations executive, the performance standard may relate to the total number or percentage of satisfied customers. For example, the standard might be that 80% of each executive's customers should be satisfied; one who satisfies only 10% of his/her customers is not likely to be considered as performing satisfactorily.

The information from a job description is used for writing a *job specification.* A job specification is a written statement of the knowledge, skills, and abilities

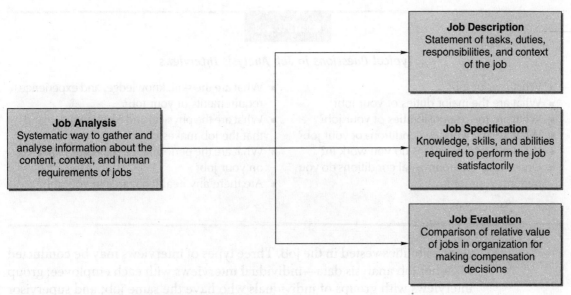

Figure 4.6: Job Analysis and its Components

(KSA) and other characteristics (human requirements) that are necessary for performing the job effectively and satisfactorily. The KSAs in a job specification include education, experience, personal requirements, physical requirements, etc. Significantly, a job specification describes the KSAs the employee needs to have to be able to perform the job satisfactorily; it does not refer to the KSAs that the current employee possesses.

Apart from providing information for job descriptions and job specifications, a job analysis also provides data for *job evaluation* and for comparing the relative value of each job in the organization. Job comparisons help in compensation administration such that jobs having similar demands with respect to KSAs are compensated similarly.

Methods of Collecting Information for Job Analysis

Information relating to tasks, duties, and responsibilities of a job as well as the required KSAs may be collected in a number of ways. The methods may be used in combination or in isolation depending on the purpose of collecting the information. A brief description of the basic methods of collecting information for a job analysis is given below.

Interviews Gathering job-related information through interviews requires the HR manager or the manager responsible for conducting the job analysis to visit the job site and talk with the employee performing the job. Sometimes the immediate supervisor of the employee performing the job in question may also be interviewed in order to obtain a different perspective of the duties and

Exhibit 4.2

Typical Questions in Job Analysis Interviews

- What is your job?
- What are the major duties of your job?
- What are the responsibilities of your job?
- What are the working conditions of your job?
- What physical locations do you work in?
- Under what environmental conditions do you perform your job?

- What are the skill, knowledge, and experience requirements of your job?
- What are the physical and emotional demands that the job makes on you?
- What are the performance standards expected on your job?
- Are there any health hazards in your job?

Source: Dessler 2005

responsibilities vested in the job. Three types of interviews may be conducted to gather job analysis data—individual interviews with each employee; group interviews with groups of individuals who have the same job; and supervisor interviews with one or more supervisors who are familiar with the job.

When many employees are engaged in performing similar jobs, group interviews provide a quick and inexpensive method of obtaining information. Usually the worker's immediate supervisor also attends the group interview session. Alternatively, the supervisor may be interviewed separately. Interviews are the most widely used method for determining the duties and responsibilities of a job. However, job analysis interviews are sometimes viewed by employees with apprehension and are seen as 'efficiency evaluations'. This apprehension prevents them from describing their jobs accurately. Therefore, before conducting interviews, it is important to ensure that the interviewee fully understands the purpose of the interview. A few questions typically asked in job analysis interviews are presented in Exhibit 4.2.

Questionnaires Another good and widely-used way of gathering data for a job analysis is to have the employees fill out a specifically designed questionnaire. Questionnaires are the cheapest method for collecting information. Typically, a job questionnaire evaluates the following factors.

- Duties, and how much time is normally spent on each specific duty or task
- Special duties performed less frequently
- Materials and equipment used
- Work coordination and supervisory responsibilities
- Knowledge, skills, and abilities used
- Working conditions

The degree of structure in the questionnaire may vary. At one end are questionnaires that are structured checklists that provide an employee with a long list of specific duties and tasks (for example, attend to customer complaints).

Each employee indicates whether he/she performs each specific task, and if so the percentage of time normally spent on each. At the other end are open-ended questionnaires that are less structured (for example, one question might be 'state the overall purpose of your job'). The open-ended format asks the job-holders to describe their job, and its major duties and responsibilities. The best questionnaire combines the open-ended format with the structured checklist questionnaire. For example, while information about 'educational qualifications' may be obtained through a checklist, details related to 'job duties' may be sought through open-ended questions.

Observations In the observation method, the manager or the job analyst directly observes the individual performing the job and notes the duties and tasks being performed. Observation may be continuous or limited to a small work sample. When work sampling is used, attention is not directed to each and every detailed action throughout the work cycle (the time it takes to complete a job). The cycle could be a minute, an hour, a day, or longer depending on the nature of the job. Typically, complex knowledge-based jobs have longer work cycles. Work sampling requires the manager to determine the content and pace of a typical workday by statistical sampling of certain actions instead of continuous observation of all activities. It is useful for jobs that are routine and repetitive in nature.

Direct observation per se is useful when a job consists of observable physical activities, such as the job of an assembly-line worker or a salesman. However, jobs requiring mental activity, which is not observable, do not lend themselves to the observation method. An example is the job of a lawyer or a manager. Observation is also not useful when an employee is required to engage in certain activities only occasionally. For example, a manager may be required to present the performance of his/her department in the governing body meeting of the firm twice in a year.

Often, observation is used in combination with the interview method. The job-holder may be interviewed after completing the observation episode to clarify certain points and also to obtain supplementary information on activities that the observer may have missed. Observation and interview may also be conducted simultaneously.

Participant diary/log Another method is to ask employees to maintain diaries and record their daily activities along with the time taken for each activity. When the employee logs details of what activities are performed, how frequently they are performed, and the time required for each activity, it provides a complete picture of the job. The diary method is supplemented with interviews with the employee and the supervisor.

Different methods may be suitable for specific situations. Each method also has its own strengths and weaknesses. The pros and cons of the various data gathering methods are presented in Table 4.3.

Table 4.3: Data Gathering Methods for Job Analysis

Data Gathering Methods	Advantages	Disadvantages
Interviews (individual and group)	■ Most widely used method ■ Simple and quick way of gathering information ■ Interviewer can explain the need for and purpose of conducting job analysis ■ Jobholder knows job the best	■ Problem of standardization: different interviewers may ask different questions about the job ■ Distortion of information: interviewer may intentionally distort the information gained to exaggerate or minimize certain job responsibilities in order to influence compensation rates ■ High cost, especially of group interviews ■ Jobholder's view of job can be biased ■ Time consuming
Questionnaires	■ Cheapest method for collecting information ■ Helps gather large amount of information in a short period of time ■ Can be done at the convenience of the jobholder	■ Employees may not always accurately analyse and communicate information about their jobs ■ Employees differ in how they perceive the job; this may lead to discrepancies in information gained from different people ■ Opportunity for follow-up questions or for clarifying information may be lacking
Observation	■ Simple and inexpensive method ■ Job analyst can see the work being performed and gets first hand information ■ Useful for routine and repetitive jobs	■ Not appropriate for jobs which do not have easily observable job duties or complete work cycle, for example knowledge-based jobs ■ Difficult to observe normal work because the jobholder may become uncomfortable when being watched ■ Observer may be biased and may ignore or on the contrary ascribe undue significance to certain aspects of the job ■ Requires that observer be trained to observe relevant job behaviours
Participant diary/log	■ Jobholder knows the job best ■ Encourages jobholders to think about what they do	■ Jobholder may be biased and may exaggerate some insignificant aspects of the job ■ Detracts jobholders from work since they have to make notes of their activities

Adapted from: Dessler 2005; Mathis and Jackson 1997; Ivancevich 2004

Any of the above methods may be used either in isolation or in combination. Employees (jobholders), supervisors, managers, and job analysts are the sources of obtaining job-related information using any one or a combination of these methods. No one method of data collection is the best. Different methods are suitable for collecting information in different situations. The choice of a method is dictated by the purpose of the job analysis and by time and budget constraints. A comprehensive multi-method job analysis is used more often since it offers significant advantages. A multi-method job analysis requires data to be gathered using a combination of data collection methods as well as sources. However, it can be time consuming and expensive.

In order to gather the range of job-related information, the job analysis process must follow certain steps.

Job Analysis Process

There are six steps to the process of job analysis (see Figure 4.7).

The first step in conducting a job analysis is to determine its purpose. For example, is the purpose to specify performance standards or to compare jobs for compensation purposes? The purpose of the job analysis will suggest what data should be collected as well as how that data should be collected. In other words, the objectives of the job analysis are stated.

The second step is to obtain an overview of how each job fits into the organization. Organization charts are reviewed. The organization charts show the division of work in the organization, how the job in question relates to other jobs, how the job fits into the overall organization, who reports to whom, and whom the jobholder reports to. A review of the existing job description, if any, also provides a starting point for preparing a revised job description.

The third step is to select some representative positions for the job analysis. When there are several similar jobs to analyse, it may be unnecessary to analyse all of them. Usually, a small number of jobs are selected and analysed.

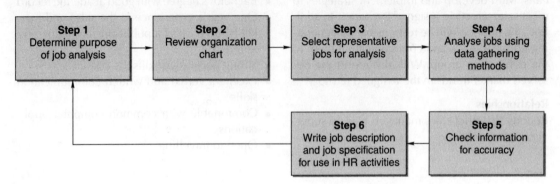

Figure 4.7: Process of Job Analysis

The fourth step is to analyse the jobs using one or more of the data gathering methods described earlier.

The fifth step is to check the job-related information gathered at step four for accuracy and completeness by verifying the information with the job incumbent.

The sixth step is to write the job description and the job specification, which are used as inputs for various HR activities. After the job description and the job specification have been applied, the results are compared with the purpose of the job analysis (determined at the first step of the job analysis process) to assess the degree to which objectives have been accomplished.

Let us now understand how job descriptions and job specifications are written for use in other HR activities (see an example in Exhibit 4.3).

Exhibit 4.3

Job Description and Job Specification—Example

Job Title: Telesales Representative

Employee Code:

Division: Higher Education

Level:

Department: Sales

Reports to:

Salary:

Job Summary

Responsible for selling college textbooks and software and multimedia products via telephone calls. Must develop and implement strategies to meet sales targets in assigned territories. In addition, the position will be responsible for generating editorial leads and communicating them to the publication group. Will also report the observed market trends in the assigned territory.

Relationships

Reports to district sales manager. Has no supervisory responsibility.

Source: Dessler 2005

Primary Responsibilities
- Achieve quantitative sales goals for assigned territories
- Determine sales strategies and develop plans for implementing these strategies
- Conduct product presentations
- Conduct at least 10 interviews with professors every day during academic session to identify product demand and market trends
- Use the telephone for selling products
- Distribute sample products to appropriate faculty

Required Knowledge and Experience
- Bachelor's degree with good academic record
- One year's experience in the sales and marketing division of a publishing company preferred
- Strong persuasive skills
- Excellent verbal and written communication skills
- Comfortable with common computer applications
- Open to travelling

Writing job descriptions A job description is a written statement of the nature and context of a job. Though there is no standard format for writing a job description, most job descriptions contain information about the following.

Job title and identification specifies the name of the job, its department/division, and grade/level of the job (for example, office executive I or II), title of the immediate supervisor, and information on salary grade or pay scale.

Job summary provides a brief description of one or two statements of the general purpose of the job, major functions or activities of the job, and the output expected from the job holders.

Relationships with others inside and outside the firm, or whom the individual reports to; whom he/she supervises directly or indirectly; and which external agencies (such as government departments) the jobholder interacts with.

Responsibilities and duties provide a list of the major duties, responsibilities, and behaviours performed on the job. This section also defines the limits of the jobholder's authority such as his/her decision-making authority and budgetary limitations.

Standards of performance and working conditions specify the standards of performance the jobholder is expected to achieve for each duty and responsibility listed in the job description. For example, an accounts clerk may be expected to make no more than three posting errors per month on an average.

Equipment and tools provide a statement of the tools, equipment, and information required for effectively performing the job.

Working conditions describe the noise level, hazardous conditions, heat, and other characteristics of the work environment.

Writing job specifications The question that needs to be addressed immediately after writing a job description is, 'What human characteristics, personal traits, and experience are needed to perform the job effectively?' Job specification information is especially useful for recruitment and selection. For example, suppose a firm is looking for an individual to fit the job description given in Exhibit 4.3. It is immediately evident from the job specification that the successful applicant would be one with good persuasive skills and strong communication skills.

The following guidelines are helpful in determining what skills, knowledge, abilities, or physical requirements are required for successfully performing a job.

- All job tasks and activities must be identified and rated for importance in performing the job using the methods of job analysis.

- A panel of experts, jobholders, or supervisors lists the skills necessary for performing each listed duty and activity successfully.
- Each skill identified should be rated for its importance. This will help determine which qualities are 'essential' for performance of the job and which qualities are just 'desirable'.
- Each identified skill should be linked to a job task or activity.
- Other characteristics such as physical requirements, personality profile, or professional certification, etc. that are necessary for performing the job should be identified.

Generally, job specifications are written as a section in the job description. Sometimes, the job specification may be a separate document. Writing job specifications for trained employees is simple and straightforward. For example, if a firm wants to hire an HR manager, the job specification might focus on factors such as length of previous experience, quality of relevant training, nature of assignments handled, etc. However, it is more complex to specify human requirements when filling jobs with untrained people because it is not possible to demonstrate proof of past performance. The firm must select the employee on the basis of those skills and characteristics that imply a potential for performing the job or potential for being trained.

Job analysis has always been viewed as a very important HR activity. In recent times, the process of job analysis is being viewed as a core or strategic management activity. In the following section, we discuss the linkage of job analysis with SHRM.

JOB ANALYSIS AND SHRM

Job analysis is the bedrock of all HRM activities of an organization. Hence, the strategic importance of job analysis cannot be over-emphasized. Since job analysis information is the basis for other HRM practices, it is not an end product. Rather, a well-conducted job analysis is important for accomplishing organizational goals. A poorly conducted job analysis may result in job specifications that do not support the accomplishment of specific tasks and duties of the job. This will result in hiring an employee whose skills may be mismatched with the job requirements. Consequently, the jobholder may not be able to reach the expected standards of performance. This will result in a sense of personal failure and dissatisfaction on the part of the employee and will also result in difficulty for the organization to achieve its goals.

It is, therefore, important to conduct a job analysis to ensure effective HR management. Job analysis directly affects recruitment and selection, performance appraisal, training, and development, safety and health, industrial relations, and compensation. Table 4.4 summarizes the input that job analysis provides for various HRM activities.

Table 4.4:   Job Analysis Input for Various HR Activities

HRM Activity	Input Provided by Job Analysis
HR Planning	• Number and types of employees that the firm will need in order to accomplish goals • Changes in the nature of job due to technology or job redesign has implications for the type of skills required by the firm
Recruitment and Selection	• The KSAs that the potential employee should be tested for and the standards of performance to be used
Compensation	• To estimate value of each job and determine its compensation • Compensation for a job depends on skills, education, knowledge, etc. required to perform the job
Performance Appraisal	• To compare each employee's performance against standards established in job analysis
Training and Development	• To determine the nature of training to be imparted based on the tasks and activities to be performed and skills required
Safety and Health	• To identify possible job hazards and working conditions associated with a job • To determine what training should be given to workers performing hazardous tasks
Industrial Relations	• Specific job descriptions reduce grievances by clearly specifying the tasks covered under a job

Adapted from: Dessler 2005; Mathis and Jackson 1997

The strategic importance of job analysis also results from the changing world of work and the changing nature of jobs.

Changing World of Work

Chapter 2 discussed several business and environmental trends that have dramatically transformed the world of work. Trends like technological change, global competition, quality initiatives, telecommuting, deregulation, demographic changes, and a service-oriented economy have forced organizations to rethink traditional job descriptions and go beyond them. These trends consequently have increased the need for firms to be responsive, flexible, and more competitive. There is a weakening of the traditional meaning of 'job' as defined earlier in this chapter. The trend is toward de-jobbing, or the 'broadening of responsibilities of a company's jobs, and encouraging employees not to limit themselves to what is specified in their job descriptions'. Dessler (2005) specified the following organizational factors that have contributed to the changing meaning of work (see Figure 4.8).

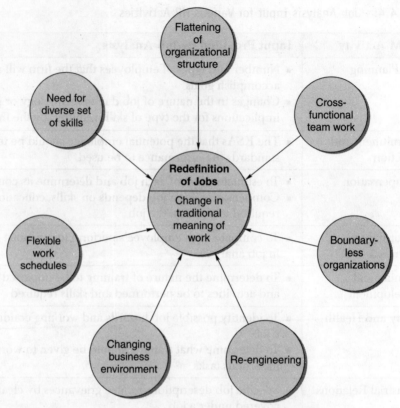

Figure 4.8: Factors Leading to Change in the Meaning of Work

Source: Dessler 2005

- Organizations are moving towards flatter structures; they have only three or four layers of management. The flattening of the organizational structure results in more people reporting to each manager. This makes it difficult for managers to supervise their subordinates closely. So, subordinates assume bigger responsibilities.
- Work is increasingly getting organized around teams. Functional areas are not as important any longer for defining an individual's job. Cross-functional teams requiring collaboration of employees from diverse backgrounds have become common. Employees no longer view their jobs as a specific, narrow set of responsibilities.
- Organizations are increasingly becoming 'boundary-less'. A boundary-less organization is one in 'which there is widespread use of teams and cross-functional task forces that reduce and make more permeable the boundaries that separate departments and hierarchical levels' (Hirschhorn and Gilmore 1992). It encourages employees to think in terms of the

overall interests of the organization rather than only in terms of the duties specified in their jobs.

- Organizations have to adapt to a continually dynamic business environment. Thus, re-engineering is not only likely to be common in organizations but a strategic HR challenge as well. Re-engineering according to Hammer and Champy (1993) involves 'fundamental rethinking and radical redesign of business processes to achieve dramatic improvements in important performance measures, such as, cost, quality or service'. Firms are likely to emphasize the combination of tasks into integrated processes and the assignation of these processes to teams of employees. Customer service is one such example. In a white goods firm, the customer service team consists of a call receptionist who logs in customer complaints and forwards them to the workshop. A mechanic then attends to each complaint. After the complaint has been attended to, an executive calls the customer for feedback on service. Customer dissatisfaction affects performance appraisals of all concerned team members. Thus, in re-engineered situations, employees share joint responsibility for the entire job process, not just a small part of the process. They become collectively responsible for overall results. Jobs may be re-engineered in many ways. Several different activities may be combined into an enlarged or an enriched job. *Job enlargement* involves assigning additional same-level activities to employees, thus increasing the number of activities they perform. *Job enrichment* involves redesigning jobs in a way that leads the employee to experience feelings of responsibility, achievement, growth, and recognition. When a teacher is assigned to teach an additional subject, his/her job is enlarged. When a teacher is assigned the responsibility of representing his/her college in an important committee working on reforms in the educational system, his/her job is enriched.

- The rapidly changing business environment also creates the need to think ahead and describe jobs that will exist in future organizations. Strategic HRM acknowledges the importance of matching HRM activities with the strategic plans of the firm. One of the important strategic roles of HR managers is to determine the knowledge and skills that will be required for the future strategic initiatives of the organization. Thus, job analysis will be strategic and focus on both the present and the future.

- The changing work environment provides employees with greater flexibility about when and how they work. As was pointed out in Chapter 2, variations of traditional work include compressed work schedules, telecommuting, flexitime, etc. Thus, job analysis will need to go beyond the traditional to cater to these new work arrangements.

- For cross-functional teams to function effectively, members need to have a diverse set of skills. Technical, interpersonal, and communication skills are important requirements of team members. They should be able to adjust their skills to match the functional requirements of the team. This is job morphing, or 'readjusting skills to match job requirements'.

As jobs go beyond narrowly defined lists of job-specific duties, employees are expected to be more flexible in their behaviour. Employees who can easily move from one job to another, adapt to new responsibilities, and be flexible, are the ones who are likely to be successful. Instead of the traditional knowledge, skills, and abilities needed to perform a job, the focus today is on competencies. Therefore, there is a shift towards new ways of describing jobs. Competency-based analysis is one such approach to job analysis.

Competency-based Job Analysis

Competencies are popularly defined as general attributes employees must possess to be able to perform well in multiple jobs. Job-related competencies are always observable and measurable behaviours. Competencies might include anything from 'leadership competencies' to 'team work' to 'technical competencies'. For example, a technical competency for the job of a systems engineer might be 'designing complex software applications'.

Competency-based job analysis means 'describing the job in terms of the observable, measurable, and behavioural competencies that an employee doing that job must exhibit to do the job well'. Thus, competency-based job analysis differs from traditional job analysis in certain ways. The differences between the two are summarized in Table 4.5.

As mentioned earlier, the concept of a 'job' is being redefined. In several industries, 'jobs' are seen as obsolete. This is primarily true for knowledge-based organizations where employees work in cross-functional teams on time-based projects. Each member of a cross-functional team has certain responsibilities and targets to accomplish. For example, a project team

Table 4.5: Comparison between Traditional Job Analysis and Competency-based Job Analysis

Traditional Job Analysis	Competency-based Job Analysis
▪ Job-focussed ▪ Describes jobs in terms of job duties and responsibilities	▪ Worker-focussed ▪ Describes jobs in terms of the measurable, observable, and behavioural competencies that must be exhibited by an employee doing that job
▪ Focusses on 'what' is accomplished	▪ Focusses on 'how' the employee accomplishes the work

Adapted from: Dessler 2005

consisting of 10 members developing software for conducting online banking transaction through credit cards will have to work on several tasks. The team members will work on these tasks either individually or as a team. On completion of the project, the team will disband and the members will move to other projects and work with a different group of employees. In some industries (such as IT or services), such shifts occur quite frequently. Hence, firms select, recruit, and compensate these individuals for their competencies and skills, and not just for a specific job or what they do. Therefore, writing an accurate job description for such a job may be difficult. It is easier in this case to identify the competencies required for successful performance on the job. Describing jobs in terms of competencies helps to

- communicate the behaviours that are valued in the firm, since competencies are described in behavioural terms;
- raise the competency levels in the organization; and
- determine the competencies that are important for achieving the strategic goals of the firm and emphasize these competencies to enhance organizational competitive advantage.

BP is an example of a firm that has abandoned the traditional job descriptions in favour of skill matrices. The reason that the firm made this shift was that it needed to be more flexible, efficient, flatter, and empowered. Skill matrices were created for both management and technical employees. Within each matrix are cells that describe (1) the basic skills needed for that job, and (2) the minimum level of each skill required for performing that job successfully. BP identified the skills that are important for the firm to enhance its performance and to be successful in the future. Thus, the emphasis is not on job duties, but on specifying and developing skills that the firm needs to give its employees broader responsibilities. The skills matrix at BP is integrated with other HR practices such as training, compensation, etc. For example, the matrices clearly communicate to the employees the skills they must improve upon. The employee can work on developing these skills. Training efforts of the firm are also directed towards developing skills like leadership, planning, etc. that may be generally applicable across the entire firm. Similarly, the reward system of the firm is linked to skill development. BP has a skill-based pay plan that awards pay raises on the basis of skills improvement. Performance appraisals also focus on skills improvements. Thus, an employee may receive a higher salary by improving his/her skills and productivity within the current role and not only by winning a promotion. A competency-based system also clarifies expectations of the employee and the organization.

Though competency-based job analysis has gained significance in the twenty-first century, the traditional job description is not entirely out of circulation. However, the rapid change in technology, products, and markets are pushing job descriptions to a corner. Firms are competing for employees who have the mix of skills they require; they may or may not write a formal job description. With the growth of knowledge-intensive industries and the high demand for knowledge workers, organizations have to develop plans and strategies to ensure that they have the right types of employees in the right numbers at the right places at the right time.

HRP HORIZONS

Human resource planning may be done organization-wide, or may be restricted to a division, department, or a specific employee group. It may be carried out regularly or tied to a major business decision of the firm or before the launch of a new product or before undertaking a major expansion exercise. Human resource planning can also extend from being long-term, general, and strategic to short-term and specific. It serves as a means for building competitive advantage. Strategic planning in a firm can take place at three levels or horizons—long range, medium range, and short range. There is a close interaction between a firm's strategic plans and its HR plans. Business planning impacts HRP. Human resource planning should be linked with business plans in order to be effective. When Gillette announced its merger with Procter & Gamble (P&G), it also decided to restructure and move from business units based on geographic regions to global business units based on product lines. The new cost-efficient structure and processes will result in redundancy of some employees. While some of the Indian staff is to be relocated to P&G Singapore, there is likely to be separation of a few employees. A voluntary retirement scheme (VRS) package and outplacement service is planned for Gillette staff made redundant.

Several firms develop explicit HR plans as part of their strategic plans. For each planning horizon there is corresponding HRP. The interaction between strategic business plans and HRP is presented in Figure 4.9.

The long-range strategic plans extend to time horizons of more than five years. These are referred to as corporate plans or business plans. Long-range plans are essential for organizational survival and growth and are primarily the responsibility of top management executives. Formulating business plans at this level involve developing a corporate philosophy and an organizational mission. The corporate philosophy identifies why the organization exists and what it expects to do. The organizational mission specifies the products or services that should be produced. At this level, planning should also include an assessment of strengths and weaknesses of the firm. There are three questions to ask:

1. From where does the organization gain its competitive advantage?
2. Are there unique features of its products that provide it with competitive advantage?

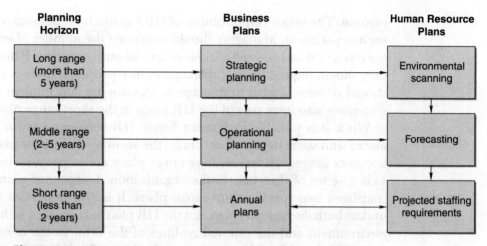

Figure 4.9:   Interaction between Strategic Planning and HRP

Adapted from: Cherrington 1991

3. Are there any weaknesses that will negatively affect the performance of the firm in the long run?

During this planning period, HRP is concerned with such issues as assessing the workforce implications of business objectives; estimating the internal supply of employees over the long run; and assessing and scanning factors external to the firm (involves analysis of labour force composition, socio-cultural changes, demographic changes, changes in labour supply, etc.). The focus of HRP is only to analyse major issues, not to make detailed forecasts. An organization cannot achieve its long-range business plans if it does not have the human resources it needs. If it finds that it may not have the human resources it will need in the future, the organization may either develop action plans to develop its human resources for future use or modify its strategic plans.

Medium-range strategic plans relate to a period of 2–5 years. These consist of formulating the specific organizational goals and objectives that the firm expects to achieve during this time. These plans are stated in terms of the number of units produced, total volume of sales, or some other index of business activity. Medium-range HRP involves detailed forecasting of the number of employees that will be needed within each job category and of the mix of skills that each employee must have so that the organization may achieve its objectives. These HR forecasts should take into account expected employee turnover during this period as well as productivity changes since these will influence the HR requirements.

Short-range strategic plans relate to a period of two years or less. Short-range plans involve developing annual business plans. Most organizations develop short-range plans even if they do not have a long term corporate mission. The major responsibility of HRP at this level belongs to managers in each department. Managers should anticipate the number of employees and the types of skills required to achieve annual business plans. If there is a deficit, they should request the HR manager to hire people. If there is a surplus, they should develop a plan to manage it. Developing and implementing succession plans also form part of the HR plans in the short-range planning period.

While it is possible to forecast future HR requirements for about a year ahead with some degree of accuracy, the accuracy falls as the planning period becomes longer. However, long-range plans are important since these provide a sense of direction to the organization. Long-range plans need to be translated into specific short-range plans. It is also important to revise and update both the business plan and the HR plan to keep pace with the changing environment and the internal realities of the firm. In the context of global competition and flexible management practices of the 1990s, firms are adapting HRP to short-range strategic business plans. J. W. Walker from the Walker Group stresses that the concern for the long-term persists and that HRP continues to address long-term issues. Whether the planning range is short-term, medium-term, or long-term, certain data is intrinsic to a firm's activity of forecasting its HR requirements.

- product/service demand (sales, etc.);
- efficiency (technological changes);
- expansion (new products, increasing capacity);
- internal supply of human resources (quality of human resources and turnover); and
- external supply of human resources.

Thus, we see that the HRP process begins with strategic plans. They are then translated into HR plans. The HRP process is discussed in the next section.

HRP PROCESS

Once the organization has taken stock of the different types of jobs that need to be performed in an organization to successfully achieve corporate plans, the firm can proceed with the HRP process. The HRP process involves matching the internal and external supply of people with the organizational demand for human resources over a specified period of time. Exhibit 4.4 lists the major activities that are part of any HRP process. The HRP process begins with an understanding of corporate strategy and business plans. Organizational goals and objectives are translated into HR objectives by determining the job categories and types of people required to be able to accomplish business plans successfully. Human resource planning involves establishing HR objectives and then assessing the extent to which the current employees of the firm meet these objectives. If the skills available within the firm do not meet the skills

---

Exhibit 4.4

Major Activities of the HRP Process

Stating HR Objectives Specifying human resource objectives of the firm on the basis of its strategic plans.

Forecasting Predicting (1) future demand for human resources in terms of the number of employees needed and the skills mix required on the basis of the firm's strategic plans and (2) internal versus external HR supply and the numbers expected to be available.

Inventorying Taking stock of the current human resources of the firm in terms of numbers as well as skills. This also involves analysing the degree to which employees are being optimally utilized and optimally employed. Some of the questions it attempts to answer are: are employees placed in jobs for which they are best suited?; what is the expected productivity of an employee?; what

is the actual productivity?

Anticipating Extrapolating present resources (number of employees and mix of skills) into the future and comparing projections with future HR demand. This helps identify demand supply imbalances, or if supply is more than the demand or vice versa.

Action Plans Developing specific HR strategies to manage demand–supply imbalances. These strategies may include recruitment, training, promotion, transfer, voluntary retirement schemes, or layoffs.

Control and Evaluation Providing feedback on the degree to which the HR action plans have successfully achieved the HR objectives of the firm.

---

required for achieving organizational goals, the firm develops appropriate action plans (hiring, training, etc.). The HRP process (see Figure 4.10) involves

- environmental scanning;
- forecasting and analysing demand for human resources;
- forecasting and analysing supply of human resources; and
- developing action plans to match human resource demand and supply.

Environmental Scanning

It is the systematic process of studying and monitoring the external environment of the organization in order to pinpoint opportunities and threats. It involves a long-range analysis of employment. The range of external environmental factors that are most frequently monitored as part of environmental scanning include economic factors, competitive trends, technological changes, socio-cultural changes, politico-legal considerations, labour force composition and supply, and demographic trends. These external environmental forces influence the availability of the workforce as discussed earlier in this chapter and in Chapter 2.

Environmental scanning is the first stage of the HRP process. Strategic planning of the firm and HRP interact at this stage. The external environment

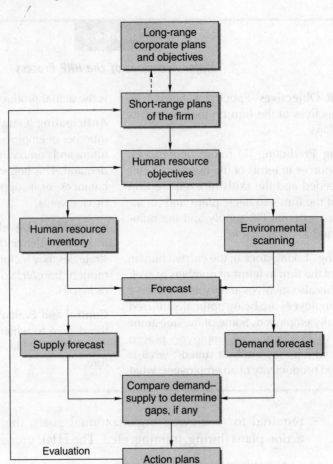

Figure 4.10: The HRP Process

directly affects the strategic plans as well as the HR strategy of an organization. The firm must be responsive to its external business environment irrespective of the business and HR strategies it chooses. For example, a firm faced with an economic downturn may respond by laying off workers. Similarly, when a firm confronts high competition, it may invest in employee training. IBM India foresees that it will be faced with a skill shortage and is taking various initiatives to bridge the gap; one of them is to expand in-house training.

Organizations should scan for changes in the external environment to align its business and HR plans with environmental demands. For example, environmental scanning may suggest that competitive pressures are likely to increase resulting in enhanced productivity requirements. The HRP objective may be 'to increase employee productivity by 5% in 2 years'. This will require the firm to determine current employee productivity. Productivity is calculated by dividing the total output of the firm by the total number of employees.

Environmental scanning assumes greater significance when changes are dynamic, as of the type witnessed in the past decade. No organization can afford to be caught off guard. Human resource supply is particularly affected by environmental changes. All organizations draw from the same labour market. As mentioned earlier in this chapter, a labour market is a particular geographical area within which forces of supply and demand interact to determine the price of labour. Demand is 'the number and characteristics (skills, abilities, pay levels, and experience) of people needed for particular jobs at a given point in time and at a particular place'. Supply is 'both the number and characteristics of people available for those particular jobs'. The environmental scanning process attempts to answer two important questions: (1) which jobs need to be filled (or vacated) during the next 12 months?; and (2) how and where will we get people to fill (or vacate) these jobs? In other words, forces of demand denote employers looking for people and forces of supply denote people looking for jobs.

In a loose labour market (a market in which supply of labour exceeds demand), employers can employ people for lower wages. In a tight labour market (a market in which demand for labour exceeds supply and firms compete for similarly qualified personnel and offer similar compensation in a particular geographical area), employers can raise compensation. Several sectors, such as ITeS, BPO, retail, aviation, construction, and steel, are faced with a tight labour market characterised by a shortage of required skills. This has led to poaching and increased attrition. The ITeS industry faces high attrition due to a labour shortage. Increased attrition has led to increased salaries and increased cost of training, which has led to an increase in the cost per transaction. A major impact of the shortage of a skilled workforce (tight labour market) in India has been on staff cost; it increased by 35% in 2005 against 25% in 2004. This can erode India's low-cost advantage and competitiveness. Fast growing sectors like BPO, IT, retail and telecom are new and do not have historical talent to bank on. These firms are hiring managers from other sectors with skill sets that are relevant to their industries. Hence, employee mobility has assumed new meaning—much movement across sectors is taking place. Cross-sector mobility results in gains for employees such as higher salaries and faster vertical movement.

However, it is not possible to define the geographical boundaries of a particular labour market precisely. Employers may recruit locally when required skills are easily available. On the other hand, for skills in short supply, an organization may extend its search nationally or worldwide (see Exhibit 4.5). Faced with an acute shortage of civil engineers in India, several construction majors, such as L&T, Punj Lloyd, and Simplex Projects Ltd, have started recruiting engineers from countries like the Philippines, Ukraine, Malaysia, Thailand, and Indonesia. India is not producing enough civil engineers to meet the current demand of the domestic construction industry. There is a serious shortage of talent and poaching engineers from other domestic companies does not help since there are not enough senior and experienced engineers. As a result, construction companies have extended the geographical boundaries of their labour market. The telecommunication revolution has transformed the relationship between geography and labour supply. The labour market has now gone global. For example, IBM, HP, Siemens, and Texas Instruments employ several skilled workers in Bangalore, India, who write software packages for these firms.

Several Indian firms are planning to set up units in China, which evokes images of a huge workforce. However, several of these firms are facing labour

---

Exhibit 4.5

The Emerging Global Labour Market

Technological advancement has made it possible to integrate global capital markets into a single market for savings and investment. Digital communication is giving rise to a 'single global labour market'; IT has made it possible for jobs to be performed at locations far removed from customers and colleagues.

There are sectoral and occupational differences in the degree to which remote employment is possible. In sectoral terms, the labour-intensive retailing sector, which employs a huge majority of employees in stores, may be able to offshore about 3% of its jobs (about 4,900,000 positions) by 2008. On the other hand, the far less labour-intensive packaged-software industry is more amenable to remote employment, and almost half the jobs (about 340,000 positions) may be performed remotely by 2008. Similarly, occupation-wise, engineering, finance, and accounting are more amenable to remote employment. The work of support staff which requires customer interaction is much less open to off shoring. However, support staff is required in every industry. Hence, these jobs in absolute terms are the highest in remote employment.

The efficiency of the emerging global labour market has strategic implications for companies as well as for countries. According to an estimate

by the McKinsey Global Institute, 11% of service jobs around the world could be carried out in offshore locations, but only a small fraction of those jobs will actually be offshored. McKinsey evaluated eight sectors—automotive (service jobs only), financial services, healthcare, insurance, IT services, packaged software, pharmaceuticals (service jobs only), and retailing. At present, about 550,000 jobs across these eight sectors are offshored to low-wage countries, such as India, China, Poland, Brazil, Hungary, etc. It is estimated that by 2008, only 1% of the total number of service jobs in developed countries will be sent offshore. There is a huge gap between the number of jobs that can move offshore and the number of jobs actually moving offshore. The reasons for this gap are regulatory barriers, management attitudes, and organizational structure.

The main reason for hiring offshore labour is the cost pressure, the strength of which varies by sector. From the perspective of the supply side of offshore labour, developing countries produce far fewer graduates employable by multinational firms than the raw numbers might suggest. According to human resource managers of multinational firms operating in 28 low-wage economies, only 13% of university graduates were found employable. They cited lack of

Contd

Exhibit 4.5 Contd

language skills, emphasis on theory in education system, lack of cultural fit, and negative attitudes toward teamwork and flexible work as reasons for rejection. The suitability of job candidates varies by occupation and by country in these low-wage economies. Multinational firms found 50% of engineers in Hungary or Poland suitable for employment but only 10% of engineers from China and 25% from India. A country's supply of suitable talent is not proportional to the size of its population. China, for example, has a population 16 times bigger than that of the Philippines, but the pool of suitable young English-speaking engineers is only 3 times as big as in the Philippines.

The availability of suitable labour is increasing fast in low-wage economies. The number of university graduates in these countries is increasing faster than that in developed countries. By 2008, the supply of young engineers is likely to be the same in the developed and the developing countries, while suitable finance and accounting professionals from the developing countries will outnumber those from the developed countries. In aggregate terms, the potential supply of talent in offshore locations will exceed potential demand in future. However, the tendency of multinationals to go to locations with a track record of providing talent is likely to create local imbalances in demand and supply and to result

in a squeeze in labour supply. This demand-supply imbalance will make these cities less attractive for many firms, especially those whose sunk costs in physical and human capital in these cities makes it difficult for them to shift location. For instance, Hyderabad is one city in India that is facing such a demand-supply imbalance. This factor has actually encouraged multinationals to scout for new offshore locations. They are now moving to Tier II or Tier III cities in India.

China, India, and the Philippines, the most popular countries for off shoring today, have the lowest average labour costs. However, the concentration of multinationals in a few locations inflates local wages. As local demand outstrips local supply, wages paid by individual firms rise. This may ultimately reduce the advantage accruing from low-cost labour.

An integrated global labour market requires that supply-side low-wage economies improve the quality of their talent, and not just their quantity. Many developing countries could become more attractive for multinationals by improving the language skills of the potential workforce. On the demand side, companies need to make more rational choices with respect to their location to ensure a demand-supply balance.

Adapted from: Diana, Martha, and Jaeson 2005

---

shortages. This is due to the concentration of industries only in certain locations in China and to the tendency of Chinese labourers to migrate to these clusters, sign one-year contracts, stay in factory dormitories, and visit home during the Chinese New Year. This is one of the HR issues that a company would need to consider before setting up a unit in China. Indian firms must also understand key issues such as intellectual property, electricity, labour laws, and the need to build relationships in China to operate a successful enterprise. Therefore, geographical area is not the only factor on the basis of which the limits of labour market may be defined. Other factors that define the labour market are industry; educational and/or technical background; union membership;

and employer competition. An organization may use a combination of these factors to define its labour market. For example, an R&D firm that needs to hire nuclear biologists must go beyond the local geographical area. Union membership is not a relevant factor for this particular labour market. However, a nuclear biologist must have the required educational qualifications and background. On the other hand, a manufacturing firm looking for unskilled labour to work on the shopfloor will define its labour market on the basis of geographical proximity. The labourer's educational background will not be a significant factor. If a firm's HR planning process succeeds, it will be able to hire all the skilled workers it needs.

Environmental scanning provides a better understanding of the context in which HR decisions are or should be made. To be effective, environmental scanning should take place both internally and externally. Scanning the external environment focusses on issues such as competitors, educational background of workers, regulations, etc. Scanning the internal environment focusses on issues such as business strategy, technology, culture, etc.

Forecasting and Analysing Human Resource Demand

Once an organization has identified the opportunities and threats in its internal and external environments, the next step in the HRP process is to forecast human resource needs in the light of organizational strategies and objectives. The objective of forecasting is to estimate future human resource requirements for specific periods. Such forecasts are of two types: (1) demand for labour—internal and external; and (2) supply of labour—internal and external.

Both supply and demand for labour are subject to several environmental factors such as global economic conditions, technology, etc. Forecasting 'makes use of information from the past and present to identify expected future conditions'. Forecasts are not perfectly accurate. As the planning horizon becomes shorter, the accuracy of forecasts increases. If there is a change in conditions based on which the projections for future are made, it may render these projections invalid. However, experienced people are able to forecast with enough accuracy for the organization to benefit.

Demand forecasting involves predicting the number and types of employees a firm will need in the future. Understanding how business strategy and needs are likely to affect HR requirement is crucial to forecasting its demand accurately. Environmental forces such as changes in technology, changes in consumer buying behaviour, the economy (local, national, and global), and government regulations are likely to influence demand for HR—both in terms of numbers and in types of employees required.

Human resource demand forecasts may be internal or external. Internal demand forecasts relate to the HR requirements of the firm for a specific time period—short term, medium term, or long term. External demand forecasts relate to the HR requirements of competitors or of those external to the firm. External demand can affect the availability of certain types of skills for a particular firm. For example, if an IT firm anticipates that there will be a general increase in external demand (by competitors or industries in sectors other than IT) for software professionals over the next 6 months, and if software professionals are in short supply, the firm is likely to find it difficult to attract this group of employees. Consider India's fast-growing energy and engineering sector. New petroleum refineries, thousands of petrol bunks, several brands of lubricants, oil, and gas, and oil and gas discoveries are creating a big demand-supply gap as far as skilled labour is concerned. Public sector oil firms such as Indian Oil, ONGC, GAIL, HPCL, and BPCL today provide direct employment to over 100,000 skilled personnel. The industry will need another 20,000 people in the next 2–3 years. This is also the time when private sector oil companies like Reliance, Shell, Essar, and Royal Dutch are setting up new refineries and planning huge investments; they require skilled manpower. Private companies are offering 4–5 times the salaries to trained and experienced employees of public sector units to lure them away (external demand). Public sector oil companies are losing 3–4 technical employees every month. They need 200–250 engineers and management graduates every year at the entry level. However, poaching by private players will result in a significant increase in the requirement of workers. Both internal and external demand forecasts depend on business plans of the firm and relate HR requirements to some factor related to business such as, projected sales, product volume etc. Demand forecasting is more of an applied art than a science.

Employee demand can be calculated either on an organization-wide basis and/or calculated based on the needs of each individual department of the organization. A demand forecast that states that 'a firm needs 200 new employees in the next year' may not indicate much, but one that states that 'there is a need for 50 new sales personnel, 50 accountants, and 10 HR personnel', clearly describes the specific skills required. Demand forecasts should take into account new job openings that are likely to occur as well as present openings that are likely to fall vacant due to promotions, transfers, resignations, etc. As people get promoted/transferred, the positions they vacate become available.

The accuracy of forecasts is linked to the stability of a firm's environment. In a stable environment (when the demand for an organization's product is steady or when the technology being used does not change over time), employment forecasts can be accurate. When the environment is dynamic, forecasts are not as accurate. However, it is at this time, that forecasts are most valuable (for example, employment projections of firms based on business growth).

There are several sophisticated techniques of forecasting HR demand. Yet, in practice, forecasting tends to be informal, judgmental, and subjective. There are two techniques of forecasting HR demand: (1) qualitative and (2) quantitative. Let us now take a look at these methods. Table 4.6 presents a summary of common demand forecasting methods.

Table 4.6: Summary of Demand Forecasting Methods

Qualitative Methods			
	Method	**Advantages**	**Disadvantages**
Estimation	People in position estimate the number of people the firm will require in the next year	Incorporates knowledge of corporate plans in making estimates	May be subjective
Expert Opinion	Panel of experts forecast HR requirements for particular future business scenarios. For this method, there may be a single expert, or the estimates of several experts may be pooled together.		
■ *Delphi*	■ Experts go through several rounds of estimates ■ No face-to-face meetings	■ Incorporates future plans and knowledge of experts related to market, industry, and technological development	■ Subjective ■ Time consuming ■ May ignore data
■ *Group Brainstorming*	■ Face-to-face discussion ■ Based on multiple assumptions about future business direction	■ Generates lot of ideas	■ Does not lead to conclusion
■ *Nominal Group Technique*	■ Face-to-face discussion	■ Group exchanges facilitate plans	■ Subjective ■ May ignore data
■ *Simple Averaging*	■ Simple averaging of viewpoints	■ Diverse viewpoints taken	■ Extremes views are masked when averaged
Sales Force Estimates	■ Used when new products are introduced by a firm ■ Sales personnel estimate the number of employees needed based on their estimate of demand of product	■ Sales personnel are familiar with the field	■ Judgmental ■ Possibility of bias

Contd

Table 4.6 Contd

Quantitative Methods			
	Method	**Advantages**	**Disadvantages**
Trend Analysis and Projection	Based on past relationship between a business factor related to employment and employment level itself		
▪ *Simple Long-Run Trend Analysis*	▪ Extrapolates past relationship between volume of business activity and employment levels into the future	▪ Recognizes linkage between employment and business activity	▪ Assumes that the volume of business activity of the firm for the forecast period will continue at the same rate as previous years ▪ Ignores multiplicity of factors influencing employment levels
▪ *Regression Analysis*	▪ Regresses employment needs onto key variables	▪ Data driven ▪ Uses multiple business factors	▪ Difficult to use and apply
Simulation Models	▪ Uses probabilities of future events to estimate future employment levels	▪ Makes several assumptions about the future regarding external and internal environment ▪ Simultaneously examines several factors	▪ Costly and complicated
Workload Analysis	▪ Based on actual content of work	▪ HR requirements based on expected output of the firm ▪ Productivity changes taken into account	▪ Job analysis may not be accurate ▪ Difficult to apply
Markov Analysis	▪ Probabilistic ▪ Based on past relationship between business factor related to employment and employment level itself	▪ Data driven	▪ Assumes that nature of jobs has not changed over time ▪ Applicable to stable environment

Source: Bernardin 2004

Qualitative Methods of Forecasting HR Demand

These are judgmental approaches to demand forecasting. Some of the judgmental methods are described below.

Estimation It is a method of demand forecasting that involves asking people in position the question, 'How many people will you need next year?' Estimation methods can be broadly classified into two approaches: (1) centralized (or top-down) and (2) decentralized (or bottom-up). The centralized approach is to have the HR department of a firm examine the business situation and estimate the staffing requirement for the firm. Though simple, this approach does not always produce accurate estimates, because the underlying assumption, that the HR department has complete understanding of business as well as the needs of each function or department, is not always true. The decentralized approach is to have the manager of each unit or function subjectively estimate its staffing needs. Estimates from all units or functions are pooled together to obtain an aggregate comprehensive forecast for the company.

Expert opinions This method uses a panel of experts or people within the firm who have an understanding of the market, the industry, and the technological developments that influence the HR requirements of the firm. The experts are asked to forecast HR requirements for particular future business scenarios. A single expert's estimate may be used or the pooled estimates of several experts. Estimates from experts may be combined in several ways.

Delphi technique This technique combines the opinions of individual experts and returns the combined opinion to each individual expert till all the experts agree. The experts do not meet face-to-face.

Group brainstorming This technique has the experts discuss the issues face to face. They make some assumptions about the future business direction. For example, the experts first examine the strategic plans of the firm for developing new products or services. Subsequently, they try to predict the future market demand for this new product or service, the percentage market share of the firm, forces such as new technology that affect the type of products or services that can be offered, and so on. The estimates are generated based on these multiple assumptions.

Nominal group technique This method requires the experts to independently and individually generate estimates, then share them with the group in a face-to-face meeting, and modify individual estimates till they reach a consensus.

Averaging This method involves simple averaging of forecasts made by individual experts.

Sales force estimate It is used when the need for additional employees arises consequent to the introduction of new products by the firm. When the new product is launched, sales personnel are asked to estimate the demand of the product (expected volume of sales) on the basis of their familiarity with customer needs and interests. This information is used to estimate the number of employees that will be needed to meet the demand. However, the method carries with it the possibility of bias. Sales personnel may purposely underestimate expected sales volume in order to earn incentives and rewards when they are able to exceed their sales beyond the forecasted sales volume.

Quantitative Methods of Forecasting HR Demand

The quantitative approach of forecasting HR demand involves the use of statistical or mathematical techniques. Different quantitative forecasting models vary in their level of sophistication. Some of the quantitative methods are discussed below.

Trend analysis and projection It is one of the most commonly used approaches for forecasting HR demand. The forecast is based on the past relationship between a business factor related to employment and the employment level. The appropriate business factor that relates significantly to employment levels differs across industries. For example, for a university, the appropriate factor may be total student enrollment; for a sales firm, it may be volume of sales; and for a manufacturing firm, it may be total units produced.

Trend projection involves certain steps (see an example at Table 4.7).

- Determine and identify a business factor that relates to the number and type of people employed. This is the most important step in making trend projections.

Table 4.7: An Example of Trend Projection for a Hypothetical Sales Firm

Calendar Year	Business Factor Annual Volume of Sales (number of units)	Total Number of Sales Personnel	Forecasted Human Resource Requirements (adjusted for productivity increase)
2000	100,000,000	5,000	5,000
2001	120,000,000	6,000	5,825
2002	140,000,000	7,000	6,598
2003	160,000,000	8,000	7,321
2004	180,000,000	9,000	7,996
2005	200,000,000	10,000	8,626

Adapted from: Ivancevich 2004

- Identify the historical trend of the relationship between this business factor and the number of people employed.
- Determine the ratio of employees to the business factor, that is, the average output per individual employee per year. This is called labour productivity.
- Determine the labour productivity ratio for the past five years at least and calculate the average annual rate of change in productivity.
- Calculate the human resource demand by dividing the business factor by the productivity ratio.
- Project human resource demand for the target year.

The historical information about the relationship between a significant business factor and the employment level for a particular firm can be used in several ways to develop trend projections. These are described below.

Simple long-run trend analysis This method extrapolates the volume of current business activity for the years for which the forecast is being made. If the volume of business activity (for example, sales, units produced, etc.) of an organization for the forecast period (2 years, 5 years, etc.) is expected to continue at the same rate as that of the previous years for which relationship has been determined, then a simple linear extrapolation can be made. Since there is a correlation between the volume of business activity and the employment level, this linear extrapolation would also indicate HR demand by job and skill category.

Regression analysis It is a statistical technique that makes a more sophisticated use of historical trend analysis by drawing a statistical comparison of past relationships among variables. For example, a statistical relationship between the number of patients (business factor) and the employment level of nurses in a nursing home may be useful in forecasting the number of employees that will be needed if the number of patients increases by, say, 20%.

Simulation models These are highly sophisticated probabilistic simulation models that use probabilities of future events to estimate future employment levels. A computer simulation may be designed that models the business environment of an organization to describe what it might look like in the future. The relationship among the variables built into the model is such that it reflects the interactions within an organization. The simulation helps determine how a particular business decision may affect the relationships among the variables and consequently the future employment needs. Several alternative assumptions about the future, such as those relating to economy, competition, etc. may be built into the model to discover their probable consequences. For each optional simulation of the firm, the effects of a business decision on the HR requirements as well as on business outcomes such as sales and profits can be tracked. The advantage of using a computer simulation is that it allows a simultaneous examination of several organizational and economic factors such as sales, market conditions, competition, etc. However, simulation techniques are used by very few firms.

Workload analysis It is a method that uses information about the actual content of work based on a job analysis of the work. Workload analysis involves use of ratios to determine HR requirements. Both the number of employees and the kind of employees required to achieve organizational goals are identified (see an example at Exhibit 4.6). The steps involved in workload analysis are to

- identify the total output the organization expects to achieve;
- translate the total output into the number of employee hours in each job category that will be required to achieve this output;
- estimate the change in employment whenever there is a change in the level of output by calculating the additional employee hours required;
- determine the total number of working hours that an individual averages in a year; and
- estimate the total number of employees required by translating the total employee hours required for the given output into the total number of employees (given that the average hours an employee works are known).

Exhibit 4.6

Example of Workload Analysis in a Hypothetical Automobile Manufacturing Firm

2006
Planned output for the year = 20,000 cars
Standard employee hours per car = 5 hours
Planned employee hours for the year = 100,000 hours (20,000 × 5)
Productive man hours per employee, per year, based on job analysis = 2,000 hours
Total number of workers required = 50 (100,000/2000)
Assume that the firm expects to increase output for the next year by 20%.

2007
Planned output for the year = 24,000 cars (20% increase)
Standard employee hours per car = 5 hours *
Planned employee hours for the year = 120,000 hours (24,000 × 5)
Productive man hours per employee, per year, based on job analysis = 2,000 hours
Total number of workers required = 60 (120,000/2,000)

* Productivity increases due to technology or other factors may reduce the standard employee hours required per car and will result in the requirement for fewer workers.

Adapted from: Cherrington 1991

An important aspect of workload analysis is the possibility of productivity change. When labour productivity increases, the demand for labour decreases. This is because an individual can work more efficiently. Productivity changes may occur due to training, experience, and, sometimes, due to improved technology. Employee demand can also be forecast by calculating average employee productivity. These forecasts are called productivity ratios. For example, a firm determines that the average number of units produced per employee per year is 1,000. If the business projection of the firm is to produce 1,000,000 units in a year, it will require 1,000 employees. Therefore, the employee requirement may be calculated by dividing the total projected number of units by the number of units an employee produces.

Markov analysis Similar to the simulation method, Markov analysis is also a probabilistic forecasting method. It shows the percentage (and actual number) of employees who remain in each job from one year to the next, as also the proportion of those who are promoted or transferred or who exit the organization. This movement of employees (internal mobility) among different job classifications can be forecast based upon past movement patterns. Past patterns of employee movements (transitions) are used to project future patterns. Markov analysis can also be used to forecast employee movement pattern that may occur among organizational units, between organizational levels, etc. The pattern of employee movements through various jobs is used to establish transitional probabilities and to develop a transition matrix. The transitional probabilities indicate what will happen to the initial staffing levels in each job category, or the probability that employees from one job category will move into another job category. Transitional probabilities also determine the forecasted employee levels at the end of the year. The transition matrix is used to forecast employment changes in future. This matrix can be used to forecast both demand and supply of labour.

For a Markov analysis to succeed, there should be enough employees in each job category; the nature of jobs should not have changed over time; and the situation should be stable.

It is not imperative for HR demand forecasts to produce accurate estimates of future HR requirements. The forecasting process itself serves an important purpose by facilitating the planning process. Requiring managers to make estimates about the future by anticipating events (economic growth, technological change, etc.) provides direction to the firm.

Forecasting and Analysing Human Resource Supply

Once HR demand has been forecast, the next logical step is to determine the availability (internal and external supply) of employees. *Internal supply* forecasts relate to conditions inside the organization such as the age distribution of workforce, terminations, retirements, etc. *External supply* forecasts relate to external labour market conditions and estimates of supply of labour to be available to the firm in the future in different categories. A discussion of methods for estimating internal and external HR supply follows.

Methods of Forecasting External HR Supply

It is a challenge for HR managers to ensure the availability of skilled talent to fulfill the needs of the firm. Therefore, it is important for a firm to estimate the external supply of potential employees available to it. Several interrelated factors must be considered in projecting external HR supply. They are

- government estimates of population available for work;
- net migration into and out of the area;
- numbers entering the workplace;
- numbers leaving the workplace;
- numbers graduating from schools/colleges;
- changing workforce composition;
- technological shifts;
- industrial shifts;
- trends in the industry (actions of competing employers);
- economic forecasts; and
- government regulations and pressures such as job reservations for certain groups.

Several agencies make projections of external labour market conditions and estimates of the supply of labour to be available in different skill categories. The Institute of Applied Manpower Research (IAMR) publishes the Manpower Profile—India Yearbook.

While forecasting the external HR supply of a particular skill available to a firm, it is important to consider the demand for this group of skills by competing organizations. This is because competition for human resources between firms places limitations on its supply to any organization. Suppose a firm wants to hire 20 MBA graduates with a first degree in engineering in 2006. In 2005, 50 firms hired 2,000 such graduates. In 2006, the number of firms looking for this group of graduates grew to 60 firms, and the total number of graduates came down by 200 to 1800. In such a scenario, there will be greater inter-organizational competition for these graduates. Each firm will have to use sophisticated recruiting practices. Therefore, it is important for firms to estimate the external labour market in order to prevent HR surplus or deficits. As a number of firms (Wipro, TCS, Infosys, Satyam, and IBM) belonging to the software industry or from different industries such as retail or hospitality recruit employees with software skills in large numbers from a talent pool that is severely limited, software professionals are in short supply.

Methods of Forecasting Internal HR Supply

Prediction of a firm's future supply of human resources begins with an estimate of the current HR supply. The factors that are considered in estimating internal HR supply are

- employee movement within the firm from current jobs into other jobs due to promotions, lateral transfers, etc.;
- employee movement out of the firm due to resignations, layoffs, or retirements; and
- changes in employee productivity and utilization as a result of training and development.

Some of the methods used for forecasting internal HR supply are discussed below.

Human resource inventory It obtains and stores information about each employee of the organization in a manner that is easily accessible because it is necessary for HRP. Employee information stored in the inventory relates to knowledge, skills, abilities, experience, and career aspirations of the present workforce of the firm. One of the major purposes of maintaining employee inventory is to make informed decisions about staffing and promotions. For example, a firm planning to diversify into agribusiness might want to know how many of its employees have the relevant experience. A human resource inventory helps to obtain this knowledge. The kind of information that is typically included in an HR inventory is presented in Exhibit 4.7.

An HR inventory may be of two types—*skills inventory* and *management inventory*. A skills inventory describes the skills and knowledge of non-managerial employees and is used primarily for making placement and promotion decisions. A management inventory contains the same information as a skills inventory, but only for managerial employees. The information in a management inventory describes the work history of employees, their strengths and weaknesses, their promotion potential, and their career goals. Thus, a management inventory describes those employees who are currently working as managers as well as those employees who have the potential of being promoted to managerial positions.

With technological advancements, HR inventories have become computerized. A computerized inventory is called a human resource information system (HRIS). The HRIS is a collection of information about each employee that is collected and stored in a way that is retrievable. An HR inventory on its own does not serve much purpose unless it is analysed in terms of future HR requirements of the firm. On the other hand, HR requirement forecasts are of no use unless it can be compared to the current and projected future internal supply of human resources. When there is clarity of the projected

Exhibit 4.7

Contents of HR Inventory

Personal Identification Information
name, personal identification number

Biographical Information
date of birth and age, gender, nationality, address, marital status, number of dependents, special case

Educational Achievements
Employment History
details of the jobs held in the last two to five years specifying (in previous as well as present firm)— job title, brief job description, number of years with that firm, salary drawn, reasons for leaving, critical skills needed in these jobs, and skills developed in these jobs, significant achievements in previous jobs

Information about Present Job
date of joining the firm, present job title, date since when the individual is in present position, salary drawn, performance appraisal, potential appraisal, training programmes attended

Present Skills, Abilities, and Competencies
- last two or three performance appraisals, self-perception of employee on skills and competencies, self-perception on areas of improvement and training required
- data about an individual's performance, skills, competencies, areas of improvement, and training required obtained from the individual's superior

Future Focussed Data
personal career goals of the employee for the next three years, data from performance and potential appraisal to identify career path for the employee, superior's views about jobs for which the employee is suitable

Specific Actions
recommendations about specific training programmes and other developmental experiences needed by employee for achieving career goals

surplus or deficits of employees in terms of numbers, skills, etc. action plans can be undertaken to manage HR problems, that is, surplus or deficit.

Human resource inventories can be used to develop employee replacement charts. A replacement chart lists current jobholders and identifies possible replacements should there be a vacancy for reasons such as resignations, transfers, promotion, etc. The replacement charts include the following information on possible replacements.

- Current job performance
- Potential for promotion
- Training experience required by replacement to be ready for the key position

The chart also details 'when' a replacement is needed for a 'job'. These forecasts are generally short-term in nature. A detailed replacement chart is presented in Figure 4.11. A replacement chart is an extremely useful tool for succession planning.

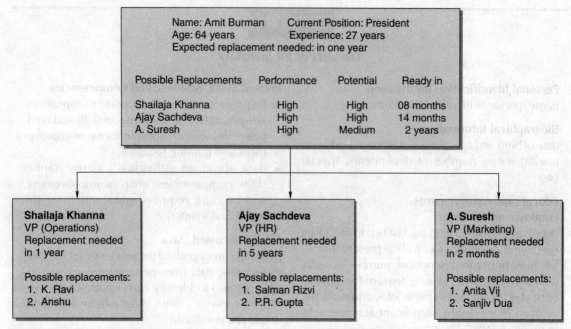

Figure 4.11: Sample Replacement Chart

Adapted from: DeCenzo and Robbins 2005

Succession analysis and planning This is another method used for forecasting HR supply for certain positions from within the organization. Succession planning is a systematic and deliberate process of identifying, developing, and tracking key individuals within the firm to prepare them for assuming senior and top-level positions in future. Take, for example, the case of Steel Authority of India Limited (SAIL). With a spate of new projects coming up, the steel sector is witnessing high attrition and consequently hiring new talent. Steel Authority of India Limited is the target of poaching from global players such as the Korean steel major Posco and Mittal Steel. As a result SAIL is now beginning to build a 'defence system' wherein a second or third line of command is being prepared. Succession planning programs known for their excellence are those sponsored by IBM, ExxonMobil, and General Electric. These firms have made large investments in integrated HRM systems. Exxon is so far ahead in the succession planning game that it has already hired its CEO for the year 2010. At present, very few family-owned firms in India have a formal succession programme. Lately, however, these firms have felt the need to have succession plans in place. Progressive firms like Godrej Consumer Products Ltd, Marico, etc. have what they call a 'drop dead' succession plan. The drop dead succession plan keeps the wheel moving. A promoter of a family-owned firm may always be around to guide the company.

However, in a competitive business environment, they also put together a team of professionals to run the business.

Succession planning is planned promotion for managerial employees. It serves as an important motivational tool for lower-level managers since it provides them with opportunities for upward movement. However, succession plans disrupt the organizational chart. One change in an upper level management position results in a vacancy at lower level, with a cascading effect (see Figure 4.12). The objective of succession planning is to provide developmental experiences for preparing managers to fill potential vacancies.

Traditionally, managers have groomed their own replacements or successors when a senior and more experienced manager provides mentoring at an informal level to a junior manager. Mentoring is discussed in greater detail in Chapter 10. Informal mentoring provides a good learning experience for the junior manager. However, a formalized mentoring has the potential of providing more extensive training experiences for the junior manager. Standard Chartered has initiated 'mentoring programmes', especially among its junior employees, in order to prepare themselves for a rise in employee turnover. Apart from mentoring, succession planning also uses developmental assignments as tools for development purposes. Developmental job assignments provide managers with special training by extending to them an opportunity to serve as managers in other departments.

Succession planning is a major step that brings together development of the present workforce and short-term HR demand forecasts. It contributes to the development of new managers and, at the same time, facilitates the promotion process. Apart from these internal HR supply forecasting methods,

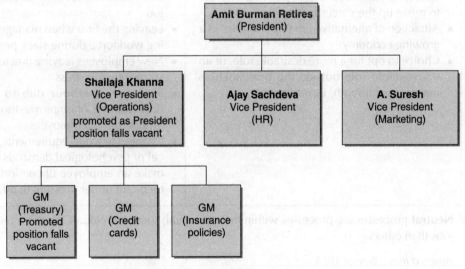

Figure 4.12:   Cascading Effect of Succession Planning

Markov analysis, discussed earlier in the chapter, also provides information for making internal supply projections.

Labour wastage analysis It is the analysis of labour wastage, or the loss of labour arising out of employee turnover. Employee turnover is the movement of employees out of an organization. Future internal HR supply of a firm is influenced by the extent of labour wastage or turnover. Hence, labour wastage should be analysed in order to determine future labour losses and to identify reasons for employee turnover. Employees may leave the organization for different reasons, such as retirement, layoffs, death or disability, terminations, promotion within the organization to a different division, or voluntary resignation. Plans for preventing such losses and for enhancing employee retention can be made once the reasons for turnover are known (see Exhibit 4.8).

Exhibit 4.8

Processes Leading to Labour Wastage

Employee turnover may be due to several reasons. Angela Bowey identified the following ten reasons or processes that lead to labour wastage and characterized them as 'push', 'pull', or 'neutral'.

Pull Processes	Push Processes
Processes outside the firm which attract the employee away from the firm	Processes within the firm which repel or push the employee out of the firm
■ Moving to another firm for higher earnings	■ Leaving the present job due to stresses, strains, and interpersonal conflicts faced in the present job
■ Changing jobs for a higher position in order to move up the career ladder	■ Leaving the firm when management is reducing workforce during slack periods
■ Attraction of alternative job opportunities in a growing economy	■ New employees leaving due to induction crisis resulting in stress
■ Choice to opt for a more desirable role, or an unavoidable role outside the firm, such as marriage, childbirth, or retirement	■ Shortage of labour due to absenteeism, understaffing, or employee turnover results in further loss of employees
	■ Changes in work requirements, such as physical or psychological demands of the job may make an employee uncomfortable who may then quit under pressure to adapt

Neutral processes are processes within the individual; some individuals are more prone to change jobs than others.

Adapted from: Bowey 1974

Traditionally, labour wastage is measured by the employee turnover index, which is also called the percentage wastage rate. The employee turnover index is calculated by dividing the number of employees who leave in a month by the average number of employees at mid-month and multiplying the figure by 100. Thus, if 25 employees leave the organization in a month and the average number of employees at mid-month is 500, the turnover rate is

$$\frac{25}{500} \times 100 = 5\%$$

Firms compute turnover rate regularly to compare different departments, divisions, or skill categories. A comparison of turnover rates helps a firm to determine if the employee turnover in a particular department or skill category is unusually high. By tracking turnover rates or pattern over time, a firm can identify the reasons for high employee turnover and take timely steps to manage the same. For example, a firm that experiences very high turnover among software professionals may find on analysis that they are moving to competitors for better pay and consider modifying compensation packages. Organizations also compare their employee turnover rates with their competitors and with the industry average.

When forecasting internal HR supply, it is important that the firm has a good understanding of employee turnover. To forecast employment levels, it is not sufficient to forecast HR demand resulting from the creation of new positions. It is also important to know and estimate the number of employees who may leave the firm during the forecasting period. The accuracy with which a firm forecasts employee turnover determines the accuracy of employment forecasts. For example, if a firm forecasts creation of five new positions by the end of two months, knows two employees will retire, and expects two employees to resign, its net HR demand will be $5 + 2 + 2 = 9$.

Turnover may be classified into two types: (1) avoidable separations (resignations and dismissals) and (2) unavoidable separations (retirement, death, and marriage).

The firm cannot do anything about unavoidable separations. However, it can manage separations that are avoidable. Employee turnover rate may be calculated to reflect only the avoidable separations. The formula for this is

$$\text{Turnover Rate} = \frac{S - US}{M} \times 100$$

where

S = avoidable separations
US = unavoidable separations
M = total number of employees at mid-month

In determining the impact of employee turnover on the potential HR supply of the firm and hence on HRP, it is important not to limit oneself to quantitative rates of employee turnover. The quality of employees who leave the organization is also important. When low performing employees leave the organization, it is called 'functional turnover'. Functional turnover is beneficial to the firm since the firm can recruit or promote those with high potential. Usually, turnover is 'dysfunctional', with high-performers leaving the organization. These employees are the ones in great demand and hence are more likely to leave when offered better conditions. Estimation of turnover levels should consider historical information and economic trends. Historical information, or the turnover rates of previous years in the various job and skill categories, is used to forecast future turnover. Firms should concomitantly analyse the effects of internal and external economic conditions on employee turnover. For example, when the external labour market is characterized by a high level of unemployment, an organization's turnover rates typically go down.

Absenteeism rate It is an important factor in internal HR supply projections. It is the rate at which employees absent themselves from work. When employees are absent from work, it results in productivity loss. A firm may have to hire more employees than required to make for the number of absences across the organization. Like turnover, absenteeism can also be avoidable or unavoidable. Unavoidable absenteeism relates to absences due to sickness, accidents, serious family problems, and so on. Avoidable absenteeism is usually reflected in the form of chronic absenteeism. This may signal that the absentee employee is facing deeper problems in the work environment that need to be addressed. Absenteeism rate is calculated by the following formula:

$$\text{Absenteeism Rate} = \frac{\text{Number of man-days lost due to absence from work during the period}}{\text{Average number of employees during this period} \times \text{Total number of days}} \times 100$$

If 300 man-days are lost due to absence during a month that has a total of 25 scheduled working days, and the average number of employees is 500, the absenteeism rate for the month is

$$\frac{300}{500 \times 25} \times 100 = 2.4\%$$

Both turnover and absenteeism result in high costs for the organization. Turnover costs are due to separation costs of the departing employee, replacement cost, and cost of training the new employee. Absenteeism cost to the organization is because of the impact of absenteeism on organizational performance, loss of man-days, and loss of productivity.

Productivity loss resulting from turnover and absenteeism has important ramifications in a competitive business environment. It is important for HR managers to translate costs of turnover and absenteeism into rupee value. Firms need to manage both turnover and absenteeism. At the same time, other measures to enhance employee productivity can also be adopted. Employee training and development is one such approach for improving employee productivity. This is discussed later in the book.

Matching Demand and Supply Forecasting

Once an organization has forecast HR demand as well as HR supply, the next step is to compare the two. Comparison of HR demand forecast with HR supply forecast helps a firm determine the action plans that should be taken to balance demand–supply considerations. Activities such as recruitment, selection, performance appraisal, training, career development, layoffs, etc. all comprise action plans. When current HR demand is compared with current supply of human resources, one of the following conditions may result:

- HR supply = HR demand
- HR supply < HR demand (deficit/shortage)
- HR supply > HR demand (surplus)

A discrepancy between demand and supply requires that action plans should be developed to eliminate it (see Figure 4.13). Out of the 3,000 B.Tech. graduates from seven IITs in 2004, more than 2,400 opted for jobs in IT, software, and BPO companies. Placement in the infrastructure sector was less than 5%. This trend towards students' preference for IT companies has created a wide gap

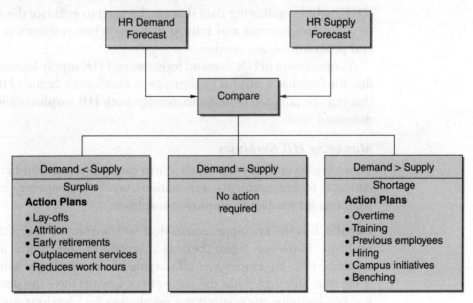

Figure 4.13:   Demand–Supply Comparison and Action Plans

between demand and supply of quality manpower in the infrastructure sector with implications for macro as well as micro level planning of human resources.

However, there may be situations when demand for as well as supply of workforce may be low. Under such conditions, the best course of action for the firm will be to focus on training of employees since demand for these skills may increase in future. Similarly, when both demand as well as supply is high, a firm can go in for recruitment and promotions.

A firm can also forecast its future employment needs by comparing future HR demand and supply forecasts. As discussed already, HR demand is based on the business and growth plans of the firm as well as future trends in business activity. Growth forecasts determine the number of new positions likely to be created. Supply forecasts determine the expected employee turnover rate in the future. The forecasted employment needs of the firm is calculated by adding the number of new positions created and the employee turnover.

As emphasized earlier, productivity improvement is an important factor influencing total employment needs. An increase in employee productivity reduces the number of employees required for the same output.

Action plans need to be developed to meet the HRP objective. They involve developing and implementing programmes such as staffing, appraising, compensating, and training to ensure that people are available with the appropriate characteristics and skills when and where the organization needs them. They may also involve developing and implementing programmes to improve employee performance or to increase employee satisfaction and involvement in order to boost organizational productivity, quality, or innovation. Finally, HRP includes gathering data that can be used to evaluate the effectiveness of ongoing programmes and inform planners when revisions in their forecasts and programmes are needed.

A comparison of HR demand forecasts and HR supply forecasts may suggest that the firm has a surplus or shortage of employees. Some of the action plans that may be adopted by firms to manage both HR surpluses and shortages are discussed next.

Managing HR Surpluses

There are several ways in which a firm can reduce the number of employees. Attrition, early retirements, terminations, layoffs (downsizing), etc. are different solutions for managing employee surpluses.

Layoffs It is the first approach to deal with surpluses, and is usually avoided by firms. However, when there is an economic downturn, usually the first response is to lay employees off. Laying off an employee is not the same as firing one, although it has the same effect. Layoffs have the potential of reducing productivity since surviving employees feel anxious and demotivated. When lay offs are a part of organizational restructuring, it is referred to as 'downsizing'. Downsizing is the reduction in jobs based on a desire to operate more efficiently, even though the demand for the products of the firm is strong. Layoffs, on the other hand, occur when there is a shortfall in the demand for products. Downsizing is also called 'rightsizing' or reduction in force. Both layoffs and downsizing result in reduction of head count. Mergers, acquisitions, competitive pressures, and economic trends have resulted in an employee surplus in many firms, or in employees who have the 'wrong' skills. In order to bridge the demand–supply gap in terms of both the number and type of employees, several companies have eliminated thousands of jobs.

Attrition Also called 'restrictive hiring', attrition occurs when firms do not replace employees who retire or resign, expecting other, existing employees to take up the extra workload. Natural attrition is a slow process unless the turnover is high. Some firms combine attrition with a hiring freeze.

Early retirement This is a process by which senior employees are encouraged to leave the organization earlier than the actual retirement age. Firms commonly offer incentives to employees if they accept early retirement. Golden handshakes (one-time bonus payments) are one example of incentives offered. In India, Fiat, Ballarpur Industries Ltd, Kinetic Engineering, Indian Overseas Bank, Crompton Greaves, and Whirlpool have announced voluntary retirement schemes (VRS). Many public sector firms such as Steel Authority of India Limited, MTNL, and the power distribution companies of Delhi offered VRS to their employees to reduce the total workforce. Dunlop announced an innovative VRS wherein it proposed what it called 'temporary VRS'—a person opting for retirement was promised to be called back as and when the need arises. In the immediate present, early retirements involve a high financial cost to the firm. However, in the long run, the firm benefits by reducing fixed employee cost. Cost-cutting remains a major factor in the implementation of VRS. Operational efficiencies brought about by the introduction of technology in old economy firms have also resulted in launching of VRS to weed out excess staff. For government firms, apart from the competitive reasons, the pension aspect is a growing concern and one that is leading to VRS. Often, firms offering early retirement schemes find that the employees who accept are those that the firms would have liked to retain. As a result, firms tend to package early retirement schemes to target those employees who are poor performers and those the firms wish would leave. Firms also may retain with themselves the decision to accept or reject requests for early retirement from employees.

Reduced work hours When there is a short-term labour surplus and the firm wants to keep all the employees, it may reduce the work hours of each employee. This strategy is usually accompanied with a reduction in employee salaries by a fixed percentage. In the long run, this strategy leads to enhanced employee commitment. Employees feel obliged that the organization took care of them during a bad phase and they, on their part, would like to reciprocate this gesture of the organization.

Outplacement Such services offer assistance to surplus employees to find alternative employment. Outplacement services include career counselling, résumé preparation, interviewing workshops, retraining for other jobs, etc. Outplacement services are most commonly used when a firm is eliminating jobs or when certain employees do not have the required skills. When Gillette India integrated its distribution with P&G, 230 of its sales employees became redundant. Gillette provided outplacement services to these sales employees. Forty of them were placed through recruitment agencies and referrals. For the rest, Gillette organized a career fair. The firm trained these employees to go through a typical stress interview and then invited a range of firms to hire them. Ten two-day workshops were held in February 2006 and the Gillette Career Fair managed to outplace 85% of the 190 employees in the first three days.

Managing HR Shortages

When HR supply is found to be less than the demand, the firm may take the following actions.

- Present employees may be made to work overtime when shortage is small and short-term.
- When there is a shortage of highly skilled employees, present employees may be trained.
- Previously laid-off workers may be recalled in case of a temporary shortage.
- Firms may hire contractual, temporary, or part-time workers to manage a temporary labour shortage or an increase in workload.
- Workers may be hired from external sources.

With the boom in the services sector, IT and ITeS firms plan to increase their global head count. Cognizant Technology Solutions (CTS) plans to increase its workforce to over 34,500 by adding 10,200 employees by December 2006. Zensar Technologies, Infosys, and IBM also have aggressive hiring projections. Hiring has become tougher with a large number of firms trying to tap into an increasingly limited talent pool. Customers demand higher quality and better value. It is therefore important for HR to train the new hires extensively.

Many firms are adopting innovative and proactive measures to tackle skill deficit and to create the skills they require. Some of these measures are described below.

Campus Initiatives Firms in several sectors undertake campus initiatives to ensure a supply of skilled workers. It is estimated, according to IBM, that

250,000 IT students graduate every year in India. The demand is for over 400,000. With projections of a future shortage in the skilled workforce, firms are adopting proactive measures to bridge the demand–supply gap. Firms in several sectors, such as banking, IT, and retail, are launching their own institutes or partnering with educational institutes to impart job-oriented training to increase the quality of manpower as well as to ensure the future supply of trained manpower. IBM and Infosys have set up in-house schools to train future manpower. The Infosys centre at Mysore has facilities to train 10,000 employees each year. IBM also runs one of the industry's biggest e-training programmes in India. The company has also launched its academic initiative programme through which the firm partners with engineering colleges and technical universities in India with a target of training 75,000 students in IBM and open-standards-based technologies. Oracle, through its Oracle Education Initiative (OEI), has undertaken several programmes. Over 150 institutions, including IITs and IIMs, are OEI members, and have received US$250 million so far. Oracle has also signed memoranda of understanding (MOU) with several institutes. Microsoft has an initiative called Project Shiksha. Pantaloon Retail India has partnered with K J Somaiya Institute of Management Research and Studies to offer specialized courses in various aspects of retailing. Those who enroll in this course are given a job offer letter by Pantaloon and the only stipulation is that they complete the course. RPG Enterprises has set up the RPG Institute of Retail Management. ICICI has tie-ups with 27 educational institutions to get 100,000 trained people in the next five to seven years. Accenture, which spends over US$400 million on training its employees, has tied up with Xavier Labour Relations Institute (XLRI) to start an HR academy.

Maintaining bench strength of employees Information technology firms use this tactic to insure against a possible, future shortage of workers. Anticipating a shortage of skilled employees in future, technology firms are recruiting engineers even when they may not have an immediate need for them, but because they think they will have work for them some time in the next several months. This is called pre-emptive hiring. Companies in the IT sector keep a large number of employees in reserve because these employees are seen as promising and can start work immediately on the firms' winning large contracts.

The reserve employees are referred to as the 'bench strength'. The term 'bench' is used to refer to the time that these employees spend off a project. Usually, this period extends from six to nine months. Mid-level professionals are on the bench between two and six months in some firms. Benching is, however, more common among freshers; 30–40% of about 70,000 new recruits are 'hired for potential'. Firms in IT compare benching to the manufacturing firms' maintaining excess capacity to take care of a spurt in sales. Most of these firms are cash-rich and do not mind paying employees to sit on the bench for a few months. However, these recruits do not always sit idle; sometimes they share job responsibility with an existing engineer. If a hire is relatively senior and on the bench, he/she would help build a team for a future project. Big firms like Infosys, Wipro, TCS, Satyam, IBM, and Accenture all have huge monthly and quarterly induction targets. However, none of these firms have an employee utilization ratio of over 70–75%.

Interface with society Firms use this tactic to persuade people to work for them. Firms in the BPO sector are faced with the dual challenge of a demand–supply imbalance and huge attrition. Some of them have been innovating to increase the supply pool and attract youngsters to choose a career in BPO. 24/7 Customer organizes parent workshops where guardians and parents are educated about the nature of work and growth opportunities in the BPO sector. The firm also organizes seminars in colleges.

The HRP process should be evaluated against HRP objectives just like any other HR activity. This requires a clear statement of HRP objectives based on environmental scanning and on HRP supply and demand forecasts. Evaluation of HRP will seek to determine the extent to which HRP objectives have been met by the action plans undertaken to manage surplus or shortage.

SPECIAL CHALLENGE: HRP AND OUTSOURCING

One would assume that when a firm decides to outsource some of its processes, such as IT or customer support, it is not responsible for the HRP of its outsourced processes. Though there is not sufficient literature on the HR aspects of outsourcing, it appears that a firm that is considering outsourcing must actively engage in HRP issues throughout the outsourcing process. Khanna and Randolph New (2005) suggested an HRP model of outsourcing. The interplay between HRP and outsourcing can be viewed in two ways.

1. It is one of many approaches of fulfilling organizational demand for human resources. Outsourcing serves primarily as a source of human resources for the firm. The organization first develops its overall HR plan or an HR plan for a particular division; the plan describes the number of people and the skills required and the roles to be executed. Next, it identifies the gaps that exist in the HR plan, or the shortage in the workforce in numbers or skills. Outsourcing is one of many ways to fill this gap. Viewed as a by-product of the overall HRP process, outsourcing is seen as a 'strategy' or a 'tactic'.

2. The decision to outsource is driven by business objectives and is made by business executives independently of the HR planner. It is not a by-product of the overall HR plan. The decision is driven by business objectives such as cost reduction, increasing flexibility, or to concentrate

on core activities and outsource the rest. According to this view, HR planners play a major role in evaluating the outsourcing relationship and supporting the changing organization after the relationship has been finalized.

Whichever of the two views is taken, it is important for HR planners to increase their involvement and leadership in the outsourcing process. Business leaders should involve HR planners early in the outsourcing process and assign them the responsibility for managing workforce planning issues throughout the implementation of the outsourcing process. The outsourcing process consists of four stages:

1. analysis and evaluation;
2. contracting and negotiation;
3. initiation and transition; and
4. stabilization and maintenance of the outsourced relationship.

These stages are part of the outsourcing of any function (IT, HR, process management), as well as of all types of outsourcing arrangements (on-shore, off-shore, near shore, and multi-shore). Human resource planners of the firm can use several best practices before, during, and after the outsourcing contract is executed. The model for HRP during outsourcing as proposed by Khanna and Randolph New is presented in Figure 4.14.

The four stages in the outsourcing process and the corresponding best practices for HR planners are briefly discussed below.

Analysis and Evaluation

The best practices for HR planners at this stage are to retain the HRP function and to consider options to pure outsourcing.

	Stage 1	Stage 2	Stage 3	Stage 4
Stages in the outsourcing process	Analysis and Evaluation	→ Contracting and Negotiating →	Transitioning →	Stabilization and Improvement
Best practices for HRP	• Retain HR talent • Do not outsource HRP • Consider alternatives to outsourcing	• Evaluate vendor organization design the internal organization to manage the vendor by developing a dedicated vendor management team, and by developing the skills and competencies required	Employ a phased approach to transition • Build a transition team	• Build in continuous improvement and flexibility at the vendor

Figure 4.14: Model for HRP during Outsourcing

Adapted from: Khanna and Randolph New 2005

Retaining the HRP function The features of retaining the HRP function are that

- only some aspects of HR administration such as payroll and benefits are outsourced;
- strategic HR aspects increase in importance and are retained;
- current internal employee strength is not reduced at this stage to ensure retention of critical skills; and
- work is extended to managing an external, dispersed workforce, in addition to managing the internal organization. For example, baggage handling, considered a non-core function, is outsourced at Heathrow airport, London; about 70,000 passengers were stranded due to a wildcat strike by baggage handlers. The strike was a direct result of a labour relations problem at British Airways' catering supplier, Gate Gourmet. People issues in an outsourced function have a direct impact on business. Therefore, the role of HR is important before, during, and after the outsourcing transition.

Considering options to pure outsourcing The key objectives of outsourcing, such as reducing costs and gaining flexibility, can be met by traditional workforce arrangements such as part-time workers, temporary workers, employee leasing, contracting, etc. These workforce arrangements will be discussed in the next chapter. Beyond these traditional approaches, several new options to structure outsourcing arrangements have emerged.

Captive (internal) shared service centres Some of the biggest companies of the world like GE, Citibank, and Microsoft have offshored their processes without outsourcing by setting up an in-house operation in a foreign country. Though this leads to loss of jobs in the country of operation of these firms, the approach allows the firm to retain control of and access to proprietary knowledge.

Joint ventures They are used to migrate to a lower wage structure.

External co-sourcing A few companies pool their operations under this arrangement.

Re-badging or re-sourcing Employees are transferred to the vendor along with the processes. A vendor is the firm to which a firm outsources its operations. It is used when work does not necessarily have to move physically.

Employee swapping A firm contracts out its idle employees to other local businesses to tide over its own business downturn.

Business transformation outsourcing The vendor engages at a strategic level with the client to influence, direct, and control business outcome. The vendor takes ownership and operational responsibility of a company's processes with the purpose of improving business performance. For example, AT&T turned over its customer relationship operations to Accenture. More recently, Unilever turned over its HR operations to Accenture.

Contracting and Negotiation

At this stage the HR planners should take the following responsibilities.

Evaluate vendor It is important to consider the fit between the two organizations and evaluate the vendor for suitability and capability. The vendor must be able to execute the work to be assigned. The outsourcing firm should guide some aspects of the vendor's organizational design, such as delivery team structure, worker job specifications and role descriptions, and training and development.

Design internal organization Human resource planning practices include designing the future internal organization for monitoring, controlling, and managing the vendor. The HR planner should focus on the organizational structure and on the skills and competencies required.

Organizational structure There should be an internal unit dedicated to vendor management that oversees outsourcing relationships. This is usually part of the function that has outsourced the process and reports to the head of that unit. For example, if the HR function is outsourced, the vendor management team would report to the Vice President of HRM. The team should be cross-functional.

Skills and competencies The skills and competencies required would be subject matter expertise, competencies in negotiations, deal making, change management, etc.

Transition

Human resource planning practices at this stage require the firm to take a phased approach to transition and to build a transition team.

Phased approach to transition A phased approach to transition is important when there is a need for a skills transfer and for large outsourcing deals. This eases the speed of organizational change and the impact on existing employees who might already foresee their almost certain departure from the firm. On the other hand, a phased approach may put the employees through a longer duration of anxiety and drain them emotionally. Human resource planners should be part of the team that works out the phased transition plan; the plan depends on the total head count, the skills transfer required, and the criticality of business continuity.

Building a transition team Human resource planning actions of the outsourcing firm require building an internal team to oversee the transition of the business process being outsourced to the vendor. The team needs to have members in different roles, such as an executive sponsor, responsible for the outsourcing decision and its success; a transition manager; a delivery manager; and a technical adviser.

Stabilization and Improvement

At this stage, HRP involves continual improvement in internal flexibility and in new technology and productivity. The size, skills, and competencies of the vendor's workforce should be regularly reviewed by the HR planner of the outsourcing firm. Human resource planning also involves having a plan for any contingency.

Summary

All firms exist to achieve certain goals and objectives. Human resources are the primary vehicle for achieving organizational goals. Therefore, it is important that firms translate all strategic business plans into human resource plans. Earlier strategic business decisions were taken in isolation without appreciating the HR implications of those decisions. Significant changes in the business, economic, and social environments have led to an integration of business planning with HRP and to a long-term, proactive perspective of HRP. All strategic decisions of a firm, such as mergers, acquisitions, and expansions, have implications for human resource issues. It is important to consider these issues right from the planning stage to the implementation stage of strategic plans. This chapter set out the relationship between business strategy and human resource planning. The significant role of external environmental forces such as globalization, new technology, economic conditions, and a changing workforce in making HRP more complex and difficult and yet more critical was highlighted. Two perspectives of HRP (macro and micro) and their objectives were outlined.

An essential prerequisite of HRP is job analysis. Job analysis was discussed with respect to the types of information obtained, its components, the methods of collecting job related information, and its process. The strategic importance of job analysis was examined in the context of the changing world of work and the changing nature of jobs. The importance of competency-based job analysis was also highlighted.

The chapter further emphasized the interaction between strategic planning and human resource planning for all planning horizons—long-range, middle-range, and short-range. The chapter examined the different stages of the HRP process. Environmental scanning, techniques of demand and supply forecasting, and matching demand–supply forecasts to identify gaps were discussed in detail. Various action plans that firms may adopt to manage surpluses and shortages of workforce were illustrated. The chapter ended with an insight into the importance of HRP during the outsourcing process.

Keywords

Absenteeism is the rate at which employees of a firm absent themselves from work; it causes productivity loss.

Bench Strength, or pre-emptive hiring, is the large number of employees kept as reserve by IT firms.

Dejobbing is the broadening of responsibilities of a company's jobs, and the encouraging of employees not to limit themselves to the specifications in their job descriptions.

Demand Forecasting is predicting the number and types of employees a firm will need in the future on the basis of the projection of how business strategy and needs are likely to affect human resources.

Employee Turnover is the movement of employees out of an organization.

Environmental Scanning is the systematic process of studying and monitoring the external environment of the organization to pinpoint opportunities and threats.

Forecasting is the making use of information from the past and the present to predict conditions in the future.

Human Resource Demand is the number and characteristics of people needed for particular jobs at a particular time and at a particular place. The characteristics are skills, abilities, pay, and experience.

Human Resource Planning is the process by which the need for human resources is analysed and identified so that the organization can meet its objectives. It helps determine the HR requirement of the firm and develop strategies for meeting those requirements.

Human Resource Supply is the number and characteristics of people available for particular jobs, or the number and characteristics of 'people looking for jobs'.

Job Analysis is a systematic process by which management gathers and analyses information related to the tasks, duties, and responsibilities of the jobs within the organization.

Job Description is a written summary of the tasks, duties, and responsibilities of a job. It also helps define performance standards of each job.

Job Enlargement is the act of increasing the number of activities performed by an employee by assigning additional same-level activities to an employee.

Job Enrichment is the act of redesigning jobs in a way that leads the employee to experience feelings of responsibility, achievement, growth, and recognition.

Job Morphing is the readjusting of skills by an employee or by the members of a team to match the requirements of the job or of the team.

Job Specification is a written statement of the knowledge, skills, and abilities (KSA) and other characteristics (human requirements) that are necessary for performing a job effectively and satisfactorily.

Labour Market is a particular geographical area within which forces of supply and demand interact to determine the price of labour.

Labour Wastage is the loss of labour arising out of employee turnover.

Macro HRP is the process of assessing and forecasting the demand for and availability of skills at the national or global level. It takes into consideration the industrial and economic growth of the country, industry shifts, and the changing nature of jobs.

Management Inventory contains information on the work history, strengths and weaknesses, promotion potential, and career goals of managerial employees.

Micro HRP is the process of forecasting demand for and supply of human resources for a specific organization to ensure that it uses its human resources optimally.

Outplacement involves offering assistance to surplus employees to find alternative employment through services like career counselling, résumé preparation, interviewing workshops, retraining for other jobs, etc.

Poaching is the hiring of employees from a competitor in a tight labour market to gain an advantage.

Replacement Chart lists current job holders and identifies possible replacements should there be a vacancy for reasons such as resignations, transfer, promotion, etc.

Skills Inventory contains information that describes the skills and knowledge of non-managerial employees and is used primarily for making placement and promotion decisions.

Succession Planning is a systematic and deliberate process of identifying, developing, and tracking key individuals within the firm to prepare them for assuming senior and top positions in future.

Concept Review Questions

1. Define human resource planning. Describe the interaction between strategic planning and human resource planning.

2. Why has human resource planning become more significant in the contemporary business environment? Discuss with examples.

3. What is the difference between macro perspectives and micro perspectives of human resource planning? What objectives does each serve?

4. Define the terms 'job analysis', 'job description', and 'job specification'. What are the pros and cons of different methods of collecting job analysis information?

5. Is job analysis the cornerstone of all human resource management practices? Explain the strategic importance of job analysis.

6. Briefly enumerate the major activities of human resource planning process. Discuss the significance of environmental scanning as the first step in the HRM process.

7. What do you understand by the terms 'human resource demand' and 'human resource supply'? Discuss the qualitative and quantitative techniques of demand forecasting.

8. Describe the methods that can be used by a firm for forecasting human resource supply. What is the importance of succession planning in managing internal human resource supply?

Critical Thinking Questions

1. Critically discuss the following statement, 'Human resource planning has become more important, though more complex and difficult, in a dynamic and global business environment'. Identify the major human resource issues that result from a dynamically changing environment. Also, explain why it is important for firms to forecast external demand for human resources when forecasting supply. What impact can external demand forecasts have on the action plans of a firm? Support your answer with examples from organizations.

2. Is outsourcing a strategy for human resource planning? When a firm decides to outsource some of its processes, is it no longer responsible for human resource planning relating to outsourced processes? Discuss the importance of human resource planning throughout the outsourcing process.

Simulation and Role Play

1. Assume you are the human resource manager of a large software firm with a global presence. The employee turnover rate of the firm has hovered around 15% for the last 3 years, compared to the industry average of 20%. Competition for quality software professionals is expected to increase as more firms from developed countries set up their operations offshore in developing economies. You foresee a shortage of software professionals in the labour market in the future at both entry and middle levels. You do not want to take chances.

- What strategies will you adopt to manage the projected shortfall of software professionals?
- Do you think succession planning as a strategy for managing internal HR supply is relevant to a software firm?
- What are the pros and cons of maintaining bench strength?

2. Assume you are the general manager of a medium-sized HR department of a small rapidly growing IT firm. Since the firm is new, it used information from secondary sources such as trade magazines and other similar firms to develop job descriptions and job specifications. You are in a meeting with all the department heads and the CEO. There are five members present in the meeting including you. During the meeting, the CEO asks you to develop job descriptions for the employees. However, before you can respond, another manager present at the meeting, Mr. Verma, says that job descriptions have no meaning in an IT firm where the nature of jobs keep changing fast. A discussion ensues in the meeting about the merits and demerits of developing job descriptions in a technology firm. The CEO is now looking to you to respond to the discussion.

Five students volunteer for the role play. The student who plays the general manager (HR) responds to the arguments by highlighting the weakening of the traditional meaning of jobs, and the factors that have contributed to the changing meaning of work in contemporary business environment. He/she emphasizes that traditional job descriptions have not become entirely redundant, but that there are new ways of describing jobs. The general manager (HR) ends by discussing the shift toward a competency-based approach to job analysis and its significance.

After the role play, the entire class participates in the discussion. The instructor leads the discussion towards identifying job-related competencies of the members of a cross-functional team in an IT firm.

Classroom Projects

The objective of this exercise is to help students understand the importance of developing appropriate action plans to balance demand–supply considerations. Divide the class into groups of four or five. Introduce the exercise to the class by clarifying the objective of the exercise. Explain to the students that matching HR demand and supply forecasts results in alternative scenarios. Human resource planning action plans should be appropriate to the particular HR demand–supply combination. For example, one combination is high demand and low supply. Each group lists the alternative scenarios and brainstorms appropriate action plans for each of these scenarios. For each identified action plan, each group attempts to give examples of firms faced with particular HR demand–supply combinations and the action plans these firms adopted. Each group also identifies the pros and cons of each action plan. Each group prepares and presents a report. The instructor then leads a general discussion.

Field Projects

1. The instructor divides the class into groups of five. Each group selects one industry and visits two firms in that industry. Group members conduct interviews with HR managers as well as a few top managers of the firms to know the total employee strength of the firms; the employee turnover trends over the past five years; the average turnover rate of the industry; the major reasons for employee turnover; and the strategies adopted by the firm to manage

employee turnover. Each group prepares a report to present in class and writes a report to submit to the instructor. The groups make presentations in the class highlighting the reasons for employee turnover in the chosen industries. Each group ranks the reasons and classifies these reasons into 'pull' and 'push' processes leading to labour wastage (see Exhibit 4.8). Each group also discusses the strategies adopted by the firms in their chosen industries for managing employee turnover. After all the groups have made their presentations, the instructor leads a class discussion on a comparison of reasons for employee turnover in industry. Specifically, the instructor encourages students to understand which of the labour wastage processes (pull, push, and neutral) played a major role in employee turnover in each industry. The discussion should be anchored in the business environment in which the particular industry operates. The class should also examine the differences between industries in terms of the strategies they adopted for managing employee turnover.

Alternatively, the instructor may ask the students to classify the reasons for turnover into functional and dysfunctional turnover.

Case Study[1]

Human Resource Issues in Private Participation in Infrastructure— A Case Study of Orissa Power Reforms

Background

In India, till independence, the generation and distribution of electricity was through private sector efforts only. Large and well-known companies managed these activities as licensees under the Indian Electricity Act 1910. Some of these organizations in Orissa were Cuttack Electricity Supply Company and Puri Electricity Supply Company. In independent India, the Government of India (GOI) enacted the Electricity (Supply) Act, 1948 which aimed at the rationalization of generation and distribution of electricity in India and created electricity boards to achieve the objective. The 1956 Industrial Policy Resolution also emphasized the need for development of the sector through state initiative and virtually barred the private utilities in adding generation capacities. State electricity boards (SEBs) were empowered to set up power generating stations (except nuclear power stations).

The Central Electricity Authority (CEA) was formed to oversee the integrated development of the sector. Subsequently, various steps were taken by the GOI, which yielded remarkable results. The achievement in the first 50 years after independence was stupendous. The installed capacity, which was only 1,363 MW in 1947, increased to 85,919 MW by 31 March 1997. As on July 2001, it is close to 99,000 MW. The total energy generation shot up from a meagre 5,000 MU to 394,800 MU per annum. During the same period the number of consumers increased 59 times with a per capita increase of consumption of power of approximately 23 times. However, in spite of such impressive results over the years, the SEBs could not fulfill the electricity needs of the country for various reasons and gradually made themselves non-sustainable in the present form. Some of the major reasons for this state of affairs were lack of

---

[1] The above case is abridged from the case study written by Prof. Pranabesh Ray, of Xavier Labour Relations Institute, Jamshedpur in July 2001. The case study was supported by the Public–Private Infrastructure Advisory Facility (PPPIAF), a multi-donor technical assistance facility aimed at helping developing countries improve the quality of their infrastructure through private sector involvement. For more on PPIAF, please see www.ppiaf.org. Used with permission.

commercial orientation and conflicting objectives; high transmission and distribution losses; unmanageable size and monolithic structure; unrealistic pricing policy, resulting in a skewed tariff structure; poor billing and collection; bad quality of service due to want of repair and maintenance activities and lack of spares; manpower-related problems like over-staffing, low skill levels and lack of training, low motivation levels coupled with low accountability; and misuse of the statutory power of the state governments to issue directives to SEBs to the extent that the political imperatives often overriding the commercial consideration.

Reform Process

In December 1991, the state chief ministers adopted a new national economic policy after several rounds of discussion. It incorporated power sector reforms to

- reduce reliance on government and raise resources from private sources for generation, transmission and distribution;

- make power available at a reasonable cost;

- ensure stable and good quality power supply; and

- supply power on demand.

This marked a reversal of the policy followed in the past as it welcomed an increasing role for the private sector in meeting the growing demand for funds and greater sector efficiency.

Orissa State Electricity Board (OSEB)

Similar to other SEBs, OSEB, established in March 1961, was the main body responsible for power sector development in the state. Along with OSEB, the Department of Energy of the Government of Orissa (GOO) was responsible for policy and planning for the power sector. Orissa Power Generation Corporation (OPGC) was created in 1984, which operated two thermal plants in the state and supplied power to OSEB. The Orissa State Electricity Board was vested with the responsibility of public power supply in the entire state as well as for regulation at the state level. It obtained the

required power for distribution either from its own generating stations or purchaed it from other generating utilities. By using its transmission and distribution network, it supplied power to the consumers.

The Orissa State Electricity Board, an organization belonging to GOO was governed by the provisions of the Electricity (Supply) Act 1948. This 1948 Act explicitly required the SEBs to operate and adjust their tariffs to achieve a minimum return after interest of 3% on net fixed assets in operation. In order to maintain this, state governments had to provide substantial subsidies to help the SEBs meet their minimum return requirements by compensating for the low tariffs charged for residential and agriculture consumers.

Performance of OSEB

In terms of plant load factor and transmission and distribution losses, the performance of OSEB during the period 1991–94 compared to other SEBs was quite dismal. A clear indication of the large transmission and distribution losses was made in the Annual Administration Report of the Grid Corporation of Orissa (GRIDCO) which listed such losses as 49.47%. During this period, Orissa also had a considerable power deficit, which was estimated to be in excess of 10%, higher than the all-India average of 8%. In 1993–94, the ratio of customers served to the employees of OSEB was 29, whereas the all-India average was around 80. The billing and collection of OSEB had been poor because a large portion of the billing was not done on the basis of meter reading but on average consumption or on load factors, which resulted in lower collection revenues. Figures available for 1998 indicated that in some of the revenue divisions, the percentage of billings collected was as low as 17%. Lack of appropriate controls and poor accounting of sales revenues had affected revenue collection. Unmetered supply to a large number of consumers and theft of power resulted in non-technical losses being as high as 20–25%. The financial performance of OSEB in the years preceding 1994 indicate that, in spite of an annual average growth of about 19% in sales revenue, it had not been able to earn the targeted statutory rate of return of 3% per cent on net fixed assets without the GOO subsidy.

HRM in OSEB

Human resource management in OSEB was also much below what may be expected from any professionally managed company. Although the Board was created to function as an independent body, its functioning indicated considerable interference by the government. 'Only a section of the HRD wing was functioning, i.e. the establishment wing. The service conditions and service benefits were regulated and guided as per the principles and policies of the Government of Orissa'. Professional HR managers were not in charges of the HR activities. Instead technocrats/engineers looked after the HR department. A glaring example of unprofessional HR management (to the extent of being ad hoc and unscrupulous) is the large number of nominal muster role (NMR) employees whose recruitment has been indiscriminate and utilization more influenced by individual concerns rather than the organization's.

Training was not thought of as an important tool in HRM. It was perceived as a cost rather than an investment. In fact, there was only one officer designated as HRD officer and industrial officer who did not have much time to spend on training and development activities. The industrial relations climate in OSEB was more antagonistic than supportive.

The erstwhile political leadership in Orissa could visualise the gravity of the situation and problems for the future. Thus, in April 1992, after elaborate discussions with the World Bank, the GOO and OSEB agreed upon a power sector reform programme. The programme envisaged substantial privatization and separation of the power utilities from government control.

As part of the Orissa power sector reform programme,

- the OSEB was restructured by separating generation, transmission, and distribution into services to be provided by different companies;
- thermal generation and distribution was privatized, and private sector participation invited in hydro generation and in the Grid Corporation of Orissa;
- new power generation was procured through competitive bidding;
- an autonomous power sector regulatory commission was developed; and
- electricity tariffs at the bulk power, transmission, and retail levels were reformed.

Grid Corporation of Orissa (GRIDCO)

The process of restructuring started in 1995. The power generation assets of OSEB were vested in a separate entity called the Orissa Hydro Power Corporation (OHPC) and the transmission and distribution assets were vested in Grid Corporation of Orissa (GRIDCO), a separate entity incorporated on 20 April 1995. The Grid Corporation of Orissa started functioning after the assets of OSEB were transferred to GRIDCO on 1 April 1996. The manpower as on 31 March 1996 was 31,654 (Table 4.8). The Grid Corporation of Orissa signed a corporatisation agreement with the GOO which gave full autonomy to GRIDCO to operate in an efficient, economic, and commercial manner. After corporatisation and the formation of GRIDCO and OHPC, the distribution function (which was with GRIDCO) was also privatized. To facilitate private participation in the distribution activity, Orissa was divided into four geographical distribution zones. Each distribution zone was initially incorporated as a subsidiary of GRIDCO (in November 1997) and then made into four independent companies (discoms) with four new managing directors during March 1998. Later, majority shares in these four companies were divested to private parties.

Table 4.8: Workforce Status in OSEB/GRIDCO as on 31 March 1996

Sl.	Category	Number[1]	
1.	Gazetted non-technical post (excluding TTPS)	167	
2.	Gazetted technical post (excluding TTPS)	1591	
	Sub-total		**1758**
	Non-gazetted		
3.	Supervisory	979	
4.	Highly skilled	975	
5.	Skilled	10513	
6.	Semi-skilled	946	
7.	Unskilled	16483	
	Sub-total		**29896**
	Total		**31654**

[1] The figures for non-gazetted officers include figures for junior engineers, junior managers (finance), and personnel assistants excluding other gazetted officers of OSEB/GRIDCO.

Effect of the Reform Process on HR

When the reform process was initiated, the OSEB had about 35,450 staff of whom about 5,000 went to OHPC and the rest 30,450 to GRIDCO (5,050 were for transmission and 25,400 for distribution). In February 1995, OSEB's Working Group on Human Resources Development concluded in their report that approximately 12,000 employees were in excess. However, in April 1996, a detailed exercise was carried out and a staff rationalization report made that considered various dimensions of the manpower status. After detailed discussions, in October 1997, the GRIDCO board accepted a report that indicated an excess of about 2800 employees. However, preliminary estimates indicated that with growth in business within five years the staff surplus would reduce to about 11% in absolute numbers, though there would be a mismatch in the skill level during the transition period. Since

any immediate reduction in staff would be disruptive to the restructuring process, and would require funds for retrenchment, several options needed to be considered for dealing with staff redundancies (in numbers as well as in skills). Surpluses in transmission were within manageable limits and potential private distribution investors were willing to accept surplus staff and deal with redundancy over a five-year period in line with GRIDCO's own staff transition plan.

The private investors had been persuaded during the due diligence process that it would not be very difficult to rationalize the surplus staff over a period of time and this did not have any significant effect on the sale price. It was also pointed out to them that manpower could be rationalised by (1) normal attrition, (2) retraining and redeployment, (3) introducing an early voluntary retirement scheme, and (4) retiring employees over 50 years of age [Rule 41(1) of Orissa Civil Services (Pension) Rules 1992]. They understood and accepted the suggestions. Hence, the surplus manpower did not have any effect on the sale price.

The private investors did not guarantee the length of time they would retain the surplus employees. However, no one has been retrenched as an outcome of reforms till July 2001. Workforce figures for 1996–2000 is given in Table 4.9. It was also decided that after the reforms each utility would have their own employee service conditions. This needed an intensive and careful study, since not only did the new terms and conditions of service need to be attractive enough to the employees to feel motivated but they also needed to be within the framework of the existing legal requirements. Thus, while the Orissa Electricity Reforms Act 1995 prescribed unbundling of the power sector, it also recommended that the terms and conditions of service should not be inferior to those existing. In the existing legal framework (especially for the non-executive category), this also implied that for all practical purposes retrenchment due to restructuring could be ruled out, although no specific guarantee was given.

Table 4.9:   Workforce Status

	GRIDCO				
	1996	1997	1998	1999	2000
Executives	1758	2218	1554	1302	1197
Non-executives	29896	28600	27724	4799	4744
Total	31654	30818	29278	6101	**5941**

Source: OSEB Annual Administrative Report 1995–96; GRIDCO Annual Administrative Report 1996–97 and 1997–98; GRIDCO papers

The officers who were working with the OSEB before it was restructured were mostly government employees. Either they were recruited by the GOO and deputed to the OSEB or they were recruited by the GOO for the OSEB. Consequently, their commitment was not toward the OSEB. This implied that since officers of the OSEB were attuned to the culture and working of a government department the process of privatization would be a culture shock for them. The restructuring of the power sector necessitated the relocation of the employees to different independent organizations; this required the identification of the organization each employee belonged to. It was therefore necessary that the status of the employees, especially the management, be clarified. The importance of status to a government employee is mainly due to the prestige and security associated with it. This need for job security is common among government employees in India and thus any restructuring would evoke strong reactions against it, if it were perceived that the need is not being fulfilled. The employees perceived power sector reforms as a blindfolded jump into the abyss of uncertainty. The business model of

Privatization → *competition* → *efficiency*

was perceived by the employees as

Privatization → *competition* → *hire and fire*
policy exploitation

Although apparently the employees were fighting against the government's decision of compulsory transfer to GRIDCO/OHPC, in essence it was a fight to ensure their future security. The objective of the reform process was to create several distinct organizations to serve the power sector effectively. Since these organizations were to be carved out by relocating the existing human resources, it was necessary to bring about a transformation in their mindset. The employees recruited and nurtured in the monolithic structure of OSEB characterised by complacency and unaccountability had to be changed into business-oriented customer-focussed personnel. This would mean a continual thrust on training. Training was needed not only for skill upgradation (for balancing the skill mismatch due to restructuring) but also for creating a sustainable training department.

Measures Adopted in Support of the Privatization Process

Although privatization of the OSEB was put into action through the Orissa Electricity Reforms Act 1995, the real transformation of the power sector needed multifaceted action implemented at various levels and stages. Given below are some of the actions and influences, which have helped Orissa power sector reforms to take firm roots in the state.

Political Support towards Power Sector Reforms

The political environment of Orissa was very supportive towards the reforms process. The political leadership and the bureaucracy supported the reform process at all stages without any hesitation. Political support also indirectly reduced the opposition from various unions/associations.

Staff Rationalization Plan

In April 1996, GRIDCO completed a staffing study that determined the staffing norms for each of the activities performed at the divisional level and within the operating, maintenance, clerical, commercial, and construction functions of GRIDCO, comprising both the transmission and distribution businesses. The staffing norms were established for the activities carried out by each of the four divisions of GRIDCO. The staffing norms gave the number of staff required in each grade for each task in each activity in terms of either work drivers or geographical locations. Separate norms were developed for each classification where geographical differences or population density affected staffing requirements. Applying the staffing norms for each activity appropriate to each division's geography and population density to the work drivers determined the total number of staff required in each grade to undertake the work of each division.

The staffing study indicated that

- labour was surplus mainly among the technical unskilled grade;
- there tended to be excess staff in the urban divisions and inadequate staff in the rural divisions;
- there was a skill shortage amongst linesmen (skilled workers whose principal tasks involve line inspection, general repair, and construction activities), with each zonal business requiring training of staff in this category; and
- there were skill shortages in some divisions, which could be met only through recruitment.

Gaining Acceptance

The staffing norms established were discussed with and accepted by the management and employees of GRIDCO. Training programmes were conducted and training centres built by GRIDCO staff to eliminate skill shortages.

Ensuring Support from the Employees

No restructuring process can be implemented effectively without the support of the employees. There were two broad categories of employees in GRIDCO—the officers and the non-officers (workers). It is imperative that both supported the reform process. Some measures adopted by GRIDCO at various stages of the reform process were

1. Creation of New Department

The OSEB was largely considered to be an engineering organization. There were about 2,500 engineers and only 200 officers from other backgrounds. Engineers performed even non-engineering functions like HR and finance. Following restructuring, people with appropriate skills were recruited to these departments. The heads of newly-created departments like HR, finance, and IT were all hired from outside the company. New appointments were made in management positions to increase the attention on these functions. For instance, new directors were appointed for corporate planning, transmission, management information systems, and distribution. Top management appointments were also made in departments like HRD and IT, which were previously headed by middle management personnel with no specialization. Thus, appointment of top specialists gave these departments more importance and a new thrust to their activities. Managing human resources was one significant area where such a thrust projected the organization's commitment towards professionalism and objectivity.

2. Management of Surplus Staff

Absence of any human resource planning, proper recruitment policy, lack of effective administration of temporary workforce and vested interests of certain groups created a large contingent of surplus workforce affecting the performance of the erstwhile OSEB. After the restructuring programme, GRIDCO introduced an early voluntary retirement scheme (EVRS) in August 1997. The first scheme had a cut-off date of June 1998, which was later extended to March 1999. The scheme received approximately 1,500 applications and as on 31 March 1999, i.e., on the eve of the privatisation of GRIDCO's distribution business, a total of 647 employees (42 executives and 605 non-executives) were allowed voluntary retirement. Although reduction of employees was the main objective, separation by way of termination under the present legal framework (ID Act 1947 debars termination because of transfer of management) is a difficult proposition. The employees could have been

redeployed in other organizations, but in a not–
so-developed economy, in which surplus workforce
was common, there were no takers. So, the only
manner in which employee separation was possible, was by adopting an EVRS. The objectives of
the EVR Scheme were to

- provide employees of the company an opportunity to seek early retirement with commen-
  surate monetary benefits;
- utilize the workforce optimally; and
- rationalize the workforce in the light of the age
  and skills mix required, and thereby increase
  productivity.

The scheme was purely voluntary and open
to all who had completed a minimum of 10 years
of continuous service or had attained the age of 40
years as on the date of the submission of application. The scheme was most beneficial and attractive to those above 53. According to the company
officials, applicants to the EVRS were mostly 55
or older; there were very few applicants who were
45 or younger. A committee consisting of the directors of finance, HRD, and transmission and distribution evaluated the applications. They
recommended to the chairman the 'right candidates' for retirement; the employees who they
wanted to retain were not recommended. In
general, officers' applications for retirement were
not accepted because there were fewer officers than
required. Although there were no specific policies
for selection of the 'right candidates', and all were
allowed to apply, the criterion was the inability to
perform due to old age, inefficiency, etc. Payment
to workers averaged between Rs 350,000 and
Rs 400,000 and to officers between Rs 500,000 and
Rs 600,000. The cost of administering the EVRS
was approximately Rs 500 million and was generated from internal resources.

One major risk of an EVRS is the loss of important and critical employees. Top managers
avoided this risk by personally and discreetly persuading certain potential EVRS applicants not to
apply since they had a bright future in the company. The unions in GRIDCO were divided in
their support to the EVRS. While they were all

officially and for their own reasons against the retrenchment of employees, few opposed it. Interaction with the union leaders made it explicit that
while some might not have agreed with the concept, they did not object to it, keeping in mind the
organization's health and the ultimate objective.

3. Regularisation of Nominal Muster Roll (NMR) employees

As mentioned earlier, absence of any HRP,
coupled with vested interests, led to the hiring of
many temporary workers in the OSEB. During the
transition of the OSEB into GRIDCO, the board
decided to regularize 4,441 NMR employees who
had completed 400 days of continuous service and
were in the regular post of helpers. Regularization
was done in phases starting from 1995–96 to late
1998 and early 1999. The number of NMR employees regularized finally totalled 5,336. Simultaneously, the semi-skilled NMR workers were paid
enhanced arrear wages with effect from 1 January
1991. It was also decided that no appointments
would be made on the NMR. The regularization
of NMR employees involved considerable expenditure; their pay increased from Rs 30 per day to
Rs 3,500 per month (approximately, after pay re-
vision; the minimum basic was Rs 2,550 and the
total pay included dearness allowance, house rent
allowance worth 20% of basic pay, and medical
allowance worth 3% of basic pay.)

Although, comparatively, regularization of the
NMR employees does not appear to be financially
beneficial, the need to carry the reform process
through compelled the management to take this
decision. They could have been terminated but this
would definitely have created the very bad impression that reform means retrenchment.

4. Regularization of Stipendiary Engineers

In 1991–92, the GOO hired many engineering
graduates in various disciplines by relaxing the
usual mode of recruitment, which was through the
Orissa Public Service Commission (OPSC). The
idea was that once the emergency recruitment had
been completed, these engineers, designated stipendiary engineers, could be regularized by issu-
ing appropriate government notifications. Around

250 of these engineers were assigned to the OSEB. Even after OSEB was split into GRIDCO and OHPC on 1 April 1996, these engineers were not regularized. They were not entitled to any service benefits, except for the fixed stipend, which had remained unaltered since 1991–92. Taking advantage of the autonomy granted to GRIDCO by the GOO under a memorandum of understanding (MOU) signed by the two, GRIDCO regularized the services of 177 stipendiary engineers in June 1997.

5. Campaigning by Management

Implementation of any process cannot be smooth unless information about it is disseminated. Management campaigned sustainedly both internally and externally during the reform process. Externally, publicity comprised advertisements in the print and electronic media. Statements were issued periodically to inform the general public and the employees about the future and to obviate any possibility of negative publicity. For example, the chairman of the corporation publicly issued statements that there would be no job losses following reform. Internally, meetings, seminars, and workshops conducted by the management with employees and their unions/associations both in public and private, and the GRIDCO newsletter, served the purpose.

Impact on Human Resources

The process of structural reforms in the power sector culminated with the privatization of GRIDCO's distribution business. Thus, the main impact on human resource appears to be qualitative. The employees have been, after privatization, pushed into developing a business-like attitude in a competitive world. As the managing director says, 'Everyone seems to think this to be a charitable organization. I want to change it.'

Questions

1. What factors prevented state electricity boards (SEBs) from fulfilling the electricity needs of the country?

2. What did the power sector reforms that started in December 1991 seek to achieve?

3. Evaluate the status and role of HRM in OSEB before privatization. In what ways did it change after GRIDCO come into existence?

4. What was the HR effect of privatization on human resources in GRIDCO?

5. What does the case suggest about the interaction between strategic planning and HRP?

6. Critically evaluate the VRS of GRIDCO for managing employee surplus. Given the culture of the firm, what optional strategies would you suggest to GRIDCO for managing surplus employees?

7. The strategy for managing the surplus employees of a firm that is going through a major transition such as privatization makes the difference between success and failure. Comment in the light of the case.

References

Bernardin, H.J. 2004, *Human Resource Management: An Experiential Approach*, Tata McGraw-Hill Publishing Co Ltd, New Delhi, p. 86.

Bowey, A. 1974, *A Guide to Manpower Planning*, Macmillan, Great Britain.

Cherrington, D.J. 1991, *The Management of Human Resources*, 3rd edition, Allyn & Bacon, Boston.

DeCenzo, D.A. and S.P. Robbins 2005, *Fundamentals of Human Resource Management*, 8th edition, John Wiley & Sons, Singapore, p. 127.

Dessler, G. 2005, *Human Resource Management*, 10th edition, Prentice Hall of India Pvt Ltd, New Delhi.

Diana, F., L. Martha and R. Jaeson 2005, 'Sizing the Emerging Global Labor Market', *McKinsey Quarterly*, vol. 3, pp. 92–103.

Hammer, M. and J. Champy 1993, *Reengineering the Corporation*, Harper Business, New York, p. 32.

Hirschhorn, L. and T. Gilmore, 1992, 'The New Boundaries of the Boundaryless Company', *Harvard Business Review*, May-June, pp. 104–8.

Ivancevich, J.M. 2004, *Human Resource Management*, 2nd edition, Tata McGraw-Hill Publishing Co. Ltd, New Delhi.

Jackson, S.E. and R.S. Schuler 1990, 'Human Resource Planning: Challenges for Industrial/Organizational Psychologists', *American Psychologist*, vol. 45, no. 2, pp. 223–39.

Khanna, S. and J. Randolph New 2005, 'An HR Planning Model for Outsourcing', *Human Resource Planning*, vol. 28, no. 4, pp. 37–43.

Mathis, R.L. and J.H. Jackson 1997, *Human Resource Management*, 8th edition, West Publishing Co., New York, pp. 198–200.

Mathis, R.L. and J.H. Jackson 2004, *Human Resource Management*, 10th edition, Thomson South-Western, Singapore.

Mello, J.A. 2003, *Strategic Human Resource Management*, Thomson Asia Pte Ltd, Singapore, pp. 135–6.

Miles, R.E. and C.C. Snow 1984, 'Designing Strategic Human Resources Systems', *Organizational Dynamics*, vol. 13, no. 1, pp. 36–52.

Mintzberg, H. 1994, 'The Fall and Rise of Strategic Planning', *Harvard Business Review*, January-February.

Porter, M. 1985, *Competitive Advantage: Creating and Sustaining Superior Performance*, Free Press, New York.

Walker, J.W. 1969, 'Forecasting Manpower Needs', *Harvard Business Review*, March-April, vol. 47, no. 2, pp. 152–64.

Notes

'China-bound Companies may Face Labour Crunch', *The Economic Times*, New Delhi, Thursday, 8 December 2005, p. 10.

'Gillette Staff to be Relocated to Singapore', *The Economic Times*, New Delhi, Tuesday, 17 January 2006, p. 6.

'Labour Reforms: Go There, Stay Off', *The Economic Times*, New Delhi, Thursday, 8 September 2004, p. 11.

'Workers' Varsity for Upgrading Skills Proposed', *The Economic Times*, New Delhi, Friday, 2 December 2005, p. 17.

Bhashyam, S., M.J. Tejaswi, and TNN, 'Bench Strength: Infotech firms on a Hiring Spree', *Business Times*, The Times of India, New Delhi, Monday, 10 April 2006, p. 17.

http://web11.epnet.com/deliveryPrintSave.asp?, accessed on 19 June 2006.

http://www.ppiaf.org

Jayaswal, R., 'Changes in Labour Norms in the Works', *The Economic Times*, New Delhi, Tuesday, 21 February 2006, p. 17.

Kant, K., 'Big Blue to set up Campus for Techies', *The Economic Times*, New Delhi, Tuesday, 21 December 2005, p. 10.

Mahanta, V. and B. Pande, 'India Inc Gives the Gate Thro' VRS', *The Economic Times*, New Delhi, Tuesday, 11 April 2006, pp. 1, 11.

Mahanti, T.K., 'Rise in Labour Productivity to Boost Industrial Competitiveness', *The Economic Times*, New Delhi, Monday, 24 January 2005, p. 16.

Markoff, J. and M. Richtel, 'Profits, not Jobs, are on the Rebound in Silicon Valley', *The Times of India*, New Delhi, Monday, 4 July 2005, p. 16.

Mathew, J. and K. Kant, *The Economic Times*, New Delhi, Thursday, 15 June 2006, pp. 1, 19.

Oberoi, S., 'BPO Staff Shortage, cost may take away India's low-cost advantage', *The Economic Times*, New Delhi, Thursday, 24 November 2005, p. 8.

Shankar, A., 'PSUs Worried as Pvt Oil Cos Up Poaching', *The Economic Times*, New Delhi, Tuesday, 31 January 2006, p. 16.

Singh, N. and TNN, 'Gillette Outplaces 190 Staffers', *Business Times*, The Time of India, Thursday, 18 May 2006, p. 15.

Sinha, V. and K. Kant, 'IT Pays not to Work too',

The Economic Times, New Delhi, Friday, 3 February 2006, pp. 1, 16.

Talwar, P. and N. Kohli, 'Post-Quota, Delhi Boys eye Non-medical courses', *The Economic Times*, New Delhi, Tuesday, 15 June 2006, p. 8.

Thanuja, B.M. and P.P. Thimmaya, 'IT Cos go Preaching Awareness', *The Economic Times*, New Delhi, Monday, 30 January 2006, p. 2.

Verma, S., 'Steel Sector Requires 1,36,000 more Hands', *The Economics Times*, New Delhi, Tuesday, 20 June 2006, p. 6.

Dutta, S., 'BPO Sob Shortage: cost may take   *The Economic Times*, New Delhi, Friday, 3 February
        away India's low-cost advantage', *The Economic   2006, pp. 1, 10.
        Times*, New Delhi, Thursday, 24 November 2005,   Talwar, R. and N. Krishna Kumar, Delhi, Patni Boss
        p. 1.

Sheshan, A., 'TCS x Worried as PE Grows Up',   Delhi, ...roup:', *The Economic Times*, New
        The ...... unt... and P.P. Thomas, 'IT Cos go
        day, 31 January 2006, p. 16.

Singh, N. and TNN, 'Offsite Outplace 190 Sta   Delhi, Monday, 30 January 2006, p.2.
        and ......Times*, The *Times*.......Thursday,   *......*
        28 May 2006, p. 18.   Humla, ...*

Sinha, V. and K. Raju(P), 'Pays me to Work too',   20 June 2006.

5

Acquiring Human Resources

After studying this chapter, you will be able to:

- appreciate the importance of human resource acquisition in the contemporary business environment
- define and distinguish between recruitment and selection
- understand the internal and external environmental factors constraining recruitment and selection efforts of an organization
- acquire an overview of the methods of recruitment and selection
- gain an insight into new approaches to recruitment and executive selection
- describe the interrelated stages of the staffing process
- understand the strategic alignment between business strategy and the recruitment and selection practices of an organization
- discuss the different forms of work relationships that provide organizations with options to the hiring of permanent workforce
- explain the issues that need to be addressed by organizations so that they can hire for diversity

INTRODUCTION

Human resource planning helps a firm determine its human resource requirements and develop action plans to meet these requirements. When organizational demand for certain skills and competencies exceed their current supply, a firm develops strategies to increase human resource supply. One way to do so is by acquiring or hiring new employees. Fast-paced economic growth, new emerging sectors, and a full-blown 'war for talent' in these sectors have created new challenges for Indian industry. Organizations are hiring more frequently and in larger numbers. As talent becomes a source of competitive advantage, organizations have been led to experiment, bend old rules, and try new approaches to cater to their growing talent needs.

This chapter begins with an overview of the relevant terminology and the importance of human resource acquisition activities in the contemporary business environment. An insight into the internal and external environmental factors that constrain the staffing efforts of a firm is presented. The chapter describes the internal and external sources of recruitment as well as the methods. A general idea of the methods of selection is also provided. Effective recruiting can be a powerful strategic weapon. Developing innovative sources through which to find the best people is as important as the selection process. The challenge is not only hiring the right people, but also hiring them before the competitor does. As firms innovate in their search for talent, new approaches to recruitment and selection are being adopted. The chapter discusses some of the new approaches to recruitment, such as e-recruitment, contest recruitment, and outsourcing of recruitment. New approaches to selection that are explored in some detail include computer-aided selection, decision support systems, competency-based approach to selection, and hiring for person-culture fit. The chapter also briefly examines the new developments in campus hiring, the executive placement industry, and the use of personality tests by industry for selection purposes. The stages of the staffing process and the different approaches to making selection decisions are also discussed. The chapter presents a conceptual framework for integrating recruitment and selection with the business strategy. The reasons that firms hire a diverse workforce are highlighted. A discussion of the issues that HR managers need to manage for adopting diversity initiatives successfully is presented. The chapter ends with an exploration of the special hiring considerations of the BPO industry.

HUMAN RESOURCE ACQUISITION: AN OVERVIEW

Today's business environment is drastically different from that a few years ago. The dominant factor for business is no longer economics or technology; it is 'demographics'. Firms and HR managers are faced with the prospect of a shortfall of qualified managerial talent because there are not likely to be enough people available to replace retiring managers. There are not only fewer people, but also fewer people with the skills in demand. Added to this is the emergence of a new employment relationship. The new relationship has shifted from the long-term relationship involving loyalty to an economic contract between the employer and employee. This whole scenario has caused an increase in employee turnover; the challenge of retaining skilled/talented employees; and more difficulty in attracting and hiring from a limited talent pool.

With human resources becoming central to business success, it is important for firms to ensure that they have the right talent in place for today as well as for the future. Thomas Jefferson's enduring words, 'No duty the executive had to perform was so trying as to put the right person in the right place', still hold true. Hiring has become tougher with a large number of firms trying to tap into an increasingly limited talent pool. As firms compete to meet their talent needs successfully, they wage what is commonly referred to as a 'war for talent'. A labour market characterized by high demand and low supply has ensured that talented employees command a high price. With firms willing to 'pay the price for talent', employees have more opportunities and change jobs more frequently. The cost of replacing an employee can be very high. Skill shortages coupled with high levels of employee turnover have resulted in firms hiring more frequently and in larger numbers than ever before. Acquisition of human resources is a strategic response by firms to gain an advantage in a competitive business environment.

Acquisition of human resources is the process by which a firm hires employees to ensure that the required number and types of employees are available to perform organizational activities and accomplish organizational objectives successfully. However, before a firm can hire new employees, it must find people who have the necessary qualifications, and generate enough interest in them to want to work for the organization. The process of finding, attracting, and hiring new employees is called 'staffing'. The staffing function of HRM is concerned with 'seeking and hiring qualified employees'. Mello defined staffing as 'the process of recruiting applicants and selecting prospective employees. Both draw upon the information culled from job analysis and human resource planning. The staffing process follows certain broad steps (see Figure 5.1). A detailed depiction and discussion of the staffing/hiring process comes later in this chapter.

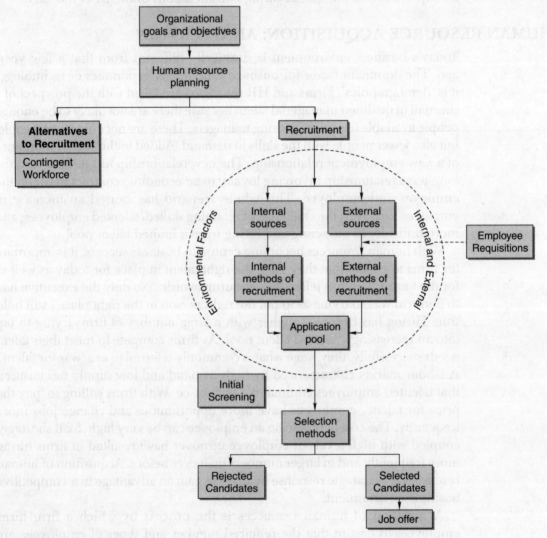

Figure 5.1:   The Staffing Process

Recruitment is the process of discovering potential candidates and of generating a pool of qualified applicants by encouraging qualified candidates to apply for actual or anticipated job vacancies within the organization. The objectives of recruitment include attracting potential candidates to the job opportunities in the firm, generating enough interest to encourage potential candidates to apply for the job, and also to project a favourable image of the company among those who come in contact with recruitment efforts. Recruitment is the first contact between a firm and potential employees. Therefore, it is important to manage the recruitment activity to create a positive first impression on job applicants. Recruitment functions as a bridge or linking activity between HRP and selection. Selection follows recruitment. The selection process involves gathering information about job applicants and using this information for making hiring decisions. The selection process is an exercise in prediction. It seeks to discriminate fairly among job applicants to predict which job applicants from the applicant pool will perform the job successfully and which ones will be unsuccessful if hired. Successful performance means 'performing well on the criteria established in job analysis for the job under consideration'. To predict the future job performance of a candidate, the selection process relies on information gathered about each candidate from selection methods such as application forms, psychological tests, interviews, etc. Not all the candidates who apply for jobs in a firm are hired or can be hired, except under extreme circumstances. Candidates who are likely to be unsuccessful on the job in question are eliminated. Selection may be seen as a negative activity or a process of elimination. Recruitment, on the other hand, is a positive activity, a process of generating an applicant pool. Table 5.1 presents a comparison of the recruitment and selection processes.

Table 5.1: Comparison of Recruitment and Selection Processes

	Recruitment	Selection
Definition	Process of generating a qualified pool of applicants for actual or anticipated job vacancies Positive process (increases the pool of available candidates)	Process of gathering information on job applicants and making the hiring decision based on the information Negative process (eliminates candidates from the applicant pool)
Objectives	▪ Making large numbers of qualified applicants aware of employment opportunities available in the organization ▪ Attracting the attention of qualified candidates	▪ Gathering information about job applicants by using a combination of selection methods ▪ Predicting which job applicants will perform the job successfully, if hired

Contd

Table 5.1 Contd

	Recruitment	**Selection**
	▪ Generating enough interest among qualified candidates so that they apply for the job and accept the job if it is offered to them ▪ Creating a positive image of the organization among those who come in contact with the firm to increase the success rate of organizational staffing activities	▪ To be able to discriminate (fairly) between job applicants likely to be successful on the job and those unlikely
Methods	▪ Company databases ▪ Job posting and bidding ▪ Advertisements, referrals, and recommendations ▪ Executive search agencies ▪ Campus recruitment	▪ Application blanks ▪ Interviews ▪ Work samples, employment/psychometric tests, and assessment centres

In the past several years, both the recruitment and selection activities have increased in importance. The recruitment and selection process is expensive and time-consuming. Therefore, firms are giving more attention to the staffing process. New methods of attracting and screening target candidates are being used by firms in order to win the talent war. Firms seek to ensure that the hired employee will perform well and make positive contributions to the firm performance as well as stay with the firm for a reasonable period of time. Several factors in the external and internal environment constrain the staffing efforts of the firm and often place limitations on a firm's ability to recruit and select a candidate of its choice (see Figure 5.2). These factors are discussed in the next section.

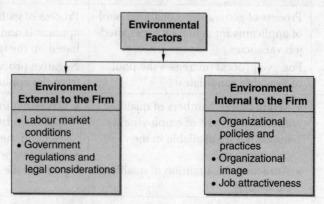

Figure 5.2: Environmental Factors Affecting the Staffing Effort of an Organization

EXTERNAL INFLUENCES ON STAFFING

These are factors that are external to the firm and have an impact on the ability of the firm to hire employees: labour market considerations; and government regulations and legal considerations.

Labour Market Conditions

Labour market conditions were discussed in Chapters 2 and 4. When there is a surplus of labour at the time of recruitment, any recruitment effort will result in many applications. This is because there are more people looking for jobs than there are jobs available. However, in a tight labour market, firms will need to develop their recruitment strategies carefully to be able to attract applicants who fulfill the requirements of the firm. Labour markets can be classified by geographic location of the firm, industry and occupation, and educational and technical qualifications.

Labour markets based on geography can be local, regional, national, or global. Local and regional labour markets differ from each other in terms of workforce availability and quality. For example, most software firms are located in Hyderabad and Bangalore because of the availability of software professionals in the local and regional labour market. Labour market conditions do not always remain the same in a particular region. When a number of employers looking for similar skills are located in a particular geographical region, it may lead to local or regional shortage of the skills in question. As a result of skill shortages, some employers may close operations and relocate to areas where there are potential employees. This exodus was witnessed in the case of BPO firms. Facing a shortage of available workforce in metropolitan cities, many BPO firms, like Dell International Services, IBM Daksh, etc. are setting up operations in Tier II and Tier III cities (non-metropolitan cities such as Jaipur and Chandigarh). Dell International Services has a centre in Chandigarh.

Besides the labour market conditions, other factors such as the type of skills and the level in the organizational hierarchy for which the firm is recruiting also determine whether a firm will recruit locally, regionally, nationally, or globally. A manufacturing firm that sets up a plant in a village will do well to hire blue-collar workers from the local labour market. On the other hand, the firm may have to recruit a senior general manager from the national labour market. For certain skills that are in short supply, firms may hire from the international labour market. For example, nursing skills were in short supply in Britain until recently. Hence, Britain's National Health Service (NHS) was recruiting about 1,000 Indian nurses annually. Now that there is a surplus of nurses, because of supply from Britain and the European Union, the British government announced a clampdown on the recruitment of overseas nurses.

The British government has invested heavily in nurse training since 1997 and is getting results now; there are more than 379,000 qualified nurses working in the NHS. This figure exceeds the 1997 figure of trained nurses in the NHS by 82,000. Moreover, there is a number of nurses undergoing training.

Occupational labour markets are based on the KSAs required for jobs. For example, engineers, doctors, accountants, and advertising professionals all belong to different occupational labour markets. The demand for different occupations may fluctuate over time. For instance, the current demand for information technology jobs or for accountants is very high. High demand for a particular occupation may lead to shortage of the available occupational workforce. Recruitment and hiring strategies will need to be more creative in order to counter this shortage. Another type of labour market is based on educational and technical qualifications. Firms may need individuals with certain qualifications, degrees, certifications, or educational attainment levels. For instance, the call for implementing caste-based reservation in private sector jobs by the government has raised apprehensions in industry that firms will have to compromise on acceptable standards related to educational qualifications. The proposal to increase student intake in the elite educational institutions of the country by 54% will require more teaching faculty, resulting in a shortage of professors with PhDs in most universities. Similarly, there are likely to be shortages of management graduates, design engineers, etc. due to the increase in demand for these skills.

Apart from labour market conditions, the state of the economy also determines the availability of workforce. In a growing economy, more jobs are created and result in higher demand and low supply (shortage) of qualified workforce.

Government Regulations and Legal Considerations

Government policies and regulations influence the staffing process of firms. For example, they prohibit discrimination in hiring and employment. No employer should discriminate between candidates on the basis of nationality, sex, race, caste, etc. Therefore, organizations analyse the composition of its workforce in order to ensure that it is representative of the relevant labour market.

In addition, there is a statutory obligation to provide opportunity for employment to the weaker sections of society. For example, government institutions and public sector firms in India are required by law to reserve some percentage of positions for people belonging to disadvantaged groups like SC/ST, physically handicapped, and children of war widows. More recently, the Ministry of Human Resource Development has proposed to reserve 27% of jobs for 'other backward classes' (OBC) over and above the existing reservations. The Government of India is also trying to persuade the private sector to follow a similar reservation policy in the interest of affirmative action. Though based on the principle of social justice, such legal requirements and government regulations directly affect the recruitment and hiring practices of a firm.

INTERNAL INFLUENCES ON STAFFING

A firm's staffing practices are influenced by internal factors like organizational policies and practices; organizational image; and job attractiveness.

Organizational Policies and Practices

Human resource management policies and practices of an organization affect the staffing process as well as who is hired. For example, several firms have a 'promote from within' policy. Firms with this policy give priority to current employees of the organization, ensuring that all positions are filled internally. These firms hire from outside the organization only at the lowest-level entry positions. The pros and cons of hiring from internal versus external sources are discussed later in this chapter.

Other organizational policies also affect staffing. Certain organizations give priority to war veterans, disabled individuals, or women, and look to these sources first when hiring. For example, all recruitment advertisements of the United Nations state that 'Women candidates are encouraged to apply'. There are other firms that follow the practice of hiring the relatives of current employees.

Organizational Image

The image of an organization held by potential candidates as well as society also affects recruitment. When the reputation of a firm is poor, it is not seen as an attractive organization to work for and potential candidates may not be interested in working for a particular firm. It is logical to conclude that 'All else being equal, firms that enjoy a positive corporate image and reputation find it easier to attract, hire, and retain employees than a firm with a negative image'. Firms that are on the top of *Fortune*'s 'Most Admired Companies' list, such as Microsoft, do not have to exert as much time and effort in recruiting high-quality employees when compared to firms that rank poorly. The same is the case for yearly corporate ratings released by *Business Today* or *Businessworld.*

If we look at campus placements, there are several students who want to get a job with firms such as Microsoft or McKinsey. These firms gain the advantage of hiring the best candidates. There are other firms that do not enjoy the same reputation on campus. For example, there are few takers for public sector jobs in the best management schools in India. This is due to the higher salaries, faster career growth, and exposure offered by multinational firms.

Job Attractiveness

Jobs that are viewed as boring, hazardous, low-paying, or lacking in career growth opportunities also find it difficult to attract a qualified pool of applicants. Jobs seen as uninteresting are not likely to attract the suitably qualified or high quality employees. For example, call centres, whose jobs are considered routine and monotonous, have had to relax employee requirements considerably since suitably qualified individuals do not prefer these jobs. Candidates who would not have been hired by these firms are now being hired after receiving pre-hiring training from the firm.

Another factor that determines the attractiveness of a job and organization is the personal preference of prospective candidates. Even though a firm may enjoy a good image and offer interesting jobs, there may be individuals who would not seek employment with the firm. Such a situation may result when, for example,

- the job is transferable and the individual does not want to be transferred (jobs in the army and the State Bank of India); or
- the candidate does not want to move to the region where the firm is located (Oil and Natural Gas Corporation in Assam); or
- the candidate wants to work for a particular sector or industry (IT or financial services and not infrastructure or heavy engineering).

The above external and internal factors place limitations on the ability of the firm to hire the candidates they prefer. Organizations must take decisions about how to generate the necessary applications as well as how to select the 'best' candidates from the application pool. Given these constraints, even if the applicant pool that results is large enough, it may not include the 'best' candidates, or the 'best' candidates may not want to work for the organization. All firms, nevertheless, must hire additional employees to increase their existing workforce, or replace employees who have retired, been promoted, or left the organization for other reasons. Let us first look at the sources of and methods of recruitment and at innovative approaches to recruitment. This will be followed by a discussion of selection methods and the selection process.

RECRUITMENT SOURCES: INTERNAL VERSUS EXTERNAL

Recruitment sources are 'the locations where qualified individuals can be found'. One of the critical questions that a firm needs to address at the outset is whether to recruit internally or externally. As mentioned earlier in this chapter,

Table 5.2:   Sources of Recruitment: Advantages and Disadvantages

Source	Advantages	Disadvantages
Internal	▪ Performance data of candidates is readily available ▪ Motivational ▪ Builds morale of employees ▪ Speed of hiring ▪ Less expensive ▪ Less time to socialize and adjust ▪ Selected individual reaches performance standards sooner ▪ Results in succession of promotions ▪ Need to hire only at the entry-level	▪ May give rise to internal politicking ▪ Morale problems for those not promoted ▪ Inbreeding ▪ Leads to a chain of promotions ▪ Perpetuates organizational culture even if it needs to change
External	▪ New people bring in new perspectives ▪ Facilitate organizational change ▪ Not aligned with any group within the firm	▪ May cause morale problems for those employees of the firm not promoted ▪ Not familiar with the culture of the firm ▪ Socialization time is higher ▪ May not get acceptability from employees of the firm ▪ Time consuming ▪ Can be expensive

certain firms prefer to recruit internally as a matter of policy. It is only when the internal search does not prove fruitful that the firm goes in for external recruitment. Internal recruitment refers to the process of recruiting from the current employee pool of the organization. External recruitment involves searching for potential employees from the external labour market. Firms necessarily have to recruit externally when they (1) expand their workforce; (2) need to fill entry-level positions; (3) need skills that are not available with current employees; and (4) need to infuse fresh ideas in the firm. Both internal and external sources of recruitment have advantages and disadvantages (see Table 5.2).

METHODS OF RECRUITMENT

Whether recruiting internally or externally, the HR manager may rely on certain methods of recruitment. Recruitment methods are the 'specific means by which potential employees can be attracted to the firm'.

Internal Methods of Recruitment

The internal recruitment methods are organizational databases; job posting and bidding; inside moonlighting; and informal methods.

Organizational Databases

Databases are records of employee-related information that all firms maintain routinely. Now, employee information is usually stored in computers in the form of human resource information systems (HRIS). These databases are commonly referred to as skills inventories or management inventories. The employee profiles available on the databases include information related to the employees' background, skills, knowledge, work history, work experience, training received, performance appraisal records, and the like. In the event of a job opening in the firm, the HR manager can access the database, key in the job requirements, and select the 'best' candidate from the list of current employees that the database provides. Databases can be used for filling vacancies through promotions or transfers from within the firm.

This is a top-down approach, which considers only those employees for a job opening who are listed by the database as meeting the requirements of the job in question. Employees not identified by the database search, but who would like to be considered for the vacancy, are not given a chance to compete for the job opening.

Job Posting and Bidding

This method requires the management to publicize and notify (post) the current or anticipated job openings in the firm and allows the current employees to bid (compete) for jobs they might be interested in. It is a bottom-up approach and provides employees with greater control over their own career. A firm may notify job openings in a number of ways, for example, by posting notices on bulletin boards, through company newsletters, or by e-mailing managers and employees. Recently, firms have been using company websites and intranets for posting job openings. Some company websites are designed to be interactive and allow an employee to match his/her skills, education, experience, etc. with the skills and other demands of the job. Computer software then highlights the gaps, if any, and also outlines the steps the employee needs to take if he/she wishes to apply for the job later.

Job posting is a legal requirement in unionized firms. However, managerial jobs are not covered under the law. Therefore, posting managerial vacancies reflects the company policy of providing opportunities to current employees before hiring from external sources. It is one of the most common methods of recruiting employees from within the organization.

Inside Moonlighting

Sometimes, firms have a temporary shortage of workforce, and at other times, there is some additional work to be done. At these times, instead of hiring new employees, a firm may encourage the current non-salaried employees of the firm to accept additional work in return for a bonus. When current employees of the firm are used to take care of additional work that arises occasionally, it is called inside moonlighting.

Informal Methods

A firm may use informal communication channels to 'spread the word' about current or anticipated job vacancies within the firm. One such informal method is the grapevine, or the process of communicating information within the firm through informal interactions between employees. Employees who indicate their willingness or interest to be considered for the job in question may then be screened for their suitability for the job.

External Methods of Recruitment

While recruiting from internal sources has its own advantages, no firm can or should meet all its HR requirements from internal sources alone. A firm may use one or a combination of external methods of recruitment: direct applicants; employee referrals and recommendations; professional associations; employment agencies; executive search firms; advertisements; and campus recruitment.

Direct Applicants

Potential candidates who apply to a firm although it has not solicited applications are called direct applicants or 'write-ins'. Their applications are called unsolicited applications, and may reach the employer by letter, telephone, or in person. Direct applicants who visit a firm to apply for a job are referred to as 'walk-ins'. Since the firm is not actively recruiting, and since there are no job openings currently available, these applications may not be immediately useful for the firm. Yet, unsolicited applications constitute a relatively inexpensive source of good job applicants. These applications become part of the database for future reference. The number and quality of unsolicited applications that are received by a firm depends on factors like size, image, reputation and location of the firm, as well as economic conditions.

Attrition and talent shortage in BPO firms has led to recruitment through an innovatively styled 'walk-in' method. Some call centres have set up groups dedicated to calling potential candidates and trying to hire them. Genpact has set up what it calls the 'Genpact Store Front' where a potential employee 'walks in' with 'qualifications' and walks out with a 'job offer letter' along with the promise of a lucrative salary. Genpact has set up six such store fronts or hiring offices, in Vizag, Kochi, Kolkata, New Delhi, Indore, and Lucknow. The firm conducts job interviews at these offices daily and hires about 40 people per week per office. ICICI OneSource also has a dedicated call centre that calls prospective candidates and offer them a job.

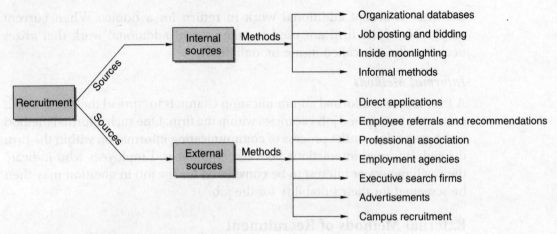

Figure 5.3:   Recruitment Sources and Methods

Employee Referrals and Recommendations

New employees are often located and hired by firms with the assistance of current employees. Before recruiting through other methods, some organizations prefer to ask present employees to recommend names of friends, relatives, or professional colleagues for a particular job opening within the firm. It is an excellent means of locating potential employees for difficult-to-fill positions or hard-to-find skills. Referrals constitute a quick, relatively inexpensive, and a powerful means of recruitment. Recommendations can be used for almost all jobs (skilled, technical, professional, and managerial). Through referrals the new employee forms realistic expectations and receives accurate and relevant information about the job. Usually, current employees recommend people only if they are sure that the person is suitable for the job. An individual whose referral results in successful hiring assumes a mentoring role to the newcomer and facilitates his/her faster adjustment to the culture of the firm. It also provides an effective screening process in terms of employee background checking.

Several firms have formalized this method of recruitment by offering rewards, either monetary or otherwise, or by recognition for employees whose recommendations result in a successful referral. The monetary reward is often in the form of a one-time bonus also called the 'finder's fee'. At Flextronics, the referral programme is called 'Head U Win'. The firm employs a person dedicated to keeping a tab on the recommended candidates. Any employee who refers at least two people becomes entitled to a lucky draw where gifts like plasma TVs, iPods, and even a Santro car are given. Cisco pays US$2000 to an employee each time it hires someone referred by the employee. This reward is not given when managers and for senior executives are hired. IBM also has a referral system that rewards employees in cash and other ways when the company hires candidates they have referred.

Due to high employee turnover, some firms have instituted a 'deferred bonus' for the referring employee. In the deferred rewards scheme, the recommender gets paid only part of the total bonus when the recommended employee joins the firm. The remaining bonus may be given in two or three instalments, and only if the recommended employee stays with the firm for a certain pre-decided time. If the recommended employee leaves before that period, the recommender forgoes the remainder of the bonus. Deferring the bonus ensures that the recommender tries to persuade the employee he/she recommended to remain with the firm. Some firms poach a senior executive from a competitor and then encourage him/her to bring over his/her team as well by promising a bonus for every employee hired.

While the traditional practice of rewarding referees continues to be popular, some innovations are happening in the referral practice. The Indian subsidiary of Juniper, a networking and security solutions company, organized a celebration for its employees at a fancy restaurant. They were encouraged to bring along friends and acquaintances the company could hire. The event was successful—the company won the attention of skilled talent in an informal environment. Intel, the microprocessor company, has created a website for referrals and pays employees Rs 40,000 in cash when it hires a referred candidate.

Sometimes, employee referrals take on negative connotations, such as when employees are 'pirated' from other firms or when employees resort to nepotism and recommend relatives or friends from their own alma mater. However, in the competitive business environment, the 'old boys' network' has been gradually replaced by 'professional networking'. A professional network is the informal interpersonal network of professional contacts that each employee establishes during the course of his or her career. When recommending a potential employee from one's professional network, an employee is guided by the skills and competence of the person rather than by family ties or friendship.

Professional Associations

Several occupational groups, such as engineers, accountants, and medical professionals, form professional associations to share new knowledge in the field and disseminate news about different aspects of the profession. Such associations publish regular newsletters, trade journals, or magazines that are circulated among members of the association. These publications also advertise job vacancies. The resulting applicant pool consists of candidates who have the necessary skills for the job.

Employment Agencies

Job seekers register themselves at employment agencies; the agencies maintain a database of jobseekers. Organizations searching for candidates can access these databases for a fee and obtain a list of eligible candidates, or they can specify their job requirements and request a shortlist of appropriate candidates. Employment agencies may be public or private. Public employment agencies are those operated by the government. In India these exist in the form of employment exchanges. Under the Compulsory Notification of Vacancies Act 1959, firms have to notify certain vacancies with these exchanges. The employment exchange then forwards a shortlist of eligible candidates to the organization when it has vacancies. The organization is required to consider the candidature of those registered with these exchanges on a priority basis. According to 2005 data, there were 998 employment exchanges in India with 12,000 employees and a database of 4.5 million registered job-seekers. Yet these exchanges manage to place only 170,000 people annually. Ma Foi, an HR consultancy firm, hopes that the government will let the private sector participate in its employment exchange infrastructure. Opening up this infrastructure for public–private partnership is likely to throw up new opportunities for the placement industry. This public–private partnership model is followed in the UK and some other countries.

Private employment agencies specialize in the skill level or the profession of the applicants that they provide, such as software professionals or nurses. An organization can access and use the database of private employment agencies for a fixed period for a fee. These agencies charge either the applicants or the organization. The fees may vary from a fixed amount to some percentage of the successful candidate's first year's salary. A good employment agency also carries out a preliminary screening of candidates, thereby reducing the firm's hiring cost. Private agencies also offer temporary help services. This method of employee sourcing will be dealt with later in the chapter.

Both public and private agencies have the same objective. However, they differ with respect to their image, quality of candidates, and the nature of applicants they provide. Private agencies enjoy a better image, provide candidates of good quality, cater to jobs that are more prestigious, and serve as a source of mid-level or high-level managerial or professional employees.

Executive Search Firms

These are also private employment agencies. However, the search firms direct their efforts to very senior or top-level managerial and professional talent. They provide a complete range of services to the client organization by a systematic process of identifying the person who will best meet the requirements of the firm. Search firms begin by unravelling the underlying company culture, clearly articulating the company's goals, vision and strategy. They also clarify the exact role that the hiring company wants a potential employee to play. While most candidates will have the technical skills required, the part difficult to assess is whether the person truly fits in with the company culture and shares its vision and philosophy. Thus, executive search firms provide a more complete line of service to the client firms.

These firms charge a very high fee; it may be as high as 30% of the employee's annual salary. Unlike private agencies, search firms often work on a retainer basis and get paid whether or not their efforts are successful. The client of a search firm is always the organization and never the potential employee. Sometimes, these firms are accused of poaching employees from competing firms, often on the request of the client organization. This has on occasions compromised the image of search firms, earning for them the title of 'headhunters'. Headhunters were tribes that beheaded its enemies and kept their heads as trophies. In the organizational context, the term 'headhunters' refers to executive search firms who recruit for top positions through informal channels. The search industry is presently going through its best phase since talent is at a premium.

With India and China on a growth path, there is huge demand for executive talent. This has resulted in new and big business opportunities for executive search firms in India. Global executive search firms are setting up base in India. Part of the interest that India is generating from global search majors is because more Indian companies—both family-owned and entrepreneur-managed—have begun demanding professional help for hiring managerial talent. See Exhibit 5.1 for new developments in the placement industry.

Advertisements

Traditionally, the most widely-used method of recruitment has been advertisements in the print media, the most common being daily newspapers. Since all households subscribe to newspapers, recruitment advertisements find a big readership and reach a large audience in a short time. Newspapers routinely advertise skilled, semi-skilled, clerical, administrative, and entry-level managerial job openings. Now there is a trend towards special recruitment editions of newspapers, for example, Ascent in the *Times of India*. Business newspapers such as *Financial Times, The Economic Times*, etc. also carry job advertisements. These advertisements, however, are targetted to the audience that reads these newspapers. The target audience includes professionals and executives from the national and global labour market. For employees with specialized skills, firms can advertise in trade and professional journals or business magazines such as *Business Today, Businessworld, Human Capital*, etc. Though radio and television are also used to advertise vacancies, an increasing trend is to use the company website to post job openings. Exhibit 5.2 describes new trends in recruitment advertising.

Exhibit 5.1

New Developments in Placement Industry

The dynamic of the Indian recruitment industry is changing. Until very recently, the recruitment services industry had low entry barriers and just about anyone could set up a 'placement service'. Now, the market has matured, and one needs scale and size in order to survive. Margins have been falling for some time and recruitments have moved beyond submitting a list of potential candidates to the client. Higher attrition rates and the war for talent are forcing MNCs to demand value-added services, globally validated recruitment tools, and best practices from placement service providers. Placement firms are expected to build end-to-end HR solutions for clients. Indian placement firms therefore have started to partner with global search firms. For example, Ma Foi Management Consultants have given 76% stake to the Dutch global search major Vedior.

Most placement firms have grown by 40–60% since 2004. Business at placement firms has grown by almost 50%. All sectors are hunting for good talent. However, three broad segments that generate the greatest demand for executive talent are (1) the entire cluster of service-oriented growth firms, which includes retail, media, and finance; (2) a few second-rung technology firms; and (3) back-office players starting their operations in India, demand for replacements from the brick and mortar companies that are poaching grounds for new sector industry.

Another area that is generating business for search firms is the demand for independent directors at the board level and various committee chairs (audit, best practices) that companies need to fulfill corporate governance norms. Another recent development is the demand for new executives for foreign acquisitions. Search firms are also approached by industries such as airlines and hospitality for globally-experienced personnel of whom there is a shortage of trained manpower in the country. The rules of engagement for executive search firms have changed in recent times. For one, the tenure of these firms has gone up as companies are willing to wait for the right candidate. Secondly, the remuneration model is changing. While the premier search firms such as Stanton Chase continue to adhere to a retainer model, there are some that use performance-based fees.

Source: Mahanta 2005; Baishya 2005

Campus Recruitment

This is one of the most popular but also one of the most expensive methods of recruiting for entry-level professional and managerial jobs. Firms also offer lateral placements on campuses to recent graduates with previous job experience. Campus recruitments require continuous interaction and information exchange between the campus and the firm during the 12-month period preceding the final selections. The college gives the firm information about the profile of students available on campus, their functional specializations, and the type of courses offered on campus. The recruiting firm on its part gives the college information about the firm, its vision, business, future plans, work culture, nature of job, career growth opportunities, reputation of the firm, etc.

Exhibit 5.2

New Age Recruitment Advertising

Recruitment advertising today is a booming business with an estimated annual growth rate of over 22%. Recruitment advertisements are often seen by analysts as an indicator of growth in the economy. The biggest spenders on recruitment advertisements are companies like Infosys, TCS, and Wipro. Earlier, recruitment advertisements used to be like statutory notice advertisements, in black and white text, plainly stating the vacant positions, pay, perks, responsibilities, and sometimes the company logo. Most jobs were in manufacturing, the numbers wanted were few, and job mobility was low. Hence, there was no need for creative recruitment advertisements. Even the simplest advertisement drew many responses. All this changed in the 1990s. This was when there was a boom in the infotech sector in particular, and the services sector in general. Even then companies like TCS and Infosys riding on their high reputation could place a plain text recruitment advertisement with a company logo and still be flooded with applications. The scenario changed with new Indian start-ups like Patni Computers. These new firms had to be creative because no one knew about them and hence these firms had to sell themselves. They had to persuade potential employees that they were stable employers offering good careers. The lesser known MNCs like IBM also faced the same recognition problem. The days when the name of an American company would result in people wanting to work for the company were long gone. Even though advertisement of such a firm may get responses because many people are out there looking for jobs, but these ads would not result in closures, that is, actual hiring.

Now, even the larger players like Infosys and TCS pay more attention to recruitment advertising to be more strategic and creative. As firms like Infosys are hiring in large numbers, the company cannot afford to wait for people to walk in. Moreover, the firm also needs to differentiate itself from others. People read recruitment advertisements. Even a person who is gainfully employed, successful, and not actively considering a change of job, is likely to leaf through the recruitment supplements just to check the market. When firms advertise a job, they are actually interested in the people who are not looking for jobs but who might be attracted by the company or its offer and apply. These candidates do not apply as soon as the advertisement appears; they consider the opportunity, discuss it with family and friends, and then apply after about a week. People who apply within the first three days of the advertisement's appearance are desperate; they are not who the firm is looking for. Thus, a firm that is recruiting is hoping to catch the eye of those people who are not really interested in the firm. Therefore, it is important to be creative in designing a recruitment advertisement. As business develops, new types of recruitment advertisements are being developed. One challenge that recruitment advertising firms are facing is to lure skilled employees to smaller markets such as Mangalore or Kerala. In such cases, recruitment advertisements are designed more like advertisements promoting tourism. Another function that recruitment advertisements must serve is to create a positive image of the company for all those who come in contact with recruitment efforts. The firm must communicate the right corporate image to potential employees, since this is critical to recruitment. Recruitment advertising is one area where corporate image is linked to very measurable results. The evolution of recruitment advertisements has been from 'situations vacant' to 'employer branding'.

Source: Doctor 2004

in its pre-placement talk (PPT) on campus as well as through brochures. Microsoft and IBM are among the most preferred companies on top campuses in the country. IBM is known for its high-performance culture, and encourages a healthy work-life balance through flexi-timing, mobility programmes, and working from home. IBM also offers career opportunities at both local as well as global level. Since campus recruitment is a high-cost method, many firms are carefully analysing the success of their recruitment efforts on various campuses. Campuses with successful recruiting experiences for a firm in the past are selected for future recruitments. 'Successful recruiting experience' refers to criteria such as the number of job offers made versus the number of job offers accepted, the cost per hire, and the turnover of recently appointed graduates. Based on these criteria, firms are identifying campuses that have been productive for them in the past. Firms seek to establish long-term ongoing relationships with these campuses to ensure a continued availability of talent (see Exhibit 5.3). Apart from recruiting from management and engineering colleges, there is a trend towards recruiting graduates from undergraduate colleges. This is especially true of call centres and BPO firms which are recruiting in large numbers.

Exhibit 5.3

Innovations in Campus Recruitment

Firms are undertaking 'branding on campus' exercises by establishing long-term ongoing relationships with selected educational institutions because this is a good strategy to attract fresh graduates and to have a pool of talent to hire from.

Industry–Academia Partnership

So far, industry–academia partnerships have been minimal and limited to big cities and premier colleges like the IITs and IIMs. High economic growth has caused firms of all sizes to establish partnerships with academic institutions across the country, even with lesser known institutions. Companies like Xansa, Wipro, Infosys, and Intel are tying up with a range of institutes in India to partner in imparting education and also to gain access to graduating classes for the purpose of hiring. ICICI, the retail banking leader is setting benchmarks. In 2005, ICICI invited 60 deans and professors to Mumbai and spent nine days discussing the change the course curriculum needs. They offered help in creating course content, and also offered to have their executives teach, as visiting faculty. ICICI Bank is also planning to provide internships for teachers for 6–8 weeks to help them understand what happens in a bank.

Visvesvaraya Technological University (VTU) in Bangalore has established a small studio from where it has been beaming live classes to 120 engineering colleges in Karnataka since 2002. This ensures that engineering education reaches remote villages as well. Under a novel programme called 'VtracU', final year students of VTU will be put through a test to determine how employable they are and their scores will be made available to companies like Intel, TELCO, and Infosys who have tied up with the university. Companies will then conduct pre-placement interviews

Contd

Exhibit 5.3 Contd

and make a final selection, all through the 'edusat' (educational satellite) network of VTU. This way, colleges even in the remotest areas with no access to campus placements become immediately accessible to the corporate world. Firms can conduct campus placements in a large number of campuses without having to physically travel to these campuses. Intel, Tesco, and Convergys have already signed up for 'VtracU'.

To address the growing requirement of IT skills, IT MNCs are entering top technology campuses with their own educational initiatives. Software design firm Autodesk has partnered with Sir J.J. College of Architecture in Mumbai and the School of Planning and Architecture in Delhi. Cadence Design has also developed educational tie-ups since 1998 with over 100 universities affiliated to their programme. While there has been a growth in the number of IT professionals in India in absolute terms, there is a huge shortfall of network professionals. As a response to this challenge, Cisco Systems has instituted Cisco's Networking Academy Programme. This programme is an alliance between Cisco Systems, educational institutions, businesses, governments, and communities. It is a worldwide initiative aimed at creating a pool of trained workers that can address the growing need of networking professionals across the world and in India. Cisco has signed a memorandum of understanding (MOU) with Jawaharlal Nehru Technological University in Andhra Pradesh to offer the programme at 250 educational institutions across the state within a year.

The dearth of trained workers is forcing major players in the organized retail industry to team up with educational institutions to formulate courses specific to the sector. For example, Hindustan Lever Limited (HLL) has formed a strategic alliance with IIM Ahmedabad to open a centre for grooming retail professionals that will develop teaching and training materials and offer retail management as an elective. Pantaloon

Retail (India) and the Mumbai-based K.J. Somaiya Institute of Management Studies and Research have collaborated to start a diploma course in retail management. Pantaloon proposes to hire all the students who get a particular grade in the course.

A new trend in India is being witnessed. Organizations are hiring fresh BA and BCom graduates from top undergraduate colleges. Firms are finding that MBA graduates turn out to be very expensive since they command very high pay packets. Moreover, they also change jobs more frequently. Top performers at the best colleges are talented, can be groomed easily, come for lower salaries, are more loyal, and are good at thinking 'out of the box'. Though these fresh graduates may leave for higher studies after working a few years, companies are willing to experiment.

Firms prefer employees with high emotional quotient (EQ), and not only intelligence quotient (IQ), to compete in the fiercely competitive global marketplace. Hence, firms are not restricting their campus recruitments to top-rung business schools, but are hiring from second-rung and third-rung institutes as well. Some companies believe that students who come from humble backgrounds and who have had exposure to tougher living conditions fare better at decision-making and risk-taking capabilities in a globalized market when compared to students from affluent backgrounds (the typical IIM graduate). Firms are also favouring students with better EQ over the toppers. The selection process on campus is dominated by group discussions and interviews. Some companies are now trying to be different. For example, Pepsi plans to introduce psychometric testing in placements. Tata Administrative Services, ICICI Bank, and HSBC follow an assessment centre approach to recruitment, involving a combination of exercises like group discussions, case presentations, aptitude tests, interviews, and personality profiling tools.

Contd

Exhibit 5.3 Contd

Recruitment Strategy

The software industry, faced with a huge hike in the wages of IT professionals, has also changed its recruitment strategy. Executives with three years' experience cost double or even more compared to an entry-level professional. Hence, as part of the hiring strategy, these firms have an increased focus on campus recruitment, recruiting as many as 50% of its workforce from entry-level professionals. Because of this strategy of recruiting at entry-level, it is noticed that even as wage bills of IT professionals have gone up by about 20%, the average employee costs of firms are not shooting up with salary hikes. Wipro, Satyam, and Infosys continue to add about 8–10% of its workforce every quarter. However, their average employee costs have started staying constant since they are hiring more fresh graduates.

Summer Internships

Due to the high cost of the campus placement method, several firms are using summer internships for hiring entry-level engineering and management students. Since summer interns work on an assigned company project, it provides the firm with an opportunity to appraise the performance and potential of the intern. Firms are viewing summer internships as a means to provide trial employment to students to determine if they would want to hire these students full-time on completion of their professional degree. Summer internships are resulting in a number of pre-placement offers (PPO) to interns during campus recruiting.

Source: *The Economic Times*, New Delhi

Organizations can no longer be sure about the success of their recruiting efforts. As competition for talent becomes intense, both within and across industry, firms are not only introducing innovations in traditional recruitment methods (see Exhibits 5.1, 5.2, and 5.3), they are developing new ways of attracting the attention of potential employees.

NEW APPROACHES TO RECRUITMENT

The new approaches to recruitment are employer branding; special events recruiting; contest recruitment; and e-recruitment.

Employer Branding

In this age of employee consumerism, the best talent is not available to a firm on demand. There are several firms vying for the best individuals, and instead of the firm choosing an employee, it is the other way round today. The best talent chooses or rejects the firm. Therefore, organizations have to make themselves attractive to likely candidates. This has led to employer branding—the intersection of the principles of marketing and brand-building and the rigour of HR practices. Companies today have to pay more attention to their 'employer brand' and how it is perceived by prospective and existing employees. Top-rated companies with strong brands have one characteristic in common—they give clear and consistent messages about themselves and that translates into a strong pull on talents. For example, Cognizant is one company that has a clearly defined employer brand called 'Celebrating Work'; the message is 'enjoyment in work, not out of work'. The company brand is built around this philosophy of making work fun. For some other firm, the main ingredient of a strong employer brand could be 'great jobs' or 'freedom and autonomy', and so on. Further, great companies send a clear and consistent message that talent is valued both before and after hiring.

Marico views former employees as brand ambassadors of the firm. The firm invited around 100 former employees from across the world to join current employees in celebrating its Rs 10 billion turnover mark. The company can hope to tap this 'alumni network' to help its recruitment efforts. A.T. Kearney threw a Valentine's Day party for students at a business school campus. Through this event the company hoped to convey to the students what it would be like working for this firm. The Valentine's Day party conveyed the firm's culture of an intellectually stimulating yet fun and down-to-earth place to work, and it stood out in the huge mêlée of pre-placement talks that are part of the placement season.

Even the biggest firms are revisiting their employer brand promise and ensuring that it is relevant to their target group of potential candidates. For example, HLL is a firm that puts in a lot of effort in building its employer brand. Several firms that are tying up with campuses for creating curricula for specific subject areas, like ICICI, Pantaloon, Infosys, etc. also serve to build their company brands on campuses.

Building a powerful employer brand requires more than aggressive hiring practices. Employer branding, rather than a conscious systematic effort, is still an unexplored and more of a default process in organizations. It is important for the brand message to be consistently woven through the company and communicated externally as well. This may be done by sharing best practices through media and ensuring that the senior management are highly visible at public fora. The responsibility for brand positioning is primarily that of top management. For example, the top management of Marico Industries regularly participate in speaker opportunities hosted by the Confederation of Indian Industry (CII) and the All India Management Association (AIMA). At Infosys and at Wipro, chairmen Narayana Murthy and Azim Premji have come to epitomize the progressive face of the companies and their values.

Special Events Recruiting

When a firm is new and hence is not likely to attract candidates, or when there is a skills shortage, firms may resort to using special events for recruiting. These include scheduling open houses or organizing career fairs to attract potential employees and to generate an applicant pool. When a firm stages an open house, potential employees are invited to the headquarters on a weekend and shown around the facility to give them an idea about the work environment of the firm. Open houses are generally arranged on a weekend since the potential candidates are usually working and may not have time to visit the recruiting firm during a weekday. Career fairs have become very popular in recent years. A career fair is conducted by a group of firms; each firm publicizes its available jobs from its own booth. In India, one of the leading national dailies regularly sponsors a career fair that gives an opportunity to hundreds of youth to explore employment opportunities. Generally, job fairs target entry-level hires. Job fairs reduce the cost of hiring since several firms are present in the same physical location and so are the potential candidates. Some colleges are also organizing career fairs as firms look for graduates to staff entry-level positions, especially in new age sectors like BPO, retail, etc.

Contest Recruitment

Certain firms announce contests for recruiting employees. Through these the firms combine their HR strategy with a public relations (PR) strategy. For example, Google has used contest recruitment with good results. In 2004, it started the contest in September and held it worldwide. A qualification round, with participants from 17 countries, narrowed the final list of contestants to 5,000. Successive competitions narrowed the contestants to 50. These 50 contestants received expense-paid trips to participate at Google's headquarters in the USA. The contest is named 'Google Code Jam' which is structured to select the winner as one who can solve a series of progressively harder programming puzzles. In the 2004 contest, held in mid-October, the contestants had to solve three puzzles within an hour. The third puzzle was the most difficult. The contestants were judged both on their speed and accuracy. The winner walked off with a prize of US$10,000 as well as a job offer. The Tata Group also launched contest recruitment for their agribusiness as part of their campus recruitment strategy. Teams of students from management schools across the country could enter the contest. Each team had to prepare a practical agribusiness plan and present it to top executives of the Tata Group. The winners got a cash reward and a job offer.

E-recruitment

The internet has dramatically altered the ways in which both job seekers and organizations think about the recruiting function. It has brought about a revolutionary change in the recruitment practices of firms. There has been a remarkable increase in the use of the internet as a tool for finding jobs (web searching) and recruiting candidates (web recruiting) in almost all sectors of the economy. The e-recruitment industry is estimated to be worth above Rs 2 billion. Key players such as monster.com, timesjobs.com, naukri.com, and jobstreet.com have shown a growth rate of 70–100%. Thanks to internet recruiting, newspaper advertisements and employment agencies may be on their exit path as the primary source of information about job openings and finding job candidates. The method is cheaper than traditional methods and provides companies with easy availability of an increasing skill-set. Employees find it easy to apply for jobs online; this gives online recruiting an added edge. Today, the print medium is being seen more as a branding medium, while the online medium is where the action is for searching jobs. Most people prefer to send resumes online even if the job advertisement appeared in print. Falling cost of broadband, rising demand for e-commerce, a record growth in the number of internet users, and affordable computers have also facilitated e-recruitment. A booming job market, the large number of internet users, and significant saving in costs are adding to the charm of online recruitment. One study estimated that 90% of the Fortune 500 companies use some on-line recruiting and that more than 18 million people post their resumes on monster.com. Web recruiting and searching are not limited to high-tech industries. Companies in emerging sectors such as FMCG, pharmaceuticals, and automotive and spare parts are also going in for e-recruitment. Many new college graduates view the internet as a major source for locating job opportunities. Until just three years ago, this medium was looked at only for junior-level employees, fresh graduates, and middle-level managers. Now, even company vice-presidents are being hired through this route, though not very often. The three most common methods used for internet recruiting are job boards or job placement websites, professional/career websites, and company websites (see Table 5.3).

Job boards provide a place for employers to post jobs as well as search for candidates. Popular job boards include www.jobsonline.com, www.naukri.com, and www.monster.com. People looking for jobs can also post their resumes on these websites as well as search and apply for jobs online. Large job placement websites report a huge increase in the number of resumes posted over the years. For example, naukri.com has over 6.5 million searchable resumes listed on the site, over 200,000 jobs attracting traffic, and over 120 million page views a month as on 24 June 2006.

Many professional associations such as the Society for Human Resource Management (www.shrm.org) or the American Society for Training and Development (www.astd.org) have employment sections at their websites. Some private corporations also maintain specialized career or industry websites. For example, the website of a private employment agency that specializes in providing IT and software professionals will focus only on jobs in this sector. Access to these websites requires candidates or recruiters to pay a fee and register.

Table 5.3: Internet Recruiting Methods

Methods	Advantages	Disadvantages
Job Boards/Job Placement Websites	▪ Useful for generating applicant responses	▪ Many individuals accessing sites are only 'job lookers', not serious applicants
Professional/ Career Websites	▪ Targets applicants interested in a specific industry or profession ▪ Reduces number of less qualified applicants ▪ Saves recruiters' time and efforts	▪ Since professionals other than the target applicants do not normally access the website, they remain unaware of the employment developments in these professions
Company Websites	▪ More effective and efficient ▪ Can be put up inexpensively compared to print ▪ Firm may be able to attract individuals otherwise inaccessible ▪ Attracts the attention of candidates worldwide	▪ Many employer websites are difficult to navigate since they do not present career and employment information ▪ May lead to negative image of the the organization if not updated regularly

Adapted from: Mathis and Jackson 2003; Mondy, Noe, and Premeaux 1999

Most organizations today have their own websites. These company websites usually have a recruitment section. A typical organizational homepage provides information about the company, its products and services, career and employment information, application procedures, qualifications sought, experience required, and benefits provided. Availability of all this information increases the quality of applicants since potential candidates tend to match their own values and qualifications with those of the firm. If the candidates find a mismatch, they self-select themselves out. Many firms have made their recruitment webpages interactive.

Many company websites also include online resume templates that can be completed and submitted through the internet, obviating the need for applicants to post, e-mail, or fax their resumes. Cisco receives a large number of resumes online through its website. IBM hires approximately 1,500 college graduates every year through its website, called 'Club Cyberblue'. The page targetting college graduates has general company information rather than job postings. Candidates who are interested can find out when IBM will recruit from their college campuses. The page also helps students prepare resumes by providing them a form that includes all the information that is important to the company.

The recruiting portion of company webpage is part of the overall recruitment strategy of the firm. Therefore, it is important that the website is designed to market the jobs available in the firm effectively. Some firms go a step ahead to include pre-screening tests as part of their online recruitment process.

On their part, job seekers have also become aggressive users of the internet, using it to their advantage in their search for jobs by setting up their own webpages or blogs, called 'websumes'. Candidates use their websumes to 'sell' their candidacy for a job. In the course of their online job search, these candidates often encourage the firms to 'check out my website'. There, the candidates may post standard resume information about themselves, supporting information, and sometimes a video where they introduce themselves to prospective employers.

The popularity of the internet as a method of recruitment has certainly skyrocketed. This trend will further expand in future. Since web-based job advertisements produce so many applicants, many firms are installing applicant tracking systems (ATS) to support their online and offline recruiting efforts. The ATS helps employers monitor applicants, collect and report applicant data, and create various recruiting-related reports such as cost-per-hire and hire-by-source.

A well-known ATS is recruitsoff.com. It is an e-recruiting applications service provider (ASP) that hosts the job sites of firms that are looking for employees and are its clients. As an ASP, recruitsoff.com posts the job openings of its client firms, collects the applications received, and provides an automated system to evaluate, rank, and match job candidates with specific job openings. In other words, it screens the resumes, compares them with the job requirements of the client firm, and identifies high-priority applicants. Thus, ASP is the electronic version of a placement agency. However, no method is foolproof. See Table 5.4 for the advantages and disadvantages of internet recruiting.

Table 5.4: Advantages and Disadvantages of Internet Recruiting

	Internet Recruiting	
	Advantages	**Disadvantages**
Organizational Perspective	■ Cost-effective compared to newspaper advertising, search firms, etc. ■ Generates more applicant resumes compared to newspaper advertisements ■ More timely; responses start coming in the day the advertisement is posted on the internet ■ Saves time, as recruiters can respond to qualified candidates more quickly	■ May get applications from more unqualified candidates ■ May create additional work for HR recruiters requiring them to review more resumes and answer more e-mail ■ Many individuals accessing websites are not looking for new jobs seriously ■ May need specialized applicant tracking software to handle increase in applicants

Contd

Table 5.4 Contd

	Internet Recruiting	
	Advantages	**Disadvantages**
	■ Recruiters can request additional candidate information ■ Job postings may be viewed worldwide; hence, the firm gets access to potential employees worldwide	
Employee Perspective	■ Allows individuals quick access to information on various job possibilities round the clock ■ Lets candidates look for jobs without taking any public or visible action ■ Helps lessen the amount of interpersonal awkwardness associated with soliciting job offers in person ■ Potential applicants from other geographic areas and countries can view job openings posted on the internet ■ Saves applicants time as they can respond quickly to job postings by e-mail	■ Individuals from disadvantaged sections of society such as lower socio-economic groups may have limited internet access; these sections may be represented disproportionately ■ Internet recruiters may not be reaching a diverse workforce

Adapted from: Mathis and Jackson 2003; DeCenzo and Robbins 2005; Dessler 2005; Feldman and Klaas 2002

OUTSOURCING THE RECRUITMENT FUNCTION

As part of outsourcing HR activities, many firms have outsourced their recruitment function. For example, firms in the retail industry, realizing the complexity of recruiting in large numbers, have increasingly begun to outsource its recruitment process to consultants. The industry is growing at 25–30% annually and is estimated to generate over 50,000 jobs per year for the next five years. Until recently, HR managers relied heavily on employee referrals and walk-ins. Since the sector has been facing the problem of getting the right people, it has begun to use skills assessment and psychometric tests. The assessment process based on these tests is largely outsourced to consultants. It is estimated that over 80% of all recruitment will shift to consultants by 2007. Company HR managers will conduct final interviews only. Consultants use tests to evaluate candidates on qualities such as confidence, communication, and personality. Role-plays in simulated sales situations are used to assess, for example, customer orientation of sales personnel. Scores on these parameters are matched with the job profile and benchmark scores to find the right candidates. Outsourcing is also cost-effective, which is one of the reasons why HR managers in retail firms are using the services of expert consultants.

Recruitment methods help a firm generate an applicant pool. The organization must then select the best candidate from those available. In making the selection decision, one or more of the following methods of employee selection may be used to obtain information about applicants.

METHODS OF EMPLOYEE SELECTION

The methods of employee selection are application blanks; employment interviews; employment tests; work sampling; reference checks and recommendations; assessment centres; and physical examinations.

Application Blanks

During recruitment, candidates are required to submit application forms, or blanks, to express their interest in the vacant position. Application forms help the organization pre-screen the candidates before a more extensive selection process can begin. Pre-screening helps in scaling down the size of the applicant pool. Some firms conduct a pre-screening interview before asking the candidates to fill a detailed application form. Application forms of different firms vary in length and sophistication. All application blanks ask for information such as applicant's name, educational qualifications, age, experience, etc. The application blanks identify the applicants who fulfill the minimum necessary conditions of the job and predict the candidates who will succeed on the job. For example, if a doctoral degree is considered essential for a lecturer's position in a university, a candidate without a doctoral degree will be eliminated from further consideration. To predict the candidates who will succeed, the weighted application blank (WAB), a variation of the traditional application blank, is used. The WAB is designed to systematically assign a score to each candidate based on the data provided in the blank. These forms help in differentiating between potentially successful and potentially unsuccessful candidates. The scoring system for the WAB is developed by comparing the high and low performers who are currently employed by the organization on a variety of characteristics (education, experience, etc.). Each item in the blank is assigned a weight based on the degree to which it differentiates between the currently high and low performing employees on some criterion of performance, such as turnover or job performance. For example, assume that the HR department of a firm is interested in developing a WAB that will predict which applicants for the job of computer operator would stay with the firm, if hired. The HR personnel would scan the application forms of those computer operators that stayed less than a year with the firm and of those that stayed at

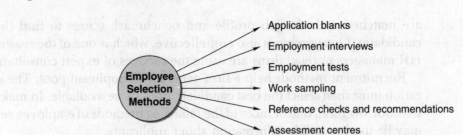

Employee Selection Methods
- Application blanks
- Employment interviews
- Employment tests
- Work sampling
- Reference checks and recommendations
- Assessment centres
- Physical examination

Figure 5.4: Methods of Employee Selection

least five years item by item to find out how each type of employee had responded to identify those items that differentiate the two groups on the performance criteria of interest, that is, tenure with the firm. Weights are assigned relative to the degree to which each item differentiates between the two groups. When there is 'no difference' between the long-tenure and short-tenure groups, that item is assigned a weight of zero. When there is just a small difference between the groups, a weight of one is assigned, and so on, with the highest weightage to the item or characteristic on which there is the biggest difference between the two groups of employees. Each applicant is assigned the final score on the application blank by totalling the weights of each item. Those who meet the minimum requirements proceed further in the selection process.

Different WABs have to be developed for different jobs. Each organization will also have different application blanks for say, technical personnel, managerial personnel, or for hourly workers. The firm should be careful to ensure that no discrimination is made on the basis of colour, caste, religion, etc., the only exception being if these are bona fide occupational qualifications (BFOQ). For example, until very recently, gender was the BFOQ for defence services, where only men were considered, except in the medical corps. The firm should also take care to ask only for information that will help the organization make a better job-related evaluation of the applicant.

Employment Interviews

Interviews are the most widely used method of selection. They let the organization meet the potential employee face to face and obtain information on various aspects such as knowledge, attitudes, communication ability, etc. Often, however, one or two attractive qualities of the candidate lead the interviewer(s) to make a decision in the candidate's favour in an interview. Interviewers often are biased toward people who are like them or who have had similar experiences. The interviewers also take the opportunity to look good rather than to know the candidate. They tend to boast that their firm has a particular culture when, in fact, it is actually the aspiration. Yet, interviews are indispensable to selection. Most firms or managers would feel extremely uncomfortable hiring an employee without interviewing him or her. Microsoft is known for asking 'not so typical' questions in a typical interview. Some of these abstract questions have no right or wrong answers but test the ability to think on the spot. Microsoft-style interviews have been adopted by several organizations across the world.

Selection interviews may be structured or unstructured. An unstructured or non-directive interview does not have any format or sequence in which questions are asked. Interviewees for the same job may not be asked the same questions. Structured or directive interviews, on the other hand, provide the interviewer with a standard list of questions to be asked of all applicants.

Interviews may also differ from each other based on their 'content' or the 'focus of questions'. *Situational interviews* present the candidate with a hypothetical or a real situation he/she might encounter on the job in question. The candidate is asked to describe how he/she would respond in such a situation. *Behavioural interviews* ask the candidate to relate an actual situation that they had encountered in the past and describe how they had reacted to that situation. For instance, a candidate may be asked to describe a situation in his/her previous job where the candidate resolved a conflict with a customer. In *job-related interviews*, questions relate to past experiences but not to a hypothetical or real situation. These are designed to assess an applicant's job performance. *Stress interviews* are designed to make the candidate uncomfortable during the course of the interview. This type of interview is used to assess the applicant's stress tolerance. There is no 'pure' form of interview. Interviewers may shift the focus of a single interview session from job-related to stress to situational.

Another point of difference between interviews is the manner in which these are conducted or administered. *Personal interviews* are one-to-one where the interviewer and interviewee are the only two participants. In a *sequential interview*, several persons interview each candidate in sequence before a decision is made. A common form of interview these days is the *panel or board interview*, in which a single candidate is interviewed by a panel or board of interviewers. The final decision is arrived at by combining the ratings of the panellists. The different types of interviews are depicted in Figure 5.5.

Employment Tests

Companies are increasingly depending on 'psychometric tools' to get the right person with the right attitude for the right job (see Exhibit 5.4). These tests supplement the findings of conventional interviews and help indicate the candidate that fits best. The tests also seek to determine certain characteristics of applicants which may not be obtainable from the resume. The characteristics assessed through tests range from personality to ability, interests, intelligence,

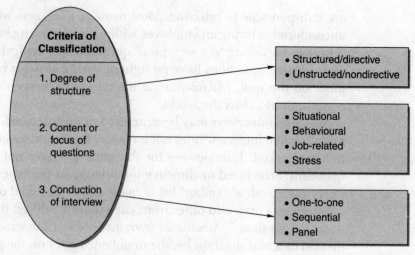

Figure 5.5: Classification of Types of Employment Interviews

Exhibit 5.4

Use of Testing in Industry

The present business scenario in which companies operate, and the high rate of attrition, make it crucial for companies to recruit candidates with the right technical skills. Along with technical skills, however, it is important that candidates demonstrate the attitude and the behavioural pattern that fits into the company culture. Firms require employees who fit job requirements very precisely, not just in terms of knowledge, skills, and background, but also in terms of personal attributes.

Psychometric tests are designed to measure one or more psychological attributes of individuals, like interests, aptitude, ability, personality, etc. These tools help employers understand how the candidate shall behave in a particular team or situation, relate to others, and approach and solve problems. The usage of psychometric tests may differ from company to company. However, the basic purpose of these tests, when applied by an organization, is to help screen candidates at the initial stage of recruitment and to understand the personality of a prospective employee at the selection stage. Information obtained from psychometric tests provides additional information that helps in recruiting the best person available for the job. Personality tests can help predict the probable success of an individual who intends to join the firm. There has been an upsurge in the use of testing in occupational selection, especially the use of personality tests, since the late 1980s and early 1990s.

Using tests reduce time and cost of hiring by screening out candidates who do not have the qualities required for organizational membership. A description or profile of the candidate is prepared on the basis of his or her answers to the psychometric test and is used to infer whether the individual is, for example, a team worker, observer, or analyst. The typical features of each description are assessed and an immediate feedback is available to the selection committee.

Personality tests are the most common form of psychometric tests employed by organizations.

Contd

Exhibit 5.4 Contd

Results of personality tests are especially useful when used during the interview. The candidate may be given the opportunity to discuss potential strengths and weaknesses during the interview and also to respond to concerns of the panelists. The National Thermal Power Corporation provides the Thomas Personality Profiles of each candidate to the panelists, who may discuss certain aspects of the profile with the candidate. However, the decision to recruit or not to recruit must not be based solely on the results of these tests.

When psychometric testing was introduced in India, it was hailed as an important tool in the recruitment process of firms. Several pharmaceutical firms (such as Eli Lilly, Lupin, Sun Pharma, Dr. Reddy's Laboratories, Glenmark Pharmaceuticals) use psychometric instruments in hiring. Glenmark uses tests also to make decisions about promotions and to provide career growth opportunities. However, it is still the big firms, the MNCs, and some ITeS firms that use tests for their recruitment process. Tata Consultancy Services, the UB Group, Bharti Airtel, LG, HCL Infosystems are some such firms.

Some tools that are popular among Indian firms are the Myers-Briggs Type Indicator (MBTI),

the Sixteen Personality Factor Questionnaire (16PF), the FIRO-B Assessment, Thomas Profiling, Picture Test, and Inkblot Test. While MBTI and 16PF are longer, Thomas Profiling tools like human job analysis, personnel profile analysis, and team analysis are quicker. Usually, firms use testing for middle- and senior-level management recruitments. However, some firms are also using these tests for entry-level selection. It is important that a trained person conducts and analyses the test results and judges the candidates.

When a person is being considered for promotion, the test can evaluate his or her readiness for the next level by identifying skill gaps and providing learning opportunities. The need for personality tests is being increasingly felt as every organization has its own culture and an individual joining the organization needs to adapt to the culture. The tests can be used to assess person–organization fit to supplement person–job fit.

Psychometric tests also help manage cultural issues in a firm. Each organization has its own unique culture and the HR department wants to make sure that only those people are hired who can adjust well. Tests help assess the culture fit of the candidate.

Source: *http://business.timesonline.co.uk/printfriendly/0,,2020-8310-987239-8310,00.html* , accessed on 18 July 2006; *http://www.expresspharmaonline.com/20060630/pharmalife01.shtml* , accessed on 18 July 2006; Jasrotia 2003

---

etc. Hence, there are personality tests, achievement tests, interest inventories, and so on. Many firms irrespective of size or the type of job obtain information about candidates through the use of employment tests. Tests are not considered the sole basis for appointments. However, they provide key information about a candidate's personality, emotional intelligence, ability to work in a team, and propensity to stay with the firm. Experts believe that use of tests during selection process helps bring down attrition. Wipro uses psychometric tests to test communication skills and analytical capabilities to hire senior staff for jobs involving people management. Some of the firms that use psychometric tests are the Tata Group, the Aditya Birla Group, Godrej, and Coca-Cola India

Ltd. The Directorate General of Shipping has introduced a psychometric test called the Merchant Marine Personality Evaluation (MMPE) with effect from 1 April 2006. All candidates for the merchant navy have to take this test. The test evaluates adaptability, emotional strength, tendency towards anger and aggression, and tolerance of frustration, anxiety, depression, and loneliness, because those applying for a sea-faring career must have the right mental make-up and attitude to withstand the vagaries of life at sea. Increasing incidents of suicides, stabbings, and of seamen reported missing or thrown overboard led the Directorate General of Shipping to introduce this test.

The process of developing a test that measures such characteristics as attitudes, for example, is difficult, time-consuming, and costly. Therefore, many firms purchase ready-made tests. Administering and scoring these tests also requires expertise. There are 'testing firms' which specialize in administering particular tests. These testing firms administer, score, and prepare a profile of each candidate for a fee. Several organizations hire testing firms to administer tests as part of their selection procedure. For example, National Thermal Power Corporation (NTPC) has a testing firm develop Thomas Profiles of candidates before it interviews them. The candidate's profile is given to the interview panel as information about the candidate.

For certain jobs, it is important to assess a candidate's honesty or his or her proneness to dishonesty. These tests may be classified as attitude tests since these seek to assess whether the candidate approves of certain behaviours like stealing, bribery, etc. Individuals seeking jobs in treasury, security services, and defence services, etc. are tested for their integrity and tolerance for dishonesty. After recent incidents of fraud involving classified data in a few BPO firms, a lot of importance is being given to the assessment of candidates' honesty. Firms are hiring professionals to check the credentials and criminal records of prospective employees.

Some recruiters pay attention to the extra-curricular activities in which a candidate is interested. Although extra-curricular talents such as quizzing, classical dancing, singing, painting, sports, etc. do not mean performance will be high, they provide clues to the personalities of candidates. For example, creative pursuits like painting may signal that the candidate may bring some of that creativity to work, and intellectual pursuits like astronomy usually make for an ability to grasp complex problems. Competitive team spirit is a personality trait that is valued by the corporate world and is reflected in a passion for competitive team sports like football, cricket, etc. At Walt Disney India, extra-curricular interests often dovetail with the job, especially if the individual is given an assignment dealing with sports, music, art etc. The firm prefers well-rounded individuals who also have an inclination for non-curricular activities.

Work Sampling

It requires the candidates to actually perform a part (sample) of the job to measure how well the candidate performs the job. Work samples measure actual on-the-job behaviour and can be used successfully to predict a candidate's actual job performance, if hired.

Reference Checks and Recommendations

Most application forms require the candidate to provide names of one or two referees whom the organization can contact to get information about the candidate. The references may be work-related (former employers and colleagues) or personal (friends and family). The purpose of reference checks is to verify the factual information provided by the applicant as well as to find out if the applicant has hidden potentially damaging information, such as a criminal record. Organizations may or may not actually check the credentials provided by the applicants. When they do, it may take many forms. Some firms prefer to verify the current position and salary of an individual by contacting the current employer of the candidate over the telephone.

As most industries hire on a large scale, companies are faced with the growing menace of fudged CVs. The problem affects the IT, BPO, retail, banking, and insurance sectors, among others. According to recent industry estimates, 10–12% of recruits submit fake CVs, fake reference letters, fake certificates, or overstate their skills and experience. Most cases of such fudging in the IT industry occur among those with one-to-three years of experience. Firms specializing in checking the background of potential employees have come up. Most of the requests received by such firms are from the IT and BPO industries; the rest are from banking, retail, and insurance. The background screening business, which did not exist a few years ago, is now estimated to be worth about Rs 750–1000 million a year.

More recently, firms have been giving serious attention to verify the antecedents of those whom they hire. Employee frauds of the kind witnessed by HSBC and other BPO firms such as Wipro Spectramind (April 2004) and MsourcE (April 2005) are the most immediate reasons for this increased emphasis on employee verification. In the HSBC case, the employee had furnished false information and false references. Inadequacies in employee verification standards are believed to be the major cause of these frauds. The cost of employee verification can range from Rs 3,000–8,000 per employee, which many firms are unwilling to pay. However, the recent scams have led the firms to think seriously about developing a good verification system. Some experts recommend going beyond verification to analysing all the data about the candidate to minimize risk. For example, if a candidate has worked in company A in a particular function, then the company B he or she is now joining can understand the risks posed by the candidate better because of the information the candidate may have gained in company A. More firms are utilizing the services of pre-employment screening firms as instances of false credentials provided by applicants increase.

Assessment Centres

These require managerial candidates to attend two-to-three day simulations in which 10–12 candidates perform realistic management tasks under the observation of experts. Each participant in the assessment centre is appraised on various characteristics such as leadership potential, problem-solving ability, and decision-making skills. Typical exercises in assessment centres include in-basket exercises, paper-and-pencil tests, presentations, interviews, group discussions, etc. An assessment centre is an effective tool for hiring employees at managerial and high-level positions. Several firms use an assessment centre as a tool for selection as well as development.

Physical Examination

Most firms require the candidate to undergo a medical fitness test once an employment offer is given. The potential employee is required to submit the medical certificate when he/she starts work or within a specified period of starting work. The job offer is conditional till the medical certificate is submitted,. One objective of pre-employment medical examinations is to ensure that the applicant does not have any medical limitations (such as a heart condition) that may affect performance on the job. A medical examination also helps establish a record of the applicant's health for future insurance or compensation claims (for example, an individual whose medical report establishes that the person suffers from some lung disorder can not claim compensation from the firm for this condition).

For certain jobs, physical standards are considered bona fide occupational qualifications. For example, those wanting to join the police services or the army must meet the criteria of minimum height. In such cases, a medical examination is conducted to screen out those who do not fulfill the minimum requirement of physical standards. Only those who clear this stage go through the rest of the stages in the selection process.

Firms use a combination of selection methods in making a hiring decision. The choice of methods depends on several factors such as cost of the method, job in question, skills on which candidate is to be assessed, time, and available expertise. These methods may be used in sequence or simultaneously. The ways in which the information obtained from different selection methods may be combined to arrive at a hiring decision is discussed later. Before that, let us look at some innovative selection tools gaining popularity.

NEW APPROACHES TO EXECUTIVE SELECTION

The quality of leadership of an organization is a critical determinant of organizational success. The selection of top management, especially that of the chief executive officer (CEO), is closely observed by shareholders, competitors, media, and business scholars. We regularly come across news items in *The Economic Times* and other business newspapers informing of top-level management exits as well as entry into new firms. The exit of a top-level executive or a succession event can influence the stock price also.

Executive recruitment and selection is a costly exercise for any firm. A large proportion of executive placements result in failure, measured in terms of either performance or turnover. Though it is difficult to estimate the total cost of selection failures, it is reasonable to believe that it may run into several hundreds of thousands in a single year. Selection failures represent selection errors. The selection errors include the cost related to the fees of the executive search firm, compensation packages, and also the high severance pay that firms sometimes have to pay to a new executive who has failed and has been asked to leave the organization. In addition to these tangible costs, there are intangible costs associated with selection errors. These include the cost of the negative impact on organizational image as well as on motivation and morale of the key people of the firm. Since the failure rate of executive selection is quite high, many firms are forced to retain under-performing executives merely because replacing this executive may be too difficult or too risky. The intense competition between firms to grow and succeed has led to an increased performance pressure on executive selectors. One factor that has contributed to the problem of finding executives who will be successful is the labour market condition. The high rate of economic growth along with demographic realities has resulted in a short supply of quality leaders. Moreover, the new economy has created a huge variety of new business sectors. Therefore, even if the numbers are available it is difficult to find leaders who have the experience of working with a particular sector for any reasonable period of time. Therefore, firms are considering alternative sources of leadership potential, such as candidates from competitors or from firms in unrelated industries. We can no longer look at executive staffing process as a 'rational' decision. More often than not, executive selections rely on organizational values and ideologies, formal and informal institutional rules, historical precedents, etc. The selection, therefore, is not necessarily linked to the strategic needs of the firm. Executive selection, like selection for other jobs, may be seen as a two-phase process. In phase 1, talented candidates are shortlisted from either the internal or the external labour market, and in phase 2, the final selection is made from the shortlist.

Organizations vary in their preferences and practices with regard to the use of formal selection tools. Given the importance as well as cost of executive

Tools for Executive Selection Decisions

Swiercz and Ezzedeen (2001) of George Washington University proposed the use of decision support systems (DSS). It is believed that using an advanced tool such as DSS helps the process of executive selection. In earlier times, managerial decision-making was considered more art than science. However, in contemporary management, decisions have become more complex and demanding. New decision tools are required to address the complex nature of decisions. The pioneering work in the field of decision science was done by Herbert Simon. With increasing complexity and a need to rationalize decision-making, new tools such as Statistical Decision Theory and Operations Research developed in the 1960s, also called the 'age of rationalism'. Management science provided a scientific and technology-supported approach to decision-making. This was far removed from the earlier approach to decision-making that was based on intuition and experience. Management science—the new approach to decision-making—begins with the formulation of a problem. Different variables related to the problem are assigned values. A mathematical model is designed that represents the decision situation in all its implications. Solutions are derived from these mathematical models. These modelling procedures have the ability to allow a better understanding of the important and relative impact of environmental variables.

For several years, the only decision tools available were of a statistical or operations research nature. It was in the 1970s that Thomas Saaty of the University of Pittsburgh began work on the mathematical foundations of a process he called the Analytic Hierarchy Process (AHP). In conjunction with computers, the AHP has proven to be a very useful executive selection decision support tool.

Source: Swiercz and Ezzedeen 2001

selection, efforts should be made to minimize selection errors or the failure rate of selection. New approaches for making selection decisions are designed to achieve the goal of making effective selection decisions. Let us now discuss four such approaches: (1) computer-aided decision support systems; (2) competency-based approach to selection; (3) virtual hiring; and (4) person–culture fit.

Computer-aided Decision Support Systems

From our knowledge of organizational behaviour, we know that decisions can be structured or unstructured. Structured decisions are possible in situations in which one can determine all the variables involved and solve the problem by using a mathematical formula. Unstructured decisions have to be taken in situations filled with uncertainties and conflicting goals. The decision to select an executive is an example of an unstructured decision. These decisions cannot be made with the help of a mathematical formula. Most decisions that a manager has to make are a mixture of structured and unstructured factors.

The statistical decision tools available lend themselves well to an analysis of structured decisions, but not to semi-structured or unstructured decisions. A useful executive selection decision tool is the Analytic Hierarchy Process (AHP). One of the applications of the AHP theory is Expert Choice (EC), a computer-aided decision support system (DSS), which is used regularly by organizations such as IBM, GM, NASA, and World Bank. The AHP requires that the various factors or criteria important for making a decision are arranged in a hierarchical form. Expert Choice helps provide an overall view of the complex relationships in a decision situation and allows the relative importance of factors at each level of the hierarchy to be compared and assessed. The steps followed in the AHP are presented in Exhibit 5.6.

The advantage of AHP is that through the mathematical process, Expert Choice clearly showcases the differences between the candidates based on the scores attained by each candidate with respect to different criteria. The main limitation of the AHP is that the pair-wise comparison process can be very tedious. However, a good facilitator can manage it well through Expert Choice. The process has the advantage of increasing the probability of decision-making by consensus.

Organizations vary in their preferences and practices with regard to the use of formal selection tools. Given the importance and cost of executive selection, efforts should be made to minimize selection errors or the failure rate of selection. The AHP tool proposes to provide a tool to improve the success rate of executive selection.

Competency-based Approach to Selection

The most common indicator of executive talent is an individual's past record of success. A firm hires an executive from another firm because of his or her performance and reputation. However, the past is not a perfectly accurate measure of future performance. Hiring experienced executives from outside the organization to fill key positions does not always result in a positive outcome. Often, new hires fail to excel in the firm. Several firms such as L'Oreal and Unilever use the competency-based selection approach to try and avoid this problem. Competency assessment helps measure an individual's accomplishment accurately. A competency is a 'set of observable performance dimensions, including skills, attitudes, knowledge, or abilities that are linked to high performance, and provide the organization with sustainable competitive advantage'. Competencies are characteristics demonstrated by superior performers. These characteristics determine people's long-term behaviour and thus their long-term performance. The competency-based approach to selection focusses on observable behaviours, which are manifestations of these underlying characteristics. Competencies are used to predict success.

Exhibit 5.6

Steps Followed in the Analytic Hierarchy Process

1. State the goal of the decision clearly. For example, the goal may be 'to select a general manager'.

2. Develop a list of criteria or factors that are important in making the decision. The criteria may be, for example, the skills of the candidates and the behaviours related to these skills. The criteria should be mutually exclusive but collectively exhaustive. They should be clearly related to the demands of the job.

3. Define the criteria in clear and operational terms. For example, 'managerial skills' may be defined as 'effectively communicating through speech and writing'.

4. Structure the problem as a hierarchy of criteria or options. The goal of decision-making is at the top of the hierarchy. In the middle are the component factors and sub-factors. At the bottom of the hierarchy are the decision options. In selection, the decision options are the candidates.

5. Follow the prioritization process. This involves assigning values or weights to the criteria and sub-criteria based on their relative importance. Criteria are compared using the pair-wise comparison process. Expert Choice helps in pair-wise comparisons. Criteria or sub-criteria are compared with other criteria or sub-criteria at the same hierarchical level with respect to the property at the next higher level of hierarchy. For example, the three main criteria for selecting a general manager (goal) may be technical skills, managerial skills, and leadership ability. These three skills (criteria) will be compared with each other through the pair-wise comparison method with respect to their relative importance for the position requirement of general manager. Pair-wise comparisons are used to compute the relative weight of each criterion assigned by each decision-maker and by all decision-makers collectively. A mathematical process compares each option (candidate) on each of the criteria and rates the options from 'most preferred' to 'least preferred'.

Source: Swiercz and Ezzedeen 2001

The competency approach attempts to identify broad executive competencies, some of which are generic and needed of all candidates by all firms while others are more idiosyncratic firm requirements. This approach incorporates situational conditions and seeks to match a candidate's competencies to the requirements of the situation, and therefore to help making a selection decision. Thus, a competency-based approach allows managers to take account of the business needs of the organization and use measurement techniques for recruitment and selection that are objective, compared to traditional methods. Changing business dynamics cause changes in the competencies required of executives. The process used to identify competencies associated with high performance on the job is based on the following assumptions.

- In every organization, some employees perform better than others.
- High performers work differently from the others.

- Differences in performance relate to specific characteristics (competencies) of outstanding performers that are often not present in others.

The best way to identify the competencies of high performers is to study them systematically, measure their performance, document their characteristics, and convert these characteristics into selection criteria for new hires. A firm may follow certain steps to develop a competency-based selection approach (see Exhibit 5.7).

It is generally believed that the competency-based selection method requires a high initial investment. However, in the long run, it results in several advantages such as lower employee turnover, faster adaptation to change by employees, and competitive advantage for the firm.

Virtual Hiring

Companies in the IT sector have a huge demand for professionals and hire in large numbers. The industry recruits around 100,000 persons annually, about 65% of whom are fresh graduates. To hire such large numbers, firms have to visit a number of campuses, sometimes as many as 100 campuses. IBM India visits 68–70 campuses each year while Wipro Technologies visits 160 colleges. Infosys received more than 10,000 resumes from 70 universities across the

---

Exhibit 5.7

Steps in Competency-based Selection

- Identify target jobs.
- Develop competency model(s) for the target jobs. This may be done by having an expert panel of people familiar with the target job requirements brainstorm to identify key accountabilities as well as the competencies employees need to perform on the job.
- Interview current incumbents of the target job(s). The purposes are to confirm the competencies identified by the expert panel as well as to record examples of these competencies as demonstrated in actual work situations. These interviews that have these purposes are called behavioural event interviews (BEI).
- Identify behaviours and personality characteristics that distinguish superior performers. Data

from the expert panel and BEIs may be used to do this.
- Validate the characteristics (competencies). This may be done by assessing a sample of superior and average performers on the competencies identified. If the assessment (ratings or rankings) show that high performers rank higher than average performers on these competencies, the competency model can be used for selection.
- Obtain data on applicants with respect to the competencies in the competency model. One or more of the various methods of selection described earlier can be used for.

Adapted from: http://www.mom.gov.sg/NR/rdonlyres/C228CEA5-B699-4E9E-B240-486ACC4950C1/1410/ 2632_RecruitmentSelection.pdf, accessed on 21 July 2006

world for 100 internships it had on offer in 2005. These firms are now looking at virtual hiring using video conferencing. It is not possible for the firms to physically visit all campuses. Infosys already hires interns through video conferencing, and also senior managers in some cases. With the cost of employee selection becoming very high, some organizations are opting for interviews through video conferencing. This saves cost as well as the travel-related time of interviewers. However, video conferencing requires that the interviewer as well as the interviewee have access to video conferencing.

Person–Culture Fit

The objective of selection is to hire the 'best' or the 'most suitable' candidate for the job in question. It is reasonable to conclude that an employee with the right skills will perform the job successfully. When employees are successful in their jobs, it results in increased productivity, lower employee turnover, and better products and services.

Until now, we have focussed on hiring employees who have the necessary knowledge, skills, competencies and other requirements identified through job analysis. This is the traditional approach to employee selection, also called the person–job fit. Person–job fit seeks to match skills and characteristics of an employee with those required for performing the job successfully and which are provided for in job specifications.

A new approach to employee selection is emerging. This approach is based on the premise that individual job performance is not a function of person-job fit alone. Rather, it also depends on the group/team he/she works with, as well as the culture and values of the organization. Therefore, it is also impor-tant to assess person-team fit and person–culture fit. For example, Southwest Airlines states, 'We value people who like to have fun'. This hiring philosophy goes beyond the individual–job fit to reflect company values. The process of selection does not take place in a vacuum. It has to be placed within the context of the job, group/team, organizational culture, and also the interna-tional culture. In selection, the following types of 'fit' should be assessed:

- person–job fit;
- person–group fit (match between the candidate and the immediate work group);
- person–organization fit (fit between the individual's personality and the cultural values of an organization); and
- person–international culture fit (fit between individual and cultural values of another country.

Work in organizations is increasingly organized around teams. For example, in the IT industry employees come together in project-based teams. The team disbands after the project is completed. Members of the disbanded team are then assigned to other project teams. Therefore, new approaches to selection are giving importance to person–group fit at the time of hiring. A person may have very good technical skills, but may be a poor team player. This may prevent this person from performing to his full potential and contributing to the firm all that he/she is capable of. Generally, when firms assess candidates for their team or work-group related qualities, they seek to determine the role the candidate can perform in the team. Each team member must take on a complementary, but not identical, role for the team to perform well. All team members cannot be leaders. This approach to hiring recognizes that each individual has strengths and weaknesses, and that the weaknesses of one can be complemented by strengths of another member of the team.

All teams that have worked together for some time develop specific cultural norms and values. These norms vary from how team members dress and how they communicate with each other, whether team meetings start on time, and so on. When a new person joins the team, unless the new member conforms with the norms, or unless the management wants to bring in a cultural change, there is potential for conflict. Usually cultural conflicts occur because of ineffective hiring. Often, during the interview process, the interviewers get carried away by a couple of qualities they like in the person, and overlook the other indicators that the person is not likely to 'fit in' the culture.

Person–organization fit includes the person–job fit and goes beyond to incorporate the fit between the personality of the individual and the culture of the organization. According to this approach, the individual–job fit is important since technical skills are important for job performance. However, social and interpersonal skills are more important for success on the job as well as for job satisfaction. For example, if teamwork is a key value in an organization, then candidates must be assessed for their ability to be team players. This approach places greater weight on social and interpersonal skills on the grounds that it is easier to train for technical skills than change or develop social skills or other aspects of personality. The 'desire to learn new skills' cannot be taught as easily to employees as job skills can be. A cultural mismatch between a new hire and the organization can lead to job dissatisfaction, poor job performance, and high employee turnover.

The emphasis on person–organization fit by firms has led to a renewed interest in the use of personality tests and increased use of job simulation exercises. Job simulations also help in hiring effectiveness by providing an opportunity to the applicant to understand what it would be like to work for the organization. However, assessing person-organization fit is expensive. The main features of the traditional (person–job) approach to employee selection and the new (person–organization) approach are presented in Table 5.5.

As firms go multinational, they send their employees to their offices in other countries. Firms also hire people from countries other than the parent

Table 5.5:   Traditional Approach versus New Approach to Employee Selection

Traditional Approach: Person–Job Fit	New Approach: Person–Organization Fit
■ Hire for 'jobs'	■ Hire for 'organizations'
■ Individual behaviour seen largely as a function of the person	■ Individual behaviour seen as a function of the situation
■ Selection attempts to capitalize on individual differences; chooses individuals best suited to the job	■ Individual can be moulded for high performance through socialization after they are hired
■ Job performance is a function of the 'fit' between KSAs and job demands	■ Job performance is a function of the 'fit' between individual and organizational culture in addition to person–job fit
■ Ignores characteristics of candidates that are irrelevant to immediate job requirements	■ Goes beyond KSAs to hire total 'people'
■ Essential for on-the-job success for jobs that demand specific technical skills and knowledge	■ People perform best when they are in an intellectually stimulating environment
■ More concerned with finding new employees	■ Concerned with finding and retaining new employees
■ Results in high quality products and services	■ Results in high commitment, job satisfaction, lower absenteeism and turnover, and high performance

Source: Bowen, Ledford, and Nathan 1991

country of the firm. It is important that an employee working overseas should have the ability to adapt and adjust to cultural differences. This issue will be dealt with in greater detail in Chapter 12.

STAFFING PROCESS: RECRUITING AND SELECTING EMPLOYEES

The process of staffing begins with human resource planning (see Figure 5.1). A firm cannot begin to hire unless the human resource requirements, in terms of the kinds of skills and competencies as well as how many employees are required, has been determined. Even then, the HR function does not begin to recruit unless it receives a formal authorization to fill positions or to increase workforce from line managers belonging to different departments. These authorizations are called employee requisitions. Employee requisitions clearly state the nature of the job the new employee will be required to perform (job description) as well as the skills and competencies required to perform the job successfully (job specification). Sometimes, the HR department may initiate the process by reminding the functional managers to send authorizations. The staffing process, as any other HR activity, is a shared responsibility between the HR and line functions.

The firm must attract suitable candidates in sufficient numbers and of appropriate quality to be able to meet its HR requirements. Whether or not the staffing process results in the selection of an employee who performs well on the job depends on how effective the process of recruitment has been. It is easy to see that the 'best' candidates cannot be selected if they are not included in the applicant pool generated through recruitment.

The process of hiring consists of seven interrelated stages:

1. clarifying hiring philosophy;
2. recruitment planning;
3. developing an effective recruitment strategy;
4. searching for job applicants;
5. screening applicants;
6. gathering information about candidates; and
7. making a final selection decision.

Let us consider each one of these stages in some detail (see Figure 5.6).

Clarifying Hiring Philosophy

It is important for a firm to be clear about its hiring mission and philosophy. This requires that there should be clarity about what the organization stands for and its future direction. This helps the firm determine the type of people it will require. For example, if a firm is going in for a culture change from a traditional family-run company to a professionally-managed high-growth firm, its hiring requirements will change.

The hiring philosophy of the firm should be aligned with company values. Let us go back to the example of Southwest Airlines that 'values people who like to have fun'. The firm should take the corporate value statement and assign adjectives to this statement to describe the type of people it wants. Once the firm knows who it would like to hire, it can develop a statement that expresses it clearly. For example, if the firm would like to hire achievers, the hiring mission may read, 'We hire achievers who love to sell'.

Recruitment Planning

Before beginning to recruit, the firm must state its recruitment objectives. In a general sense, the goal of recruitment is 'to attract the best people with the right skills who can create maximum value for the firm'. Recruitment objectives are derived from the statement of job vacancies. The objectives specify 'what

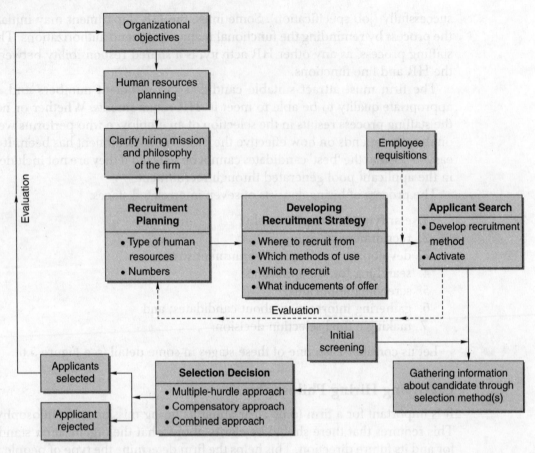

Figure 5.6: Stages in the Staffing/Hiring Process

type' and 'how many' of potential applicants to be contacted to fulfill all HR requirements with qualified applicants. The information about the 'type' of applicants required is readily obtained from job specifications.

A firm must always recruit more candidates than it actually seeks to hire. Some of the candidates may not be suitable for the job while others may not be interested in accepting the job offer. However, too large an applicant pool has a negative impact on recruitment efficiency. As firms seek to maintain competitiveness through cost advantage, most firms maintain a careful vigil on hiring budgets. It is difficult to determine the number of candidates to be contacted precisely. However, a firm can make some estimates. A tool that helps an organization decide how many applicants to recruit for each job opening is the yield ratio (YR).

The YR is the relationship between the number of applicants at one step of the hiring process relative to the number of people who move to the next step. An example of YR is presented in Exhibit 5.8.

Exhibit 5.8

An Example of Yield Ratio

To hire 10 new employees, the hiring process proceeds as depicted. Yield ratio at each step is identified.

Stage of the Recruiting Process	Applicants Screened Out	Yield Ratio
Total Applicants	120	0
Initial Screening Interview	60	2:1
Selection Interview	40	3:2
Physical Examination	30	4:3
Job Offer	15	2:1
Job Offers Accepted	10	3:2
Overall Yield Ratio	120:10	12:1

To select 1 candidate the firm will have to recruit 12 candidates. Therefore, to select 10 employees, the firm must recruit 120 candidates.

Adapted from: Mello 2003

Yield ratios are available generally for employee groups for which the firm has hired in the past. However, YR will not be available for employee groups being recruited for the first time (for example, a firm that is hiring women for the first time, such as when the Indian Navy began to recruit women on the Short Service Commission) or for recruiting methods being used for the first time (for example, personality tests). In such cases, the organization has to either rely on guesses or develop estimates based on the hiring experiences of other firms.

Recruitment objectives are also influenced by government regulations and/or internal policies of the firm. As we discussed earlier, there may be legal requirements with respect to hiring quotas based on considerations such as caste, gender, region, etc. (reservations) in order to correct prior discriminatory practices, or a firm may prefer to hire from a particular region because its previous hiring experiences from that region have been good. For example, global IT majors hire professionals from Bangalore and Hyderabad. These external and internal factors constrain the recruitment efforts of a firm.

Developing an Effective Recruitment Strategy

Company philosophy and recruitment objectives must be converted into tactics or strategy. The recruitment strategy involves making decisions about

- where to recruit from;
- which recruitment method(s) to use;
- when to recruit; and
- how to attract people to apply.

Where to Recruit From

As we have discussed earlier, a firm may recruit from internal or external sources. When recruiting externally, firms may recruit from the local, regional, national, or global labour market. In deciding where to recruit, the following general criteria may be applied by firms.

- Unskilled labour may be recruited locally, whereas for skilled workforce, a firm may recruit regionally or nationally.
- Local shortages of unskilled labour may require organizations to recruit from a larger labour market. For example, shortage of nurses in the UK or the Gulf countries resulted in the recruitment of nurses from India.
- The location of the organization may influence the decision. A firm in a metropolitan city may be able to hire managerial employees from the local labour market. However, a similar firm in a backward region may have to broaden its search for the same employee group.

Generally speaking, however, firms recruit from areas where there is a high probability of success, and/or where past experience dictates likely success. Most of the fast growing sectors like BPO, IT, telecom, and retailing are new and do not have historical talent to hire from. Hence, they hire managers from other sectors with skill sets that are relevant to their industries. As firms tap unconventional labour markets for hiring some skill sets, mobility is being given a new meaning in Indian industry. Cross-sector movement is increasing and walls between departments are blurring. For example, the marketing head of an automobile major may today join a pharmaceutical company, and an executive from a soft drink major may move into the insurance sector. Executives are not just switching sectors, they are also shifting departments as well as job functions with equal ease. In many cases, when a firm is looking for a specific skill set, the industry a candidate has experience in is immaterial. In this case, it is the experience in handling a particular situation that becomes important. Sometimes, a firm wishes to hire a person who has experience in managing, for example, acquisitions, turnarounds, joint ventures, or even a particular company exposure. For example, FMCG executives with strong marketing skills have become a source of marketing talent for almost all sectors. Similarly, hospitality industry employees who have good communication skills are being sought after by BPO firms and hospital chains. Even within the firm itself, companies like IBM, Infosys, and Accenture are investing in retraining and 're-skilling' employees to help them move up the corporate ladder, gain multi-dimensional knowledge, and in the process build their own talent pool across functions. This is in line with the bigger changes that are taking place in the corporate world. Domain knowledge and technical skills have become relatively less critical. Companies are realizing that technical skills can be developed and groomed by the firm, but it is the leadership and entrepreneurial skills that firms need to recruit for. However, as cross-sector movement becomes more common it will be a challenge for organizations to manage the diversity due to employees coming from different sectors and with different functional backgrounds.

Which Recruitment Methods to Use

A number of recruitment methods are available for a firm to choose from. Some methods are better suited than others for recruiting specific employee groups. For example, the campus recruitment method is a good source of entry-level managerial professionals. The choice of recruitment method(s) is based on the following considerations.

- Type of job or employee group. Unsolicited applications are a good method for recruiting unskilled labour but may not work well for recruiting managers.
- Cost of method. Some methods like media advertisements are costly.
- Time taken for results. Different recruitment methods differ with respect to the speed with which they provide the firm with a new hire. Newspaper advertisements may take as much as three or four months before the selected candidate actually reports for work. On the other hand, recommendations may result in a new hire almost instantaneously. If a firm would like the new hire to report at work as soon as possible, then newspaper advertisements are clearly inappropriate.

A firm needs to weigh all the three considerations in choosing the method of recruitment for a particular job. Firms often tend to use more than one method of recruitment simultaneously.

When to Recruit

As the ongoing war for talent worsens, the winners will be separated from losers only if they can get the best talent on board the fastest and the earliest. As discussed above, recruitment methods differ in how much time they take to generate an applicant pool. Based on HRP, every organization has a fair idea about when the vacancies are likely to occur due to business expansion, retirements, promotions, resignations, etc. except in cases of unexpected vacancies. The decision about when to initiate the process of recruitment depends on the time the hiring process will take. Due to competition for executive talent, firms are hiring far ahead in advance of the position falling vacant. Companies are also hiring in advance for positions much lower in the hierarchy where the turnover rate is higher and the cost of keeping them without work (benching) is lower. Almost all sectors, from IT to IteS, telecom to retailing, and media to financial services, are resorting to advance hiring or proactive hiring. Headhunters call such proactive hiring 'lighthouse appointments' by headhunters. Companies are hiring even if they do not need these people immediately. For example, at Reliance, Pantaloon, etc. the search time for top positions has more than doubled from three to four months two years ago to six to twelve months now.

How to Attract People to Apply

One of the most important aspects of a firm's recruitment strategy is the way it plans to attract potential candidates. To strengthen and increase the probability of the success of its recruitment efforts, the firm should determine what 'inducements' it has to offer to potential candidates. The recruitment effort should be preceded by an assessment of the strengths and weaknesses of the firm that may attract or repel applicants. The analysis of strengths and weaknesses should include the reputation or image of the firm; location of the office or plant; the compensation package; the working conditions; the nature of the job; security of employment; opportunities for career progression; and the culture of the firm.

The firm can use its strengths as inducements to attract candidates. Attracting candidates is like 'selling' the organization. The firm should identify its strongest selling points and publicize those since they would appeal to the applicants. For example, if a firm has unique practices, they should be publicized. Flexible work arrangements, promotional opportunities, and performance-based rewards are some unique practices. If a firm provides fast-track career growth, this factor may be highlighted during the recruitment effort.

A firm such as Microsoft that enjoys a good corporate image and reputation may not have to put in much effort in building inducements in developing its recruitment strategy, all other things being equal (see Exhibit 5.9). However, in highly competitive markets, the same firm may have difficulty in attracting highly skilled employees. During these times, this firm will have to increase its recruitment efforts.

However, in trying to attract candidates, a firm must guard against overselling. When a firm oversells some of its features, it increases the likelihood of unrealistic expectations on the part of candidates. Problems occur when these candidates are hired and join the organization. On confronting reality, they may realize that things are very different from what they were led to believe during recruitment. The candidate may end up feeling cheated and respond by leaving the firm.

Exhibit 5.9

Inducements: How to Attract Candidates to Opportunities in the Firm

With several sectors facing a serious mismatch between demand and supply of skilled manpower, talent acquisition is being reported across sectors, especially in sunrise sectors such as insurance, aviation, hospitality, retail, media, research, and banking. The emergence of new industries and the opening of an industry to new players results in the poaching of talent. New entrants to a sector usually offer a hike in salaries to the tune of about 50% to employees to leave their existing jobs. For example, with the advent of Kingfisher and SpiceJet, the aviation sector witnessed job-hopping in a big way. Pilots who were being paid Rs 150,000 a month got a raise of 25–33% for changing jobs. Apart from such monetary inducements, the new players are also offering opportunities to fly bigger and newer aircraft. Flight engineers and cabin crew are also being hired on higher salaries. Media is another sector in the middle of a poaching drill with 100% salary hikes in some cases. In the retail sector, there is not a big hike in base salary. The focus is on attracting talent with other inducements, such as employee stock ownsrship plans (ESOP) and bonuses with balanced scorecard system. Expatriates in the retail sector are being offered very lucrative packages. For example, the compensation of an expatriate hired for the retail sector included an all-expenses-paid holiday in India for two months every year. Start-ups are also selling the idea of working for something exciting and new. In the banking sector, there has been a movement of top management from established organizations to new banks such as Yes Bank. In this case, the compensation is benchmarked against the industry average, but it is the 'chance to create something new' and 'performance-linked ESOPs' that is being used as inducements for top managers to change jobs. Top managers do not change jobs for money alone but also for challenging assignments. Some even accept a lower hike while switching jobs in return for a larger job responsibility or better working contracts, such as a European shift instead of an American one that calls for late night working hours, in the case of a BPO operation.

Many firms also offer a salary hike to senior managers to the tune of about 30% on the previous pay packet, and in addition, also offer a guaranteed cash bonus in the first year. This bonus is called the signing-in bonus and ranges from one-and-a half to two months' salary, which could mean Rs 800,000–1,200,000 for a typical senior executive or Rs 500,000–800,000 for a middle level manager.

A special case is of the recruitment of chief executive officers (CEO). There are few really good CEOs available in the country and hence they are a prize catch that no firm wants to lose. High-performing CEOs are also the ones who are the target of poaching. This has led companies and executive search firms to try and make offers attractive enough for a successful CEO to accept and stay on. While the innovative structuring of CEO compensation is prevalent, there has also emerged a new vocabulary in relation to CEO compensation. The new vocabulary includes 'collapsible ESOPS', 'underwriting of options', 'market premium bonus', 'staying-on bonus', 'forgivability of loans', and so on. So, apart from a sign-on bonus, there is a joining bonus (for furnishings etc.) plus a pre-joining holiday at company expense. Moreover, companies are willing to make CEOs partners in wealth creation, so equity is offered to the candidate at this level. While ESOPs have been around, the latest trend is toward 'underwriting of options', which means that if at the time of investing, the CEO is not making any money, he will be given a certain sum. Often, when an MNC executive joins a family business, the CEO's contract has a

Contd

Exhibit 5.9 Contd

clause that states that if the company fires the CEO, it will have to pay a hefty severance package to the fired executive.

While the company is 'selling' its strengths to attract potential candidates, the latter also seek to assess what the firm has on offer in relation to their own needs. Values and need patterns of the society and of people change over time. Hence, different factors attract potential candidates at different times and at different stages of their careers. Earlier, while executives were in awe of Hindustan Lever Limited, considering a job with them a dream job, they are no longer in awe. Rather, they are looking for the best career prospects and study their job responsibilities and growth opportunities before accepting the job offer. In recent times, the trend indicates that all

things being equal, executives would now rather work for a fast-growing Indian company or a local group rather than for an MNC. This is because many Indian businesses provide the same monetary benefits and work environment as MNCs. As Indian companies scale up and go global, they are also willing to pay more than MNCs for the same job in some cases. Salaries, perquisites, and work environment are not the only variables in the decision matrix of an executive looking for a career move. Intangible factors like the work challenge, their relative position in the organizational hierarchy, and the company's work ethic and corporate culture are also things that executives look for. These are the factors on which Indian firms score over their MNC counterparts.

Source: Sinha and Kant 2005; Mahanta 2005

Inducements or attracting candidates is not a one-way process. While the firm sells itself, the potential candidate is also evaluating what the company has to offer against what he is looking for. For example, one person may be driven by money while someone else wants a job with challenge and responsibility. Younger workers want career advancement while older workers may be more concerned with security.

An important aspect of developing an attraction strategy is to understand what candidates from a particular employee group are looking for and then customize the recruitment message to provide the desired information.

Searching for Job Applicants

After recruitment plans and strategies have been developed, recruiting can begin. However, strategy cannot be immediately put into practice. First, the HR manager cannot initiate recruiting activities unless there is a requisition from the concerned functional department. Secondly, most recruitment methods require considerable development work before they can be activated. For example, a firm cannot just visit a business school during placement time to recruit from campus. For campus recruiting, developmental activities begin months ahead of the actual campus visit. These include, for example, preparing and distributing company brochures, contacting campus placement officers, holding pre-placement talks, etc. The HR manager starts recruiting activities after receiving the authorization. Depending on whether the firm is recruiting internally or externally, appropriate recruitment methods are used to generate the applicant pool.

Initial Screening of Applicants

The applicant pool needs to be scaled down. A firm will select only some candidates, the 'best' candidates, from the applicant pool. Initial screening is the part of the staffing process that signifies the last stage of recruitment and the first stage of selection. Based on job descriptions and job specifications, candidates who are obviously unqualified for the position in question are eliminated. For example, candidates with inadequate or inappropriate experience or education are screened out. Some firms may conduct an initial screening interview. An initial screening interview also provides another opportunity to the firm to communicate the expectations it has from potential employees clearly. This helps the candidates consider whether they are really serious about the job opportunity or whether they would like to withdraw their candidature. Initial screening may also be based on information provided by applicants in application forms. However, when the applicant pool is very large, screening interviews may be impractical and costly. At the end of initial screening, the applicant pool reduces in size. However, firms must be careful not to screen out potentially successful employees.

Gathering Information about Candidates

We have already discussed that selection involves assessing the applicants against the criteria established in the job analysis. The criteria against which applicants are assessed include educational qualifications, work experience, past performance, personal characteristics, and physical characteristics. A firm must gather as much information as possible about the candidates to make these assessments and to be able to make effective selection decisions. All selection methods discussed earlier help the firm gather job-related information about the applicants. Each method is best suited to obtain a particular kind of applicant-related information. For example, interviews help understand how an individual handles stressful situation, the ability to handle interpersonal situations, the communication ability of the candidate, etc. Personality tests are designed to measure certain characteristics of individuals such as aptitude, emotional resilience, the ability to work in teams and so on. Firms can use reference checks to verify the information provided by the candidate. Reference checks have become important in certain sectors, a recent example being the BPO sector. Like recruitment methods, the choice of selection method(s) by a firm will vary depending on considerations such as cost, expertise required, time available, etc. (see Exhibit 5.10).

Exhibit 5.10

Factors Determining Choice of Selection Method(s)

- **Type of job** For blue collar workers, interviews may not serve any purpose. However, a firm may be uncomfortable hiring a manager without conducting an interview.
- **Cost of selection method** The assessment centre approach is expensive. It is appropriate when hiring for top positions. The hiring budget of a firm may not permit the use of assessment centres.
- **Expertise required** Some selection methods such as personality profiling require considerable expertise and can be administered only by a person trained in its use.

- **Time available** When a firm needs to hire immediately, an interview may be the most suitable.
- **Skills and competencies** These need to be assessed.

Based on the requirements and constraints, a firm will use one or more of the selection methods to gather information on candidates. Once the firm has this information, it seeks to use this information to select the candidates with the highest probability of success on the job.

Making a Final Selection Decision

Information about candidates may be combined in different ways to reach a selection decision. The way a firm will use the information will depend on the particular selection approach of the firm. A firm may follow one of three approaches to selection: (1) multiple-hurdle approach; (2) compensatory approach; and (3) combined approach. These three approaches are depicted diagrammatically in Figures 5.7a, b, and c. In the multiple-hurdle approach, each selection method is seen as one step of the discrete selection process (Figure 5.7a). The approach, as the name suggests, is made up of multiple hurdles. It begins with the initial screening interview and ends with the final selection decision.

Any candidate who 'trips over' any hurdle goes 'out of the race' of job candidacy. For example, if the job requires five years of work experience and the initial screening shows that a candidate has only two years of work experience, the candidate is rejected. Thus, in the discrete selection process, there is progressive elimination of candidates at each step (where each step is a data-gathering method) until the firm locates the individual who has all the skill and other human requirements at the 'minimum acceptable level' as provided in the job specifications. However, this approach may result in the elimination of a potentially good candidate just because he/she received a poor evaluation at a particular step.

All individuals have strengths and weaknesses. It may be difficult to locate a person who has all the skill requirements at a certain acceptable level. This

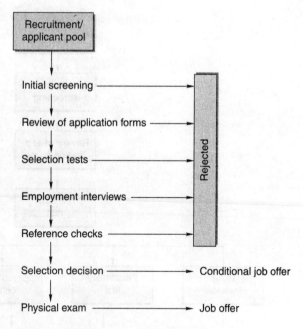

Figure 5.7a: Multiple-hurdle Approach to Selection

is especially true when recruiting for managerial and professional jobs, for which multiple qualities are required for success on the job. The compensatory approach (Figure 5.7b) recognizes this limitation and is therefore more realistic. As the name suggests, the lack of certain qualities may be compensated by the presence of certain other qualities. Hence, information about all aspects is gathered for all candidates.

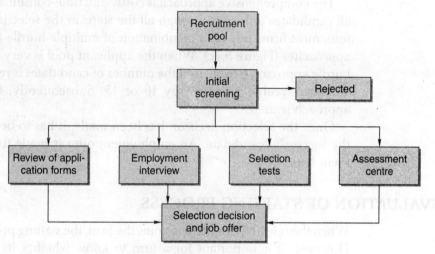

Figure 5.7b: Compensatory Approach to Selection

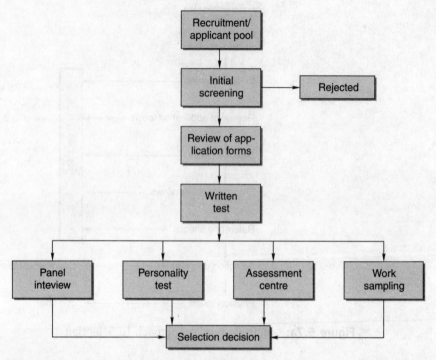

Figure 5.7c: Combined Approach to Selection

The information gathered for each candidate is combined comprehensively for making a selection decision. In combining information, different qualities measured may be assigned weights to reflect their relative importance for the successful performance of the job in question.

The comprehensive approach is costly and time-consuming since it requires all candidates to be put through all the steps in the selection process. Therefore, most firms rely on a combination of multiple-hurdle and compensatory approaches (Figure 5.7c). When the applicant pool is very large, the multiple hurdle approach is used until the number of candidates is reduced to a smaller and manageable number, say 10 or 15. Subsequently, the compensatory approach is used.

Once the selection decision has been made, it has to be communicated to the successful candidate. An employment offer is made through an employment letter.

EVALUATION OF STAFFING PROCESS

When the selected candidate(s) joins the firm, the staffing process is completed. However, it is important for a firm to know whether its efforts have been worthwhile. Every organizational activity should add value and contribute to improving firm performance. This is true of all HR activities and hence of recruitment and selection also. Evaluation of the staffing process involves two activities—monitoring and feedback.

Both the recruitment and selection processes are monitored for efficiency and effectiveness by tracking various indicators. The main performance indicators are quality, quantity, and efficiency of the process. Table 5.6 gives the commonly used indicators for measuring efficiency and effectiveness of recruitment and selection.

Table 5.6: Measuring Efficiency and Effectiveness of Recruitment and Selection

Performance Indicators	Recruitment	Selection
Quantity	■ Size of applicant pool ■ Yield ratio (comparison of the number of applicants at one stage of the recruiting process to the number of applicants at another stage) ■ Number of job vacancies filled	■ Are all job vacancies filled with qualified candidates ■ Selection rate, or the percentage hired from a given group of candidates (number hired * 100/ number of applicants)
Quality	■ Number of job offers made ■ Qualifications of candidates vis-à-vis job specifications ■ Percentage of applicants offered jobs ■ Number of job offers made versus number of vacancies ■ Job performance of selected candidates (new hires) after six months on the job ■ Number of selected candidates who stay with the firm at the end of one year	■ Quality of job performance of selected candidates ■ Rate of acceptance of job offers (number of offers accepted/total number of offers made)
Efficiency	*Cost/Benefit* ■ Cost-per-hire (recruiting costs/number of vacancies) ■ Cost-benefit per recruitment method (comparison of cost of hiring from a recruitment method with the length of time the applicant hired on the basis of that method stays with the firm) ■ Cost-per-hire by recruitment method (number of job acceptances by method/number of candidates interviewed)	■ Staffing efficiency ratio (total staffing costs/total compensation of those hired)

Contd

Table 5.6 Contd

Performance Indicators	Recruitment	Selection
	Time ■ Time-to-fill (length of time taken to fill job opening, that is, number of days between the date the position was approved for staffing and the date the new employee started work)	■ Time it takes for the new employee to report to work from the time of the first day of recruitment
Effectiveness	■ Comparing recruiting efforts with past patterns ■ Benchmarking recruiting efforts with those of other organizations ■ Information on job performance, absenteeism, cost of training, and turnover by recruitment method indicates relative effectiveness of each method	■ Tracking the success rate of applicants where success rate is the quality of the employees hired and who perform well on the job ■ Success base rate (number of past applicants who were selected and who became successful employees based on historical data) ■ Benchmarking (comparing the success rate of the firm with that of other employers in the area or industry)

Modified: http://www.mom.gov.sg/NR/rdonlyres/C228CEA5-B699-4E9E-B240-486ACC4950C1/1410/ 2632_RecruitmentSelection.pdf, accessed on 21 July 2006; Mathis and Jackson 2003

The data obtained from performance indicators can be used to improve the recruitment and selection process. This data helps determine whether there is a need to change recruitment methods, whether inducements offered have been effective, and whether the appropriate selection methods have been used. Exit interviews of departing employees also provide feedback about different aspects of HR activities. For example, a new hire who resigns from the job within six months may reveal in the exit interview that the job he was required to do was vastly different from what he was led to believe. This may help the firm improve upon its strategy for attracting talent.

SELECTION OUTCOMES

As mentioned earlier, selection involves predictions. It seeks to predict which job applicants are likely to perform successfully on the job, if hired. Prediction is a 'best guess' process; it can never be perfect since it is based on future probabilities. Selection decisions may result in correct outcomes or selection errors (see Figure 5.8). A correct selection decision may either select a candidate

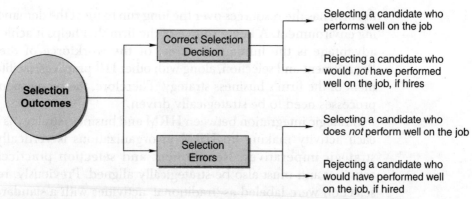

Selecting a candidate who performs well on the job

Rejecting a candidate who would *not* have performed well on the job, if hires

Selecting a candidate who does *not* perform well on the job

Rejecting a candidate who would have performed well on the job, if hired

Figure 5.8: Selection Outcomes

who performs well on the job or reject a candidate who would not have performed well on the job.

While the importance of the former is obvious, the significance of the latter is not readily evident. It is only when the firm has clearly stated hiring policies, objectives, and criteria that it will be able to discriminate (fairly) among candidates and predict their success or failure on the job.

An evidence of selection error is poor performance of the selected candidate on the job. However, several factors, such as low motivation and lack of facilities for job performance, may contribute to poor performance. All performance failures cannot be traced to faulty hiring. Another type of selection error takes place when a potentially good candidate, who would have performed well on the job, is rejected. Though there is no way a firm can determine this error, it is important to be aware of the possibility of rejecting a candidate who should have been selected.

The purpose of designing the staffing process carefully is to increase the chances of correct selection decisions and minimize the chances of selection errors. Recruitment objectives, recruitment strategy, choice of selection methods, etc. all contribute to the quality of selection decisions. However, it is prudent to recognize that 'to err is human'. It is not possible to eliminate selection errors entirely. As media baron Ted Turner once remarked, 'After all, Jesus Christ only had to make 12 appointments, and one of them was a bummer'. It is important to expect errors and to plan to minimize them.

STRATEGIC RECRUITMENT AND SELECTION

It is important to ensure that the recruitment and selection processes are strategic. A dynamic business environment has resulted in greater strategic behaviour on the part of organizations as they strive for competitive advantage. An important aspect of organizational strategic orientation is to ensure that the firm has the resources over the long run to meet the demands of the changing environment. A key resource of the firm that helps it achieve competitive advantage is the human resource, or the workforce of the organization. Recruitment and selection, along with other HR practices, facilitate the achievement of the firm's business strategy. Therefore, the recruitment and selection processes need to be strategically driven.

Strategic integration between HRM and business strategy is achieved when each activity making up HRM in organizations is vertically aligned with strategic imperatives. Recruitment and selection practices are key HR activities and must also be strategically aligned. Previously, recruitment and selection were labeled as 'traditional' activities with a standard approach. In the traditional approach to recruitment and selection, the first step is to identify the type of person who will perform a particular job effectively. Subsequently, applicants are assessed against the defined personal attributes in order to determine a person–job fit. In recent times, however, the central focus of recruitment and selection have become more driven by business strategy. Instead of hiring employees solely on the basis of person/job fit, firms place a premium on person–organization fit. Therefore, applicants are selected against organizational rather than job-specific criteria. Also, strategic orientation in recruitment and selection has led to the increased use of sophisticated selection techniques and greater involvement of line managers in the entire process of selection.

The above developments in the process of recruitment and selection provide for a greater integration between employee resourcing and business strategy. Millmore suggests that for recruitment and selection to be classified as strategic, they must demonstrate three primary features: (1) strategic integration, (2) long-term focus, and (3) a mechanism for translating strategic HR demands into appropriate recruitment and selection specification.

Strategic Integration

As suggested above, recruitment and selection are powerful means of aligning employee behaviour with the business strategy of the firm. Recruitment and selection play an important role in the success of organizational strategy. Strategic recruitment and selection (SR&S) involves an alignment of hiring practices with the strategic planning process of the firm. It also involves translating the strategic plans of the firm into those employee attributes that are critical to successful accomplishment of strategic plans.

Long-term Focus

Strategic recruitment and selection also represent a long-term focus. The objective of SR&S is to develop recruitment and selection practices so that the firm has the HR attributes that are critical to the future and long-term success of the firm.

Mechanism

Staffing is concerned with choosing people who will contribute to the long-term success of the firm. To accomplish this, it is important to forecast the HR requirements necessary for the successful achievement of the strategic plans of the firm. It is also important to develop various staffing activities to find such people.

Strategic recruitment and selection that satisfy the above three features cause recruitment and selection to become more important to the firm and also make it more sophisticated and complex. The outcomes of SR&S have a significant impact on organizational practice in several ways.

First, the effort and cost of effective recruitment and selection is preferable to the cost of managing poor performers.

Secondly, greater effort and financial investment made in the recruitment and selection process will certainly lead to an emphasis on evaluating (1) the effectiveness of the process as well as (2) the contribution of recruitment and selection to the attainment of strategic objectives.

Thirdly, higher investment in the process as well as greater complexity in person specification focusing on person-organization fit will require the use of a combination of several methods of selection to assess potential recruits.

Finally, the complex and critical nature of SR&S requires a multi-stakeholder approach and recognizes recruitment and selection as a two-way process.

As a multi-stakeholder approach, the recruitment and selection process is seen as best served by the active involvement of all relevant stakeholders, that is, the firm and the candidate. Being a two-way process, SR&S encourages the participation of candidates and is sensitive to the impact of the process on candidates. The firm also provides enough information to the candidates about the vacancy and its context so that the candidates can make their own informed self-selection decisions.

These four features of recruitment and selection, however, are seen only as secondary features and are not considered to be sufficient on their own to result in SR&S. The three primary features of strategic integration, HRP, and long-term focus are important. When the primary features are taken together with the secondary features, they can be depicted as an explanatory framework of SR&S practices (see Figure 5.9).

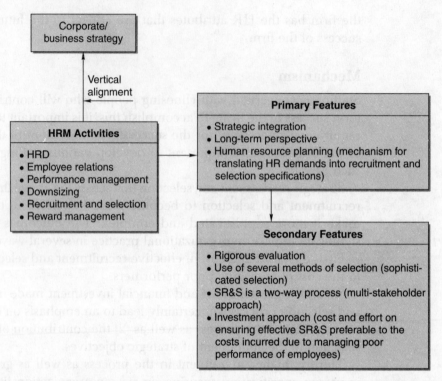

Figure 5.9: Conceptual Framework of Strategic Recruitment and Selection

Adapted from: Millmore 2003

Staffing Effectiveness

Staffing effectiveness may be influenced by several factors. For example, situational variables that may impact staffing effectiveness include labour market conditions, type of vacancy, time and cost constraints, and characteristics of the people involved in the hiring decision. More recently, there have been suggestions emphasizing the importance of organizational characteristics in determining staffing outcomes. These organizational characteristics include structure, size, and strategy. As mentioned earlier, recruitment and selection have moved beyond the traditional person–job fit emphasis to the strategic approach that focusses on person–organization fit. The question being raised in organizational staffing is, 'What skills, aptitudes, behavioural styles etc. are most compatible with future organizational objectives and strategy?'

The staffing process has several stages as has already been pointed out earlier in this chapter. These stages are:

- choice of selection criteria;
- selection of recruitment method;

- development of marketing strategy;
- choice of selection technique; and
- final decision.

Chapter 1 discussed various classifications of business strategies. The typology put forth by Miles and Snow (1978) has received recent empirical support and seems to have implications for staffing effectiveness. According to Miles and Snow, even within the same industry, effective organizations may adopt different structures, processes, and strategies in the pursuit of organizational goals. Let us now use Miles and Snow's typology to illustrate linkages between business strategy and effectiveness of the recruitment and selection process (see Table 5.7). Using Miles and Snow's typology, Olian and Rynes assessed the appropriateness of particular staffing practices at each stage of the selection process for each business strategy.

Table 5.7: Linkages between Business Strategy and SR&S Effectiveness

	Business Strategy Typology		
	Defender	**Prospector**	**Analyser**
Business Strategy	■ Function in relatively stable markets ■ Depend on development of efficient technology and production ■ Find change threatening ■ Focus on improving efficiency in technological and transformational processes ■ Devote few resources to research and development	■ Identify and exploit new product and marketing opportunities ■ Decentralized authority, informal procedures ■ Thrive on change	■ Seek to match new ventures with the present business set-up ■ Operate in stable as well as dynamic markets ■ Frequently organized into matrix structures that combine both functional and product groups
Hiring Managerial Talent	■ Managers have narrow specialized skills ■ Almost always promoted from within	■ Often acquired from outside	■ Drawn from internal promotions, external recruitment, mergers, and acquisitions
Dominant Power Coalition	■ Consists of financial and production experts	■ Individuals with backgrounds in marketing or product research and development	■ Experts in marketing, applied research, and production

Contd

Table 5.7 Contd

	Business Strategy Typology		
	Defender	**Prospector**	**Analyser**
Staffing Practices	▪ Individuals hired at low level, receive considerable on-the-job training, and slow, steady promotions if they show promise in their functional areas	▪ Employees face relatively frequent changes in job duties and assignments ▪ More likely to hire appropriately experienced individuals, since speed is important for moving into new product lines	▪ Some employees are hired at low levels and moved to positions of higher responsibility within functions ▪ Some employees are brought in at higher levels to provide quick, ready-made expertise
Recruitment Methods	▪ Internal sources	▪ External sources	▪ Mixture of sources, including cross-divisional or cross-product transfers, external recruitment, and internal promotion
Effective Recruitment Messages	▪ Convey information about centralization of control, emphasis on internal promotion within well-defined functions, importance of meeting cost and production goals, and high investment in employee development ▪ More formal dissemination of information through the use of recruitment brochures, videotapes, or standard presentations by the firm's representatives	▪ Indicate dynamism in job and project assignments, decentralized control, risk-taking in work procedures, and emphasis on technological and marketing innovations ▪ Convey recruiting messages informally, and make use of line managers who are more aware of the changing requirements and characteristics of vacancies	▪ Messages similar to defenders' in stable areas of the organization, and more like prospectors' in change-oriented sectors ▪ Also emphasize likelihood of transfers across product or divisional lines ▪ In stable parts of the firm, formal, standardized recruitment channels are used; change-oriented divisions use less formal channels and rely more more on line managers to transmit information

Contd

Table 5.7 Contd

	Business Strategy Typology		
	Defender	**Prospector**	**Analyser**
Criteria for Hiring	▪ Less weightage given to past achievements ▪ More emphasis on future aptitudes or potential ▪ Individuals with high need for security and low tolerance for change and ambiguity more well suited ▪ Emphasize relatively narrow range of specialized skills ▪ Clearly articulate selection criteria	▪ Focus on past achievement in desired knowledge, skills, and abilities ▪ Seek individuals with high tolerance for ambiguity and a willingness to incur risk ▪ Wider and more general range of aptitudes and abilities for adapting to their more rapid production or service shifts ▪ Less likely to formalize selection criteria because job requirements change with changes in strategic direction	▪ Focus on both, past achievement and future potential ▪ Wider and more general range of aptitudes and abilities ▪ Clearly articulate selection criteria
Selection Methods	▪ Use future-oriented tests such as aptitude tests and seek to assess potential promotability	▪ Rely on methods that emphasize the applicant's work history, such as ability tests, reference checks	▪ Use combination of methods
Selection Decision	▪ Involve HR specialists in final hiring decisions ▪ Greater corporate control over final hiring	▪ Greater line influence in hiring decisions ▪ Less corporate control over final hiring	▪ A mix of the two ▪ Fall somewhere in between, with corporate representatives providing guidance but not having the final authority to make a final decision

Source: Olian and Rynes 1984

HIRING FOR A DIVERSE WORKFORCE

An important HR challenge faced by organizations is the management of a diverse workforce. There are more women, older workers, minorities, and disabled workers in the workforce today. Diversity has become a part of the vocabulary of firms and their management, especially since the 1990s. There is no standard definition of diversity. In general, the term implies 'differences'. (see Figure 5.10) Organizations undertake workplace diversity initiatives to (1) abide by the law and to avoid the legal consequences of violating these laws; (2) adhere to their philosophy of social responsibility; (3) reap the benefits of a heterogeneous workforce; (4) manage the shortage of available talent; and (5) conform with social expectations.

1. The law in India requires 22.5% reservation of government jobs for SC/ST candidates, 5% reservation for children of war widows, and 3% reservation for the physically handicapped. Public sector firms in particular are called upon to ensure adequate representation to those sections of society who are historically or socially disadvantaged. It is part of affirmative action to support the weaker sections of society. Both public and private sectors are required to ensure that there is no discrimination or differential treatment based on race, gender, caste, etc. in the hiring process.

2. Many firms take special steps to recruit a diverse workforce to conform to their philosophy of social responsibility or altruism.

3. Global competition requires that firms be creative in their approach to hiring talent. A diverse workforce helps the firm to innovate and to expand into new markets.

4. Organizations are facing a shortage of skilled talent. Hiring from non-traditional sources provides them with optional sources of talent and helps them bridge the talent gap. Hiring older workers, women, minorities, and employees with different racial or cultural backgrounds also reflects a response to the demands of the changing demographic situation in most societies across the globe.

5. Organizations sometimes hire a diverse workforce in response to external factors such as image development, public relations, and the pressure to conform because 'everyone else is doing it'.

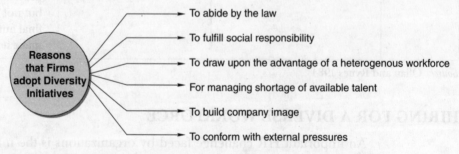

Figure 5.10: Organizational Motives for Adopting Diversity Initiatives

To hire a diverse workforce, organizations need to take specific actions to attract workers from different backgrounds and develop HR programmes to retain them. Certain categories of the workforce, such as women and minorities, may not respond to traditional recruitment efforts because of unequal opportunities in the past. These groups may go completely unrepresented in a typical recruitment process. Therefore, specific actions should be taken to attract these sets of workers. Recruitment programmes should be made more inclusive.

As a first step, a firm should analyse its current recruitment procedures. For example, a firm that recruits primarily from employee referral programmes or unsolicited applications may need to reconsider their use. Most referrals are of candidates who are similar to the existing employees of the firm. For example, an employee may recommend candidates from his alumni network or on the basis of regional or race considerations.

Secondly, firms may use qualified members from these diversity groups in key recruitment activities. For example, a firm may send a female employee for campus recruitment, or portray pictures of women or minority employees in advertisements to lend credence to the firm's claim of being an 'equal opportunity employer' or 'encouraging diversity at the workplace'. The product advertisements of Benetton, the global retail chain, are an example of how they may be used effectively to convey the image of an employer of a diverse workforce.

Several MNCs, such as HLL, Procter & Gamble, Cadbury, and Sony, are breaking the old mindset of treating certain jobs such as sales and marketing as male bastions and are hiring and grooming more women to prepare them for future leadership roles. Global research suggests that a diverse organization leads to more innovation and better performance in the workplace. Hence, gender diversity is a focus area in the Indian context as well. Hindustan Lever Limited is making sure that there are more women in their 'listers' (high-potential employees). Procter & Gamble grooms women performers for top jobs by offering them location-free jobs and roles, extended leave to address personal issues, and flexi-time. Hindustan Lever Limited also supports diversity through its women-friendly work policies. For example, it has a sabbatical policy that lets women managers take up to five years' leave in two intervals; it also lets women to work part-time or consult. Almost 16% of middle management positions are occupied by women. Sony also initiated a gender diversity project to promote the careers of women employees. The company believes that a diverse workforce that appropriately reflects the demographics of a company's consumer base and fulfills their talent needs will keep it competitive and successful.

Though there is a need to recognize workplace diversity issues, it is important to recognize that diversity can be a double-edged sword. Diversity initiatives can lead to significant conflict between employees as well as harm, if not managed strategically. Therefore, when a firm seeks to undertake diversity initiatives, it will do well to answer the following questions.

- Why is diversity important for the organization? A firm may initiate diversity initiatives for a number of reasons, as discussed earlier, but they will be successful if the objective or purpose for adopting these is clearly understood.

- How does diversity relate to the mission and to the strategic objectives of the organization? It is important for the firm to understand how diversity relates to the current state of the organization as well as its intended future direction. For example, if a firm wants to expand its markets internationally, a culturally-diverse workforce can be a facilitating factor. How inclusive will the diversity initiatives be? This relates especially to those minority groups that are not protected from discrimination by law. For example, people who have serious mental illnesses or who abuse drugs may be classified as disabled. However, in the absence of laws providing for equal opportunity for these groups of people, firms do not consider them for employment.

- Should the firm undertake special efforts to attract a diverse workforce? There is a need to analyse the present recruitment sources and methods of the firm. However, this will also depend on whether the firm is adopting affirmative action to redress past discriminatory practices or, alternatively, to treat everyone equally in present and future employment practices and decisions. A firm is likely to adopt more inclusive and intense recruiting efforts when the aim is to make amends for past discrimination.

- How do the current employees feel about diversity? Whenever a new policy or programme is adopted by an organization, it has the potential to disrupt the status quo. This is likely to result in some resistance within the organization. At the same time, these efforts are also closely watched by those outside the firm, such as customers, potential employees, etc. Firms must identify potential obstacles to promoting diversity, such as employee attitude, resistance, cultural factors etc. Adequate and appropriate actions need to be taken to anticipate resistance to diversity actions and manage it. For example, the ongoing debate in India about extending caste-based reservations in jobs to be extended to private sector firms is being met with resistance on the part of industry associations, current managers and employees of these firms, as well as certain sections of the society who are likely to be potential candidates. Further, there are fears being expressed that such reservations may have an adverse impact on the credibility and reputation that Indian firms enjoy in the international business community.

- What specific type(s) of diversity initiatives will be undertaken? The specific initiatives should be consistent with the motive for adopting these initiatives as well as with the strategic objectives of the firm. The firm also needs to address the issue of how much time and money will be invested in these initiatives and how these efforts will be measured for effectiveness.

Diversity is a buzzword today in management circles but one that can be extremely dangerous if adopted as a fad. It is important to understand the factors necessary for the success of diversity efforts.

An important kind of diversity in contemporary business environment is the cultural diversity brought about by a globally diverse workforce. A telecommuting firm in Delhi accesses audio records of doctors' prescriptions from a toll-free number in the US, transcribes them, and delivers the transcribed prescriptions back to the doctor overnight. British Airways tracks frequent-flyer mileage out of Mumbai. Ernst and Young may be filing a company's income tax with an Indian or a European accountant. Coca Cola India has moved several of its managers into global assignments.

As firms scan the globe for the best resources and talent, they manage their talent globally. Apart from the benefit of cost saving, a global workforce can bring additional value to the firm in improved quality, skills, market access, and productivity. The firm can tap the world's best talent and hence needs a holistic approach to managing talent. The HR leadership needs to work with the top leadership of the firm to develop the strategy for sourcing global talent for the firm. The sourcing of talent from across the globe has emerged as a fundamental change in the way business is conducted. Firms need to evolve appropriate HR strategies to ensure the adaptation of employees from different cultural backgrounds. Issues related to global talent are dealt with in greater detail in Chapter 12.

ALTERNATIVES TO HIRING PERMANENT EMPLOYEES

Much of the discussion in this chapter implies that recruitment and selection processes in a firm are designed to locate and hire permanent employees in order to fulfill the HR requirements of a firm. However, environmental trends such as globalization and high competition have created pressure on firms to seek cost advantage. Changes in the business environment have also resulted in management trends such as rightsizing and a re-defined employer–employee relationship. The growing trend of hiring and retaining a contingent workforce was discussed in Chapter 2. In the past two decades, there has been a lot of debate about temporary or contingent workers as alternatives to permanent employees. Many companies are hiring temporary employees. The main goals of hiring a temporary or contingent workforce are staffing flexibility and lower long-term labour cost. Organizations seek to reduce the fixed cost of hiring through these alternative work relationships. However, there are concerns being expressed that these goals often come at the cost of two other important organizational goals—employee productivity and loyalty. Contingent arrangements take the forms of independent contractors, temporary agents, leased employees, temporary help services, re-hiring former employees, and hiring from the non-traditional labour pool (see Figure 5.11).

Independent Contractors

Companies may hire independent contractors, also called consultants, to do specific work for the organization either on-site or off-site. For example, when medical transcription is contracted out, consultants can perform the job at home. The nature of work that is contracted out may range from routine jobs that constitute the non-core activities of the firm to highly specialized jobs for which the firm may lack adequate skills. For example, jobs such as marketing research or payroll administration are often contracted out.

Employee Leasing

This is also called staff sourcing. A firm may lease employees from a leasing company for a fee. When a firm needs certain skills that are not available in-house or are in short supply, it may seek trained employees from the leasing firm. The leased employees are employees of the leasing company which performs all personnel functions for them such as payroll, employee benefits,

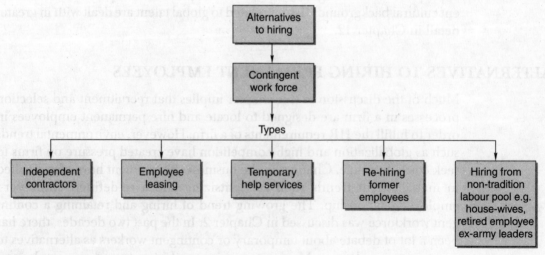

Figure 5.11: Types of Contingent Workers

and other HR functions. The client firm simply pays a fixed fee to the leasing company. Leased employees remain with the client firm for a longer duration than temporary employees. When the project gets over, the leased employees return to the leasing firm. Thus, the client firm saves fixed costs and cost of lay-offs and simultaneously benefits by getting well-trained employees. Firms may lease out cleaning and security services. Skilled workers are also leased by firms. For example, additional tax accountants may be needed by a firm during tax season. Since there is strong fluctuation in the demand for accountants, a firm may not want to hire accountants on a permanent basis. At such times, the firm may lease accountants from an accounting firm. Many firms do not employ workers on jobs such as project implementation; instead, they prefer to employ workers under a third party which takes care of monthly salaries of the employees for a management fee. Some firms which hire in this manner are Tata Iron and Steel Company, Hindustan Zinc, Bharat Heavy Electricals Limited, and Bank of India.

Temporary Help Services

Traditionally, temporary staffing services were seen only as a source of semi-skilled clerical workers. Today, however, temporary services extend to skilled workers such as nurses, programmers, etc. Temporary services provide trained and experienced personnel who can be put to work quickly and also removed. Temporary help firms often specialize in the kind of skills they make available to firms. For example, there are temporary firms providing software engineers. There is also a trend toward hiring stop-gap CEOs. Ma Foi Management Consultants Limited offers the highly specialized service of providing interim managers. Interim managers are highly skilled professionals at or above the rank of functional heads who work with a company on a specific project and then move on. Temporary workers get their salaries from the client firm, unlike leased employees. However, the client firm does not have to pay fringe benefits or provide training to temporaries.

Re-hiring Former Employees

Another option to external recruiting is to hire former employees, although, strictly speaking, it also constitutes recruiting from external sources. However, the cost of re-hiring a former employee is half that of hiring a new person. Re-hires become productive on the job immediately since they are familiar with the firm. Since former employees are familiar entities, the risk of a costly mis-hire is almost completely eliminated. Former employees may also be used as a source of referrals. Some firms offer former employees a reward for referrals who are hired. Agilent Technologies and McKinsey are examples of firms that invest significantly in cultivating and managing the network of and relationships with former employees. Today, less than 5% of the 3,000 engineers graduating from premier Indian Institutes of Technology every year work with the infrastructure sector. Most of these engineering graduates are attracted towards the IT sector. Earlier, Larsen & Toubro, the country's biggest heavy engineering and infrastructure development company, used to attract the best talent. With the boom in the IT sector and very high salaries and performance bonuses, the firm is finding it difficult to hire from campus. In order to fulfill its human resource requirements, the firm revoked the policy against re-hiring former employees, and is getting in touch with former employees who left the company five to ten years ago and are open to returning. Already, about 4% of ex-employees have returned to the firm. Several IT and BPO firms are willing to re-hire former employees. The companies are showcasing employees who have returned to encourage others to follow. This trend of re-hiring former employees is being promoted by firms to appear as an employer of choice. 'Ex-employee' may also refer to retirees of the firm.

Hiring from Non-traditional Labour Pool

Another way in which firms avoid incurring the cost of permanent employees is by hiring from the non-traditional labour pool. Among them are women who are entering the working world at a late age without experience and have no work experience and housewives who are stepping out of their homes in search of a career for the first time or who can work from home. Amway, for example, has successfully tapped this labour market. An MNC bank has retained a consulting agency to recruit over 100 women employees of the above descriptions for part-time permanent jobs. These candidates are expected to have a good command of English and the right attitude. With just a brief orientation, they are able to perform in industries like banking, BPO, etc.

Other non-traditional sources of talent include retired personnel who are willing to work a few hours a day but are not interested in full-time employment. The firm can employ people from these groups when there are seasonal work fluctuations or even for a longer duration, at a lower cost.

Several firms are hiring former defence personnel to serve as independent directors on their boards. While ex-army personnel have traditionally been hired by industry in the HR and security functions, appointing them as directors is a new trend. The qualities for which firms are keen to have former army officers on their board are strategic and tactical thinking ability, experience with high-technology systems and huge logistics and supply chain machinery, operational thinking ability, ability to withstand pressure, high values, leadership skills, and ability to motivate others. An important responsibility of independent directors is the selection of top executives. The defence services are considered to have one of the best selection processes in India, so their officers are believed to be able to judge candidates well. Wipro, Videocon, East India Hotels, Hero Honda, Reliance Energy, Jet Airways, and Ballarpur Industries Limited are some of the firms that have defence personnel on their boards.

Apart from the different types of contingent arrangements, the skill levels of contingent workers may also vary. Contingent workers may be less-skilled or highly-skilled. The highly-skilled contingent workers (SCW) differ from the less-skilled contingent workers in the level of training and education required for a job. Highly-skilled contingent workers perform jobs requiring higher levels of education and experience, such as in the IT industry. Less-skilled contingent workers are clerical workers and manual labourers, whose jobs require less education or experience. Highly-skilled contingent workers work at a firm as long as their skills are required and then move to another firm. Since SCWs are temporary workers and not regular or permanent employees, they are hired without incurring some of the commitments associated with regular employees. Until recently, it was assumed that firms benefit from hiring SCWs because they do not have to pay employee benefits or maintain a long-term employment relationship. It was also assumed that hiring SCWs did not result in any negative reaction from similarly-skilled regular employees because their jobs were secure. Recently, this assumption has been challenged. It has been argued that in organizations where regular employees work alongside SCWs, regular employees may experience inequity because SCWs earn substantially more in direct compensation than they earn in direct and indirect compensation combined. The SCWs are paid a wage premium because of their unique skills, which are not available in the hiring firm, and to compensate for the inconvenience of contingent work, lack of benefits, higher risk of unemployment, and, sometimes, poor working conditions. This premium is called compensating wage differential (CWD). The CWD often makes the direct compensation of SCWs significantly higher than the average employee's total compensation. This results in feelings of inequity on the part of regular employees. In certain situations, the inequity may result in regular employees' quitting the firm, and therefore companies are concerned about retaining their skilled regular employees. If these employees quit the firm, it results in loss of company knowledge and training. It is more difficult to replace highly-skilled regular employees compared to the less-skilled ones. To counteract the effects of hiring SCWs, HR managers of the hiring firm can adopt and implement certain HR approaches to reduce turnover and increase productivity of high-performing regular employees. Some of these approaches are described below.

- Develop systems to enhance organizational commitment of regular employees, such as training leaders to instill loyalty and increase employee commitment.

Table 5.8: Advantages and Disadvantages of Skilled Contingent Workers

Advantages	Disadvantages
■ Most included in benefits programmes ■ Reduce the firm's recruiting and selection costs ■ Allow access to specialized skills without incurring training costs ■ Are easier to dismiss than regular employees ■ Increase companies' ability to hire a flexible workforce that grows and shrinks with product and service cycles ■ Help the company reduce long-term labour costs ■ Help acquire specialized skills that will be too expensive to develop in-house	■ May become a source of information for regular workers about opportunities in external labour market as well as an aid to regular employees for entering contingent employment ■ Firm has little control over contingent employees; this threatens organizational quality standards ■ Compensating wage differentials paid to SCWs results in perceptions of inequity by the regular employees; the latter may leave the firm if SCWs are hired for the long term when these skills may be needed only for a limited time or are skills that change rapidly ■ Provide firms with an opportunity to witness work of potential employees before hiring them as regular employees, and so satisfy a requirement of the hiring strategy of the firm

Source: David 2005

- Focus on work relationships with supervisors to enhance productivity. These can be enhanced significantly by training supervisors to improve these relationships. Relationships with co-workers may be strengthened through employee empowerment, cross-training, participation, decentralization, etc.
- Create ways, such as ESOPs, internal promotions, and skill-based pay, to reduce the probability of employee turnover.

See a synopsis of the advantages and disadvantages of hiring skilled contingent workers at Table 5.8.

Exhibit 5.11

Temporary Staffing

Temporary staffing, or temping, has become common in India over the past few years, especially in the services sector. Since 2000, there has been a significant growth in temporary employees. Insurance, telecom, IT and IteS companies currently employ over 50,000 temps. Global temping majors like Adecco and Vedior, and Indian temporary service firms like Ma Foi, Peopleone Consulting, and Teamlease have over 10,000 employees each on their rolls. In India, the growth of temporary staffing has been driven by the services sector rather than by the manufacturing sector. Globally, it is the industrial segment that accounts for about 70% of temps.

Contd

Exhibit 5.11 Contd

Labour market liquidity, or the ease with which a company can add or remove labour depending on its need, is the key to investment. Temporary staffing firms, who employ temporary workers, offer this flexibility. These firms hire the employees out to other companies for a few months. On the completion of the assignment, the temporary employee is moved to another company by the temporary staffing firm. An assignment may not be followed by another assignment immediately; there may be a break of a couple of months. The temporary worker may even receive statutory benefits like provident fund for the duration of his assignment. Temporary jobs have existed in India for years, but primarily in the unorganized sector; the phenomenon of workers being employed temporarily in the organized sector is new. However, only 5% of the workers in the organized sector are temporary employees; labour laws, which currently stand in the way of a temping boom, need to be modified to extend the benefits of flexi-staffing to manufacturing firms also. A new trend is that of mid- to top-level corporate executives taking on temporary assignments. They are called 'floaters' or 'on-contract hires' and move from one company to another with assignments as short as three to six months. For example, a family-owned business may hire a temporary CEO to fill the gap till the heir apparent takes over the reins. Similarly, a multinational firm might hire a CEO for six months with the mandate to set up its office in India. The trend is more prevalent at the middle level than at the top level. Executives who take temporary assignments are not 'has-beens' or those who 'do not have jobs'; on the contrary, they are most successful in their specific field of activity and are experts to the core. They use temporary assignments as an opportunity to encash on their expertise before they settle down in another job with a long-term commitment. These are typically the executives with the IIT-IIM tag in the age group of late 30s and 40s,

driven by the variety and flexibility in working hours, and the challenge of short deadlines. These executives earn more from temporary assignments than they would in similar permanent jobs. They are also motivated by the desire to spend time with their family without retiring. Firms hire temporary managers at the middle or senior level for certain reasons, which are detailed below.

Subsidiaries of multinational corporations hire floaters because they follow very strict headcount ratios and need to show a significant revenue jump to their parents even if they add a single extra manager or a front-end sales force.

Many companies abroad hire interim managers to reduce their pension liability.

Companies hire temporary workers when the requirement is for a specific project or assignment.

Some firms use the opportunity of a temporary assignment to see if they would like to have a longer association with the executive. These firms put an 'absorption clause' in the contract that provides for the hiring of the executive as a full-time employee after the project ends if both parties wish it.

Sector-wise, IT is the biggest user of temporary managers, because project-specific assignments are far greater in number. The concept is also catching up in the manufacturing sector. In FMCG firms, it is often used for branch or regional managers to achieve a sales target in a short period or for the launch of a product or service. Usually, the process of hiring temporary managers begins with the company's contacting its HR agency, which has a list of floaters who are then deputed for the assignment. The company pays the contract amount to the agency, which pays the manager after keeping its fee. The HR consulting agency may recruit some permanent temporary staff in different domains. Most of them get paid irrespective of the work flow. Client firms who make use of services of these HR agencies are required to pay an honorarium

Contd

Exhibit 5.11 Contd

even when it is not using the services of the agency.

Temporary staffing at senior management and strategic levels is beginning to catch on in India. Temporary managers are on the payroll of various HR agencies. It is believed that increasing attrition rates at top levels in some sectors have triggered this trend. In India, internal interim CEOs have been common. However, now firms are open to having external interim CEOs. While the interim CEO operates like a permanent CEO, he/she is generally hired for a short term, ranging

from three months to two years. The interim CEO is given a clear assignment with a clearly defined tenure specifying start and finish dates. Interim CEOs are used by firms for business turnarounds and restructuring, filling urgent senior- and board-level vacancies, change and culture management, IT systems implementation, programme and project management, new product launches, merger and acquisition management, team development, and crisis management. However, firms in India do not yet like to openly admit that they have an interim CEO.

Source: Sinha and Kant 2004; Ramnath 2005; Goyal and Rajawat 2006

HIRING CONSIDERATIONS IN BPO FIRMS

The dramatic growth of the BPO industry is a worldwide phenomenon. Business process outsourcing firms in India have experienced spectacular growth in the past five years. This rapid growth has also brought managerial challenges with respect to recruitment, staffing, training, and retention of workers and managers with the requisite skills and abilities to provide quality service. The BPO industry is among the largest recruiters in India, hiring over 70,000 people every year. The top 10 BPO firms hire an average of 40,000–48,000 people annually at an expense of Rs 400–480 million. The average cost per hire in the BPO sector is approximately Rs 10,000–12,000. At the current growth rate of 50% per year, the BPO industry is expected to double its employee strength every two years. The employee costs of IT and BPO firms have risen by 41% over the fiscal year 2005–2006. Almost 35–40% of the revenue of IT firms goes into workforce costs. Attrition for the top IT majors has risen by 2–3% in 2005–2006. Let us look at some issues related to recruitment and selection faced by the BPO industry.

Skill Requirements

Flawless verbal communication and service orientation are the most important skills required in call centres. At the time of selection, agents/associates go through voice/accent, language, and typing speed tests. The organization structures of call centres change rapidly and new roles keep getting created. Processes such as loans, stock trade, and insurance claims offer high-end jobs because they require risk profiling, analysis of credit limits and creditworthiness of customers, and decision-making skills. For these jobs, BPO firms hire

MBA graduates and accountants. For the technology help desk, firms hire engineers, science graduates, and those with Microsoft certification. High-end BPOs employ post-graduates. Evalueserve recruits from the IIMs, IITs, FMS, and XLRI. Their talent pool comprises MBA graduates, chartered accountants, doctors, and lawyers.

Inducements Offered

To attract and retain talent, BPO companies are taking several measures, such as paying higher base salaries, night shift, and overtime allowances; and offering cash and non-cash incentives to employees. The variable cash component in the salary is based on performance and offered across all levels. Non-cash incentives include company-sponsored education policy, health/life/accident insurance, free transport, subsidized meals and free concierge services that employees can use to pay their telephone, electricity bills, and insurance policy payments. Firms also maintain help-desks for discounted loans, free credit cards, and for filing tax returns. Business process outsourcing firms are also offering skill allowances that take into account criticality (size/training) and complexity (error tolerance level/process complexity). Skill allowances may range up to Rs 2,400 per month. Performance bonuses are also paid.

External Labour Market

Many companies are facing skill shortages and facing extreme difficulty in finding candidates with either back-office or call centre experience. Since the back-office and customer care industry is fairly new in many emerging economies, the availability of supervisory and/or managerial candidates is often quite limited. This is because people have had limited opportunities to obtain the experience that is traditionally necessary to handle a second- or third-level managerial position. It is expected that the industry will need about 300,000 managers and supervisors by 2008. That is about 30% more than the entire industry today. This suggests that every single individual in the BPO industry today can become a supervisor within four years, and that there will still be a shortage of executive talent. For many companies, these labour shortages are driving firms to hire employees away from other organizations, often using higher wages and signing bonuses as the primary lures to attract workers from other firms. The industry is also likely to recruit from a number of related industries and professions. such as accounting and financial services and customer service (hotels, airlines, etc.). However, the BPO industry will also seek to meet the demand from the internal labour market by identifying good performers and promoting them up the ladder more rapidly than normal.

Until recently, software and BPO companies in India had developed in clusters like Bangalore, Gurgaon/NCT region, and Mumbai/Pune. Some companies are realizing that large clusters in a single location or region may be harmful since it leads to higher attrition, battle for talent, and puts pressure on the city's infrastructure. Firms cannot afford the knowledge loss (due to high training costs), nor can they continue to increase salary (since the basic premise of offshoring is the low-cost advantage). They have found the solution in de-urbanization, or shifting from metros to smaller, Tier II cities like Hyderabad, Chennai, Kolkata, Chandigarh, Ludhiana, etc. Business process outsourcing companies will move to towns that will have better educational infrastructure to ensure supply of workforce. The main reason for moving to smaller cities is the difficulty in retaining talent in metropolitan cities in the face of increasing scarcity of skilled personnel. Dell International Services (DIS) has set up a centre in Chandigarh. Wipro is planning to move into cities like Mangalore, Mysore, Kochi, Vishakapatnam, and Goa. Wipro has started identifying towns and cities where it can build IT development centres or BPO service centres. Some cities are more suitable for BPO firms than for IT companies. The reason is that BPO companies require graduates with either language skills or financial and other process-related skills. On the other hand, IT firms require engineering or science graduates who can be trained in programming. Though Goa does not have a high talent base, migration to the state is much more likely from the metros due to its climate, beaches, and international environment. This does not hold true for cities like Mysore or Vishakapatnam.

Some organizations are looking at the global labour market and targetting expatriates as an important source of talent. One US-based MNC has a 'return home' programme that targets individuals who were educated in the US and worked with it there for a number of years. By seeking out employees, often with young families, who are looking to return to their native countries, firms can retain talented employees and have corporate talent migrate to their operations in emerging economies. Spouses of expatriates and US retirees who are interested in part-time work may also be a good source. Both programmes are aimed at individuals who have a combination of work experience and strong English language skills and are interested in working in a new and dynamic work environment.

Government Policies

This is an external environmental factor that may affect the hiring effectiveness of a firm. The government's proposals, to increase reservation in elite educational institutions, and to impose job quotas in the private sector, have resulted in certain apprehensions in the BPO sector. According to players in the BPO industry, there is already a dearth of qualified workers, and any additional restriction on who to hire is likely to worsen the situation. Further,

BPO firms are required to perform according to global standards. Hence, irrespective of caste, creed, etc., firms seek employees who meet global standards. The top management of the BPO industry is in support of affirmative action and feel that companies should make efforts to hire candidates from backward classes and deprived communities, but they should be given the freedom to hire a candidate with suitable skills, rather than being forced to hire someone who is not good at work. During selection interviews in BPO firms, caste-related information is neither asked for nor stored in the employee database. Hence, employees belonging to OBC and SC/ST communities are currently employed not because of their caste, but because of their merit.

Recruitment Methods

The sheer number of potential candidates often places limitations on the capacity of firms to screen and evaluate the candidates. Yet, despite the large number of candidates, the ability to hire the right employees for potentially stressful, customer service positions remains critical. To address the problem of hiring a few employees from many candidates, employment agencies often conduct the initial screening, evaluating candidates on a variety of dimensions including voice, problem-solving capabilities, teamwork skills, the ability to work within a Western-style organization, and computer literacy, to name a few. However, the final interviews and decisions often remain with the hiring company.

Business process outsourcing firms are trying to meet the challenge of keeping hiring costs to a minimum through the use of new recruitment methods, such as job portals on the internet, walk-ins, career offers on homepages of company websites, and employee referrals. Referrals are the most popular method; companies pay cash incentives to employees who refer potential hires. Referral hiring costs are half that of traditional hiring methods like advertisements or third-party hiring firms. While recruiting bonuses may provide a short-term incentive, employees may want to demonstrate to peers and families the 'validity' of their new profession. By recruiting others to work in the same location and industry, employees are able to demonstrate that call centre and back-office work is not only financially rewarding but also socially acceptable. Progeon, the BPO outfit of Infosys, is experimenting with several innovative methods that will bring the right candidate to the firm. One method is called the 'campus ambassador programme', where an identified student in a college gets a thorough briefing on the BPO industry—how it works, the career path it offers, its future growth opportunities—and on Progeon. The student then spreads the word about the industry and the company to peers in the college. This reduces hiring costs.

Campus Recruitment

Campus recruitment is an integral part of the recruitment strategy of BPO firms, as it allows access to a large pool of candidates. In many countries, on-campus recruiting at the university level is just beginning to be used to attract potential employees. While less valuable in high-growth markets that require large numbers of candidates in a short time-frame, university relations can help attract a regular volume of candidates, particularly in markets where foreign language skills are important. Managers in BPO firms suggest that the government should set up institutes where candidates, irrespective of their caste, can be trained, and hired from. Dell International Services, which has a centre in Chandigarh, has recently partnered with the Chandigarh administration to train potential employees in skills relevant to the BPO industry under the Chandigarh Training on Soft Skills (C-TOSS) programme. To make students industry-ready and employable immediately on graduation, the IteS industry has developed programmes for long-term partnership with educational institutions. These programmes include providing training to the teaching community on various aspects of the BPO industry and introducing optional subjects in teaching curricula. For example, 24/7 Customer recently launched its education programme called '24/7 Varsity' in Andhra Pradesh, designed for lecturers and professors of educational institutions to equip students to leverage career opportunities in the BPO industry. In the first phase of this programme, English professors from over 25 colleges in Tier II cities of Andhra Pradesh were trained on various facets of communication. Other campus recruiting activities include guest lectures at universities, centre tours, and mentoring efforts. Overall, campus recruiting appears to be an emerging method for attracting candidates for call centre and back-office work in many locations.

Selection Methods

Global firms are outsourcing processes that involve sensitive information about credit cards, bank accounts, and insurance policies and give employees of BPO firms direct access to customer assets and, therefore, the potential to steal them. Recent incidents like fraud at Mphasis' Pune operations have raised the issue of data security and protection and brought new dimensions to the selection process of the BPO industry by increasing the sensitivity of companies towards employee selection, psychological profiling, as well as socio-behavioural risk assessment.

Psycho-profiling is not a new idea. It has been a part of industry selection procedures. Firms in BPO are now planning to use psychologists to adminis-ter tests to candidates and judge the likelihood of their committing a crime on the job. These are called the 'G' tests, where 'G' stands for greed. These G tests classify persons who test negative on aspects like handling data and managing boundaries as threats. However, tests that can establish criminal intent or state of mind of a potential employee also need to be developed, and they have to take into account many socio-economic and other conditions. With incidents such as an employee of a BPO firm being caught selling sensitive information to an undercover journalist in 2005, and the arrest of another employee in September 2005 for allegedly stealing data, assessment of behavioural risks has gained currency.

Socio-behavioural risks were not paid any attention in the initial wave of outsourcing to India. However, firms are now approaching consultancy organizations for socio-economic and behavioural assessment of employees at BPOs and call centres while offshoring/outsourcing work to India. Through this method of risk assessment, these firms seek to predict employees' attitude towards protecting confidential information and probability of giving in to pressure. Firms also ask their consultants to check the credentials, including criminal records, of employees who are likely to work on a project. Consultancy firms are being asked to make an assessment of the likelihood of data theft in BPOs as well as crime and conviction rate in cities where work will be done to get an idea of overall risk.

Frequent hiring by the IteS and BPO firms makes it difficult for them to obtain all the essential information about the candidates. In most BPO firms, an interview lasts for an average of 4–7 minutes, which is extremely inadequate to know the person. Most companies conduct checks on employees by doing a five-year police track record search, a financial background check from the regulatory bodies, and a reference check from past employees.

However, there is evidence of high incidence of resume fraud in the BPO industry, which has increased the significance of pre-employment screening. As many firms have migrated from BPO to high-end knowledge process outsourcing (KPO), they have raised the hiring standards since KPO needs higher skills. The change in hiring standards is one reason for the increasing incidence of resume fraud by aspirants for BPO jobs. A Hill and Associates Survey reveals that 56% of the candidates provided false information at the hiring stage, 2% provided incorrect details about both education and employment, and more than 4% candidates gave false education-related credentials. There were discrepancies in the employment details of around 18% of candidates, and in several cases candidates gave mobile numbers that were hard to track. The most common misrepresentations in resumes were about work history and additional skill sets to enhance their chances of being hired. It is also possible to provide fake certificates and degrees.

To counter these frauds, BPO firms are hiring specialized agencies called pre-employment screening (PES) service providers to check the background and references of prospective employees. These service providers check personality, expertise, people skills, attitude, and beliefs with previous employers, peers, and friends; verify academic and professional qualifications with educational institutions; and look for social credentials such as dowry indictments, alcoholism, and sexual harassment claims. In some cases, they monitor employees after employment as well. Earlier, BPO firms resorted to selective checks only, but now they conduct checks on all prospective employees. These background checks have raised recruitment costs by about 15%. For example, iGate Global Solutions, a Hyderabad based technology and operations firm, pays about US$300–400 per person for carrying out checks on applications. Technology-intensive MNCs in security and risk analysis, banking, and finance are relying on third-party PES service providers. The phenomenon is spreading across sectors due to globalization. Pre-employment screening is a legal requirement in other countries, though not in India. The trend is catching up in India as many IT and IteS jobs are being created in India, and because of the limitations of 'reference checks'. Some firms have their HR teams work closely with screening agencies to double-check bona fide certificates and references. Firms are also hiring detectives to do an impartial background scrutiny, in addition to the first-level checks by their own recruitment teams. More recently, companies are approaching universities as well as police departments for verification requests. Universities and police departments charge a fee to provide the necessary information.

The incidents of data theft by some employees of Indian BPO firms has led the National Association of Software and Services Companies (NASSCOM) to propose a national registry of BPO and call centre employees. This registry will be a database of trained and certified personnel and trainers for the IteS/IT industry maintained by a common national body and will be shared with industry players as required, and run by a third party for a 'marginal fee'. The database is being prepared by National Securities Depository Limited (NDSL). It will include employment background and biometrics details like fingerprints as well as details like police checks and photographs. This registry, when ready, will allow the details of BPO employees across the country to be available at the click of a mouse. However, employees have the option of refusing to be in the registry. The database will supplement background and reference checks since they have traditionally not been very useful. Besides curbing electronic crimes by listing 'history-sheeters' of the industry, the list is also expected to help curb attrition by pointing out frequent movers.

The National Association of Software and Services Companies has taken a quality control initiative that is likely to change the hiring process of BPO firms. It has proposed a single national-level examination for entry-level jobs at BPO firms to replace the tests they give. The examination, called 'NASSCOM Assessment of Competence' (NAC), shall be given online and shall test the aptitude of candidates on different skill sets. The NAC shall build a supply of the IteS/BPO workforce that shall be certified and available to meet the present and future requirements of the industry. Though the proposal is still in the pilot stage, all the big names in the industry such as Genpact, Convergys, Progeon, Wipro, ICICI One Source, etc. have already signed up with NASSCOM for using NAC. The NAC shall be made mandatory if its pilot succeeds.[1] It is expected that companies will benefit from this since hiring costs will go down significantly because the recruitment process will be shorter and training requirements will be reduced. It is also likely to standardize hiring benchmarks. The efforts of NASSCOM are expected to result in the prescription of a profile of the 'successful BPO employee'.

Hiring Process

Another challenge faced by the BPO industry is to make the hiring process smoother and faster. Effectively managing the entire hiring process—scouting for talent, attracting prospective employees to job opportunities, and bringing them on board while keeping a tight watch on cost—is becoming similar to the way successful manufacturing firms identify suppliers, source raw material, and produce goods. For example, Accenture treats hiring as a scientific method and not as a functional process. In the BPO industry, the conventional process, in which one team conducts the entire process from sourcing CVs to fixing interviews to meeting candidates till getting people into the company, is not practicable. Hence, Accenture has divided the hiring process into three activities: (1) generate CVs; (2) take candidates through multiple stages of assessments; and (3) measure the recruiting process on key matrices.

Quality of Hires

The BPO industry hires in large numbers and faces high attrition. It is a challenge to find the right kind of personnel in such large numbers and to hire them. The high demand for and the urgency of hiring people that characterize BPO firms has resulted in many firms compromising on their selection process and criteria. The degree of selectivity employers practise is an indicator of their attempt to compete on the basis of quality service. The 'select rate' is the percentage of the total pool of applicants that is hired. The lower the select rate, the more selective the employer is in hiring new applicants. The industry average of the interview-to-hire ratio varies between 100:8 and 100:12 for the voice business and between 100:12 and 100:16 for the non-voice

---

[1] NASSCOM planned to start administering the NAC in November 2006, according to a NASSCOM press release, http://www.nasscom.in/Nasscom/templates/NormalPage.aspx?id=50359, accessed on 3 November 2006.

business. The interview-to-hire ratio is also called the yield ratio. The yield ratio of 100:8 for new hires suggests that out of every 100 candidates who turn up for a walk-in interview, only about eight are worth hiring. Call centres serving global customers hire one of every ten applicants on an average while those serving domestic customers hire one of every four. This suggests that global call centres are considerably more selective in hiring than domestic call centres. The select rate is highly influenced by labour market conditions. The rapid growth of call centres in India has caused demand to outstrip supply and the select rate to be relatively high.

To meet the huge demand for people, some firms have devised a novel method of meeting its requirements. Firms like 3Global and Wipro BPO are hiring people through pre-hiring training (PHT). Pre-hiring training is for those applicants who did not clear the selection process but are likely to meet hiring requirements if trained. Firms believe that such borderline candidates tend to be more loyal. The duration of PHT is for a minimum of two weeks, but may extend to two months. During the PHT, the candidates are paid a small stipend. Training of borderline candidates focusses on improving communication skills (grammatical skills, written English, and spoken English) and computer skills (using a computer to sort data, typing speed, and basic knowledge about different software packages). At the end of the training, the skills of these candidates have to be at par with those who were hired in the first instance. These candidates get the final offer of employment only after they clear another round of interviews. Firms are using PHT to hire at least 50% of the candidates they reject in the first instance.

The IBM Institute for Business Value conducted a research study to understand opportunities and unique human capital cost challenges faced by companies in relocating a number of business processes to lower wage countries. One of the messages that came across clearly is the importance of addressing HR issues as part of the strategy for locating a service centre. First, companies need to understand the composition of local labour markets in terms of their size, education levels, and the availability of language skills. While there may be large labour pools, those with specific language capabilities or managerial skills may be in relatively short supply.

Companies also need to review their experience in managing existing operations and their corporate reputation in the area. An existing local presence, even in a non-related line of business, can have a strong positive impact on recruiting new employees, retaining existing talent, and attracting in-house expatriates. Finally, companies need to be cognizant of the overall business environment, which includes the current regulatory structure, tax incentives, the role of organized labour, and the transportation infrastructure. There is currently little direct involvement of government and organized labour in the BPO industry, but as it matures, additional scrutiny could be placed on issues such as working conditions, contractor benefits, and exit decisions. Local employment laws and practices may govern or limit the combined use of contractors and regular employees performing similar activities. There exist challenges of recruiting and selecting employees for call centres in emerging economies.

Summary

The chapter discussed the context of the increasing importance of human resource acquisition strategies. The objectives of and differences between recruitment and selection activities were highlighted. The role of environmental factors, both internal and external, in determining the success of a firm's efforts to recruit and select a candidate was discussed. The internal and external sources and methods of recruiting qualified individuals were examined. The chapter also presented a general discussion of various selection methods a firm may use for gathering information about job applicants to select the 'best' candidate. New approaches being used by firms for recruitment and selection were also discussed. These included e-recruitment, contest hiring, competency-based approach to selection, and person-culture fit approach, among others. Various stages of the staffing process—clarifying the hiring philosophy, recruitment planning, developing the recruitment strategy, searching for and screening applicants, gathering data about applicants, making the final selection offer, and evaluating the staffing process—were illustrated. The chapter also outlined the different approaches to making selection decisions as well as the types of selection outcomes.

The importance of the strategic alignment of recruitment and selection activities was emphasized. Miles and Snow's typology of business strategies was used to illustrate the linkages between business strategy on one hand and recruitment and selection activities on the other. The chapter acknowledged the challenge of hiring for a diverse workforce. The specific issues confronted by firms when they adopt diversity initiatives and also how they can manage these issues were explored. When a firm faces talent shortage, hiring more permanent workers may be the most obvious response, though not always the best or most preferred one. Different types of contingent or alternative work arrangements that firms may enter into were discussed. These include independent contractors, employee leasing, temporary help services, re-hiring former employees, and hiring from the non-traditional labour pool. The chapter also examined the advantages and disadvantages of hiring skilled contingent workers. The chapter ended with an insight into the special hiring issues faced by the BPO industry and its response to these issues.

Keywords

Acquisition of Human Resources is the process by which a firm hires employees to ensure that the required number and types of employees are available to perform organizational activities successfully and accomplish organizational objectives.

Compensating Wage Differential (CWD) is the wage premium paid to skilled contingent workers as compensation for bringing unique abilities not available in the hiring firm and for the lack of

benefits, higher risk of unemployment, and, sometimes, poor working conditions.

Competency-based Approach to Selection is an objective approach to recruitment and selection, and seeks to match candidate competencies to the requirements of the situation in making the selection decision by focussing on observable behaviours.

E-recruitment is the use of the internet to find jobs (web searching) and recruit candidates (web recruiting).

Employee Leasing, also called 'staff sourcing', is the leasing of trained employees of the leasing company to the client firm for a specific period when certain skills are not available in-house or are in short supply for a fee.

Employer Branding is the process by which organizations make themselves attractive to prospective candidates and involves the intersection of the principles of marketing and brand-building and the rigour of HR practices.

Employment Agencies are agencies that help individuals at the middle level or below find job opportunities and also help organizations search for candidates.

Executive Search Firms recruit top-level executives for client firms on a retainership basis.

Independent Contractors, also called consultants, are hired by firms to do specific work on-site or off-site.

Inside Moonlighting is the performance of additional work that arises occasionally in a firm by its employees.

Job Boards are websites that let employers to post jobs and search for candidates.

Person–Organization Fit is the fit between the individual's personality and the cultural values of an organization.

Person–Job Fit seeks to match the skills and characteristics of an employee with those required for performing the job successfully and which are provided for in the job specification.

Psychometric Tests are designed to measure one or more psychological attributes of individuals, like interests, aptitude, ability, personality, etc. to help employers predict how the candidate might behave in a particular team or situation, relate to others, and approach and solve problems.

Recruitment is the process of discovering potential candidates and of generating a pool of qualified applicants by encouraging qualified candidates to apply for actual or anticipated job vacancies in the organization.

Recruitment Methods are specific means of attracting potential employees to the firm.

Recruitment Sources are the locations where qualified individuals can be found.

Selection is the process of gathering information about job applicants and using it to make hiring decisions by predicting which job applicants, if hired, will perform the job successfully and which ones will not.

Skilled Contingent Workers (SCW) are temporary workers who perform jobs requiring high education, experience, and training.

Staffing is the process of finding, attracting, and hiring new employees.

Virtual Hiring is the use of video conferencing by firms to hire candidates when they cannot meet.

Websumes are webpages or blogs that candidates set up and use to 'sell' their candidacy for jobs.

Yield Ratio is the relationship between the number of applicants at one step of the hiring process relative to the number of people who move to the next step.

Concept Review Questions

1. Define the terms 'recruitment' and 'selection'. Describe the linkage between business strategy and the effectiveness of the recruitment and selection process.
2. What factors in the external environment place limitations on the ability of a firm to recruit and select a candidate of choice? Give examples.
3. Discuss the advantages and disadvantages of recruiting internally versus externally. List and briefly discuss any two external methods of recruitment.

4. Discuss how the internet has changed the way companies recruit. Enumerate the advantages and disadvantages of e-recruitment.

5. Explain the competency-based approach to selection. Why has this approach gained importance in the current business environment?

6. Discuss the relative merits of person-job fit and person-organization fit. Why do firms today hire for 'culture fit'?

7. Briefly discuss the various stages of the staffing process.

8. Discuss any two forms of contingent work arrangements that provide the firm with alternatives to permanent hiring. What are the pros and cons of hiring contingent workers?

Critical Thinking Questions

1. Have organizations changed the way they hire from educational campuses? What factors have led to these changes? Discuss the innovations that have been introduced in campus hiring in recent times, citing examples. Critically evaluate the campus placement strategy and process followed by any two organizations that visit your campus. Can it be said that these organizations had 'successful recruiting experience' in your campus? What criteria did you use to make this judgement?

2. What do you understand by the term 'diversity'? Which groups of employees constitute a diverse workforce? What initiatives can a firm adopt to attract and retain a diverse workforce? Enumerate the reasons that firms adopt diversity initiatives. Give examples of diversity initiatives of some firms you are familiar with. Do you think diversity is a double-edged sword? Why?

Simulation and Role Play

1. Go through daily newspapers, business magazines, or special editions of newspapers carrying advertisements for job vacancies. Select two recruitment advertisements, one traditional and one contemporary. Identify and compare the features of the two types of advertisements. Also check the websites, if any, of these two firms.

   • Did you find the new contemporary advertisement to be more creative? Why?

   • Do you think the new advertisement creates a positive image of the company and results in 'employer branding'?

   • Describe the online recruiting process followed by these firms. Compare and evaluate the effectiveness of online recruitment process of each of these firms.

   • Which of these firms is likely to be more successful in hiring quality talent? Why?

2. A leading software firm has recently faced high employee turnover at the middle management level. Most of those who left this firm moved across industries for better pay as well as faster career progression. The firm is at the moment scouting for a general manager (projects). The firm had approached a placement agency. The agency shortlisted five candidates. Mr Biswas, the HR manager, screened out three candidates, and is not too satisfied with the other two candidates either. Mr Biswas is meeting Mr Singh, vice president (projects) to discuss the candidates shortlisted by the placement agency and to explore other possibilities.

   Two students should volunteer for this role play. One assumes the role of the vice president (projects) and the other that of the HR manager. The discussion should begin with Mr Biswas's apprising Mr Singh of the shortlist of candidates forwarded by the placement agency. Mr Singh wonders what options the firm has in order to fill the vacancy with a qualified candidate and in good time. The two will discuss the pros and cons of using the placement agency for recruitment. Exploring various recruitment methods and their pros and cons, the two should finally agree on one or a combination of recruitment methods. The role play should be followed by a class discussion to evaluate the potential usefulness of a placement agency as a tool for recruitment. The instructor should also steer the discussion to explore the most suitable method of recruitment in this case. The class should also be encouraged to discuss the pros and cons of hiring a temporary manager in a software firm.

Classroom Projects

1. The objective of this exercise is to help students understand the factors that should be taken into consideration in developing a recruitment strategy. The exercise is introduced to the class by clarifying its objectives. The class divides into groups of four or five. A brief lecture is given to students about the decisions that need to be made when developing the recruitment strategy. Each group is assigned the task of developing a recruitment strategy for one of the following organizations: the Indian Armed Forces, a BPO firm in a metropolitan city, a luxury hotel in a hill station, a retail firm, and a central university. Groups make assumptions about various aspects, such as the external environmental factors, target employee group for which the strategy is being developed, their level in the hierarchy, and so on. Each group prepares and presents a report followed by a general discussion led by the instructor. The discussion should centre on the factors each group took into consideration while developing the strategy and why. Attention may also be drawn to how recruitment strategy may differ across different types of organizations and why.

Field Projects

The objective of this project is to help students gain an insight into the various hiring issues of the BPO industry. Students form groups of three or four. Each group chooses two BPO firms, one Indian and one international, for a field visit, and interviews the HR managers to obtain information related to various hiring issues. Four or five line managers in each of these organizations may also be interviewed to understand their perception of staffing practices and major hiring challenges confronting these firms. Students are encouraged to read the section on 'Hiring Considerations in BPO Firms' as well as newspapers and business magazine reports on the BPO industry to get a general idea. Each group prepares a report on major hiring issues that confront the BPO industry in general, and the firms they visited in particular. The group must also include in the report their recommendations for enhancing the effectiveness and efficiency of the hiring process (recruitment and selection) in the BPO industry. The instructor may ask each group to make a class presentation of their reports. The presentations may be followed by a class discussion on the issue led by the instructor.

Case Study

Hiring for Excellence at Cisco Systems

Background
Cisco Systems Inc. was founded in 1984 by Leonard Bosack and Sandy Lerner, a husband-and-wife team working in computer operations at Stanford University. They invented a technology to link the separate computer systems at Stanford. Cisco's

products enable computers to communicate with each other, offering customers end-to-end network solutions. Cisco has been at the heart of many historic changes in technology. The company helped catalyse the industry's move toward internet protocols and is now at the centre of fundamental changes in the way the world communicates; it is the worldwide leader in networking for the internet. It is leading the transition to a network-centric technology environment. Almost 14 billion devices will be connected to the internet by 2010. As the network evolves into a platform, users will be able to communicate from any device and in whatever mode they choose.

A $12 billion high-technology company, Cisco went public in 1990. Its revenue growth has been nearly a hundredfold in seven years. It is the fastest-growing company of its size in history, faster even than Microsoft, with a market capitalization of over $200 billion. Cisco competes in markets where hardware is obsolete in 18 months and software in six. Cisco's stock has risen roughly 50,000 percent during the decade between 1990 and 2000. In fiscal 2005, Cisco achieved record performance across almost all financial and operational metrics and generated $7.6 billion in cash. The annualized revenue per employee, a measure of productivity, was approximately $700,000 in 2005, up from approximately $450,000 in fiscal 2001. This is significant given that the firm also increased headcount in fiscal 2005 by 12 percent, primarily in sales. Cisco is one of America's great success stories.

Cisco's Leadership, Culture, and Values

John Chambers, Cisco's CEO, has an energetic, self-effacing manner; 'my definition of leadership is, don't ask someone else to do something you wouldn't do'. John Chambers' kindness is never mistaken for weakness. Three things that can get someone fired at Cisco are (1) not producing business results; (2) not recruiting and developing the right people; and (3) not being a team player. Cisco defines its mission to 'be the supplier of choice by leading all competitors in customer satisfaction, product leadership, market share, and profitability'.

Its business purpose is 'to shape the future of global networking by creating unprecedented opportunities and value for our customers, employees, partners, and investors'. Cisco's culture was founded on the principles of open communication, empowerment, trust, integrity, and giving back to the community. These same values thrive at Cisco today.

Cisco espouses five core values: (1) dedication to customer success; (2) innovation and learning; (3) partnerships; (4) teamwork; and (5) doing more with less. Each of these values is continually articulated and reinforced in the mission statement, current initiatives, policies and practices, and culture of the company. Not many companies take their culture as seriously as Cisco in managing the business and in hiring. Ross Fowler faced 18 interviews before he was hired as managing director, Australia. Many of these interviews were conducted to ensuring that the culture and values fit between Cisco and Fowler was good. Cisco sees it as a two-way process; both company and candidate are encouraged to assess each other. According to Fowler, the key elements of Cisco's culture are having stretch goals, fun, teamwork, the ability to drive change, and giving back to the community. Cisco values the ability to sense when the market has moved and the ability to adapt accordingly very highly. The single most important value at Cisco is competence—one has to be good at what one does—and is enforced more by peer pressure than by management. If one cannot do one's work, one gets pushed out fairly quickly. Another important value is frugality; all Cisco employees, from the top down, always fly economy class. This is to ensure that the value is delivered to the shareholder. However, frugality at Cisco is not about being cheap, but about getting the 'best value'.

Cisco's values are considered very important for continued success. Therefore, its HR group ensures that the culture is aligned with the business strategy and continually reinforced. Talk about the culture is backed up by actions. A range of mechanisms is used to reinforce values. 'All hands' meetings are held quarterly to communicate the company values and to ensure that everyone feels included. The culture and values are also emphasized in communications through the company intranet. Important events are delivered to the desktop computers of employees. Attempts are made to create an exciting environment, characterized by high levels of motivation, empowerment, and recognition. Cisco has parties, including a Christmas bash with 100 food stations and entertainment. They also provide other employee services, such as onsite stores, dry cleaning services, fitness centres, ATMs, automobile oil changes, and mobile dental clinics with appointments made via e-mail.

Decentralization is encouraged. Employees do not have to take permission on every little thing. At Cisco, senior management gets cubicles in the centre of the fluorescent-lit space while employees get the windows. All offices are of the same size. Consistent with its emphasis on people management, the company was ranked 24th on *Fortune's* list of the '100 Best Companies to Work for in America' in 1999, and was ranked fourth on *Fortune's* list of America's most admired companies in 2000.

People at Cisco

In 1999, the company had more than 26,000 employees operating in over 54 countries; in 2005, 38,056; and today, more than 47,000. Women who were vice presidents or even more senior numbered 33 at last count. Cisco has a voluntary attrition rate among employees of about 8%, much lower than the average 30% employee turnover at Silicon Valley. Working with Cisco is an experience in itself. Its employees believe that 'It's addictive to work for Cisco. It can take over your life if you let it'. Cisco employees are always smiling, because it is a great place to work and they are all getting rich from stock options.

Recruitment and Selection

Effective recruiting can be a powerful strategic weapon. Developing innovative sources to find the best people is just as important as the selection process. The challenge is not only hiring the right people, but to find them before the competitor. Cisco is known for its non-traditional recruiting methods. To attract the highest calibre people, Cisco's recruiting team targets what they call passive job seekers—people who are happy and successful where they are—because the most sought-after employees are not very accessible. As Barbara Beck, vice president for human resources, says they 'usually are not cruising through the "want ads"'.

For the past several years, Cisco has averaged over 1,000 new hires every three months, an achievement by any standard, since Silicon Valley is one of the tightest job markets in the US. The recruiting team at Cisco first identified the kind of people they needed to hire, their ideal recruitment targets. They then held focus groups with the ideal recruitment targets, such as senior engineers and marketing professionals from competitors. Through these focus groups, the recruiting team found out where these people spent their time and how they hunted jobs. The team then innovated a hiring process that reached these potential applicants through a variety of routes not usually used in recruiting, such as infiltrating art fairs and microbrewery festivals and other places they frequented. Silicon Valley's annual home and garden show has been a particularly fruitful venue. The first-time homebuyers that the event attracts also tend to be young achievers at successful high-technology companies. Cisco recruiters work the crowd, collecting business cards from prospects, and speaking with them informally about their careers.

Cisco continues to place newspaper help-wanted advertisements, but rather than listing specific job openings, the advertisements feature its internet address and an invitation to apply. Beck notes that Cisco is a high-technology company and 'if you don't leverage the technology, you won't be able to leverage HR's capabilities'. On the internet, it can post hundreds of job openings inexpensively and lots of information about each one. The website has a built-in monitor that measures important aspects of its recruiting programmes, such as the number of visits to its site. Since most prospects visit the website from their workplaces, the company can even tell where they work.

Besides this, Beck also notes, that the top 10% of the highest-performing employees are not typically found in the first round of layoffs from other companies. Moreover, the top performers are not likely to be usually cruising through the 'want ads'. Therefore, the strategy for recruiting the high performers relies heavily on the internet.

E-recruiting at Cisco

The company's website (http://www.cisco.com/jobs) has become a turbo-charged recruiting tool. An individual looking for a job at Cisco can search by keyword to match one's skills with the job openings. One can also file a resume or create one online using Cisco's resume builder. By monitoring the website, the recruitment team realized that their jobs page recorded over 500,000 hits per month, with the heaviest load occurring between 10 am and 2 pm. This meant that people were looking for jobs on company time. To help facilitate this practice, Cisco is developing software to make life easy for stealthy job-seekers. It will let users click on pull-down menus and profile themselves in 10 minutes. If the boss walks by, users can hit a button that activates a screen disguise, changing it to 'Gift List for Boss and Workmates' or 'Seven Successful Habits of a Great Employee'. The website has caused 30–50% of all resumes to be submitted electronically and routed automatically into a database that can be accessed immediately.

The website actively targets passive job seekers by making it fun and easy to match personal skills and interests to job openings. Through focus groups, Cisco sought to learn how happily employed people could be enticed to interview for a job. The firm goes beyond technology. Focus group results showed that referrals from friends were a powerful factor in the job search process. The response 'I'd do it if a friend told me he had a better opportunity at Cisco than I have at my current employer' caused Cisco to launch an initiative— the 'friends' programme—to help prospects make a friend at Cisco who could describe what it was

like to work there. The Friends programme on Cisco's website involves potential recruits by allowing them to pair up with a volunteer 'friend' from within the company. Cisco establishes connection with a potential employee on their website. Their 'Make Friends @ Cisco' button begins the process of establishing an 'e-mail pal'. The objective is to connect potential recruits to real people in the company. The recruits are then swept into the recruiting pipeline. Cisco employees are matched with people who have approached the company as prospects and who have similar backgrounds and skills. They then call these prospects, or 'visitors' as they are called at Cisco, to tell them in their own words about life at the company. The new friend teaches the visitor about Cisco, introduces the visitor to the right people, and leads the visitor through the hiring process.

It works like this. A designer of printed circuit boards clicked on the 'Make Friends @ Cisco' button at the website. She received a call from a printed circuit board designer at Cisco, the volunteer friend, who talked about life at Cisco. The volunteer referred her to his boss and a few days later she visited Cisco. After five interviews, she accepted a job, even though she had been with her earlier firm 11 years and was not really looking to leave. Having a 'friend' made the difference. When a recruit is invited to visit the company, the volunteer friend/host may pick the recruit up at the airport, show them around the area, escort them through the interview day, and generally be the 'at-ease-link' in the recruitment process. According to *Fortune*, 1,000 Cisco employees have volunteered for the programme, enticed by a generous referral fee and a lottery ticket for a free trip to Hawaii for each reference hired. Referees are eligible for other prizes such as stainless steel commuter mugs and athletic bags. Though the programme is advertised only in local movie theatres, Cisco receives 100–150 requests each week from applicants wishing to be introduced to a friend at Cisco. This source provides about a third of Cisco's new hires.

It is believed that about 60% of the people who join Cisco do so because they have a friend there.

Every time a referral is hired, the Cisco employee gets $500–2,000. Referral rates at Cisco are twice the industry norm. Cisco uses internal communication tools such as newsletters and the intranet to update employees about the referral programme. The real power of Cisco's website is not that it helps active job seekers move more quickly; it is that the website sells the company to people who are happy and satisfied in their current jobs and have never thought about working at Cisco. The firm targets the passive job-seeker.

Cisco is also making their managers' time-consuming recruiting process easier by hiring in-house headhunters. Since hiring a new salesperson six months earlier can mean several million dollars in incremental revenue, expediting the hiring process far outweighs the expense of the additional staff. Based on performance reviews conducted three months after employees start work, and a continued low turnover rate, the networking giant believes its talent pool remains undiluted. Chambers says, 'Our philosophy is very simple—if you get the best people in the industry to fit into your culture and you motivate them properly, then you are going to be an industry leader'.

Cisco Networking Academy Program

To help foster access to education and professional opportunities worldwide, Cisco founded the Cisco Networking Academy Program in 1997. This is a global e-learning programme that offers students an opportunity to pursue IT curricula through online instructor-led training and hands-on laboratory exercises. Since its creation in 1997, over 1.6 million students have enrolled at more than 10,000 academies located in high schools, technical schools, colleges, universities, and community-based organizations in more than 163 countries.

The programme trains students to design, build, and maintain computer networks. By combining education and the internet, Cisco Networking Academies help students acquire the skills needed for IT-related jobs and for higher education in engineering, computer science, and related fields.

Diversity Initiatives at Cisco

Cisco is dedicated to connecting businesses, people, and communities. As a leading global company, it recognizes that inclusion and diversity of thought is a business imperative. Achieving business objectives is seen as directly related to the advantage of having an inclusive workforce and a diverse group of suppliers. Employees at Cisco come from different cultures and geographies, with a variety of viewpoints and styles of interacting, unique backgrounds, experiences, and values. Cisco believes that such a diverse workforce gives the company access to new ideas, promotes better decision-making, and helps the firm understand the needs of the customers better. A workforce of inclusion also allows the firm to be well-positioned to anticipate important market changes, and be more responsive to customer needs. Cisco's Equal Opportunities Policy commits the company to recruit, promote, re-assign, and train people, regardless of race, colour, religion, gender, sexual orientation, age, disability, or nationality.

Cisco boasts of a global workforce. In 2005, 71% percent of the employees at Cisco were based in the US, 15% in Europe and the Middle East, 9% percent in the Asia Pacific region, 2% in Japan, and 3% in central and South America. To promote and foster an environment that supports diversity, Cisco encourages networks that enable employees to connect with other employees who share cultures, identities, or career goals.

Gender Initiatives

Cisco recognizes that women are under-represented in IT and has a team dedicated to develop a number of avenues to encourage and promote professional roles for women in the technology industry. It established the Gender Initiative in 2000 to recruit women, ensure that women have access to the same career opportunities as men and prevent them from being channeled into low-paid IT jobs, and provide women with the IT skills necessary to participate in all aspects of the global economy. Two gender initiatives at Cisco are Girls in Technology Initiative or Women's Initiative and Employee Women's Access Networks (WANs). The Girls in Technology Initiative or Women's Initiative encourages girls and young women to consider careers in engineering and technology, and supports them in their pursuit of high-technology education. It also aims to increase career opportunities for women in high-technology industries and encourage more girls to consider technology careers and focusses on providing advancement and development opportunities for women employees. This initiative is further supported by the Women's Networks, by connecting members—women who work in engineering and technology jobs—with students in high schools and universities, with the hope of ultimately increasing the number of future women engineers. Employee Women's Access Networks (WANs) seeks to empower women employees at Cisco to grow professionally. The

WANs offer networking, mentoring, and career development resources to women employees throughout Cisco's global operations. This serves to increase Cisco's competitive advantage and helps it achieve its mission by capitalizing on the talents and skills of its women employees. In 2005, there were 27 active WANs throughout Cisco worldwide.

This is a company that has repeatedly reinvented itself. It is indeed intriguing to work out what Cisco has that others do not, how it has been able to be so flexible and fast. These are times when it is hard to find people and to get the people you find to become productive quickly. How has Cisco managed this startling growth in an industry where technology is constantly changing, intellectual capital is scarce, financial capital for new start-ups is abundant, and the competition is brutal?

This case study has been constructed on the basis of inputs from the following sources: www.cisco.com, accessed on 28 July 2006; Depp, D. 1998, 'Hire Power', http://www.fenemoregroup.com/newsletters/1998/fall.htm, accessed on 18 July 2006; O'Reilly III, C.A. and J. Pfeffer 2000, 'Cisco Systems: Acquiring and Retaining Talent in Hypercompetitive Markets', *Human Resource Planning*, vol. 23, no. 3, pp. 38–52.

Questions

1. What is the hiring philosophy of Cisco? How has it contributed to Cisco's becoming an employer of choice? How does Cisco leverage its recruitment process to enhance its 'employer brand'?

2. Based on the information provided in the case, reconstruct and evaluate the recruitment strategy followed by Cisco Systems. What is it about Cisco that makes people want to work for it?

3. Is 'culture' highly valued at Cisco? Do you think that Cisco's 'recruiting for culture' or

'person/organization culture fit' approach has been successful?

4. Based on evidence from the case, discuss the importance and advantages of e-recruitment.

5. What objectives and goals does Cisco seek to achieve through its diversity initiatives?

6. Do you think Cisco's gender initiatives are directed towards increasing the supply of talented workforce to the firm? What other initiatives at Cisco increase the probability of continued supply of adequately trained workforce to the firm in future?

References

Athley, T.R. and M.S. Orth 1999, 'Emerging Competency Methods for the Future', *Human Resource Management*, vol. 38 no. 3, pp. 215–26.

Batt, R., V. Doellgast, H. Kwon, M. Nopani, P. Nopani, and A. DaCosta 2005, 'The Indian Call Centre Industry: National Benchmarking Report

Strategy, HR Practices, & Performance', Working Paper Series, School of Industrial & Labour Relations, Cornell University, *https://www.ilr.cornell.edu/ depts/ cahrs/downloads/PDFs/WorkingPapers/WP05-07.pdf*, accessed on 18 July 2006.

Bohlander, G.,S. Snell, and A.Sherman 2002, *Managing Human Resources*, 12th edition, Thomson South-Western, Singapore.

Bowen, D.E., G.E. Ledford Jr., and B.R. Nathan 1991, 'Hiring for the Organization, Not the Job', *Academy of Management Executive*, vol. 5, no. 4, pp. 35–51.

Capelli, P. 2001, 'Making the Most of On-line Recruiting', *Harvard Business Review*, vol. 79, no. 3, pp. 139–46.

David, J. 2005, 'The Unexpected Employee and Organizational Costs of Skilled Contingent Workers', *Human Resource Planning*, vol. 28, no. 2, pp. 32–40.

DeCenzo, D.A. and S.P. Robbins 2005, *Fundamentals of Human Resource Management*, 8th edition, John Wiley & Sons, Singapore, pp. 155–6.

Dessler, G. 2005, *Human Resource Management*, 10th edition, Prentice Hall of India Pvt Ltd, New Delhi, p. 175.

Feldman, D. and B.S. Klaas 2002, 'Internet Job Hunting: A Field Study of Applicant Experiences with On-line Recruiting', *Human Resource Management*, vol. 41, no. 2, pp. 175–92.

Gandossy, R., Kao, T., and Hewitt Associates 2004, 'Talent Wars: Out of Mind, Out of Practice', *Human Resource Planning*, vol. 27 no. 4, pp. 15–19.

Ivancevich, J.M. 2004, *Human Resource Management*, 9th edition, Tata McGraw Hill Publishing Co Ltd, New Delhi.

Mathis, R.L. and J.H. Jackson 2003, *Human Resource Management*, 10th edition, Thomson South-Western, Singapore, pp. 217–19.

Mello, J.A. 2003, *Strategic Human Resource Management*, Thomson Asia Pte Ltd, Singapore, p. 241.

Millmore, M. 2003, 'Just How Extensive is the Practice of Strategic Recruitment and Selection?', *Irish Journal of Management*, vol. 24, no. 1, pp. 87–108.

Mondy, R.W., R.M. Noe, and S.R. Premeaux 1999, *Human Resource Management*, 7th edition, Prentice Hall International Inc., USA, pp. 191–2

Olian, J.D. and S.L. Rynes 1984, *Industrial Relations*, vol. 23, no. 2, pp. 170–83.

Saaty, T. 1990, 'How to Make a Decision: The Analytic Hierarchy Process,' *European Journal of Operational Research*, vol. 48, pp. 9–26.

Sertoglu, C. and A. Berkowitch 2002, 'Cultivating Ex-Employees', *Forethought, Harvard Business Review*, June, pp. 20–1.

Simon, H.A. 1948, *Administrative Behaviour: A Study of Decision-Making Processes in Administrative Organizations*, Macmillan, New York.

Simon, H.A. 1960, *The New Science of Management Decision*, Harper, New York.

Sinha, V. and Kant, K. 2005, 'Most Wanted Uncork the Bubbly', *The Economic Times*, New Delhi, 29 July 2005, p. 3.

Swiercz, P.M. and S.R. Ezzedeen 2001, 'From Sorcery to Science: AHP, a Powerful New Tool for Executive Selection', *Human Resource Planning*, vol. 24, no. 3, pp. 15–26.

Notes

Baishya, D., 'Hunting Season', Corporate Dossier, *The Economic Times*, 14 October 2005, p. 3.

Bhargava, A., 'BPO Express: Fast Track or Slow Coach?', *The Economic Times,* New Delhi, 15 November 2004, p. 7.

Dang, C., 'BPO Rejects Get Second-time Lucky', *The Economic Times*, New Delhi, 23 June 2006, p. 8.

Dang, C., 'BPOs Oppose Q-word in Private Sector, Call for Affirmative Action a la US', *The Economic Times*, New Delhi, 4 May 2006, p. 10.

Doctor, V. 2004, 'In the Hiring Line', Brand Equity, *The Economic Times*, 1 December 2004, pp. 1, 3.

Duttagupta, I., 'IT MNCs Moot Steps to Enter Top Technology Campuses', *The Economic Times*, New Delhi, 4 May 2006, p. 10.

Ganguly, D., 'All Work and Play', Corporate Dossier in *The Economic Times*, New Delhi, 3 March 2006, p. 3.

Goyal, M. and K.Y. Rajawat, 'Never Panic if Your CEO says Bye', *The Economic Times*, New Delhi, 2 May 2006, p. 8.

Goyal, M., 'Cos Look Beyond IITs, IIMs to Assist, Educate and Hire', *The Economic Times*, New Delhi, 4 May 2006, p. 10.

Goyal, M., 'Delivery Boy to Top Gun, Talent Finally Arrives', *The Economic Times*, New Delhi, 15 May 2006, p. 1 and p. 12.

Goyal, M., 'Lighthouse Hiring: India Inc Discovers Biz Code', *The Economic Times*, New Delhi, 5 April 2006, p. 10.

Hay Group Pvt. Ltd. 2004, 'Recruitment and Selection', A Case Study Commissioned by the Ministry of Manpower, Singapore, January, http://www.mom.gov.sg/NR/rdonlyres/C228CEA5-B699-4E9E-B240-486ACC4950C1/1410/2632_RecruitmentSelection.pdf, accessed on 21 July 2006.

IBM Institute for Business Value, *Back-office and Customer Care Centres in Emerging Economies: A Human Capital Perspective*, www.ibm.com/services/us/imc/pdf/g510-3945-emerging-economies.pdf, an IBM Institute for Business Value executive brief, IBM Business Consulting Services, accessed on 18 July 2006.

'In Pursuit of "the" Personality', http://www.expresspharmaonline.com/20060630/pharmalife01.shtml, accessed on 18 July 2006.

Jasrotia, P. 2003, 'Psychometric Tests Still to Catch on', http://www.expressitpeople.com/2030120/cover.shtml, accessed on 18 July 2006.

Jayaswal, R., 'GenY Clocking Out of BPOs', *The Economic Times*, New Delhi, 23 February 2005, p. 17.

Kumar, V., 'Dream Merchants', Corporate Dossier in *The Economic Times*, New Delhi, 2 September 2005, pp. 1, 2.

Mahanta, V. and B. Pande, 'Old Battle Hands on Board', *The Economic Times*, New Delhi, 27 June 2006, pp. 1, 19.

Mahanta, V., 'Dangling the Bait', Corporate Dossier in *The Economic Times*, 23 July 2004, p. 3.

Mahanta, V., 'The Hunters and the Hunted', Corporate Dossier, *The Economic Times*, 29 July 2005, p. 3.

Nagaraj, S., 'IteS, BPOs on Pre-hiring Recce to Spot Bad Apples', *The Economic Times*, New Delhi, 10 August 2004, p. 18.

Nayani, S., 'Ex-staffers get Return Call', *The Economic Times*, New Delhi, 6 April 2006, p. 6.

Oberoi, S., 'BPO Recruitments to be Streamlined', *The Economic Times*, New Delhi, 12 October 2005, p. 15.

Oberoi, S., 'Resume Frauds Worry IteS Cos', *The Economic Times*, New Delhi, 19 October 2005, p. 4.

Pratap, R., 'Foreign Firms Making Sure BPO Staffers Above Board', *The Economic Times*, New Delhi, 4 May 2006, p. 10.

Rajawat, K.Y. and R. Parwan, 'BPO or IT? Indian Cities Getting Sorted Out', *The Economic Times*, New Delhi, 9 May 2006, p. 6.

Rajawat, K.Y., 'Honey, When You Get Shrunk, Just Call the Shrinks', *The Economic Times*, New Delhi, 29 June 2005, pp. 1, 31.

Ramnath, N.S., 'Archaic Labour Laws Blocking Temping Boom', *The Economic Times*, New Delhi, 31 January 2005, p. 5.

'Recruitment: Psychometric Testing', *Times-online* 2004, http://business.timesonline.co.uk/printfriendly/0,,2020-8310-987239-8310,00.html, accessed on 18 July 2006.

Shahane, P.S., 'Non-IT Cos Drive E-recruitment Mart', *The Economic Times*, New Delhi, 24 February 2006, p. 10.

Shahane, P.S., 'Perked up Packages', *The Economic Times*, New Delhi, 3 November 2005, p. 11.

Shankar, A., 'Engineers' Love for IT makes L&T Woo NRIs', *The Economic Times*, New Delhi, 28 November 2005, pp. 1, 15.

Singh, A., 'Walk in with Your CV, Walk Out With a Job', *The Economic Times*, New Delhi, Monday, 6 February 2006, p. 11.

Singh, S., 'IT May Tech a Call for Hiring', *The Economic Times*, New Delhi, 27 January 2006, pp. 1, 13.

Sinha, K., 'Indian Nurses Bear Brunt of British Ban', *Times of India*, New Delhi, 4 July 2006, p. 9.

Sinha, V. and K. Kant, 'Yearning for a Fling? Call up Stop-gap CEOs', *The Economic Times*, New Delhi, 12 October 2004, pp. 1, 10.

Subramanyam, R., 'Get Them Fast, But at Lower Cost', *The Economic Times*, New Delhi, 4 August 2005, p. 7.

Subramanyam, R., 'IT Pays to be Friends: Suggest a Name to Your Boss and Get Paid', *The Economic Times*, New Delhi, 1 June 2005, p. 17.

Thanuja, B.M., 'Outsourcing of Hiring in Retail Next Big Thing', *The Economic Times*, New Delhi, 9 August 2005, p. 15.

The Economic Times, 12 June 2006, 'Part-time Permanent Jobs Beckon Women' New Delhi, p. 9.

The Economic Times, 13 February 2006, 'Psychometric Tests Made Compulsory for Pre-sea Cadets, New Delhi, in Shipping Bureau, p. 18.

The Economic Times, 25 October 2004, 'Contest Recruitment: Doing it the Google Way', New Delhi, p. 4.

The Economic Times, 27 June 2006, 'Plug-n-play Recruits for BPOs', New Delhi, p. 6.

Verma, P., 'BPO Staff Details to be Made Public', *The Economic Times*, New Delhi, 18 July 2005, p. 11.

Verma, P., 'Software Cos Reprogram Recruitment', *The Economic Times*, New Delhi, 10 September 2004, p. 9.

Vijayraghavan, K., 'Multinationals Turn Fair and Lovely', *The Economic Times*, New Delhi, 17 May 2006, pp. 1, 19.

Zachariahs, C. and M. Sabarinath, 'Retail Players Tie Up with B-schools to Groom Execs', *The Economic Times*, New Delhi, 1 November 2004, p. 19.

6

Training and Development of Human Resources

After studying this chapter, you will be able to:

- understand the need for training and development
- define training and development and understand some related concepts such as education, experience, and learning
- understand the purposes and benefits of employee training and development
- appreciate the significance of training and development in contemporary business organizations
- understand the linkage between business strategy and training
- understand the four phases of the process of training and development
- acquire an insight into training and development methods
- gain a perspective on the special forms of training and development and on the role of technology in training
- understand the competency-based approach to training and development

INTRODUCTION

Since the 1990s, the economy has been characterized by intense global competition and rapid technological advance. Dramatic changes in the economy and the consequent corporate restructuring are bringing forth significant transformation in organizational structure and work practices. There are changes taking place in the structure of jobs, skill requirements, and the labour–management contract. New job skills and greater levels of workforce skills are required due to changing job profiles and organizational structures. Changes of this magnitude in the corporate world have significant implications for training and development of the workforce. It is increasingly being felt that the best way for both organizations and employees to develop a competitive advantage in the global economy is to improve the level of workforce skills. Organizations must continually readjust the size and skill composition of their workforces.

This chapter begins with a conceptual overview of the terms 'training' and 'development'. The differences between the two terms are highlighted and related terms such as 'education', 'experience', and 'learning' are explained. The purposes that training and development programmes serve within an organizational context are also discussed. The chapter explores the growing significance of training and development in a business environment characterized by competitive pressures, technological advancement, and changes in organizational and work structure. These changes have created the need for expanded skills and continuous skill upgradation to prevent obsolescence. Within this context, the reasons for training and development (T&D) becoming a strategic organizational activity are discussed.

The chapter also examines the linkage between business strategy and training. It is emphasized that for T&D to be strategic, it is important to develop T&D activities to support the business strategy of the firm. Miles and Snow (1978) gave a typology of business strategies to explain this linkage. This chapter describes the four phases of the training process, viz. needs assessment, programme design and development, programme implementation, and evaluation.

Cost–benefit approach, return on investment approach, and benchmarking are discussed as methods to determine the value of training for business performance. Special forms of training relevant for organizations characterized by changes in nature of jobs and organizations are also discussed. These include team training, diversity training, training for global assignments, training for leadership skills, and new employee training (orientation). The chapter ends with a discussion of some recent developments in training and development. These include the role of technology in training (e-training) and the competency-based approach to management development.

THE NEED FOR TRAINING AND DEVELOPMENT

In the contemporary business environment, organizations and managers are faced with several types of changes in their environment. These include, for example, a dynamic business environment, new technologies, new competitors, fluctuating productivity, changing nature of jobs, employee turnover, etc. To successfully manage such changes, managers must make the right choice while making decisions. Therefore, they must keep themselves informed and updated in their field. Managers also have the responsibility of managing an ever-changing workforce operating in a dynamic environment. In order to achieve their goals, organizations require employees who have the relevant skills, knowledge, and competencies. Firms seek to ensure that they have the 'right type' of human resources by hiring people with the required skills and competencies. The IT services industry hired about 70,000 employees in 2005 and is estimated to add approximately 100,000 new employees by the end of 2006. Though there is no dearth of people available, certain skills are in short supply. For example, the industry is finding it difficult to get technical architects, functional ERP professionals, semiconductor design engineers, and animation and program management engineers.

Even if an organization finds the right skills, there is no guarantee that these skills will continue to be relevant and important for organizational goals. An individual who enters the workforce today with certain skills is unlikely to have these skills go unchallenged through the rest of his/her work-life. Similarly, many jobs that exist today were not there 50 years ago. The nature and content of jobs evolves and changes as discussed in Chapter 2. The coming years are likely to herald new jobs that will require new set of skills. For example, no one had heard of the job of a web designer about 20 years ago. Professionals with new technology skills, such as those with experience in a specific SAP module, are hard to find. Moreover, a large percentage of the work force will need new or significantly expanded skills to match the growing demands of their job. This includes technological skills, customer relations skills, etc.

With the resurgence of the manufacturing sector, the country is faced with a shortage of vocationally trained workforce. It is estimated that in India approximately only 6% of the workforce is vocationally trained. Hence, leading firms are investing on re-training the force with multi-skills. All of these changes and their consequences have made it imperative for firms to make considerable investments in HR training and development. Organizations have no choice but to put the recruits through long training programmes. Typically, IT services firms are spending upwards of Rs 30,000–40,000 for training one engineer. In the last quarter of the year 2005, Infosys spent 1.1% of its total revenues on training. The company places great emphasis on regular upgradation of skills. It also holds regular value workshops to reinforce articulated values and has also set up a Global Education Centre and Infosys Leadership Institute in Mysore. The firm will invest upto Rs 12 billion in this centre by the end of 2006.

TRAINING AND DEVELOPMENT: BASIC CONCEPTS

Training is a process that attempts to improve employee performance on a currently held job by providing the employee with the knowledge and skills needed for their present job. It is designed to bring about changes in specific knowledge, skills, attitudes, or behaviour. An ideal training effort is one that meets the goals of the organizations well as those of the employees. *Development* refers to learning opportunities directed toward helping employees grow. Generally, the term development is used to refer to new learning experiences provided to managerial employees, and hence, it is also called management development. The development opportunities are not limited to improving employee's performance on their current jobs; rather, development represents efforts to help an individual acquire capabilities beyond those required by the current job. Management development consists of all learning experiences provided by an organization to upgrade knowledge, change attitudes, or increase skills in order to improve current or future management performance. Employees with appropriate capabilities enhance organizational competitiveness and its change adaptability. At the same time, for the employees, development extends opportunities for career growth. Thus, development is future-focussed and benefits both the organization and the individual.

Taken together, T&D refers to a planned, continuous effort on the part of the organization to improve employee competency levels and firm performance. Training and development activities are designed to align employees of a firm with its corporate strategies. The two terms, 'training' and 'development' may be used interchangeably, but sometimes a distinction is made between the two. Table 6.1 highlights the main points of difference between training and development.

Distinction is also made between 'general training' and 'specific training'. Training that helps employees gain skills that can be used at most workplaces is called general training. Communication skills training is an example of general training. *General training* is equally useful in many firms. It raises worker's productivity at other employers by the same amount as at the employer that provides the training. Workers can take their acquired transferable skills to other employers. Therefore, general training is a risk for the employer providing it. This risk is often referred to as the poaching or 'cherry picking' problem, that is, other organizations may hire trained workers away with better salaries and positions. Since general training benefits the employees by increasing their future wages, the employees are often willing to pay the cost of general training. *Specific training*, on the other hand, is training that increases the worker's productivity only at the employer's workplace. The employees gain information and skills that are directed specifically to the employee's own workplace. For example, non-transferable skills that are

Table 6.1: Training and Development: A Comparison

Training	Development
■ Process designed to bring about a relatively permanent change in employees' skills, knowledge, attitudes, or behaviour in order to improve their performance on currently held job	■ Process designed to impart learning experiences in order to help employees acquire skills and competencies for future responsibilities
■ Imparts technical skills	■ Imparts managerial skills
■ Focus on small number of technical skills specific to the current job	■ Focus on broad range of skills applicable more generally across different situations
■ Directed towards non-management personnel	■ Directed towards managerial personnel
■ Present-focussed, short-run	■ Future-focussed, long-run
■ Activity designed to manage an existing performance problem	■ Activity designed to be a continuous process

organization-specific include understanding the processes and computer systems that are peculiar to a particular organization or a proprietary system specific to the organization. Thus, if two companies merge and one set of processes and systems is phased out, some non-transferable skills become obsolete. Training on these skills is beneficial only to the current employer because workers cannot use the acquired skills in other organizations. Due to these reasons, employees are generally not willing to pay for specific training costs, unless there is a contract between employers and employees to share the benefits.

Managers need a broad variety of skills, such as leadership and supervisory, communication, general business, organizational, and technological skills. They need a solid understanding of the industry in which they operate and the structure and functions of the organization. They also need to be familiar and comfortable with finance, marketing, and operations, regardless of their particular area of expertise. Employees need to clearly understand the culture, philosophies, policies, and procedures of the organization. Training and development, therefore, should be both general and organization-specific. Given the talent crunch today, organizations today are willing to provide their employees with opportunities to develop their general skills too. Several firms today sponsor their employees for higher education. Computer Sciences Corporation (CSC) encourages its employees to upgrade their skills. The company funds any course that an employee might want to take to the extent of two months' salary, and grants paid leave to pursue the course. Some employees have joined the IIMs to pursue a management programme on paid leave and their course is funded partly by the company.

Some Related Terms

Apart from the terms 'training' and 'development' there are other terms that result in changes in an employee's skills and competencies, and therefore, must also be explained. These terms are 'education', 'learning', and 'experience' (Figure 6.1). Let us understand the meaning of these terms and how they are different from 'training'.

Training and education Education is broader in scope than training. It does not always have an immediate or a specific application. For example, education provided in a management institution aims at developing an individual's knowledge, skills, and competencies in a comprehensive manner so that they are applicable across several situations rather than developing skills relating to a single job. Thus, education increases the range of possible responses available to an individual. Education prepares an individual to assess situations and select the most appropriate response from the range of responses available.

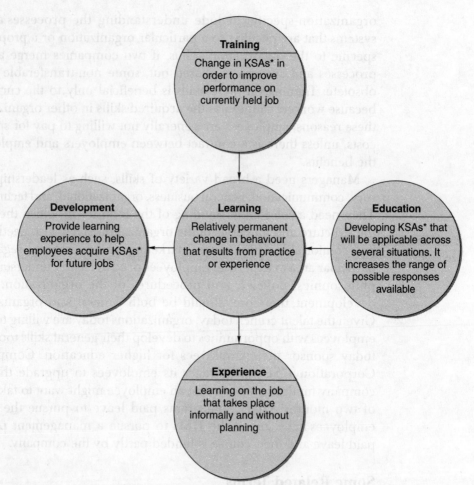

Figure 6.1: Terms Related to Training and Development

* KSA: Knowledge, skills, and attitudes

Training, on the other hand, is designed to help an employee learn the most appropriate response to a situation. It, therefore, limits the range of responses available to an employee. An example of training is the firefighter's drill. The firefighter must precisely follow the steps in case of a fire. However, when a manager has to allocate funds for different organizational activities, there is no 'best' way. Rather, the manager must use his/her judgement and gather information to reach optimal budget allocation decision.

The term 'training' is used to refer to activities designed to improve the job performance of non-supervisory personnel. Managerial positions, on the other hand, require elements of education. In recent times, the distinction between training and education has blurred. As decision-making responsibility gets delegated, training programmes too come to incorporate elements of education.

Training and experience Training is a planned and systematic process, whereas experience results in learning on the job, without planning. The importance of learning by experience is extremely high. However, training has certain advantages over experience. Training reduces the time it takes for an individual to reach maximum efficiency. Left to oneself to learn through experience by doing, an individual may take longer to reach the same standards of performance. Moreover, learning by experience can sometimes prove to be costly. For example, a pilot cannot be left to learn to fly an aircraft through experience. In such cases, training is important.

Training and learning Learning refers to any relatively permanent change in behaviour that results from practice or experience. Hence, learning can be formal as well as informal. Informal learning takes the form of 'learning' through experience. Formal learning occurs during a training episode. The process of learning is inherent to training, development, education, and experience, in that each seeks to bring about a change in the behaviour of an individual.

Training programs serve several organizational functions beyond direct skill development.

PURPOSES OF TRAINING AND DEVELOPMENT

Training and development serves important purposes other than providing an efficient way to obtain needed skills at higher levels (Figure 6.2). For example, firms that include training as a way of career mobility may use it to communicate 'fairness' and commitment by the firm to its employees and as a means of having employees internalize the norms of the organization, particularly as job structures move away from direct supervising or control mechanisms. The major purposes served by T&D of managerial and non-managerial employees are described below.

Performance improvement The main purpose of training is to improve individual and organizational performance. When employees are unable to perform in accordance with expected standards due to deficiency in skills, training often becomes instrumental in minimizing those problems. For example, an otherwise competent manager may be ineffective due to lack of interpersonal skills. Imparting interpersonal skills training may help the manager perform more effectively on the job. Training is also useful to help a new recruit or a newly promoted individual to reach performance standards sooner than they would otherwise. Often, organizations hire new employees who have the aptitude to learn but may not be immediately ready for the job. After hiring organizations train these newcomers to perform specific tasks. By improving the job performance of employees, training contributes to organizational performance improvement also. However, not all performance

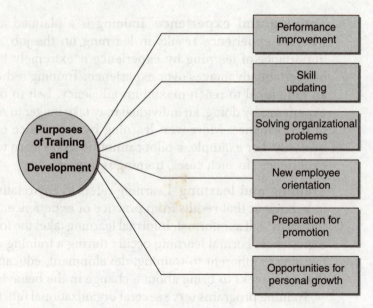

Figure 6.2: Purposes of Training and Development

problems may be due to skill deficiency and therefore training may not be needed. Training may not be a solution to motivational problems resulting from dissatisfaction with the immediate superior.

Updating skills Technological advances result in changes in the nature of jobs. This results in new skill demands for these jobs to be performed successfully. Employees who fail to adapt to changes in the nature of jobs and the way jobs are performed become obsolete. Managerial obsolescence is the failure to keep pace with new methods and processes that enable employees to remain effective. Training helps in upgrading employee skills to meet the challenges of technological advancements and prevents managerial obsolescence. Training and development programmes concern all aspects of an organization like finance, manufacturing, general management, IT, etc.

Solving problems Organizations face several problems such as scheduling delays, inventory shortages, absenteeism, employee turnover, union management disputes, etc. Training provides one means for solving these problems.

New employee orientation New employees come to the organization with certain expectations. They experience anxiety and discomfort when they find that reality is different from their expectations. Their interactions with other organizational members lead them to form impressions about the organization and its employees. Moreover, for some time, the new employees perform below their potential since they are still getting familiar with the job and with the organization. Orientation training helps new comers adjust faster to the organization in their run-up to become fully functional members of the firm.

Preparation for promotion Promotions serve to motivate and retain personnel. When people perceive career growth opportunities in a firm, they are attracted to jobs in the firm. Organizations design their training and management development programmes to prepare and enable employees to acquire the skills needed for a promotion. Thus, T&D facilitates employee movement from the present job to a job with higher responsibilities.

Opportunities for personal growth Many employees strive for continuous growth and seek challenges in their present job. Training and development serves to help employees in their quest for personal growth. Employee growth leads to improved job performance as well as greater organizational effectiveness.

It is evident that T&D leads to both individual and organizational performance improvement. As mentioned earlier, T&D benefits both the employee and the organization, causing a win-win situation (Figure 6.3). Training should be analysed in its organizational context and in the context of its having multiple determinants in addition to its technical function of increasing efficiency. Recently, there has been a growth and expansion of the notion of training to include a broader focus on those skills that may not contribute directly to efficiency or productivity but are general skills and thus more transferable.

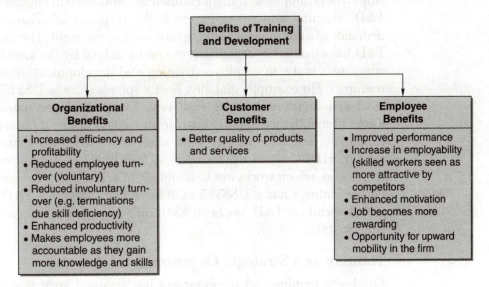

Figure 6.3:   Benefits of Training and Development

SIGNIFICANCE OF TRAINING AND DEVELOPMENT

Globalization of business, advancement in technology, increase in skills at workplace, and constant change has made learning very important for organizations. Significant changes have occurred in organizations as a result of downsizing, technology, and customer demands for new and better products and services. Competitive pressures have made firms more conscious of productivity levels. The result is that firms often expect more work to be accomplished by fewer people. In the process, decision-making is delegated down the line. Changes in technology, products, and methods have had a major impact on job requirements. All these changes translate into more emphasis on training and development within the company and into the need for employees to constantly upgrade their skills. Providing training and learning opportunities for employees is especially important in the services economy. Service providers, across all sectors, cover large and small firms who attempt to communicate and then satisfy customer expectations through tangible and intangible benefits. The context for providing services to customers is characterized by the difficulty in achieving homogeneity; the personal contact between customers and staff during the delivery of the service; and the difficulty in correcting faults and service quality breakdowns.

In such a context, training of employees and managers is considered the key element of business strategy for building successful service encounters. Organizations must keep on learning if they want to maintain or improve competitive advantage. The most important source of competitive advantage for an organization is its workforce, that is, its human resources. To ensure that employees continue to remain competent, firms need to engage in continuous T&D. Training and development is the response of organizations to the demands of a constantly changing business environment. The significance that T&D has assumed in organizations can be judged by the kind of investment companies make in employee training and development infrastructure and resources. For example, globally, FedEx spends close to US$155 million and 1523 man-hours on training each year. Every employee spends four to six weeks in mandatory training apart from 15 days optional classroom training. Employees are also entitled to an additional US$2,500 annually as tuition refund. HDFC gives upwards of 35,000 hours of formal training to its employees, which works out to about six to seven days of training a year per person. Infosys has a US$125 million annual outlay for T&D. Accenture's global spend on T&D has been $546 million between September 2004 and August 2005.

Training as a Strategic Organizational Activity

Employee training and development has assumed great significance in the past few years. In a knowledge economy, it is no longer sufficient to get employees to attend an occasional training module a few times a year. Firms operating in a globally competitive market need to train and re-train their employees. The emergence of training as a strategic organizational activity is due to several reasons (see Figure 6.4).

Advances in technology Technological advances render many skills obsolete and simultaneously develop new skill requirements. As skill requirements change due to technological advances, training is required to help the workforce learn the new skills. Technology impacts jobs across all hierarchical levels. For example, those who draw their expertise from a knowledge base, such as surgeons, computer programmers, etc. will be challenged by the advancements in this knowledge base during their careers. At the other end, typists must now learn use of computers for performing daily activities. To remain competitive, organizations must continue to train their employees to learn and use the latest available technologies. Continuous learning has become important for managers and workers alike in such a dynamic environment.

Work redesign The redesign of work has brought in jobs that assign broader responsibilities to employees. Employees are required to take initiative, develop interpersonal skills to be able to perform well, and work in teams. Therefore, they need to acquire a broad range of skills, such as team work,

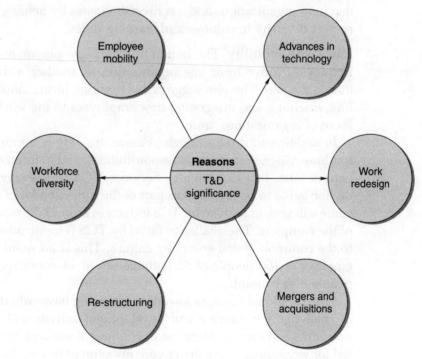

Figure 6.4:   Emergence of Training as a Strategic Organizational Activity: Reasons

collaboration, and conflict management. Another change in organizations is towards cross-functional teams. Cross-functional training is required to facilitate the employees to broaden their range of skills to enable them to meet new job demands.

Mergers and acquisitions With mergers and acquisitions, rules of corporate competition are being rewritten, and change has become inevitable. A major challenge during mergers and acquisitions is to integrate employees of two organizations that have different cultures. At these times, training becomes a strategic tool.

Restructuring Organizations are downsizing, or reorganizing with regularity in order to remain competitive. Whenever a firm restructures itself, training issues are likely to emerge. Common training needs during restructuring include new job skills, morale, outplacement, change management, etc.

Workforce diversity Diversity of workforce has increased, as already discussed in earlier chapters. Moreover, globalization of business operations requires managers to acquire knowledge related to cultural differences and develop skills to manage them. Therefore, diversity and cross-cultural training becomes important, to ensure that cultural differences are understood and managed effectively. Trainers need to design and deliver training modules that help organizations address diversity issues by helping managers learn to respect diversity in cultures and learning styles.

Employee mobility The notion of lifetime employment stands challenged. Employees move from one organization to another with higher frequency than in the past. This also suggests that firms are hiring more frequently. Therefore, orienting and integrating new employees to the workplace is taking up more of organizations' time.

In addition to these strategic reasons, training is important for new hires, for those assigned to new job responsibilities, and to improve performance on current jobs. Tata Consultancy Services (TCS) is working on developing an on-line game to be included as part of the induction kit of a new recruit. This game will seek to familiarize TCS inductees around the world with the culture of the company. The challenge faced by TCS is to introduce every employee to the common global company culture. This is no small task, because TCS employs 71,200 people of 53 nationalities in 34 countries and recruits 2,500 people every month.

Organizational changes toward outsourcing have ushered in different kind of challenge for training and development activities of the firm. As firms outsource and increase their use of contingent workers, there exists the potential for weakening of the firm's core investment in workforce skills. Segments of the workforce that were formerly considered part of the organization are now either contingent workers or are located in external supplier firms that are usually smaller and have less capacity and fewer resources to train. These workers are not considered for training and skill development opportunities within the firm. In this context, individuals have to assume greater responsibility for their own skill development in order to remain employable.

Although T&D is highly significant in today's competitive environment, traditionally it was seen as a solution to performance-related problems after they occurred and was thus reactive in nature and imparted as an afterthought. It was neither strategically aligned nor viewed as an important contribution to organizational goals. Many firms continue to conduct ad hoc training programmes or consider training as a fad. However, firms are increasingly recognizing the value of training for accomplishing organizations' strategic goals. Training and development is seen as proactive (see an example in the context of sales at Exhibit 6.1). Strategic goals and objectives of the organization

Exhibit 6.1

Upgrading Sales Training: A Proactive Approach

Firms are investing in initiatives to improve customer satisfaction; one such initiative is sales training.

Maruti's sales training budget has grown 35–40% every year. If senior management time and resources spent on training are factored in, this figure would double. Reliance Industries reportedly spent Rs 170 million to acquire NIS Sparta, a Delhi-based sales training institute. Companies like Godrej, Mahindra & Mahindra, and Eveready have set up sales academies. LG organizes around 20 workshops in its branches every year at a cost of a few million rupees. These workshops are aimed at arming its sales and marketing team with the skill sets to handle trade and customers.

Other companies that have been traditionally known for their sales training programmes, such as HLL and Maruti Udyog, are moving their programmes to the next level. Maruti trains 6,000–7,000 people at its dealer outlets every year. In 2003, HLL rolled out 'Project Dronacharya' to impart continuous training for about 5,000 stockists' salesmen to improve their capabilities and skills.

Retail formats are changing and old relationship-based selling is transforming into a more fact-based and customer-focussed activity. The changes in demographics, expectations, as well as in the retail landscape have pushed firms to re-look at the skills needed by the frontline salesforce. The increasingly competitive scenario has led to the realization that the company's relationship with distributors and dealers is the most important. Hence, a proactive sales force becomes very important. Therefore, sales training programmes need to be carefully designed.

With retail becoming more demanding, Gillette India has increased the number of training personnel in the firm. The training function at Gillette India has one head-office based national sales training manager. In 2004, the company appointed four regional trainers to assist the national sales training manager. The budget for sales training was also hiked. The firm is also outsourcing some training to specialists.

Source: Pande and Banerjee 2004

are translated into HR terms to identify the type of skills that the firm will require to achieve these goals. In its proactive form, T&D focusses on anticipating the skills that the firm will require and on ensuring their availability by designing appropriate interventions. This suggests that training has become strategically aligned with the business goals of the organization.

HRM APPROACHES TO TRAINING AND DEVELOPMENT

Several changes have taken place over the years in corporate strategy as well as in the training provided by firms to their employees. During the era of crafts-based enterprises, apprentices worked alongside their master who was a skilled and an experienced craftsman, and gradually learned the skills. In the manufacturing age, workers started working together in factories. The workers no longer owned the machinery but they were still the masters of the production process because they possessed the skills and expertise. The fragmentation and separation of activities began with Adam Smith's idea of the division of labour. This saw the advent of increasing task specialization and began to lead to a continuing disqualification of the worker. This process of fragmentation of expertise became the basic feature underlying the classic organization theories of 'Taylorism' and 'Fordism'. Taylorism proposed the 'one best and only way' that implied training the worker in the 'best way' of accomplishing a task. Fragmentation of expertise is, however, characterized by a short-term nature, fragmented and shallow content of knowledge, and transmission of skills that can be immediately applied to measure work tasks. There are three HRM approaches towards T&D in organizations, as explained in Figure 6.5.

Human capital approach It views training as an investment in human capital that gives returns in the form of increased productivity. The strategic framework of Jackson and Schuler (1989) considers human resources a significant factor of sustained competitive advantage for a company. This implies that when the capabilities and skills available to an organization in the form of the skills and competencies of its individual employees are superior to those of its competitors, the firm gains an advantage over its competitors. In this context, training becomes invaluable, since it results in the development of the human resources of the firm into a valuable and unique resource that cannot be copied and is not substitutable.

Contingent approach A theoretical approach that has received maximum attention is the contingent approach. It views training (or any other HRM practice) and the business strategy of a firm as interdependent. It does appear, then, that training is related in a systematic manner to the generic business strategies formulated by the organizations. However, one problem with the

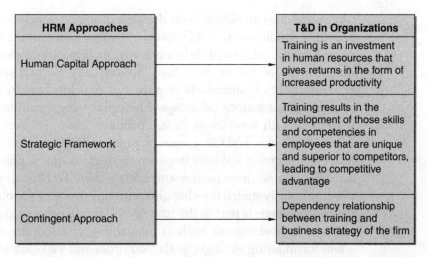

Figure 6.5:   HRM Approaches and Training and Development in Organizations

relationship between strategy and HRM practices is the diversity of typologies of strategies proposed in the literature (see Chapter 1). Some conclusions, however, can be drawn based on the contingent approach. For example, in firms that follow the *innovation strategy* and the *quality strategy*, training is likely to be oriented towards developing multiple skills. Innovation strategy is also likely to be linked with training oriented to providing skills needed in the future and for better group co-operation and results. When a firm follows a *dynamic growth strategy* or a *cost strategy*, training is likely to be highly specialized and oriented towards a short-term pay-off. Firms following a *profit strategy* emphasize training the individual.

Strategic framework   Using T&D and management development programmes as a competitive weapon has emerged as an option in recent years. To do this there is a need to strengthen the link between business strategy and T&D. To ensure that training adds value to an organization, the training strategy should be linked to organizational objectives and the business strategy. Strategic training is concerned with developing training plans and activities that are aligned with organizational strategic plans and decisions and human resource planning (HRP) efforts. Hence, strategic training interventions and activities focus on developing those competencies and skills among employees that improve their job performance and also result in competitive advantage for the organization.

LINKAGE BETWEEN BUSINESS STRATEGY AND TRAINING

For training efforts to be strategic, it is important to develop training programmes and activities to support the business strategy of the firm.

Organizations can obtain skills through hiring or develop skills through T&D activities. Traditionally, T&D practices focussed on training individuals to overcome specific job-based deficiencies or to impart knowledge and skills predicted to be of use in the future. Strategically aligned staffing and training activities help organizations acquire and develop human resources required to achieve *competitive advantage*. Exemplary organizations recognize that a workforce with superior skills is a primary source of competitive advantage. These firms use T&D to create change-readiness in the organization. They also ensure strong linkages between strategic business plans, goals, and T&D activities. These firms review and update their T&D goals on an annual basis to continuously match the changing strategic needs of the business units. Training professionals is part of the strategic planning process to ensure that human resource considerations such as availability of talent are taken into account when formulating strategic goals. Motorola and P&G are examples of organizations that undertake such exercises.

Another way in which organizations can establish strategic linkage of T&D activities is by having a clear statement of training policy. Some organizations establish training as a prerequisite for consideration for promotion. Companies like P&G require employees to undergo training each time they receive a promotion. Some other aspects of policies relate to number of hours each employee is to spend annually in T&D, and budget allocations for T&D. Some organizations assign the responsibility for seeking T&D opportunities to the employees.

Organizations invest huge amounts in employee T&D as pointed out earlier. This investment of effort, time, and money will be futile if training does not result in creating skills that are important for an organization in achieving its strategic objectives. Hence, it is important to match the training practices and strategic objectives of a firm. At FedEx, investment in training is seen as a cost-saver and a revenue-generator. Unless clearly linked to strategy, even the best-designed and -implemented training will remain ineffective. This assumes that the organization has a clear business strategy to link training to. Take the case of a firm that may be trying to distinguish itself from its competition on the basis of the quality of its customer service. To support the strategic objective of the firm, significant customer service training will be needed. The example suggests that the training focus and activities must parallel business strategies.

Miles and Snow (1984) provide a conceptual basis for linking training practices with business strategy by identifying four types of business strategies based on how firms adapt to their environments. As mentioned in earlier chapters, the basic strategic types are—defenders, prospectors, analysers, and reactors. The prospector and defender strategies are distinct in their characteristics. The analyser strategy is a combination of these two approaches. Let us focus on the defender and prospector strategies to compare training practices linkages with business strategies (Table 6.2). To explain this linkage, Raghuram and Arvey (1994) addressed two issues:

- Buying versus building skills (skill source)
- Types of functional skills (skill type)

The business strategy of a firm will influence the decision to buy skills or to build skills from within. Moreover, different strategies will place emphasis on different functional skills.

Defender strategy is associated with production and process efficiency. Therefore, skill types that lead to improving efficiency of processes are likely to be

Table 6.2: Linkage between Business Strategy and Staffing and Training Practices

Type of Business Strategy	Characteristics	HRM Requirements	Staffing and Training Practices
Defender Compete on the basis of low price and high quality; stable environment	■ Limited product line ■ Single capital-intensive technology ■ Skills in production efficiency, process engineering, and cost control ■ Emphasize technical efficiency ■ Long-term perspective ■ Functional structure ■ Division of labour	■ Skill specialization ■ Emphasis on production and finance functions ■ Build skills	**Skill Type** ■ Staff and train for narrow skills ■ Staff and train for production and finance functions **Skill Source** ■ Internal staffing ■ Much training ■ In-house training
Prospector Compete on the basis of new markets and new products; unstable environment	■ Diverse product lines ■ Multiple technologies ■ Skills in product research and development and product engineering ■ Emphasize product/ market innovation ■ Rapid growth ■ Decentralized structure ■ Low formalization ■ A product or geographically divisionalized structure	■ Skill flexibility ■ Emphasis on marketing/sales and on research and development ■ Buy skills	**Skill Type** ■ Staff and train for broad marketing skills ■ Staff and train for research and development **Skill Source** ■ External staffing ■ Little training ■ External training when required

Source: Raghuram and Arvey 1994

more important for these firms. Thus, these firms are likely to place more emphasis on selecting and training employees in the functions of production process, finance, accounts, and quality control. Since defenders compete on the basis of low price and high quality, they are more likely to build skills internally through training and internal staffing (skill source). This strategy helps these firms refine their skills toward greater efficiency. It also provides the firm with competency continuity. Over time, these skills become organization-specific, unique, and non-imitable and hence become the source of competitive advantage for the firm.

Prospector strategy is associated with the preference to buy new and diverse skills from external sources. Since the nature of technological change is unpredictable, firms cannot project the specific skills they would require in future. When requirement for such skills does come, it is difficult and expensive for these firms to develop them internally at short notice. Under these circumstances, the prospectors resort to external sources for acquiring these skills. With respect to skill type, the prospectors are likely to value expertise in research and development, functions that emphasize growth, and marketing. Consequently, these firms are expected to emphasize employee selection for these functions. The emphasis of training in firms that follow the prospector strategy is also on skills required by the marketing, sales, and research and development functions.

The variations in the skill sources and skill types of business strategy discussed here are based on the assumption that different staffing and training practices are important for achieving different strategic objectives. However, this relationship between source and type of skills may not always hold. This is because effectiveness of staffing and training practices may be influenced by several factors, such as the climate for transfer of training, compensation system, etc.

Among the more recent theoretical developments, the resource-based view (as discussed in Chapter 1) contributes further to an understanding of how firms acquire and shape their human resources to establish a sustainable competitive advantage. The resource-based view suggests that organizations achieve competitive advantage through their human resources that are unique, valuable, and that are not imitable. Some of these resources are difficult and expensive to replace or to acquire when needed. Some resources cannot be traded. Firms that have resources that are difficult to replace or develop must work with existing resources rather than attempt to create them. Firms ensure that they have the required human resource through their staffing and training practices. Moreover, firms achieve competitive advantage to the extent they are able to create a pool of unique human resources based on its staffing and training practices.

Strategic linkage of training activities results in several benefits for the firm:

- Human resource and training professionals become business partners and work with operating managers to help solve their problems
- Human resource professionals contribute to organizational results through various activities
- Rather than chase latest training fads, human resource professionals design need-based programmes
- Reduces the mindset that training can solve most employee or organizational problems. The focus is on assessing what approach—training or non-training—will help manage the performance issue at hand.

THE PROCESS OF TRAINING AND DEVELOPMENT

In a broad sense, T&D activities are designed to help the organization achieve its overall goals. Organizational goals and objectives should, therefore, be the starting point of T&D programmes. The first step in a T&D programme should be to clearly determine and specify the organizational goals, objectives, and strategies. It is important for the entire training process to be oriented and aligned with organizational goals and strategies. For example, if the strategic objective of a fast food restaurant chain is 'customer delight', the business strategy that the restaurant should choose is one that facilitates the overall organizational goal. The training programme should also be directed towards building upon and improving skills and competencies that will further the organizational goal. In this case, the skills may be related to customer service excellence. Through enhancing individual employee skills, T&D results in improved individual and organizational performance.

A strategically aligned T&D process represents the systems approach to T&D. Unfortunately, many organizations do not establish the linkage between strategic objectives and training programmes. Instead, they prefer to adopt training fads or copy whatever the competition is doing. Too often management development is informal and disjointed rather than part of a strategic training plan. Training is offered or managers are encouraged to take advantage of training opportunities, but these opportunities are not part of a formal programme that is linked to organizational goals and long-range objectives. Such an approach results in T&D programmes that are misdirected, poorly designed, and inadequately evaluated. While much organizational investment is directed to such ad hoc T&D activity, they do not offer much return to the organization.

A schematic diagram of the process of training is presented in Figure 6.6. The systems approach to T&D involves the following four phases.

1. Needs assessment (diagnostic phase)
2. Programme design and development

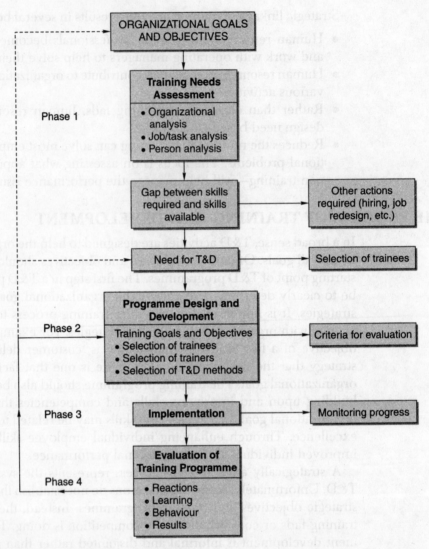

Figure 6.6: The Training Process

3. Programme implementation
4. Evaluation

Needs Assessment Phase

Needs assessment is a systematic, objective determination of training needs based on data. It involves placing training within an appropriate organizational context. The goal of needs assessment is to determine whether a need for training actually exists in the organization. A training need is said to exist when there is a discrepancy between what is desired and what exists. Needs assessment takes the form of comparing the skills required with the skills available. To the extent that there may be a skills shortfall—that is, more skills are required than are available—training may be required. If a firm decides to install a new computer system in its main office, it would first determine the level of skills required to use the system. Subsequently, through a skills inventory, the firm would determine whether the relevant group of employees have the requisite skills. A gap between the two suggests the need for training. Comparison between the expected level of performance (as specified by job analysis) and the current level of performance of the individual may indicate performance discrepancy. If the performance discrepancy is due to a skill or knowledge deficiency that is trainable and can be met by training, it suggests the need for training.

An organization should commit resources to T&D activities only if it expects to achieve some goals. For example, training needs have increased in the IT services industry today as the average graduate does not possess the required skills. Training has assumed particular importance in the BPO industry. With thousands of fresh graduates handling customer queries, there is an ongoing need to train them on soft and specialized skills. As BPO firms look towards moving up the value chain, cultural and value training and training to gain understanding of the industry in general and of the organization in particular has become important. Firms that conduct T&D programmes without conducting needs assessment may be investing money where it will not result in returns. For example, needs assessment may suggest that instead of conducting training, the organization would be better off if it chooses less costly options, such as hiring new employees, job redesign, etc.

There are certain indicators in a firm that suggest the need for training. The most obvious indicators come from productivity measures, such as reduced productivity, or poor job performance. Other indicators may be high wastage, accidents, poor product quality, etc. However, these outcomes may not always be the result of skill deficiency. If the employee has the required skill, yet is not performing as expected, the performance problem may be due to factors such as low motivation. In this situation, some other intervention such as new incentives or rewards instead of training may prove to be more effective. Therefore, systematic needs assessment is important to determine that training is the solution to the concerned problem. Needs assessment is the most important step in the T&D process. The entire process flows from the needs identified. If needs are incorrectly determined, the training programme will also be inappropriately directed. Despite its importance, very few organizations conduct a systematic needs assessment in the context of their strategic plans.

Information with respect to T&D needs assessment is collected by conducting three primary types of analyses. These analyses are organizational analysis, job/task analysis, and person analysis (see Table 6.3). Figure 6.7 shows the types of need analysis.

Organizational analysis Training does not exist in a vacuum. The context in which training occurs has an impact on training effectiveness. The first step in needs assessment is to identify the forces that can influence the need for training. Organizational analysis is an examination of the environment, strategies, organizational goals, resources of the organization, personnel inventories, performance data, and climate and efficiency indices to determine where the training emphasis should be placed in the organization and what factors may affect training. Companies like Motorola and IBM conduct annual surveys to assess training needs in the context of the company's short and long-term goals.

The strategic initiatives and the short-term and long-term goals of the organization are reviewed to channelize the training towards specific issues of importance to the firm. For example, a firm that is participating in a strategic merger or a strategic acquisition will have to manage employees coming together with different cultures. Thus, the firm may emphasize training on managing cultural diversity and on understanding different ways of conducting

Table 6.3: Source of Needs Analysis Data

Types of Analyses in Needs Assessment	Sources of Data
Organizational Analysis An examination of the environment, strategies, organizational goals, resources of the organization, performance data, personnel inventories, etc. To determine where the training emphasis should be placed in the organization	▪ Economic and policy issues ▪ Strategic initiatives of the organization ▪ Technological change ▪ Technological, financial, and human resources available to meet training objectives ▪ Data about turnover, accidents, absenteeism, etc.
Job Analysis Job description and job specifications to determine the content of the training programme to ensure that the trainee performs well on the job	▪ Job descriptions ▪ Job specifications ▪ Competency assessment
Person Analysis To determine which employees need training and which do not	▪ Attitude surveys ▪ Group discussions ▪ Questionnaires ▪ Performance appraisals ▪ Skills tests ▪ Exit interviews ▪ Employee performance documents

Adapted from: Bohlander, Snell, and Sherman 2002

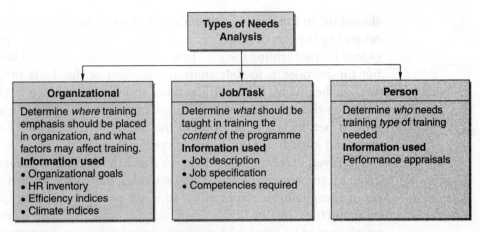

Figure 6.7: Types of Needs Analysis

business. Similarly, globalization, technological change, and restructuring of organizations all influence the way work is done and hence the types of skills required by the firm. When faced with employee surplus, IBM tried to reduce layoffs by retraining employees to be sales representatives. IBM minimized layoffs and through its larger sales staff achieved another goal, that is, to improve customer satisfaction.

Organizational analysis also involves examining the HR inventory. The HR or skills inventory is helpful in determining retirements and turnover and in projecting employee mobility. Inventories also indicate the number of employees available in the organization in each knowledge and skill group. This information is compared to the skills needed as determined by the HRP process, thus indicating which skill groups are deficient.

Efficiency indices, such as cost of labour, quality of the product, wastage, late deliveries, customer complaints, repairs, etc., may also be examined to find discrepancies between desired and actual performance. The climate index can also identify problem areas that can be managed with training. Climate indices include records on turnover, accidents, productivity, attitude surveys, employee suggestions, etc. Apart from these factors, it is also important to identify any organizational constraints on training efforts. Adequate facilities and resources may not be assigned for training effort if the top management is not convinced of the benefits of training.

Job/task analysis Job analysis is concerned with determining what should be taught in training to ensure that the trainee performs the job satisfactorily. Job descriptions and job specifications are of great help at this step. By listing the specific duties and skills of a job, job description and job specifications provide the basic reference point in determining the training required. *Task analysis* is the process of determining what the content of a training programme should be on the basis of the study of tasks and duties involved in the job. By reviewing the job description, task analysis determines the specific skills required for performing the job. Task analysis is more detailed than job analysis, but the purpose is to determine the content of the T&D programme. Task analysis begins by listing all the tasks and duties included in the job. It then identifies the steps performed by the employee to complete each task. The type of performance required on the task is then identified followed by the skills and knowledge necessary for performance.

However, in recent times, there is a shift in both job analysis and task analysis. From a fixed sequence of tasks and activities, this shift is toward a more flexible set of competencies required for superior performance. Competency assessment focuses on the analysis of sets of skills and knowledge needed by employees to be successful, particularly in knowledge-intensive jobs. Training programmes based on task analysis become dated as the nature of jobs change. On the other hand, competency-based training programmes are more flexible. Competency-based approach to T&D is discussed in more detail later in the chapter.

Person analysis This is the third step in needs assessment. Person analysis determines which employees require training, and, equally importantly, which do not. It answers the question of who needs training in the firm and the specific type of training needed. Person analysis involves comparing the actual performance of individuals, groups, or departments (based on performance appraisal data) to the expected performance standards. The performance appraisal data helps determine which employees (or groups of employees) have been successful in performing the job according to performance standards, and which employees are not meeting expectations. However, performance data typically do not reveal the reasons for performance deficiency. While performance discrepancy indicates areas that need attention, it is important to determine whether the discrepancy is due to knowledge or skill deficiency or due to lack of motivation as emphasized earlier. Training will be beneficial for people who lack certain 'trainable' skills. Thus, person analysis helps organizations avoid the costly mistake of sending all employees into training when, in fact, some do not need it. It also helps determine the present skill levels of employees entering training so that the programme can be designed to emphasize those skills on which they are deficient. To obtain person analysis information, companies may use self-assessment, customer feedback, peers and subordinate feedback, performance appraisal data, etc.

If training is needed, managers and HR personnel should determine what kind of training is needed, where in the organization training is needed, what specific knowledge, skills, abilities, etc. the employees need, and what methods will best deliver the needed knowledge, skills, and abilities.

Programme Design and Development Phase

After identifying training needs, the next step in the training process is to design the learning environment necessary to facilitate learning and to develop the training programme. Design and development of training programme includes the establishment of training goals, selection of trainees, trainee potential and readiness, focus on principles of learning, selecting training methods for use in the programme, and choice of instructors or trainers.

Establishing training goals and objectives Once training needs have been assessed, goals and objectives of T&D should be defined. Training goals should be integrated with the training needs of the organization in order to ensure that these needs will be served when training goals are achieved. Since the entire training programme will be designed to accomplish the training goals, it is important to align training goals with organizational objectives. As training goals are accomplished, the training needs should be met, and the objectives of the organization should be served. Training goals also provide direction to the training programme.

Training goals and objectives specify what the training programme should accomplish and the specific performance the trainees should be able to exhibit at the end of the training programme. These are the desired outcomes of the training programme. Training goals should be clearly stated in behavioural terms. Well-written training goals have the following characteristics:

- Specify observable actions (e.g., time on target, error rate, etc.) What is to be achieved?
- Specify measurable criteria (e.g., percentage correct, percentage error, etc.) How it is to be measured?
- Conditions of performance. When the behaviour should occur.

The training objective 'Learn to manage time' is vague, and does not demonstrate the above characteristics. However, when the objective is stated as, 'Will make a list of things to be done, assign a priority to each item, and schedule time for various activities 100% of the time, and follow this schedule at least 80% of the time', it reflects a clearly stated training goal.

Organizations often conduct training programmes without stating objectives in specific terms. When they do so, they lose out on the following advantages of establishing training goals.

- Objectives help determine criteria for evaluating training programmes.
- They help determine the content of the training programme.
- Objectives ensure that the issues identified through strategic planning are being addressed.
- Ensure that training function becomes more accountable and clearly linked to other HR activities.

- Objectives help training managers demonstrate the strategic value of training and gain more support for training activities.

When establishing objectives, it is also important to consider how the accomplishment of these objectives will be measured. Therefore, evaluation should be built into the training process right from the early stages of planning a training programme. Follow-up measurement should be designed to directly evaluate the impact of training activities on meeting the stated objectives.

Selection of trainees Person analysis helps identify the individuals or groups that require training. For example, customer feedback may indicate that customers are dissatisfied by the manner in which sales personnel interact with the customers. In this case, the target employee group that should receive training is obvious. However, not all sales personnel may be selected for training. This may be due to several reasons:

- all sales personnel may not need training (if we use the performance discrepancy logic);
- some sales personnel may lack the ability to learn the skills required and to subsequently use them; and
- imparting training to employees who are unlikely to gain from training results in feelings of personal failure on the part of such trainees. It also leads to unproductive expenditure of resources on training.

Training potential and readiness Employees selected for T&D programmes should have the *ability* to learn as well as *motivation* to learn from the training, that is, the individuals selected to undergo a training programme should be 'trainable' (ready to learn). Trainee motivation can be enhanced by

- demonstrating the value of training and how they can use new skills on their jobs; and
- informing trainees of the benefits of attending the training. These benefits may be intrinsic (or towards personal growth) or extrinsic (or towards promotion).

Preparing employees, typically high performers, for higher responsibility within the firm is a major input for selecting who will be sent for training. At J. Walter Thomson, the best training programmes are skewed towards the star employees—those identified as high performers and future leaders. Similarly, Ogilvy and Mather and GroupM extend training to young talent to provide them an opportunity to grow. At GroupM, there is a programme called 'Fast Trackers' for young achievers through which they are groomed to take on additional responsibility. Senior executives identified for greater responsibilities are also given special training. For example, at J. Walter Thomson, top-level managers who have been identified to head offices are nominated for the international programme. The firm has also introduced a top achiever's programme.

It is common to encounter resistance from managers when providing management development opportunities. They may be hesitant to admit to areas of weakness or that they need additional training, which may give rise to many barriers to participation, most commonly 'lack of time'. Resistance to change and fear of failure are natural. When T&D is positioned as a prerequisite to growth within the organization, employees are extended an incentive for participation. At the same time, it also develops a form of a self-selection process for identifying employees interested in advancement within the organization.

Focus on principles of learning Training is a learning situation aimed at imparting skills, knowledge, or competencies to the learner, that is, the employee. There are certain conditions in which learning is effective. The training environment should be designed to maximize learning. This can be achieved by incorporating principles of learning in the training programme. The success or failure of a training programme is linked to these learning principles. These principles of learning are briefly described in Table 6.4.

Selection of trainers In designing the training programme, decision needs to be made regarding who will conduct training, that is, the choice of trainer. The success of a training programme in large part is guided by the skills of the instructor (trainer). Certain characteristics separate good trainers from bad trainers. Some of the characteristics of good trainers are sincerity, sense of humour, knowledge of subject, interest, enthusiasm, ability to give clear instructions, and ability to adapt style to match trainees' preference and learning ability. Trainers are also required to keep updating their skills and knowledge. Many firms like TCS have 'train the trainer' programmes in place.

Another issue related to the selection of a trainer relates to whether the training will be in-house and conducted by internal training staff member(s) or will be external to the organization and conducted by a consultant or training specialist. Whether the training is internal or external, the trainer should demonstrate the above-mentioned qualities. In several firms like ICICI, Infosys, Wipro, Genpact, and in the IT services industry, in-house training has become crucial to the growth of the firm. IBM Daksh, the BPO firm considers training the most important means to deliver high quality talent that has a direct impact on client satisfaction. The company has a separate in-house training group that has been rechristened the Talent Transformation Business Unit (TTBU). The TTBU is run like a separate business with its own finance controller, quality head, an administration and transport wing, and a dedicated HR representative. The TTBU is held accountable for output measures of its trainees, such as voice quality, rejection rates, cost of delivery, and customer satisfaction metrics.

Table 6.4: Principles of Learning

Goal-setting	When the goals and objectives of training are clearly stated and communicated, trainees are motivated to make efforts towards goal achievement.
Meaningful presentation, practice and repetition	Material to be learned should be meaningfully arranged so that each subsequent information builds upon the previous information. Trainees should be given an opportunity to practise what has been learned in the training situation. Active and repeated practise leads to greater efficiency in job performance.
Feedback and reinforcement	Feedback provides the trainees with knowledge of results, so the trainees know the areas in which they have done well and the areas which need improvement. Feedback is also motivational. Knowledge about how well one has performed is motivating. Verbal encouragement or other extrinsic rewards also reinforce desired behaviour.
Whole vs part learning	Complex jobs should be broken down into its parts. Trainees should learn each part separately, starting from the basic to the difficult ones. After mastering each part separately, the trainee should be shown how these parts fit together.
Massed vs spaced learning	Practice is important for learning a new skill. Practicing a new skill with rest pauses in between (spaced practice) is more effective than practicing without breaks (massed practice).
Individual differences	People learn at different rates and in different ways. Trainees differ in their learning style. For example, some trainees learn best by actually doing (activists). Some others learn by listening to others. Still others learn by observing others.
Transfer of learning	Transfer occurs when trainees use on their job what they have learned in training. One way to achieve this is to ensure that training situation has elements of the actual job context.

Source: Bohlander, Snell, and Sherman 2002

Many firms are outsourcing part of their training requirements, while several others believe in developing an internal talent pool of trainers. The latter believe that the best trainers are the line managers and executives who have spent time with the organization and understand the business first-hand. Accenture has outsourced cross-cultural and communication training to vendors. However, for technical training, it develops trainers from within through what it calls a 'leaders teaching leaders' approach. In order to encourage senior managers to take an active interest in training others, some firms link their performance appraisals and upward growth to investing time in training others. At ICICI bank, senior executives are required to spend time training others. The company has a 'Leadership Talent List' of potential fast trackers. In order to make it to this list senior executives are required to spend time training others. Infosys too links training to individuals' performance.

The quality of internal training capability is expected to be a key driver of business success in the future. It is therefore not surprising that firms are investing heavily in training infrastructure. At the same time, firms such as Accenture, Infosys, and TCS are building external partnerships with educational institutions, as discussed in Chapter 4.

Selecting training and development methods A significant decision in designing the training programme relates to the choice of selection method(s) to be used for imparting training. A range of training methods are available for training employees at all levels. These differ from each other primarily in terms of the degree to which they allow and encourage active involvement of trainees in the process of learning. On a continuum of 'degree of trainee participation', lecture methods fall at one end (where there is no participation by the trainee, only one-way-communication), and on-the-job training falls on the other end (where trainee learns by doing). Figure 6.8 depicts this continuum. It is generally believed that training methods that encourage trainee participation in the learning experience are more effective than those that limit trainees' involvement.

Knowledge, skills and abilities that need to be learned are major consideration in choosing training methods. Different methods are suitable for imparting different kinds of skills. For example, for giving the factual information, one-way communication using lecture methods may serve the purpose. However, when behavioural or attitude change is required, methods requiring greater employee participation, such as simulations, may be more appropriate. Training methods can also be categorized as on-the-job and off-the-job. The relative merits and de-merits of on-the-job and off-the-job methods are presented in Table 6.5.

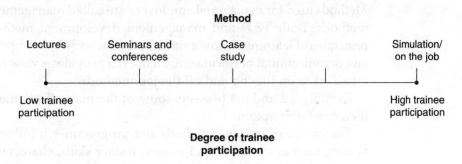

Figure 6.8:   Continuum of Training and Development Methods

Table 6.5: Pros and Cons of On-the-job and Off-the-job Methods

On-the-job method	Off-the-job method
Employee is placed in the real work situation. Employees learn through actual practice and experience. An experienced employee or the supervisor demonstrates the job and teaches the tricks of the trade. Employee learns by doing the job.	Employees learn by listening or observing others in a learning situation away from work. Conceptual knowledge and certain skills are learned in this way. These methods supplement the experience gained on the job.
Pros • Simple and less costly • Provides hands-on experience under normal working conditions • Manager/senior employee providing training can develop good relationship with new employees • High trainee motivation since training is relevant • Good transfer of learning	**Pros** • More appropriate for certain skills where learning on the job may be risky • Trainees are free from worries of performing the job and can focus on learning
Cons • Training environment is not well-structured • Managers may lack training skills and willingness to impart training • May be costly due to lost production and mistakes if not handled properly • May have frequent interruptions due to job demands	**Cons** • Problems may arise in transfer of learning to work situation • If trainees do not clearly understand the relevance of training for work, they may lack motivation to learn • Costs the organization in terms of man hours when employees are away for training

Some training methods are more appropriate for use with non-managerial employees while others may be better suited for managerial employees. Methods directed at non-managerial employees are called training methods. Methods used for managerial employees are called management development methods. Both T&D and management development methods incorporate principles of learning, follow a similar process, and aim at improving individual and organizational performance. Figure 6.9 provides a view of T&D methods classified as on-the-job and off-the-job methods.

Exhibits 6.2 and 6.3 presents some of the major T&D methods including their brief description.

The choice of training methods and programmes is influenced by several factors, such as availability of trainer, trainer skills, characteristics of participants, sociocultural environment, programme objectives, principles of learning, and available infrastructure (Table 6.6).

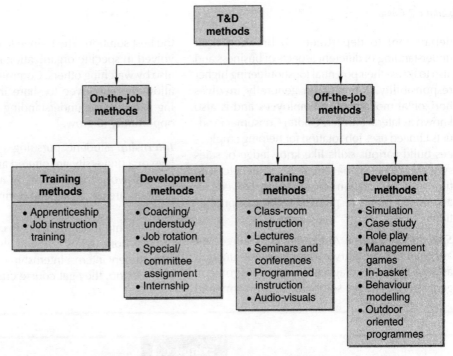

Figure 6.9: Classification of Training and Development Methods

---

Exhibit 6.2

On-the-job Employee Training and Development Methods

Training Methods

Apprenticeship Training Individuals entering industry, particularly skilled workers such as laboratory technicians, electricians, plumbers, carpenters, etc. are given thorough instruction and experience in both theoretical and practical aspects of work by an experienced worker. It involves some off-the-job training also. Apprentices earn a stipend during the training period.

Job Instruction Training A systematic method of on-the-job training where an experienced employee teaches the job to the newcomer in a stepwise manner. It consists of four steps—preparation of the learner, presentation of skill or knowledge, performance try-out by the learner, and follow-up by trainer to assess learning.

Management Development Methods

Coaching/Understudy or Assistant to Positions The trainee works directly with the person he/she is to replace. The latter is responsible for the trainee's coaching. The trainee relieves the executive of certain responsibilities, performs several duties under the coach, and in the process learns the ropes of the job. Some companies like P&G have a coaching programme as part of their management development method.

Job Rotation It involves moving employees or management trainees to various positions from

Contd

Exhibit 6.2 Contd

department to department to broaden their understanding of different aspects of business and also to assess their potential for shouldering higher responsibility. Job rotation generally involves horizontal movement of employees and is also known as lateral transfer. Godrej Consumer Products Limited uses job rotation for helping employees build various skills like knowledge of sales system, project management, IT skills, etc. The firm uses job rotation to prepare employees for assuming a higher responsibility through promotions.

Special/Committee Assignments Trainees are assigned to temporary committees that function as a taskforce to diagnose a specific problem, generate alternative solutions, and recommend the best solution. The trainee learns by being involved in specific organizational problems, and also by watching others. Committee assignments allow the employee to share in decision-making, broaden the understanding, and provide an opportunity to grow.

Internship Students pursuing a course in a college or a university are offered an opportunity to get real-world experience by an organization. Students are paid a stipend during the internship period.

Internship programmes help organizations get projects done at low cost and also get new ideas from student interns. Internship programmes help students too; they get course credits.

Exhibit 6.3

Off-the-job Employee Training and Development Methods

Training Methods

Classroom Instruction Training has been generally seen as synonymous with classroom instruction. Classroom instruction allows a single instructor to impart training simultaneously to a large number of participants. This method is particularly useful for presenting information through lectures, demonstrations, films, audiotapes, videotapes, or through computer instructions. For example, an audiotape of a conflict between managers from two functional areas can be played to an audience. After listening to the audiotape, the behaviour of the two managers may be discussed by the trainees, who may be assisted by the trainer. This helps develop an understanding of skills in handling interpersonal situations.

Lectures They are the traditional form of instruction that involves one-way presentation of knowledge/concepts. Lectures are a quick and simple way to provide knowledge to large groups of trainees. Lectures also are the best means to introduce other more participative methods of training as well as to summarize the learning generated through other methods. Firms are using technology for imparting training. There is a growing trend towards holding lectures and seminars through distance learning.

Seminars and Conferences Like lectures, seminars and conferences bring groups of people together for training and development. These provide a vehicle for communicating ideas and procedures and for a debate and discussion on relevant issues.

Programmed Instruction This is a step-by-step self-learning method in which the trainee can learn at his/her own pace. It consists of three parts: presenting facts and new knowledge (stimulus) to the trainee followed by a question, allowing the trainee to respond to the question, and

Contd

Exhibit 6.3 Contd

providing feedback on the accuracy of the answers. The trainee cannot proceed to the next step without mastering the information presented in the previous step. It is also called self-directed learning. It incorporates most principles of learning.

Audiovisual Methods Films, PowerPoint presentations, videoconferencing, audiotapes, and videotapes are widely used in training. These serve as effective accompaniment to lectures, seminars, role plays, case studies, etc. These are more expensive but the cost is far outweighed by the interest they generate, by the trainee involvement in the learning process, and by the greater retention of learned material. These are useful to demonstrate how to perform a job in a stepwise manner, such as assembling electronic equipment or working with a problematic employee. Advancement in technology, such as CDs, video discs, DVD, etc. has taken audio-visual technology a step further by providing interactive capability to trainees.

Management Development Methods

Simulation Method This method develops a training or learning situation that is designed to closely resemble the actual work situation the trainee is likely to work in. This increases the likelihood of transfer of learning to the work situation. It is especially useful when it is unwise or impractical to train employees on the job or on the actual equipment used on the job. For example, learning the skill to provide feedback to a subordinate through on-the-job training may prove to be too costly in terms of likely consequences.

Case Study Approach A class-room learning situation, the case study approach presents the trainee with a written description of an organizational problem. The trainee proceeds to analyse the case, define the problem, and generate possible solutions in discussion with other trainees.

This approach is most useful for imparting analytical, problem-solving, and critical-thinking skills.

Role Play It creates a realistic situation in which one or more trainees assume the role of a specific person in the given situation. This provides an opportunity to the trainee to try out and experiment alternative behaviour (autocratic and democratic leadership behaviour, for example), in order to develop sensitivity to the limitations of the other person, group, or functional area (workers and management, marketing and production, line and staff, for example). Role plays are most useful for training managers to handle conflict situations, performance feedback, etc. By assuming the role of the other person, they improve their ability to understand and cope with others.

Management Games They present the trainees with the task of making a series of decisions in a hypothetical organization. Each decision impacts some part of the organization. The trainee makes further decisions in a continuously evolving situation. The task of the trainees is to decipher what makes the model underlying the management game to react in the manner that it does, that is, the impact on the hypothetical organization. Several environmental and business factors are built into the game. This ensures that the training situation closely approximates the functioning of an organization. Management games lead to a high degree of trainee participation. The use of management games has become pervasive in the industry and the games have become highly sophisticated and computerized. Companies like GE and Motorola use industry-specific games for training.

In-basket The trainee is given materials that include items from a manager's typical work-day. These include mail, e-mail, and other pressing matters such as customer feedback, demand for

Contd

Exhibit 6.3 Contd

a report from a senior, etc. The trainee is required to take a series of decisions on each item in the in-basket within a limited time period. The trainee is given feedback on the quality of decisions taken, the manner in which items were prioritized, and how well the time was utilized.

Behaviour Modelling   This is an approach to improve interpersonal skills and is also called interaction management. Trainees learn through observing. The method involves four steps: modeling of effective behaviour (often by use of films), role playing the behaviour by trainees, reinforcement of effective role playing, and transfer of

learning to the job. Several firms like AT&T, IBM, GE, etc. have introduced behaviour modelling in their management development programmes.

Outdoor-oriented Programmes   Also called wilderness or survival training, their purpose is to develop interpersonal skills, team skills, skills for handling conflict, interpersonal trust building, etc. through participation in adventure games like river rafting, rock climbing, etc. These games challenge an individual's potential and reinforce the importance of working together and of succeeding as a group.

Table 6.6:   Factors that Influence Selection of Training Methods

Factor	Training Method
Trainer's knowledge and experience	▪ Case study: trainer needs to have high level of analytical skills ▪ Role play: trainer should be experienced in handling interpersonal problems
Trainee characteristics	▪ Intellectual level, educational background, age, and experience of trainees influence choice of training method ▪ Case studies more appropriate for experienced managers
Sociocultural environment	▪ Lectures most appropriate with people culturally used to lectures ▪ Team training methods more suitable in participative culture
Programme objectives	▪ Group exercises: for motivating trainees toward learning ▪ Role play: to enhance communication effectiveness ▪ Case study: for problem-solving, analytical, and diagnostic skills
Principles of learning	▪ Motivation, active involvement, and feedback: business games ▪ Sequencing and structuring of training material: lecture ▪ Individualized approach, transfer of learning: project assignment
Available infrastructure	▪ Group training: several discussion rooms ▪ Lecture: a classroom, whiteboard, audio-visuals ▪ Computer based training: sophisticated and costly technology

Employee development, however, is not viewed as the sole responsibility of the firm. Employees are being encouraged to assume responsibility for their own development. For instance, HP, besides providing formal training to employees through various training programmes, also reimburses employees for formal courses they might want to take, and ICICI offers its employees sabbaticals of up to four years.

An interesting development in management development is to provide an opportunity to employees to earn an MBA degree from a prestigious business school. Now several business schools are designing customized degree-granting MBA programmes around the needs of specific companies. This trend has been around in India for some years. For example, IIM Ahmedabad runs special programmes for public sector employees. LG Electronics has signed a five year contract with Thunderbird, the Gavin School of International Management in the US, to educate about 150 LG executives. LG employees will participate in week-long modules held every four weeks at the company's headquarters in South Korea. All courses are taught in person by members of Thunderbird's faculty. It is a 13-month programme and is designed to culminate with a month-long capstone session at the Thunderbird campus in the US.

Programme Implementation Phase

Once the learning objectives have been specified, a learning environment designed, trainees and trainers selected, and choice of training methods been made, the training can be conducted. While the training is in progress, the progress of the trainees in the direction of learning objectives should be monitored. The monitoring is usually done through periodic skill or knowledge tests, observation, or feedback from trainees themselves.

Evaluation Phase

After the training episode is over, and the trainee returns back to job duties or takes independent charge of given tasks, it is expected that this employee will perform more effectively on the job or will be better prepared for additional responsibilities. Evaluation is the process of systematically collecting information and using the information to determine the effects and value of a training programme. It seeks to determine the degree to which the programme has done what it was supposed to do. The question that remains to be answered at this stage is: Was training effective in meeting the stated objectives? This question is most important to determine the value of training. Yet, this is the question that remains frequently overlooked by several organizations. Firms that do address this question often limit it to assessment of trainee reactions, such as how well trainees liked the programme, whether trainees think the programme was useful, and whether it will help them perform their jobs better. Though trainee feedback offers some insight about the usefulness of the training programme, it does not indicate the extent to which training goals were met.

While everyone recognizes the importance of evaluating training, it is a phenomenon that is very difficult to study. This is especially true for on-the-job training, which is mostly informal and, therefore, hard to measure and its effects on productivity even more difficult to quantify. Since organizations assign a large percentage of budget for employee training and development activities, it would be prudent on their part to assess whether all of the investment has been worth it. Evaluation ensures that T&D programmes are accountable and are meeting the needs of employees and the organization in the most cost-effective manner. This has gained greater significance in a competitive business environment when organizations seek to improve quality and achieve cost advantage.

Formal evaluation of T&D programmes serve to demonstrate the contribution these programmes have made to individual and organizational performance improvements. In the absence of such evidence, T&D budgets become the first casualty of a cost leadership business strategy.

Evaluation of T&D programmes should assess

- the amount of change—degree to which change has occurred in skill, ability, or job performance; and
- the source of change—whether the change can be attributed to a specific T&D programme.

Stages of Training Evaluation

The evaluation phase requires the identification and development of criteria against which the T&D programme will be assessed. The criteria include participants' reactions to the programme, learning, and job performance measures such as accidents, productivity, absenteeism, sales figures, etc. The choice of these criteria is made before conducting the training programme. The formal evaluation is related to training objectives. Hence, the criteria for evaluation are determined when the objectives of the programme are established. Evaluation is, therefore, not something that is tagged to the end of the actual process of the T&D programme; instead, how a T&D programme will be evaluated is planned fairly early in the process. Evaluation begins right from the time that the T&D programme begins and continues through till the end and beyond. There are three stages at which information is gathered to evaluate a T&D programme (see Figure 6.10).

Pre-training evaluation This involves evaluation at the time that the T&D programme is inaugurated. At this stage, the objective of evaluation is to clearly communicate the objectives of the programme to the trainees. It also seeks to understand the expectations the trainees have from the programme. Pre-training evaluation is useful in ensuring that trainee expectations are aligned

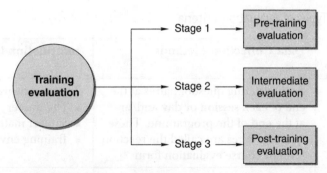

Figure 6.10: Stages of Training Evaluation

with the objectives of the T&D programme. In certain cases, the content and scheduling of the programme may be modified to match trainee expectations.

Intermediate evaluation As mentioned earlier, the T&D programme should be monitored while it is in progress in order to ensure that it is progressing as expected. Evaluating the programme while it is being conducted helps find out if it is going off-course. Mid-course corrections may be introduced to realign the programme with its objectives. For example, a programme aimed at enhancing communication skills of a group of employees may be found to impart theory about communication, rather than the skill. Intermediate feedback from trainees may be useful to modify the instructional method.

Post-training evaluation A T&D programme should at the end assess its effects. It serves the purpose of assessing whether

- trainees have acquired new knowledge or skills or have improved their skills and competency levels;
- training objectives have been met;
- learning from training has led to improvement in job performance; and
- organizational performance has improved when measured against criteria such as absenteeism, productivity, employee satisfaction, product quality, etc.

Criteria for Training Evaluation

Generally, four types of criteria are used to evaluate training programmes.

- Reactions
- Learning
- Behaviour
- Results

The types of data collected for each of these criteria when evaluating training programmes are summarized in Table 6.7. Most training programmes limit themselves to assessing trainee reactions to the programme. Relatively few

Table 6.7: Types of Evaluation Criteria

Evaluation Criteria	Data Collection Methods	Information Obtained
Reactions	Administering questionnaires at the end of each session or day and/or at the end of the programme. These questionnaires are called the reaction form or course evaluation form	Trainees' degree of satisfaction with ■ The trainer ■ Subject matter and content ■ Training environment
Learning	■ Paper and pencil tests (multiple-choice) ■ Performance tests ■ Simulation exercises	Trainees' level of understanding before and after the training to determine gains in knowledge
Behaviour	■ Performance appraisal ■ Observation of trainees on the job ■ Interviews with trainees and their managers	Ratings of trainees before and after training to assess the degree to which training has changed their performance
Results	■ Productivity data records ■ Tracking performance measures such as productivity, turnover, grievances, absenteeism, sales targets, etc. ■ Annual reports of the company	Before and after data on performance criteria measures

Source. Bernardin 2004

organizations seek data related to changes in business results due to training. Though reactions and learning are easier to measure, each criterion is important for assessing the success of the programme.

Reactions Participant reaction measures seek to assess trainees' opinions about the training programme. Reactions indicate more than whether the trainees liked the programme. Trainee reactions help gain insights into aspects of the programme that they found useful as well as aspects that need to change. For example, trainees may be critical of the training methods used, or the depth of coverage of certain topics. This feedback helps in making modifications in the training design and implementation. Moreover, if trainees do not like the programme, they are unlikely to be motivated to learn, or to participate in the learning process. However, positive reactions do not necessarily indicate that learning has occurred, or that training has been successful. Reactions in any case do not provide complete information about the effectiveness of the programme.

Learning Learning measures assess the degree to which trainees have acquired new knowledge, skills, or competencies. In order to assess the learning that has occurred, the knowledge and skill levels of trainees should be tested before beginning the training programme. This then serves as a baseline standard against which the level of trainee knowledge and skills measured after the training is compared to determine improvement.

Behaviour The degree to which training has resulted in a change in trainees' job performance is assessed through their behaviour or performance on the job. This is, in fact, the main purpose of training. Comparison of employees' job performance before and after the training programme can be made to determine the impact of training. Unfortunately, much of what is learned in a training programme is never used on the job. This does not suggest that the training was ineffective, though it probably was a waste of resources. Trainees may have liked the programme (reactions) and also gained knowledge (learning) from it. However, there are many factors that may prevent the transfer of learning to the work situation. As principles of learning suggest, it is important to design the programme to maximize transfer. This is likely when, for example, the training situation is similar to the trainees' work situation, and there is a climate that supports transfer and application of learning. Xerox assesses the transfer of learned skills to the job through multiple methods such as observation of trainees when they return to their jobs, post-training performance appraisals of trainees, etc.

Results This criterion seeks to determine the impact of training on the performance of the organization. HR professionals are under increasing pressure to demonstrate how T&D programmes have contributed to the 'bottom line' results of the firm. Data on measures such as productivity, sales volume, profits, is obtained before and after the training. The phrase 'business performance' needs to be understood as more comprehensive and not limited to financial data such as profitability ratios. There is now an emerging consensus that given the nature of the service sector business, business performance measurements must be different for the manufacturing and services sectors. Hence, a number of approaches to performance measurement have been developed which incorporate 'hard' measures such as financial performance and 'soft' measures such as employee satisfaction.

The balanced scorecard approach discussed in Chapter 1 has gained popularity in recent years as a means of measuring business performance. Fitzgerald et al. proposed that there are six dimensions of business performance. These are competitiveness, financial performance, quality of service, flexibility, resource utilization, and innovation. These six dimensions are further divided into two categories—*resultants* and *determinants.* Competitiveness and financial performance are seen as the result of other factors, and hence these are resultant dimensions of business performance. Quality of service, flexibility, resource utilization, and innovation are the determinants of the financial performance of the firm. Training is most likely to impact upon the determinant measures and thereby influence competitiveness and financial performance. However, estimating the benefits of training for improving business performance is a complex issue because business performance depends on several other factors such as economic climate, level of investment, marketing, etc.

JWT evaluates its training programmes based on trainee reactions (feedback) and learning. The employees who underwent training learnt to network and bounce off ideas better, and junior and middle managers also learnt to communicate with top managers of the firm (behaviour). At JWT, it is believed that training helps improve the quality of output and increase employee satisfaction (results). Contract, another advertising agency, considers training to be of help in stemming attrition (results).

Apart from these four criteria of evaluation, additional methods can be used to assess the value of training (Figure 6.11). These include

- return on investment (ROI);
- utility analysis or cost-benefit approach; and
- benchmarking.

Return on investment and cost benefit approach The ROI and cost-benefit approaches both seek to compare the monetary benefits of training with the cost of training. In effect, these approaches determine the value of training in rupee terms, that is, for every rupee spent on training, what does the company gain in rupees? If the cost of training is high and the benefits are

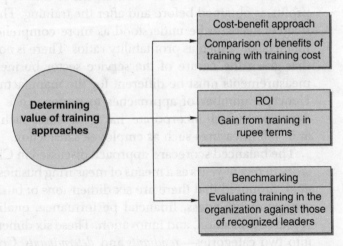

Figure 6.11: Approaches for Determining Value of Training

low, the utility of training and ROI may be low. The ROI is calculated by using the following formula:

$$ROI = \left\{ \frac{\text{net benefits of training}}{\text{training costs}} \right\} \times 100$$

where,

net benefits = total benefit of training – cost of training

Ford Motor Company, British Airways, and Motorola are some companies that calculate ROI for training programmes. Usually the benefits are the 'amount saved' or 'amount gained' in the year after the training is completed. Some costs of training programmes that should be measured are listed below.

- One time costs such as needs assessment cost, trainers' salaries, cost of training material and equipment (computers, handouts), programme development costs, etc.
- Costs associated with each training session, such as costs associated with trainer, facilities rental, etc.
- Costs associated with trainees, such as trainee salaries for the training period, non-reusable training materials, cost of boarding and lodging of trainees, total man-hours spent away from work, etc.

However, it is difficult to measure an investment in training and the benefits resulting from training. Though the cost of training can be measured, the precise financial benefit resulting from investment in training is difficult to establish. The linkage between training aspects such as the level of training activity, average training man-hours, and factors such as business performance is difficult to establish because business performance depends on several factors and varies across sectors and service types.

The utility model is not so commonly used for training evaluation since it is based on subjective measures. The utility of a training programme is seen as a function of measures such as the total cost of the programme, number of employees trained, value of the job for which training was provided, effect of training on employees, etc.

Benchmarking *Benchmarking* is the process of evaluating a company's own practices against those of recognized leaders in order to identify areas of improvement. A majority of firms engage in some informal form of benchmarking. As T&D becomes more strategic and important for organizational success, benchmarking is gaining popularity. To use benchmarking effectively, managers must clearly define measures of competency and performance, assess the current situation objectively, and identify areas of improvement. By learning what are the best practices of organizations that excel on these measures of competency and performance, managers implement specific changes in their own organizations. The American Society for Training and Development (ASTD) has established a project that allows organizations to measure and benchmark T&D activities against each other. Benchmarking data that is compared across organizations include data on training costs, training cost per trainee, average training hours per employee, etc. These data relate to three broad areas namely, training activity, training results, and training efficiency (Table 6.8).

McDonald's invests more than one billion dollars annually in training. As early as in 2001, Infosys spent 2.65% of its turnover on education and research. Every employee at Infosys receives an average of 47 hours of training. ICICI clocks an average of 62 hours of training per employee. The HR functions of IBM India and Accenture India are manned by around 300 people, each looking after hiring and training needs. Genpact spent close to $8 million on training, has 313 trainers along with 70 part-time specialists who also conduct domain-specific training for its 25,000 strong workforce across the world. JWT clocked 2,030 mandays of training and spent Rs 1.2 crores on training between January and June 2006. The total monetary allocation for training for the full year is Rs 2.25 crores. These are examples of measures of training activity. The average training per staff member per year for JWT currently stands at 3.46 days. O&M has 30 to 40 man-hours of training per employee.

Table 6.8: Measures Used for Benchmarking Training

Type of Data	Measure used for Benchmarking Data
■ Training Activities	■ Percentage of payroll spent on training ■ Average training hours per employee ■ Rupees spent on training each employee ■ Percentage of employees trained per year ■ Training staff per 1000 employees
■ Training Results (bottom-line)	■ Average percentage of satisfied trainees ■ Average percentage gain in learning per course ■ Average percentage of job performance improvement ■ Cost savings as a ratio of training expenses ■ Profits per employee per year ■ Revenues per employee per year
■ Training Efficiency	■ Training cost per student per hour ■ Time on task

Source: Bernardin 2004; Bohlander, Snell, and Sherman 2002

Some writers on the topic have emphasized the importance of understanding the 'cost of not training'. Sometimes, the decision to slash training budgets is aimed at reducing business costs but fails to recognize that cutting back on training is not without costs. For instance, reduction in training budget and training activity may result in reduced productivity and service quality, dissatisfied customers, lower employee commitment, and increased staff turnover. In such a case, the business incurs extra costs that can far outweigh the savings made from reduced training activity.

SPECIAL FORMS OF TRAINING AND DEVELOPMENT

Changes in the business environment have thrown up new and unique HR challenges and new forms of work and organizational structures, as has been pointed out. In response to these challenges, special forms of training programmes have been developed by organizations (Figure 6.12). Let us discuss some of these.

Team Training

Organizations may conduct training programmes for individuals or for work teams. Teams are becoming increasingly important in achieving an organization's operational and strategic goals. For example, members of

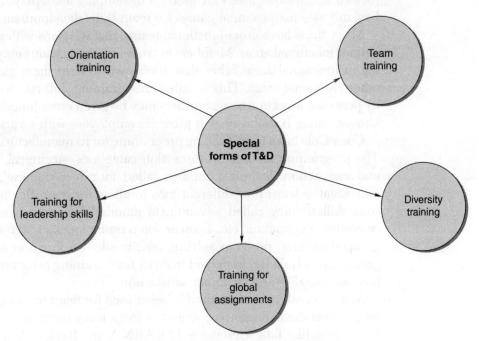

Figure 6.12:   Special forms of Training and Development

air-crew, a unit of the army, a research team, a manufacturing unit, a project team, etc. are all work groups or teams. In each of these groups, the contribution of each individual member is a function of the skills and knowledge of the individual as well as of the interaction of team members. Therefore, firms are extending training to teams. Team training is concerned with helping team members learn how to work more efficiently and effectively in teams. Some of the components of team training are team building; problem-solving; trust building, meeting skills; communication skills; conflict management; etc. HP provides a two-week training to team members to familiarize everyone with the processes of the organization and the needs of the business. GE also sends teams of employees for training, where they participate in business games that deal with the company's strengths and weaknesses. Mudra Communications focusses on 'team creativity'; the agency continuously forms and disbands cross-functional teams from different departments. Training for creativity at Mudra Communications is based on energizing team-members to work with one another in producing workable novel solutions.

A range of training methods may be used in the conduction of team training. These include in-baskets, group discussions, role plays, simulations, video films followed by discussion and lectures to impart information, etc. More recently, adventure training (wilderness training) is also being used to build effective teams. At Ramco Systems, outdoor training exercises such as para-sailing and rock-climbing expeditions are used for developing team-playing skills. Ashok Leyland uses management games for team skills development.

Many firms have cross-functional teams, that is, teams with members from various functional areas. Members of cross-functional teams may require training in functional areas other than their own to help them gain insight into other functional areas. This is called cross-training. Job rotation and training by peers are ways in which members may be given cross-functional exposure. Cross-training is useful since it provides employees with a variety of skills.

Coca-Cola has a team-training programme for its manufacturing employees. The programme focuses on three skill categories—technical, interpersonal, and team action. Technical training, called 'four deep training', requires each individual to learn four different jobs to allow for team flexibility. Interpersonal skills training, called 'adventure in attitudes', focusses on listening, conflict resolution, negotiation, etc. Team action training focusses on team leadership, group dynamics, problem solving, etc., needed to function effectively as a group. Coca-Cola has benefited from its team training programme by way of increased quality and customer satisfaction.

More recently, a new method is being used for team training. This method emphasizes the experience quotient to forge team bonding in organizations. Companies like Tata Teleservices Ltd, ABN Amro, Bank of America, Standard Chartered, Wipro BPO, and Hutch have adopted this method. It involves activities that simulate situations that test the individual and the team, and focusses on analysis, feedback, accountability, and ownership resulting in a personal action plan (PAP). At the end of it, the challenge of the game is just 20 per cent of the exercise, the rest focusses on charting a plan for a successful team whose members can rely on one another in adverse situations. The activities assigned to teams include, for example, delivering piping hot lunch boxes to 25 addresses using local transport in a specified time, feeding 1,000 impoverished people in a day armed with a few telephones and yellow pages, earning money in two hours in an unknown city, etc. These games are believed to act as a facilitator towards understanding the organization and its people, creating a comfort zone, and reducing attrition. Teams learn to manage time, existing leaders become more open to accepting their limitations, and real life pressure creates unlikely leaders.

Diversity Training

In Chapter 2, we discussed that workforce diversity has increased significantly. There are more older workers, women, minorities, regional groups, etc. in the workforce today. Moreover, the values and attitudes of generation Y also have implications for the design and conduct of T&D programmes within organizations. One aspect of SHRM is the internationalization of management development. This means learning how to do business internationally, understanding cross-cultural/diversity issues, international finance and strategy, and international human resource practices. Some organizations like Motorola, Coca-Cola, HLL, P&G, and IBM have been proactive about hiring employees from diverse backgrounds. Some other organizations, however, consciously try to minimize diversity of workforce, unless forced to do so by legislation. A global environment characterized by diverse workforce has made diversity management a crucial managerial responsibility. Managing or valuing diversity encompasses a range of activities aimed at making managers more aware that women and members of other cultures or subgroups may hold different values and assumptions which can affect the way they co-operate, compete, communicate, plan, organize, and are motivated.

Managing diversity in an organization refers to two broad categories: cross-national and international. Cross-national management of diversity refers to managing the interface between people of two countries. International diversity management involves managing an increasingly diverse workforce within a given country. South African, Malaysian, Indian, and American societies, for example, are diverse, and the workforce is multi-cultural. Managing such diversity requires skilful, informed, and extensive training in interpersonal skills and appropriate systems, and an understanding of both ethnic and corporate cultures.

Organizations conducting business across the world and operating from multiple locations sponsor some sort of diversity training. The prevalence of diversity training has increased to a great extent in the globalized business world. Diversity training involves training for generating awareness about the diverse workforce. The adoption of diversity training programmes by an organization is likely to be determined by several factors. The following types of organizations are more likely to adopt diversity programmes:

- Firms that are large in size.
- Firms that consider diversity as a strategic priority relative to other objectives.
- Firms having a diversity manager.
- Firms having other diversity-supportive practices.

Diversity training is of two types:

- Awareness building training designed to help employees understand the benefits of a diverse workforce, with the objective of increasing acceptance of diversity among employees.
- Skill building training designed to provide the KSAs necessary for working with people who come from diverse backgrounds.

In the design of a diversity-training programme, all types of diversities should be considered. These include difference of race, gender, age, culture, education, backgrounds, etc. A gender diversity-training programme in a firm might help employees accept a higher number of women in workforce, and also to respect them as an equal and as a professional. Skill building programmes may teach male supervisors how to mentor female employees to prepare them for career growth, and teach male employees how to interact with and conduct themselves when working with female colleagues.

Carefully planned international assignments, exposure to relevant induction programmes, and satisfying work experience are important in ensuring development and transfer of learning. Many companies have instituted multicultural value-sharing workshops (for imbibing soft approaches). Educative workshops, conferences, and awareness training programmes are necessary, but not sufficient for addressing structural inequalities, technical and skills inequalities, and reward differentiation.

Diversity training programmes are expected to improve the productivity and competitiveness of the firm, reduce conflicts, change stereotypes about certain groups, improve communication, improve work relationships, and enhance the satisfaction of minority groups at the workplace. However, relatively few diversity training programmes are designed independent of other training programmes. Most organizations combine diversity training programmes with other trainings. For example, at Honeywell Inc. diversity training is part of the week-long advanced management programme as well as the sales training programme. This integration of diversity training with other T&D programmes is indicative of the recognition of diversity as a strategic issue. Xerox, American Express, Disney, Texas Instruments, and AT&T offer diversity-training programmes to their employees. American Express conducts diversity learning labs for their employees. At Texas Instruments, all employees are required to take the 'valuing individuals class' at least once, preferably within the first year of being hired. The success of diversity training programmes depends on

- top management support and participative implementation—for example, at HP, diversity initiatives are driven by its diversity leadership council, which is comprised of senior executives;
- support of immediate supervisors and peers;
- reward for trainees when they show positive changes in their behaviour;
- mandatory attendance for managers in diversity programmes;
- long term evaluation of training results; and
- managerial rewards for increasing diversity.

Valuing diversity goes beyond understanding and co-operation between diverse sub-groups. Rather, it should seek to improve managerial and organizational effectiveness. The goal of valuing diversity is to build upon the strengths of each individual or subgroup to ensure that the whole is greater than the sum of the parts. A failure to understand cultural and other differences can lead to misguided assumptions, poor working relations, underperformance, and discrimination. Performance, level of contribution, and personal growth are partly a function of how people fit into and are treated in the work environment. Individual level changes in managing diversity through management development programmes will not have an enduring effect, if these are not accompanied with concomitant changes in other organizational and HRM practices to remove employment discrimination. Training for valuing diversity might then be regarded as just a deflection from a failure to successfully address the issues of development and advancement. This could result in exactly the opposite of what is intended.

Training for Global Assignments

A large number of firms are competing in the global marketplace. As international boundaries become permeable, organizations are setting up projects overseas. Firms are posting employees overseas to manage these projects. Individuals who are sent overseas need to have more than just technical skills and a proven track record. In order to be successful in overseas assignments, individuals need to have cultural adaptability, language skills, understanding of cultural values, customs, codes of conduct, etc. of the country in which they are posted. T&D programmes for international assignments have become very common today. This aspect will be discussed in greater detail in Chapter 12.

Training for Leadership Skills

Globalization, deregulation, e-commerce, and rapid technological change have resulted in companies re-evaluating the way they operate. Approaches that have worked for years are no longer effective. In an environment where firms are competing for human resource talent in order to achieve a leadership position, the ultimate source of sustainable competitive advantage may be the leaders who continue to learn. Development of leaders who think strategically is the new strategic reality and increasingly a source of sustainable competitive advantage.

Many companies today invest heavily in leadership development. Leadership development programmes focus on helping key executives learn leadership skills. As early as 1993, *Business Week* estimated that $17 billion was being spent annually on helping managers develop decision-making and company-specific skills that could enable them to move up and lead their business areas. *Training magazine* estimates that in 1998, U.S. companies spent $60 to 70 billion on training. FedEx founded its Leadership Development Institute in 1984 to ensure development and understanding of, and commitment to, the immediate corporate strategic objectives. Godrej Consumer Products Limited (GCPL) has created a talent management system that helps it to build leaders and plan for succession. Good performers are rated on leadership potential by superiors and an independent assessor. The short-listed people get a career choice between general management and domain expertise. The person who chooses general management will 'rotate' in functions, whereas the person who chooses to remain in a function, say, marketing, gets exposed to cutting-edge technology and practices in it. These employees receive training in foreign universities and their developmental needs are addressed by coaches. Based on the talent management system's succession plan, GCPL grooms a successor. Xerox, Eicher Group, Indian Rayon and Industries, TCS, and HCL Ltd are some other firms that have instituted formal leadership development programmes. Ashok Leyland and Ramco use management games and outbound training exercises to identify leadership potential and build leadership skills among their employees.

Apart from investing money in leadership development, top executives are investing significant amounts of their time personally guiding and mentoring future leaders. According to them, leadership development is not a luxury but a strategic necessity. Narayana Murthy, the non-executive chairman of Infosys, had changed his designation to 'chief mentor' to communicate the importance of building leaders. Increasingly, programmes that focus on developing future leaders are seen as providing firms with an edge over competitors.

A study by Fulmer, Gibbs, and Goldsmith (2000) attempted to understand how winning companies developed leaders. What processes transform managers into strong leaders ready for strategic action? How do the organizations known for their leadership development programmes design, manage, and deliver world-class programmes? It was found that the winning firms tied leadership development closely to business strategy and invested financial resources in it. The CEOs of these firms supported the leadership development programmes because they had a conviction that such programmes can assist in aligning functional areas with corporate strategy. For example, Johnson and Johnson (J&J) revised succession planning and performance-management systems to reflect the qualities anticipated by a 'leader-of-the-future' exercise in a leadership-development conference.

Leadership development has become too specialized to be relegated entirely to the human resource department. In winning companies such as HP, J&J, Infosys, Wipro, etc., top-level managers support and get involved in the leadership process. If these programmes produce business results, the corporate leaders are more likely to offer support. Although firms known for their leadership development efforts differ in their emphasis on making leadership development strategic, there are some similarities across these firms. The leadership development programme of each of these firms includes the following five critical steps:

- building *awareness* of external challenges, emerging strategies, organizational needs, and what leading firms do to meet the needs,
- employing *anticipatory* learning tools to recognize potential external events, envision the future, and focus on action the organization can take to create its own future,
- taking *action* by tying leadership-development programmes to solving important, challenging business issues,
- *aligning* leadership development with performance assessment, feedback, coaching, and succession planning, and
- *assessing* the impact of the leadership-development process on individual behavioural changes and organizational success.

Exhibit 6.4 presents some examples of leadership development programmes.

Orientation Training

When new employees join an organization, they lack familiarity with the organization, their supervisors, and co-workers. New employees are also unsure of their work and the expectations that others have of them. They are therefore, likely to perform below their potential for the time it takes for them

Exhibit 6.4

Examples of Leadership Development Programmes

General Electric (GE) Tremendous growth, reductions in the number of its employees worldwide, and significant delayering of the organization in the 1980s and 1990s caused an enormous cultural shift in GE. With fewer layers of management, individuals received fewer vertical promotions and hence fewer opportunities to practice being leaders. A new approach was called for. Today, in the human resource department's 'Session C' meetings, senior executives assess key GE personnel. After an initial meeting in March, there are two or three additional meetings and a wrap-up session in June or July to select employees who will attend the executive development courses at Crotonville. At the end of the year, corporate leadership development, like all corporate functions, is measured by whether it was able to support GE initiatives. Steve Kerr, GE's chief learning officer, remarked jokingly, 'Crotonville is GE's only unbudgeted and unmeasured cost centre'. He goes on to add seriously, 'Everyone would know if we weren't delivering strategic value.'

Hewlett-Packard (HP) HP, under the leadership of CEO Carly Fiorina, is rushing to reclaim its status as a top high-tech innovator. The CEO must convince the public and HP employees that HP is the hottest new company of the Internet era, and continues to have the same old-time commitment to quality and integrity. Past HP glory led many excellent engineers to focus on what used to be important, instead of on the future. Once HP started to improve leadership development, the company could make better business decisions. Today HP's senior executives actively participate in leadership development. Fiorina uses management meetings and leadership-development programmes to articulate her vision of making the company 'represent the next decade rather than the past one.' Her predecessor, Lewis E. Platt, showed his support for leadership development by making personal appearances at all HP Accelerated Development Programs, opening and closing them with an opportunity for participants to have a dialogue with him. Senior HP executives have served as faculty in part of every core programme. Fiorina's early commitment to communication with her management team has led to an expectation within the company that she will continue using leadership development for strategic change.

Source: Fulmer, Gibbs, and Goldsmith 2000

to 'settle down' and adjust to their new environment. Left on their own to make sense of their surroundings and carve out an identity for themselves, the new employees might take longer than if they are helped formally in this adjustment process. Orientation training is the planned introduction of new employees to the company, their job, and the work group to help them perform their jobs satisfactorily. Orientation programmes may range from brief, informal introductions to extended, formal sessions lasting a few days to few months. New employees are informed about their roles and responsibilities (what is expected of them), performance expectations, the organization's mission, goals and objectives, and policies and procedures of the organization.

The entire programme is directed towards facilitating new employee transition from being an outsider to being an insider. Orientation programmes are important for new employees at any level in the organizational hierarchy. However, orientation is most significant for an employee who is making a transition from a non-work life (student) to work life (employee). Typically, orientation for entry-level employees is more formal and lengthy, involving both off-the-job and on-the-job methods. At senior levels, orientation may be brief and focus more on company history, mission, goals, strategies, and meeting key executives.

Orientation training in some organizations Orientation programmes serve the following main purposes:

- To have the new employee become productive on the job as quickly as possible.
- To provide the new employee with information about company policies and procedures. This may include providing an employee handbook to the newcomer.
- To provide information about the reward system.
- To familiarize the newcomer about company culture and 'the way things are done here'.
- To communicate what is expected of the newcomer and what is important in the firm to advance in the job or for promotion.
- To reduce the anxiety of the newcomer with respect to job performance and belongingness to the firm by taking measures to integrate the person into the formal aspects of the organization.

PricewaterhouseCoopers (PwC), IBM, and McDonald's are examples of companies having extensive formal and well-designed orientation programmes. At PwC, there is a two week long orientation programme for new employees. The programme is attended by employees around the world and focusses on topics such as team-building, ethics, benefits, etc. After the two week programme, the new employees are assigned a coach who assists them in their career within the firm and their job assignments.

Every new recruit at Intel Technologies, India undergoes an intensive culture integration programme. Managers and team leaders get training on how to lead by example and uphold the values. The learning at Intel is not just in classrooms, employees are measured regularly on how they are doing on the core values.

Exhibit 6.5 discusses the induction programme at Sapient Corporation. Citibank has a well-designed orientation training programme which is a combination of off-the-job and on-the-job methods. The first phase of orientation training at Citibank for management associates (MAs) focusses on job rotation.

Exhibit 6.5

Induction at Sapient Corporation

Sapient Corporation, the global business consulting and IT services firm, inducts newcomers with a coaching programme. At Sapient, there is a team called 'quality start' that ensures that every new hire has an excellent on-boarding and integration experience. The 'quality start' process begins two weeks prior to the new entrant's joining date and continues till about three months post joining. All new hires at Sapient have to go through the Sapient induction, called the Sapient readiness programme, on the day they join the firm. The programme manager helps the newcomer map out his/her career, and also clearly spells out what the newcomer must deliver for

the company. In the first week itself, newcomers from different departments are grouped together and assigned to a project (called Sapient start), which will be eventually presented to the existing employees of the firm. The newcomers' performance is closely monitored. It is a great learning experience since it gives the new entrants the feel of an actual project as it is executed, just like a live project. At the end of the project, the newcomer is given feedback. Performance is linked to promotion. Though instant feedback may be unnerving for newcomers, at Sapient it works because the employees don't have to wait till the year-end to be told if they have not performed.

Source: Guha 2006

This phase also includes active simulation through role plays. For example, trainees are made to role-play the clearance of an overdraft cheque. In the third week of orientation training, the trainees at Citibank are given a specific job or a long project. The trainees get the first feel of responsibility and importance and are assigned mentors at this stage. Citibank reserves the theoretical class-room teaching to the end of the orientation programme since all inputs can now be related to the job by the trainee who has already been exposed to the real job.

It is of immense value if the top management of the firm takes part in orienting the new recruits, especially the entry-level employees. Information about the history, significant achievements, and key executives of the firm are best 'told' to newcomers by the top management. This serves a motivational purpose since this makes the newcomer feel important.

At Honeywell Technology, the managing director meets all new employees, talks individually to all newcomers during the induction, and signs all certificates given to the employees. Most orientation programmes consist of the following three stages:

1. general introduction to the organization (given by HR department)
2. specific orientation to the department and the job (given by new employees' immediate superior)

Exhibit 6.6

Benefits of a Well-designed Orientation Programme

- Lower turnover
- Increased productivity
- Improved employee Morale
- Lowering of employees anxiety

- Higher employee job satisfaction
- Facilitate learning
- Lower costs of training
- Lower start-up cost for new employee

Source: Bohlander, Snell, and Sherman 2002

---

3. follow-up meeting to verify that the important issues have been addressed and employee questions have been answered (meeting between newcomer and supervisor).

Exhibit 6.6 shows the benefits of a well-designed orientation programme. A well-integrated orientation programme rests on co-operation between line and staff. The HR department is responsible for coordinating orientation activities and for providing information about conditions of employment, pay, benefits, and other areas of general nature. The supervisor's (line manager) role is to prepare the work group to receive the new employee to facilitate the newcomer's adjustment. The supervisor also gives information about the newcomer's responsibilities, duties, the sub-culture of the work-group, co-workers, etc. Figure 6.13 presents the roles of HR and line managers in orientation training programmes.

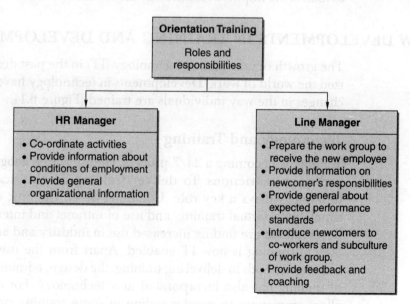

Figure 6.13: Roles of HR and Line in Orientation Training Programmes

---

Exhibit 6.7

Checklist of Topics in an Orientation Programme

- Company history
- Organizations purpose and strategy
- List of chain of command
- Who are the key executives
- Introduction to other employee
- Expectations for attendance, conduct, and appearance

- Conditions of employment
- Explanation of job duties, standards, and appraisal criteria
- Safety regulations
- Rules, policies, and procedures (standard operating procedures manual)

Orientation programmes have a significant impact on the newcomers' adjustment to the organization and their subsequent performance. Therefore careful consideration needs to be given to the goals of the orientation programme, content, and method of presenting information to the new comer. Generally speaking, the information that should be given as part of an orientation programme is listed in Exhibit 6.7.

Some organizations are using technology during orientation training. IBM has eliminated paper in the classroom by giving instructions to students on the web and facilitating their discussion of the material. This is in line with IBM's commitment to teach new employees the technology it sells. Technology has, in fact, invaded most training programmes. In the following section, let us look at the impact of technology on the conduction of training programmes.

NEW DEVELOPMENTS IN TRAINING AND DEVELOPMENT

The growth of information technology (IT) in the past decade has revolutionized the world of work. Developments in technology have also brought about changes in the way individuals are trained (Figure 6.14).

Technology and Training

Training is becoming a 24/7 process, cutting across geographical boundaries and time restrictions. To deliver training on this scale and frequency, technology plays a key role. Computer-based training, computer-supported simulations, virtual training, and use of intranet and internet for training and development are finding increased use in industry and academia. At Infosys, 30% of training is now IT enabled. Apart from the use of high-technology training methods in delivering training, the design, administration, and support of training has also incorporated new technology. For example, companies allow employees to register online in some training programmes, conduct

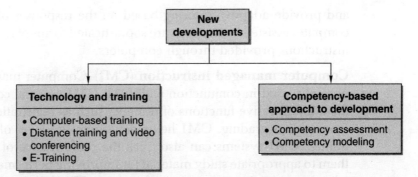

Figure 6.14:   New Developments in Training and Development

certain tests online, and may even monitor learning progress electronically. Some of the ways in which technology is used to impart training are discussed below.

Computer-based Training (CBT)

Organizations use computers to train employees especially in technical skills. Computer-based training is used more often by IT firms like Microsoft, IBM, Oracle, SAP, etc. In CBT, the trainee uses computer-based and/or DVD systems to interactively increase his/her knowledge and skills. Computer-based training uses the speed, memory, and data manipulation capabilities of computer systems to make instruction flexible and learning interactive and realistic. When CBT is structured such that it is available to employees on the job whenever they need it, it is called 'just-in-time' training. It may also utilize multimedia, which is a computer application that enhances learning with audio animation, graphics, and interactive videos and photos. Interactive multimedia training produces a complex training environment with which the trainee interacts. For example, in training a medical student, an interactive multimedia training system will present a hypothetical patient. The medical student will then take the medical history of the hypothetical patient, conduct a medical examination, and analyse lab tests. If the medical student wishes to conduct a chest examination, he/she can click on the 'examine chest' button and hear the sounds of the person's heart. The medical student will interpret these sounds and draw conclusions on which to base the patient's diagnosis. The student may then be given feedback about the accuracy of the conclusions drawn and diagnosis made. There are two types of techniques used in CBT. These are as follows:

Computer assisted instruction (CAI)   CAI delivers training material directly to the trainee through a computer terminal in an interactive format. These are expert systems that are used to tutor the trainee, monitor trainee knowledge, and provide adaptive tutoring based on the responses of the trainee. Thus, computer assisted instructions are sophisticated forms of individualized tutorial instructions provided through computers.

Computer managed instruction (CMI) Computer managed instruction is normally used in conjunction with CAI. CMI uses the computer to manage the administrative functions of training, such as registration, record keeping, scoring, and grading. CMI helps determine the level of proficiency of the trainee. CMI systems can also track the performance of trainees and guide them to appropriate study material for improving performance. The computer takes up some routine aspects of training. This helps provide the instructor with an opportunity to spend more time on course development or on individualized instruction. CMI, thus, is an efficient means of managing the training function.

Virtual reality training takes the realism of CBT a step further. Virtual reality is an advanced form of computer simulation. It places the trainee in a simulated situation, which is 'virtually' the same as the physical environment. Thus, the artificially simulated environment exactly simulates the events and situations that might be experienced on the job. The trainee wears special equipment such as goggles and auditory and sensory devices. The sensory devices transmit how the trainee is responding to the computer and the trainee sees, feels, and hears what is going on. The trainee learns by interacting with objects in the electronic environment to achieve some goal. Motorola is an example of a firm using virtual reality for training. The armed forces often use simulation-based training programmes for soldiers and officers. For example, to train soldiers in combat skills, war-game simulations may emphasize real-time leadership and decision-making skills. Pilots also train through virtual reality simulation. This type of training is especially useful when it would be too costly to impart skills through on-the-job training. Though virtual reality training and multimedia training are both interactive, the difference lies in the degree to which the learning situation approximates reality. Multimedia training is not a simulation of the actual job environment.

Multimedia is sometimes criticized for lack of 'human touch' in training delivery. Even though the cost of software and hardware can be a disadvantage, when there is a large number of trainees, cost is not a major issue. One way to manage costs is by firms coming together in a consortium, like the one 3M, GM, and Motorola have formed along with three universities. They have combined resources to buy the multimedia equipment. Though in different businesses, these firms have similar training needs. For example, diversity training needs are the same for each firm, whatever their business. Together the cost of training is much less than if they were to go for it alone.

Distance Training and Video Conferencing

Today firms are using various forms of distance learning methods for training. Common distance learning methods include the traditional correspondence courses, video conferencing, and tele-training. *Tele-training* involves offering training programmes over a satellite-based network. The trainer is in a central location and teaches groups of employees at remote locations via television hookups. The heaviest users of tele-training are universities, but lately organizations are also using tele-training. For example, an IBM subsidiary offers training programmes over a satellite-based network. At each of the 44 sites, there is a 25-inch monitor on the student desk, which is equipped with a student response unit. These units allow inter-connection with other classrooms and the instructor. The response unit has a microphone that allows the student to ask questions and answer questions from the instructor. Direcway and Reliance Infocomm offer courses from leading management institutes. Reliance Infocomm offers connectivity across its network of 241 outlets in 105 cities. Up to 60 locations can be hooked up simultaneously across India. Recently, it held a virtual classroom for 750 people organized by the Institute of Chartered Accountants of India. It has also tied up with the Xavier Institute of Management, Bhubaneshwar (XIMB) and Xavier Labour Research Institute (XLRI), Jamshedpur, for offering specialized management education programmes to working executives. *Videoconferencing* is used for training employees who are geographically separated from each other or from the trainer. Through audiovisual equipment, videoconferencing allows people from geographically dispersed locations to communicate live with each other. Firms are using videoconferencing for conducting selection interviews too. Several firms such as AT&T, DuPont, Ford, GE, etc. have used distance learning programmes for their employees. Gillette and HLL are using modern technology tools like videoconferencing and other satellite-based communication systems for conducting sales training on a new product or promotion for its sales force spread across the country. Reliance Webworld makes extensive use of video-conferencing for communicating with its retail team about tariff changes, or when new applications or services are launched. Videoconferencing helps communicate changes like new schemes and tariffs in the mobile services industry faster and more effectively. Typically, training for tariff change is conducted over 4–5 days, during which sales people undergo assessment tests, are ranked, and, if necessary, re-tested. Recently, when Reliance Infocomm tied up with Air Deccan to sell tickets through its webworld outlets, employees went through a series of training sessions and assessment tests to ensure that they were up to the mark in the new area of airline ticketing. BPOs and IT companies, however, are the ones which are the largest users of video-conferencing for internal communication and training.

Global companies particularly benefit from this new technology. Since frequent travel to far-flung locations is expensive, distance learning programmes help reduce the cost of delivering T&D programmes. Citigroup India has tied up with Direcway for conducting induction programmes for new employees from across its branches. The benefits are savings in terms of travel time and cost. Use of technology also makes training more accessible to employees and ensures consistency of instruction. A great deal of training is beginning to take place using videoconferencing and satellite technology.

E-training

A new term is on the round, that is, cyber learning. The term cyber learning refers to high-tech training methods. E-learning is a high-tech training method and is defined as the use of the Internet or the intranet of an organization to conduct training online. Internet-based learning programmes are becoming increasingly popular with firms. Intranet is similar to the Internet, but is a private network of an organization which is behind a 'firewall' software that restricts access to authorized users. As more numbers of employees have access to the internet, firms are looking at the world wide web as a means of providing training to employees located in distant locations. According to the ASTD, firms in America deliver 8.4% of their training via the Internet. Delta Airlines has achieved significant reductions in its training costs through the use of e-training. This reduction has come about since training now takes less work time and employees do not have to travel to centralized training facilities. Many organizations have full fledged 'learning portals' to satisfy their employees' training needs. Hewlett-Packard has developed such a portal for its employees. FedEx has tied up with SkillSoft, an e-learning portal, to provide its employees a choice of 800 short courses on a range of topics, from communications to project management to strategic planning. All these courses are specifically designed to fill all vacancies at FedEx from within. The knowledge portal of ICICI is called 'Wise Guy' and is accessible to all employees. 'My knowledge corner', one section of the portal, contains an inventory of employee skills, which helps share expertise across the group. Employee training is also managed online and e-learning is used for skill upgradation. The firm conducts 190 e-learning programmes annually. ICICI links training hours completed to the performance score of the individual. E-Training, like other forms of training, should also be tracked and evaluated for its effectiveness. Table 6.9 presents some advantages and disadvantages of technology-based training.

Table 6.9 Advantages and Disadvantages of Technology-based Training

Technology-based training method	Advantages	Disadvantages
Computer based training (CBT)	■ Self-paced—allows different individuals to learn at their own comfort level ■ Adaptive—can be customized for different employees ■ Easy to deliver information ■ Flexible—can be imparted at home or at work ■ Trainers and trainees need not be in the same physical space ■ Less expensive when employees are geographically dispersed ■ Can be conducted whenever convenient to trainee ■ Can be undertaken without advance scheduling ■ Increased speed of presentation ■ Decreased dependence on instructor ■ Standardized—instructional consistency ■ Mastery of learning—trainee cannot move to next step if previous step has not been learned	■ Learners should be self-motivated, take initiative, and responsibility for their learning ■ High cost of producing online, interactive methods ■ Content becomes outdated very quickly and requires redesign frequently ■ Lack of two-way communication and human touch may be demotivating
E-learning (web based training)	■ Self-paced—trainees proceed at their own pace ■ Interactive—trainee is an active participant ■ Allows for consistency in the delivery of training ■ Easy for trainers to update content ■ Can be used to enhance other instructor-led training methods ■ Enables quick scoring of questionnaires and provides feedback immediately ■ Built-in guidance for employees when needed ■ Saves travel and classroom costs	■ Trainees unfamiliar with the Internet may experience anxiety ■ Not all trainees may have uninterrupted access to computers and the internet; not appropriate for all types of skills, especially behavioural skills such as leadership ability, cultural change, etc. ■ Requires significant cost and investment ■ Has not demonstrated a significant increase in learning over that of traditional training methods ■ Requires top management support

Contd

Table 6.9 Contd

Technology-based training method	Advantages	Disadvantages
	■ Trainees do not have to wait for scheduled training sessions ■ Anytime and anywhere training results in employee assuming greater responsibility for one's own training	■ Internet users tend to 'surf', which distracts attention from training

Source: Bohlander, Snell, and Sherman 2002; Mathis and Jackson 2003; Mello 2003

Competency-Based Approach to Management Development

In a competitive corporate world, it has become very important to identify characteristics for successful performance. These behaviours are called 'competencies'. One comprehensive definition of competency is 'a cluster of related knowledge, skills, and attitudes that affects a major part of an individual job, that correlates with performance on the job, that can be measured against well-accepted standards, and that can be improved via training and development' (*Training Magazine*, July 1999). A competency may be comprised of knowledge, a single skill or ability, a personal characteristic, or a cluster of two or more of these attributes. The performance of most tasks requires the simultaneous or sequenced demonstration of multiple competencies.

Knowledge is awareness, information, or understanding about facts, rules, principles, guidelines, concepts, theories, or processes needed to successfully perform a task. A *skill* is a capacity to perform mental or physical tasks with a specified outcome. An *ability* is a demonstrated cognitive or physical capability to successfully perform a task with a wide range of possible outcomes. Personal characteristics include attitudes and traits, values, work habits, ways of interacting with others, or manner of conducting oneself that contribute to effective work performance.

Management competencies are used to build a framework for analysing the resources available to achieve business strategies and to forecast areas of risk. Competencies form the foundation for many human resource functions and are an integral part in maintaining a competitive edge. Organizations develop competency frameworks as a basis for the design of their management development, appraisal, and recruitment programmes, and detailing the technical and behavioural competencies required. Competencies are the components of development programmes to supply shortfalls in management competencies for the future. Effective management development programmes identify common competencies and design approaches capable of delivering focussed common management competency training. Patni Computer Systems has a structured process called Leadership Excellence at Patni (LEAP), which incorporates a competency framework. This process is an end-to-end framework that begins right at the time of recruitment and helps in recruiting the right professionals. The firm also defines the gold standard for leadership based on LEAP such that every employee understands the contents of the standard.

Competency Assessment and Competency Modelling

Competency based approach uses competency assessment and competency modelling to determine the competency requirements for effective performance.

Competency assessment is the process of identifying the competencies among a group of employees, typically by department, job category, or hierarchical structure. There is a difference between competency assessment and task analysis. Task analysis bases training on what people do, whereas competency assessment bases training on who the successful performers are. Traditional job analysis includes all employees and does not differentiate between good and excellent performers. Task analysis typically focuses on jobs with an emphasis on psychomotor skills whereas competency assessment conducts training for employees who perform decision-making tasks and are knowledge workers such as managers and professionals.

A *competency model* is a success profile created on the basis of competency assessment. This profile describes the behaviour relevant to success at a firm and is called the 'competency model'. A competency model is an organizing framework that lists the competencies required for effective performance in a specific job, job family (i.e., group of related jobs), organization, function, or process. These competencies are associated with exemplary performers and tied to the corporate culture. Individual competencies are organized into competency models to enable people in an organization or profession to understand, discuss, and apply the competencies to workforce performance.

The competencies in a model may be organized in a variety of formats based on organizational needs. A common approach is to identify several 'core' or 'key' competencies that are essential for all employees and then identify several additional categories of competencies that apply only to specific subgroups. Some competency models are organized according to the type of competency, such as leadership, personal effectiveness, or technical capacity. Other models may employ a framework based on job level, with a basic set of competencies for a given job family and additional competencies added cumulatively for each higher job level within the job family.

Competency assessment and modelling are used heavily in performance management, selection, reward, training and development. The theory is that if companies can identify the knowledge, skills, and behaviour of their most successful employees, they can train other employees to acquire and apply the same attributes to yield better results. Management development is a priority at FedEx, and central to it is an initiative called SPEED, which stands for succession planning executive education. SPEED is a fully automated, intranet-based competency assessment and succession planning system for use by senior management at FedEx. SPEED allows vice-presidents and senior vice presidents to regularly rate the competencies, readiness, and promotability of their direct reports. These direct reports, in turn, create plans to strengthen their competencies through, among other things, formalized executive education programmes.

With increasing competitive pressure, new business strategies that require management re-structuring emerge with increasing rapidity. Implementing an organizational re-structuring requires an assessment of the management competencies needed and available to manage the business resources in a different way. Hence, the competency approach has gained considerable popularity in business and industry in recent years. There are several reasons for the increasing use of competency assessment by organizations:

- The speed of change in the business environment has led to an increase in interest in assessment because of the nature of task analysis. Compared to task analysis, competency assessment is much more flexible and does not get dated quickly.
- The changing nature of work implies that workers rely less on psychomotor skills. Workers are beginning to make more decisions these days. Employees are becoming empowered. Hence, competency assessment is used more as job responsibilities include more of decision-making.
- Widespread corporate downsizing requires training and development professionals to move to more flexible definitions of jobs, and away from the bureaucratic job definition.
- Competency assessment can become the basis for an entire corporate HR department's activities such as recruitment, selection, orientation, training, compensation, performance appraisal, career paths, etc.

The premise behind the use of the competency framework for management development is that if an organization's managers are equipped with the right competencies to carry out their jobs effectively, corporate success should, all things being equal, not only be improved, but accelerated. There are seven steps to the successful development of a competency model (Exhibit 6.8).

Exhibit 6.8

Developing Competency Modelling Process

The process has seven steps.

1. *Define objectives:* The following questions must be answered—why is there a need to develop a competency model? What problems will be solved, benefits gained? What is the unit of analysis? Is it a specific job, job family, a single work group, a function, or an entire organization? How will the model be applied, that is, for selection, strategic workforce planning, promotion, performance management, and T&D?

2. *Obtain support of a sponsor:* A sponsor is a person of some influence in the organization, such as a CEO. The sponsor helps gain commitment and participation of employees and managers from whom data will be collected.

3. *Develop and implement a communication and education plan:* Success of the competency model depends on convincing those who will participate of the value of the model. A communication strategy must be developed. All stakeholders should be informed of the initiative early in the process, and should be kept informed of the progress through communication at periodic intervals.

4. *Plan the Methodology:* A methodology to develop the competency model is designed. This involves selecting a sample and data collection methods. The high performers are used to collect data in developing competency model. The goal is to identify competencies required for excellent job performance, not average or poor performance.

5. *Identify the competencies and create the competency model:* This step involves three inter-related tasks. (a) Developing a complete understanding of the job through JD and JS

to acquire a job definition. The definition includes job responsibilities, its place in the organization and profession, and the education and experience required. (b) Identifying competencies for each element of the job. (c) Assemble the competence model by clustering together similar KSAs and personal characteristics. Each competency is accompanied with a definition and behavioural example. The same competency for different jobs will have different behavioural examples. The completed competency model includes a list of competencies organized by type, with a definition and several behavioural examples at three or more levels of proficiency.

6. *Apply the competency model:* This is done for purposes of selection, recruitment, training and development, and other HR practices. With respect to 'training and development', the application involves the use of competencies to design a curriculum for training and other developmental activities, developing a multi-rater feedback instrument to assess employee needs for competency development, providing development planning guides that provide employees with specific suggestions on how to strengthen each competency.

7. *Evaluate and update the competence model:* The competency development process must be evaluated to determine the value of the model.

Competency development is a continuous process. Required competencies must be revised with changes in job design, contextual conditions, etc.

Adapted from: Marrelli, Tondora, and Hoge 2005

Strategic Approach to Competency Assessment

There is a need for a stronger link between management development programmes and corporate strategy. This link is growing these days for several reasons. For one, there is the emergence of new organizational structures to cope with competition. In such a scenario, the HR function is seen as being able to understand business objectives and the actions that need to be taken to achieve these objectives. Therefore, competency assessment is viewed as the bridge between strategy and MD. A strategic approach to competency assessment was highlighted by Laura Tovey (1994) as one vehicle which management development practitioners can use to strengthen the management development–corporate strategy link. This approach consists of five main building blocks.

The strategic review Stage one of the review process is concerned with gaining a full and clear understanding of the strategic requirements of the business, business environment, corporate mission, and the business strategy being pursued. This represents the starting-point for defining the strategic areas of competence for the business. For competency identification, development, and assessment to be successful, that is, to have an impact on job and therefore on business performance, it needs to be built around a sound strategic understanding of an organization's business. The first stage is the stage when competencies are assessed, and is therefore, also called the competency assessment stage. At this stage the following questions are asked:

- What is the nature of the organization? Is it hierarchical, operating in a stable industry, or is it fast-moving and high-tech?
- What is the objective of competency assessment? Will it be the basis of all activities such as selection, etc.?
- For which levels do you want to identify competencies—supervisory, managerial, top-level, middle level, etc.?
- How will competencies be defined to be meaningful in the context of the organization?

Strategic areas of competence In the next stage, critical success factors for business strategy are clarified and confirmed so that areas of strategic competence can be identified. A strategic area of competence is defined as an area in which the organization must be competent, if it is to succeed in its mission, and which has implications for individual capabilities. For the organization to succeed, it is necessary for it to possess capabilities in each strategic area of competence. Together they are sufficient to achieve the mission. The list must therefore reflect the absolute minimum number of areas in which capabilities are required to accomplish the mission.

Determining competency requirements Common competencies are identified by examining all competencies that managers possess and exercise to achieve business results. Competency requirements refer to the discrete dimensions of behaviour which lie behind success or failure in a particular job or job category. Such dimensions may include knowledge, skills, behaviour, and other factors which can be precisely defined and assessed for management development purposes and will be influenced by the organizational level and culture. Competency requirements are derived from three sources:

- The requirements of the business, as reflected in the strategic areas of competence.
- The job itself, in terms of business, professional, and technical requirements as well as in terms of personal and managerial competencies.
- The organization, in terms of the culture and therefore, the behaviour required and the level at which the individual operates.

It is evident that the ideal scenario is to have specific and meaningful job-related competencies which are also related to the strategic needs of the business. These competencies are then classified under a number of cluster headings in order to be tested and prioritized against the strategic areas of competence.

Assessing competency requirements By measuring the difference between competency requirements and the extent to which these are possessed by employees (whether by self assessment, peer/subordinate assessment, or through assessment centres), the size of the training and development gap can be established and compared with the organization's current training provision. Assessment of requirements helps with developing training and development needs. There are two forms of assessment,

- assessment of current job performance, which is an ongoing responsibility and culminates in the formal annual appraisal; and
- assessment of the employee's potential, which guides career direction and planning.

Application The competencies are tested in the fourth stage—the 'application' stage. Every line manager should engage in at least four sequential activities which relate to the performance of job holders under his/her supervision, selection, assessment, development, and succession. Selection will have an impact on job performance and relies on a clear definition of critical competencies, which must be derived from the strategic requirements of the business. Job performance too needs to be assessed. The next step is to design training interventions that develop common competencies. Development of individuals is based on the assessment of their performance and potential. It impacts directly on current job performance as well as preparing them for succession for future positions. Finally, planned development leads to individuals being ready to occupy identified positions on a reasonable time-scale. Individual performance of the job impacts business performance and it is imperative that the job and the organization's strategic goals are aligned.

Summary

The chapter discussed the role of training and development of human resources in organizations for attaining a competitive edge in an increasingly dynamic business environment. The meaning of the terms 'training' and 'development' and the differences between the two were explained. The importance of training and development activities for both individual and organizational performance improvement was highlighted. Training and development activities are important for upgrading skills, new employee orientation, solving performance problems, and for providing opportunities for personal growth. The increasing significance of continuous learning and training in organizations was traced to several reasons such as technological advances, work redesign, mergers and acquisitions, restructuring, workforce diversity, and employee mobility. The chapter also detailed the process of training. The activities within each of the four phases of the training and development process, that is, needs assessment, programme design and development, programme implementation, and evaluation were explained. The discussion emphasized that the training programme should be anchored in organizational goals and strategies.

The chapter presented a brief overview of the methods of training and development. Linkage between training and development strategy and the business strategy of the firm was examined. Miles and Snow's typology of business strategies was used to illustrate the linkage. A discussion of special forms of training focussed upon new skill demands was also presented. These included team training, diversity training, training for global assignments, training for developing leadership skills, and orientation training for new employees. Technology has revolutionized the world of work with training being no exception. The impact of technology on the design, delivery, and administration of training and development was discussed. The pros and cons of e-training and computer-based training were also presented. In the end, the competency-based approach to training and development was discussed. The discussion dwelt upon the importance of competencies in determining effective managerial performance, the steps in developing a competency modelling process, and the strategic approach to competency assessment.

Keywords

Benchmarking is the process of evaluating one's own practices against those of recognized leaders in order to identify areas of improvement.

Competency Assessment is a process of identifying the competencies of successful performers, typically by department, job category, or hierarchical structure.

Competency Model refers to an organizing framework that lists the competencies required for effective performance in a specific job, job family (i.e., group of related jobs), organization, function, or process. These competencies are associated with exemplary performers and tied to corporate culture.

Computer Assisted Instruction (CAI) refers to expert systems that are used to tutor the trainee, monitor trainee knowledge, and provide adaptive tutoring based on the responses of the trainee by delivering training material directly to the trainee through a computer terminal in an interactive format.

Computer Based Training (CBT) involves the use of computers to train employees especially on technical skills.

Computer Managed Instruction (CMI) uses the computer to manage the administrative functions of training, such as registration, record keeping, scoring, and grading. CMI is normally used in conjunction with CAI and helps determine the level of proficiency of the trainee.

Development is a process designed to impart learning experiences in order to help employees acquire skills and competencies for future jobs.

E-learning refers to a high-tech training method that makes use of the Internet or intranet of an organization to conduct training online.

Education prepares an individual to assess situations and select the most appropriate response from the range of responses available by increasing the range of possible responses available to an individual.

Evaluation is the process of systematically collecting information and using the information to determine the effects and value of a training programme.

General Training helps employees gain skills that can be used at most workplaces.

Learning is any relatively permanent change in behaviour that results from practice or experience. Learning can be either formal or informal. Informal learning takes the form of 'learning' through experience. Formal learning occurs during a training episode.

Multimedia Training produces a complex training environment with which the trainee interacts through the use of a computer application that enhances learning with audio animation, graphics, and interactive videos.

Needs Assessment is a systematic and objective determination of training needs based on data gathering that takes the form of comparison between 'skills required' and 'skills available'. A training need exists when more skills are required than are available.

Organizational Needs Analysis is an examination of the environment, strategies, organizational goals, resources of the organization, personnel inventories, performance data, and climate and efficiency indices, in order to determine where the training emphasis should be placed in the organization and what factors may affect training.

Orientation Training refers to a planned introduction of new employees to the company, their job, and the work group to help them perform their jobs satisfactorily.

Person Analysis determines who needs training in the firm and the specific type of training needed. It involves comparing the actual performance of individuals, groups, or departments to the expected performance standards.

Return on Investment (ROI) is calculated by dividing the net benefits gained from training by the cost of training. Net benefits are obtained by subtracting the costs from the total benefits of the training.

Specific Training increases worker's productivity in the organization that is providing the training.

Tele-training refers to training programmes offered over a satellite-based network by trainers who are in a central location and teach groups of employees at remote locations via television hookups.

Training is a formal learning process that attempts to improve employee performance on a currently held job by providing the employee with the knowledge and skills needed for their present jobs.

Videoconferencing uses audiovisual equipment for training employees who are geographically dispersed. It allows trainees and trainers to communicate live with each other.

Virtual Reality is an advanced form of computer simulation that places the trainee in an artificially simulated situation that exactly simulates the events and situations that might be experienced on the job. The trainee learns by interacting with objects in the electronic environment to achieve some goal.

Concept Review Questions

1. Define 'training' and 'development'. What is the difference between training, development, education, experience, and learning?

2. Why is training a critical strategic issue for organizations? What purposes are served by training and development programmes?

3. Diagrammatically explain the four phases of the training process. Why is it important to align training and development programmes with the goals and strategies of the organization?

4. Explain why orientation training is important for new employees.

5. Discuss the advantages and disadvantages of on-the-job, off-the-job, and e-training. For what types of training is each most appropriate?

6. Why is it important to evaluate training programmes? How can training and development programmes be evaluated for results and effectiveness?

7. Why has diversity training become an important component of corporate training programmes? What are the benefits of diversity training?

8. What do you understand by competency assessment and competency modelling? Discuss why the competency-based approach is being increasingly used by organizations for management development, and what advantages this approach has over the traditional management development methods?

Critical Thinking Questions

1. Do you agree with the statement, 'Training is the solution to all performance problems'? What factors other than skill or knowledge deficiency may lead to a gap between expected performance and actual performance of an employee? Within this context discuss the significance of training needs assessment. Explain the three types of analyses involved in conducting training needs assessment and give examples.

2. Briefly discuss how changes in corporate strategy over the years have been accompanied with changes in the training provided by firms to their employees. Should training activities be strategically aligned? What are the benefits of strategic linkage of training activities? Explain the business strategy–training linkage with respect to the business strategy typology given by Miles and Snow.

Simulation and Role Play

1. Assume that you are the HR director of a large software firm with headquarters in Bangalore. The firm has offices in almost 15 countries around the world and is the top performing software company in the industry. The employees of the firm are routinely targeted for poaching by competitors. Yet, the firm has been able to maintain the employee turnover rate at a low of 10% where the industry average is about 20%. This year when you conducted the annual employee survey, you found that most software professionals wanted the firm to provide them with more training than what was currently provided. Since skills in software industry become obsolete very quickly, the software professionals also wanted regular training

on continuously evolving skill sets. The survey therefore, suggested some dissatisfaction among software professionals with respect to training practices. You discuss the issue with the CEO of the firm and both agree that the concerns of software professionals should be addressed by giving them greater opportunity for training. Since the employees are geographically dispersed, you believe that e-training will be more cost-effective in the long-run. However, the CEO is not convinced. A discussion on the pros and cons of computer-based, distance training, and Internet training ensues between the two of you.

Two students volunteer for role-play. The student who plays the Director (HR) presents arguments in support of e-training. The student playing the role of CEO is more concerned about the high cost. The discussion ends with both agreeing to gather more information about the experience of other firms already using Internet-based training.

After the role play, the entire class is encouraged to participate in the discussion on the merits and demerits of e-training. Students are encouraged to share examples and experiences of firms using e-training. The instructor further encourages the students to suggest alternative training approaches for this group of employees.

2. Form groups of students and ask them to discuss and analyse the orientation programme they participated in when they joined their current college/business school. The discussion should veer around the content, duration, degree to which it was formal, the extent to which it satisfied their concerns as a newcomer, as also the concerns it did not address. Each group is asked to design a model orientation programme that they believe the college should adopt for future batches of students and make a presentation. How is the suggested orientation programme better than the current one? The instructor facilitates the group discussion to identify the similarities in the suggestions of different groups to determine the common concerns faced by a majority of new students of the college.

Classroom Projects

1. The purpose of this exercise is to understand the significance of training and development activities in the contemporary business environment. Ask half the students in the class to take Position 1 and the other half to take Position 2 with respect to the significance of training in contemporary business environment:

   Position 1: 'Investment in training and development activities by a firm is a wasteful expenditure given the high rate of employee turnover'.

   Position 2: 'Investment in training and development is imperative for improved business results and for gaining competitive advantage over competitors'.

   Each student should individually develop and write ideas in support of the position taken. Divide all the students of the class into two groups according to the position they took. Ask members of each group to share their individual ideas and develop arguments in support of their chosen position on the topic. Allow 15 minutes time for group discussion and 10 minutes time for presentation to each group. An open discussion with the class follows highlighting the pros and cons of each position. The

students are also encouraged to cite examples of firms that emphasize employee training and development.

Hint: The discussion may incorporate the following issues among others—nature of changes in business environment, organizational and work structures, technological advancement, change in skill requirements, changing employer–employee contract and the growth of contingent workforce, outsourcing, and general vs specific training.

2. This exercise will help students to gain an insight into the design and evaluation of the training process. The focus is on facilitating an understanding of the linkages between training objectives, training methods, and training evaluation. The exercise needs out-of-class preparation time.

Steps:

Day 1

- Divide the class into groups of four or five.
- Introduce the exercise to the class by clarifying the objectives of the exercise. Present a brief overview of the training process to the students.

- Distribute Form 1 to all the students. Each student should complete form 1 individually before coming to the class. The task for the students is to identify which training methods are most appropriate for achieving each of the training objective(s) listed in Form 1.

Day 2

- Since each student would have different ideas about the most appropriate method for each training objective, allow the groups about 15 minutes to discuss and reach a consensus. Each group fills up Form 1 again based on discussion by placing a 'x' to reflect the method that is most appropriate for achieving a particular objective.
- Present the following situation to the students: 'Assume you are the training manager of a global retail chain. The chain has recently hired sales associates. You as the training manager have to design a training programme for the recently hired sales associates for the retail chain.' (Instead of all the groups focus on sales associates in a retail chain, encourage the

groups to choose different occupational groups from different sectors).

- Each group specifies the particular occupational group they have chosen.
- Ask each group to determine two or three important training needs for the selected occupational group. Each group then chooses only one training need.
- Groups now are asked to develop specific training objective(s) for the identified training need.
- Having determined the objectives, the groups then select a combination of training methods (from Form 1) that would be most appropriate for meeting the training objectives. Training objectives are likely to fit into one of the major objectives listed in Form 1.
- Now the groups must determine what criteria they will use to evaluate the training programmes. The criteria may be reaction, learning, behaviour change, or results.
- Each group prepares and presents a report followed by a general discussion led by the instructor.

Form 1: Training Methods and their Effectiveness in Achieving Different Training Objectives

Training* Methods	Knowledge Acquisition	Knowledge Retention	Attitude Change	Problem-solving Skills	Interpersonal Skills	Participant Acceptance
Lecture method						
Seminars and conferences						
Job instruction training						

* See Figure 6.9 for a complete list of training and development methods.

[1] *Adapted from*: Nkomo, S.M., M.D. Fottler, and R.B. McAfee 1992, *Applications in Human Resource Management: Cases, Exercises, and Skill Builders*, 2nd edn, PWS-KENT Publishing company, Boston, pp. 170–177.

Field Projects

1. Divide the class into groups of five each. Ask each group to select one industry, that is, BPO/ITeS, FMCG, travel and tourism, aviation, retail, automobile, etc. Each group makes a field visit to two organizations from the chosen industry. Group members conduct interviews with HR managers as well as a few top-level managers of the firms to obtain the following information for each organization:

   • Dominant business strategy of the firm using Miles and Snow's typology.

   • Training practices of these firms with respect to skill type and skill source.

   • How the firms assess training needs.

   • Whether training is aligned with organizational goals and objectives.

   • Average training hours per employee.

   • Training staff per employee.

   • Cost of training per employee.

   • Training methods used for different skill groups.

   • Criteria used for evaluating training effectiveness.

   • Other training-related information that is available.

   Each group prepares a report for class presentation as well as a written report for submission to the instructor. Group presentations should highlight the similarities and differences between the two organizations visited, in respect of various aspects of training.

   After all the groups have made their presentations, the instructor should lead a class discussion on training needs assessment, training practices, linkage between business strategy and training, and evaluation of training. The discussion should revolve around the business environment in which the particular industry operates, the impact (or lack of it) of business strategy on training strategy, and how decisions related to training and development activities are taken by organizations. The instructor should also encourage the class to examine industry differences in various aspects of training.

Case Study

McDonald's

McDonald's is a leading global foodservice retailer with more than 30,000 local restaurants serving nearly 50 million people in more than 119 countries each day. It is the world's largest restaurant chain with outlets in every continent and in almost every country. McDonald's serves the world some of its favorite food—French Fries, Big Mac, Quarter Pounder, Chicken McNuggets, and Egg McMuffin. The first McDonald's restaurant opened by Ray Kroc was the Des Plaines restaurant at Illinois, USA in 1955 and the first day's revenues of the restaurant were a whopping $366.12! No longer a functioning restaurant, the Des Plaines building is now a museum containing McDonald's memorabilia and artifacts.

McDonald's went public in 1965 with the company's first offering on the stock exchange. A hundred shares of stock costing $2,250 dollars that day would have multiplied into 74,360 shares, worth over $1.8 million on December 31, 2003. In 1985, McDonald's was added to the 30-company Dow Jones Industrial Average. It holds a leading share in the globally branded quick service restaurant segment of the informal eating-out market in virtually every country in which it has a presence. As a 50 year old company, McDonald's today is one of the two most well-known, powerful, and valuable brands in the world, the other being Coca-Cola, the only soft drink supplier to McDonald's.

Values of the Company

McDonald's has one agenda; providing 100% total customer satisfaction. The formula through which McDonald's seeks to achieve this goal in the restaurant operation is the long-standing commitment to Q, S, C, and V, that is, quality, service, cleanliness, and value. Well-trained crew and managers are the first step to achieving these standards. It is a company policy to provide career opportunities that allow employees to develop their full potential. This includes a comprehensive training programme for crew and career progression that enables a 'first job' employee to progress through to a senior management position through merit-based promotions.

People at McDonald's

Each McDonald's restaurant is structured as an independent business, with restaurant management responsible for accounting, operations, inventory control, community relations, and training and human resources. McDonald's is a large-scale employer with a typical McDonald's restaurant employing about 60 people. Most employees are paid by the hour and are referred to as 'crew members'. Their primary responsibility is to prepare the food, serve customers, and carry out tasks for the efficient running of the restaurants. Crew members have to work hard and learn quickly. Other hourly-paid employees who work alongside them include training squad members, dining area hosts, party entertainers, administrative assistants, security coordinators, maintenance staff, night closers, floor managers, and shift running floor managers. Although these employees carry out more specific job functions, their overall role is to ensure that the restaurant runs efficiently. McDonald's is representative of the wider growth in temporary, part time service sector work. 55% of McDonald's hourly paid staff are students, usually in further or higher education. Many McDonald's employees have been recruited from both short and long-term unemployment. Most crew members have additional demands on their time, whether through studying or caring responsibilities. There are people who don't last long amidst the intense demands of the McDonald's workplace and development programmes. But there are also many who see these through and go on to have successful and rewarding careers.

The remaining company employees are salaried managers working in either the corporate or regional departments. It is their responsibility to manage the restaurant's operations, crew, and business performance. 20 of 50 top managers started in McDonald's restaurants, including the CEO, Jim Skinner. 67,000 McDonald's restaurant managers and assistant managers started as restaurant staff. McDonald's was voted the 'best place to work for minorities' by *Fortune Magazine* in 2005, and 'one out of five best places to work in Latin America' by *America Economic Magazine* in the same year.

Commitment to Training

McDonald's is an organization that demonstrates a strategic commitment to training 'as the way we do business around here'. From the very early days, Ray Kroc, the founder of McDonald's as we know it today, was prepared to invest a great deal of money (and way before McDonald's came close to turning a profit) in training staff. The company's attitude to training and development today can be traced straight back to Kroc's philosophies and beliefs about learning and work. McDonald's, with a strong tradition of and belief in training, invests more than $1 billion annually in training. However, it is not always training as we know or might expect it. McDonald's Hamburger University first opened in the basement of a restaurant in Elk Grove, Chicago, in 1961. It was initially aimed at Kroc's growing number of franchisees, a learning process through which he could assert control over his cherished standards of quality, service, cleanliness, and value. At the time, the idea of a university for the still fledgling industry of fast food franchising was scoffed at but Kroc didn't care. The first graduates were awarded a Bachelor of hamburgerology degree with a minor in french fries. Hamburger University® has more than 275,000 graduates worldwide and, with training, eligible for college credits.

When Ray Kroc was initially expanding McDonald's in the 1950s and 60s he avoided employees or franchisees with direct experience or formal training in the food preparation, restaurant, or service business. They were the people who wanted to do it their way, the way that they had learned through their formal training in catering. But Kroc never saw that as the right preparation for making McDonald's do well. Instead, he saw a different mix of dedication, entrepreneurship and wider skills in service and quality as the right type of skills mix. He freely admitted to 'putting the hamburger on the assembly line'—a process where traditional catering and restaurant skills were obsolete. This new fast food revolution could not be encumbered by traditional beliefs—rather Kroc was convinced that new abilities and a 'try anything' philosophy would better deliver the national brand that he craved. But, in the 21st century service sector, the skills process has changed. The company invests in its people and—these are all formal learning processes that McDonald's utilises—they are perhaps a better reflection of Kroc's philosophy than existed in the US in the 1950s. However, despite this, McDonald's still sets great store by its training procedures. Just like Kroc in the 1950s, they are always prepared to tear up their own systems and start again with all of its development procedures. There is a major paradox that exists at the heart of perceptions about the job at McDonalds, called McJob. If it takes only a few minutes to be fully up to speed in the deskilled environment that is a McDonald's kitchen, why does the company claim to invest so much time and money in training and development? At crew level, there is considerable initial and ongoing training that is consistently applied to everybody in the business, whether part, full time, hourly paid staff, or salaried managers undergoing their compulsory in-restaurant training.

Orientation and Induction

The first stage of training at McDonald's is at the Welcome Meetings. All new employees are inducted into the business through a Welcome Meeting, which they must attend. These set out the company's standards and expectations. The Welcome Meeting gives an overview of the company, including job role, food, hygiene and safety training, policies and procedures, administration, benefits, and training and development.

Welcome Meetings are followed by a structured development programme that provides training in all areas of business. Crew trainers work shoulder-to-shoulder with trainees while they learn the operations skills necessary for the running of each of the 11 workstations in each restaurant, from the front counter to the grill area. All employees learn to operate state-of-the-art foodservice equipment, gaining knowledge of McDonald's operational procedures. The majority of training is floor based, or 'on-the-job' training because people are more likely to retain information if they are able to practise as they learn. All new employees have an initial training period. Here they are shown the basics and allowed to develop their skills to a level where they are competent in each area within the restaurant. The time scale for this depends on their status, that is, full or part-time. They also attend classroom-based training sessions where they complete workbooks for quality, service, and cleanliness. New employees also meet their trainer and tour the restaurant. The company operates a three week probationary period, after which employees are rated on their performance and are either retained or have their employment terminated.

Training and Management Development

After inductions and team orientation sessions, every employee embarks on his/her individual training plans. All employees receive ongoing training. There are no set timescales as there are many crew working for a handful of shifts each week.

The leisure retailing industry is unique in that the customers know what they are looking for, the quality of service they received on their last visit, and what service they expect on this visit. In such a situation, extreme variations in standards gets noticed and 'punished'. McDonald's places great emphasis on employee training to ensure the highest standards of service across all outlets globally, regardless of the restaurant or the continent. The tightly controlled process is called the 'one best way'. It covers all areas of business, from meeting and greeting, to food preparation, to cleaning the floor. In order to relieve monotony, crew members are rotated through a number of different roles. It takes an average of 44 shifts to become competent in all areas.

Training is delivered and assessed through a variety of methods. Much is done 'shoulder to shoulder' with a manager or training squad member from the restaurant. However, training is also delivered through attending classes in the crew room or in the restaurant itself. Additionally, e-learning modules can also be completed during allotted times in the crew rooms using the crew computer station and by accessing the company intranet site.

Once in a restaurant manager position, employees continue with further intensive development. All the development plans at McDonald's stem from the same essential principles that Kroc introduced in the 1950s, i.e., quality, service, and cleanliness. Through a combination of time in restaurants and at a management training centre, managers progress through hundreds of training days. Courses for management development include:

- Employee relations training
- Time management
- Staff retention and discipline
- Personal leadership and effective coaching
- Employee communications
- Learning to manage shifts
- Community image
- Managing staff development
- Optimizing restaurant food cost
- Accounting and financial procedures

The operations and training manual weighs just over 4 kg and is more than 800 pages long. General Managers at McDonald's are expected to complete further programmes, such as a Diploma in Management from Nottingham Trent University (in UK outlets), a far cry from Ray Kroc's partly

mischievous degree in Hamburgerology that he first awarded in the early 1960s.

The restaurants also promote crew members to hourly-paid management positions that carry accountability for areas within the restaurant, or responsibility for a shift. All members of the restaurant crew are trained on the job by a training squad. The training approach at McDonald's is based on developing competencies using a Personal Development Plan (PDP). Training is monitored by the use of 'Observation Checklists' (OCLs) for the station they are working at. Ratings from these checklists are used in appraisals of employees. Successful completion of a range of OCRs across various job tasks leads to a small pay increase.

In addition, the participants (crew members) attend regular development days. On successful completion of a management entrance exam, employees attend a training course held by the training department at the regional office before returning to the restaurant in a management position. The McDonald's management development curriculum takes new recruits from trainee manager to restaurant manager. This consists of on-the-job training and open learning development modules, supported by courses and seminars at the company's national and regional training centres. The management development curriculum is aimed at persons aged 21 or over, either graduates or individuals with some previous management experience. It offers a direct route into restaurant management, through an intensive structured training programme.

The management development curriculum is divided into four key programmes:

- *Shift Management:* Developing trainee managers in the skills and techniques required to become effective in all aspects of running a shift.
- *Systems Management:* Targeting second assistant and newly promoted first assistant managers. This programme covers all areas of McDonald's systems, thus increasing the manager's business knowledge. It also develops individual techniques.

- *Restaurant Leadership:* Introducing managers to the key skills needed to become effective restaurant leaders, e.g., team-building, communication, decision-making.

- *Business Leadership:* Focussing restaurant/general managers on the need to develop a business strategy that encompasses both internal and external factors.

Most departments in the regional offices offer restaurant managers opportunities to work in the regional office. This gives an experienced manager the opportunity to develop and learn new skills, to see a different side of the business, and to experience how each department's strategies have a role in achieving the company's goals.

McDonald's Diversity Initiatives

McDonald's is the world's community restaurant. It has a long-standing commitment to a diverse workforce. Diversity at McDonald's is seen as understanding, recognizing, and valuing the differences that make each person unique. McDonald's is committed to recognizing the talents and job performance of all employees and values the contributions that come from people with different backgrounds and perspectives. Some of the diversity initiatives at McDonald's have resulted in it having the largest number of minority and female franchisees in the quick service industry, with more than 40.7% of all McDonald's US owner/operators being women and minorities. More than 25% of company officers are minorities, more than 24% of company officers are women, 26% of middle-management employees are minorities, and 46% of middle-management employees are women.

The company has employee networks such as Women's Leadership Network, Asian Employee Network, McDonald's African American Council, etc. These networks help the company achieve its diversity vision by improving processes like performance feedback and employee development, recruitment and retention of excellent employees, and maintaining a better connection with the diverse customer base. McDonald's is committed to diversity education and has developed a framework to provide it throughout the organization through formal presentations, workshops, and seminars. Seminars and workshops like Winning with Diversity and Inclusion, GenderSpeak, Asian Career Development, Black Career Development, and Women: Enhancing Personal and Professional Effectiveness, serve as the cornerstone for bringing diversity to life in the organization. Presentations and customized and informal training materials are provided for integration into team and department processes. Diversity education is an ongoing process, creating awareness and building skills for managing an inclusive and diverse workforce.

Evaluation of Training

The managers of each unit are responsible for training and also for monitoring training effectiveness based on OCLs through a computerized log. The results are used by the head office to track restaurant performance, resulting in what is called a 'training grade'. This serves as a key indicator in measuring the unit managers' performance. This linkage ensures that training is prioritized. Restaurant's performance with respect to training is measured by the following indicators:

- Overall training audit grade
- Proportion of fully trained staff
- Number of OCLs awaiting completion
- Employee satisfaction levels

To measure the quality, service, and cleanliness of restaurants McDonalds uses mystery shoppers who pay a monthly visit to each site. The results from these visits indicate that restaurants in the above average training category have higher scores across the board, especially on 'service'. This means that when staff are well trained and motivated, customer service improves, and long queues and delays are less likely.

McDonald's provides a real justification for training, through real evidence that directly explains the impact of training investment on the bottom line. It has been observed that the restaurants where the manager or their second-in-command takes a hands-on approach to training tend to perform better. Yet, the company does not look for immediate financial benefits from training, the impact of which may be more medium to long-term. Fundamentally, though, McDonald's knows that skills do create better businesses and with it, better jobs and opportunities for their workers. Apart from measuring the success of training by its impact on bottom line or profits, McDonald's links a number of other benefits to ongoing training. These include improved employee morale and productivity.

Effective and regular training is seen as bringing cascading benefits, such as employee satisfaction, which in turn enhance customer ratings. McDonald's believes that the success of the restaurants and the company is achieved through the people it employs. The company aims to recruit the best people, to retain them by offering ongoing training relevant to their position, and to promote them when they are ready. Training is inherent in McDonald's work culture, and the link between training and progression within the company is explicitly communicated.

Restaurants with high levels of training also have lower staff turnover. A more consistent crew, in turn, delivers higher levels of service to the customer, resulting in more profits and so on. The staff turnover rate at McDonald's is low, with the average length of service of a McDonald's manager currently at over ten years.

Training and development at McDonald's really works. According to McDonald's, some 70% of their current management team (in head and regional offices and in restaurants) began as crew members. These findings suggest that training plays a primary role in the delivery of the three major business objectives of quality, service, and cleanliness and also in achieving better employee and customer satisfaction and a drastically reduced staff turnover rate. All have direct impacts on the bottom lines of each restaurant and of the company as a whole. McDonald's may be regarded as a model employer keeping in view the importance it attaches to employee training and the set of indicators it uses to measure training success.

This case has been constructed on the basis of secondary information from following sources: http://www.mcdonalds.com (accessed on 18 August 2006); http://www.mcdonaldsindia.com, accessed on 18 August 2006; http://mcdonalds.net.in/mcd/corp/index.htm, accessed on 18 August 2006; http://www.thetimes100.co.uk/case_study.php?cID=28&csID=194&pID=5, 06 July 2006; Christine 2002; Westwood 2003; http://www.theworkfoundation.com/Assets/PDFs/are_we_beingserved.pdf, accessed on 18 August 2006.

Questions

1. Do you think McDonald's training initiatives are aligned with business strategy? Explain the reasons for it. Why is it important to establish business strategy–training linkage?

2. Discuss how McDonald's strategic commitment to training has contributed to its position as a 'leading global foodservice retailer'.

3. Examine Ray Kroc's training philosophy. How has McDonald's gained from this philosophy?

4. How relevant is training and development for a company like McDonald's which is seen as 'deskilled'?

5. Describe the orientation training at McDonald's. What purposes does it serve?

6. Discuss the training and management development process at McDonald's with respect to its design, purpose, methods, and content. What organizational goals does it help McDonald's achieve? Evaluate McDonald's T&D process based on your understanding of the process of training.

7. What purposes are served by diversity training for McDonald's? What initiatives does McDonald's take for diversity inclusion in its workforce and with what benefits?

8. What criteria are used to evaluate training effectiveness at McDonald's?

References

Bernardin, H.J. 2004, *Human Resource Management: An Experiential Approach*, 3rd edn, Tata McGraw Hill Publishing Company Limited, New Delhi, pp. 180–2, 185.

Bohlander, G., S. Snell, and A. Sherman 2002, *Managing Human Resources*, 12th edn, Thomson South Western, Singapore, pp. 225–8, 231–3, 243, 254, 255.

Carrell, M.R., N.F. Elbert, and R.D. Hatfield 1995, *Human Resource Management: Global Strategies for Managing a Diverse Workforce*, Prentice Hall, Englewood Cliffs, NJ.

Christine, T. 2002, 'Systematic Training makes McDonald's Number One', *Training and Management Development Methods*, vol. 16, p. 909.

DeCenzo, D.A. and S.P. Robbins 2005, *Fundamentals of Human Resource Management*, 8th edn, John Wiley & Sons, Singapore.

Dessler, G. 2005, *Human Resource Management*, 10th edn, Prentice Hall of India Pvt. Ltd, New Delhi.

Fulmer, R.M., P.A. Gibbs, and M. Goldsmith 2000, 'Developing Leaders: How Winning Companies Keep on Winning', *Sloan Management Review*, Fall, pp. 49–59.

Horwitz, F.M. 1999, 'The Emergence of strategic training and development: the current state of play', *Journal of European Industrial Training*, vol. 23, no. 4–5, pp. 180–90.

Ivancevich, J.M. 2004, *Human Resource Management*, 9th edn, Tata McGraw Hill Publishing Company Ltd, New Delhi.

Jackson, S. and R.S. Schuler 1989, 'Organizational Characteristics as Predictors of Personnel Practices', *Personnel Psychology*, vol. 42, pp. 727–86.

Kossek, E.E. and R.N. Block 2000, *Managing Human Resources in the 21st Century: From Core Concepts to Strategic Choice*, South-Western College Publishing: Thomson Learning, USA.

Marrelli, F.A., J. Tondora, and M.A. Hoge 2005, 'Strategies for Developing Competency Models', *Administration and Policy in Mental Health*, vol. 32, no. 5–6, pp. 533–61.

Mathis, R.L. and J.H. Jackson 2003, *Human Resource Management*, 10th edn, Thomson South-Western, Singapore, p. 293.

Mello, J.A. 2003, *Strategic Human Resource Management*, Thomson Asia Pte Ltd, Singapore, p. 277

Miles, R.E. and C.C. Snow 1978, *Organizational Strategy, Structure, and Process*, McGraw Hill, New York.

Miles, R.E. and C.C. Snow 1984, 'Designing Strategic Human Resources Systems', *Organizational Dynamics*, vol. 13, no. 1, pp. 36–52.

Mondy, R.W., R.M. Noe, and S.R. Premeaux 1999, *Human Resource Management*, 7th edn, Prentice Hall, USA.

Nkomo, S.M., M.D. Fottler, and R.B. McAfee 1992, *Applications in Human Resource Management: Cases, Exercises, and Skill Builders*, 2nd edn, PWS-KENT Publishing company, Boston, pp. 170–7.

Raghuram, S. and R.D. Arvey 1994, 'Business Strategy Links with Staffing and Training Practices', *Human Resource Planning*, vol. 17, no. 3, pp. 55–73.

Ron, Z. 2002, 'FedEx', *Training*, 39 (3), 67, http;//web.ebscohost.com/ehost/delivery?vid=34, accessed on 18 August 2006.

Sims, R.R., J. Veres, and S.M Heninger 1989, 'Training for Competence', *Public Personnel Management*, vol. 18, no. 1, pp. 101–7.

Tovey, L. 1994, 'Competency Assessment: A Strategic Approach–Part II', *Executive Development*, vol. 7, no. 1, pp. 16–19.

Valle, R., F. Martin, P.M. Romero, and S.L. Dolan 2000, 'Business Strategy, Work Processes and Human Resource Training: Are they Congruent?', *Journal of Organizational Behaviour*, vol. 21, no. 3, pp. 283–97.

Westwood, A. 2003, 'Are we Being Served? Career Mobility and Skills in the UK Workforce', Report by The Work Foundation commissioned by McDonald's.

Notes

Business Today, 21 January 2001.

Business Today, January 7 to 21 1996.

Business World, 6 December 2004.

Coutinho, A., 'When it Trains it Pours', *Brand Equity*, The Economic Times, New Delhi, 9 August 2006, pp. 1–2.

'Does Training Trigger Turnover... Or Not? The impact of formal training on young men's and women's job search behaviour', http://www.eale.nl/conference2006/Papers%20Saturday%2014.00%20-%2016.00/add12582.pdf, accessed on 11 August 2006.

Grensing-Pophal, L. 2002, 'Management Development: A Strategic Initiative', Society for Human Resource Management, http://www.ispi.org/pdf/suggestedReading/Grensing_Pophal_No2.pdf, accessed on 11 August 2006.

Kumar, V. 2005, 'Connecting People', Corporate Dossier, *The Economic Times*, Friday, 23 September 2005, New Delhi, p. 1.

Kumar, V., V. Mahanta, and P. Rao 2006, 'Licence to Skill', *The Economic Times*, New Delhi, 4 August 2006, pp. 1–2.

Lee, A., 'Competency Assessment', Centre for Collaborative Organizations, University of North Texas, http://www.workteams.unt.edu/literature/paper-alee.html, accessed on 14 August 2006.

Salzman, H., P. Moss, and C. Tilly 1998, 'The New Corporate Landscape and Workforce Skills', National Centre for Postsecondary Improvement, School of Education, Stanford University, CA, http://www.stanford.edu/group/ncpi/documents/pdfs/2-07_newcorplandscape.pdf, accessed on 11 August 2006.

Singh, S., 'IT Services Industry to add Lakh Jobs in '06', *The Economic Times*, New Delhi, 30 December 2005, p. 8.

The Economic Times, 30 June 2006, 'Made-to-Order MBAs', New Delhi, p. 2.

Training Magazine, July 1999.

7 Performance Management and Development Systems

INTRODUCTION

Competition has become a way of life for most organizations. To survive and be successful, it is important for organizations to remain competitive. Since human resources are a unique and valuable source of competitive advantage, organizations must ensure the most effective and efficient utilization of these resources. It is also important to ensure the continued viability of human resources in the face of technological growth, changes in the nature of jobs, and changes in the demands that jobs make of the employees. To ensure that the organization has competent and motivated employees, there should be a fair basis for rewarding employees. Employees should also have opportunities for growth and development. Employee performance management system provides one such mechanism for employee development as well as for making personnel decisions.

The present chapter begins with a conceptual overview of the terms commonly used to refer to the performance management process. The differences between the traditional and contemporary performance appraisal systems are highlighted. The objectives served by the performance management process within an organizational context are discussed. The chapter discusses the steps in the design and development of a performance management system. The steps include the identification of job performance dimensions; defining performance standards and sources of appraisal; choice of performance appraisal methods; and communication of appraisals to the employees. The main problems and characteristics of performance management are discussed. The chapter also discusses the special features and aspects of performance management such as the team based approach, assessment centre approach, and the 360 degree appraisal feedback. The significant role of technology in supporting various aspects of performance appraisal is also presented. In the end, the chapter examines the linkage between business strategy and performance management. It is emphasized that for performance management to be strategic, it is important to align performance management with organizational strategies at different stages of the organizational life cycle.

PERFORMANCE MANAGEMENT

A major concern of organizations centres on the performance of employees. 'Performance' refers to what an employee does or does not do on the job. Employee performance includes, for example, quantity of output and quality of output. When employees do not perform according to expectations, or when they under perform, it is difficult for a firm to achieve its objectives. Under such conditions, the firm will not be able to achieve competitive advantage. Therefore, organizations seek to determine and evaluate the performance of all employees on a regular basis. Several terms such as *performance assessment, performance appraisal, performance evaluation,* and *performance management* are used commonly and interchangeably to describe the process of employee performance evaluation. Let us understand the meaning of each of these terms.

Performance assessment is the process by which data about an employee's past and current job performance in the organization is collected and reviewed. Assessment suggests a top-down judgmental approach where the manager takes the role of a judge who makes decisions about the adequacy of employee performance. *Performance appraisal* is the system by which an organization assigns some 'score' to indicate the level of current and/or past performance of a target person or group. The individual's performance is compared to a set of performance standards when assigning the score. The term performance appraisal includes assessment too. Both the terms, that is, performance appraisal and assessment, are combined and are synonymous in many organizations. The term *performance evaluation* is used to describe the process used to determine the extent to which an employee performs the work effectively. Some other terms that have been used to connote the same meaning are performance appraisal, merit rating, performance review, and employee evaluation. *Performance management* is a broader term than performance appraisal, performance evaluation, or performance assessment. It is defined as an integrated process that consolidates goal setting, employee development, performance appraisal, and rewarding performance into a single common system. The aim of performance management is to ensure that employee performance supports the strategic goals of the organization. Thus, performance management includes practices through which managers (superiors) work with their employees (subordinates) to define the goals of the latter, develop employee capabilities through training, measure and review employee performance in order to reward performance, all with the ultimate aim of contributing to organizational success. Performance management integrates management of organizational and employee performance. Baron and Armstrong (1998) emphasized the strategic and integrated nature of performance management by stressing that it focuses on increasing the effectiveness of organizations by improving the performance of employees and by developing individual and team capabilities. Performance goals of each employee are linked with the strategic goals of the firm. Performance management is a continuous process and not an annual event. It involves performance reviews focussing on the future rather than the past. An effective performance management system requires the manager to work together with the employees to set performance expectations by defining excellent performance, reviewing performance, providing feedback to employees, and planning for future performance. Determining what constitutes good performance and how different aspects of high achievement can be measured is an important component of an effective performance management process. Performance appraisal or evaluation is, therefore, an integral part of performance management process.

From Performance Appraisal to Performance Management

Performance management was first introduced by Michael Beer (Beer and Ruh 1976) as an innovative appraisal and development system. It was intended to be an improvement on the traditional performance appraisal system that was generally seen as subjective and plagued by rater problems. A comparison of the traditional performance appraisal systems and the new performance management systems is presented in Table 7.1.

Performance appraisal represents an isolated, mechanistic, and HR-driven approach. Performance management, on the other hand, is a comprehensive, integrated, business-driven system aimed at organizational and people development. The performance management process gained popularity in the 1980s with the advent of the total quality management (TQM) programme. Total quality management emphasized the use of all management tools, including training and performance appraisal, in order to achieve performance goals.

As it stands today, performance management as a process recognizes that, in a globally competitive business environment, it is essential that the efforts of every employee of the firm are focussed on helping the firm achieve its strategic goals. Therefore, it is important to integrate individual goals with organizational goals. It is easy to see that if employee performance does not

Table 7.1: Comparison of Performance Management and Performance Appraisal

Characteristics	Performance Management (PM)	Performance Appraisal (PA)
Types of objectives	Emphasis on integrating organizational, team, and individual objectives	Individual objectives
Types of performance measures	Competency requirements as well as quantified measures	Qualitative and quantitative
Frequency	Continuous review with one or more formal reviews in a year	Annual appraisal
Rating system	Joint or participative process, ratings less common	Top-down system, with ratings
Reward linkage	Does not have direct link to reward	Often linked to pay
Ownership	Owned by line management	Owned by human resource department
Corporate alignment	Integrated business-driven system aimed at organizational and people development	Isolated system not linked to organizational goals
Focus of performance reviews	Future focussed	Focus on past performance
Questions asked	What can be done to help employees perform as effectively as possible?	How well was the work done?

Source: Spangenberg and Theron 2001; Armstrong and Baron 1998

help the firm accomplish its goals, then the very survival of the firm is threatened. At Pfizer, the managing director defines the annual objectives, that is, the business performance measures. These objectives then get translated down the hierarchy. The measures include, for example, budgeted sales, net profits, operating profits, etc. Managers set their own objectives to match organizational objectives and their superiors ensure that these are stretch targets. Employees also carry out self-assessment exercises every quarter to gauge where they stand with respect to their annual objectives. At the end of the year, the employees are rated as outstanding, good, satisfactory, below average, or poor. The company's business performance is also calculated on the same poor-to-outstanding scale. Thus, individual objectives and the business objectives of the organization are aligned.

Formal and Informal Performance Appraisal Systems

Performance appraisal is easily the oldest management tool available. In fact, performance appraisal is an inevitable part of any superior–subordinate relationship, be it a teacher–student, master–servant, or father–children relationship. In each such relationship, the superior in the dyad forms opinions about the 'worth' of the subordinate. This occurs even when a formal system of performance appraisal does not exist. When a formal appraisal system does not exist, appraisal goes on informally. Take the case of a household helper. The wages of the helper are fixed based on the quantum of work he/she is required to do. The master also expects a particular level of performance from the helper. When the helper 'performs' the work according to the expectations of the master, he/she is rewarded with a token money or gift over and above the wage.

Performance appraisal as an informal process has existed in organizations since time immemorial. *Informal performance appraisal* takes place when managers frequently think about how well employees are performing on their jobs, even when they are not officially required to do so. Day-to-day interaction of the manager with an employee allows the former an opportunity to appraise the employee's performance. Informal appraisals are often communicated by the manager to the employee over coffee or immediately when his performance is observed. Informal appraisals have the following advantages:

- They help provide immediate feedback to employees, resulting in high motivation.
- Frequent informal appraisals prevent surprises during the annual formal appraisal.

The formal process of performance appraisal began to be increasingly used in the 1940s. *Formal appraisal*, on the other hand, is systematic appraisal. It is a system set up by the organization to evaluate the performance of an employee. Almost all organizations have some variation of formal appraisal in place. Infosys, LG, AV Birla group, ICICI, Gillette, Godrej, and HP are some of the companies in India having a formal appraisal system. Today, almost all organizations have two evaluation systems existing side by side—the formal system and the informal system. In the present chapter, we are concerned with the formal process of evaluating employee performance. A formal system serves multiple purposes or objectives for the organization.

Objectives of Performance Management Systems

Performance appraisal data is potentially viable for use in almost every HRM activity. Figure 7.1 depicts the various uses and objectives of a performance management system.

A well-designed formal performance management system helps accomplish the following objectives.

Human resource planning Performance appraisal information provides a valuable input for skills inventories and human resource planning (HRP). By providing information about the human resource strengths and weaknesses of the organization, the performance appraisal system helps determine the promotability and potential of all employees. It, therefore, constitutes an important information base for developing succession plans, replacement charts, and creating new positions in the organization.

Recruitment and selection Performance appraisals can be used to validate or evaluate decisions related to employee recruitment and selection. By comparing employees' performance appraisal with their test scores as job applicants, it is possible to determine the effectiveness of the recruitment and selection system. For instance, employees who received about the same scores on the selection tests should perform similarly on the job. However, if these employees show a significant difference in their job performance after one year on the job, then the selection system is not considered successful.

Personnel decisions Apart from validating selection procedures, performance appraisals also serve as a guide for other personnel decisions such as promotions, layoffs, etc. Performance data helps make rational personnel decisions. In the absence of this information, personnel decisions become subjective. Performance data also helps defend promotion decisions once the decision is made.

Training and development Appraisal data helps an organization determine specific training and development needs based on an assessment of the deficiencies in performance levels and skills. It helps to identify employees and departments in need of training. However, not all performance deficiencies may be overcome through training. Performance appraisal should clearly determine whether the reasons for performance deficiency are due to the lack of skills or because of low morale.

Feedback, motivation, and personal development Performance appraisals help provide performance feedback to employees. They also help in the development of action plans for individual performance improvement and facilitate learning of new behaviour. All employees want to know how they are performing on the job, what their manager thinks of their performance, and where they need to improve. Performance feedback is a primary developmental need and serves to motivate employees. Performance appraisals help determine employee strengths, weaknesses, potentials, and training needs. When providing feedback to employees, the manager can inform employees

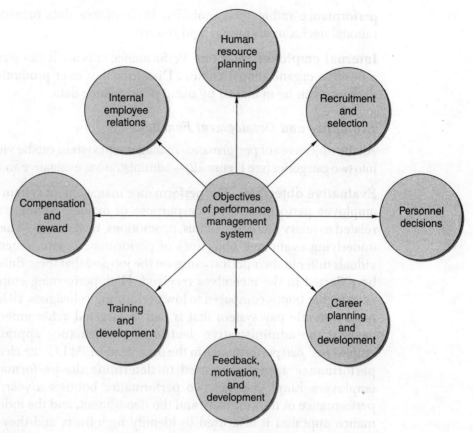

Figure 7.1: Uses and Objectives of Performance Management System

about their performance, discuss what aspects need improvement, and also identify what direction employees should take to improve performance.

Career planning and development Appraisal data also helps in identifying employee potential and in planning future growth opportunities for the employee. Information about the strengths, weaknesses, and potential of employees can be used to counsel and assist them in developing and implementing realistic career plans.

Compensation and reward A fair and objective performance appraisal system helps in making differential reward decisions, such that the most productive workers or teams are rewarded accordingly. In the absence of performance data, everyone gets the same bonus, is rewarded equally, or rewards are subjectively distributed. Such a situation results in perception of inequity on the part of high performers. When rewards and compensation are linked to performance, it reinforces the belief that pay raises should be linked to performance rather than seniority. Performance data provides a basis for rational decisions about pay and rewards.

Internal employee relations Performance appraisals can serve to maintain a positive organizational culture. Dissatisfaction over promotions or reward decisions can be managed by using performance data.

Evaluative and Development Functions

All the objectives of performance management system can be viewed as falling into two categories (see Figure 7.2)—administrative/evaluative and development.

Evaluative objectives The performance management system measures past employee performance for the purpose of making administrative decisions related to salary increases, bonus, promotions, rewards, etc. The basic premise underlying evaluative objectives of performance management is that individuals differ in their performance on the job and that these differences should be reflected in the incentives received. High-performing employees should get a higher bonus compared to low performing colleagues. IBM, for instance, has a variable pay system that is tied to targeted achievements. In making each of the administrative decisions, performance appraisals focus on employees' *past* performance in the organization. At LG, the electronics major, performance appraisal is used to determine the performance bonus of employees. Employees get two performance bonuses a year, based on the performance of the company and the department, and the individual. Performance appraisal is also used to identify high-flyers and they are rewarded with double-promotions.

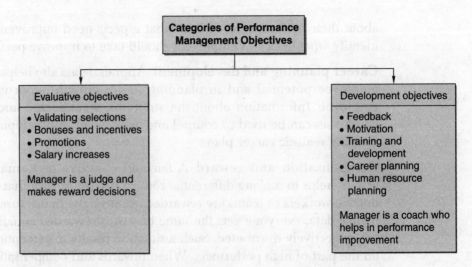

Figure 7.2:   Two Categories of Performance Management Objectives

Development objectives Another objective of performance management is to facilitate the development of employee skills and motivation for *future* performance. Development objectives focus on employee career growth and potential development.

American Express has a Performance Management Process (PMP) that is used to identify and facilitate career moves within the organization. National Panasonic, the Japanese white goods major, has developed a performance assessment system that is based on key result areas (KRAs). Key result areas describe business, functional, and behavioural performance goals with a time-frame defined for each performance goal. The employee and the manager jointly decide the KRAs in the beginning of the year. These KRAs are then used to map the employee's progress. Based on employee performance, the organization identifies performance gaps and designs relevant training inputs to plug performance gaps. National Panasonic places a lot of emphasis on re-skilling its employees, hence the company focusses on developmental performance appraisal objectives. Cadbury India, Sandoz, Pfizer, Mafatlal, Philips, GlaxoSmithKline (GSK), and Procter & Gamble (P&G) are some of the companies in India to have redesigned their systems shifting from pure performance orientation to a potential and performance-based appraisal system. Bangalore-based Silicon Automation Systems (SAS) has a comprehensive performance, planning, review, and development module. The company clearly explains to its employees what their targets are, whether they have achieved them, and based on the results, where they can expect their career paths to lead. At GSK, there is a small section on potential appraisal within the performance appraisal form that is to be filled in by the employee's superior. This section lists out certain attributes such as attitude, accountability, initiative, drive, etc. At Cadbury, the insights received on the potential of employees are through the review system by immediate appraisers, departmental heads, or the functional Vice Presidents. Godrej Consumer Products Limited (GCPL) has a talent management system that helps to develop leaders, facilitates succession planning, and provides a clear career path to employees. The system requires good performers to be rated on their leadership potential by superiors and an independent assessor. The short-listed people get a career choice between general management and domain expertise.

Traditionally, performance appraisals primarily served evaluative or administrative objectives. These objectives continue to be important reasons for conducting formal performance appraisals in organizations. A leading financial institution in India has a system for spotting high performers through its performance appraisal system. There is a performance appraisal form that is filled by each employee and his/her immediate supervisor. A moderating committee comprised of members of cross-functional teams takes the decision on performance bonus. The score-sheet (performance appraisal form) is then returned to the employee's immediate boss who then shares the appraisal feedback with the employee and discusses career options with him/her. The Central Government of India recently outlined initiatives for re-orienting the performance appraisal system for IAS officers. The performance appraisal system is designed to provide opportunity for mid-career exit for inefficient officers and fast-track rewards for the high performers. The main purpose of the performance appraisal system is stated to make civil servants accountable and responsive. The system proposes an intensive review of the officer's per-formance at two stages in the career—after every 15 and 25 years of service. Those who receive high scores on evaluation measures will get promotions and recognition. Those who do not qualify on these appraisal measures will not be promoted and will have the option of choosing voluntary separation from service. The officers will be assessed by a group of eminent persons who will be selected by a high-level committee. The annual confidential reports of civil servants are being replaced by the performance appraisal reports. The latter system is expected to provide a more objective evaluation.

In several organizations, performance appraisal these days is viewed as being much broader in scope. Performance management serves both evalua-tive and the development purposes. However, the two purposes are often conflicting. Evaluative performance appraisal requires the manager to be a *judge* of employee performance and make differential reward decisions. How-ever, in developmental performance appraisal, the manager assumes the role of a *coach* or counsellor. A coach rewards good performance with recognition, explains where improvement is necessary, and shows employees how to improve. Evaluative performance appraisal requires managers to make judg-ments that affect the future of employees. These decisions relate to promo-tions, bonus, rewards, etc. On the other hand, developmental appraisal requires employees to participate in their own appraisal in order to identify those aspects of their performance that need improvement. These two purposes have an inherent conflict with each other.

A major mistake that organizations commit while designing and imple-menting a performance management system is to seek to achieve both evalu-ative and developmental objectives at the same time. Providing feedback about performance to employees and identifying areas of improvement while making evaluative decisions at the same time leads to ambiguity and defensiveness on the part of employees. This defeats the very objective of a performance man-agement system. Hence, it is important that organizations have at least two formal appraisals, instead of only one, in a single year. One appraisal should focus on developmental goals, while the other appraisal should focus on evaluative goals. It is important for an organization to strategize the main purpose for which performance management is being used—evaluative or developmental. The organization should ensure that in a performance management system that is designed to serve multiple purposes, these purposes do not conflict with each other. Organizations are moving toward a system of more frequent and multiple formal appraisals in a year, though the appraisals essentially remain evaluative in nature. Hewlett-Packard has a system of monitoring and rewarding employee performance thrice a year. Samsung India, the consumer electronics company and Mantra, an internet service provider and portal, have instituted quarterly performance reviews. Gillette India has introduced a Hall of Fame review system in its sales function whereby performance is measured against a given target every two months. The firm uses the performance review to keep employee morale high and to recognize extraordinary performance in the short run.

DEVELOPING PERFORMANCE MANAGEMENT SYSTEMS

The specific design and implementation of performance management differs from one organization to another. However, certain steps need to be followed in the development of a performance management system. These steps are common across all organizations (Figure 7.3). The steps that constitute the performance management process include

1. identifying dimensions of job performance;
2. defining and communicating performance standards;
3. determining who will conduct the appraisal;
4. choosing appropriate methods of performance appraisal; and
5. communicating appraisals to employees.

The steps in the performance management process are summarized in Exhibit 7.1.

It is important to remember that the performance management system should be aligned with organizational objectives. Therefore, the long-term as well as short-term objectives of the firm should be identified first. This will help determine the type of jobs, skills (human resources), and nature of employee performance that the organization will require to achieve its objectives. This becomes the basis for specifying performance measures against which employee performance will be assessed. MindTree Consulting provides a good example of how organizational values and objectives can be integrated with performance management systems. The core values at MindTree are called CLASS (caring, learning, achieving, sharing, and social conscience). These values represent the firm's values and are the guiding principles for the employees of the organization. The firm has tied CLASS to its employee performance appraisal system. Every employee is evaluated on 100 points. Out of a total of 100 points, 60 come from job objectives and 40 points are related to how an employee is doing with respect to CLASS. Employees are

Exhibit 7.1

Steps in Performance Management Process

The following steps constitute the performance management process in organizations:

1. Conducting job analysis and developing job descriptions and job specifications. These help define the broad performance dimensions or activities of an employee, ensuring that each employee's goals are aligned to accomplish organizational goals.
2. Developing performance standards for each performance dimension. Performance standards specify the expected levels of performance. Setting performance expectations involves:
   - Checking individual or group performance standards or goals against department and organizational goals to ensure that they support the latter.
   - Specifying measures for appraising how well an employee accomplished each

objective or goal. Measures may be related to quality of performance, cost/budget, and time taken to accomplish the objective. For instance, a measure for evaluating sales persons' performance may be reaching a particular sales target within a six month period.
   - Developing a plan to monitor employee performance. This helps in tracking employee performance and taking corrective action at the right time.

3. Appraising employee performance and holding performance review discussions with the employee.
4. Using performance management information to make administrative decisions, identify and solve problems, and develop action plans for performance improvement.

---

required to fill a self-appraisal form and demonstrate through anecdotes and personal experiences how they acted on some of the values. The immediate superior adds his/her input to the self-appraisal. Let us now discuss each of these steps of the performance management system.

Dimensions of Job Performance

Before conducting any appraisal, the important elements in a given job, that is, the job criteria, should be identified. Job criteria are also called the evaluation criteria or dimensions of job performance. These are the factors for which the employee is paid by the organization. At Escotel, the telecom company, along with individual performance, company goals, country performance, operating margin, and customer satisfaction are woven into senior managers' appraisals. PepsiCo India uses unit performance, volume growth, and market share to calculate incentives for senior level executives.

Some performance dimensions are common to most jobs, for example, quantity of output. Beyond these general dimensions there are other dimensions of job performance too. For example, important evaluation criteria in a college professor's job are—teaching and research. A college professor is paid to do

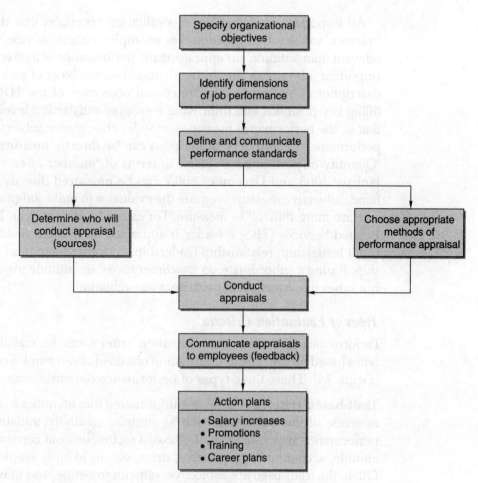

Figure 7.3: Process of Performance Management System

research and teaching and therefore, the performance of college professors on these job criteria should be measured. It is quite possible for an individual to demonstrate better performance on some job criterion than others. A college professor may be a good researcher but not a good teacher or vice versa. It is also possible that some criteria are considered more important than others by the organization. One department of a university may consider teaching to be a more important job criterion when compared to research. Another department may place higher value on research as a job criterion. By assigning weightages to different job criteria, it is possible to show the relative importance of several criteria in one job. Going back to the college professor's example, in a particular teaching institution, teaching may be given a higher weightage of 50%, research a weightage of 30%, organizing seminars 10%, and presenting conference papers 10%.

An important characteristic of evaluation criteria is that they should be 'relevant' to the job in question. For example, 'volume of sales' may be more relevant than 'attitude' for appraising the performance of a direct sales person. Important job criteria should be identified on the basis of an employee's job descriptions. At Amtrex, the functional objectives of the HR manager are filling key positions and improving employee satisfaction levels. Job criteria, that is, the performance measures, may be objective or subjective. Objective performance measures or dimensions can be directly measured or counted. 'Quantity of performance' stated in terms of 'number of cars sold between January 2005 and December 2005' can be measured directly. On the other hand, subjective measures require the evaluator to make judgments and therefore are more difficult to measure. For example, at American Express Travel Related Services (TRS) a leader is appraised on thought or idea leadership, result leadership, relationship leadership, customer focus, and people leadership. Rating a subordinate on 'customer focus' or 'attitude towards customer' is a subjective measure of performance evaluation.

Types of Evaluation Criteria

Performance dimensions or evaluation criteria can be classified into three types based on the type of information obtained about employee performance (Figure 7.4). These three types of performance dimensions are as follows:

Trait-based criteria These seek information that identifies a subjective characteristic of the employee, such as attitude, creativity, initiative, etc. In the performance appraisal form of Glaxo, a section lists out certain attributes like attitude, accountability, initiative, drive, etc. to identify employee potential. Often, the traits used are subjective, difficult to define, and may be altogether unrelated to job performance. Performance evaluations based on traits are vague and are not the best for making performance-related HR decisions.

Behaviour-based criteria Such performance measures focus on specific behaviours that lead to success on the job. For example, for a manager an appropriate behaviour to evaluate might be 'developing others', or for a salesperson it could be 'customer service orientation'. Behaviour-based information

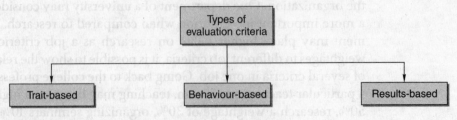

Figure 7.4: Types of Performance Evaluation Criteria

helps to clearly specify the type of behaviour that is considered desirable or appropriate in an organization. When using behavioural information as criteria for performance evaluation, an organization rewards and recognizes employees for behaving in certain ways that produce results. This leads to the repetition of desired behaviour on the part of employees. Behaviour measures are also useful when it is difficult to specify outcomes or goals in a particular job. For example, it may be difficult to clearly specify and measure the outcome of a college teacher's job since the outcome may be influenced by several factors. In such a case, it is more appropriate to evaluate an employee's task-related behaviour. The teacher's performance may be evaluated on the basis of criteria such as, whether a teacher is regular in taking classes, conducts regular tests for students, etc. Sometimes, however, several different types of behaviour may all lead to successful performance in a given job. For instance, different salespersons may use different types of behavioural approaches to make successful sales. It may then become difficult or inappropriate to specify one particular task-related behaviour as leading to desired performance outcomes.

Results-based criteria This criterion is appropriate for jobs in which measurement is easy and obvious, and where there is a tangible output. When *ends* are considered more important than the *means*, results-based measures are the obvious choice. The focus of all employees shifts toward producing 'results'. To emphasize the importance of outcomes, large tasks are divided into smaller, more specific, and time-bound projects. Criticality of processes followed is also rated. For instance, the AV Birla group rates performance on specific and critical tasks in its rating system. In HCL Technologies, individuals are rated on their performance on each project. One problem with this type of information occurs when the results or outcomes are influenced by multiplicity of factors and are not within the control of the employee. In such a case, an employee may work very hard, yet may not produce results. Another problem arises because of emphasizing results at the cost of quality. Employees may use unethical means to achieve results. For example, if a teacher is evaluated on the basis of the total number of students who pass the course, the teacher may not take regular classes (behaviour) and may become very lenient in grading to ensure that all students pass. Thus, overemphasizing outcomes may result in low quality and even the use of unethical means to achieve goals.

On the other hand, overemphasizing behaviours may lead to very good quality products but the product delivery may overshoot deadlines and result in lost business for the firm. It is, therefore, important to balance both behaviour (quality or doing it the right way) and results (accomplishing goals and meeting deadlines).

The three evaluation criteria for evaluating employee performance should not be considered mutually exclusive. In fact, most appraisal systems incorporate all three types of criteria (information) in various degrees. At ICI India, performance ratings are decided by individual performance as well as business performance and gauged against budget compliance, profit maximization, volume growth, and innovation. Whirlpool's performance excellence plan assesses performance using shareholder value, customer value, and employee value to fit the employees on a salary grid. Appraisals of top management at HP take into account the business performance as well.

For each job, therefore, there exist multiple criteria in order to measure performance completely. As already mentioned, some criteria may be more important than others for successful job performance. For example, Godrej & Boyce is structured around business divisions such as, office equipment, locks, machine tools, etc. Each business division is a team. Performance measures used for each team (business division) are volume of business growth, net contribution of the division, and net working capital returns. For support services such as finance, HRD, etc. the parameters for achievement include staying within budgets, company profits, manpower costs, success at meeting deadlines, and internal customer satisfaction. The company measures the performance of its teams on these parameters using three benchmarks—levels 1, 2, and 3. Level 3 refers to minimum acceptable performance on the parameter. The other two levels represent stretch targets, with level 1 signifying extraordinary performance that surpasses all expectations. At the beginning of each year, the quantifiable indices corresponding to each of the three levels are set, but only level 1 targets are actually communicated. Unless a division reaches level 3, there is neither a team reward nor an individual one. Thus, achieving the benchmark of level 1 is more important at Godrej. The top performers of each division are determined by the divisional head and they get additional rewards for their individual performance. Employees also have their annual bonuses tied to performance. Members of business divisions receive 20% of their consolidated basic salary as bonus if both the company and the division make a profit. If either does not, the bonus drops to 10%. The support services earn bonus if the organization makes profits.

Multiple criteria must be judiciously combined to obtain a single performance measure. One must also be careful to evaluate both behaviour and results.

Performance Standards

Identifying job or evaluation criteria is only the first step in performance management. We still need to know the expected level of performance on each of these criteria. To specify teaching and research publications as the evaluation or job criteria for college teachers is not enough. It is important to specify the 'standards' by which performance on these two job criteria will be evaluated. Performance standards define the expected levels of performance, goals, or targets. The performance standard with respect to the research publication criterion for college teachers may be defined as, 'publish two research papers in referred journals in a year'. Thus, performance standards, simply stated, define what constitutes satisfactory job performance. Performance standards should be determined before the work is performed and communicated to the employee. This ensures that employees know what level of performance is expected from them. At Reckitt and Coleman, all managers have a well-defined job description listing all the key result areas (KRAs) that their job profile requires them to achieve. Each KRA is a parameter for productivity review. Key result areas are broken down into micro-activities and performance standards are set for each activity. A manager's record on each of these activities is measured. Typical KRAs for a manager in the sales department include, for example, simplifying a customer oriented process, maintaining sales expenditure at 5% of total sales volume, etc. However, sales volume is not considered in isolation when measuring a sales manager's productivity. The aggregate of the achievements under each parameter is presented in a performance development and review document filed by the manager and his/her immediate superior. This system helps the organization achieve corporate objectives while enabling individuals to set and meet the KRAs during the course of the year.

Standards or performance goals should be realistic, specific, and clearly stated in quantifiable, measurable terms. For example, resolving customer complaints is not a clearly stated performance standard. When stated as 'resolving customer complaints in first instance 98% of the time', it presents a clear picture of the standard that an employee is expected to demonstrate in job performance. For example, at Hinduja Finance, the manager in the corporate finance department has a target to bring Rs 15 crore worth of underwriting assignments a year. However, bringing in the business is not enough, the decision to accept an underwriting offer must be cleared by a committee since the business carries some risk. Thus, the manager's productivity is actually determined by whether the business he/she has brought in is of acceptable quality.

However, for certain jobs, it is not always possible to specify performance standards in quantifiable terms. For example, one performance criteria for teachers may be to evaluate students objectively and without bias. The performance standard in this case will be non-numerical and may be stated as 'a teacher will be considered to be unbiased and objective in evaluating a student when all the guidelines for evaluation have been followed'.

Determining who will Conduct Performance Evaluation

In performing the job, an employee has to interact with several other individuals in the organization. These include peers, subordinates, superiors, customers, and employees from other departments. The nature of interaction of an employee with each of these people differs. Therefore, it is unrealistic to assume that one person can observe and evaluate all aspects of an employee's performance. The performance of an employee can be evaluated by anyone who is familiar with his/her work. The sources of information about employee performance may include superior, subordinate, peers, team members, customers, and self (Figure 7.5). Each of these sources provides unique information about the performance of an employee. Nevertheless, each source is fraught with advantages and disadvantages (Table 7.2). A brief description of these appraisal sources follows.

Appraisal by supervisor and/or manager This is the traditional approach to evaluation of an employee's performance. The immediate superior has the legitimate authority as well as the responsibility to evaluate the performance of employees, and to communicate this assessment of performance to the employee concerned. Often, however, managers do not have the opportunity to fully observe the performance of the employee they are evaluating.

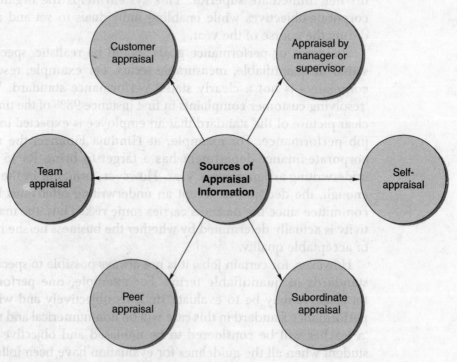

Figure 7.5: Sources of Appraisal Information

Self-appraisal Most organizations require employees to evaluate themselves on the performance appraisal form prior to the performance interview. This leads to greater involvement of the employee in his/her own performance. The employee is also encouraged to think about his/her strengths and weaknesses as well as the barriers to effective performance. Self-appraisals are best used for development purposes rather than evaluative purposes. Used with other sources of appraisal, self-appraisals provide important performance related information.

Subordinate appraisal This type of appraisal is also called upward appraisal. It involves performance appraisal of a superior by his/her subordinate. Evaluation of a teacher by students is an example of upward appraisal. Certain dimensions of a manager's job, such as planning and organizing, analytical ability, etc. are not usually considered appropriate for subordinate appraisal. Performance dimensions that are considered most appropriate for subordinate appraisals include leadership, oral communication, delegation of authority, etc. Subordinate appraisals serve the purpose of giving feedback to managers on how they are perceived by their subordinates. These are, therefore, appropriate for developmental purposes rather than for administrative purposes. Pepsi has devised the People Engagement Index through which employees can evaluate their superiors on 15 parameters every quarter. The firm essentially uses upward appraisal to recognize junior and mid-level managers and to give them an opportunity to be a part of the decision-making process. At FedEx, employees rate their managers through a voluntary survey called the 'survey-feedback-action'. The survey has only two parameters, satisfied or not satisfied. Any manager rated as unsatisfactory by his employees is put on notice. The management and the HR constantly evaluate these managers over the next quarter. The managers are expected to improve during this time. However, if they continue to fair poorly on their appraisals over the next few quarters, they are asked to leave the organization. Upward appraisal at FedEx, therefore, combines developmental and evaluative purposes.

Peer appraisal Peers are individuals who work together and are of equal rank. Peer appraisal is an employee's appraisal done by fellow employees. Information obtained from peer appraisal is different to some extent from appraisals done by superiors, subordinates, etc. Peers see different dimensions of performance of their co-workers, such as leadership skills, interpersonal skills, and their strengths and weaknesses. Peer appraisals are better used for developmental rather than for evaluative purposes. This source, however, has not been used very frequently because it has the potential of negatively impacting the interpersonal relations among co-workers, resulting in rivalries, hostility, and retaliation.

Team appraisal Such an appraisal is an extension of peer appraisal. While peers are individuals in the same rank, they may not be working together very closely. A team consists of employees who work together in pursuit of a specific task or project assigned to the team. In a team it is difficult to isolate the individual contribution of an employee. Team performance is usually linked with team incentives or group variable pay.

Customer appraisal Internal and external customer appraisals are used as a source of performance appraisal information. External customer feedback is often used in the service industry, for example, banking services and restaurants. However, companies such as Maruti Udyog Ltd and AT&T have also begun utilizing feedback from external customers. Managers establish performance measures related to customer service and specify goals for the employee. These individual goals are linked with company goals. For example, one performance dimension is to treat customers with courtesy and promptness. A performance standard or goal related to this performance measure may read, 'attends to the customer within two minutes of his/her arrival'. A questionnaire survey is conducted on customers. The survey items reflect various performance measures related to customer service. The feedback obtained from customers becomes part of employee appraisals and is used to enhance employee effectiveness and organizational performance.

Internal customers are employees within the organization who depend on the work output of the employee being evaluated. For instance, for the human resource department of a firm, employees belonging to other departments are its internal customers. These employees depend on the HR department for their training and, therefore, evaluate the training services provided by the HR department.

Multisource feedback Many companies combine the above appraisal sources to provide multisource feedback or rating. When all sources of appraisal are combined together it is called 360 degree appraisal. As mentioned earlier, different people see different facets of an employee's performance. Thus, an individual employee's performance is appraised by his/her superior, peer, subordinate, and customer. It may also include self-appraisals. Hence, a comprehensive view of an employee's performance is obtained by combining inputs from all those with whom the employee interacts in performing the job. Multisource feedback is useful for both evaluative and developmental feedback. However, most firms prefer to use it only for developmental purposes. The AV Birla Group, Gillette, and Ballarpur Industries have 360 degree feedback for senior level managers. A more detailed discussion of 360 degree feedback is discussed in a later section in this chapter.

Table 7.2:   Advantages and Disadvantages of Appraisal Sources

Appraisal Source	Advantages	Disadvantages
Supervisors	▪ Are often in best position to evaluate employees directly under them ▪ Can observe improvements in employee performance over time ▪ Are in a position to provide immediate feedback about aspects of performance	▪ Often do not have time to fully observe the performance of employees ▪ Very little opportunity for feedback or input from the employee ▪ Often do not have appropriate information to provide informed feedback ▪ Not the best source for evaluating subordinates on technical dimensions of work since supervisors may not necessarily be up to date on those aspects ▪ View it as an administrative burden ▪ Several biases and errors are inherent ▪ Appraisal may have negative impact on supervisor–subordinate relationship ▪ May manipulate evaluations to justify their decisions concerning pay increases and promotions
Peer/Team	▪ Useful for developmental purposes ▪ Provide more valid and accurate information compared to superiors ▪ Peer/team members have a more realistic picture on fellow employee's performance ▪ Peer pressure is a powerful motivator for team members ▪ Not dependent on one individual's views	▪ Can be very political and self-serving in organizations where employees compete with each other formally or informally ▪ Peers are often reluctant to appraise each other ▪ Since peers are in competition, peer appraisals are preferably not used for administrative decisions ▪ Those receiving low ratings may retaliate against peers ▪ May lack objectivity when there is personal loss or gain at stake ▪ May lead to lower morale ▪ May negatively affect teamwork and future work relationships ▪ Often end up as popularity contest
Subordinates	▪ In frequent contact with their superiors and hence in good position to evaluate superiors	▪ Employees avoid appraisal by subordinates, especially when it is used as a basis for compensation decisions

Contd

Table 7.2 Contd

Appraisal Source	Advantages	Disadvantages
	■ Brings power into more favourable balance as employees get power over their superiors ■ Provides insight into interpersonal and managerial styles and leadership potential of employees ■ Helps organization address developmental needs of high-potential employees ■ Help in identifying competent managers ■ Manager becomes more responsive to subordinates	■ Suffer from political problems as subordinates may use it for retaliation ■ Managers may focus on 'being nice' to subordinates in order to get good feedback, especially if it is linked to personnel decisions such as promotions ■ Subordinates fearing reprisals from managers may not give objective feedback ■ Managers may get caught in a popularity contest
Customers	■ Provide feedback that is most free from bias ■ Feedback is critical for facilitating employee development and determining rewards	■ May not know important demands within the organization ■ May have unrealistically high expectations and hence give poor evaluation
Self	■ Encourages employees to think about their strengths and weaknesses ■ Leads employees to set goals for themselves ■ Employees with unique skills may be the only ones qualified to rate themselves ■ Increases employee's involvement in review process	■ May try to present oneself in highly favourable light

Choosing Methods of Performance Appraisal

When designing a performance management system, an important strategic decision relates to the choice of appraisal methods. Performance appraisal methods have evolved over time and today there are several methods to measure it. They have been variously classified and a brief overview of three classification approaches is presented in Table 7.3. For our discussion, we will follow the trait, behaviour, and results classification of performance appraisal methods (Figure 7.6). This approach classifies performance appraisal methods on the basis on 'what' is measured, that is, traits, behaviour, or results.

Table 7.3:   Classification Approaches of Performance Appraisal Methods

S. No.	Classification Approaches	Methods of Performance Appraisal
I	*Absolute measures* evaluate employees relative to performance standards of the job	Graphic rating scales, forced-choice method, critical incident technique, checklists, and BARS
	Relative measures evaluate employees in comparison to co-workers	Ranking, paired comparison, and forced-distribution method
II	*Category rating methods* evaluate employees against a standard	Graphic rating scales and checklists
	Comparative methods evaluate employees by comparing the performance of employees against one another	Ranking and forced-distribution
	Narrative methods assess employees by describing their actions or behaviour	Critical incident techniques and essays
	Behavioural methods evaluate employees' behaviour instead of their characteristics	BARS
III	*Trait-based methods* measure the extent to which an employee possesses certain characteristics viewed as important for the job in particular and the organization in general	Graphic rating scale, forced-choice method, essay method, ranking method, and forced-distribution method
	Behaviour-based methods describe which actions or behaviour should (or should not) be exhibited on the job	Critical incident techniques, checklists, and BARS
	Results-based methods evaluate employees' accomplishments, that is, the results they achieve through their work	Productivity measures, MBO

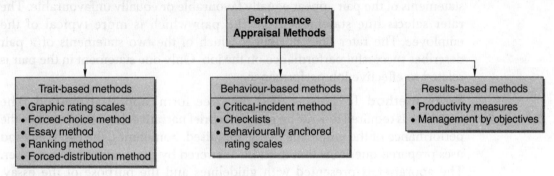

Figure 7.6:   Methods of Performance Appraisal

Trait-Based Methods

These appraisal methods are designed to measure the extent to which an employee possesses certain characteristics that are important for performing the job successfully.

Graphic rating scales This is the oldest, simplest, and perhaps the most widely used appraisal method. The rating scale allows the rater to represent each trait, characteristic, or judgment about performance on a continuum or a scale. The scale is divided into categories—usually five to seven in number. These points or categories on the scale are defined by adjectives such as outstanding, average, or poor. The rating scale requires the rater to indicate the degree to which an employee possesses a particular trait, characteristic, or demonstrates a type of performance, by circling the point on the scale that best describes the employee being evaluated. The values assigned by the rater on each trait or characteristics are added to obtain an overall evaluation score for an employee. The method allows for the use of more than one performance dimension. However, an overall rating may be provided. Two types of factors are typically included in rating scales:

- Job-related factors such as quantity and quality of work, attendance, etc.
- Personal characteristics such as initiative, dependability, etc.

Rating scales differ in the degree to which various performance dimensions (such as quality of work, initiative) are defined for the rater. Some scales may be anchored simply by 'initiative', while others may provide a definition of the term for the rater. Rating scales also differ in the degree to which each point on the scale is defined. For example, point five in a five-point scale may be stated only as a number or it may be labelled as 'outstanding', or the term outstanding may be defined as 'consistently maintains good quality'.

Forced-choice method This is an alternative form of rating method. Forced-choice method requires the appraiser to choose from a set of descriptive statements about an employee. These statements are often given in pairs. Both statements of the pair appear equally favourable or equally unfavourable. The rater selects one statement from the pair which is more typical of the employee. The rater does not know which of the two statements of a pair describes successful performance on the job. Only one statement in the pair is related to effective job performance.

Essay method It is also called the 'free form' appraisal method. The appraiser is required to write an essay or a brief narrative that best describes the performance of the employee being appraised. Sometimes, the essay method uses prepared questions that must be answered by the manager or appraiser. The appraiser is presented with guidelines and the purpose of the essay. Usually, the appraiser is asked to describe employee strengths and weaknesses.

Managers also provide feedback to the employees and suggest performance improvement plans.

Ranking method This method requires the manager to rank or list all employees from highest to lowest on a trait or dimension of performance. For example, on the dimension of 'quality of performance—performance meets highest standards', out of a group of ten employees the manager will rank as number one that employee who demonstrates the highest quality of performance. At rank ten will be the employee whose quality of performance is worst relative to the rest of the employees.

Forced-distribution method The rater is required to assign employees in the work group to a limited number of categories so as to approximate a normal frequency distribution. A predetermined percentage of employees are placed in each performance category. For example, 10% of employees may be in the 'outstanding' category, and 60% of the employees may be in the 'average' category. Thus, in a group of 60 employees, six employees will be placed in Grade A+, and 36 employees will be in Grade B. Even if there are two more employees who demonstrate the same quality of performance, they are assigned a lower grade. Several firms such as GE, Sun Microsystems, etc. use forced ranking of their employees. At LG, employee performance is evaluated based on the performance of the company, the department, and the individual. About 15 to 20% of employees get a 500% bonus, while a minimum of 5% are given zero bonus. Even though an employee may have met the targets, he/she will get zero bonus if everyone else exceeds their targets.

Behaviour-Based Methods

These methods obtain descriptions of employee behaviour and place them along a scale. This helps identify those actions which need to be improved.

Critical-incident method Critical incidents are descriptions of job-related behaviours that represent either effective or ineffective performance for each employee being evaluated. The HR manager, in consultation with operating managers, prepares a list of critical incidents. These incidents range from highly effective to highly ineffective behaviour for job performance. The manager observes the employee at work and keeps a written record of both highly effective (favourable) and ineffective (unfavourable) actions demonstrated by the employee when performing the job. The method is best used for developmental purposes and for developing other behaviour-based measures.

Checklists A checklist is a set of descriptive statements. Each statement describes a job-related behaviour. It is prepared on the basis of the critical incident method. The behaviour descriptions on a checklist range from those that are related with effective job performance to those related with ineffective job performance. The rater is required to check those statements that are most representative of the characteristics or performance of the employee. A variation of checklists are the 'weighted' checklists. These assign weightages to each statement on the checklist. The weightage reflects the degree to which a statement is related with effective job performance. High weightage signifies that the behaviour is very effective for job performance. The weightages of the statements that are checked by the rater to describe the employee are summed to obtain a numerical score of the employee's job performance. The rater does not know the weight assigned to a particular statement. Checklists also serve developmental goals of performance appraisal.

Behaviourally anchored rating scales (BARS) These are a combination of traditional rating scales and the critical incident method. A BARS rating form consists of a certain number of dimensions relevant to job performance, usually six to ten. These performance dimensions include salesmanship skills, customer service skills, job knowledge, etc. A BARS is constructed for each performance dimension. Each BARS is typically a seven or nine point vertical scale. Each point on the scale is anchored in behavioural terms. Point one on the scale represents unfavourable job performance and the highest scale point represents favorable job performance. The rater reads the behaviour anchors on each scale and checks on the point that is most descriptive of the employee. BARS is very useful for providing developmental feedback and identifying training needs.

Result-Based Methods

These methods focus on the accomplishments of the employees, that is, the results they achieve through their work. Measures such as sales figures, production output, etc. are more objective criteria for assessment.

Productivity measures A number of results-related measures are available that can be the basis for performance evaluation. For example, sales people are evaluated on the basis of volume or value of sales and production workers are evaluated for the number of units produced. The functional objectives of the HR manager at Amtrex are, not keeping key positions vacant and improving the employee-satisfaction level. At Amtrex, company profits or growth rate frequently become the criteria for measuring the productivity of executives. Productivity measures directly link employee goals and accomplishments with the results that are significant for the organization. Several firms like PepsiCo, Escotel, ICI, Whirlpool, and HP use measures such as profit maximization, shareholder value, customer value, business performance, etc.

Management by objectives (MBO) This concept was proposed by Peter Drucker in 1954. The management by objectives approach requires employees to establish objectives for themselves. It involves developing a cascading set of objectives beginning with the organization, then for departments, individual managers, and employees. This is a participative process and objectives are time-bound and set by employees in consultation with their superiors. The goals are realistic but challenging. Frequent reviews are conducted to assess the progress towards objectives and to make any modifications in the original objectives. There is a linkage between the objectives at each level such that if each employee, manager, or department achieves their objective, the organizational objectives too will be met. Several firms such as Pricewaterhouse Coopers, Ernst and Young, etc. use MBO for performance appraisal. Objectives based performance management systems are based on goal-setting theory. Goal-setting theory, proposed by Edwin Locke (1989), states that when employees work towards specific goal(s) and are provided with feedback about their progress, their motivation is enhanced. Though objectives may be set for six months or for a year, it does not mean that performance feedback should be provided only at the end of this time period. Rather, informal feedback should be given on a regular basis immediately following a particular behaviour. Immediate knowledge of results enhances motivation to a higher extent than a formal feedback provided annually.

An objectives-based performance management system results in higher commitment and motivation on the part of employees due to the following reasons:

- Employees participate in setting goals for themselves rather than having objectives determined for them by the organization.
- Employees discuss important organizational goals and clearly perceive how they contribute to these goals.

Table 7.4 presents the pros and cons of the three performance appraisal methods discussed here. It is important to know which method or combination of methods to use in conducting performance appraisal.

Table 7.4: Pros and Cons of Performance Appraisal Methods

Methods	Pros	Cons
Trait-Based Methods Graphic Rating Scale	▪ Simple ▪ Most widely used ▪ Easy to develop ▪ Provides numerical score for performance ▪ Allows comparison of scores between individuals	▪ Each point on the scale may have different meaning for different raters ▪ May result in subjectivity ▪ When combining ratings on various characteristics into a total score, high scores on one characteristic may compensate for low score on another, resulting in an average performance score

Contd

Table 7.4 Contd

Methods	Pros	Cons
Forced-choice Method	▪ Helps discriminate between good and poor performers ▪ Reduces bias and subjectivity ▪ More objective	▪ Difficult to construct pairs of favourable or unfavourable items
Essay Method	▪ Provides opportunity to highlight unique characteristics of the employee being appraised ▪ Allows for more flexibility for the rater ▪ Most effective when combined with other methods	▪ Time consuming ▪ Quality of performance appraisal is influenced by the writing skills of the manager ▪ Tends to be subjective since manager may not focus on relevant aspects of job performance
Ranking Method	▪ Simple and uncomplicated	▪ Size of difference between two ranks is not well-defined. Difference between ranks one and two may not be the same as difference between ranks three and four ▪ Difficult to use with large groups of employees ▪ Employee's rank is relative to others with whom he/she is compared. An employee ranked at one in one group may be at rank ten in another ▪ Employees ranked at number one in respective groups may show wide variation in performance
Forced-distribution Method	▪ Reduces rater biases and errors	▪ Assumption that the bell-shaped normal curve of performance exists in every group does not always hold in a distribution of performance ratings ▪ Forces some employees to be placed in lowest group even if they do not belong there
Behaviour-Based Methods Critical Incidents	▪ Covers the entire appraisal period and therefore guards against errors related to behaviour sampling or focussing on last few weeks of performance only	▪ Difficult for the evaluator to observe and note down all instances of favourable and unfavourable employee performance ▪ Managers must be trained observers in order to be objective

Contd

Table 7.4 Contd

Methods	Pros	Cons
	■ Focus on specific incidents help in employee feedback and development ■ Contributes to the development of checklists and bars	■ Process is time-consuming for the evaluator
Checklists and Weighted Checklists	■ Minimizes biases and errors ■ Facilitates comparison of performance between employees ■ Helps in identifying training needs of employees	■ Require time and effort to develop ■ Checklist items have to be changed as the nature of jobs change over time ■ Raters do not know the weights assigned to each statement, creating a barrier to effective performance feedback
Behaviourally Anchored Rating Scales (BARS)	■ Describe specific examples of job behaviours ■ Less biased ■ Based on observable behaviour rather than subjective perceptions ■ Help give specific behaviour-based feedback to employees ■ Help in identifying performance improvement areas	■ Time and effort required to develop and maintain BARS ■ Different appraisal forms are needed for different types of jobs in an organization
Results-Based Methods Productivity Measures	■ Directly align individual goals with organizational goals	■ Employee results such as productivity may be influenced by factors beyond the control of the employee ■ May encourage employees to focus on short-term results to get good appraisals, thus ignoring long-term objectives ■ Employees would focus on those performance aspects which are the focus of appraisals ■ When focus is on productivity measures, important factors such as initiative, cooperation, etc. may be ignored

Contd

Table 7.4 Contd

Methods	Pros	Cons
Management by Objectives (MBO)	▪ Participative goal-setting enhances employee commitment ▪ Ongoing feedback and coaching results in higher motivation ▪ Employees know how they are contributing to overall organizational performance	▪ Time-consuming ▪ Superior and subordinate may collude to set easy targets ▪ Fails in an autocratic system ▪ May lead to emphasis on short-term objectives

Communication of Appraisals

A good performance management system is one that allows the employee (appraisee or ratee) to participate and contribute in his/her own performance evaluation, in partnership with the manager (appraiser or rater). Once the information about an employee's performance has been obtained, it is the responsibility of the manager to communicate the evaluation to the employee. This is done by holding an evaluation or appraisal interview with each subordinate. The appraisal interview is the most important part of the appraisal process. It serves the following basic purposes:

- discussing the subordinate's performance record
- exploring areas of possible improvement and growth
- determining subordinate's feelings and attitudes about the appraisal
- assisting the subordinate in setting objectives and personal development plans
- providing positive feedback on accomplishments as well as help to overcome shortcomings
- rewarding good performance so that it will be maintained

The manner in which the appraisal interview is conducted depends upon the specific purpose of the interview. Exhibit 7.2 explains the characteristics of an effective appraisal interview. Appraisal interviews are typically of three types. These are discussed below.

One-way communication (tell and sell approach) The supervisor is in a dominant position and communicates the appraisal as well as the action plan for improvements to the subordinate. The subordinate must accept both the appraisal and the developmental plan. The subordinate can neither disagree with the supervisor nor express his/her feelings about the appraisal. Therefore, this type of interview results in lowered motivation and high defensiveness on the part of subordinate. It also threatens the supervisor–subordinate

Exhibit 7.2

Characteristics of an Effective Appraisal Interview

- In addition to one formal appraisal, supervisor should provide ongoing, continuous feedback to subordinates on an informal basis.
- Should be structured so that it is viewed by both the superior and the subordinate as a problem-solving session.
- Schedule interview soon after the end of the appraisal period. Delaying the interview results in heightened anxiety on the part of employees.
- Conduct two separate interviews—one for discussing employee performance and development, the other for making evaluative or personal decisions.

- Focus the discussion of performance problems on the performance deficiency itself, not on the person.
- Minimize threats to self-esteem of the person
- Handle employee mistakes or problems related to job performance on an ongoing basis. Do not defer them for appraisal interview at a later date.
- Clearly outline specific plans for improvement of the employee's future performance in discussion with the employee.
- Allow employees an opportunity to present their ideas and feelings during the interview.

relationship. These outcomes are more likely to emerge when both developmental and evaluative purposes are being served by the same appraisal and the ongoing supervisor–subordinate relationship is not very good.

Two-way communication (tell and listen approach) The supervisor communicates appraisals and developmental plans to the employee. Subsequently, the subordinate has the opportunity to express his/her feelings about the information provided. The subordinate may also express disagreement with the appraisal. The supervisor lends a sympathetic ear to the subordinate. However, expression of feelings by the subordinate does not result in change in the appraisal and developmental action plan of the subordinates. This type of post-appraisal interview results in lowered defensiveness since the subordinate gets a chance to disclose true feelings about appraisal feedback. Though it maintains supervisor–subordinate relationship it does not lead to performance improvement. At Reckitt and Coleman, appraisals are conducted once a year. Appraisals include both self-appraisal by the employee and appraisal by a superior. The average ratings of both appraisals yield a measure of the productivity over the year. In case there is a discrepancy between self-ratings and that of the supervisor, the employee and the supervisor meet. However, in case of a deadlock, the superior's opinion prevails.

Mutual problem-solving This approach also involves two-way communication, but it is more effective than the former type of interview discussed earlier. Subordinate performance is defined as a mutual problem. The subordinate plays an active role in appraising his/her own performance as well as in developing action plans for performance improvement. The supervisor assumes the role of a helper and encourages the subordinate in reaching a realistic evaluation of self-performance by asking exploratory questions. This method reduces defensiveness and improves subordinate motivation as well as the supervisor–subordinate relationship. At ICICI, for example, based on the performance appraisal, the immediate supervisor discusses the career options with the appraisee. For different purposes, different types of interviews are considered effective. Choice of interviews will also depend on the maturity of the employees and skills of the supervisor.

PROBLEMS IN PERFORMANCE MANAGEMENT

It is important that the employee's experience of the performance management process is positive. However, in practice, it often turns out to be negative. Majority of employees are usually dissatisfied with their evaluations. The manner in which evaluations are communicated to employees is an important determinant of how subordinates experience the performance management process. Problems in performance management arise due to three sets of factors (Figure 7.7). These are discussed in detail in this section.

Ambivalence The appraisal process is an emotional experience for both the manager and the subordinate. The manager (superior) is responsible for the performance of his/her subordinates. He/she must ensure that employee performance contributes to the achievement of organizational goals and targets. Therefore, it is part of a manager's job to appraise subordinate performance, provide feedback, make decisions about pay increase and promotion based on performance appraisal, and facilitate employee performance improvement. When employee performance has been satisfactory and rewards are in abundance the superior has no difficulty in appraising the subordinate. Problems arise when subordinate performance has been less than satisfactory. No individual likes to be the harbinger of bad news, especially when it is

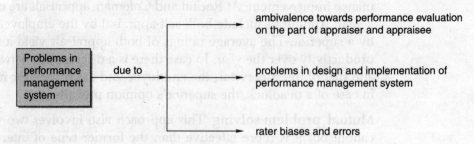

Figure 7.7: Factors Leading to Problems in Performance Management Systems

likely to significantly impact the career growth of the individual. The manager (appraiser) feels uncomfortable when communicating negative feedback. Moreover, managers may find it difficult to handle the difficult interpersonal situation that may arise when negative feedback is communicated. The supervisor–subordinate relationship can be adversely affected due to negative feedback. Since the superiors must work with the subordinate in future, he/she may be reluctant to engage in performance evaluation and discussion. The supervisor's ambivalence is thus a result of the conflicting demands of fulfilling the two roles of a judge and a coach. Performance appraisals require supervisors to assume both the roles simultaneously. In the role of a judge, supervisors make evaluative decisions about the subordinate's career. In the role of a coach, they encourage subordinates to discuss their performance problems. This results in ambivalence because it is difficult for the two roles to co-exist simultaneously.

The subordinates too are ambivalent about performance appraisals. On one hand, all employees would like to get an objective feedback about their performance so that they can improve their performance. On the other hand, when performance feedback is negative, employees find it difficult to accept it since it leads to a sense of failure and lowering of self-esteem. Moreover, if performance appraisal is tied to valued organizational rewards such as promotions, pay increases, and incentives, subordinates would not like their appraisals to be negative and hence would like to avoid appraisals. Under such circumstances, negative feedback results in defensiveness on the part of subordinates and this may get manifested in several ways. These include, for example, blaming others for their own poor performance, casting doubt on the source of performance data, and validity of the performance appraisal method.

If both the superior and the subordinate are uncomfortable about performance evaluation and performance feedback, both may seek to avoid engaging in the process. Therefore, superiors may go through the process mechanically by routinely filling the evaluation form and avoiding serious discussion of performance with the employee. As long as the subordinate perceives the appraisal process as not affecting his/her career or rewards in any significant way, he/she is quite agreeable to go along with the supervisor in conducting performance appraisal in a routine and mechanical way. Performance appraisal interviews in such cases get reduced to small talk and rarely serve the purpose for which they were conducted.

System design and implementation problems Often, problems in conducting performance appraisal can be traced to poorly specified performance criteria, use of inappropriate performance appraisal approaches, poorly constructed performance appraisal methods, or lack of top management support to the process. For instance, a performance evaluation system may focus only on personality traits. This may result in dissatisfaction because when this performance appraisal data is used, actual job performance gets ignored. Some supervisors and even subordinates may resent the time it takes to carry out formal appraisals. It is thus important to institutionalize the performance appraisal process as an ongoing system. The formal appraisal is then less likely to be viewed as a cumbersome process.

Rater biases and errors Even the most well-designed system can fail if the people using the system are not well trained in its use. They may deliberately distort appraisals or hold negative attitudes about the performance appraisal process. This may render performance appraisals as highly subjective. A brief description of performance appraisal problems that may arise due to rater biases and errors is presented in Table 7.5. One of the major sources of *rater errors* is the mistakes made by the appraiser. It is not possible to completely eliminate rater errors, but training raters to make them aware of these errors is helpful. *Rater biases* occur when the values and prejudices that the appraiser holds distort the ratings. Biases may be either unconscious or intentional. For instance, an appraiser may deliberately give high scores to an employee belonging to his/her own domicile state or region.

Table 7.5: Rater Errors and Biases

Rater Errors	Brief Description
Varying Standards	Managers appraise different employees by using different standards and expectations. This often results when performance criteria are ambiguous and standards are not clearly specified.
Recency Effect	Manager gives higher weightage to most recent instances of performance, good or bad, when appraising an individual's performance.
Primacy Effect	Information about individual performance obtained first gets the highest weightage in appraisal. This is the opposite of recency effect.
Central Tendency Error	When the appraiser avoids using high or low ratings and rates all employees as falling in a narrow range, that is, everyone is average. Even the poor performers receive an average rating.
Leniency Error	Appraiser rates all employees at the higher end of the scale as good performers. Low performers also receive high ratings even though they do not deserve that.
Strictness Error	All employees are assigned low ratings. The rater is unduly critical of employee performance.
Personal Bias Error	A manager may have a personal bias against a particular caste, nationality, or region and assign low ratings to an employee belonging to that group.

Contd

Table 7.5 Contd

Rater Biases	Brief Description
Halo Effect	A manager rates an employee high on all performance criteria because of high performance on a single criterion. For example, an employee who is very punctual may be rated higher in team participation as well.
Contrast Error	Employees are rated relative to others rather than to an objective standard. If other employees are average, a slightly better employee (as compared to the employee just evaluated) may be rated as excellent because of the contrast effect.
Similar to or different to me	Managers compare the employees against their own characteristics. Those employees who are seen as similar to themselves by managers are rated higher.
Sampling Error	The rater sometimes observes only a small sample of an employee's work. If 95% of the work of the employee has been very good, but the boss saw only the 5% that was unsatisfactory, the supervisor is likely to rate the employee as a poor performer.

EFFECTIVE PERFORMANCE MANAGEMENT SYSTEMS

The problems inherent in a performance management system can be dealt with if the system is designed to possess certain characteristics. The characteristics that help reduce subjectivity in implementation of performance management system and make it more effective are explained in this section.

Separate evaluation and development appraisals Problems are likely to emerge when the same performance appraisal is used for making evaluative decisions as well as for identifying development needs. Problems of defensiveness and avoidance can be minimized by having two separate formal performance appraisals in a year—one that focusses on evaluation and the other that focusses on development. Decisions about pay increase, rewards, and promotions should be scheduled at a different time of the year rather than in the meeting that engages the subordinate in a dialogue for identifying performance problems and developing plans for performance improvement. The performance appraisal should not require the manager to be simultaneously a judge as well as a helper.

Use job-related performance criteria To ensure that the criteria used in appraising performance is job related, it should be determined through job analysis. Even subjective criteria such as loyalty, initiative, etc. should be used only when they can be clearly shown to be related to the job.

Specifying performance standards It is important to specify performance standards for each criteria of performance. These performance standards or expectations must be mutually agreed upon by managers and subordinates before the beginning of the appraisal period. If subordinates do not know what they are supposed to accomplish on the job, they are not likely to get there.

Use appropriate performance data Appraisals that use behavioural data result in greater acceptance on the part of the subordinate of his/her performance evaluation. For instance, rating a person low on 'customer orientation' is likely to send the subordinate on the defensive. However, presenting the subordinate with specific instances of behaviour that suggest a lack of customer orientation is likely to be accepted more readily by him/her. This feedback also helps the subordinates in improving their performance. Performance appraisal methods such as BARS and critical incidents methods use behaviour-based performance measures.

Improving supervisor–subordinate relationship The outcomes and quality of appraisal process depends on the ongoing supervisor–subordinate relationship. If the relationship is good the supervisor will provide feedback and coaching to the subordinates on an informal ongoing basis. The formal appraisal interview in this situation will only be a review of issues already discussed. There will be no surprises in store for the subordinate. Moreover, the subordinate will not be defensive and will be more open to discussing performance problems.

Provide ongoing feedback All employees like to know how well they are performing their jobs. Principles of learning suggest that immediate feedback is more effective than delayed feedback. When delayed, the subordinate may not be able to associate the feedback with a specific behaviour. Hence, regular performance discussions conducted on an informal basis provide the subordinate with an opportunity to improve performance before the scheduled formal appraisal. Ongoing feedback is inherent to the MBO approach.

Upward appraisals One factor that contributes to subordinate defensiveness in performance appraisal is that the supervisor has authority and controls rewards such as promotions. This results in submissiveness on the part of the subordinate in order to gain rewards. Moreover, subordinates are reluctant to discuss performance problems with superiors who have the power to decide their career. In order to manage this unequal power distribution between the managers and their subordinates, the latter may be asked to appraise their supervisor. This brings power into a more favourable balance and results in higher participation of the subordinate in the appraisal process.

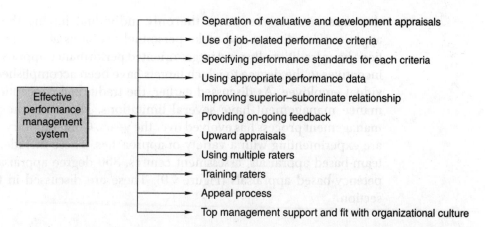

Figure 7.8: Characteristics of Effective Performance Management Systems

Use multiple raters To manage rater errors and biases in the appraisal process, multiple raters should be used. Use of multiple raters involves obtaining ratings on the same individual from more than one rater, such as peers, customers, superiors, and self. When multiple raters are used to evaluate an individual's performance, it is called the 360 degree appraisal or multi-source feedback. This concept will be discussed in detail later in the chapter.

Train appraisers By extending training to raters, it is possible to minimize errors such as halo, leniency, strictness, etc. if not eliminate them entirely. A poor appraisal is worse than no appraisal since it can demoralize employees, leading to reduced productivity. Training should focus on areas such as how to conduct appraisal interviews, how to rate, purposes of performance appraisal, ethics of performance appraisal, etc.

Appeal process Each organization should ensure that subordinates get an opportunity to appeal against appraisal results if they see them as inaccurate or unfair.

A performance appraisal, no matter how well-designed, will be unsuccessful if it does not fit with the prevailing culture of the organization, lacks support from top management, or if the employees do not hold positive attitudes about the process and its effectiveness.

DEVELOPMENTS IN PERFORMANCE MANAGEMENT

When discussing the performance management process, it is the individual employee's performance that is generally referred to. This reflects the historical belief that employees are the building blocks of an organization and hence are the basic unit of analysis in performance management systems. Moreover, the supervisor is viewed as the only individual having the mandate to appraise subordinates and make personnel decisions about them. Organizations have traditionally used target-oriented performance appraisals and linked incentives to the degree to which targets have been accomplished by the individual employee. As discussed earlier, the traditional conceptions of performance management have several limitations. However, the performance management process has evolved over the years. Contemporary organizations are experimenting with a variety of approaches. These include, for instance, team-based appraisals, assessment centres, 360 degree appraisals, and competency-based appraisals (Figure 7.9). These are discussed in the following section.

Team or Work Group Appraisals

Though literature on performance appraisal has focussed largely on appraisal of an individual employee's performance, there has been an emergence of interest for evaluating group or team performance. It was in the early 1990s that there was a movement toward team-based structures. A large number of organizations began to restructure themselves around teams. A team consists of individuals who work collaboratively and take the responsibility for the performance of the team rather than just their own individual performance. A team is more than the sum of the individual members. Members of the team are assigned a specific role depending on their skills for the benefit of the team performance. The primary focus is on the team and not the individual. A team is different from other groups in an organization because of the following distinctive characteristics.

- Teams have a common purpose.
- They have agreed norms and values that regulate behaviour.
- Team members have interdependent functions.
- Each member has a team identity (specific role).
- Members possess complementary skills.

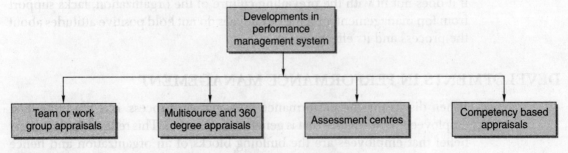

Figure 7.9: Developments in Performance Management Systems

- Teams have shared leadership roles.
- Teams have mutual accountability.

There are different types of teams.

1. Teams may be *temporary* or *permanent.* Temporary teams are set up to solve a specific problem or for a specific project. Temporary teams are also called project teams. These teams disband after the problem is solved or the project is completed. Committees formed in organizations for a specific purpose are also an example of a temporary team. Project teams have a limited future since members come from different functional areas, have different skills and knowledge bases, and return to their functional areas on completion of the project. Lupin Laboratories has both cross-functional project teams and task-oriented teams. Employees in TCS also work in project teams, when one project finishes, the team working on that project disbands, and each individual then gets attached to a new project as per the organizational and individual needs. Some teams in certain departments such as production are permanent teams. Permanent teams are ongoing and do not disband.

2. Teams may also differ on the basis of types of skills required of members. Some teams require each member to learn all relevant skills. This results in interchangeability of skills. Production teams work on the interchangeability principle. This suggests that each member of the production team will be able to take on the role of some other team member should the latter quit. Some teams, however, have members who bring their specialist skills for the benefit of the team. These are cross-functional teams, for example, surgical teams, new product development teams, etc. Otis Elevators has self-managed cross-functional management teams at senior levels. The teams deal with matters relating to people, customers, and the organization.

3. Teams may also be intact or virtual. An intact team attends to the core work in an organization and is also called a work team. A work team is a well-developed social system, where task interaction between members is predictable. Work teams engage in routine manufacturing or service jobs. Intact work teams have static membership. A functional department such as finance and accounting department is a work group or work unit, or work team. On the other hand, a virtual team that is geographically or organizationally dispersed may attend to more complex tasks. Network teams are virtual and their potential membership is not constrained by time and space. Virtual team members interact primarily through telecommunications and IT, rather than face-to-face. Contingent workers, customers, consultants, and employees become part of the network teams.

The same organization may have a diversity of team forms. This trend has accelerated with the shift from a manufacturing to a knowledge-based economy. The emergence of team-based structures has raised new questions about the efficacy of traditional appraisal systems. Questions relate to, for example, whether individuals or teams should be appraised in a team-structured organization. Should appraisals focus on measuring specified outcomes, on behaviours to achieve outcomes, or on acquiring competencies and skills? From whom should the data about team performance be obtained—from team members, customers, or from other teams? How should organizations evaluate team performance?

Several firms have begun to use team appraisal systems. Hindustan Lever Ltd has a team-based assessment and compensation system. Amtrex links individual assessments to the company's team appraisal system. Moreover, each functional team assesses the other teams as a customer (for instance, the manufacturing department is the materials department's customer). Only one team is ranked as the top performer. Then the departmental head rates the managers within his/her team individually. Hence, an employee's final assessment and reward is on the basis of his/her individual appraisal, team rating, and individual rating within the team.

Since different forms or types of teams possess different characteristics, each presents a different challenge to the performance management system. It is important to ensure that the performance appraisal characteristics built into the performance management system are appropriate to the specific type of team, such as work team, project team, or network team. Employee performance appraisal has become more challenging today than in the past due to the pervasive use of teams in today's organizations. Extrapolating the individual performance management process to evaluate team performance may not be the right approach. Many performance appraisal systems do not lead to anticipated benefits when applied to team-structured organizations. There is no single performance-appraisal system that is applicable across all types of organizations or work units. A generic system, when applied across the entire organization, ignores important differences between teams.

Designing effective performance appraisal systems for teams requires careful consideration of differences in team characteristics such as team membership configuration, team task complexity, and the nature of the interdependencies among the team and external groups. A brief description of these dimensions is presented in Exhibit 7.3.

As the complexity of interdependence increases, it is important for teams to manage extensive interactions with others inside the organization. It is important to ensure that performance measurement systems focussed on team performance do not result in teams trying to optimize their own performance at the expense of other teams. Team-focussed outcome measures serve

---

Exhibit 7.3

Dimensions of Team Characteristics

Membership Configuration	■ Expected tenure of a team, stability of its membership, and allocation of work-time of team members. ■ Varies from static to dynamic. ■ *Static* teams have full-time team members, constant membership throughout the existence of a team, and common level of involvement of members throughout the life of the team. *Dynamic* teams have shorter tenure and floating membership since members come and go depending on the task demands. Members of dynamic teams also work on other teams simultaneously. Members of a college governing body are an example of a dynamic team.
Task Complexity	■ Refers to the fact that organizational teams engage in a wide variety of work that varies from the routine to the non-routine. ■ *Routine* tasks are those that are well defined, the required time needed to finish one complete unit of work (cycle time) is specified in advance, cycle time is of short duration, there are well-defined quantifiable criteria, and outcomes are easily assessed soon after task completion against these criteria. *Non-Routine* tasks are not well-defined. The outcome and the means to accomplish these are not defined in advance: It requires application of multiple skill sets acquired through training or education; cycle time is longer and difficult to determine.
External Interdependencies	■ Interdependencies exist when a team is dependent on contributions and non-members to complete tasks and goals. ■ May range from high to low. High interdependence exists when teams are dependent on several outsiders for information and support. Low interdependence implies that teams are dependent on only a few outsiders.

Source: Scott and Einstein 2001

---

important purposes when team-development is a major objective. However, when team interdependencies become high, there is a need to balance outcome measures.

Based on membership configuration and task complexity dimensions, three types of teams can be identified—work teams, project teams, and network teams (see Table 7.6). Though the three types of teams do not cover the entire range of teams possible in organizations, they do indicate the importance of matching performance appraisal with team characteristics.

Table 7.6: Fit between Team Characteristics and Performance Appraisal Characteristics

Type of Team and Dimensions of Team Characteristics	Team Characteristics	Performance Appraisal Characteristics
Work or Service Teams Low on both membership configuration and task complexity	■ Engage in routine manufacturing or service tasks ■ Been in existence for a long time and membership stability is high ■ Members have similar skill sets ■ Cross-training of members ■ Team tasks are standardized, there is short cycle time and multiple task cycles in each performance appraisal period ■ Team output is easily and objectively evaluated ■ Feedback on performance provided by task itself ■ Well-developed social system and interpersonal trust ■ Needs, preferences, and goals of all members are similar ■ Engages in team-building and training as an intact unit	■ Both individual and team appraisals are recommended ■ Peer ratings useful as supplement to manager's evaluations ■ Feedback from peer ratings used only for development purposes ■ Feedback provides for a dialogue among members on how to improve team functioning ■ Outcome-based performance appraisal for the team but not for individual members of the team ■ Teams held accountable for monitoring their own performance against standard goals, team goals, and for results ■ Feedback to individual team members on their own task accomplishment to help them regulate their own performance ■ Individual performance information used for identifying training and development needs, planned development exercises for each member ■ 360 degree feedback sometimes used for team as a unit (not for individual members)
Project Teams Medium on both membership configuration and task complexity	■ Engage in work that is less routine than that of work or service teams ■ Assemble for a specific project and disband after project completion ■ Not permanent or intact like work teams	■ Limited usefulness of outcome-based assessment because project cycle and appraisal cycle are different. Team is dissolved by the time outcomes are reached

Contd

Table 7.6 Contd

Type of Team and Dimensions of Team Characteristics	Team Characteristics	Performance Appraisal Characteristics
	▪ Difficulty and pace of team tasks varies across the life of the project ▪ Focus more on tasks than on team members ▪ High goal interdependence among members for achieving project goals ▪ Training of members does not take place as an intact unit ▪ Members apply and integrate individual training with team experience	▪ Use measures related to various stages of a project so that teams can self-correct before things go too far off-course. These measures include continuous tracking of time, cost, and return on investment (ROI) ▪ Multisource performance appraisal most appropriate here because members of project teams are working simultaneously in more than one team and/or projects. Therefore, no single manager, set of peers, or team leaders have observed employee behaviour across all work situations ▪ Feedback from peers and project leaders used by functional managers to identify developmental needs and schedule training ▪ Training focusses on development of behaviours and competencies that are transferable from one team assignment to another ▪ Members rated on the employee's individual performance and his/her contribution to team role
Network Teams High on both membership configuration and task complexity	▪ Work is extremely non-routine ▪ Team engages in one task cycle that is not repeated again ▪ Membership is dynamic and shifting in response to changing task needs ▪ Timing and intensity of members' participation, nature of interaction, and level of exchange among members is not fixed. It depends on task needs	▪ Performance cycle is different from annual performance appraisal systems ▪ Performance of the team as a whole is not assessed in any formal way ▪ Emphasis of performance for team members shifts from what they did in the past to what they are willing and capable of doing in future

Contd

Table 7.6 Contd

Type of Team and Dimensions of Team Characteristics	Team Characteristics	Performance Appraisal Characteristics
	■ Primary competency is the ability to rapidly select and assemble the most appropriate member configuration for the task at hand	■ Appraisal focusses on developing individual capacity to initiate, participate, and lead improvement plans, rather than on assessment of past outcomes ■ Competency-based appraisal systems are most appropriate for assessing potential of network team members ■ Competencies appraised and used for evaluation as well as development purposes ■ Behaviour-based appraisals can be used to assess employee participation in learning activities during performance cycles (self-paced programme or in-house training), involvement in collaborative communication, and teamwork behaviour when participating in network teams ■ Multi rater behavioural assessment since members work in multiple performance settings during any given performance cycle

Source: Scott and Einstein 2001

As firms move from the stable and routine end of the continuum to the dynamic, emergent, and interdependent end, performance appraisal systems must also move from outcome-based (work teams) to competency-based (network teams). Performance management systems are more effective if designed with careful attention to the characteristics of the team as well as the characteristics of performance appraisal (type, source, and purpose). Such an approach towards performance management results in employee behaviour that leads to organizational goal attainment. This by far suggests a strategic approach to performance appraisal design. It also ensures that team structures will lead to greater organizational effectiveness. Some firms following this approach are Xerox, HP, etc.

Evaluation of work-group performance suggests that performance ratios (i.e., measures of key outputs in relation to critical inputs of the work unit) can be tracked for evaluation purpose. Outputs are the services or products that the work unit produces and are measured in terms of total units produced, number of clients served, etc. Inputs refer to whatever resources (material, capital, energy, etc) the work unit consumes to produce a product or service. To establish these performance ratios or performance measures for a work unit, it is important to begin with the mission or goals of the work unit. Subsequently, the main customers of the unit are determined along with identifying the products and services produced by this work group (outputs) that are most valued by these customers. Performance measures of these outputs become part of performance criteria (indicators) of the work group. An exhaustive list of performance measures is created for each work group. For the HR department, for example, the performance measures may include the ratio of number of individuals trained to total training costs, grievances settled satisfactorily, or the total number of grievances. For the marketing department, the performance measure may include ratio of market share to total promotional expenditures.

When specifying output performance measures of the work group, an analysis of the transformation process of the work group (those that transform inputs into outputs) is also undertaken. This helps determine what the work group should be doing and what it is actually doing. The use of input–output statistical ratios as measures of work-group (team) performance result in certain advantages over the traditional performance appraisal focussed on individual employee performance. These are as follows.

- Issues related to rater biases and errors (for example, leniency, halo, etc.) are rendered irrelevant. Even deliberate distortion is unlikely since evaluation is based on objective data.
- Focus on work unit performance helps avoid judgmental problems arising out of the necessity of identifying degrees of performance at the individual level for making performance comparisons among employees.
- Since evaluation is at the work unit level, individual defensiveness is greatly reduced. This is because no single individual is singled out for poor performance.
- Feedback focusses on task-related information. The quality of feedback is independent of supervisory interpersonal skills.
- Work-group appraisals can be conducted with higher frequency than individual appraisals.
- Members are rewarded or punished collectively based on unit performance. This encourages work group members to think of achievement of the unit's mission and objectives instead of focussing on tasks that result in individual level rewards.

- Since work group goals are set in consultation with the group members, it results in high levels of intrinsic satisfaction among members.
- Work group evaluation enhances group cohesion.

However, use of work group or team performance indicators may raise certain concerns. For one, these pointers tend to ignore individual performance. High performers of a work group may get demotivated because their efforts go unrewarded in an average performing work unit. Thus, work unit performance measurement fails to reward individuals in proportion to their contribution. This raises the question—is it the individual or the team/work group which is the elementary unit of an organization? An organization hires *individuals*, not *work groups* or teams. Yet, the success of the firm depends on the performance of teams. Individuals see themselves as contributors distinct from the work unit. A high performing employee cannot single-handedly steer the organization or department to its goals. Therefore, it is important that instead of the employee, the organization must make the work-group central to its rewards system. Under this system, high performers need to focus not only on their own accomplishments but also on helping others perform well.

Secondly, problems regarding dissatisfaction with appraisal of individual performance emerge at the group level too. Certain teams may complain about the differences in the difficulty levels of targets between work groups.

Some unintended consequences occur when work group level performance measures are used. For example, if the performance measure for employees in a five-star hotel is the ratio of rupee amount of food served/number of employees per shift, then employees may find ways to encourage customers to order more dishes and more expensive dishes.

Adopting an individual performance appraisal or a work-group appraisal is not mutually exclusive. An organization should develop a system that combines the individual and the group appraisal, since both serve useful purposes. Systems having both individual rewards and group rewards linked to performance often create confusion and conflict. Hence, it is important for firms to carefully manage the situation and also ensure the compatibility of work-group appraisals with organizational culture and employee expectations. A gradual and complete transition to work-group appraisals facilitates team-building.

Assessment Centres

The discussion on the purposes of the performance management system presented earlier in the chapter emphasized that performance appraisal serve both evaluative and developmental purposes. Thus, performance appraisal systems evaluate not only an employee's past performance but also his/her potential for career advancement. Some organizations have developed an independent approach designed for exclusively assessing employee potential.

This approach is called the 'assessment centre' approach. Some firms use assessment centres for selection purposes too.

The term 'assessment centre' refers to an approach and does not refer to a physical place. Assessment centres require the participants to complete a range of tests and exercises which simulate the activities they might encounter in the target job. Each assessment centre consists of approximately six to twelve participants. Participants engage in a combination of group and individual exercises over a period of two or three days spent away from the job. These exercises may include case discussions, in-basket exercises, group discussions, psychological tests, management games, role-play, etc.

Assessment centres are simulations because the exercises used represent situations that require the use of managerial skills and behaviours that the participants will actually need for performing the job assigned to them. The fundamental idea behind the assessment centre approach is that the best way to predict future job performance is to get the individual to actually perform the set of tasks which sample and resemble those required in the job. A team of trained assessors observe the employees as they participate and engage in various situational tests and activities. Assessors evaluate employee performance. They are usually experienced line managers from the organization who have volunteered to be observers and have been specially trained for observation and evaluation of employees. They are usually at a higher level in the organization than the candidates being assessed. Assessors can also be independent consultants or outsiders who have been trained to conduct assessments. Each assessor compiles judgments from all the exercises to form a summary evaluation report for each candidate or participant of the assessment centre. All the assessors pool their evaluations and assign a rating to each participant. Assessment centres provide information about a variety of job-related skills, such as planning, as well as, more generalized skills in dealing with others (for example, oral communication), in addition to information about values and preferences of examinees. Assessment centres evaluate individuals along a number of dimensions, such as personal style, ability to handle stress, decision-making, flexibility, leadership potential, etc. These dimensions refer to those behaviours that are specific, observable, and are drawn from job analysis information. Hence dimensions assessed in an assessment centre will depend on the target job. However, certain dimensions, such as communication and leadership, are common across jobs. Assessment centre programmes vary in purpose and use. Assessment centres serve the purposes of

- determining management potential of employees;
- assessing promotability of employees; and
- identifying training and development needs for improving employee job performance.

Assessment centres help an organization arrive at an informed decision on the strengths and weaknesses of its employees in relation to specific jobs for determining employee suitability as well as for employees' career development. Assessment centres have been found to be a more effective way of predicting performance than the traditional performance appraisal interviews. Exhibit 7.4 shows the historical perspective of the assessment centre approach. There is no such thing as a 'standard' assessment centre. Assessment centres vary across organizations with respect to the *length* of the assessment process (which may vary from one day to one week), the ratio of assessors to those being assessed, the number, and the type of assessment instruments and exercises that are used for assessing participants. One of the exercises commonly used in assessment centres is the *leaderless group discussion* which is used to evaluate an individual's emergent leadership and social skills. In this activity, participants first consider an issue individually and make specific recommendations. Subsequently, they assemble together in a group to discuss the issue or assigned topic. No one is designated as the leader of the group. However, a leader usually emerges in the course of the group interaction. The participants are given no instructions on how to approach the topic or what decision to reach. Two or more assessors observe the group as members attempt to reach a consensus. Participants are evaluated on leadership skills, initiative, communication, and ability to work in a group.

Several organizations such as AT&T, IBM, Ford, Crompton Greaves, Eicher, HLL, Xerox, and P&G use assessment centres for various purposes. The assessment centre scores are taken into consideration during promotions by GAIL and the organization has mapped the potential of several senior officers through the process. Though more effective than traditional performance appraisals, well-designed assessment centres are very expensive. For small

---

Exhibit 7.4

History of Assessment Centres

Assessment centres were first used by the German military forces in World War II. In the US, the Office of Strategic Services (OSS) of the Central Intelligence Agency began to use the assessment centre approach in the mid 1940s. The CIA used assessment centres to select spies for World War II. The first industrial application of assessment centres can be traced to 1956, when psychologist Douglas Bray implemented assessment centres as part of a research study involving AT&T. The study was longitudinal and demonstrated that assessments done early in a manager's career were a valid predictor of performance even twenty years later. In the UK, assessment centres can be traced to 1942 when they were first used by war office selection boards. Several firms today use assessment centres for identifying high potential employees who can be groomed for future leadership responsibilities.

organizations the cost of developing an assessment centre may be prohibitive. Developing an assessment centre that serves the purpose of several organizations provides a potential solution.

The assessment centre data helps the organization to plan, acquire, and develop the competencies that it will need in the future. With organizations going multinational, it has become important that assessment centres reflect the global work culture practices. Hence, it is not appropriate to have a universal leadership competency model or to design assessment centres around those behaviours and competencies that are representative of the culture where the organization has its headquarters.

In recent times, some distinction is being suggested between assessment centres and development centres. Assessment centres are seen as formal processes where the individuals being assessed have the feedback in the context of the selection decision. Development centres stress the developmental aspect of assessment. More recently, there has been a rise in the use of 'pure' development centres. The reasons for this separation of assessment centres and development centres and growth in the use of the latter are as follows:

- to prevent the demoralizing effect on those individuals who were pronounced unsuccessful based on assessments in the centre that had an element of selection decision-making
- the importance of continuously investing in employee development to equip them to respond to an uncertain environment
- growth of the idea of 'behavioural competencies' in the practice of HRM—development centres provide for an effective means of assessing employee competencies because they use simulations

The main points of difference between assessment centres and development centres are given in Table 7.7. Since assessment centres and development centres focus on the assessment of employees, it is good to think about assessment centres as being applied to both selection and development.

Lately, assessment centres have become competency-based. When assessments are competency-based, the information available on individuals can be aggregated. This aggregated information provides data on the overall level of competencies or capabilities available in the organization. This data can be compared with the future competency requirements of the firms relative to the business needs of the organization

- to make managerial selection and decisions;
- to assess how individuals function in a group; and
- to provide feedback to employees on specific behavioural dimensions such as communication skills, interpersonal skills, etc.

Software companies with an emphasis on speed and quality use competency assessment centres. Assessment centres are most effectively used for

Table 7.7: Differences between Assessment Centres and Development Centres

Assessment Centres	Development Centres
■ Used purely for selection purposes	■ Primary purpose is development
■ Have a pass/fail criteria	■ Do not have a pass/fail criteria
■ Focussed on immediate need of the organization	■ Focussed on long term needs of the organization
■ Have fewer assessors than participants	■ 1:1 ratio of assessor to participants
■ Involve line managers as assessors	■ Do not involve line managers as assessors
■ Focus on candidate's performance here and now	■ Focus on candidate's potential
■ Focus on meeting organizational needs	■ Focus on meeting both individual and organizational needs
■ Assessors take on role of judge	■ Assessors take on role of facilitators
■ No departmental feedback or follow up with participants	■ Provide developmental feedback and follow up to participants
■ Used with external candidates	■ Used with internal candidates

Source: http://www.psychometrics.co.uk/adc.htm, accessed on 21 April 2006

succession planning and filling up functional head positions. Companies such as Infosys, Wipro, Cognizant, and Satyam have assessment centres. Cognizant Technologies has been using the assessment centre approach since 1998 for the purpose of objectively identifying leaders from within the organization. It has also used assessment centres to assign these leaders with the roles and responsibilities that fit with their leadership competencies. In Cognizant's assessment centre programme, employees are put through a series of individual and group exercises designed to measure proficiency in distinct leadership competencies and dimensions using a battery of tools. Assessment centres measure an individual's current and future potential in each competency. At Satyam Computer Services, competency assessment is an integral part of the annual appraisal system for employees. All the approximately 22,000 associates, irrespective of hierarchy, at Satyam are assessed on the basis of three critical parameters of thinking, doing, and communicating. If the score of present employees on assessment centres is below 83 out of 100, Satyam externally recruits people who are above this score.

Multisource Feedback and 360 degree Appraisals

Many firms have combined the different sources of performance appraisal into a 'multisource' appraisal and feedback system, popularly called the 360 degree appraisal. The use of 360 degree performance appraisal systems gained popularity in the 1990s. The process implies that an employee is appraised and receives feedback from supervisors, subordinates, peers, and/or customers (see Figure 7.5). The feedback is generally provided anonymously to the appraisee (the employee whose performance is being appraised).

One of the main purposes served by the 360 degree appraisal system is to obtain information about an employee's performance in multiple roles and from different perspectives. In traditional top-down performance appraisals, superiors evaluate their subordinates, i.e., performance is evaluated from only one perspective. An employee may be performing well when viewed by his/her supervisor. However, the same individual may receive a very different evaluation when evaluated from the perspective of his/her subordinate. Similarly, the employee's peers may also have a different evaluation. For example, Amway, a direct selling organization, practices a group appraisal system where a manager is appraised by his management team as well as customers. At Lupin Laboratories, self-evaluation and colleague evaluation is used to assess several characteristics such as ability to recall, concept retention, seriousness, etc.

Each job is multi-faceted and an individual assumes different roles at different times when performing the job. The 360 degree feedback approach seeks to provide employees with as accurate a view of their performance as possible by obtaining feedback from all angles—subordinates, peers, customers, supervisors, etc. Feedback from multiple sources may reinforce and support the feedback provided from the supervisor, thus making it harder to discount negative feedback from the supervisor (manager) as one person's feedback that is perhaps biased.

The traditional top-down appraisal systems appear to be increasingly inconsistent with recent developments in management thought and practice. For example, as organizations eliminate boundaries vertically across hierarchies, horizontally across departments, and organizationally between firms and their customers, 'the boundary-less appraisal', that is, 360 degree appraisal, has emerged as a more viable alternative to traditional appraisals. Several firms such as Shell, Exxon Mobil, IBM, AT&T, Levi Strauss, FedEx, etc. have started using 360 degree appraisal and feedback systems. The AV Birla Group, Gillette, and Ballarpur Industries have 360 degree feedback systems for senior level managers. It is expected that the 360 degree system will result in a more comprehensive picture of an employee's performance and developmental needs and since ratings are anonymous, a more honest evaluation is possible.

The 360 degree appraisal approach is more appropriate for developmental purposes than for evaluative purposes. Feedback from multiple sources helps employees in self-development. It may also reduce prejudice since performance feedback comes from multiple sources. Though 360 degree appraisals may serve both developmental and evaluative purposes, most organizations begin by using 360 degree appraisals exclusively for developmental purposes, focussing on management and career development. However, 360 degree appraisals have also begun to be used for making evaluative or administrative decisions. For instance, an employee's incentives may be linked to customer feedback. Reliance Industries Ltd, Crompton Greaves, Godrej Soaps, Wipro, and Infosys all use 360 degree feedback primarily for self-correction and fact-finding purposes. However, it is also being used for promotion and reward decisions. For example, American Express uses target-based performance appraisal to award a performance bonus at the year-end. The leadership rating of the 360 degree assessment at American Express is linked to promotions and increments. When used for evaluative decisions (pay increases, promotions, etc.) 360 degree appraisals may lead to certain problems (see Exhibit 7.5).

It is more appropriate to use 360 degree feedback for developmental purposes at first. When managers and all others participating in the process have become comfortable with the system, when employees and managers feel that the information from the 360 degree system is helpful, they will gradually lower their apprehensions about the use of 360 degree feedback for making evaluative decisions. Some firms like GE have become disenchanted with 360 degree appraisals and discontinued its use.

Any firm that seeks to implement the 360 degree system should follow certain general guidelines, such as

- determine the potential cost of the programme;
- focus feedback on specific goals;
- train employees giving and receiving feedback; and
- ensure that the feedback is productive, unbiased, and development oriented.

Exhibit 7.5

Potential Problems of 360 Degree Appraisal Feedback

- Considerable anxiety for the employee (appraisee) when appraisals are negative. The employee may get a feeling that everyone is 'ganging up' against him/her.
- Customers, subordinates, and peers can also be biased. Their lack of accountability can further affect appraisals.
- Anonymity and breach of privacy can become a major issue. Since several employees are involved in 360 degree appraisal systems, it is likely that evaluators may discuss an employee's appraisals and violate privacy.
- Peers may deliberately evaluate a manager lower than he/she should be in order to increase their own chances of promotion. This tendency is enhanced because the 360 degree appraisal system is anonymous.
- There is greater likelihood that rater biases will influence evaluations because multiple evaluators are involved. It is important to train all evaluators to provide valid evaluations.

Source: Greer 2002

An important aspect of 360 degree appraisals relates to the 'acceptability' of the system, that is, what factors influence whether people are willing to participate and use 360 degree feedback data? Acceptability is defined as the willingness to provide unbiased feedback by raters, or to receive and utilize 360 degree data by the appraisee. When the purpose of 360 degree feedback is development, and when the feedback is shared only with the appraisee, the appraisee may have little interest in using the feedback for self-improvement. Since pay and promotions do not get affected, the appraisee may also perceive little accountability for using the results. When the appraiser feels that the appraisee or the organization will not make use of the appraisals, there will be little incentive to take time to do the appraisal or to provide accurate or complete information. Thus, acceptability is an important factor in the effective implementation of 360 degree appraisals.

Factors impacting 360 degree appraisal

Some factors may impact the acceptability of 360 degree appraisals by both the appraiser and the appraisee. These are as follows.

Organizational cynicism When employees in an organization hold the common belief that potentially fixable problems cannot be resolved due to factors beyond the control of the employees, it results in 'organizational cynicism'. Cynicism with regard to new initiatives results from past implementation failures or incompetence (or both) resulting from lack of commitment of leaders. Both the appraiser and appraisee may nurture cynicism about the 360 degree appraisal system. Appraisees may be unsure about the management's intention in adopting 360 degree appraisal. The appraiser may feel that it will result in no changes. To manage cynicism, it is important to first implement 360 degree as a pilot project and allow organization members to experience the process.

Purpose of appraisal Employees who are evaluated by peers and managers who are evaluated by subordinates all prefer that feedback from 360 degree appraisals should be used solely for development and feedback. However, appraisees prefer that upward appraisals should have an evaluative component, but they should be kept anonymous. This controversy pertains to the age-old issue regarding the use of performance appraisal for evaluative as opposed to developmental purposes. Those who appraise may find the 360 degree appraisal system more acceptable when ratings are used for evaluative purposes, but the appraisee may not find this acceptable. The latter would like to use 360 degree for only developmental feedback. Organizations are moving in the direction of making 360 degree appraisals more evaluative in nature. However, too hasty a movement towards evaluation may compromise acceptability. When appraisals are used for making administrative decisions, appraisers are likely to manipulate ratings of appraisees, such that they are different from the ratings they would give in a purely developmental appraisal. Bias in ratings reduces the acceptability of the 360 degree system. Hence, evaluative processes should be implemented gradually to increase acceptability.

Anonymity This becomes an issue in 360 degree appraisals. With traditional appraisals, anonymity is not an issue. The supervisor evaluates and shows the written appraisal to the subordinate, only to file it in personnel records. 360 degree appraisals, on the other hand, incorporates upward appraisals, that is, appraisals of employees by those who are lower than them in the organizational hierarchy. This may result in power differentials and hence it is important that appraisals are anonymous. This is to protect subordinates who provide appraisals from backlash from the superiors whom they appraise. Peers or external customers also may fear repercussions if their appraisals are identified. For example, a customer service executive may disrupt or withdraw the service to an external customer.

Peer appraisal Acceptability of 360 degree appraisals is also affected by the extent to which work is designed around teams. Traditionally, performance appraisals are designed around the jobs that are not related or dependent on other jobs or tasks. Since co-workers are at the same organizational level, within the same group, they are likely to have closer interpersonal relationships and to be in direct competition for organizational rewards. Generally speaking, co-workers are not comfortable appraising each other. However, acceptability of co-worker appraisals increases when the group tasks and activities are highly interrelated and the group is operating as a team for solving problems and improving performance. The interrelated nature of the work situation makes it possible to observe co-workers or their cooperativeness and helpfulness. This increases the likelihood that co-worker appraisals are seen to be fair.

Competency of appraisers Appraisees may find it difficult to accept ratings or feedback when they perceive that the appraiser does not have the competence to appraise and hence any ratings provided by them will be perceived as biased or unfair. Appraisees may perceive the appraiser to be lacking in competence when

- the appraiser is not familiar with the work of the appraisee, as in the case of external customers who may not be aware of various work-related pressures of the appraisee—moreover, appraisees may also believe that the appraisers do not observe their performance frequently enough and hence are not competent to rate them; and
- appraisees are unwilling to be appraised by those who they believe cannot themselves perform the task.

The issue of acceptability of appraisals has generally been overlooked in the design and implementation of appraisal processes. While 360 degree appraisal and feedback is based on the premise that it will lead to positive behavioural change, this expectation is not always fulfilled. Rather, it is accompanied by potential risks such as negative reactions, reduced effort, dissatisfaction with raters, etc. It is important to give careful consideration to the 'how' of the implementation of the 360 degree feedback process in order to maximize its benefits. An organization can make multisource and 360 degree appraisals more effective by following certain guidelines (Exhibit 7.6). Thus, 360 degree appraisal provides a valuable approach to performance appraisal, but its success depends on how the system is introduced, how information is used, and how fairly employees are treated.

Competency-based Performance Management System

Traditionally, the emphasis in performance management systems has been on performance—the 'what' of behaviour, that is, the specific quantitative monetary or productivity results achieved in the past. The appraisals were used to make decisions about rewards such as performance-based bonuses, merit awards, etc. Recent years have seen greater efforts directed towards devising more effective ways of managing the performance of key managerial employees (Exhibit 7.7). Several organizations are becoming

---

Exhibit 7.6

360 Degree Appraisal—Some Suggestions to Maximize Benefits and Minimize Risks

- Provide training to employees to enhance self-awareness. This minimizes inflation in ratings and also results in more accurate self-ratings.
- Provide orientation to all employees about the implementation of the 360 degree appraisal process.
- Assess degree of organizational cynicism among employees prior to implementing 360 degree appraisal. Take steps to reduce cynicism to make employees more inclined to embrace feedback and personal change.
- Follow-up negative feedback with encouragement and coaching.

- Integrate 360 degree feedback with other training and development efforts. Providing feedback to suggest changes, without providing training or assistance, will result in lower motivation on the part of recipients of feedback.
- Institutionalize 360 degree appraisal as part of the organizational culture. This requires multiple administrations before the results will be fully realized. Over time, employees adapt to the process and organizations tailor the process to fit their needs.

Source: Atwater, Waldman, and Brett 2002

> ### Exhibit 7.7
>
> #### *Corporate Examples of Competency-based Performance Management System*
>
> **Larsen and Toubro**, the engineering major, has developed a competency matrix which lists 73 competencies to measure performance and assess the developmental needs of its employees. These competencies vary across managerial levels. Each competency has associated knowledge, skills, and attributes. Individual employees are appraised on the listed competencies. Based on this assessment, functional, managerial, and behavioural skill gaps are identified. The competency matrix is linked to business strategy on one hand and training needs on the other. The development policies are driven by the strategic needs of the organization ensuring that the process of re-skilling is focussed.
>
> **Hughes Escorts**, the subsidiary of US headquartered telecom company, Hughes, uses a competency-based performance enhancement model. Each position in the organization is defined in terms of 23 key competencies. These competencies are categorized into four groups: attitude-based, knowledge driven, skill centred, and value-based. These competencies are used to measure gaps. Relevant training inputs are given based on the competency gaps identified. The objective is to maximize productivity as well as to help individual employees understand their professional status with respect to these competencies.
>
> *Source*: http://www.themanagementor.com/kuniverse/kmailers_universe/hr_kmailers/perf_best.htm, accessed on 26 September 2006

---

interested in the management and appraisal of competence—the 'how' of performance. The assessments are qualitative, developmental, and future focussed. Competency assessment has been adopted as an increasingly powerful tool in the implementation of many contemporary HRM practices. Competency assessments help determine job-related characteristics and desired levels of performance, thereby providing a basis for many HRM practices. Levi Strauss, one of the most famous names in the clothing business, focusses on paying the person, not the job. Hence, across-the-board pay increases are smaller than the pay increases given to employees with critical skills sets. Competency-based performance management systems offer organizations the ability to manage performance from a quantitative output-based perspective as well as from a process-based perspective, that is, how the output gets generated.

The traditional performance appraisal systems appraised managers against a range of technical job function requirements and in relation to quantifiable performance criteria or metrics. They focussed on the performance requirements (standards) of job positions and not on the job-holders themselves. It was assumed that the job-holders possessed the characteristics required to perform the job. In competency-based approaches, on the other hand, it is the observable and measurable characteristics of managers that are used as the basis of performance management activities. This approach focuses on the person-related variables that the individual brings to a job. One problem with traditional performance management systems that focus exclusively on performance or outcomes is that they do not consider the fact that employees' ability to achieve job-specific outcomes are not always within their control. Factors such as economic changes, changes in the organizational structure, and market-related changes, all impact an employee's ability to perform and produce desired results. The competency-based approach helps the organization overcome this problem by increasing the importance of the 'process' and rewards employees for skills (skill-based pay) rather than outcomes. This system helps employees to know *how* to improve current performance if their performance is not meeting expected standards. For instance, Cadbury rates its managers on six generic competencies which must manifest in a high performing manager. Several public sector undertakings (PSUs) such as IOC, GAIL, BPCL, etc. have instituted competency-mapping of employees and devised development programmes based on a competency gap analysis. BPCL has identified competencies for all levels of jobs in its management cadre and runs its own development centre for competency profiling. Competency assessments are used by the company to make decisions about strategic assignments.

Measuring Managerial Performance

Performance management is a core strategic HRM activity where both performance standards and competency based approaches can be applied. A manager's performance can be reviewed against both the performance criteria (that is, performance standards) and competencies or desired behaviours for determining rewards and developmental needs. It is important to recognize that performance takes place in a unique social and cultural context. This context should be understood since it may affect the evaluation of the manager's performance.

Holmes and Joyce (1993) suggested three approaches to measuring managerial performance. These are as follows:

1. Job-focussed approach
2. Person-focussed approach
3. Role-focussed approach

Job-focussed approach This is the traditional approach to performance appraisal that concentrates on identifying the key tasks of a managerial position. The job is viewed as independent of the job-holder. This represents the competence-based (not competency) approach to performance appraisal. Competence is a 'description of something which a person who works in a given occupational area *should* be able to do, it is a description of an action, behaviour, or outcome which a person should demonstrate' (Training Agency 1988). Competence is expressed in terms of the *purpose of the job* and the *standards of performance* expected to be achieved. This has been called 'micro-competence' (Elkin 1990). This approach has been criticized on the following grounds.

1. It promotes inappropriate and inflexible performance standards for management positions and does not take into account the complex and dynamic context in which managerial performance takes place,
2. Managerial performance is a process of implementation of knowledge. It is not limited to the practice of measurable skills.
3. Several soft skills like leadership, creativity, etc. are important for success in a managerial job.
4. The job-focussed approach is not helpful in the face of new job demands that emerge in managerial positions.
5. The approach is focussed only on past performance.

Person-focussed approach This approach focuses on person-related competencies that employees bring to a job, thus relying mainly on input-based criteria for performance evaluation. This is the competency-based approach to performance management. It considers a manager's performance in terms of how it relates to his/her personal background, personality, values, motivation, etc. This approach views competencies as 'macro' in nature and distinct from the task-specific 'micro' competences of the job-focussed approach. Macro competencies are important in the performance of managerial work, which involves non-routine and complex situations. Moreover, certain general abilities are common for different managerial jobs. These are required for performing managerial work across all jobs. Hence competencies are not seen as the functional tasks of the job, rather they refer to those actions and behaviours which help managers to carry out their jobs effectively. Personal qualities are central to this approach. It focusses on identifying characteristics that distinguish superior from average managerial performance.

Role-focussed approach This approach is one that focusses on the social context in which performance occurs. When performing a job, an employee enacts a role. This role emerges out of the interaction between the employee (role holder) and the others in the social situation (colleagues, boss, and subordinate) with their varying perceptions and expectations. The role approach is more realistic since it relates to managers' situations, rather than what any manager *should* be doing. The approach focusses on examining the various demands made on the manager by others and the extent to which the manager accepts them. It also examines the extent to which managers' performance meets the demands imposed by themselves as well as by others in the multiple roles occupied by them. The approach acknowledges the extent to which an individual's performance meets imposed demands of various roles. It also acknowledges the factors that impact on job performance (for example, leader behaviour, co-workers, organizational values, etc.). This approach goes further than either the job or person–focus perspectives. This perspective is particularly appropriate for managers whose performance is contingent on the particular circumstances of the project or task at hand.

Hybrid approach The three performance management approaches discussed in this chapter should be viewed a complementary rather than mutually exclusive. Thus, there should be a systematic combination of both micro competencies and macro competencies within a new framework and underpinned by role-focussed measures. This leads to a holistic managerial performance perspective, which may be labelled as the *hybrid approach*. The hybrid approach uses the following measures to assess job performance of an individual:

- A clear description of the work tasks managers should be competent in (micro competencies)
- Factors enabling them to complete those tasks effectively (macro competencies)
- Specific role-focussed criteria for performance excellence (social context)

The hybrid approach represents a radical departure from the performance appraisal strategies currently dominating several project-based sectors such as the IT industry. The traditional approaches to performance appraisal are appropriate for an organization operating in a slowly changing environment. However, project-based organizations are faced with higher rates of change in their external environments. A single focus—job or person—performance management approach is not appropriate for such an environment. The hybrid approach is both past and future oriented, and combines quantitative and qualitative assessments of performance. It aligns employee competencies with the performance improvement requirements in the social context of the organization and the job demands. The multifaceted approach is useful for a range of HR functions including recruitment, training, promotion, rewards, etc. It results in a more participative, developmental approach to the HRM function and leads to sustained performance improvements in the future. The multidimensional competency-based performance management or the hybrid approach is most appropriate for the following organizations and teams:

- Organizations operating in an uncertain and changing environment. When results (outcomes) are not under the control of the manager and are difficult to measure. Evaluation is, therefore, based on whether they demonstrated the right behaviours rather than on achievement of specific targets.

- Team-based environments where work is team based and it is not possible to identify individual contributions. Contribution to group processes is more important that individual results.
- Dynamic environment and organizations in which managers' potential to contribute to the company in the future is more important than their past performance.
- Jobs which have no measurable outcomes. For example, service-oriented jobs are not easily measured in terms of outcomes. In this case, an employee's performance may be measured in terms of competencies.
- Future and development-oriented organizations must evaluate and develop relevant competencies.
- When workforce is highly variable and dynamic. For example, project-based work requires continually changing skill sets. When workforce is dynamic, employees are required to assume multiple competency-based roles in their work.

Different jobs are best managed by different performance management approaches. For service jobs, the competency-based approach may be more appropriate, and therefore, a higher weightage would be assigned to the competencies rather than to the output.

TECHNOLOGY AND PERFORMANCE MANAGEMENT

We have discussed in an earlier chapter, the important role that technology has played in revolutionizing the workplace as well as the significant impact it has had on HRM. Like other HR practices, technology can support performance appraisal in aspects such as providing ongoing feedback, annual appraisals, and employee development. Technology can be used to enhance the positive outcomes of a well-administered performance management system. Technology-supported performance appraisal will not be successful if employees are not satisfied with the appraisal process. In discussing how technology interacts with performance management systems, the role of appraisal satisfaction is important for organizations. Satisfaction with the appraisal process has an impact on productivity, motivation, and organizational commitment. Technology may contribute to the performance appraisal process in two ways:

- Technology may perform the function of measuring an individual's performance through computer performance monitoring (CPM) activities. These activities are mechanical and do not require any input from employees except task performance. Jobs for which such an appraisal technology is used are the ones that are repetitive and involve little personal judgment or discretion.

- Technology may be used as an aid by managers to write performance reviews or for generating performance feedback. For example, supervisors or team members can generate multi-rater appraisals online or readymade appraisal software packages may be used to construct an evaluation. Jobs for which this kind of technology is used involve discretion, personal judgment, and are open-ended.

Computer Performance Monitoring (CPM)

The CPM technology helps in collecting performance data by counting the number of work units completed in a time period, error rates, time spent on various tasks, etc. The organization can use this data for workforce planning, evaluating worker performance, controlling performance, and in providing performance feedback to employees. Computer performance monitoring has positive aspects as well as drawbacks (see Exhibit 7.8).

Online Evaluation and Appraisal Software

While CPM helps generate the actual content or data, online evaluation and/or appraisal software helps generate appraisals and the accompanying narrative and also facilitates the delivery of performance feedback. The Internet or the Intranet of the organization can be used for administering the performance management process. Indian Oil Corporation (IOC) has instituted an online performance management system. In GAIL, another PSU, the key performance areas (KPAs) and key performance indicators (KPIs) are captured electronically.

Increasingly, Intranets are preferred by organizations for implementing multi-rater or 360 degree feedback. For example, a performance evaluation process may begin with an e-mail message to all employees giving them information about the process. Subsequently, in a multi-rater system employees (appraisees) can nominate potential raters from whom they want to obtain performance feedback. All nominations go to a central e-mail where they are sorted. Raters are then sent an e-mail message, giving a list of employees they will evaluate. Raters, therefore, receive one e-mail rather than several individual requests from all those employees who would like to be rated by them. Using assigned passwords to enter a secure site, raters complete evaluation questionnaires online. It allows raters to click buttons on the screen for each rating and if the rating is high or low on a factor, the programme prompts the rater to review the rating and to add his/her own comments to the evaluation. Feedback from multiple raters is then centrally collected and a report is generated. This report is sent electronically to the employee being evaluated. PepsiCo India has developed an e-HR software called Connect Survey, which enables employees to rate their bosses on parameters like whether they

Exhibit 7.8

Benefits and Drawbacks of CPM

Benefits

- Provides objectives and timely feedback to employees
- Enhances fairness of a performance evaluation system
- Feedback is seen as more clearly related to work output (and hence fair) and less associated with the biased impressions of the superior

One way to pursue objectivity in CPM is by making it a part of a broader 'management by objectives' (MBO) format. When employees participate in goal determination, they respond with greater trust to an appraisal system.

Drawbacks

- Reduced face-to-face interaction within an organization lowers interpersonal trust. Reduced trust leads to lower productivity, which has negative implications for performance management. Computer performance monitoring results in diminished trust when
  - it occurs in a telecommuting or distance environment that reduces face-to-face interaction; and
  - when an individual believes that the purpose of CPM is to monitor and control performance rather than to coach and develop.

  For feedback to be effective the appraisee should accept feedback and respond by performance improvement. However, lowering of trust results in reduced acceptability of the performance data and feedback based on the data generated by CPM.

- Computerized monitoring may lead to a dehumanizing work environment and become a cause of stress and health problems.
- Acceptability of computer-generated performance and feedback is reduced when it is supervisor-generated. It tends to be more effective and is received positively by an individual when it is self-generated.
- Individuals who lack computer literacy are more likely to reject computer-generated feedback.
- It is restricted to delivery of performance data. This falls short of a truly developmental approach that includes devising a plan for monitoring progress and achieving high performance.
- CPM raises concerns about how to measure quality of performance. When the CPM process provides for acknowledging the situational constraints on performance, it is likely to enhance employee satisfaction with the appraisal process.
- A CPM system overemphasizes quantitative performance measures. These measures do not take into account various contextual factors that potentially influence an individual's performance. For example, CPM may track the 'number of customer calls' made in a day for a customer service representative. However, it will not be able to track the difficulty level of each customer call. An employee with more difficult calls may not be able to meet the target of total number of calls in a day. This may lead to negative evaluation of this employee's performance.

Source: Miller 2003

recognize the efforts of subordinates, enable them to strike a good work–life balance, or interact with them beyond day-to-day work. Web-based appraisal technology has certain benefits as illustrated in Exhibit 7.9.

Exhibit 7.9

Benefits of Web-based Appraisal Technology

- Organizations can evaluate more employees simultaneously.
- More frequent evaluations become possible.
- Feedback recipients can get online suggestions for development and information relating to training opportunities within the organization as well as on the web.
- Employees can track their own progress over successive evaluations.
- It allows performance management to become paperless thus simplifying the administration of the process.
- Some software may include a coaching utility that provides information to raters about coaching the individuals whom they evaluate.
- The process becomes less daunting for scientists, engineers, and others who sometimes have little background in evaluating others, and resist spending time and effort on performance evaluations.
- Appraisee satisfaction with the appraisal process increases when the use of appraisal software leads to a rise in coaching and development efforts.
- Appraisers can compare their ratings with aggregated ratings provided by other appraisers for the same individual. This helps in reducing rater distortions.
- Appraisers can also compare their ratings with independent feedback provided by each of the other individual raters (appraisers). This allows them to see how closely the appraisers agree on the evaluations of an employee. This helps develop a frame of reference resulting in higher accuracy in evaluations.
- Makes the appraisal process less tedious, easy to administer, results in ongoing feedback, and increases accuracy.

Source: Miller 2003

All organizations cannot replace the traditional performance appraisal systems with online performance management. An organization must evaluate the following factors prior to implementing technology-based appraisals:

- Organization must have a culture which supports technology.
- Organization must have appropriate technological sophistication and adequate IT resources.

Understandably then, the earliest adopters of technology to enhance the value of HR delivery in organizations have been organizations in the IT, BPO, and retail banking sectors where employee numbers run into several thousands. These organizations implement their e-HR systems for all human resource practices. For instance, at Infosys, use of technology has ensured that appraisals are not a one-time event. Appraisals are ongoing as the appraisee's performance is recorded electronically on various parameters for every project that the appraisee executes throughout the year. At the time of the annual appraisal, all performance details are available on the system, for both the manager and the appraisee to discuss. The entire appraisal process at Infosys is built around the work processes.

Satyam Computers Limited is a firm where HR professionals have come to rely on IT for almost all HR activities, be it recruitment, retention, performance management, or other administrative tasks. The performance appraisal process at Satyam Computers has been automated. Each associate from a particular strategic business unit (SBU) has two assessors who fill the appraisal form online. The online performance management system at Satyam draws on the concept called numeric management. At a very fundamental level all business concerns can be expressed in numbers. The manager's role is to manipulate 'reality' to achieve the 'desired' state on the specified number. Vision Compass is a software product developed and marketed by Satyam. This software draws upon the philosophy of numeric management and provides a framework for implementing numeric management within an organization. Numeric management helps Vision Compass to capture performance through performance dashboards, and handle specific management frameworks such as MBO, balanced scorecard, etc. Vision Compass allows the user to generate various types of predefined reports. It makes it possible for a manager to access his/her subordinate's performance sheets and get an instant insight into the major work of their subordinates, as well as the major concerns that they were facing. The software also helps managers to clarify job expectations and roles to their subordinates and helps minimize ambiguity in that respect. Additionally, the software also enables associates to manage their own performance with facts and data. It provides information and feedback on performance or efforts of people throughout the organization, on a day-to-day basis. This allows the manager to make necessary interventions to change the course of performance in the desirable direction.' Vision Compass helps in translating the vision, mission, and strategy of an organization into a comprehensive set of performance and action plans. Performance is measured at the business unit level, team level, and individual level. It also aligns individual and team goals with those of the organization. This provides for a comprehensive approach to HR solutions.

As with other HR practices, performance management should also be aligned with the strategic goals of the organization.

STRATEGIC LINKAGE OF PERFORMANCE MANAGEMENT

In earlier chapters we discussed the relationship between business strategy and HR strategy. The best-fit approach emphasized the importance of linking HR strategies with business strategies. The 'fit' perspective suggested that HR strategies should match the stages of development of the firm, namely, start-up, growth, maturity, and decline. Different dimensions of HR practices are important at various stages of the organizational life cycle. Since performance appraisal is an HR activity, it should also be aligned with business strategies.

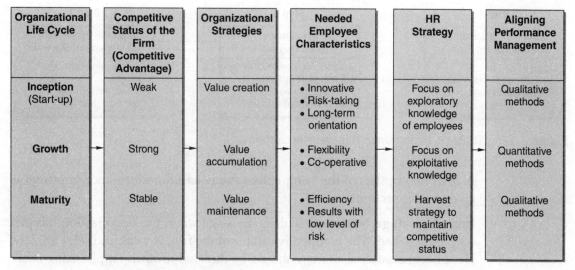

Organizational Life Cycle	Competitive Status of the Firm (Competitive Advantage)	Organizational Strategies	Needed Employee Characteristics	HR Strategy	Aligning Performance Management
Inception (Start-up)	Weak	Value creation	• Innovative • Risk-taking • Long-term orientation	Focus on exploratory knowledge of employees	Qualitative methods
Growth	Strong	Value accumulation	• Flexibility • Co-operative	Focus on exploitative knowledge	Quantitative methods
Maturity	Stable	Value maintenance	• Efficiency • Results with low level of risk	Harvest strategy to maintain competitive status	Qualitative methods

Figure 7.10: Linkage Between Organization Life Cycle, Competitive Status, Organizational Strategy, and HR Strategy

As the organizational life cycle moves from start-up to growth to maturity, the competitive status of the firm also changes, from low to rapid growth to lower but stable growth across these stages. Organizational strategies adopted should be appropriate to the competitive status of the firm at each stage of organizational life cycle. The various stages of organizational life cycle will require different employee characteristics in order to successfully implement organizational strategies at each stage. The HR strategy may be developed to align with organizational strategy, competitive status of the firm, and the required employee characteristics, at each stage of the organizational life cycle. Performance appraisal approach will be contingent on the competitive status of the firm and will change as its competitive status changes (Figure 7.10). Before designing the performance appraisal system, the competitive status and organizational strategies of the firm should be specified. Performance appraisals should therefore be aligned with organizational strategies. Determining organizational strategies requires an assessment of the strengths and weaknesses of the organization.

The strategic performance management system includes the following steps:

- Identify competitive status of the firm
- Determine organizational and HR strategies
- Align the performance management system

For each stage of the organizational life cycle, these three steps are likely to help determine the appropriate performance appraisal strategy (Figure. 7.11).

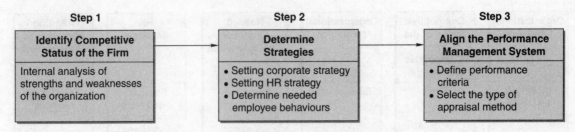

Figure 7.11: Strategic Performance Management System

A brief description of the competitive status based performance appraisal is given in this section.

Inception stage (start up) This is the stage when the organization has just been established. The competitive status of the firm is weak and sales are low. Hence organizational strategy should be directed towards emphasizing R&D and product development. Since competitive advantage results from creating value, the organizational strategy focusses on *value creation*. This can be achieved through employees. The employees, at this stage, should have an innovative approach, be focussed on long-term goals, and be open to risks if required. Performance criteria should incorporate these characteristics. It is important that those knowledge and skills of employees that are easy to develop and assess are included in performance appraisal and also continually measured. Since employee performance on the characteristics important at the inception stage are easy to measure, qualitative performance appraisal methods are more appropriate for employee appraisals.

Growth stage This stage is characterized by a very strong status of competitive advantage. The organization follows the strategy of value accumulation and placing higher emphasis on production and support service. Employees at this stage should be flexible to change, look for short-term survival, and work in close co-operation with each other. The HR strategy should focus on utilizing employee competence. The performance criteria measure the degree to which employee competence appears and converts to actual behavioural performance on the job. At this stage quantitative performance appraisal methods are more appropriate for appraisals.

Maturity stage The competitive advantage status of the firm becomes stable at this stage. Sales, though stable, are at low level at this stage. The organizational strategy moves towards value maintenance by attempting to maintain its market in a highly competitive scenario. Desirable employee characteristics at this stage are efficiency, an ability to yield results, and take on tasks that involve a low level of risk. The HR strategy should focus on 'harvesting' in order to maintain its competitive status through its employees. This strategy encourages low-risk and highly repetitive behaviour. The performance output criteria measure employee performance, that is, whether work behaviour is converted into performance. Qualitative performance appraisal methods are likely to be more appropriate.

The life-cycle typology suggests a helpful approach on the basis of which HR managers may decide the appropriate strategy for more effective performance appraisal.

Summary

Performance appraisal is an inevitable aspect of organizational life. All organizations without exception have a system for evaluating employee performance. However, performance appraisal systems across organizations differ in the degree to which they are formal, objective, or participative, how they are implemented, and the purposes they are designed to serve. The chapter clarified the terms that are used interchangeably when describing the process of employee performance evaluation and also examined the differences between the traditional performance appraisal and the contemporary performance management system. The uses and objectives of the performance management system were outlined. The steps in the design and implementation of the performance management system were discussed. These included-identification of performance dimensions, defining and communicating performance standards, determining the sources of appraisal information, choice of selection methods, and communicating performance feedback to employees. Often employees experience performance evaluation as a negative process. Problems in performance appraisal may result from several factors.

The chapter discussed three sets of factors that may lead to problems in performance appraisal–ambivalence on the part of manager and subordinate towards appraisal, system design and implementation problems, and rater biases and errors. The characteristics of effective performance management system were highlighted. Developments in the approach to performance management were also discussed. These included team or work-group appraisal, assessment centre approach to performance management, multisource and 360 degree appraisals, and competency-based approach to performance management. The advantages and areas of concern of team appraisals are discussed. The chapter suggests that careful attention should be given to the characteristics of the team when designing the performance appraisal system. The chapter also dwelt upon how technology can support various aspects of performance appraisal. Two ways in which technology may contribute to the performance appraisal process were presented. These include computer performance monitoring and online evaluation and appraisal software. The chapter ended by providing an overview of the strategic linkage of performance appraisal.

Keywords

360 Degree Appraisal takes place when all sources of appraisal are combined together. A 360 degree appraisal system helps obtain information about an employee's performance in multiple roles and from different perspectives.

Assessment Centre is an approach that requires the participants to complete a range of group and individual tests and exercises which simulate the activities they might encounter in the target job. Each assessment centre consists of approximately six to twelve participants and may extend over a period of two or three days.

Behaviour-based Methods of performance appraisal obtain descriptions of employee behaviour and place them along a scale to identify those actions which lead to good performance as well as actions which need to be improved.

Competence describes what a person who works in a given occupational area should be able to do and is expressed in terms of the purpose of the job, and the standards of performance, expected to be achieved. It is a description of an action, behaviour, or outcome which a person should demonstrate. It is different from competency.

Computer Performance Monitoring helps in collecting performance data by counting the number of work units completed in a time period, error rates, time spent on various tasks, etc. The data can be used for workforce planning, evaluating worker performance, controlling performance, and in providing performance feedback to employees.

Formal Appraisal is a system of appraisal set up by the organization to evaluate employee's performance systematically. All organizations have some variation of formal appraisal in place.

Informal Performance Appraisal takes place when day-to-day interaction of the manager with an employee allows the former an opportunity to appraise the employee's performance on his/her jobs, even when the manager is not 'required' to do so. Informal performance appraisal provides immediate feedback, and results in high motivation.

Multisource Feedback takes place when an organization combines two, more, or all of the available appraisal sources for providing an individual's performance information.

Online Evaluation and/or appraisal software help generate appraisals and the accompanying narrative, and also facilitate the delivery of performance feedback. The Internet or the Intranet of the organization can be used for administering the performance management process.

Performance Appraisal is the system by which an individual's performance is compared to a set of performance standards to assign a 'score'. The score indicates the level of current and/or past performance of the individual. The term includes assessment.

Performance Assessment is the process by which data about an individual employees' past and current job performance are collected and reviewed. The manager adopts a judgmental approach and makes decisions about the adequacy of the employee's performance.

Performance Dimensions are the job criteria or evaluation criteria that are the most important factors of the job. These are the factors for which the employee is paid by the organization.

Performance Evaluation is the process that determines the extent to which an employee performs the work effectively. Other terms that connote the same meaning are performance appraisal, merit rating, performance review, and employee evaluation.

Performance Management (PM) is an integrated process that consolidates goal-setting, employee development, performance appraisal, and rewarding performance, into a single common system. Performance management aims to integrate employee performance with the strategic goals of the organization. It is a broader term than performance appraisal, performance evaluation, or performance assessment.

Performance Standards define the expected levels of performance, goals, or targets by which performance on job criteria is evaluated.

Rater Biases occur when the values and prejudices that the appraiser holds distort the ratings of the appraisee, either unintentionally or intentionally.

Rater Errors are the mistakes made by the appraiser when appraising an employee.

Result-based Methods of performance appraisal focus on the accomplishments of the employees, that is, the results they achieve through their work, such as sales figures, production output, etc.

Teams are made up of individuals who are assigned to a specific role depending on their skills. Teams work collaboratively, and take responsibility for the performance of the whole team rather than just individual performances.

Trait-based Methods of performance appraisal are designed to measure the extent to which an employee possesses certain characteristics that are important for performing the job successfully.

Work Team is a well-developed social system, where task interaction between members is predictable. These teams engage in routine manufacturing or service jobs and have static membership. These teams are also called intact teams.

Concept Review Questions

1. Explain the term performance management. Identify the major points of difference between traditional performance appraisal and the new performance management system.

2. What are the major objectives of performance management? Why are performance management objectives often contradictory?

3. Describe the general guidelines for the development of a performance management system. What decisions must be taken by the organization at each step?

4. What are the characteristics of an effective performance management system? What major problems are inherent in most performance management systems?

5. Describe the assessment centre approach to performance management.

6. Are behaviour-based methods more effective than trait-based methods? Describe any two methods of each type, citing their advantages and disadvantages.

7. What are the different sources of appraisal information? Discuss the pros and cons of each source.

8. Discuss the advantages of competency-based performance management over traditional appraisals. Under what conditions are competency-based performance management systems most appropriate?

9. Explain how the performance management system can be aligned with the business strategy of the organization.

Critical Thinking Questions

1. Why have team appraisals become significant since the 1990s? Is it appropriate to apply the individual performance management process to evaluate team performance? What advantages do team-based appraisals have over the traditional individual performance appraisal? What are some of the limitations of team-based appraisals? What factors must be considered in the design of an effective team performance management system?

2. What is 360 degree appraisal? What advantages does it have over the traditional performance appraisal systems that use only downward appraisals? What factors may impact the acceptability of 360 degree appraisals by both the appraiser and the appraisee?

3. Think of two teachers who have taught you—one whom you consider very good and one whom you consider a poor teacher. What specific behaviours distinguish the two teachers? In your opinion what is the best source of obtaining performance data for appraising performance of teachers? What are the merits and demerits of appraisal of teachers by students?

Simulation and Role Play

1. The objective of this role-play exercise is to compare the three types of appraisal feedback interviews for their effectiveness. The three types of appraisal feedback interviews are one-way communication, two-way communication, and mutual problem-solving.

Situation: The subordinate (appraisee) has not been able to meet the performance targets. Hence the appraisee is neither going to receive incentives nor will be considered for a promotion. The task of the appraiser is to communicate the appraisal to the appraisee.

Exercise: The exercise requires some out-of-class preparation by participants. Six students have to volunteer for the role-play. These students are to be formed into 3 dyads. In each dyad, one student has to play the role of the appraiser and the other student has to play the role of the appraisee. Each dyad is assigned to role-play one type of appraisal feedback interview. The instructor should brief each dyad about the manner in which the feedback interview is to be conducted.

Each dyad role has to play the assigned type of appraisal interview in front of the entire class. No discussion or questions should be permitted when the role-play is in progress. The class is encouraged to make notes about their observations on each type of appraisal interview. After all the three role-plays are over, the instructor has to invite observations and questions from the class. The students who played the appraisee in each dyad share their feelings during the course of the feedback session. The instructor leads the discussion on the relative merits and demerits of each type of appraisal interview. The discussion ends by outlining the characteristics of effective appraisal interviews.

2. Assume you are the General Manager (HR) of a reputed IT services firm with business in several countries. The organization operates in a dynamic business environment. The organizational structure is relatively flat with only four hierarchical levels. Almost all employees are required to work in project-based teams. The rate of employee turnover of the firm is not very high by industry standards. However, there have been times when a member of the project team has quit before the completion of the project. The firm on such occasions found it difficult to replace the team member. The firm presently has a results-based performance management system in place. You, as the GM (HR), recently attended a workshop on the competency-based performance management system. You are convinced that your firm should change over to a multi-dimensional competency-based performance management system. As GM (HR) your responsibilities are the following:

- To convince the top management of the importance of adopting the multi-dimensional competency-based performance management system.

- To suggest how the development of competency profiles of employees will help in quickly replacing a member of the project team if the person leaves in the middle of a project.

Classroom Projects

1. The purpose of this activity is to debate the following proposition:

   'Performance management is an important HR activity and plays a significant role in the achievement of individual and organizational objectives'.

   Steps:

   - All students sitting on the left side of the room will take the 'pro' position; those

sitting on the right side will take the 'con' position.

- Students have to form groups of five or six and develop arguments in support of their position. The instructor should allow fifteen minutes time for group discussion.

- Both the sides should then develop a master list of arguments supporting their positions. The master list is developed by having a representative from each subgroup meet with one another and compare lists. Thus there will be two master lists.

- The subgroup representatives from each side will become the debate teams.
- Each team will get ten minutes time to present its arguments. At this stage the arguments of each team should focus only on supporting its own position (not to rebut the arguments of the other team).
- The 'pro' team goes first.
- Each team gets five minutes to rebut the arguments given by the other side and reconstruct and re-emphasize its own arguments, as needed. The rebuttal should directly address the arguments of the opposite side. The purpose of rebuttal is to question and cast doubt on the arguments of the opposite team. The 'con' side has to present its arguments first.
- The rest of the students are given ten minutes to cross-examine members of either team. The students are also encouraged to cite experiences of organizations with their performance management systems.
- The class ends with a vote on which position they hold.

- The instructor has to then close the discussion with comments and observations.

2. The objective of this exercise is to help the students gain an insight into the design and implementation of the performance management process. Introduce the exercise to the class by clarifying the objectives of the exercise. The instructor presents a brief overview of the steps in the design and implementation of the performance management process. Divide the class into groups of four or five. Each group is asked to select one occupation from the following suggestive list and design a performance management system for this position.

- University professor
- Software engineer
- Customer relations executive
- HR manager of a firm
- Sales executive of an FMCG firm

Each group has to prepare and present a report followed by a general discussion led by the instructor. The discussion centres on the steps in the design and implementation of performance management process, the decisions that need to be made at each stage, potential implementation issues, and differences in appraisal criteria across different occupational groups.

Field Projects

1. The objective of this field project is to help the students appreciate the role of technology in supporting performance management systems. The instructor should divide the class into groups of five each. Each group is asked to visit any two organizations. Group members have to conduct interviews with HR managers as well as a few middle-level managers of the firms to obtain the following information:

- Whether the organizations have incorporated technology in any aspect of their performance management process.

- When was technology introduced in implementation of performance management?

- For what aspects of performance management do these firms use technological support (for example, feedback, online filling of appraisal forms, identifying training needs, etc.)?

- Benefits that have resulted for the firm as a result of use of technology-based performance management.

Each group has to prepare a report for class presentation as well as a written report for submission to the instructor. The groups have to make presentations in the class highlighting the trends in the use of technology supported performance management systems. When all groups have made their presentations, the instructor should engage the entire class in a discussion about the importance of technology supported performance management and web-based appraisal technology. The

discussion should also focus on industry differences in the use of technology for performance management, aspects of performance management for which use of technology is more pervasive, degree of satisfaction of employees with the web-based appraisal technology, and potential problems of technology supported appraisals.

Case Study

Performance Appraisal at Amber Limited

Amber Limited is a multinational pharmaceutical firm with its headquarters in Mumbai. Incorporated in the year 1940 as a family-owned firm, it is today a professionally managed firm. However, Mr Naik, the President of the company, comes from the family of the founders. The first manufacturing unit of the organization was set up at Ankleshwara. At present, the firm has ten such units across India. The company started by manufacturing ready-to-use surgical dressings. Gradually it expanded into pharmaceuticals (1950s) and medical devices (1960s). In recent years Amber Ltd has expanded into toiletries (1990s), personal healthcare products, and consumer products (2002). The consumer division of the company is located in Pune. Amber has 50 subsidiaries with operations in about 20 countries across three continents, that is, Europe, North America, and South Asia. The company is listed on the National Stock Exchange and recently, it was also listed in the New York Stock Exchange. With an annual turnover of Rs 250 crore, it is a Fortune 700 company. Today, many brands of Amber Ltd are household names.

The employee strength of the company stands at 6000 employees, with about 500 employees located at the company headquarters in Mumbai. Of the total 1800 executive and managerial employees in Amber Ltd, approximately 30% are women. There are about 300 executives and managers in the consumer division at Pune. Since the year 2002, Amber Ltd has consistently figured in the top 20 companies in the *Business World* list of

'Best Employers' based on survey conducted by top management consultants. It was also voted as the 'Most Preferred Employer for Women' in 2001 based on an *Economic Times* survey. From the very beginning the promoters of the company have demonstrated a people-oriented and humane approach. This philosophy continues to govern the organizational functioning even today. The Human Resource (HR) department is a strategic function at Amber Ltd. The function is headed by the Executive Director (HR), Mr Seshadhiri, who is also a member of the organization's strategic planning team. Mr Seshadhiri is positioned at the company headquarters in Mumbai. The HR team at the headquarters consists of, apart from Mr Seshadhiri, Director, organizational development group, Director, performance and career management group, and Director, human resource planning and administration group. The total strength of staff in the HR department at headquarters is 70. The HR function at each manufacturing unit is headed by a General Manager (HR). The total staff strength of HR department ranges from eight to twelve employees in each unit.

Mr Patel was appointed as the Director, performance and career management group, at the headquarters in 1996. He was an alumnus of one of the top business schools in India, having graduated in the same year. He contributed substantially in transforming the HR policies and practices at headquarters. When Patel joined Amber Ltd in 1996, he found that the firm continued to use a traditional performance appraisal system at the headquarters. The appraisal form consisted of a rating scale to obtain performance scores on employees. There were two sets of factors on the rating scale, the job factors and the behavioural factors. These factors were determined on the basis of job analysis information. An example of the rating scale used for the performance appraisal of the marketing manager at the headquarters is given in Table 7.8.

The performance appraisal form consisted of one page. It was filled up by the superior and signed by the subordinate in the presence of the superior. When the subordinate disagreed with the rating given by the subordinate on a particular factor, it was discussed between the superior and subordinate. The rating could be modified if the superior was convinced about the arguments of the subordinate. The superior gave recommendations about the salary increase or promotion for the appraisee. The reviewing officer, who was a manager senior to the supervisor conducting the appraisal, then signed the form. Finally, the performance appraisal forms were submitted to the HR department. Appraisal was an annual exercise and the appraisal cycle was from January to December each year.

Mr Patel felt that this appraisal system had its limitations. A major drawback according to him was that it provided no information regarding company expectations, leaving the employees in the dark as to what they needed to do to achieve favourable ratings. Moreover, due to its impact on salary and promotions, the appraisal system generated considerable degree of emotions during and after appraisals. To resolve these problems, Mr Patel considered introducing changes in the design and implementation of the appraisal system at the headquarters. His initiative was completely backed by Mr Seshadhiri and the President of the company.

Mr Patel designed and conducted training for all managers in the use of the new performance review system before it was implemented in 1997. The new appraisal system was now called 'Annual Performance Review' and it consisted of three parts.

Specific performance objectives This consisted of identifying Key Performance Areas (KPAs) for each job. The KPAs constituted the job criteria. Specific measurable performance objectives (targets) were identified for each KPA. The KPAs and the objectives were jointly negotiated by the supervisor and the subordinate, at the beginning of the rating period. The supervisor had to ensure that the objectives contributed to the achievement of the strategic goals of the organization. Self-appraisal was built into the form. Employees had to rate themselves on the degree to which they had achieved the specified objectives within the given time period. If they had not been able to achieve the targets, they also had to record the reason for this. Subsequently, the supervisor rated the employees on the degree of task accomplishment.

Behavioural standards This consisted of a rating form listing several positive and negative job behaviours (for example, 'takes initiative in group meetings', 'gets along well with colleagues', 'is closed to new ideas', etc.). There was no self-appraisal on this form. The supervisor rated the subordinate and it was directly sent to the supervisor's boss (reviewing officer). The aspects on which the employee needed to improve were discussed during the feedback meeting.

Salary and promotion recommendations Based on the employee's strength, weaknesses, and accomplishments, the supervisors recommended salary action and promotion status for each employee. The reviewing officer reviewed these recommendations and forwarded them to the HR department for final approval.

In 1999, business environment for the pharmaceutical industry underwent a major transformation. The changes in international regulations with respect to pricing, patenting, etc., led pharmaceutical firms to pay greater attention to margins in order to ensure their presence in the market. The pharmaceutical industry was also faced with a highly competitive business environment with a spate of mergers and acquisitions. Amber Ltd itself has acquired two small companies within India and is poised to make a major acquisition in

Table 7.8: Rating Scale for Performance Appraisal of Marketing Manager

	5 Exceptional: Consistently exceeds requirements	4 Good: Frequently exceeds requirements	3 Average: Consistently meets requirements	2 Below average: Needs improvement. Requirements not met occasionally	1 Unsatisfactory: Does not meet requirements
Job Factors					
Quantity of work (volume of work achieved)					
Quality of performance (process in handling duties)					
Clarity about duties and responsibilities					
Behavioural Factors					
Dependability (can be relied on to meet work requirements)					
Initiative (resourcefulness and willingness to accept responsibility)					
Adaptability (ability to respond to changing conditions)					
Communication skills (ability to put across ideas to subordinates)					

Europe. Such an environment has ensured that the performance of the company and all its employees is closely monitored.

The company therefore, began to place greater emphasis on performance orientation and performance target achievements. In this year, a new dimension was added to the performance appraisal form. On the basis of ratings in Part I of the performance appraisal form, all employees were classified into three categories–those who had exceeded the specified performance targets by more than a specified percentage, those who had met the performance targets, and those who had not achieved the targets. Decisions about annual bonus and career movements were based on this classification, with the employees who exceeded the targets classified as 'high performers' getting the maximum rewards. Those who had not met the targets were called for a counselling session to help them improve their performance next year. The tacit understanding was that those who got classified in this category for three consecutive occasions should find alternate employment. This year, a formal appraisal feedback system was also introduced. Though appraisal feedback gave the employee an opportunity to discuss his/her performance with the supervisor, the final decision still rested with the latter. Part II of the form continued to be used for identifying areas of improvement.

On a sunny winter morning in December 2001, Patel was mentally reviewing his stint with Amber Ltd. He felt he had accomplished reasonably well. He had just returned after attending a four day conference on 'the use of technology in HR'.

Amber still did not use technology for several practices; though employee records such as leave, absenteeism, training, etc. were computerized. Patel decided to make the performance review system available online. Having made his decision, Patel got up to get a cup of coffee. He was taken aback when Mr Das, his marketing manager, walked in looking visibly upset. When Patel asked him what the matter was, Mr Das expressed his dissatisfaction with the performance review system. Das had just got to know that he had not been classified as a 'high performer'. Das had been with Amber Ltd for the past 15 years. He had a consistently good performance record, got along well with all his colleagues, and the firm trusted his decisions. This year, however, he had faced some personal problems and had not been able to give undivided attention to official assignments. He told Patel that he felt betrayed since he had expected the company to be understanding. Das felt that the performance review system itself needed a review urgently. Patel listened to Das, giving an empathetic ear, and assured him that he would take up the matter with the top management. Patel sought an appointment with Seshadhiri to discuss the matter. He knew that Das would have no dearth of offers, should he decide to leave. Patel wondered whether it was time to revamp the performance review system. How could a firm be performance oriented and yet show concern for the personal problems of employees? How can a performance system be designed and implemented to ensure appraisal objectivity as well as employee satisfaction with the system?

Questions

1. What were the main drawbacks of the traditional appraisal system of Amber Ltd that was in place until 1997? Did the new performance review system overcome these drawbacks? Explain citing examples from the case.

2. Evaluate the 'annual performance review' as it was implemented in 1997. Do you think the modifications introduced in the performance

review system in 1999 at Amber Ltd helped it to become more performance-oriented? Give reasons for your answer.

3. Is Amber Ltd ready for a technology supported performance review system? Why do you think so? What will be the best way for designing an online performance appraisal at Amber?

4. Do you think Mr Das's reaction is justified? What problems do you see in the current performance review system at Amber Ltd?

5. Give suggestions for making the current performance review system at Amber Ltd more effective.

6. Do you think that implementing a competency based performance management system will help Amber Ltd overcome some of the problems of the current performance review system?

References

Armstrong, M. and A. Baron 1998, *Performance Management: The New Realities*, Institute of Personnel and Development, London.

Atwater, L.E., D.A. Waldman, and J.F. Brett 2002, 'Understanding and Optimizing Multisource Feedback', *Human Resource Management*, vol. 41, no. 2, pp. 193–208.

Baron, A. and M. Armstrong 1998, 'Out of the Box', *People Management*, vol. 23, pp. 38–41.

Beer, M. and R. Ruh 1976, 'Employee Growth through Performance Management' *Harvard Business Review*, vol. 54, no. 4, pp. 59–66.

Bohlander, G., S. Snell, and A. Sherman 2002, *Managing Human Resources*, 12th edition, Thomson South-Western, Singapore.

Campbell, D.J., K.M. Campbell, and Ho-Beng Chia 1998, 'Merit Pay, performance Appraisal, and Individual Motivation: An Analysis and Alternative', *Human Resource Management*, vol. 37, no. 2, pp. 131–46.

Carrell, M.R., N.F. Elbert, and R.D. Hatfield 1995, *Human Resource Management: Global Strategies for Managing a Diverse Workforce*, Prentice Hall, Englewood Cliffs, New Jersey.

Chen, Hai-Ming and Tung-Sheng Kuo 2004, 'Performance Appraisal Across Organizational Life Cycles', *Human Systems Management*, vol. 23, pp. 227–33.

Cheng, Mei-I and A.R.J. Dainty 2005, 'Towards a Multidimensional Competency-based Managerial Performance Framework–A Hybrid Approach', *Journal of Managerial Psychology*, vol. 20, no. 5, pp. 380–96.

Copithrone, K. 2001, 'Case Study of a Competency based Performance–Management System', Thesis submitted to the Faculty of Graduate Studies in partial fulfillment for the degree of MBA, University of Calgary, Alberta, www.proquest.com, accessed on 1 September 2006.

DeCenzo, D.A. and S.P. Robbins 2005, *Fundamentals of Human Resource Management*, 8th edition, John Wiley & Sons, Singapore.

DeNisi, A.S. 2000, 'Performance Appraisal and Performance Management: A Multi-level Analysis', in K.J. Klein and S. Kozlowski (eds), *Multilevel Theory, Research and Methods in organizations*, Jossey-Bass, San Francisco, pp. 121–56.

Dessler, G. 2005, *Human Resource Management*, 10th edition, Prentice Hall of India Pvt Ltd, New Delhi.

Drucker, P.F. 1954, *The Practice of Management*, Harper and Brothers, New York.

Elkin, G. 1990, 'Competency Based Human Resource Development', *Industrial and Commercial Training*, vol. 22, no. 4, pp. 20–5.

Greer, C.R. 2002, *Strategic Human Resource Management: A General Managerial Approach*, 2nd edition, Pearson Education, Singapore.

Hartog, Deanne, P. Boselie, and J. Paauwe 2004, 'Performance Management: A Model and Research Agenda', *Applied Psychology: An International Review*, vol. 53, no. 4, pp. 556–69.

Holmes, I. and P. Joyce 1993, 'Rescuing the useful Concept of Managerial Competence from Outcomes back to process', *Personnel Review*, vol. 22, no. 6, pp. 37–52.

Ivancevich, J.M. 2004, *Human Resource Management*, 9th edition, Tata McGraw Hill Publishing Company Ltd, New Delhi.

Kossek, E.E. and R.N. Block 2000, *Managing Human Resources in the 21st Century: From Core Concepts to Strategic Choice*, South-Western College Pub, Thomson Learning, USA.

Locke, E. 1968, 'Toward a Theory of Task Motivations and Incentives', *Organizational Behaviour and Human Performance*, vol. 3, pp. 157–89.

Mathis, R.L. and J.H. Jackson 2003, *Human Resource Management*, 10th edition, Thomson South-Western, Singapore.

Mello, J.A. 2003, *Strategic Human Resource Management*, Thomson Asia Pte Ltd, Singapore.

Miller, J.S. 2003, 'High Tech and High Performance: Managing Appraisal in the Information Age', *Journal of Labour Research*, vol. 24, no. 3, pp. 409–24.

Mondy, R.W., R.M. Noe, and S.R. Premeaux 1999, *Human Resource Management*, 7th edition, Prentice Hall International Inc., USA.

Scott, S. and W.O. Einstein 2001, 'Strategic Performance Appraisal in Team-based Organizations: One Size Does not fit All', *Academy of Management Executive*, vol. 15, no. 2, pp. 107–16.

Spangenberg, H.H. and C.C. Theron 2001, 'Adapting the Systems Model of performance Management to Major Changes in the External and Internal Organisational Environments', *South African Journal of Business Management*, vol. 32, no. 1, pp. 35–47.

Spencer L. and S. Spencer 1993, *Competence at work models for superior performance*, John Wiley and Sons Inc., New York.

Training Agency 1988, 'The Definition of Competences and Performance Criteria', Guidance Note 3 in *Development of Assessable Standards for National Certification*, Training Agency, Sheffield.

Waldman, D.A. and D.E. Bowen 1998, 'The Acceptability of 360 degree Appraisals: A Customer-Supplier Relationship Perspective', *Human Resource Management*, vol. 37, no. 2, pp. 117–29.

Notes

Business Today, 12 January 1996.

Business Today, Anniversary Issue, 21 January 2001.

Business World, 6 December 2004.

'Finally, an Exit Plan for Non-Performing Babus', *The Times of India*, 17 February 2006, New Delhi, p. 8.

http://www.expresscomputeronline.com/cgi-bin/enprint/MasterPFP.cgi?doc, accessed on 21 April 2006.

http:/www.humanlinks.com/manres.htm, accessed on 27 September 2006.

http://www.psychologymatters.org/assessment center.html, accessed on 21 April 2006.

http://www.psychometrics.co.uk/adc.htm, accessed on 21 April 2006.

http://www.themanagementor.com/kuniverse/kmailers_universe/hr_kmailers/perf_best.htm, accessed on 26 September 2006.

'Never Too Old to Rock and Roll', *Corporate Dossier*, The Economic Times, 26 August 2005, New Delhi, pp. 1–2.

'Now, IAS Officers can't take their Jobs for Granted', *Times of India*, 17 December 2005, New Delhi, pp. 1, 16.

'The Man Machines', *Corporate Dossier*, The Economics Times, 10 February 2006, New Delhi, pp. 1–2.

'The Technical (IT)ies of Assessment', *The Economics Times*, 4 August 2005, New Delhi, p. 7.

Vaneevich, J.M., 2004, *Human Resource Management*, 9th edition, Tata McGraw Hill Publishing Company Ltd, New Delhi.

Kossek, E. et al., 'Career Aspirations in the 21st Century', Sage Pub., Thousand Oaks, USA.

Locke, E. 1976, 'Towards a Theory of Task Motivation and Incentives', *Organisational Behaviour and Human Performance*, vol. 3, pp. 157–89.

Maus, R.L. and L.L. Jackson, 2002, *Human Resource Management*, 10th edition, Thomson South-Western, Singapore.

Scott, S. and W.O. Einstein 2001, 'Strategic Performance Appraisal in Team-based Organisations: One Size Does not fit All', *Academy of Management*.

Spangenberg, H.H. and C.C. 2006, 'Administering a Model of Performance Management to Major Changes in the External and Internal Organisational Environments', *South African Journal of Business Management*, vol. 42, no. 1, pp. 39–47.

Spencer Land
Jhar Son,
Inc, New York,
Singapore.

8

Compensation and Rewards Management

OBJECTIVES

After studying this chapter, you will be able to:

- define 'compensation' and understand its objectives
- gain an overview of the components of financial compensation
- understand the ways in which organizations recognize employees
- understand the determinants of financial compensation and rewards
- discuss four approaches to pay-for-performance
- understand the role of equity perceptions in the design of compensation and reward systems
- understand new developments in compensation and rewards
- understand the linkage between business strategy and compensation strategy
- appreciate the significance of a total compensation and rewards strategy

INTRODUCTION

Organizations achieve their objectives through their employees. Employees expect to be rewarded by the organization for their contribution. Compensation plays an important role in the organization's ability to attract and retain high-performing employees; it is the key reason that an employee chooses to work for one organization and not for another. Employee perception of the adequacy of organizational rewards is an important determinant of their satisfaction and subsequent performance. Compensation or rewards management is a key aspect of human resource management (HRM).

This chapter begins with the definition and objectives of compensation and rewards systems. It classifies compensation and rewards into two types: 'financial' and 'non-financial'. The components of financial compensation—base pay, variable pay, and benefits—are discussed. The chapter discusses various individual, group, and team incentives offered by organizations to reward employees. The types of benefits, changes in the nature of benefit offerings, and the flexible benefit approach are highlighted. The role of recognition in motivating employees toward high performance is examined. The determinants—internal and external—of compensation and rewards are examined. The chapter compares the traditional and contemporary approaches to compensation. An overview of the different pay-for-performance approaches is presented. The chapter examines in some detail the competency-based and team-based approaches to compensation and rewards. Compensation and rewards trends for top management are explored. The linkage between business strategy and compensation strategy is examined based on the typology of business strategy, type of industry, and organizational life cycle stage. In the end, the chapter discusses the importance of a total compensation and rewards strategy.

COMPENSATION AND REWARDS

Compensation is the sum total of all forms of payments and rewards provided to employees for performing tasks to achieve organizational objectives. Compensation and rewards management is a complex process that includes decisions regarding benefits and variable pay and is one of the most significant and dynamic of HR practices. Like any other HR practice, it involves the design, development, implementation, communication, and evaluation of the reward strategy and processes of the organization. It suggests an exchange relationship between the employee and the organization. The compensation an employee receives determines one's standard of living and purchasing power. Employees seek to maximize their rewards to meet their aspirations. They also expect to be compensated fairly and rewarded for the effort, skills, knowledge, etc. that they contribute towards the achievement of organizational goals. For the organization, pay and rewards are important since these affect its profitability. Compensation constitutes the major cost of doing business, since it determines the employee cost. An *Economic Times* survey (Economic Times 2005) of 200 large private sector organizations found that their wage bill went up by 23.5% in the first half of 2005 over that of 2004. Organizations also view compensation and rewards as a means to reinforce desirable employee behaviour. Compensation and rewards offered by an organization is an important determinant of an individual's performance, decision to join a company, motivation to improve performance, desire to undergo training, and desire to continue to work for the organization. Thus, compensation and rewards serve several objectives for both the employee and the organization (Exhibit 8.1).

Exhibit 8.1

Objectives of Compensation and Rewards

- Pay each employee fairly, in line with his or her effort, skills, or competencies
- Attract and retain high-performing employees
- Motivate employees towards higher performance
- Reinforce desirable employee behaviour

- Communicate to the employee his or her worth to the organization
- Align employee efforts with achievement of organizational objectives
- Enhance co-operation and collaboration among team members
- Provide employee social status

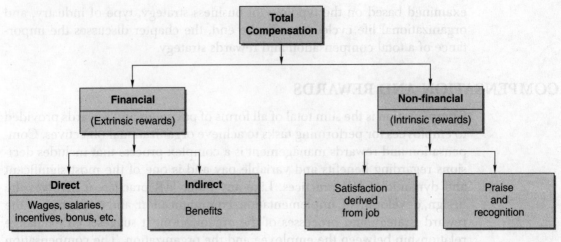

Figure 8.1:   Classification of Rewards

Types of Compensation

Compensation or rewards can be financial or non-financial. Financial compensation can be of two types—direct or indirect.

Direct financial compensation and rewards   These refer to monetary payments made to employees in exchange for work. These include basic wage or salary, bonus, incentives, merit increases, overtime payments, variable pay, and commission.

Indirect financial compensation and rewards   These include benefits such as pensions, insurance, paid time off work, etc. These rewards are received by all employees on the basis of their membership in the organization. As part of indirect compensation, employees do not receive actual cash; rather, they receive the tangible value of the reward.

Both direct and indirect financial compensation are called *extrinsic rewards*.

Non-financial compensation is the satisfaction that an individual derives from the job or from the environment in which he/she performs the job. If the job provides an individual variety, challenge, responsibility, etc. and allows him/her to establish close friendships with colleagues, it provides non-financial compensation to the employee. Praise and recognition for good performance or for completing a project also constitute non-financial compensation. These are also called *intrinsic rewards*.

The classification of rewards is depicted in Figure 8.1.

Financial Compensation Components

The components of the financial aspect of a compensation and rewards programme (Figure 8.2) are as follows.

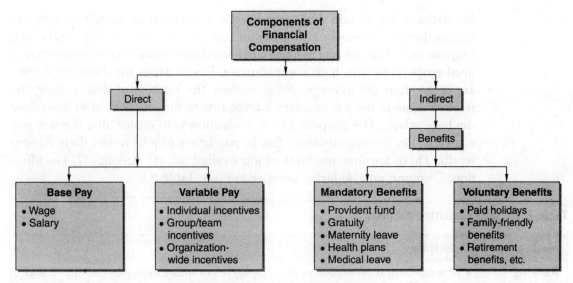

Figure 8.2: Components of Compensation and Rewards

- basic salary, or base pay, that is adjusted for length of service and for cost of living;
- variable pay or incentives, that take the form of pay-for-performance; incentives may be individual or aggregate (group); and
- benefits, or employer-provided rewards, other than wages, salaries, or incentives.

If organizations wish to retain high performers, they will have to focus on compensation strategies such as performance-based incentives. A competitive salary is a hygiene factor, that is, it is essential to prevent dissatisfaction, but is unlikely to motivate employees. Therefore, components such as bonuses, incentives, and variable pay, are being structured into compensation packages.

Base Pay

Base pay is the direct financial compensation an individual receives based on the time worked. The calculation of these payments may differ. Generally, organizations have two base pay categories—hourly and salaried. When employee payments are calculated on the number of hours worked, that is, on an hourly basis, they are called wages. When employees receive consistent payments at the end of a specified period regardless of the number of hours worked, they are said to receive a salary. Salaries have typically been associated with jobs higher in the hierarchy of the organization compared to wages. Many organizations have moved towards an all-salaried approach for all categories of employees. To attract and retain high quality personnel, the base pay or salary must be market-driven. Market demand for different skills varies. When the demand for certain managerial skills is higher than supply, employees having these skills may be paid a higher base pay to attract the top candidates. Organizations that operate in uncertain environments and face constant change need employees with high competencies. Base salaries for these employees are more than the average. *Job evaluation*, the process of determining the relative value of the job to assign a wage rate to the job, is used to determine the base salary. The purpose of job evaluation is to ensure that there is pay equity within the organization, that is, pay levels of jobs reflect their relative worth. There are four methods of job evaluation: (1) ranking; (2) classification; (3) point; and (4) factor comparison (see Table 8.1).

Table 8.1: Job Evaluation Methods

Method	Description
Ranking	■ Management representatives and employees examine each job description and arrange the jobs in order of importance ■ Simplest and oldest method
Classification	■ Jobs are classified and grouped. Each successive grade or class requires increasing amounts of job responsibility, skill, ability, etc. Class/grade descriptions reflect the differences of groups of jobs at various difficulty levels. Evaluators compare each job description with its grade/class description. Each job is classified in the grade whose description most closely agrees with the job description. ■ Also a simple method
Point	■ The job is broken down into specific components/criteria such as skill, effort, responsibility, etc. and numerical values are assigned to each of these components. Weights are assigned to each job component depending on the relative importance of each criterion to performing the job. The sum of these weights/points provides a quantitative assessment of the relative worth of the job. Jobs with similar point totals are placed in the same pay grade. ■ Expensive and time-consuming, but widely used.
Factor Comparison	■ Evaluators do not evaluate the complete job, but separate factors of the job. These factors are called compensable factors. It is assumed that there are five universal job factors: mental effort, skill, physical effort, responsibility, and working conditions. Compensable factors of the job being evaluated are compared with the compensable factors of key jobs within the organization. ■ Key jobs are the benchmark jobs within the organization, which are widely known in the labour market and are used for wage determination purposes. Experts establish the relative degree of the difficulty of each of the compensable factors for each key job. Monetary rates of pay are assigned to each compensable factor of each key job based on the relative importance of the respective factor to the job.

Contd

Table 8.1 Contd

Method	Description
	■ A factor comparison scale reflecting ranking and money allocation is developed. Job evaluation is done on a factor-by-factor basis. Each job to be evaluated is compared factor by factor with key jobs on the factor comparison scale. The monetary rates assigned to each job on each factor are added to obtain the total monetary value of the job.

Incentives

Incentives are another form of direct financial compensation. The terms 'variable pay' and 'pay-for-performance' are often used synonymously with 'incentive plan'. Incentive, or variable pay, is defined as 'any plan that ties pay to productivity or profitability usually as a one-time payment'. It is the compensation linked to individual, team, or organizational performance, not to time worked. Pay-for-performance plans pay employees based on their performance; one such plan is merit pay. The incentive component of the compensation package is usually considered most critical for the successful achievement of organizational goals and business strategies. Bonuses, profit-sharing plans, variable pay, and stock options are examples of incentive pay. In the calendar year 2005, LG paid an average bonus of 1200%, and 15% of the top performers received 2100%. Call centres such as WNS, Progeon, and Wipro BPO offer cash and non-cash incentives to employees. The cash component is part of the variable pay and is performance-linked for all levels of employees. This ranges from 10% at the agent level to beyond 20% for higher levels. There are three types of incentives. These include individual incentive plans, group incentive plans, and organizational incentive plans. *Individual incentives* are given to reward the effort and performance of individuals. For sales personnel, individual incentives form a large part of the salary. Incentives are also used by organizations as a tool for employee retention. For example, Infosys has evolved a new incentive tool for executives in 2006. It is called the 'deferred compensation/bonus scheme'. The company plans to create a compensation fund and use it to reward employees for their performance. The reward will be staggered over a period of time. The objective of this scheme is to communicate to employees that the longer they stay with the firm the better their rewards will be. However, this scheme is likely to be limited to senior management, and cover only a small percentage of Infosys's over 50,000 employees. Retail majors and IT firms are offering retention bonuses to employees. For example, Wipro asks fresh campus recruits to make a bank deposit of Rs 75,000 on signing the employment contract. If the employee leaves before 15 months, the money is paid to Wipro by the bank and the employee loses the whole amount. However, if the employee stays for 15 months, the employee gets back the principal amount with interest as well as Rs 6,000 as retention bonus. Fearing high attrition levels, BPO firms also introduced loyalty bonuses for employees in 2004 in the form of white goods, PCs, and free study packages. With growth in the outsourcing business resulting in fast-paced hiring and poaching in BPO firms, employees get a loyalty bonus for every quarter they spend with the company. For example, HCL offered loans for PCs to its employees that were to be partly written off every year the employee spent with the organization. Organizations are increasingly moving toward use of work teams to accomplish objectives. Therefore, *group/ team incentive plans* are being designed to encourage team collaboration and co-operation. Team members' compensation includes rewards based on team performance in addition to individual salaries. *Organizational incentives* compensate all employees for the organization's performance that year. The objective of organization-wide incentives is to enhance organizational performance by rewarding co-operation. Stock options and profit-sharing plans are common forms of organization-wide incentives. A brief description of some common types of individual, team, and organizational incentives is presented in Table 8.2.

Table 8.2: Types of Incentives

Type of Incentives	Description
Individual Incentives	
Piecework Plans	The oldest individual incentive plan and still widely used, its origin can be traced to Taylor's Scientific Management. In the *straight piece-rate system,* wages are determined by multiplying the number of units produced by an employee in a unit of time (for example, garments stitched) by the rate per unit. A *differential piece-rate system* pays employees one piece-rate wage for a standard number of units produced in a given time, but a higher piece-rate for units that exceed the standard output. For example, if an employee is expected to stitch five garments in a day, he or she gets the standard rate for five garments. However, if he/she stitches seven garments, the employee will get a higher rate per garment.
Merit Pay	Also called merit raise, it is the salary increase that the employee receives for his/her performance. The increase becomes part of the base salary. Thus, merit increases become cumulative, and lead to significant increase in payroll cost. In each subsequent year, base pay goes on increasing on a permanent basis. Recently, organizations have begun to tie merit pay to both individual and organizational performance.

Contd

Table 8.2 Contd

Type of Incentives	Description
Bonus	The additional compensation payment made to employees, it is a one-time payment and does not become part of the employees' base pay, and hence is less costly. When an employee performs well, he or she may be given a bonus equivalent to two weeks' pay.
Individual Incentives for Sales Personnel	
Salary Plan	Sales personnel are paid fixed salaries with occasional incentives which include bonuses, sales contest prizes, etc. This plan is most useful when the main job is to find new clients or to execute training programmes for a customer's sales force rather than to 'make the sale'.
Commission	Salespeople are paid for results. These establish a clear link between effort and rewards. Commission is the compensation calculated as a percentage of sales in units or rupees. In *straight commissions*, a salesperson receives a percentage of the value of sales made. If the person makes a sale of Rs 100,000 in a year, he or she receives a percentage of this amount as a commission.
Combination Plan	The most frequently used form of compensation for salespeople, it is a combination of salary and commission. The salary/commission split is usually 80/20, that is, salary and incentives make up 80% and 20% of the compensation respectively, though other combinations are possible. The salary component is fixed, while the 20% incentive component is variable and tied to achievement of sales targets or other specified performance criteria.
Group/Team-based Incentives	
Work-team Plan	All members of the team may be rewarded equally on the basis of group performance, measured in terms of output, cost savings, etc. For example, in a service firm, all employees may receive a fixed incentive for each percentage decrease in customer complaints. Each team member also continues to draw a fixed salary.
Gain-sharing	An organization may share with employees greater-than-expected gains in profits and/or productivity. The rewards may be distributed in various forms: a flat amount for all employees; a percentage of base salary for all employees; percentage of gains according to employee categories; or a percentage based on individual performance. To encourage teamwork, the first two methods of gain-sharing are more appropriate.

Contd

Table 8.2 Contd

Type of Incentives	Description
Organizational Incentives	
Profit-sharing Plans	Employees receive a share of the firm's annual profit. The percentage of profit to be shared is agreed on a year before actual distribution. Employees may receive their share of profit at the end of the year, or on retirement, or in part (the rest is deferred). Deferred profit-sharing also serves as a retention tool for the organization.
Employee Stock Option Plans (ESOP)	Allow the employees to gain stock ownership in the organization for which they work. This allows employees to share in the growth and profitability of their firm and results in higher motivation.

Benefits

Benefits are employer-provided rewards other than wages, salaries, or incentives. These make up the indirect financial compensation component of the total compensation plan. Benefits differ from incentive plans since benefits and services are not contingent on performance of individual, team, or organization. Benefits and services accrue to all employees of an organization by virtue of their membership in the organization. Employees continue to avail of benefits as long as they work for the organization, regardless of seniority or performance. Benefits are of two types: (1) mandatory; and (2) voluntary.

Mandatory benefits These benefits are legally binding on the employer. Provident funds, gratuity schemes, health plans, maternity leave, medical leave, etc. are examples of mandatory benefits. All employers to whom the Employees' Provident Fund and Miscellaneous Provisions Act 1952 applies are statutorily liable to subscribe to the Employees' Deposit Linked Insurance Scheme 1976 to provide life insurance to all their employees. MetLife India has launched a group term life insurance product called Met Group Life in lieu of the EDLI that insures employees and their families as well. The cover amount is fully tax-free in the hands of the beneficiary and the coverage starts from the first day irrespective of the PF balance. For the employer, the premium paid is treated as business expense for income tax purposes. All employees who are members of the employee provident fund scheme of the employer are eligible for Met Group Life.

Voluntary benefits These are discretionary and are provided by the employer voluntarily. These include compensation for time not worked, for example, paid holidays, family-friendly benefits, retirement, etc. Organizations today offer their employees benefits such as paid sabbaticals, childcare centres, the option to work from home—especially for expectant mothers, a job search facility for spouses of employees, language courses, etc. Call centres offer benefits such as company-sponsored education policy, health/life/accident insurance, free transport, subsidized meals, and free concierge services where employees can pay their telephone, electricity bills and policy payments. The majority of call centres also offer night shift and overtime allowances. The biggest reason for attrition in BPO firms is that young employees leave for further studies. To retain these employees, BPO firms offer to refund the course fee of employees who pursue studies if the employee stays with the organization. More private sector organizations offer career breaks and sabbaticals today; these were earlier limited to government jobs. Previously, such HR practices and benefits were seen as welfare measures, but now these are considered essential retention tools. Table 8.3 provides examples of benefits that organizations offer their employees voluntarily today.

Table 8.3: Voluntary Benefits

Nature of Benefit	Examples
Educational	■ Motorola India offers educational assistance to employees' spouses for getting a suitable job abroad when the employee is given an international assignment. ■ NIIT gives employees paid sabbaticals for six months every five years. ■ ONGC is planning to allow paid sabbaticals of three to seven years for its employees who wish to enhance their qualifications. ■ The Aditya Birla Group offers sabbaticals informally and is likely to formalize them. ■ HLL offers a career break to employees who wish to study.
Family	■ Motorola India provides childcare centres to working mothers and flexible working hours to certain employees. ■ HLL, HCL Technologies, Yes Bank, Genpact, Mocha, etc. offer paternity leave. ■ Bharti Telecom has several programmes for families of employees. Family trips and a 'family day at office' are organized. The firm also conducts employee fairs, summer camps for employees' kids, kids' days out, etc. ■ NIIT offers wedding anniversary allowance. ■ LG Electronics has a new initiative called the 'Joyful Working Team' where employees and their families are taken for lunch or sporting activities like rafting. There is also a 'Happy Moments Board' to share positive happenings in the members' lives. ■ Infosys allows employees leave without pay for a year to allow them to join their partners abroad. However, the firm requires that the employee complete a year of service before availing this benefit.

Contd

Table 8.3 Contd

Nature of Benefit	Examples
	■ HLL offers a five-year career break for diverse reasons, such as taking care of children, or even to join one's spouse who may be working elsewhere. ■ A differential leave strategy is also being offered to older employees in the form of reward. HLL offers six months instead of three month maternity leave for women who have worked with the organization for at least two years.

Structuring benefits This has become important. The changes in the work environment have brought about significant changes in the employer–employee relationship. A job for life is no longer a reality. Hence, the nature of benefits offered by the organization should match the expectations of employees. Traditionally, organizations have adopted a 'one-size-fits-all' approach to rewards in which individuals have little choice about the benefits they receive. This approach works well with a homogeneous workforce. However, for a diverse workforce, this approach does not work. This is because the traditional approach runs the risk of giving rewards to individuals that they do not value, and often fails to reward them with what they value. It is important to find out how employees perceive their benefits and whether they value them. *Flexible benefits*, or a *cafeteria approach*, gives choice to individuals. Benefits need to be relevant if they are to be valued. A young workforce may expect and value benefits such as childcare, paid holiday for the whole family, maternity leave, etc. For the older workforce, health-related benefits, pension plans, etc. are more relevant. Hence, organizations seek to offer a flexible benefit plan that allows employees to choose the benefits they value most from a basket of offerings. For example, a firm may have the following benefits in its basket—healthcare, life insurance, cash reimbursement for some purchases, paid holidays, and childcare. Each benefit in the basket has a money value attached to it. The employee may be given the option to choose any two or three benefits from the package such that the total money value of the chosen benefits does not exceed a specified amount. As a variant, the organization may extend one or two benefits to all employees and allow flexibility in choice for a certain number of additional benefits. Organizations are also modifying their leave policies for the purpose of using holidays as a differentiator. Instead of increasing the number of holidays, the private sector is thinking innovatively and giving the employees greater flexibility in structuring their leave. Traditionally, most organizations divided annual leaves into three categories—paid, casual, and medical. An increasing number of firms are adopting the bouquet approach. For example, Genpact and ebookers offer a consolidated leave basket to employees. Employees of ebookers are offered 30 days of leave annually and may divide it the way they prefer.

Earlier, executives were entitled to many benefits in the form of cash reimbursements, like driver allowance, perquisites under different heads, and so on (see Exhibit 8.2). The variable salary component was small. Moreover, almost

Exhibit 8.2

Fringe Benefit Tax

Benefits and perquisites are benefits over and above the salary received by an employee and are major components of an employee reward strategy. Traditionally they were viewed as aspects of compensation that could facilitate the employee in effective tax planning. Fringe benefits include gifts, car allowance, use of club facilities, reimbursements of credit card expenses, etc. Perquisites include accommodation, cars, interest on loans, educational facilities, use of laptops, computers, entertainment expenses, personal attendants, electricity and water, concessional education, gift vouchers, etc.

However, with the fringe benefit tax (FBT) introduced under the Income Tax Act 1961 as amended by the Finance Act 2005, benefits and perquisites have become taxable and have lost their tax advantage to a great extent. The FBT is to be paid by the employer on the value of fringe benefits and expenses like training and development, free medical samples, conferences, and travel between two different offices. Free holidays given to employees and their families or airline tickets for a weekend getaway, whether as a reward for high performance or as an incentive extended to select or senior level employees to stay with the organization, are also covered. Earlier, such privileges did not attract any tax either for the employee or for the employer. Organizations usually booked the cost incurred on such employee benefits under conveyance and travel or tour expense. The FBT will now apply to such LTA that is over and above the salary package. Employers will have to pay FBT on all expenses incurred to provide facilities to employees. These include facilities such as garden, library, TV set, school, cable connection,

reimbursement of expenses on books and periodicals to employees. These affect employees at all levels.

The FBT has led organizations to rethink and rework the new costs of benefits and design the compensation package/salary structure so that its impact is minimized in both monetary and administrative terms. Organizations need to analyse the manner in which the employer calculates the cost-to-company (CTC) figure. This is important because the compensation figure quoted to employees is the CTC while the gross salary figure is different, resulting in a different inflow for employees. If the CTC figure includes the FBT element, then, in effect, the employee bears the expense, as the tax liability on the employee goes up. Though the FBT is to be paid by the employer, there is thus likely to be an indirect impact on the employees.

Organizations might structure employee salaries to avoid paying FBT and, so, to reduce tax liability. Flexible compensation packages, which are seen as providing flexibility to the employees to structure their own salaries as well as to optimize their tax liability, could see a major rationalization in the items of pay allowed in the package. It is likely that employers shall consolidate salary heads to avoid FBT. Until now, the consolidated pay packet under one broad head was restricted to the top management of an organization as they got more perquisites that were taxable under the FBT. Any change from a reimbursement to an income in the structuring of salary will lead to an increased tax burden for the employee. If reimbursements are converted into a direct payment, then the tax on the employee will increase.

every executive at the same level in the organization received the same salary. This type of compensation structure has undergone a change. Reimbursements under different heads have virtually ended. The variable component has increased, sometimes being as high as 35% of the total compensation. However, in a BPO firm, the salary is uniformly structured, and consists of a basic salary and a bouquet of allowances—house rent (HRA), leave travel assistance (LTA), and medical—that employees have the flexibility to allocate. The fringe benefit tax has affected the structuring of benefits.

Segmentation This is a new approach to designing or structuring employee benefits. Organizations are beginning to recognize that different employees have different preferences, work for different reasons, and are motivated by different things. It is, therefore, important to customize not only the benefits but also the compensation packages. Organizations segment the employees into categories and customize the compensation package based on what employees of that category want. A 25-year-old employee may be open to risk in salary and prefer stock options; a 45–year-old may prefer a more stable income and hence avoid stock options. Young employees want work–life balance, and would not like to wait for retirement to go on an adventure vacation. In mid-career, employees prefer training and education. Retired employees, if they continue, prefer to work part-time. It is important that organizations adjust their compensation and benefits to these realities. A Boston-based consulting firm proposed six categories of employees and identified their characteristics and reward preferences (see Table 8.4).

All these employee categories exist in every organization in almost equal proportion. Generally, traditionalists form the largest proportion. Human resource departments of organizations cannot create benefit packages for each of these six categories, especially because they are scattered across the organization, and therefore should customize packages for different functions and business units, where one or the other of these employee categories dominates. For example, in BPO 'stalled survivors' dominate. Hence, the benefit package of BPO firms should be high on flexibility and low on security. The organization may want a certain type of individual in sales and another in R&D. There should be compensation and benefit packages designed to suit each one of them.

Non-financial Compensation: Components

The non-financial component of the compensation package is an important aspect; financial compensation is no longer the only differentiator. Intrinsic motivators, such as getting a challenging assignment, chance to do something worthwhile, etc. are as important as the financial package. These are the psychological rewards that employees get when they feel that others have

Table 8.4: Reward Preferences

Category of Employee	Characteristics and Reward Preference
Self-powered Innovators	▪ Impassioned and energized by their work ▪ Prefer to be given work that empowers them and enables them to learn and grow ▪ Less motivated by traditional rewards like additional compensation and vacation time
Fair and Square Traditionalists	▪ Reliable and loyal family people who desire traditional rewards ▪ Least interested in risky compensation packages containing bonuses and stock options ▪ Less interested in soft benefits like stimulating work, enjoyable workplaces, or flexible work arrangements
Accomplished Contributors	▪ Take pride in what they do, are team players ▪ Value comfort and security and prefer an environment that is co-operative, congenial, and fun
Maverick Morphers	▪ Young and restless, want flexible work schedules that allow them to pursue their own interests ▪ Prefer bonuses and stock options ▪ Organizations have to make efforts to retain them
Stalled Survivors	▪ Work is not the most important or satisfying part of their lives ▪ Younger employees who are getting married, having children, exploring alternative career avenues and viewing their current job as a temporary phase ▪ Prefer flexible work arrangements, added pay, and vacation time
Demanding Disconnects	▪ Feel disgruntled and dead-ended by lack of opportunity ▪ Struggle to make ends meet, hence place high value on traditional compensation and benefits

Source: The Economic Times, 12 August 2005

recognized their skills and contributions. For example, employees at the middle and senior levels want control over shaping the organization and making a difference to it. Top-level executives desire empowerment and clarity in the organization's vision. Information technology professionals prefer to work on high-end technology since their worst fear is to stagnate at a point in the learning curve and become redundant. Hence, the design of rewards for these employees should build in these factors. A major factor of employee retention is the quality of work that is being done by an organization. Technology companies that focus on R&D can offer their employees an opportunity to work on cutting-edge technology, which serves as an intrinsic motivator. This is one of the reasons that employee attrition in R&D firms is very low. Other than the quality of work, which serves the important objective of attracting and retaining scarce talent, it is also important to provide opportunities to develop careers. Intel is an example of a firm that provides such career development opportunities.

Recognition is the most reliable of all rewards. Recognition schemes are significant because they are a symbolic way of reinforcing the 'new' behaviour and performance desired by the organization. Also called 'special incentive awards', they are usually linked to the achievement of performance targets, and can be developed for groups, or for entire organizations. Recognition schemes often focus on rewarding high-performing employees. Organizations recognize employees by means of (1) awards; (2) recognition awards; and (3) service awards.

Awards

Awards may include cash merchandise, gift certificates, movie tickets, parties, dinner coupons for the family, travel awards to popular destinations, plaques, etc. Awards have a positive impact on performance on their own as well as when given in conjunction with financial incentives. Non-financial incentives have a higher motivational value than financial incentives. At NIIT, rooms in office buildings are named after employees chosen as high achievers.

Recognition Awards

Recognition award programmes recognize employees for their performance. For example, several organizations have 'employee of the month' and 'employee of the year' awards. In service industry enterprises such as hotels, restaurants, etc. guest comment cards are used as the basis for giving recognition awards to hourly employees. Recognition awards work best when the organization can demonstrate clearly how an employee was selected for the award, and when recognition is given to recognize specific performance that is important for the organization. Blue Dart declares the star performer of the month from among the operations staff for their monthly performance. 'Bravo Blue Darter' is an on-the-spot award given by the manager to his people for outstanding achievement in the course of their day-to-day work.

Service Awards

These reward employees for length of service, not for performance. For example, some organizations have long-service awards for which those employees who have completed a specified number of years of service in the organization become eligible.

Organizations are devising a range of reward and recognition programmes for employees. IBM has a global recognition programme called 'The Best of

IBM'. The programme rewards exploration, collaboration, and risk-taking behaviours. 'The Best of IBM' focusses on recognizing these behaviours, which IBM employees value most, and provides a way to reward, inspire, and motivate individuals. IBM employees can recognize each other through a 'Thanks Award' or an 'Appreciation Card'. Ideas and achievements that have an impact on business lead to a management reward, such as a 'Bravo Award' or an 'Ovation Award'. A few select employees get a Corporate Award for exceptional technical accomplishments that have value to IBM. Intel recognizes employees who have given their time to community service. Employees get a token of appreciation, either a plaque or a practical gift, at an event held in their honour. At Sasken, the recognition programme is built around goal achievement at three levels: individual, team, and organization. If an individual makes a contribution beyond the call of duty and if this contribution has a significant impact on business, customer or employee, then the individual is chosen as the 'achiever of the quarter'. A similar award is given to the 'team of the quarter'. Spot awards are also there for tasks that are appreciated by customers or peers.

COMPENSATION AND REWARDS—DETERMINANTS

The compensation received by an employee is proportional to the effort exerted by the employee, the nature of the job, and the skills of the employee. However, these are not the only factors that influence compensation. Several external and internal factors determine pay levels, that is, the individual financial compensation (Figure 8.3). For example, at Infosys, salary revisions are determined based on factors such as company philosophy, internal parity, external equity, and market dynamics.

External Determinants of Pay Levels

There are six external determinants of pay levels: (1) labour market conditions; (2) economic conditions; (3) area wage rates; (4) government controls; (5) cost of living; and (6) union influences.

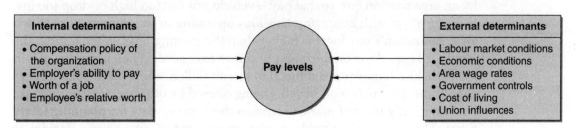

Figure 8.3: External and Internal Determinants of Individual Financial Compensation

Labour market conditions The forces of demand and supply for qualified people within an area influence wage and salary rates. When demand for human resources is high and supply is limited, wages and salaries are higher in order to attract and retain qualified employees. Employees with skills that are rare and valuable are in a strong bargaining position and command high compensation. A demand-supply mismatch in the market for software developers in India, especially at the entry and the middle level, has led to increase in salaries over the years. Salaries at the middle management level have grown by 15–18% for the past two years since 2004. When supply of human resources exceeds demand, organizations may lower wage rates or compensation levels. However, the full impact of supply and demand of human resources gets reduced under certain conditions. For example, even though supply of human resources may be high in a region and there may be high unemployment, unions may not allow employers to reduce compensation. Government regulations also ensure that employers do not reduce pay levels below a certain established minimum.

Economic conditions They are another external determinant of pay levels. For example, the degree of competitiveness of the industry affects an organization's ability to pay. The ability of the organization to pay reduces as the competitiveness of the industry grows. An organization's ability to pay is also a consequence of the relative productivity of the organization and of the industry. An organization that has high productivity will be able to pay more. Advanced technology, higher operational efficiency, a skilled workforce, or all of these can increase productivity.

Area wage rates The rates being offered by other organizations for similar jobs in the same geographical area influence an organization's wage rates, and therefore its ability to attract, recruit, and retain competent employees. IBM is a firm that offers competitive salaries. Wage surveys—the means of obtaining data about the wages and salaries paid by other firms for a particular job in a given labour market—provide the organization with the means to ensure that pay levels offered by it are equitable with other organizations competing for the same HR in the surrounding labour market. Wage surveys conducted by an organization ensure that pay levels do not rise too high or drop too low in comparison with other organizations operating in the same region. When an organization's pay level is higher than the existing level in the region, the employee cost of the organization becomes excessive. When its pay level falls too far below, it may find it difficult to recruit skilled employees. Wage surveys should also obtain data on benefits being offered by other organizations. Pepsi has historically utilized market remuneration survey data for planning salary hikes. The organization tracks market movement of salaries and decides to hike the salary of its employees based on market survey data. The salaries of managers may be moved to a higher percentile to stay competitive.

Government controls These influence the rate of pay through legislation such as the Minimum Wages Act 1948 and the Payment of Wages Act 1936 that establish minimum wage rates for certain categories of employees and also prevent discrimination. Taxation policies of the government with respect to executive compensation also affect the level and structure of compensation by providing guidelines. For example, organizations are offered allowances under different sub-heads to minimize their tax liability. However, several Indian firms use cost-to-company (CTC) pay packets. This is partially driven by lowering of tax rates, removal of tax exemption in many such allowances, and a rising interest among organizations to turn good citizens. Due to changes in the fringe benefit tax (FBT) in 2006, employers are looking at consolidating cash salary under one head rather than breaking it under various heads such as HRA, conveyance, medical, LTA, etc. (see Exhibit 8.2).

Cost of living Increases in the cost of living raise the cost of goods and services. Compensation rates are revised upward periodically to help employees maintain their purchasing power. These changes in compensation rates are made on the basis of the consumer price index (CPI). The CPI measures average change in prices of some fixed goods and services such as food, clothing, fuel, medical services, etc. over a period of time. Changes in CPI affect pay levels. Firms in IT that differentiate pay based on locations (though most IT firms do not have a high differentiation across locations) align it to differences in the cost of living and to the challenges of attracting employees to a particular location and retaining them there.

Union influences These are another determinant of pay levels. Union negotiations tend to establish the wage patterns for the region. Unions bargain collectively over working conditions and wage rates to obtain increases that are larger and more favourable than the established pattern in a geographic region. Wages are generally higher in those areas where organized labour is strong. This has an escalating effect on the compensation of other segments of employees.

Organizations are seeking help from compensation analysts to ensure that their compensation is at par with the external environment such as competition, geography, and industry growth rate (see Exhibit 8.3).

Internal Determinants of Pay Levels

There are four internal determinants of pay levels: (1) compensation policy of the organization; (2) employer's ability to pay; (3) worth of a job; and (4) relative worth of an employee.

Exhibit 8.3

Determinants of Compensation: Examples

Globalization Globalization has ushered in an era of higher compensation levels, restructuring of compensation packages, steep hike in annual salaries, and a trend towards competitive salaries. As Indian business houses go global, they are reworking their salary structures to make them comparable to those of MNCs. Examples include Bharti, Pantaloon, etc. This is primarily because Indian companies are hiring expatriates and also going global. Many of these firms are also willing to pay more for the same talent than MNCs.

There is a salary boom in almost all sectors, for example, retail, IT, and even hospitality. Depending on the sector, the average annual wage earnings of workers grew by 15–35% in 2005–06, and the aggregate salary bill of computer hardware companies rose by 36%. Software firms witnessed a rise of more than 35% in their salary bill in 2005–06 and the share of salaries in total expenditure was estimated at 56% in the same period. The rise in the salary bill of software companies is also because workers are better qualified than their counterparts in other industries. The IT majors in India such as TCS and Infosys reported growth in revenues in 2006. However, employee expenses also increased. The increase in staff costs have kept the operating margins of the big IT firms stagnant between December 2004 and December 2005, even though there has been a healthy increase in revenues. Salaries are likely to go up by 10–15% in 2007 and raise labour cost to over 55% of an organization's budget. If wage increases are not accompanied by productivity gains, India will lose her cost advantage.

Cross-sector employee movement Executive movement is no longer restricted to organizations within one sector. Competition for talent has gone beyond being sector-specific to being cross-sector. Cross-sector movement has made salary benchmarking more complicated. Earlier, a hotel benchmarked the salaries of its staff with other hotels to avoid attrition. Now, hospitality sector employees are being hired by airlines, BPO firms, healthcare companies, and even the telecommunications sector. Hence, salary levels have begun to reflect this cross-sector movement of executives. Benchmarking is being done across sectors to make the job offer financially lucrative. In some sectors, such as IT, organizations are benchmarking globally to retain talented employees because some MNCs with regional headquarters in India are offering globally comparable salaries to their employees and because many top managers being wooed for overseas postings have to be offered comparable salaries.

Characteristics of employees The changing profile of employees has also resulted in a change in the salary structures of organizations. The average age of employees has come down and hence organizations are searching for ways to structure salaries better suited to the needs of the employees. For example, younger employees may prefer cash in hand rather than retiree benefits. Organizations are factoring this aspect into their design of salary structures.

Compensation policy of the organization It determines the organization's ability to attract and retain employees. Organizations adopt different policies for compensating employees. The compensation policy of one firm may be to be an industry leader in pay while another firm may seek to be wage competitive.

An organization that pays higher wages and salaries than competing firms is the pay leader and attracts better workers and so achieves lower cost per unit of labour. Every organization should have a compensation policy that is related to what the competition is paying and to the internal wage relationship among jobs and skill levels. A firm may adopt the policy of paying the market rate, which is the average pay that most employers offer for the same job in a specific market or region.

Employer's ability to pay An employer's ability to pay employees and provide them benefits is an important determinant of pay levels. It is influenced by factors such as the budget available, profit of the organization, economic conditions, competition faced by employers, etc. Competition and recessions in the market result in cheaper goods and services, which, in turn, result in reduced income and hence limit an employer's ability to pay. Examples include the competition faced by internet service providers, mobile phone companies, etc.

Worth of a job It continues to be an important determinant of compensation levels in some organizations apart from market forces and internal company policies. When the job is the criterion for pay levels, organizations pay for the duties, responsibilities, working conditions, and effort required on the part of employees. The relative worth of jobs is determined and jobs with higher worth are paid more. Organizations that base their pay levels on the worth of the job rely on job evaluation. However, some organizations do not have a formal compensation programme. These organizations base job worth on the subjective opinion of people who are familiar with the jobs. In such a case, the pay rate is influenced by the labour market or by collective bargaining.

Employee's relative worth It determines pay levels and influences the notion of equity. In most organizations, merit raises are granted to all employees irrespective of performance. In such cases, employees are rewarded for being present physically on the job rather than for performance. However, many organizations have begun to link employee pay to performance. When individual compensation and reward is linked to employee performance, performance appraisal data provide the input for determining employee pay levels. The appraisal system differentiates high performers from low performers. High-performing employees are assigned higher worth relative to low-performing employees and are paid higher. An employee may be recognized and rewarded through promotion or other incentive systems for good performance. Table 8.5 outlines the pros and cons of linking individual rewards to employee performance. We shall discuss various pay-for-performance approaches in the next section.

Table 8.5: Performance–Reward Linkage

Pros	Cons
▪ Each employee is rewarded on the basis of individual output ▪ Individual performance–rewards linkage is motivational ▪ Employee has some control over total compensation	▪ May be counterproductive if appraisals are seen as unfair ▪ Increase in pay is not meaningful after pay for non-performance factors such as seniority and cost of living is subtracted from the increase ▪ Timing of rewards is tied to budget rather than to task accomplishment, reducing the motivational value of the rewards

Source: Bohlander 2001

COMPENSATION AND REWARDS—APPROACHES

Compensation and rewards are used by organizations as an important tool for attracting, recruiting, motivating, and retaining high-performing employees. Over the years, compensation approaches have undergone tremendous change. Organizations may choose one of two compensation approaches—traditional and contemporary—to achieve these goals (Figure 8.4).

Traditional compensation approach This approach compensates employees through job-based pay systems. These systems use job evaluation to determine the relative worth of each job, which helps determine the salary for the job. The advantage of the traditional compensation approach is that it is more defensible legally since compensable factors of the job are scientifically determined. However, the traditional compensation system has certain limitations. Employees are paid only for the performance of a specific job. This tends to limit workforce flexibility, especially when an employee is assigned some work outside of his or her job classification. The traditional compensation has

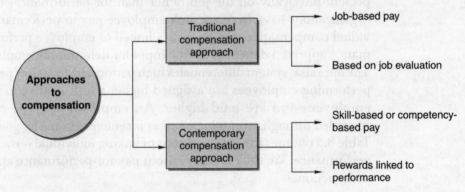

Figure 8.4: Compensation Approaches

several components, such as base pay, merit pay, market-based salary increases, incentives, and benefits. These programmes come to be viewed by employees as their entitlement and not something they can influence by their performance. The message conveyed is that pay has no connection with organizational performance. This results in a workforce that lacks motivation.

With changes in the nature of the organization, work, employee skills, etc. and with the interest of organizations in improving performance, the compensation approach should move beyond the traditional. In a competitive market that places high emphasis on productivity, traditional forms of compensation are no longer very attractive. The competitive business environment presents HR challenges relating to attracting, retaining, and motivating the workforce.

Contemporary compensation approach This approach attempts to place value on individuals rather than on jobs. Compensation in this approach is skill-based or competency-based. The need for the new approach is especially significant in the knowledge economy, where competitive edge results from HR. There is a need to compensate knowledge workers for their potential and for what they are capable of rather than what they actually do. The new approach links performance to reward strategies. The employees can influence their compensation through their performance. Compensation is no longer seen as entitlement. Compensation and reward systems have become less complicated, more homogeneous, transparent, and a lot more performance-driven.

PAY-FOR-PERFORMANCE APPROACHES

There are four pay-for-performance approaches: (1) merit pay; (2) variable pay; (3) skill-based pay; and (4) competency-based pay (see Figure 8.5). Merit pay and variable pay are the traditional approaches to compensation. Skill-based pay ad competency-based pay are examples of contemporary compensation approaches.

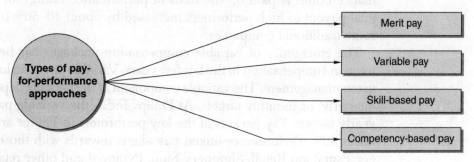

Figure 8.5:   Pay-for-Performance Approaches

Merit Pay

Merit pay is the pay increase given to employees based on their performance as indicated in the appraisal, and is the most widely used approach to reward individual performance. It is usually extended to reward an employee's performance over a period. The best performing employee gets the highest merit pay. Rewarding the best performer with the largest pay is highly motivating for the performer. In 2004, Shriram Pistons and Rings (SPR) rewarded its top performers with salary increases of 25–30% besides cash pay-outs and bonuses. LG has linked performance to pay to encourage a results-driven culture.

However, the approach has certain disadvantages. If the performance appraisal is perceived to be biased, merit pay will result in feelings of dissatisfaction and inequity. Another major disadvantage in merit pay increase is that it gets added to an employee's base pay permanently. Even if the employee's subsequent performance falls, he or she continues to receive the merit pay every year. Although several companies have merit pay, there is a movement toward variable pay.

Variable Pay

With high levels of competition confronted by organizations, it has become important that organizations control labour costs and also maintain high levels of employee performance. Variable pay meets these objectives by rewarding high performance. Rewards provided for good performance during a previous employment period are not added to the base pay; instead, a lump sum amount is given. Thus, apart from offering increases in basic salaries, organizations are offering cash incentives and year-end bonuses to high performers. Bonuses and incentive plans are a form of variable pay. This amount is not automatically carried over into subsequent performance periods. Variable pay, therefore, reduces the fixed cost related to employees' pay. Since many benefits, such as life insurance, retirement, etc. are tied to the base salary, variable pay also helps reduce the total cost of benefits. At WNS, a call centre, the performance bonus is paid on the basis of performance ratings for a period. The total payout to high performers increased by about 40–50% in 2004 even in some traditional companies.

The emergence of variable compensation packages has been the biggest trend in compensation in the last few years. Variable pay is no longer restricted to top management. The variable component of the package depends on yearly, quarterly, or monthly targets. At Philips India, the variable pay package has yearly targets. Pay packets of the key performers in Philips are increased by about 30%. Performance-linked pay aligns rewards with those of shareholders. Pantaloon Retail, Shoppers' Stop, Pyramyd and other retail majors have increased performance-linked incentives for their employees in 2006.

One problem associated with variable pay is that it places a percentage of an employees' compensation at risk. If employee performance exceeds the standard, variable rewards lead to significant increase. However, if performance is below standard, an employee's rewards get reduced. This risk of losing significant rewards if performance is below par leads to financial insecurity among employees and likely affects employee morale. Therefore, most organizations use variable pay as a supplement to merit pay and not exclusively.

Skill-based Pay

Skill-based pay is premised on the belief that employees who possess more knowledge and skills are more valuable to the organization and therefore should be rewarded accordingly; it compensates employees for job skills and knowledge and not for job titles. When skill-based pay is in place, employees performing several different types of jobs may receive the same pay rate or rewards. As employees acquire more skills, their compensation increases. Thus, skill-based pay encourages employees to learn continuously and gain additional skills. When they obtain additional skills relevant to the jobs, it results in an advantage for both the employee and the organization. For the employee, acquiring new skills leads to both tangible and intangible rewards, that is, pay increase, increase in employee worth, etc. Employees can increase their earnings as they increase their skills repertory. Several factors in the changing business environment have enhanced the importance of skill-based pay. Rapid technological changes and the need for flexible assignment of work require employees to have a broad range of skills. Moreover, downsizing and de-layering of the organizational structure have severely limited the promotional opportunities. Hence, it is important for organizations to provide growth opportunities within jobs and to find ways to motivate employees in ways other than promotions. Several firms have adopted this approach. These include both manufacturing and service companies such as GE, HP, Xerox, etc. At WNS, a call centre, skill allowances range up to Rs 2,400 per month. Often, skill-based pay is implemented as part of the 'job enrichment' programme. *Job enrichment* is the process of making a job more rewarding and satisfying by increasing the level of responsibility, promoting variety, providing more autonomy, and giving opportunities for personal growth. Job rotation—moving an employee from one job to another—is one approach used to enrich jobs. Employees are rotated through different jobs to acquire a range of skills. After employees master the skills in one team, they are rotated to jobs in another team and acquire more skills. Skill-based pay

- makes employees more flexible;
- enables employees to do each other's work by requiring them to learn a range of skills;
- increases variety in employees' tasks;

- increases employee motivation for training;
- bases pay and promotion on skills instead of seniority; and
- improves productivity and quality.

However, skill-based pay presents some challenges to the management.

- It requires an organization to have a well-designed training system to provide employees opportunities to enhance their skills.
- It increases the average rate of payment (although higher employee productivity offsets higher wages and salaries).
- It raises the challenge of continued motivation of employees who have reached their maximum level in a skill-based pay system.

Employees reach their maximum skill levels in about three years and begin to feel dissatisfied. Organizations may motivate them by providing incentives such as gain-sharing, or passing on to these employees, or savings from cost reductions or increased productivity, with them.

Competency-based Pay

As discussed in earlier chapters, competencies include not only skills and knowledge, but also factors such as motives, traits, attitudes, etc. Competency-based pay rewards employees for the expertise they bring to the organization. While other pay-for-performance plans focus on results, competency-based pay focusses on how the objectives are accomplished. Competency-based pay is discussed in more detail later in the chapter.

Apart from pay-for-performance plans, other employee-related factors determine pay and rewards (see Exhibit 8.4). Companies in IT and IteS are

---

Exhibit 8.4

Factors of Employee Rewards

Seniority It is the relative length of time an employee has been associated with an organization or job. Traditionally, compensation was linked to seniority. In contemporary times, however, performance is given priority over seniority. But, government organizations continue to use seniority as the basis.

Experience Employees are compensated for experience. Experience has the potential to enhance an individual's performance. However, this is possible only when the experience is relevant to the job in question.

Membership in the organization Some aspects of financial compensation are extended to all employees of the organization, irrespective of their performance, simply because they are part of the organization. Vacation days, life insurance, etc. are some examples.

Potential Some employees are paid for their potential to contribute, not for actual performance. When recruiting fresh graduates who have no experience, organizations offer compensation for the potential they bring to the organization.

basing and differentiating total rewards on specialized skills. Salary structures in these firms are a derivative of factors like skill, complexity of job, experience, productivity goals, and special domain or process expertise.

EQUITY IN REWARD DECISIONS

An organization that bases its compensation and rewards on employee performance or job evaluation would expect that it would result in employee satisfaction. It also appears logical to assume that higher the pay, higher the satisfaction. This, however, is far from the truth. The amount of pay is often less important than the perceived fairness or 'equity' of the pay or reward as a determinant of employee satisfaction. Equity is the perception of an employee that he/she is being treated and compensated fairly for what he/she does. A major determinant of an employee's productivity, satisfaction, motivation, commitment, and performance on the job is the degree of fairness (equity) and unfairness (inequity) that an employee perceives at work in comparison to others. Therefore, it is important that individuals responsible for designing compensation and reward systems understand how perceptions of equity and inequity are formed. J. Stacy Adam's Equity Theory helps understand the formation of these perceptions. According to the Equity Theory, people form perceptions based on two factors—inputs and outcomes. *Inputs* refer to the perception that an individual has regarding what (skills, knowledge, effort, and performance) he or she contributes to the job. *Outcomes* refer to the perception that an individual has regarding the returns he/she gets for the work he/she perform (pay, prestige, and recognition). Perceptions of equity and inequity result from a comparison of an employee's outcomes-to-inputs ratio (O/I) with another employee's O/I ratio. The person with whom an individual compares his or her own O/I ratio is called the 'significant other'. The significant other is usually a peer holding a similar job in the same organization, but sometimes also a person outside the organization; for example, a former classmate working in another organization. Consider a film actor who is dissatisfied with an offer of Rs 10 million for acting in a film, and demands more, not out of need or greed, but out of a perception of inequity, because another film star, who is not as successful or as acclaimed (or whom the first actor does not perceive to be as successful or acclaimed), commands Rs 20 million per film.

A common grievance in organizations relates to the perception of inequity. Often, an employee feels that he or she contributes the same effort compared to the significant other or better, yet receives a lower salary, bonus, or reward.

It is important that employees feel that their compensation or rewards are fair relative to their co-workers' who are in similar jobs in the organization as well as in other organizations. This holds true for base pay, variable pay,

	Self	**Significant other**
• Equity perception	$\dfrac{\text{Outcomes}}{\text{Inputs}}$ =	$\dfrac{\text{Outcomes}}{\text{Inputs}}$
• Inequity perception		
▫ Undercompensation Inequity	$\dfrac{\text{Outcomes}}{\text{Inputs}}$ <	$\dfrac{\text{Outcomes}}{\text{Inputs}}$
▫ Overcompensation Inequity	$\dfrac{\text{Outcomes}}{\text{Inputs}}$ >	$\dfrac{\text{Outcomes}}{\text{Inputs}}$

Figure 8.6: Perceptions of Equity and Inequity

benefits, etc. Since the performance of employees is often contingent on whether they perceive their compensation or rewards to be fair, organizations must strive for equity in compensation and reward. Equity in compensation and rewards exist when the O/I ratios of the individual and the significant other are perceived as equal. When the two ratios are perceived as unequal, an employee experiences inequity (Figure 8.6).

The key to understanding equity and inequity is *perception*. Comparisons of O/I ratios are based on individual perceptions. They may not be based on facts or reality, and are often based on incomplete or inaccurate information. Nonetheless, these perceptions affect employee motivation and performance. When employees perceive that their O/I ratios are less than that of their significant other, they feel underpaid. This is called *under-compensation inequity*. When their O/I ratios are higher than that of the significant other, they feel they are being overpaid. This is called *overcompensation inequity*. When an employee's O/I ratio is equal to that of the significant other, there exists a state of balance or equity.

Perceptions of inequity result in feelings of discomfort on the part of the individuals concerned. This, however, is true only of under-compensation inequity. Individuals who are overpaid experience little discomfort, and feel no need to reduce the discomfort, if any; they justify their outcomes by enhancing the symbolic value of their inputs. For example, an individual may not be assigned any job by the organization but may get the same bonus as other members of the organization. This individual may believe that the organization is gaining a lot by having him as a member, thereby inflating his own value.

When employees experience under-compensation inequity, they engage in certain behaviours to restore equity (Adams 1963); they

- decrease their inputs by reducing effort for performance; or
- attempt to increase outcomes by seeking a raise in salary; or

- distort their perceptions of their inputs and/or outcomes by persuading themselves that their O/I ratio is equal to that of the significant other; or
- attempt to change the inputs and/or outcomes of the significant other; or
- leave the organization.

Types of Equity

An equitable compensation and reward system must incorporate three types of equity: (1) internal; (2) external; and (3) individual (see Figure 8.7).

Internal Equity

It 'exists when employees are paid according to the relative value of their jobs within the same organization'. Employees should feel that differences in compensation levels between jobs are fair given the differences in job responsibilities. Job evaluation forms the basis for determining internal equity. If the sales manager feels that his pay is fair when compared with that of the production manager, there exists internal equity.

External Equity

It exists when the employees of one organization feel that they are paid comparably to employees who perform similar jobs in another organization. When a sales manager in a firm feels that his salary compares well with a sales manager, there exists external equity in another firm rates. To address external equity, an organization needs to determine the market relative to the industry, geographic region, or professional group. Market rates are determined by compensation surveys. The surveys should focus not only on base pay, but

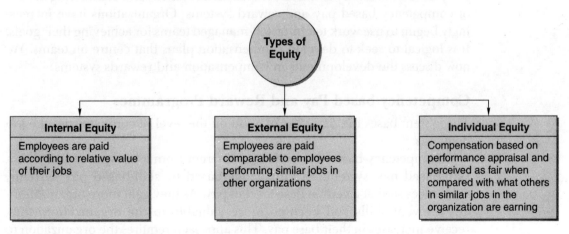

Figure 8.7: Types of Equity

also on other forms of compensation such as bonus, benefits, and incentive plans. This information on other forms of compensation is especially important for executive and managerial positions, though more difficult to obtain.

Individual Equity

It exists when an employee perceives that his or her pay is fair when compared with what co-workers are earning for similar jobs within the company, based on each individual's performance. Thus, individual equity is different from internal equity. Individual equity relates to performance differentials in job and is addressed through performance appraisal and various types of incentive pay. Pay differentials among employees in similar jobs can be based on several criteria. These may include experience, etc. Employees performing the same job may draw different salaries because of differences in seniority or years of job experience or tenure within the organization. Salary differentials may also be based on performance. Merit pay and variable pay are examples of the pay-for-performance approach, as already discussed. Skill-based and competency-based differentials in pay are other ways to address individual equity issues.

COMPENSATION AND REWARDS—NEW DEVELOPMENTS

Traditionally, compensation programmes were designed to reward employees for performing a set of assigned tasks, duties, and responsibilities. The specific requirements of the job determined the employees who would be paid more than the others. Employees who performed jobs that require greater variety of tasks, responsibility, more skills and knowledge, and more demanding work conditions received higher pay. However, many organizations are moving away from traditional job-based compensation systems and considering the use of competency-based pay and reward systems. Organizations have increasingly begun to use work teams or self-managed teams for achieving their goals. It is logical to seek to develop compensation plans that centre on teams. We now discuss the developments in compensation and rewards systems.

Competency-based Pay and Reward Programmes

The system bases the pay rates of a job on the level of competencies the job demands.

A competency-based pay system is different from a knowledge-based or a skill-based pay system. In knowledge-based or skill-based pay systems, employees start at a certain base level of pay. As they gain more organizationally-relevant skills and become more valuable to the organization, they receive increases in their base pay. This approach requires the organization to place a high emphasis on training and rotate employees through jobs.

A competency-based pay system is one in which employees are paid for the range of skills, knowledge, motives, attitudes, etc. that they bring to the job rather than for the job title they hold. Employees are paid for what they can do even if they do not have to do it now. It is people-based, not job-based. Competency-based system allows the top performers of an organization to be distinguished from other employees. Pay differentials are related to differences in level of competencies; they are not related to hierarchical levels. Thus, a competency-based system supports a flatter and more flexible organization.

The strategic goals of an organization are achieved through the employees, more specifically through the utilization of skills and competencies of employees. These skills and competencies, thus, become very important. All HR practices (training, appraisals, and rewards) should focus on nurturing these competencies in an integrated fashion. Competency-based pay is aligned with business goals. If an organization's emphasis is on developing a particular type of product, then the organization should reward employees based on the skills and competencies they develop for meeting the organizational goal. Thus, an employee is not paid only on the basis of the jobs to which they are assigned.

When an organization moves to a competency-based pay system, it must identify the required competencies for various jobs and then assign a value to various competencies. The steps that are usually followed in setting up a competency-based pay system are presented in Exhibit 8.5 and Figure 8.8.

Organizations still do not have a pure competency–development–pay increase programme. Progression through pay bands still relates to a mix of merit pay increase, job promotion increase, and development pay increase. A competency system needs to have a system to certify employees that they acquire certain competencies, and then to verify the maintenance of those competencies.

Competency-based pay has its detractors. The system is laborious and time consuming. Identifying competencies, their proficiency levels, and assessing employee competencies requires considerable investment of time and commitment on the part of the management. Another problem relates to implementation of the system. Competency-based pay results in higher HR cost since it involves paying employees for knowledge and skills they have even if these skills are not used. A competency-based pay system must communicate a clear link between new competency learning and pay increases to motivate employees. Its success will also depend on the value employees place on the increased pay associated with the new skills acquired. If competency development seems to be unrelated to pay, employees may not feel motivated to learn new competencies. Employees will do whatever they expect will most influence their pay than emphasize on an HR learning experience (competency development) that is difficult and seemingly unrelated to pay.

Exhibit 8.5

Steps in Designing Competency-based Pay System

1. Identify competencies and distinguish between proficiency levels
   - Identify competencies relevant to carrying out a particular function, for example, leadership, marketing skills, decision-making skills, etc.
   - Differentiate between competencies
     - Identify competencies that are important for excelling in the function.
     - Identify proficiency levels for each competency. For example, proficiency level 1 on a particular competency may indicate the employee has limited ability and knowledge of only basic facts. Level 2 may indicate partial proficiency. Level 3 may suggest that the employee is fully competent in the area.
   - Differences in the proficiency level of competencies are determined by establishing a relationship between competencies and variations in employee performance. The correlations help determine the relative impact that each competency has on performance.
   - Proficiency levels of competencies help establish a highly performance-oriented pay and reward system.

2. Assess the competency levels of job-holders
   - Assessing individual employee proficiency levels on different competencies by good measurement tools may be made through job simulation, behaviour rating scales, feedback from customers, self-report system, etc.

3. Create pay bands
   - In a competency-based pay system, pay bands replace salary grades.
   - An organization may have 5 to 8 bands. Each pay band is broad enough to contain a relatively wide range of jobs and salary levels.
   - Pay bands reflect the proficiency level of each competency.
   - These bands may reflect increasing levels of proficiency on competencies, increasing number of competencies, or a combination of both.

4. Develop a pay delivery system
   - In a competency-based pay system, pay increases are related to competency development.
   - When individuals enhance proficiency levels of their competencies, or learn more organizationally-relevant competencies, they progress from one pay band to another.

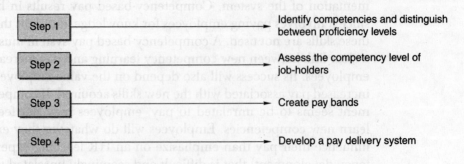

Figure 8.8: Steps in Developing a Competency-based Reward System

Team-based Pay and Rewards

Organizations have increasingly begun to use work teams or self-managed teams for achieving their goals. It is logical to seek to develop compensation plans that centre on teams. Changes in organization, such as lateral organizations, employee involvement, etc., have led to greater popularity and prevalence of team-based pay-for-performance or reward systems. These provide financial rewards to individual employees working within a formally established team. Team objectives or goals are specified and payments to each team member are linked to team performance. Thus, each team member gets a reward if the team achieves or exceeds its goals. The rewards may be in the form of cash, such as bonuses, or in the form of indirect compensation such as vacation, time off from work, stock ownership, etc. Team-based pay-for-performance plays an important role in motivating team performance. Team-based cash bonuses can also motivate individual performance. Compensation plans centred on teams serve as an incentive for team members to co-operate with each other and to be more adaptable when working with others in the pursuit of group and organizational objectives.

However, a team-based reward system may affect group dynamics, lead to intra-group conflict, and dampen enthusiasm if certain team members feel that certain other members are not doing their share of the work. Therefore, it is important to design and implement a team-based reward system carefully. When everyone in the team is paid the same amount, even though they possess different levels and types of competencies and demonstrate different levels of performance, many employees feel concerned about equity. It becomes important to determine how to compensate the individual team member for his or her personal contribution as well as the team's achievement. The three elements that constitute a team-based reward system are the

- individual, that is the basic pay that is linked to individual performance or skills/competencies;
- team, that is, linked to the achievement of team objectives; and
- organization, that is related to business performance measured as profit, or such criteria.

Many organizations use team rewards as a variable pay above the base pay. To determine base pay, individual compensation is based on skills or competencies. Hence, base pay will differ for different team members. Variable pay rewards for teams are linked to the achievement of team objectives and are paid annually. These are fixed amounts and not a percentage of base pay. To design a successful team-based reward system, base pay should be determined on the basis of skill or competencies of the individual employee, and variable pay should be based on the business performance of the organization, distributed among team members, and be of a fixed amount.

A team-based rewards system should focus on rewarding team performance beyond the satisfactory level, be constituted of add-on incentives, and should not substitute for base pay programmes. Some organizations couple individual and team incentives. A team-based rewards system may be implemented in an organization that values sharing, collaboration, cooperation, and open communication. It does not fit into hierarchical structures. Team culture cannot evolve if individual members of the team concentrate on promotions. Table 8.6 presents the advantages and disadvantages of team-based rewards.

A team-based rewards system requires the organization to determine the weights of team, individual, and organizational performance in the calculation of overall individual compensation. A combination of individual, team, and organization pay-for-performance plans works well when

- individual performance can be measured;
- individuals are part of a team;
- team performance is measured well; and
- the organization encourages individuals to participate in decisions affecting the entire organization.

If individual performance is difficult to measure, such as in situations where teams are highly interdependent, the focus should be on team and organizational performance.

There have been marked changes over the years in the way executive compensation is structured. Demand for executives, competition, increase in performance-based compensation, ownership ideas, etc. have contributed to these new trends in executive compensation.

Table 8.6:   Team-based Rewards System

Advantages	Disadvantages
- Overcomes the difficulty inherent in measuring individual contributions - Facilitates co-operation - Establishes a strong link between desired behaviour and rewards by awarding bonuses shortly after a project is completed - Motivates high-performing members to train other members when the team performs below the bonus-winning standard until all members are cross-trained and thus leads to skill development	- May foster unhealthy inter-team competition and conflict - May de-motivate hard workers if individual pay is perceived to be lower than proportionate to effort and also if under-performers earn as much as high achievers

TRENDS IN TOP-LEVEL EXECUTIVE COMPENSATION

Compensation for top executives has increased to unbelievable levels in the past few years. The compensation of chief executive officers (CEO) in India has touched global levels. There has also been a big shift in the way senior executives and CEOs are paid. There has been much innovation in structuring CEO compensation. It is also being benchmarked against other firms in the industry.

The employment contract between the organization and top-level executives is becoming complex and lengthy. Earlier, the contract did not look beyond compensation and standard working conditions. However, with increasing risks, both the organization and the employee are building in safeguards for themselves. For example, an organization introduced a penalty clause in the employment contract that required the candidate to pay Rs 1 million if he/she did not join the firm after having committed. Senior executives today demand that a 'golden parachute' clause be included in the contract when they believe that the project is too risky, or involves serious regulatory issues beyond the control of management, or when there is a risk that the company may change its business plan mid-way. Organizations are also using several techniques to retain executives. There is the 'retention bonus', which is worth approximately Rs 450,000–900,000. It is paid in advance and is for a 2–3 year period. If the employee leaves before that time, he/she has to return the allowance. Chief executive officers have begun to negotiate hefty severance pay packages when accepting a job offer from an organization. Severance pay is the compensation that an organization contracts to pay the CEO if it asks him/her to leave.

A CEO's compensation includes

- an employee stock option plan (ESOP);
- underwritten stock options;
- a retention bonus;
- a free residence (if the employee stays on, the organization gifts to the employee the house that he/she is living in);
- a sign-on bonus, to ensure commitment;
- a joining bonus or a 'golden hello' (to compensate the loss of the existing job);
- severance pay (if one party decides to rescind the contract, it will pay a certain amount to the other); and
- a pre-joining holiday.

The new FBT (2006) has brought about some changes in the bouquet of executive allowances (see Exhibit 8.2). Some CEO allowances (annual holidays, retention bonus, and ESOPs) that were outside the salary structure have now been included as part of salary or of CTC.

A look at the trends in CEO compensation suggests that it is structured to reward executives when the organization grows in profitability and in market value over the years. Chief executive officers are being offered a 'market premium bonus'. Such a bonus is a small percentage of revenue paid to the CEO if the company is listed in the top 25% of the stock market. Since CEO compensation falls in the high tax bracket, the structuring of the package is more important than the base pay per se. Organizations are providing long-term wealth creation opportunities in the form of incentives, retention pay, ESOPs, and deferred bonus plans. The components of executive compensation package include the base pay (salary), short-term incentives, long-term incentives, benefits, and perquisites. A brief overview of these components of executive compensation is presented in Exhibit 8.6.

The most popular form of performance-based long-term incentives for executives and CEOs is the ESOP. It gives them the option to buy a specific number of shares of the company stock at an advantageous/concessional price during a specified time. An ESOP has four stages: (1) the actual granting of the option; (2) vesting; (3) exercise (conversion of the options into shares); and (4) sale. The vesting period is the length of time that the restriction to sell the shares, levied at the time the options are given, applies. An executive can make a huge profit by exercising his/her stock option if he/she buys the shares in 2006 at a 2004 price, for example, if the price goes up. The rationale for

---

Exhibit 8.6

Components of Executive Compensation

Salary Executive salaries tend to vary by region, industry, size of the organization, type of job, etc.

Short-term incentives These are designed to motivate the short-term performance of managers and are tied to company profitability. The annual bonus is a short-term incentive. The bonus component of the compensation is tied to some performance measure. In a sales-driven firm, the bonus of the sales manager or business unit manager may be tied to the increase in sales territory, sales volume, or market share. Bonus payments may be as high as 35% of the manager's salary.

Long-term incentives These are designed to motivate executives to stay with the organization for a longer period. These allow executives to accumulate capital that can be encashed only after a few years, thus resulting in retention.

Benefits These may include health insurance, vacations, etc. However, executive benefits are often packaged differently from other employees'. For example, executive health plans may allow the executive to charge all medical bills (with no limit specified) to the company. The organization may also allow complete freedom to the executive in the choice of hospital or physician.

Perquisites Some special benefits for executives come in the form of non-cash perquisites. They serve to retain the executive by enhancing his/her status by means of visible symbols.

offering an ESOP is an assumption that the manager will work towards ensuring that the price of the stock rises. The stock price is a measure of organizational performance. However, stock price is not always in the management's control. General economic and market conditions play an important role. The senior executives generally negotiate for ESOPs during the hiring stage. Employee stock option plans

- make employees aware of the significance of creating value;
- align rewards with the creation of value as reflected in the market valuation of the company's stock;
- attract and retain talent;
- help organizations compete in the market for talented employees; and
- align individual goals with organizational goals.

Employee stock option plans became popular in the 1990s. Infosys was among the first Indian firms to introduce ESOPs as an incentive tool. The scheme was very successful as stock prices of technology firms soared. However, stock market fluctuations made ESOPs a less lucrative HR tool for attracting or retaining employees, particularly in the IT industry. Stock options were replaced by a highly flexible compensation package for high fliers in 2004, when organizations began customizing compensation packages and began asking employees how they would like to be paid. Infosys suspended the ESOP scheme in May 2003 and renewed cash rewards for employees. However, stock options made a comeback in 2006, and are being recognized as an integral part of senior executive compensation in industry. The advent of the FBT has contributed to this trend in some measure.

Several organizations, particularly large recruiters in the retail and telecommunications sectors, have started to rely on ESOPs to attract and retain talent. Though the term has come to be associated with young and new companies, several old and established organizations are also offering ESOPs. Punj Lloyd, GATI, Nagarjuna Constructions, etc. have announced ESOPs. The Government of India proposed in 2006 to offer liberal ESOPs when the entity that emerges from the merger of Air India and Indian Airlines makes its initial public offering (IPO). Most private sector banks that started operations in India in 1994–95, have liberal ESOPs. In the Indian banking industry, HDFC Bank and IDBI Bank used this compensation tool to attract senior executives from foreign banks during their initial years of operation. A proposal for ESOPs for public sector banks to reward and retain talent is on the anvil.

Organizations are also innovating ways to implement ESOPs. *Phantom stock option plans* allow executives to hold shares without owning them physically. These shares are held in 'units' and accumulate over time. These are also performance-based. At some time in the future, the executive can encash these units by receiving the value of the appreciation of the 'phantom' stock they own.

A *restricted stock option plan* allows the executive to hold shares without paying for it. The employee can sell the stock after it vests. If the executive leaves during the vesting period, he/she gives up the right to these shares.

Another innovation in ESOPs is one in which options come with assured returns, that is, the employer offers to pay the differential amount if the stock price is below the allotment price at the time of vesting (see Exhibit 8.7).

Exhibit 8.7

Innovative Stock Option Schemes

Phantom Stock Option Plan This is a form of deferred compensation. Each employee who participates in the plan is granted a certain number of stock units. One share in phantom stock has the same value as one share of the company's common stock. The employee does not earn anything from the phantom stock account for the vesting period. This promotes retention of employees. After the vesting period ends, the employee is paid a cash bonus on the basis of the appreciation of the stock or the growth in value of the company. However, while the employee is taxed on the cash bonus, the company gets a tax deduction. If the stock was valued at Rs 10 per share when the options were granted, and was worth Rs 20 per share when the bonus was paid, the employee must pay income tax on the gain of Rs 10 per share. Phantom stock options give benefits of stock options to employees without giving them the actual stock. One benefit of phantom stock is that the ownership rights of existing shareholders do not get diluted. These are beneficial when companies are unable or unwilling to alter their ownership structure but want to give employees incentive compensation tied to the length of time they stay with the company and how well the business performs. With phantom stock, employees receive the financial benefits of stock ownership without owning stock. However, phantom stock benefits are generally paid out in cash, therefore, they pose the problem of cash drain on the company.

Restricted Stock Option Plan In such a plan, stock is given to the employee in the form of a grant; he/she does not have to pay. Restricted stock options are called so because the executive is restricted from vesting them until he/she achieves certain revenue and profitability targets. If the restricted stock is awarded on the condition that the employee remains with the company for two years, those two years are the vesting period. If the stock is to vest when gross sales exceed Rs 1 billion, the vesting period will be as long as it takes for that target to be reached. At the end of the vesting period, the value of the stock is paid to the employee. For example, in a five-year scheme with 1,000 stock units, one-fifth, or 200 restricted stock units, each representing an equity share, shall vest at the end of every year. When the employee exercises the option, he/she gets the market value of 200 shares as cash in the salary at the end of each year. Restricted stock was popular in the early 1990s, later overridden in popularity by stock options, regained popularity in 2004.

The use of restricted stock options as a retention tool has led to changes in compensation models for IT companies. Stock options were awarded to almost all employees. However, restricted options are given to select employees. The selection of employees for restricted stock options is based on the performance of the employee. Only top performers are likely to be given restricted stock. Thus, this becomes the means of rewarding high performers. At the end of the vesting period, the restricted stock gets converted into equity and a tax liability arises in the hands of the employee, as these are counted as income.

Apple Computers and ExxonMobil are among companies that give its CEOs restricted stock and no stock options. At Apple, the CEO's compensation package for 2004 was US$75 million; however, all but US$1 was in stock that the CEO could not sell until 2006. Wipro introduced 'restricted stock awards' in 2004. It granted six million stock options to its middle level managers, who constituted 10–12% of its total workforce. The options had a vesting period of five years (encash 20% allotment each year) and a nominal exercise price. It was estimated that about 2000 employees of Wipro would be entitled to options worth Rs 20 lakh over a five-year period. Wipro's objective was to reward employees and to have a deferred salary component that locks the employee for some years. The scheme was believed to help the company retain the middle level managers. Other Indian software companies like Satyam, HCL Technologies, and Infosys are expected to introduce restricted stock units by the end of 2006. Microsoft announced a stock award scheme in 2004. HLL, the FMCG major, has also introduced a variation in the implementation of stock option plan. The scheme at HLL, introduced in May 2006, is called the 2006 HLL Performance Share Scheme. The objective of the scheme is retention of talent. The restricted stock scheme at HLL provides for conditional grant of performance shares free of cost to eligible management employees. Employees are prevented from immediate sale of shares. Unilever and American Express also offer similar stock grants to their employees. Information technology and multinational companies have also adopted stock award schemes. Under these schemes, shares are given at concessional rates to employees. Stock awards differ from ESOPs in that the base for stock awards is the real value of shares rather than the perceived value of options, as in ESOPs. See two examples of innovative stock option schemes in Exhibit 8.7.

It is important to link rewards to business strategy of the firm. Incentives provided to executives give signals about what will be rewarded by the organization. This is likely to make an impact on the success of business strategy. Let us now discuss the linkage between business strategy and compensation.

BUSINESS STRATEGY AND COMPENSATION

The past few years have been witness to an increasing alignment of HR strategy with business strategy. In earlier chapters, we have discussed the linkage between the HR practices of an organization and its business strategy. There is a growing recognition that compensation and reward strategy must also complement organizational strategy. The objectives of an organization's reward strategy are to motivate employees to perform better and to reinforce those employee behaviours that contribute to the achievement of organizational objectives. This linkage has always been implicit in discussions of compensation and reward strategy. However, it is only recently that systematic efforts have been made to identify appropriate compensation and reward strategies for different organizational strategies. The linkage between reward strategy and business strategy focusses on identifying behaviours needed to achieve organizational objectives. In turn, compensation and reward systems that elicit these behaviours can be identified and implemented. For example, an organization that achieves its objectives through work groups or self-managed teams should have team-based pay and reward systems. The design of an effective reward system requires a close association and relationship between HR strategies and pay strategies and between compensation strategy and organizational strategy. The linkage assumes that individuals direct their effort toward achieving the strategic objectives of the organization through the compensation system. When properly designed, the compensation system contributes to organizational effectiveness. Thus, it is important to understand the role that compensation can and should play in the strategic plan of the organization.

Gomez-Mezia and Welbourne (1988) defined compensation strategy as 'the repertoire of pay choices available to management that may, under some conditions, have an impact on the organization's performance and the effective use of its human resources'. In other words, the compensation strategy of an organization determines the conditions under which employees are rewarded. The degree to which various compensation or pay choices will be successful will depend on the conditions or contingencies facing the organization at a given point of time. The repertory of pay/compensation choices can be grouped into three strategic compensation dimensions: (1) the criteria or bases for determining pay levels; (2) the design of the compensation system; and (3) the administrative framework. Table 8.7 details these dimensions, as well as the compensation choices relevant to each dimension.

Table 8.7: Dimensions of Compensation

Compensation Dimensions	Description
1. Bases for Determining Pay Levels	
Job or Skill	The traditional job-based system is based on job evaluation. Skill-based pay focusses on individual skills rather than on the job.
Performance or Seniority	Rewards may be based on performance or on seniority.
Individual Performance or Group Performance	Rewards and pay may be based on individual performance or on group performance. Organizations prefer to use both as the basis.

Contd

Table 8.7 Contd

Compensation Dimensions	Description
Short-term Orientation or Long-term Orientation	Rewards may be based on the short-term objectives and performance of the organization or on its long-term objectives and performance.
Predilection to Risk or Aversion to Risk	High-growth firms may use rewards to encourage individual risk-taking, while mature firms may align rewards with risk aversion.
Compensation Level or Market	Comparison of the total compensation package with the competition through wage surveys, benchmarking, etc.
Internal Equity or External Equity	Rewards may be designed to ensure internal equity or to ensure external equity.
Hierarchy or Egalitarianism	An organization may link money and perquisites with movement up the corporate hierarchy or de-link the two and pay for performance and capabilities.
Fixed Pay or Incentives	Mature firms may emphasize higher fixed pay and offer more security. High-growth firms may encourage more risk by offering higher incentives and low base pay.
Quantitative or Qualitative Measures of Performance	Firms may use objective (quantitative) or subjective (qualitative) measures to measure organizational performance. Firms growing through mergers and acquisitions should use objective performance measures, while firms trying to be 'first movers' in new product and market areas should utilize subjective measures of performance.
2. Design of Compensation System	
Bonuses or Deferred Compensation	Firms that focus on short-term performance may pay frequent bonuses. Firms that focus on long-term performance may defer compensation.
Intrinsic Rewards or Extrinsic Rewards	Firms may focus on intrinsic rewards (achievement, recognition, and job satisfaction) or on extrinsic rewards (incentives).
3. Administrative Framework	
Centralized Pay Administration or Decentralized Pay Administration	Pay decisions may be controlled by corporate headquarters (centralized pay administration) or by plants, divisions, etc. (decentralized pay administration).
Open Pay or Secret Pay	Firms may keep pay issues open (thereby encouraging communication and involvement) or secret (thereby diminishing trust).

Contd

Table 8.7 Contd

Compensation Dimensions	Description
Inclusion of Employees in Pay Decisions or Exclusion of Employees from Pay Decisions	Firms may or may not encourage employees to participate in pay decisions. Firms that employ non-traditional compensation systems and highly knowledgeable workers include employees in the process to decide pay; firms that are bureaucratic do not.
Bureaucratic Pay Policies or Flexible Pay Policies	Compensation system may be highly formalized and inflexible or it may be flexible. Compensation system should be formalized, but flexible enough to allow for changes. However, too frequent a change in pay system can lead to lack of alignment with organizational strategy.

Source: Gomez-Mejia and Welbourne 1988

Some of these compensation dimensions are associated with each other; when they are, basic combinations or patterns of compensation or pay decisions result. Gomez-Mezia and Welbourne (1988) created a typology of compensation dimensions based on relationships among the three compensation dimensions. Two clear compensation patterns were identified: (1) mechanistic; and (2) organic (see Table 8.8). These strategic patterns of compensation may apply to a variety of organizations and environmental conditions.

Table 8.8:   Strategic Compensation Patterns

Mechanistic Compensation Strategies	Organic Compensation Strategies
▪ Make pay decisions routine ▪ Applied uniformly across the entire organization	▪ More responsive to changing conditions, contingencies, and individual situations
Basics for Pay ▪ Pay for job performed, not employee skills ▪ Emphasis on seniority-based pay ▪ Base salary related to individual performance appraisals ▪ Internal equity ▪ Foster hierarchical emphasis ▪ Minimum risk-taking ▪ Quantitative performance measures ▪ Short-term focus	**Basics for Pay** ▪ Pay for skills ▪ Pay for performance ▪ Both group and individual appraisals ▪ External equity ▪ Egalitarian ▪ High risk-taking ▪ Long-term focus

Contd

Table 8.8 Contd

Mechanistic Compensation Strategies	Organic Compensation Strategies
Design to Pay ■ Pay higher than the market rate ■ Fixed pay more than incentives ■ Frequent bonuses ■ Intrinsic rewards	**Design of Pay** ■ Pay less than the market rate ■ High incentives in pay mix ■ Use of bonuses and deferred income ■ Extrinsic rewards
Administrative Framework ■ Centralization ■ Secrecy of pay ■ Lack of employee participation ■ Bureaucratic policies	**Administrative Framework** ■ Decentralization ■ Open pay policies ■ High employee participation ■ Flexible compensation programmes

Source: Gomez-Mezia and Welbourne 1988

It is necessary to pay attention to certain issues to understand the linkage between compensation strategy and organizational strategy. For example, it is necessary to understand the relationship between strategic employee groups in an organization and the compensation strategy. The strategic significance of different employee groups varies according to industry and firm characteristics. Scientists and engineers may be crucial in influencing compensation strategies of high-technology firms. However, this employee group may not be as important when designing pay systems for mature manufacturing organizations. It is also likely that compensation strategy may differ for different functional areas such as marketing, finance, or R&D. Similarly, pay and reward systems for professional, semi-skilled, and unskilled employees can be quite different.

We have already emphasized that the compensation strategy must complement the business strategy of the organization. Efforts to identify appropriate compensation systems for different organizational strategies have focussed on the (1) typology of business strategy; or (2) type of industry; or (3) organizational life cycles.

Typology of Business Strategy

The most common approach to theorizing about compensation strategy is to categorize organizations by business strategy, based on a chosen typology (such as that of Miles and Snow or of Porter). Subsequently, the compensation features most appropriate for firms in each category are delineated. The question that needs to be answered is: which organizational strategies are related to mechanistic and organic compensation strategies? The *mechanistic compensation strategy* is likely to be used by organizations that are secure in their present business and current product. When expanding, these organizations prefer to grow into a similar business by utilizing their expertise. Mechanistic pay patterns are associated generally with organizations following the defender and maintenance business strategies. As discussed in Chapter 1 (Miles and Snow typology of business strategy), defenders are concerned with maintaining their current market share. Organizations following a maintenance strategy are also concerned with retaining their current position in the market. The primary concern of the business unit is with existing products and markets.

The *organic compensation strategy* is likely to be used by organizations that are at a stage of early growth and are preparing for rapid expansion along a narrow product line. It is also used by organizations that are in a stage of mature growth when they acquire businesses unrelated to their current business or product through acquisitions and mergers. Organic compensation patterns are associated with the prospector and dynamic growth strategies. The prospector strategy involves searching for new products and markets and pursuing opportunities both within and outside the existing domains of expertise. The dynamic growth business strategy is to take on significant and frequent financial risks. Thus, the prospector and dynamic growth strategies are opposite to the defender and maintenance strategies associated with the mechanistic compensation strategy.

The mechanistic and organic compensation strategies represent the two ends of a continuum. There is also the possibility of a third compensation strategy, which is at the mid-point of this continuum, called the mixed *compensation strategy*. It is associated with the 'analyser' business strategy. The analyser strategy is used by firms operating in both stable and growing markets. The mixed strategy is also associated with firms that follow the dominant product strategy. The dominant strategy is followed by organizations that are not very diversified and that earn their revenue primarily from a single dominant product. These firms may be in a transitional stage. Therefore, they need a compensation strategy that can provide both control and autonomy. A summary of the linkage between business strategies and compensation strategies is presented in Table 8.9.

Many compensation theorists propose the concept of 'fit' between corporate strategy, HR strategy, and compensation strategy. According to this perspective, optimal conditions for organizational success result from a best fit between business and compensation strategy. However, the 'fit' perspective may suggest rigidity. Determining compensation features most appropriate for firms in each category of business strategy results in an 'ideal' type in terms of pay strategies for each strategic grouping (e.g., prospectors, defenders, analysers, etc.) One drawback in the use of typology of business strategy in compensation strategy is that few organizations can be neatly classified by business strategy. Most organizations use a combination of business strategies. Hence, business strategy

Table 8.9: Business Strategy and Compensation Strategy Linkage

Business Strategy (Miles and Snow Typology)	Compensation Strategy
Defender Strategy (maintain current market share) **Characteristics** ■ Maintenance strategy ■ High commitment to existing product ■ Expand in current product areas and in related areas of expertise ■ Obtain high percentage of revenue from a single business or product ■ Mature companies	*Mechanistic Strategy* ■ Provide pay package and policies to maintain in-grown talent needed to enhance the existing business ■ Reward work experience with the firm or seniority because long tenure with the organization provides expertise to preserve the current business strategy
Prospector Strategy (actively search for new products and markets and pursue opportunities both within and outside current area of expertise) **Characteristics** ■ Dynamic growth strategy ■ Take financial risks ■ Use acquisitions and mergers for expansion ■ Use unrelated business strategy to grow ■ Diversify by entering new markets	*Organic Strategy* ■ Seek external equity in compensation strategies ■ Reward patterns control outcomes (achievement of goals) rather than evaluate behaviour used to attain goals ■ Seek to minimize fixed costs due to fast growth and risks associated with business ■ Higher level of incentive pay
Analyser Strategy (limited diversification and dependence on a single product) ■ Dominant product strategy	*Mixed compensation strategy* ■ Provides both control and autonomy

Source: Gomez-Mejia and Welbourne 1988

typology linkage with compensation strategy at best provides a general direction; it cannot be prescriptive. Though a fit is desired, strategies that are appropriate today may become inappropriate tomorrow. Therefore, management should be careful when developing ideal compensation strategies since these could easily become obsolete. This issue is especially significant, because once a reward system is in place, employees develop a set of expectations. This makes it difficult to change the reward systems.

For a particular business strategy, there are a variety of approaches that can be used to achieve the goals of that business strategy. For example, an organization operating in a very competitive environment and manufacturing a standardized product may follow a cost leadership strategy. Several approaches are available to achieve the goal of cost leadership. For example, one firm may adopt the lowest price approach. Another firm may develop innovative product and process changes that reduce manufacturing costs. Thus, the same goal of cost leadership may be achieved by following different ways. When an organization follows the cost reduction business strategy, rewards should be linked to improved profit margins. Reward systems for the same business strategy, that is, cost leadership strategy, will then have different emphases, depending on the approach to achieve cost leadership. This view supports the contingency perspective.

Another aspect of business strategy and compensation strategy linkage and one that supports the contingency view relates to the components of a compensation programme, that is, base pay, incentives, and benefits. The *base salary*—the fixed component that is adjusted annually—must be market-driven to attract and retain employees. However, managers with different abilities command different prices in the pay market. Different organizations require different levels of expertise depending on their strategy and their environment. Organizations that have an environment of uncertainty and change need to give greater attention to their staffing. These organizations must pay higher-than-average base compensation in order to attract the top candidates, that is, those who have high technical competency and can cope better with uncertainty.

The *incentive component* plays a key role in the successful achievement of business strategies. Incentives have the potential to motivate managers to carry out the activities that are significant for accomplishing organizational goals. Incentives should be tied to behaviours that are critical for achieving organizational strategy. The same business strategy, for example, cost leadership strategy or the differentiation strategy, might require differences in approach by different organizations. The incentive programme must be designed to support the particular approach of the business strategy followed by the organization.

Type of Industry

Firms in technology-intensive industries, and in emerging and rapidly-growing industries, adopt different compensation strategies.

Technology-intensive Industry

High-technology firms develop compensation strategies that are congruent with the culture of innovation. Some attributes are characteristic of high-technology firms (see Exhibit 8.8).

The business strategies followed by high-technology firms are of innovation or creative destruction in order to be the first to the market. The attributes of high-technology firms pose several challenges for the HR function, such as

---

Exhibit 8.8

Attributes of High-technology Firms

- The product is at the cu tting edge of technology
- High priority is given to R&D personnel
- High rate of turnover for R&D personnel
- Innovations introduced at frequent intervals
- Concentration in geographic 'technology centres' (Hyderabad, Bangalore, Silicon Valley)

- Profile of employees characterized by high need for achievement, drive to succeed, willingness to take risks, high tolerance for ambiguity, and weak loyalty to the firm

---

attracting and retaining R&D personnel when turnover rates are very high, rewarding the performance of R&D personnel, etc. The attributes of high-technology firms and their business strategies require a compensation strategy that will facilitate the successful management of these firms in the light of the constraints and challenges that they face. High-technology firms that adopt a certain profile of compensation strategies have a more effective pay system than those high-tech firms that do not adopt this profile. This profile of compensation strategies is characterized by greater emphasis on the individual rather than the job, more risk sharing, an external market orientation, discretion in making pay decisions, emphasis on aggregate incentives, and a longer time orientation. Thus, the compensation strategies most likely to be utilized by these firms are individual-based compensation; risk-sharing; market-driven pay; higher discretion; aggregate incentives; and time-orientation (Figure 8.9).

Individual-based compensation strategy It rewards employees in high-technology firms for their skills, knowledge, and ideas. Compensation strategy is, thus, employee-based. Knowledge workers should be rewarded for their contribution to innovation and not for their position in the organizational hierarchy.

Risk-sharing compensation strategy It is used by high-technology firms to reduce risk by having employees share part of the performance uncertainty with the organization. Employees do this by accepting less secure income, that is, by earning a large percentage of their salary in the form of variable pay and incentives. This helps the organization reduce labour costs. Risk sharing is reflected in compensation strategies such as, performance-related pay, variable pay, and market pay policy.

Market-driven pay It enables high-technology firms maintain external equity in their pay system by paying their employees based on external comparisons. High-technology firms depend heavily on human capital, or knowledge workers. It is important for these firms to be responsive to the market

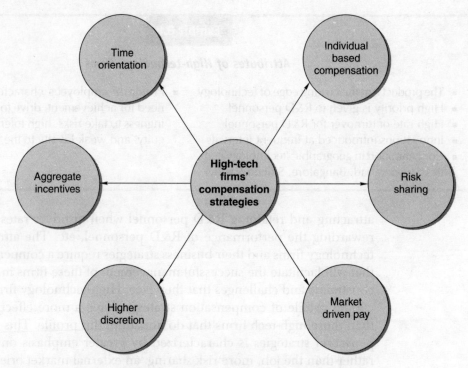

Figure 8.9: Compensation Strategies of High-technology Firms

value of each individual. If best performers are not paid according to their market value, they may leave the organization for more lucrative offers made by competitors. The market for high-technology talent evolves rapidly. Therefore, the firm needs to respond quickly to attract critical employees and retain high performers.

Higher discretion Higher discretion in compensation strategy is appropriate for high-technology firms. This suggests higher latitude in decision-making when making pay allocations. Rigid compensation systems that do not permit exceptions to existing norms are not applicable to these firms. When judging the performance of R&D workers, many factors need to be considered. These include difficulty of task, ideas generated, integration in a team, etc. A centralized rigid system does not allow a consideration of these factors.

Aggregate incentives These are appropriate to the characteristics of high-technology firms. Aggregate incentives are financial rewards linked to the performance of teams as opposed to individual incentives that depend on individual employee performance. Most high-technology firms are work-group based where employees work in teams for accomplishing a project. Therefore, it appears more natural to link rewards to group performance.

Time orientation It is used by high-technology firms to reward employees. These firms emphasize long-term incentives. Long-term incentives serve some purposes for the organization. These include increase in employee retention since an employee who changes the organization has to forfeit certain accrued gains. This makes it expensive for employees to change jobs.

Thus, the compensation strategies of high technology firms are unique and distinguish them from that of other companies.

Emerging and Rapidly-growing Industries

Emerging and rapidly-growing industries are defined as 'those industries that are newly formed or revitalized industries that have been created by technological innovations, changing cost factors, or new consumer demands that elevate a new product or service into a potentially attractive business opportunity' (Porter 1980). For example, in the 1980s, financial services and personal computing were emerging industries. In the 1990s, IT and ITeS were emerging industries, and in the decade starting 2000, the retail sector, insurance, and outsourcing are emerging industries. The characteristics of emerging industries are presented in Exhibit 8.9.

Rapidly-growing firms have certain characteristics that place some constraints on HRM programmes. All HRM practices, including rewards, must support the organization's growth goals. These attributes of rapidly-growing firms have an impact on the design of the reward system (see Table 8.10).

Exhibit 8.9

Characteristics of Emerging Industries

- Operate in growing markets where most potential consumers do not have the product, but there is an increasing demand for the product
- Growing market opportunities attract many competing firms
- Intense competition among rival firms creates risk and uncertainty
- Few firms survive till the industry reaches maturity
- May follow an internal growth strategy by expansion within a single product line or by diversification into a related product line
- Firms are in the growth stage of the organizational life cycle

- Competitive strategy focusses on increasing market share in a high-growth market, getting there first by creating an entry barrier for rivals (having a dominant comparative position in relation to competitors in the market), and/or holding relative position in a high-growth market (meeting the growth in demand for the product or service produced by the firm)
- Short-term profits sacrificed for higher long-term profits
- Fast- or rapid-growth firms
- Small to medium in size

Table 8.10:   Rapidly-growing Firms and Reward Systems

Characteristics of Rapidly-growing Firms	Characteristics of Reward Systems
▪ Business decisions must be made quickly and under conditions of incomplete information because the organization is new ▪ Organization must foster teamwork to facilitate information-sharing and making it available to decision-makers ▪ Involves taking risks under conditions of uncertainty because decisions must be made quickly	▪ Foster risk-taking by providing rewards proportional to the risks assumed by the employee ▪ Rewards should be market driven ▪ Foster teamwork and cooperation
▪ Expanding job demands as new responsibilities are added to jobs ▪ Result in long work hours	▪ Rewards tied to unit or company success
▪ Change is inevitable. Employees need to adjust to changing work relationships, working conditions, products, etc.	▪ Flexible reward system ▪ Rewards should recognize growth goals
▪ Scarce resources	▪ Provide for long term rewards contingent on company success and times for when resources are more plentiful

Source: Balkin 1988

The reward system for rapidly-growing firms consists of base salary, benefits, short-term pay incentives, and long-term pay incentives. The incentives component is an important part of the overall reward package for a rapidly-growing firm, but not for a mature firm. The incentives are tied to the growth of the firm since it is growing rapidly. The general characteristics of the pay/reward components of rapidly-growing firms are presented in Table 8.11.

Organizational Life Cycle

Organizations in the birth, growth, mature, or decline phases choose different strategic directions at each phase because they confront different opportunities in their external and internal environments. Table 8.12 suggests that compensation strategy has to be adapted to the overall business strategy of each stage of the organizational life cycle. The pay mix (base salary, incentives, and benefits) varies as an organization moves from the growth stage to the mature stage.

Table 8.11: Reward System Components of Rapidly-growing Firms

Reward System Components	Characteristics
Base Pay/Salary	■ Pay level at market rates to successfully recruit new employees and to attract experienced employees from mature firms ■ External pay equity, that is, competitive pay ■ Job evaluation used only to rank jobs based on internal worth, not for pricing the jobs
Benefits	■ Competitive with other benefits programmes available in the market ■ Profit-sharing plan to fund retirement benefits. Profit-sharing plan puts a portion of employee benefits 'at risk' which fits with the moderate risk-taking expected of employees during rapid growth. Mature organizations fund retirement benefits based on a fixed funding formula. Fixed funding can drain the resources of fast-growth firms ■ ESOPs
Short-Term Pay Incentives	■ Place a significant portion of the employees' total compensation 'at risk' ■ Individual pay incentives such as merit-pay ■ Aggregate or group-level incentives such as cash-bonus ■ Team-based incentives such as group bonus to reward and reinforce teamwork and high productivity work norms within the group. It is a one-time cash payment (given as a percentage of base salary) and is tied to a significant group accomplishment ■ Profit-sharing to reward organizational performance. Useful as a cash reward distributed to employees so they can share in company success
Long-term Pay Incentives	■ Recognition and reward of key employees who make major contributions to the success of the firm ■ ESOPs

Source: Balkin 1988

When a firm is at the growth stage, product innovation is viewed as the best way to get established in a particular industry. High-technology firms that are in the growth stage search for new products that are based on technology that is more advanced than the existing technology with the objective of penetrating markets controlled by mature firms, and in which mature companies have invested heavily in existing routine technologies. Firms at the growth stage invest significant time and money in R&D since these firms are focussed on launching new products in the market. Therefore, these firms rely heavily on

Table 8.12: Organizational Life Cycles and Compensation Strategy

Organizational Life-Cycle	Compensation Strategy
Start-up Stage	■ Low base pay (to conserve cash) ■ High emphasis on incentive pay (to emphasize performance and to share results of growth) ■ Low benefits (to control costs)
Growth Stage	■ High dependence on incentive pay to attract and retain R&D scientists and engineers ■ Stock options, profit sharing, bonus
Mature Stage	■ Less likely to use incentive pay strategy
Decline Stage	■ High base salary and benefits (high fixed costs) ■ Less flexibility to offer pay incentives

incentive-based compensation for scientists and engineers involved in R&D, to attract and retain this employee group. Employees in R&D may be willing to accept the short-term risks inherent in working for a firm that is not yet established in expectation of long-term rewards.

Firms that have reached the mature stage are less likely to use an incentive pay strategy. Mature organizations use well-established and routine technologies which they are reluctant to change because of high associated risks. These firms are conservative and growth is less rapid. At this stage, product innovations do not play a major role. In the last stage, that is, the decline stage, organizations face declining product demand in the external market(s) (Table 8.12). They are likely to pay a high salary and benefits but less likely to offer pay incentives.

TOTAL COMPENSATION AND REWARDS STRATEGY

A compensation and rewards strategy aims to attract, retain, and motivate workers. It is a subset of an organization's HR strategy, which is aligned with business strategy. Therefore, the compensation and rewards strategy should also be aligned with business strategy so that it facilitates the accomplishment of organizational goals by reinforcing the behaviours needed to achieve these goals.

A total compensation and rewards strategy defines the compensation and rewards programmes, the individual elements of these programmes, and the ways in which the elements relate to each other to fulfill compensation and rewards objectives. A total compensation and rewards strategy is a statement of an organization's HR philosophy related to rewards, or the organization's compensation and rewards philosophy. It is important that organizations have a well-conceived total compensation and rewards philosophy that embodies the values and benefits of the organization. This philosophy should serve to guide the design of reward programmes as well as to measure their effectiveness. When a new compensation and rewards programme is being developed by an organization, or when the organization is refining the existing reward programme, the proposed design of the compensation and rewards programme should be viewed within the context of the total rewards strategy. This is to ensure that the design of the compensation and rewards programme does not conflict with the reward philosophy of the organization. For example, if the compensation and rewards programme strategy of an organization emphasizes teamwork as its core value, it will be incongruent with a compensation and rewards programme that rewards individual achievements exclusively. This incongruence will then not permit the reinforcement of desired behaviours (teamwork) that are important for achieving business goals. International organizations also extend their total rewards strategy to their global operations across several countries. In doing so, the underlying compensation philosophy remains constant across the countries. However, specific country offerings, in terms of individual elements of the compensation programme, may differ. Thus, various reward programmes are integrated with a common philosophy underlying them.

It is rare to come across companies that have a clearly articulated total compensation and rewards philosophy. Many organizations that do articulate a compensation philosophy in writing still fall short of incorporating other types of rewards into their compensation strategy. Organizations generally adopt individual elements of the compensation programme, such as different types of incentives, variable pay, etc. piecemeal, without considering how these individual elements fit strategically into the total compensation and rewards programme. Sometimes, the individual elements may even conflict with each other, and render the strategy counter-productive. In such a situation, the compensation programme neither helps the organization achieve its objectives nor helps meet the employee's needs and aspirations.

It is also imperative for organizations to examine their total compensation package to ensure that it reinforces the HR strategy and the business strategy. From the HR perspective, it is important to evaluate whether the various reward programmes are achieving their objective of motivating employees. Evaluation should also focus on the return on total expenditure on compensation and rewards. To improve the ROI, the cost structure should be realigned by redesigning the rewards programme.

Components of Total Compensation and Rewards Strategy

The design of the total compensation and rewards strategy requires that decisions must be made regarding the overall objectives of the reward programme;

the competitiveness of reward programmes; and the types and mix of rewards. These decisions are influenced by several internal and external factors. Therefore, the formulation of the total compensation and rewards strategy should incorporate (1) a comprehensive audit or assessment of current programmes; (2) internal business factors; and (3) external environmental and market factors.

Audit of Current Programmes

Auditing an organization's existing reward programmes helps to

- determine which programmes have achieved their objectives;
- review the competitive posture of the current total compensation package in relation to the market by determining the value of each element or component of cash and non-cash compensation such as basic, incentives, benefits, perquisites, pension, etc.; and
- rate each element of the programme on the degree to which it supports key objectives.

By doing these, an audit examines the combined effect of the total package and identifies gaps between programmes and objectives. For example, the annual bonus may be seen as important for retaining employees, providing them recognition, and motivating them through short-term incentives. An audit will help determine that the bonus is meeting these objectives.

Assessment of Internal Factors

This is most significant for ensuring an alignment between rewards strategy and business strategy. It involves examining the key elements of business strategy; the organization's mission, vision, values, culture; and management philosophy; life cycle position of the organization; and workforce demographics. Possible internal factors are business strategy (growth objectives, life cycle stage); management philosophy/values; and workforce demographics (turnover rate, age profile, and family status profile). These factors determine the reward strategy of the firm. A start-up technology company with limited cash flow may emphasize variable pay and long-term rewards over base salary. However, a mature financial institution may favour a larger benefits package over a variable pay programme. Company demographics play an important role, too. The needs of a young workforce differ from those of a mature workforce. The younger employee may value rewards such as skill development, career development, and cash rewards. Older workers may prefer a mix of cash and estate-building vehicles, etc. Similarly, gender plays a role. Women may favour different benefits and types of flexibility compared to men. As mentioned earlier, it is important to align rewards with organizational philosophy and values so that rewards convey them.

Assessment of External Factors

External factors such as economy, supply–demand, resources, stakeholder demands, etc. influence the total compensation and rewards strategy. For example, if there is a shortage of certain specialized skills, this will influence the rewards package needed to attract and retain employees who possess these skills. External factors include, economic environment (globalization, unemployment rate, supply–demand situation in labour market), market compensation trends (trends in increase in salary and in financial rewards), tax/regulatory environment, and demographics/social trends (trends in workforce demographic and in societal trends and values). These have been discussed earlier in this chapter.

Assessment of external factors requires that the organization identifies the key factors and then aligns compensation elements with these factors. For example, an organization may consider the salary trend an important factor. This organization will develop a total compensation programme that is attuned to salary trends. Tracking market trends and monitoring economic forecasts and legal developments are all important to the development of compensation strategy.

Internal factors and external factors need to be balanced by the organization when designing the compensation package. This is likely to result in closer alignment between compensation and business strategy and with other important internal and external factors. Three types of assessments help develop a total compensation and rewards strategy. The total strategy helps determine the changes that are required in the design, delivery, and administration of reward programme to align these programmes with business requirements.

A total compensation and rewards strategy helps the organization

- align its compensation and rewards strategy with its HR and business strategies;
- develop new compensation and rewards programmes or update existing ones by serving as a guide for HR practitioners;.
- compete better when recruiting new talent;
- moderate its labour costs by trading off some components; and
- enhance performance.

Summary

The design and implementation of a compensation and rewards system is one of the most challenging of HRM activities. Compensation and rewards play an important role in attracting, retaining, motivating, and enhancing employee performance as well as in the achievement of organizational goals. Employees expect to be rewarded and recognized for the contribution they make toward the achievement of organizational objectives. At the same time, employees expect rewards to be fair. When rewards are perceived as unfair or inadequate, employees feel dissatisfied and reduce effort; performance is, therefore, impaired. There have been several changes in compensation trends over the years: the variable component of pay has increased; rewards have become performance-linked; there is a trend toward team-based rewards; and rewards are linked to organizational performance. Average salaries have been increasing continuously over the past several years. The chapter categorized rewards into two—financial and non-financial. The basic components of compensation and reward programmes—base pay, variable pay or incentives, and benefits—were discussed. Three types of incentive plans—individual, group, and organizational—were also described. The chapter dwelt briefly upon the role of intrinsic motivators and of recognition schemes in rewarding employees. Two approaches to compensation—traditional and contemporary—were presented. The internal and external factors in the determination of individual financial compensation were highlighted. The chapter also discussed the four types of pay-for-performance approaches for rewarding individual employees: (1) merit pay; (2) variable pay; (3) skill-based pay; and (4) competency-based pay. The important role that employees' perception of equity plays in their satisfaction was discussed. Team-based reward systems and their advantages and disadvantages were also discussed. The components, trends, and innovations in compensation of top management were examined. The linkage between business strategy and compensation and reward strategy was discussed with respect to typology of business strategy, stage in organizational life-cycle, and type of industry, viz. technology-intensive and fast-growth industry. The linkage between two compensation patterns—mechanistic and organic—and a variety of organizational and environmental conditions were highlighted. The chapter ended with an overview of the total compensation and rewards strategy and by emphasizing its importance in guiding the design of the compensation and rewards programme in an organization.

Keywords

Base Pay is the direct financial compensation an individual receives based on the time he/she has worked for the organization. It includes wages and salaries.

Benefits are employer-provided rewards other than wages, salaries, or incentives that accrue to all employees by virtue of their membership in the organization. Benefits are a form of indirect financial compensation and are not contingent on the performance of an individual, a team, or an organization.

Compensation is the total of all forms of payments and rewards given to employees for performing tasks to achieve organizational objectives.

Compensation Management is a process that includes decisions regarding benefits and variable pay.

Compensation Strategy is the repertoire of pay choices available to management that, under some conditions, have an impact on the organization's performance and the effective use of its human resources.

Competency-based Pay System is one in which employees are paid for the range of skills, knowledge, motives, attitudes, etc. that they bring to the job, not for their job titles.

Contemporary Compensation Approach places value on individuals rather than on jobs and pays for skills and competencies.

Direct Financial Compensation or Reward is the monetary payment made to employees in exchange of work. It includes basic wage or salary, bonus, incentives, merit increases, overtime payments, variable pay, and commissions.

Employee Stock Option Plan gives an individual the right to buy a specified number of shares of the company stock at an advantageous price during a specified period.

Equity is the employee's perception of fairness of the compensation and rewards he/she receives compared to what he/she does. Equity in compensation and rewards exist when the output/input ratios of the individual and the significant other are perceived to be equal.

External Equity exists when the employees of one organization are paid comparably to employees who perform similar jobs in another organization.

Flexible Benefits or **Cafeteria Approach** gives employees a bouquet of benefits to choose from.

Indirect Financial Compensation or Rewards are benefits (pensions, insurance, paid time off work, etc.) given to all employees on the basis of their membership in the organization.

Individual Equity exists when an employee perceives that his or her pay is fair when compared with what co-workers are earning for similar jobs within the company, based on each individual's performance.

Individual Incentives are given to reward the effort and performance of individuals.

Internal Equity exists when employees are paid according to the relative value of their jobs within the same organization.

Job Evaluation is the process that determines the relative value of a job in order to assign a wage rate to the job.

Mandatory Benefits are those benefits that are legally binding on the employer. Provident fund, gratuity, health plans, maternity leave, medical leave, etc. are examples of mandatory benefits.

Merit Pay is the pay increase given by an organization to employees based on the organization's appraisal of employees' performance during a previous period.

Non-financial Compensation, also called intrinsic rewards, is praise and recognition for good performance and the satisfaction that an individual derives from the job or from the environment in which he/she performs it.

Organizational Incentives compensate all employees of the organization based on its performance that year. Stock options and profit-sharing plans are common forms of organization-wide incentives.

Phantom Stock Option Plan allows executives to hold shares in the form of units without physically owning them and to encash the units to receive value equal to the appreciation of the phantom stock they own at a specified time in the future.

Restricted Stock Option Plan allows an executive to hold shares without paying for it but restricts him/her from selling them for a specified period.

Salary refers to a consistent payment made to employees at the end of a specified period regardless of the number of hours worked.

Skill-based Pay compensates employees for their job-related skills and knowledge, and not for their job titles.

Team-based Pay Plans link individual financial rewards to team performance or to the achievement of team objectives/goals.

Total Compensation and Rewards Strategy is a statement of an organization's compensation and rewards philosophy. It defines the objectives of the rewards programmes, the individual elements of these programmes, and the ways in which those elements relate with each other to fulfill reward objectives.

Traditional Compensation Approach is to use job evaluation to determine the relative worth of each job, which in turn, helps determine the salary for the job.

Variable Pay is the compensation linked to individual, team, or organizational performance, not to the time worked. It is a form of direct financial compensation.

Voluntary Benefits are discretionary and provided by the employer voluntarily. Compensation for time not worked, paid holidays, sick leave, family-friendly benefits, retirement, etc. are examples of voluntary benefits.

Wages refer to employee payments directly calculated on an hourly basis.

Concept Review Questions

1. What is compensation? Differentiate between direct and indirect financial compensation. Also, outline the major objectives served by a compensation and reward system.

2. What are the basic components of a compensation and rewards system? What innovations have organizations introduced in each of these components because of an increasingly competitive business environment?

3. Compare the two major approaches to compensation and rewards. Discuss the importance of a total compensation and rewards strategy.

4. What is incentive pay? Distinguish between individual incentives, team-based incentives, and organizational incentives.

5. Under what circumstances is it appropriate to link individual payment to team performance?

What are the advantages and disadvantages of team-based rewards?

6. Compare performance-related pay, skill-based pay, and competency-based pay. What steps should be followed in designing a competency-based pay system?

7. 'Recognition is the most reliable of all rewards'. Critically examine the statement. Identify two or three ways organizations commonly use to recognize and reward employees through non-financial means.

8. What is compensation strategy? Explain the difference between mechanistic and organic strategies of compensation.

9. Explain the business and compensation strategy linkage in organizations.

Critical Thinking Questions

1. What is merit pay? How is it different from variable pay? What are the main advantages and disadvantages of the following two forms of pay-for-performance: (1) one-off bonus payment and (2) salary increments linked to high performance? Which of the two, in your opinion, has a higher motivational value for an employee? Explain your answer with suitable examples.

2. What is the role of equity in compensation and rewards decisions? What leads to perceptions

of inequity in compensation and rewards decisions? Describe the three types of equity that should be a part of an equitable compensation and rewards system.

3. Do you think that the compensation and rewards strategy of a high-technology firm will be different from that of an emerging fast-growth firm? Why? Enumerate your answer giving examples from organizations you are familiar with.

Simulation and Role Play

1. Turnstar is a leading consumer durables MNC headquartered in the US. It is a well-respected firm with a well-established brand name. It is one of the most sought-after firms during campus recruitments at all prestigious management institutes. Fresh management graduates consider the firm one of the best training grounds for starting one's career. Those who begin their

career with this firm command high respect in their professional circles. Until about five years back, most of the management graduates who began their career with Turnstar stayed with the firm for seven or eight years at the least. Lately, however, Mr Mishra, the HR manager, observed that many employees were leaving the firm after about two years. The compensation and reward structure at Turnstar has followed a fixed salary plan. High performers were rewarded with merit pay increases. The salary levels at Turnstar were lower than other firms' in the geographical region. However, the CEO had consistently refused to increase its executive salaries stating that the executives who worked for the firm received non-financial compensation that more than made up for lower rates. For example, Turnstar recognized skills and contributions, provided challenging assignments, chances to do something worthwhile, and opportunities to develop a career. Mr Mishra conducted several exit interviews with employees who were leaving the organization. It emerged that the majority were leaving because other firms were offering them higher salaries and performance-based incentives. Mr Mishra would like to restructure the reward and compensation plan at Turnstar to include performance-linked incentives.

Assume you are Mr Mishra, the HR manager. Design a variable rewards and compensation plan for Turnstar to be presented to the CEO for approval. While designing the new pay plan, incorporate the following: percentage of total pay that will be fixed and variable, pay rates of other firms operating in the region, etc. Also, develop arguments in support of variable pay over merit pay.

The situation may also be used for a role play exercise. Two students should volunteer with one student taking on the role of Mr Mishra, and the other that of the CEO. Both Mr Mishra and the CEO are concerned about the reasons for the increase in employee turnover and debate them. They search for solutions and deliberate upon several different reward, bonus, and incentive schemes. Mr Mishra suggests that the firm should offer executives an ESOP to retain them. The student volunteers should discuss the pros and cons of changing the reward structure of the organization from a merit-based system to a variable pay system.

After the role play is over, the instructor invites observations and questions from the class. The instructor leads the discussion on the importance of performance-linked variable pay system, external equity in compensation, the need to have a competitive salary structure, the merits and demerits of ESOPs, and innovative approaches to the implementation of ESOPs.

Classroom Projects

1. Working in teams of three or four, list the range of benefits that are offered by organizations to their employees. Classify these benefits into 'mandatory' and 'voluntary'. Discuss the voluntary benefits that are of greatest value to employees. Are all voluntary benefits equally relevant to employees of all age groups in an organization? Give reasons for the differences in benefits preferences across different age groups.

   Assume your team has been hired as a benefits consultant to an IT firm. Your job is to

   - list the benefits that employees belonging to different age groups—20s, 30s, 40s, etc.— will find valuable and relevant;

   - customize flexible benefit packages for three groups of employees: (1) new graduates recently hired; (2) employees in their early 30s; and (3) employees around 50;

   - assign a money value to each benefit in the flexible benefit package and calculate the total cost of benefits for each of the three employee groups;

   - discuss the impact of FBT on the structuring of executive compensation packages as well as the manner in which the employer calculates cost-to-company; and

   - discuss the objectives that organizations seek to accomplish by customizing benefits packages for employees.

Each team prepares a report for presentation and discussion in the class. The instructor facilitates the discussion emphasizing the importance of customizing benefit packages and the role of benefits in attracting, motivating, and retaining employees.

2. This exercise requires some out-of-class preparation. The students are required to gather information from newspaper articles, business magazines, and company websites about the changes in the structuring of executive compensation packages. Students also obtain examples of organizations that have modified their reward and compensation packages. In the class, students are asked to form groups of 4 or 5 students. Based on the information each

student has, the group discusses the nature of changes that have occurred in reward and compensation structuring and the reasons for the changes. The discussion centres on the increase in variable pay, competency-based pay, and skill-based pay. The significance of ESOPs in executive compensation packages is also discussed. Each group presents a summary of the discussion to the rest of the class. When all groups have made their presentations, the instructor should engage the entire class in a discussion on the trends in executive compensation. The discussion should also focus on the pros and cons of factoring in individual, team, and organizational incentives in executive compensation packages.

Field Projects

1. The objective of this field project is to help students appreciate the role of internal and external determinants of compensation and rewards. The instructor should divide the class into groups of five. Each group is asked to visit one organization belonging to one of the following industries: retail, insurance, BPO, IT and ITeS, and hospitality. Group members conduct interviews with HR managers as well as few middle-level managers of the firms to find out

   - the compensation and rewards structures for different groups of employees in the organization;

   - the internal and external factors that influence reward and compensation decisions;

   - if the firm conducts salary surveys, how often it conducts them, and how it uses the results; and

   - if the firm benchmarks salaries in the same sector or across sectors, and why.

   Each group prepares a report for class presentation as well as a written report for submission to the instructor. The groups make presentations in the class highlighting the

internal and external determinants that influence compensation decisions. When all groups have made their presentations, the instructor should engage the entire class in a discussion about the relative importance of various factors that influence compensation decisions in the contemporary business environment. The discussion should also focus on industry differences in the determinants that are important for compensation decisions.

2. The objective of this group exercise is to appreciate the strategic linkage between organizational life cycle and compensation strategy. Students form groups of five members each. Each group identifies one organization and determines the life cycle stage of the selected organization. Group members visit the selected organization and conduct interviews with HR managers as well as a few line managers to obtain information about the business strategy that the firm follows at its current stage in organizational life cycle. Students also obtain details of the compensation strategy of the firm. Each group prepares a report for presentation in the class as well as a written report for submission. After all groups have made their

presentations to the class, the instructor leads the discussion to demonstrate how the pay mix (base salary, incentives, and benefits) varies at different stages of the organizational life cycle.

Industry differences as well as specific compensation features unique to particular industry are also emphasized.

Case Study

Rewards System of a University

A shift in the culture of any organization is effective only if employees change their behaviour to support the change. For this to happen, rewards must be designed to reinforce desirable behaviour. Employees must be able to see a clear connection between their everyday work and their rewards. At the Central University, however, achieving these objectives seems too farfetched.

Central University is one of the leading universities of the country. There are about 30 postgraduate departments, and almost 500 teachers. The university was established in 1950, and has enjoyed a reputation of academic excellence. Several of the teachers have been very well known in their fields, nationally as well as worldwide. Some of them have been leading scientists and have won prestigious awards. However, the well-acclaimed and highly qualified first set of professors have all but retired. In the past decade, the academic standards at the University have gradually eroded. Students have become apathetic. Teachers' commitment has declined. They no longer take pride in being associated with the University. According to the teachers, the root of the problem is the culture, which is not oriented towards performance. Whatever the reason, it is evident that the University has slipped from its elite position of academic excellence.

The new head of the university, Dean Puri, who assumed office in early 2003, was worried and keen to reinstate the university to its former glory. He felt that teachers' responsibilities included teaching classes, writing and publishing research papers, presenting research papers in conferences, and administrative work assigned from time to time. According to Dean Puri, promotions of teachers

should be linked with the academic contribution of teachers. He also felt that the salaries of teachers should have a variable component, linked to research publications, courses offered/taught, training programmes conducted, research projects undertaken, resources generated, etc. If promotions and salary increases of teachers were made contingent on such criteria, these rewards would reinforce desirable behaviour and a performance-oriented culture.

Accordingly, when promotion interviews were held, promotions of several teachers belonging to various departments were not approved. This resulted in much discontent among the teaching community, because of which the university administration came under severe attack from the teachers' associations. They argued that since there were hardly any avenues of career growth in the profession, time-bound promotions should be given to everyone as a right. Moreover, they felt that the implementation of academic criteria for assessment of teachers should have been preceded by communication to this effect. Since the university did not have a system of performance-linked promotions or performance-linked financial incentives, it was unfair to link promotions or salary increases to academic criteria without formalizing such a system. It was clear that the teaching community was not ready for a change in the reward system. Change of such a magnitude required a university-wide communication programme.

Dean Puri took the initiative to diagnose what was ailing the university. Hence, at his behest, a university-wide survey was commissioned to determine the levels of satisfaction, motivation, and commitment among the teachers. To obtain an objective feedback, the survey was conducted anonymously. What emerged was unbelievable: almost 90% of the teachers were dissatisfied with various aspects of their job, had low levels of motivation, and felt emotionally detached from the university although they felt morally committed to the system of education. This was highly disturbing and something needed to be done urgently. Hence, a follow-up survey was undertaken to diagnose the reasons for this state of affairs, during which many teachers were interviewed in depth. The survey found that satisfaction, motivation, and commitment of teachers was low because

- automatic salary increments did not discriminate between high performers or poor performers;
- teachers who taught sincerely were not rewarded, and teachers who did not teach sincerely were not penalized;
- there were no incentives for research, publications, paper presentations at conferences, or other such academic criteria;
- promotion decisions were based on seniority and/or length of service rather than on merit;
- there was no assessment of or formal feedback on performance;
- benefits given to teachers were mandatory only; and
- the university lacked a performance culture.

Thus, the findings suggested that the major source of the problems confronting the university was the absence of a formal compensation and rewards system. Until 2003, there was no reward strategy; only a time-bound promotion system based on years of service rather than on performance. There was no system for appraising performance of the teachers along any of the specified criteria. Salaries of teachers were according to grades and increased annually. The university followed the traditional compensation philosophy—it increased the salary of all every year according to salary grades and increased the salary for performers and non-performers equally.

Since performance was not linked to rewards or promotions, nor recognized, teachers who had a good performance record and showed high potential gradually reduced their effort. The feeling was that since everyone was promoted with time, extra effort would not lead to higher rewards. This resulted in the institutionalization of a non-performing culture, a culture in which there was no motivation to excel or perform well.

Dean Puri was keen to orient the culture toward higher performance. He constituted a committee to recommend a reward system that would help achieve this objective. The committee recommended, among other things, to

- differentiate the salary increase for average and excellent performance, so that past performance is rewarded and future performance is motivated;
- assign weightage to criteria such as publications, number of courses taught, and other contributions for rewarding performance;
- base rewards such as promotions less on seniority to avoid demoralizing teachers and being perceived as unfair;
- extend more benefits to teachers, such as transport services, subsidized housing, admission of teachers' children in the university, etc.;
- base a component of the salary on various criteria mentioned already;
- compensate and reward teachers for job-related skills and knowledge, not for job titles, because a skill-based pay and reward system will encourage teachers to learn continuously and gain additional skills, and will help reduce stagnation and monotony among teachers, and also ensure that the university has competent teachers;
- institute a competency-based pay system that rewards teachers for the skills, knowledge, motives, attitudes, etc. they have and pay for what they can do even if they do not have to do it now;
- recognize achievements; and

- extend some voluntary benefits based on requirements.

Dean Puri has the committee recommendations with him at this time. He has several questions:

- How should these recommendations be incorporated to design a total rewards system for the university?
- What criteria can be used to appraise teachers' performance?
- What weightage should be assigned to each

of these criteria when determining merit pay increase?

- How should incentives be linked to performance?
- Will the teachers accept the proposed reward structure?
- Will the rewards system be successful when implemented?
- What is the significance of recognition relative to financial incentives for stimulating high performance in the case of education?

Questions

1. Analyse the existing reward system of the university for the teacher community.
2. Do you think that the earlier reward system of the university was equitable? Explain your answer with a suitable rationale.
3. What criteria can be used for assigning points to teachers' performance along various dimensions? How much weightage should be given to each criterion? Explain.
4. Develop an incentive plan for the teachers.

5. Do you think recognition will play an important role for motivating teachers? What kind of recognition schemes can the university develop for the teachers?
6. What, in your opinion, will the teachers of the university value more—extrinsic rewards or intrinsic rewards?
7. Design a total compensation and rewards strategy for the university.

Notes

The Economic Times, 14 September 2006, 'Leave your Worries at Office', New Delhi, p. 6.

The Economic Times, 26 July 2006, 'Paid Holiday: You're Free to Date, Wed & Have Child', New Delhi, p. 6.

The Economic Times, 16 June 2006, 'Industrial Wages Rise 7.5% annually During 1998–99 to 2003–04', New Delhi, p. 25.

The Economic Times, 8 June 2006, 'Infy Moots Deferred Compensation Package for Senior Management', New Delhi, p. 10.

The Economic Times, 8 June 2006, 'Infy Moots Deferred Compensation Package for Senior Management', New Delhi, p. 10.

The Economic Times, 31 May 2006, 'Cos to ink New Contract Norms for Honchos', New Delhi, p. 6.

The Economic Times, 30 May 2006, 'Pay Under Different Heads Now History', New Delhi, p. 10.

The Economic Times, 18 May 2006, 'IT cos Move Beyond Stock Options', New Delhi, p. 6.

The Economic Times, 11 May 2006, 'HLL Shifts Focus to Stock Grant Scheme', New Delhi, p. 11.

The Economic Times, 19 April 2006, 'Top Execs Want Cos to Walk the Talk', New Delhi, p. 10.

The Economic Times, 6 April 2006, 'Old Economy now Takes to ESOPs', New Delhi, p. 8.

The Economic Times, 14 March 2006, 'IT Pays to be Skilled', New Delhi, p. 6.

Human Capital, March 2006, 'All About Accolades', New Delhi, pp. 20–3.

The Times of India, 8 February 2006, 'Desi Firms Beat MNCs in Pay Hikes, Says Study', New Delhi, p. 17.

The Economic Times, 1 December 2005, 'Competitiveness Conundrum', New Delhi, p. 15.

The Economic Times, 8 November 2005, 'Support for CMP: Surprisingly from Salary Hikes', New Delhi, Editorial page.

The Economic Times, 3 November 2005, 'Perked up Packages', New Delhi, p. 11.

The Economic Times, 26 September 2005, 'Employer must Pay FBT on all Staff Welfare Costs', New Delhi, p. 12.

The Economic Times, 1 September 2005, 'FBT Slap on Bank Pension', New Delhi, p. 4.

The Economic Times, 1 September 2005, 'With FBT in, Employers Likely to Club Cash Salary Under one Head', New Delhi, p. 4.

The Economic Times, 22 August 2005, 'Ringside View: It Helps to be Paycheck Savvy', New Delhi, pp. 1, 9.

The Economic Times, 12 August 2005, 'What Employees Want', Corporate Dossier, New Delhi, p. 3.

The Economic Times, 6 April 2005, 'Soxed IT cos Find ESOP Backup', New Delhi, pp. 1, 33.

The Economic Times, 11 October 2004, 'Wipro to Grant 6m Stock Options to Staff', New Delhi, p. 11.

The Economic Times, 16 August 2004, 'Cash Reward: High-Fliers get Bonus Points', New Delhi, pp. 1, 13.

The Economic Times, 23 July 2004, 'Dangling the Bait', Corporate Dossier, New Delhi, p. 3.

The Economic Times, 7 June to 13 June 2004, 'More the Merrier', New Delhi, p. 2.

The Economic Times, 5 May 2004, 'ESOP Umbrella Widens: Another Move towards Liberalization', New Delhi, p. 8.

The Times of India, 3 May 2004, 'Companies Change the Way CEOs are Paid', New Delhi, p. 15.

References

Adams, J.S. 1963, 'Toward an Understanding of Inequity', *Journal of Abnormal and Social Psychology*, vol. 67, pp. 422–36.

Balkin, D.B. 1988, 'Compensation Strategy for Firms in Emerging and Rapidly Growing Industries', *Human Resource Planning*, vol. 11, no. 3, 207–13.

Balkin, D.B. and L.R. Gomez-Mezia 1984, 'Determinants of R&D Compensation Strategies in the High Tech Industry', *Personnel Psychology*, vol. 37, pp. 635–50.

Bohlander, G., S. Snell, and A. Sherman 2002, *Managing Human Resources*, 12th edn, Thomson South-Western, Singapore.

Carrell, M.R., N.F. Elbert and R.D. Hatfield 1995, *Human Resource Management: Global Strategies for Managing a Diverse Workforce*, Prentice Hall, Englewood Cliffs, New Jersey.

Carroll, S.J. 1988, 'Handling the Need for Consistency and the Need for Contingency in the Management of Compensation', *Human Resource Planning*, vol. 11, no. 3, pp. 191–6.

DeCenzo, D.A. and S.P. Robbins 2005, *Fundamentals of Human Resource Management*, 8th edn, John Wiley & Sons, Singapore.

Dessler, G. 2005, *Human Resource Management*, 10th edn, Prentice Hall of India Pvt Ltd, New Delhi.

Gibson, V.M. 1995, 'The New Employee Reward System', *Management Review*, February, pp. 13–18.

Gomez-Mezia, L.R. 1997, 'The Effectiveness of Organization-wide Compensation Strategies in Technology Intensive Firms', *Journal of High Technology Management Research*, vol. 8, no. 2, pp. 301–16.

Gomez-Mezia, L.R. and D.B. Balkin 1989, 'Effectiveness of Individual and Aggregate Compensation Strategies', *Industrial Relations*, vol. 28, no. 3, pp. 431–45.

Gomez-Mezia, L.R. and T. Welbourne 1988, 'Compensation Strategy: An Overview and Future Steps', *Human Resource Planning*, vol. 11, no. 3, pp. 173–90.

Greer, C.R. 2002, *Strategic Human Resource Management: A General Managerial Approach*, 2nd edn, Pearson Education, Singapore.

Haigh, T. 1989, 'Aligning Executive Total Compensation with Business Strategy', *Human Resource Planning*, vol. 12, no. 3, pp. 221–7.

Ivancevich, J.M. 2004, *Human Resource Management*, 9th edn, Tata McGraw Hill Publishing Company Ltd, New Delhi.

Kaplan, S.L. 2005, 'Total Rewards in Action: Developing A Total Rewards Strategy', *Benefits and Compensation Digest*, August, pp. 32–7.

Kleiman, L.A. 1997, *Human Resource Management: A Tool for Competitive Advantage*, West Publishing Company, New York.

Mathis, R.L. and J.H. Jackson 2003, *Human Resource Management*, 10th edition, Thomson South-Western, Singapore.

Mello, J.A. 2003, *Strategic Human Resource Management*, Thomson Asia Pte Ltd, Singapore.

Miles, R.E. and C.C. Snow 1984, 'Designing Strategic Human Resources Systems', *Organizational Dynamics*, vol. 13, no. 1, pp. 36–52.

Mondy, R.W., R.M. Noe, and S.R. Premeaux 1999, *Human Resource Management*, 7th edtion, Prentice Hall International Inc. USA.

Nemerov, D.S. 1994, 'How to Design a Competency-based Pay Program', *Journal of Compensation and Benefits*, vol. 9, no. 5, pp. 46–53.

Porter, M.E. 1980, *Competitive Strategy*, The Free Press, New York.

9

Managing Careers

OBJECTIVES

After studying this chapter, you will be able to:

- discuss the significance of career planning and development in the contemporary business environment

- define 'career' and understand the difference between 'career planning', 'career development', and 'career management'

- identify the career stages through which individuals progress during their work life

- describe the career planning practices and career development interventions appropriate for each career stage

- appreciate the individual and organizational perspectives of career management

- describe the guidelines for the design and implementation of a successful career management system

- understand the significance of adopting a strategic approach to career management

INTRODUCTION

In the contemporary business environment, the traditional notions about career and career management have taken on entirely new dimensions for both employees and organizations. Business decisions such as mergers, acquisitions, lay-offs, and restructuring all have influenced the way individuals and organizations view *careers* and *career management*.

More opportunities have become available for the high performing employees who are valuable to the firm. High performers, who are in short supply, get many job offers from other companies due to their competencies and skill sets. Employees are changing jobs more often than in the past and job-hopping has become an acceptable reality today. Employee loyalty today extends more to the individual's 'career' rather than to the 'organization'. If an individual's career aspirations are not fulfilled by the organization, he/she is likely to seek fulfillment in some other organization. Therefore, organizations are confronted with the challenge of attracting and retaining this group of employees.

Job and *career* are not viewed as equivalent any more. Employees are no longer content with just having a secure *job* with time-bound upward mobility. Today, employees are looking for a 'career' and are not willing to take any chances with it. Employees do not let their careers just 'happen', instead, they want a more active control over their careers. They also want their firms to provide them with career development opportunities. Changing workforce expectations and the changing psychological contract between the employer and the employees have led organizations to direct more attention towards career management interventions.

The present chapter discusses various aspects of career management—both from the employee and the organizational perspective. The career stage model, career planning, and career development issues related to each stage have also been explored. A perspective on the design and implementation of career management programmes within organizations is also explored. A typology of organizational career management practices has been discussed. The chapter goes on to offer a strategic view of career management as well as some creative career practices that firms may adopt to manage contemporary HR challenges.

CAREERS—CONTEMPORARY NOTIONS

The nature of the world of work, as it exists today, is fundamentally different from what it was a generation ago. Earlier, individuals were expected to work for only one organization during their entire work life. The individuals belonging to today's generation, on the other hand, are likely to work in many different organizations during the course of their careers. These individuals are also unlikely to remain in one job or occupation, leave alone one organization, for their entire work lives. Recently, it was reported in a national newspaper that the country manager of Oracle India quit the firm after a stint of 12 years to pursue other interests. In the next phase of his career he is expected to join academics where he feels his experience with Oracle will give him an advantage. Such shifts are likely to become more common in the near future. Globalization, mergers, acquisitions, lay-offs, technological advancements, and other such trends have significantly contributed to this trend.

Changing economic and market conditions have led many organizations to take some tough decisions, such as cutbacks, manpower reduction, and de-layering. For example, Delta Airlines Inc. had announced plans for reducing workforce in thousands as part of the company's plans to save $5 billion a year by 2006. The growing concern on part of organizations to lower costs has reduced opportunities as firms adopt measures such as downsizing and restructuring. In the face of such cost constraints, career paths often collapse, resulting in employee dissatisfaction. At the same time, the limited supply of high-talent employees ensures that firms compete for this scarce resource. By offering career development opportunities, organizations may be able to improve their ability to attract and retain this group of employees. Many firms incorporate 'career growth' as part of their recruitment strategy. In a study conducted by AC Nielsen ORG-MARG, for identifying the most preferred company in the top campuses in India in the year 2004, IBM emerged among the top three. According to the study, students chose IBM because it offers individuals with career opportunities, at the local as well as global level, along with a high-performance culture and a healthy work–life balance. The recruitment campaign of e-Serve, a member of Citigroup, talks about the opportunities that the company offers its employees, such as an opportunity to do an MBA programme while working.

Volatility of environmental conditions has placed a question mark on the relevance of long-term business decisions. These have, in turn, also affected how individuals perceive organizations. The employee–organization relationship has been re-defined, as discussed earlier in the book. Organizations realize and accept the reality that employees may leave the organization for more challenging or lucrative jobs. The educational level of the workforce has increased along with their career aspirations. Employees are no longer content with only good pay cheques and secure jobs. They want greater challenge, autonomy, better quality of work-life, and an opportunity to fit their work harmoniously with other priorities such as family, health, etc. Career planning and development help employees achieve this balance between different priorities. Thus, career management helps employees achieve these concerns and also ensures that organizations have a productive and committed workforce.

Careers are a late entrant in the field of management study. According to Boerlijst (1984), career as a whole began to receive real attention only in the 1970s. Although a more systematic study of careers has arisen since, the organizational aspect in career theory still lacks a comprehensive framework.

The term *career* has been used to connote several different meanings. In day-to-day usage, career is used to refer to the choice of a profession ('she has chosen a career in management') or vertical advancement in the organization ('he is moving up in his career'). In management parlance, a career refers to the series of work-related positions occupied by an individual throughout life and the associated activities, behaviours, attitudes, values, and aspirations. A *job*, on the other hand, refers to the grouping of tasks, duties, and responsibilities that is assigned to an individual as part of work at a particular point of time. This grouping may change over time and hence jobs assigned to individuals may also change. The sequence of jobs that an employee performs during the span of work life, not necessarily with the same company, may constitute his/her career. However, an individual's career does not consist of an unrelated sequence of jobs. Rather, the concept refers to a visible progression through objectively defined stages or steps.

Today, the definition of career itself has undergone a change (Figure 9.1). 'Career success' is no longer measured in terms of vertical advancement in the hierarchy or increasing salary levels. It is now characterized by the achievement of one's full potential, and the ability to face challenges and assume greater responsibility, along with increased autonomy. More than salary and security, individuals today look for interesting and meaningful work. Though career success may be objectively measured in terms of promotions, it may

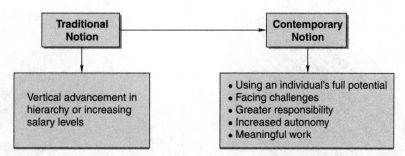

Figure 9.1:   Changing Notions of Career Success

also be subjectively defined in terms of satisfaction. The socially acceptable connotation of what constitutes career success may depend on how each individual defines personal career success. For a university teacher, career success may be defined in terms of a promotion from lecturer to reader after the stipulated number of years. On completion of the requisite number of years of experience, if one teacher gets promoted while another does not, then, in social terms, the former may be considered to be more successful than the latter. However, if the latter intrinsically values academic and research contribution instead of the designation, then this individual may be viewed as more successful in terms of the internal subjective valuation of success. Let us take another example—if person A is working to earn as much money as possible so that his/her family can have all luxuries and if person B works as a social worker in order to help the less privileged sections of society, in internal subjective terms, person B is likely to be more successful. Due to these differences in viewpoints and definitions of career success, individuals are likely to respond to different motivational tools.

CAREER PLANNING, DEVELOPMENT, AND MANAGEMENT

Career planning involves establishment of individual career objectives based on an assessment of career goals, aspirations, performance, and potential. Career planning is concerned with the choosing of occupations, organizations, and jobs by individuals. It is a personalized and ongoing process whereby an individual establishes career goals and identifies the means for achieving these goals. A fresh management graduate hoping to start an independent financial consultancy firm may first choose to work for such a firm for some years to gain experience. Individuals may identify a sequence of positions they need to move through to achieve their career goals. These sequences of positions may extend beyond the organization. Career planning should focus on matching personal goals with opportunities that are realistically available. Since the number of positions at senior levels are scarce, upward mobility

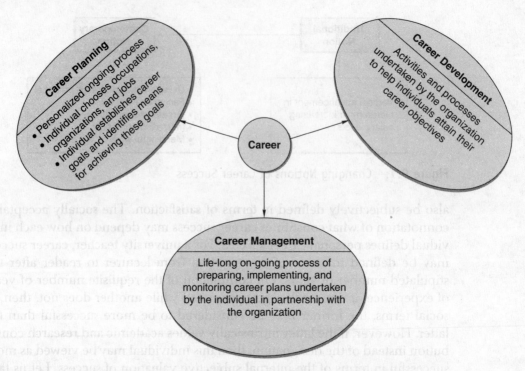

Figure 9.2:   Career Planning, Career Development, and Career Management

cannot be a reality for every employee. Hence, career planning need not focus only on success related to promotions.

Career development, as opposed to career planning, refers to the activities and processes undertaken by the organization to help employees attain their career objectives. It is the process by which an individual's career plans are accomplished. For example, an organization may provide developmental training to employees to help them perform better in their jobs. Career development, however, is different from employee development. Employee development focusses on improving work effectiveness and performance in the immediate or intermediate time frames. Career development is oriented towards long-term career effectiveness and success of the employee.

The two concepts, however, are closely linked. Employee development should be compatible with an employee's career development in the organization. However, a successful career programme should not only match individual aspirations with the needs of the organization, it should also develop employees for the long-term needs of the organization.

Career management is a continuous process that involves setting personal career goals, developing strategies for achieving these goals, and revising the goals based on work and personal experiences. McMahon and Merman (1987) defined career management as 'an ongoing process of preparing, implementing, and monitoring career plans undertaken by the individual alone or in concert with the organization'. Since careers are made up of exchanges between individuals and organizations, career management incorporates a partnership between individuals and organizations. Baruch and Peiperl (2000) defined 'organizational career management' (OCM) as the design and implementation of activities relevant to the career development of its employees. They proposed that OCM was distinct from career management as practiced by individuals. However, the two were not mutually exclusive, rather, OCM can complement career management. Figure 9.1 presents the concepts of career planning, career development, and career management.

Several sources have suggested lists of OCM practices. These include lists by Walker and Gutteridge (1979), Baruch (1996), and Bowen and Hall (1977), among others. The most exhaustive list of OCM practices is perhaps the one suggested by Gutteridge, Leibowitz, and Shore in 1993 in their study of OCM practices in the United States. Baruch and Peiperl gave their list of OCM practices based on a pilot study and a review of the sources cited above. This list is presented in Exhibit 9.1 and according to the researchers; it may be taken as covering the whole range of OCM practices.

The individual and the organization have different perspectives on careers. Depending on whether career is viewed from the perspective of the employee or of the organization, the study of careers takes on different orientations.

From an employee's point of view, concerns such as technological advancement, slow rate of economic growth, opportunities for personal advancement, ageing, and organizational restructuring have a long-term impact on career

Exhibit 9.1

Organizational Career Management Practices

- Performance appraisal as a basis for career planning
- Assessment centres
- Peer appraisal
- Upward (subordinate) appraisal
- Career counselling by direct supervisor
- Career counselling by HR department
- Formal mentoring
- Career workshops
- Common career paths

- Dual ladder (parallel hierarchy for professional staff)
- Written career planning (done by the organization or jointly)
- Retirement preparation programmes
- Succession planning
- Books and/or pamphlets on career issues
- Postings regarding internal job openings
- Formal education as part of career development
- Lateral moves to create cross-functional experience

Source: Baruch and Peiperl 2000

related issues. For instance, computerization and automation are accompanied by skill obsolescence. When economic growth is slow, fewer jobs are created, and, therefore, individual careers are affected. Further, as firms restructure and reorganize, employees have lesser opportunities for career advancement. As people grow older, they have fewer career options and opportunities.

Therefore, for individuals, there exists a personal interest in their own careers. Individuals wish to satisfy their personal needs through the careers they pursue. When they experience a sense of psychological failure and lack of accomplishment in their careers, they may look for career change.

On the other hand, organizations' perspective on careers is directed towards ensuring a people–career match and smooth employee succession when managers need to be replaced due to retirements, resignations, or other such movements. The main concern of organizations is to ensure high levels of performance and lower levels of employee turnover. Therefore, it is in the interest of organizations to ensure that employees pursue careers in which they are interested and for which they are properly trained.

Although individuals and organizations clearly have different perspectives on careers, both can benefit from working together to improve career management (Exhibit 9.2).

Effective career planning and development take into consideration both the individual-centred and the organization-centred perspectives. When an organization provides opportunities to employees for integrating personal

---

Exhibit 9.2

Individual and Organizational Benefits of Career Management

Benefits for the Individual
- Enhanced career and job satisfaction
- Development of competencies and personal skills
- Enhanced opportunities for growth in the organization
- Improved performance
- Development of potential
- Enhancement of status
- Increase in salary
- Maintenance of the individual's marketability in a changing employment market
- Achievement of personal career aspirations

Benefits for the Organization
- Improved productivity
- Reduced employee turnover
- Increased retention of high talent employees
- Creating a positive recruitment image
- Ensuring availability of promotable employees within the firm
- Better individual–organization match
- More effective utilization of employee skills
- Promoting organizational goodwill (when employees become brand ambassadors)

Adapted from: Nelson and Quick 1994

---

career goals with its objectives, it needs to recognize that each individual's career moves through several stages. Employees change as they grow older and move into higher positions. Therefore, these employees view their careers differently at various stages of their lives. An individual at the age of 28–30 years may be extremely ambitious and focussed on upward mobility. The same individual at the age of 45 years is likely to be content with career achievements and satisfied with a slower pace of career growth. One way to analyse careers is to discuss their various stages. Each stage of an individual's career is characterized by unique concerns, needs, and challenges. The next section discusses the four-stage typology of careers.

CAREER STAGES

Career stages are gradual changes that occur over time in careers. Moorhead and Griffin (1995) define career stages as periods in which an individual's work life is characterized by distinctive needs, concerns, tasks, and activities. Several models of career stages have been proposed by various researchers. Dalton, Thompson, and Price (1997) suggested that there are four stages in a career—apprentice, colleague, mentor, and sponsor. Hall (1976) presented a five-stage model that was proposed by Erikson (1963). However, the most commonly used career stage typology identified four distinct but inter-related career stages—establishment, advancement, maintenance, and withdrawal (Figure 9.3).

Huse and Cummings (1980) proposed that as individuals move from one stage to another, needs and expectations evolve and change. Each stage is also marked by significant personal life transitions. Individuals enter and exit each stage of their career at different ages. The age ranges shown here for each stage of career are approximations.

Establishment stage (age 20–26 years) The first stage of an individual's career marks the onset of his/her career. At this stage, individuals are often unsure of their capabilities, competence, and potential. Hence, they show high levels of dependence on their superiors for guidance, support, and feedback. Being newcomers, they may be unsure about their choice of career and may continue to explore alternative career options and available choices regarding organizations and jobs. Their main concerns, however, are directed towards learning the job and adjusting to the organization. Towards the end of this stage, newcomers manage to adjust within the organization.

Life transitions In the establishment stage, individuals move from educational institutes school to work, that is, from non-work to work life. They also become less emotionally and financially dependent on their parents.

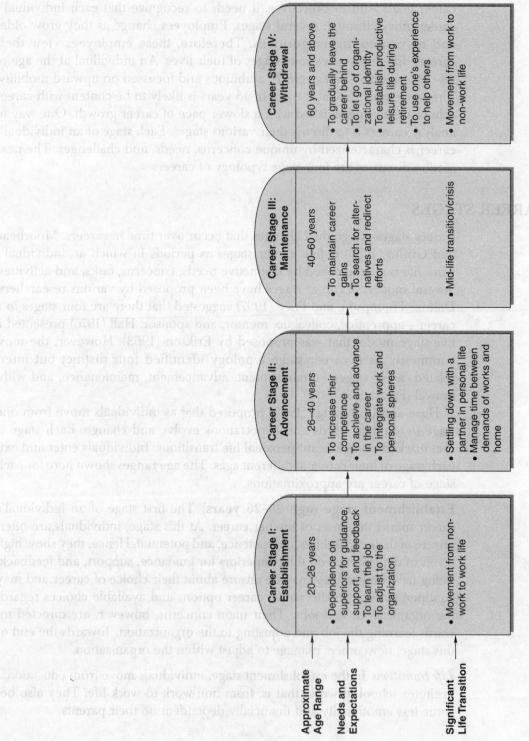

Career Stage I: Establishment	Career Stage II: Advancement	Career Stage III: Maintenance	Career Stage IV: Withdrawal
Approximate Age Range 20–26 years	26–40 years	40–60 years	60 years and above

**Needs and
Expectations**
• Dependence on
  superiors for guidance,
  support, and feedback
• To learn the job
• To adjust to the
  organization
	• To increase their
	  competence
	• To achieve and advance
	  in the career
	• To integrate work and
	  personal spheres
		• To maintain career
		  gains
		• To search for alter-
		  natives and redirect
		  efforts
			• To gradually leave the
			  career behind
			• To let go of organi-
			  zational identity
			• To establish productive
			  leisure life during
			  retirement
			• To use one's experience
			  to help others

**Significant
Life Transition**
• Movement from non-
  work to work life
	• Settling down with a
	  partner in personal life
	• Manage time between
	  demands of works and
	  home
		• Mid-life transition/crisis	• Movement from work to
			  non-work life

Figure 9.3: Four Career Stages

Advancement stage (age 26–40 years) In this stage, individuals become independent contributing members of the organization and are no longer dependent on their superiors or on co-workers. Advancement is a highly achievement-oriented stage during which employees are mainly concerned with increasing their competence and achieving and advancing in their careers. The employees also seek to advance in life. Developing closer ties with peers and integrating career choices (such as promotions or transfers) and personal spheres also emerge as important concerns for employees in this stage. Vertical (promotions) and lateral (transfers) movements frequently occur during this stage. These movements broaden the sphere of experience for the employees as they learn different jobs.

The employees who fail to make the necessary adjustments in the organization during this stage, may respond by changing jobs. Job hopping has become a characteristic of the advancement stage in recent years, because of greater career opportunities for high performers.

Life Transitions When individuals reach and cross the age of 30, it marks an important personal life transition. It is during this stage that most individuals settle down with a partner, necessitating several adjustments in personal life. These include working out dual career partnerships (when the employee has a working spouse) and managing time between the demands of work and home.

Maintenance stage (age 40–60 years) By the time an employee reaches this stage, he/she has usually achieved career ambitions and created a place in the world of work. Individuals are, therefore, no longer concerned with advancement. Most of their efforts are directed towards maintaining the career gains. Some people, however, continue to grow during this stage, though not at the same rate as in the advancement stage. Typically, this stage involves levelling off or reaching a *career plateau*, i.e., the point where the probability of moving up the hierarchy is low. Not all individuals, however, manage career plateau equally well. Some employees may become frustrated and dissatisfied with their jobs and achievements. These individuals go through what may be termed as 'mid-career crisis', wherein they perceive a threat to their career identity. These individuals experience this career stage as one of conflict and crisis. In an organization, these employees may be identified as those who have not achieved their career goals probably because of a mismatch between their aspirations and the reality. Newcomers to the organization are perceived as threats by these employees. Reappraising circumstances, searching for alternatives, and redirecting efforts assume great significance during the maintenance stage.

Life Transitions Individuals experience mid-life transition approximately around forty-five years of age. This is the time that people realize that they are no longer young and they are mortal. This transition also involves assessing the extent to which they have been able to realize their dreams. Individuals who believe that their dreams have been stalled experience mid-life crisis, which also contributes to mid-career crisis.

Withdrawal stage (age 60 and above)   During this stage, individuals seriously begin to consider and plan withdrawal from active employment. This stage involves gradually leaving the career behind, letting go of the organizational identity, and establishing a productive leisure life during retirement. Career needs of individuals in this period are limited to using their experience and wisdom to help others.

The decision to retire varies from person to person. Some individuals welcome this stage. They view retirement as a signal that a long period of continuous employment will soon come to an end, providing them more time for their leisure activities like gardening, golf, music, or socializing. Others, however, may prefer to gradually withdraw from work by scaling down their work hours or by working part-time. For instance, after retirement, a manager may accept the position of a consultant in his/her organization. In such a case, the organization derives the benefit of the senior employee's experience. At the same time the individual's need to continue to be useful is fulfilled. For individuals who have had a satisfying career, this period results in greater willingness to leave the career behind.

Life Transition   This stage signals a major personal life transition from work to non-work life. This also encompasses the possibility of income uncertainty, declining physical capacity, failing health, and the fear of losing one's family members and friends. The individual seeks to establish a meaningful post-retirement life and achieve a sense of integrity.

The duration of each stage and the timing of transitions between career stages vary greatly from one individual to another. Individuals are likely to face and experience specific personal and career issues differently at each stage. For instance, one person may experience the withdrawal stage as a positive opportunity to indulge in leisure time activities. Another person, on the other hand, may view the withdrawal stage as signifying the beginning of a meaningless existence. An understanding of the personal and career issues confronted by individuals at different stages of their career can contribute to effective career planning.

CAREER PLANNING

Career planning, as defined earlier, is about individuals' choice of occupations, organizations, and jobs. In planning their careers, individuals set career objectives and determine the methods to achieve those objectives. Individual career planning generally includes the following:

- individual's assessment of his/her own interests, abilities, and goals
- examining alternative career opportunities
- establishing personal career goals
- developing a career path
- planning how to progress through the career path

Career path refers to a line of progression through which an individual moves during employment within an organization. Career paths are the logical sequence of job progression tracks for employees to follow. For example, the progression of a sales representative to account director to sales manager to vice president (sales) constitutes one such track.

While planning their careers, individuals determine the types of training and development they would require at different stages to be able to successfully achieve their goals. At the same time, they need to monitor their progress towards their goals. They also need to determine the relevance and appropriateness of their career goals in a dynamically evolving environment and may revise their career expectations from time to time. For instance, a fresh management graduate may choose to join a consumer goods firm, but, two or three years later, the same person may feel disenchanted with the industry and its pace of work. This may propel the individual to change his/her career track. He/she may then choose to go for further studies and join the world of academics.

Traditionally, career planning was considered to be the responsibility of the employee. However, employees may lack the information required for determining their career goals. They may also lack the skills to develop suitable career plans. This situation can lead to blocked ambitions, frustration, and lowered motivation. Therefore, it is important that organizations provide resources and support to help employees identify their career paths and plan their careers accordingly.

Career Planning Methods/Practices

Organizations may use various ways to support employees in deciding their career goals and career plans. The career planning methods that may be used by organizations to help individuals in career planning include communication, counselling, career planning workshops, self-development materials, and assessment programmes (Figure 9.4). The objectives of these methods are described in Table 9.1.

These career planning practices may be used by organizations in isolation or in combination. For example, an organization may provide self-development materials to the employees as part of career planning support. Another organization may organize career planning workshops and disseminate career-related information on a regular basis. For example, JPMorgan Chase offers a

Table 9.1:   Objective of Career Planning Methods/Practices

Career Planning Methods/Practices	Objectives
Communication	▪ To provide career-related information to employees ▪ Give information about career opportunities and career paths available within the organization ▪ Disseminate information about the resources available to employees, such as educational assistance, training and development options, etc.
Counselling (may be conducted by company counsellors, external experts, or by managers)	▪ To help employees with their personal assessment of interests, aptitudes, and capabilities ▪ To facilitate employees' interpretation of self-assessment in the context of their career plans
Career planning workshops	▪ To help employees assess their own interests and abilities ▪ To help employees set personal career goals and plans for development
Self-development materials	▪ Providing employees with materials such as workbooks, reading material, and other media aimed at career planning ▪ These materials may be integrated with other career planning practices such as workshops and counselling
Assessment programmes (include a battery of tests on interests, abilities, aptitudes, etc.)	▪ To facilitate employees in setting their career goals ▪ To provide employees with a basis to assess how well their personal abilities may fit with their career paths ▪ To identify specific developmental needs required for achieving employees' career goals

Source: Huse and Cummings 1980

wide range of programmes and services globally to help its employees improve their skills, grow in their career, and meet their personal and professional commitments. JP Morgan Chase has a set of tools and resources that help its employees around the world assess their strengths, set career goals, improve skills, and identify growth opportunities within the firm. Employees can establish a concrete plan for career growth. Learning Connect is a career management programme at JPMorgan Chase that provides employees with ready online access to all types of global firm-wide training as well as business-specific learning, from instructor-led training and virtual classrooms to web-based programmes, and ordering self-study materials. Employees are able to follow a comprehensive and personalized learning path.

Since unique needs and concerns are associated with each career stage, career planning practices and activities need to be customized to the specific

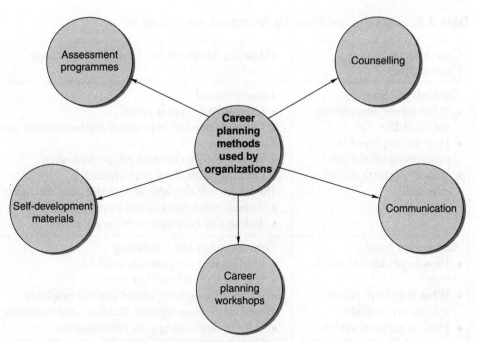

Figure 9.4: Career Planning Methods Used by Organizations

concerns of each career stage. This requires, first, diagnosing the career stage in which an employee presently is. Secondly, it involves designing the career planning practices to help the employee address the concerns and issues relevant to that career stage.

Table 9.2 presents the main career planning concerns and how each of the career planning methods may be appropriately used for each career stage.

The career planning practices used by firms are directed towards meeting the employee needs and expectations associated with each of the four career stages. A number of career planning practices are adopted by firms for their employees at the establishment stage. Infosys, for example, maps out a software engineer's future the day the individual joins the firm. Using a combination of training and small simulated projects, the company assesses each newcomer's abilities and strengths. The career plan is then determined accordingly. The manager provides constant feedback to the newcomer. Sapient Corporation, LG Electronics, and Modi Xerox are a few of the several firms which assign mentors to newcomers. Noida-based ST Microelectronics provides its employees in the first career stage with a great deal of freedom to work. The firm also ensures that the newcomer works on critical projects right from the beginning. This gives an opportunity to the new employees to demonstrate their potential and experience a sense of achievement. HCL Technologies also provides newcomers with tremendous operational freedom and the constant stimuli of working with cutting-edge technology. At ICICI,

Table 9.2: Concerns and Planning Methods at each Career Stage

Concerns at Each Career Stage	Planning Methods for Each Career Stage
Establishment Stage • What career alternatives are available • How an employee is performing on the job • How to perform more effectively	*Communication* • On available career paths • On skills needed to progress on these career paths *Counselling* • To give feedback about job performance • On how to improve performance *Workshops, Self-development Materials, and Assessment Centres* • To help employees in self-assessment • To link this information to career plans
Advancement Stage • How to advance in one's career • What long-term career options are available • How to integrate career demands like transfers with personal lives	*Communication and Counselling* • Challenging assignments available • Feedback on where they stand • Range of long-term career options available *Workshops, Self-development Materials, and Assessment Centres* • Help in developing peer relationships • Identifying effective mentors • Help in integrating life and career spheres
Maintenance Stage • How to help new employees in their careers • Reassessment of self and career • How to redirect efforts to continue to contribute, such as by helping newcomers • Mid-life crisis for some employees	*Communication* • About how the employee's new role fits with the organization *Workshops, Self-development Materials, Counselling and Assessment Centres* • Develop skills in order to train and coach others • Develop mentoring skills • Reassess circumstances • To identify new roles and develop in new directions • Help individuals confront identity issues • Emotional counselling for those experiencing crisis
Withdrawal Stage • Stress about work to non-work transition • How to secure a productive leisure life • How to be financially secure	*Communication and Counselling* • Financial security • Acknowledge the importance of employees' experience *Retirement Planning Materials and Workshops* • Develop skills and gain relevant information • Facilitate transition from work to non-work lives • Help develop other interests

Adapted from: Huse and Cummings 1980

empowerment of employees, who are fresh from a business school or university programme, is very swift. Immediately after the orientation, the employee is given an assignment and may be required to take decisions in the very first week.

For employees in the advancement stage, organizations provide fast track growth, career counselling, and lateral movements. Polaris Software Labs identifies high performers, who are called 'konarks'. These employees are treated as mini CEOs and are invited to participate in strategic thinking sessions. They also enjoy accelerated career development. The 'high flyer' concept of LG rewards exceptional performers with double promotions. The HLL tradition of identifying high potential managers as 'listers' has been a much talked about practice. The listers are managers who are given more responsibility. Several firms such as Ashok Leyland and Marico provide opportunities for job rotations to employees in the advancement career stage to provide opportunities for skill development. Eicher, HLL, Modi Xerox, BILT, and Crompton Greaves are some of the firms who are using assessment centres for development purposes. General Electric (GE) believes in assessing performance and aligning performance with meritocracy. Towards this end, GE has a well developed system of continuously measuring its people and providing them feedback. Based on performance and potential, GE works with-employees in helping them map their career and move ahead. PricewaterhouseCoopers (PwC) has an independent career counselling service to help employees recognize their development needs and develop action plans.

Organizations offer opportunities for cross-functional movements for their employees in the maintenance stage of their careers. Several organizations offer opportunities for skill upgradation through specialized training programmes or sponsoring employees to enroll for management development programmes in reputed business schools. Aviva Life Insurance sends its high-performing middle-level managers to IIM Ahmedabad on an 'accelerated leadership programme'. The firm also selects some middle-level managers for 'rotational development programmes' to provide them cross-functional avenues of growth. Wipro, L&T, HCL Infosystems, and FedEx Corporation are some other firms that encourage employees who are in this stage to go for development programmes in order to provide them opportunities for cross-functional movements.

Bharat Heavy Electricals Ltd (BHEL) provides reading material to employees who are nearing retirement, i.e., in the withdrawal career stage. As support for these employees, BHEL also organizes workshops for providing guidance for financial planning.

All of these career planning methods are used by organizations to assist employees in their career planning efforts. Yet, the primary responsibility for establishing career goals and career paths still rests with the employees. Organizations can adopt a more active role in helping individuals attain their career goals. This idea is explained in detail in the next section.

CAREER DEVELOPMENT

As mentioned earlier, career development is a formal approach taken by an organization to help employees in achieving their career objectives. Thus, career development includes all those activities undertaken by the organization which prepare an employee to meet the current and future needs of the organization. Career development, therefore, benefits both the employee and the organization. While employees become better equipped to meet their goals, they also add value to the organization through superior performance, higher motivation, and commitment. Career development may include various organizational practices such as skills training, performance feedback, coaching, planned job rotation, etc. Like career planning, career development activities too need to be integrated with specific career needs of the employees at each career stage. As mentioned earlier, each career stage is characterized by specific career issues relevant to career planning. Career development practices should be geared towards helping employees implement these career plans. Career development needs are likely to evolve as an employee progresses from one career stage to the next. Therefore, different career development practices are likely to be relevant and effective at different career stages. Table 9.3 depicts the specific career development needs associated with each career stage and the career development interventions that organizations can adopt to facilitate career development.

Table 9.3:   Career Development Interventions for each Career Stage

Career Stages	Career Development Needs	Career Development Interventions
Establishment Stage	• Challenging initial job • Variety in job activities • Opportunities for development of relevant skills • Feedback on performance and potential	• Realistic job preview • Job pathing • Performance feedback and coaching
Advancement Stage	• Opportunity to do challenging work • Exposure and visibility in the firm • Opportunity to demonstrate potential • Balance career with outside interests • Dual career concerns	• Challenging and visible assignments • Mentoring • Assessment centres • Dual career accommodation

Contd

Table 9.3 Contd

Career Stages	Career Development Needs	Career Development Interventions
Maintenance Stage	■ Levelling off and maintaining careers ■ Redefine role in company ■ Opportunities to develop others ■ Autonomy	■ Developmental training ■ Assigning mentoring roles ■ Rotation to jobs requiring new skills ■ Mid-career counselling
Withdrawal Stage	■ Adjust to role of retired person ■ Continue to use experience to help others ■ Establish a meaningful life outside the organization	■ Consultative roles ■ Phased retirement ■ Retirement counselling

Adapted from: Huse and Cummings 1980

Establishment Stage

The career development interventions for the establishment stage are explained in this section.

Realistic job preview (RJP) Employees often develop unrealistically high expectations about their jobs and the organization. This usually happens when employees get 'good news only' information about the organization from various sources such as business magazines, company communications, and so on before joining for the organization. On joining the firm, if their high expectations are not fulfilled, they may suffer from 'reality shock' resulting in reactions such as reduced motivation, performance, and even employee turnover. Firms may prevent such unproductive reactions by providing employees with realistic expectations about the job prior to signing the employment contract. During the establishment stage, it is important even for newcomers to assess whether the company and job are likely to be consistent with their career plans. Therefore, they need objective information about organizations and jobs. For example, Texas Instruments (TI) hires only those individuals who have the specific skills the centre needs. Hence, employees joining TI know about the company and their job profiles well in advance. This practice, according to the manager (staffing) at TI, helps in managing employee expectations. Tata Telecom has recently introduced some changes in its mode of recruitment, the key priority being to get the right candidate. Before calling candidates for an interview, it sends a CD to them which contains information about the company, its work environment, and HR policies.

Job pathing It refers to the planned movement of an individual through a carefully developed sequence of job assignments to develop his/her skills, knowledge, and competencies. The jobs in the sequence are at the same organizational level. Job pathing provides challenging job assignments to employees fairly early on in their careers. Employees move through selected jobs of increasing challenges and responsibility, thus allowing for gradual stretching of their talents. Effective job pathing requires the following steps:

1. Identifying a target job for the employee
2. Identifying the skills and experience an employee needs to reach this target job
3. Laying out a sequence of jobs that provides experience in those skills
4. Assigning the employee to each job in this sequence one at a time. When the employee gains experience and performs well on one job he/she is moved to a more demanding job sequentially.

Each subsequent job in this career path requires more advanced skills and knowledge. The sequence is arranged to provide skills and experience in small enough increments so as not to overload the individual, but in large enough jumps so that the person is always being stretched. For job pathing to be successful, different jobs should provide enough challenge to stretch an individual's learning capacity. Moreover, the target job should not be withheld for too long. Job pathing helps in minimizing the time the employee takes to reach the target job. Quite similar to job pathing is the practice at Infosys to map a software engineer's future the day he/she joins the organization. Infosys uses a blend of training and simulated projects to assess each new employee's abilities and strengths. This is used to determine the career plan of the newcomer. Constant feedback from the employee is used to modify the career plan. For example, when the engineers in the firm complained that they were progressing only as engineers but not as managers, the HR department initiated management development programmes for developing the leadership skills of these engineers.

At Hughes Software Systems (HSS), the 'people action plan' is steered by the CEO. In this plan, managers work with employees who have spent at least one year at HSS to understand their career aspirations and develop plans to provide opportunities to fulfil these.

Performance feedback and coaching Career establishment can be facilitated by a superior by providing performance feedback, coaching, and on-the-job training. This, by far, is one of the most effective interventions during the first career stage. Through performance feedback and coaching, employees are helped in getting the job done, while, at the same time, meeting their career development needs. Silicon Automation Systems (SAS) uses a comprehensive performance, planning, review, and development module to clearly explain to its employees their targets, whether they have achieved them, and where they can expect their career paths in the company to lead.

General Electric believes in continuously measuring performance and giving feedback. Based on performance and potential, GE helps employees map their career and move ahead.

Advancement Stage

The various career development interventions in the advancement stage are explained here.

Challenging and visible assignments Such assignments include transfers into new areas after an individual has demonstrated competence in one area. Such rotations provide employees with the challenge and visibility they need for advancing further in their careers. Firms like Procter and Gamble (P&G) and Hewlett-Packard (HP) have such interventions in place. Hewlett-Packard, for example, identifies 'comers'. Comers are managers who are under forty years and demonstrate potential for assuming top management positions. These employees are provided with cross-divisional experiences in the form of cross-divisional job transfers or promotions. For example, a 'comer' who is in advancement stage, may be transferred from the consumer products division to the industrial products division. This provides an opportunity to employees to acquire a broad range of skills and knowledge to display their managerial talent to the top executives of the firm.

General Electric provides global opportunities across different businesses for its high-performing and high-potential managers. This offers a unique opportunity for learning and experience. These are typically six-month to two-year assignments at client locations. After completing these stints, these employees return to the business and share their knowledge and expertise.

The Global Leadership Program at GE identifies high potential external and internal individuals for its leadership development. The headership programme members belong to a core area of expertise, for example, HRLP for human resources, FMP for finance, and IMLP for information management. The individuals progress through multiple locations across businesses, locations, and sometimes functions to prepare them for substantial roles at the end of the programme.

To prevent the possibility of an employee in the advancement stage from becoming trapped in a new job assignment that is neither challenging nor visible, it helps to have fallback positions. The fallback position assures the individual that there is a position equal in status and pay to the original job to which the individual can move if things do not work out in the new position. Procter and Gamble is one such firm that has employee fallback positions. Fallback positions are identified before an employee is transferred and employees are assured that they can return to them, without negative consequences, if transfers do not work out.

Mentoring It involves establishing a close relationship with a superior who takes a personal interest in the employee's career and guides and sponsors the employee. A mentor ensures that the hard work and skills advancements of the protégé get noticed and rewarded. It has been observed that most successful people have had a mentor or mentors. Several firms, such as Modi Xerox, JPMorgan Chase, Eicher, Infosys, and Ashok Leyland have started formal mentoring programmes. Mentoring is dealt with in more detail later in Chapter 10.

Assessment centres Traditionally used for the selection of high potential managers, assessment centres use a battery of psychological tests, in-basket exercises, simulations, interviews, group discussions, etc. over a period of four to five days. Each assessment centre is facilitated by trained observers. At the end of the assessment centre workshop, a detailed assessment report of each individual is prepared. More recently, assessment centres have been used for purposes such as performance evaluations, promotions, career development, etc. When assessment centre approach is used for career development purposes, the organization becomes a partner in individual development by providing employees with the support and direction needed for career development. The emphasis is on providing feedback on assessment centre results to participants and on counselling them about career advancement training required by them to aid their advancement. IBM, AT&T, and General Motors are some firms who have assessment centres. Many firms in India who have established assessment centres include Cadbury, Aditya Birla Group, Eicher, RPG, TISCO, Wipro, and Castrol (India).

Dual-career accommodations It is during the advancement stage of their careers that most individuals are likely to settle down with a partner. More women are entering the workforce today. Hence, dual-career couples have become more prevalent. A major career issue confronted by individuals in this career stage is that of job transfer to another location. When both the husband and wife are working, the transfer of either one of them would mean that the spouse also relocates. For instance, if the wife gets transferred to another city, then the company employing her husband must either lose one employee (the husband may change the job to be with the wife) or may arrange for the husband to be transferred to the same location as his wife. Career development interventions that may be adopted by firms for helping employees cope with the problems inherent in dual careers include help with relocation, flexi-time, and day-care centres. These initiatives make it easier for both the husband and the wife to work outside the home. These issues have been discussed in detail in Chapter 11 which deals with work–life integration.

Maintenance Stage

The career development interventions for the maintenance stage focusses on development training, mentoring, job rotation, and mid-career counselling. These are explained briefly in this section.

Development training Employees at the maintenance stage have usually reached the highest possible level in their career. In this stage, the attention of most employees is focussed on developing and grooming less-experienced employees for higher responsibilities. Therefore, career development programmes help employees gain the skills and knowledge for training and coaching others. In-house programmes for training managers to develop skills to train and coach others include reading material, lectures, experiential exercises, and case studies on topics such as active listening and supportive relationships. These practices are rotated with on-the-job experiences and workshops for developing coaching skills. Ashok Leyland uses questionnaires and management games to develop team spirit, leadership qualities, and feedback skills among middle managers. Ramco Systems, BPL, and ITC also focus on developing skills required for the role of middle managers.

Assigning mentoring roles A manager in this career stage can also be assigned the role of a mentor. As mentors, such managers assume responsibility for mentoring younger employees who are in the establishment and advancement stages of their careers. A mentoring role offers opportunities to mid-career managers to satisfy one of their major career concerns of the maintenance stage—to share their knowledge and experience with those who are less experienced than them. It has been observed in Crompton Greaves that performance level of middle managers rise when they are given mentoring assignments. Philips Software too trains its managers to become mentors for younger employees.

Rotation to jobs requiring new skills It has been observed that when individuals remain in one job for three years or more, they become unresponsive to job features such as autonomy, responsibility, skill variety, and other job enrichment characteristics. It is only during the first one to three years that jobs are seen as challenging and motivating. Then they lose their motivational value. Hence job rotation is an important developmental tool. When employees are moved to a new job, it provides them with new challenges and opportunities for learning and contribution. By providing mid-career alternatives in the form of rotation to new and more challenging jobs at about three year intervals, organizations can prevent the loss of motivation among this group of employees. Job rotations for this group of employees assume importance since they are likely to remain in jobs for longer periods of time than employees in the establishment and advancement stages. At times, redesigning the current job can also serve the function of sustaining employee motivation. The middle level managers in the Tata group who have completed about fifteen years in their existing functions are provided cross-functional exposure. They are encouraged in decision-making and their span of responsibility is increased. Some companies encourage employees who are not promoted to make lateral moves that can broaden their experience. Companies also provide assignments to these employees that are different from those they have had in the past. At GE, middle level managers are encouraged to take a foreign assignment or take positions that they could not hold at a younger age. The employees who reach mid-level in organizational hierarchy are usually more settled in life and have grown up children. General Electric encourages these employees to take advantage of the greater flexibility and personal mobility that they have at this age. The organization actively recruits seasoned managers for jobs overseas. For instance, a middle level manager who had spent most of his career in the US was transferred to Budapest after his children grew up. Recently, this manager moved again to China, where he helps local employees understand GE procedures and culture. Phillips has effectively redeployed mid-career managers to the company's overseas operations to retain this group of managers whose experience makes them ideal candidates for handling sensitive situations. Overseas posting rescues them from their comfort zones, rejuvenates them, and makes them productive again. Similarly, New York apparel maker Phillips-Van Heusen provides new career opportunities for its seasoned employees. For instance, a manager of a branded business may be given an option of moving to a design business. At Marico, employees at mid-career stage are provided frequent inter-functional movements and are involved in the strategic business planning of the firm.

Mid-career counselling Employees in the maintenance stage are also likely to confront mid-career crisis as mentioned earlier in the chapter. Mid-career crisis leads to lowered job performance as employees' upward mobility levels off. Providing counselling to help the plateaued employees (those with little chance of further advancement) accept their new role in the company can help them continue to have satisfying and productive careers. For example, Marico organizes value experiential workshops for mid-career employees. The workshops are designed to help these employees understand and accept that promotion is not the sole criterion for measuring growth. It is communicated to them that being assigned to leadership or problem-solving tasks is a measure of the trust that the organization has in their abilities. It is one of the ways that the organization redefines their role in the firm.

Withdrawal Stage

Organizations have not been very proactive in helping employees cope with the withdrawal stage. Traditionally, career development interventions have focussed on younger employees who are likely to contribute to the firm for longer periods. However, more recently, a few firms have been helping employees manage their withdrawal from active work life.

Consultative roles Employees in their late career stages can be assigned the role of consultants. This provides them the opportunity to apply their wisdom and knowledge to help others in solving organizational problems. Consultative roles are different from mentoring roles. In consultative roles, employees help in dealing with complex organizational problems or projects. Mentors, on the other hand, focus on guiding and helping a younger manager's career. Moreover, in consultative roles, senior managers' credibility is based more on wisdom and experience rather than on managerial authority vested in that position. Hence, older managers can apply their years of experience and skills in a more supportive way. Consultative roles provide a smooth transition for pre-retirement managers to more support-staff positions. Some public sector firms in India follow this practice. Eicher Goodearth Ltd is one of the firms that retains its retired managers in consultative roles.

Phased retirement An effective way to withdraw from active work life and establish a productive leisure life is to reduce the time devoted to the organization gradually. For example, an employee nearing retirement may be given time off work to enroll for certain courses and gain new skills to create a productive post-retirement life. Alternatively, they may be required to work part-time so that they may make a gradual transition from organizational to retired life. An important advantage of phased retirement is that it lessens the reality shock for employees nearing retirement and allows them to withdraw emotionally from the organization. Various universities in India have been following the practice of phased retirement. Professors who attain the retirement age of 62 years are re-employed for the next three years. The retiree in such cases can gradually withdraw from work life.

Retirement counselling By providing counselling to employees who are about to retire, organizations can facilitate a smooth work-to-non-work transition. Some of the practices adopted by firms to manage the concerns associated with the withdrawal stage include retirement workshops, providing material on post-retirement financial planning, and organizing alternative skills training programmes. The pre-retirement workshops of BHEL are designed to offer the employees guidance for financial planning and attitude change towards life. The workshops have a spiritual element too with discourses by spiritual leaders. The firm also provides a retirement planning booklet to these employees. HSBC Bank also offers pre-retirement counselling to its employees.

CAREER MANAGEMENT SYSTEMS

The basic unit in career management is the individual. As mentioned earlier, career management refers to a collaborative effort between the employee and the organization, which results in career development. It is the process by which organizational career planning is implemented. Therefore, there exists an interaction between the organizational and individual approaches to career planning and development. Career management is best viewed as a partnership between the individual and the organization and, therefore, as a shared responsibility. For instance, at JPMorgan Chase, it is believed that career management will succeed only if it is a partnership between employees, their managers, and the firm. While each employee is expected to take a leadership role in managing his/her own career, it is critical that employees, managers, and the firm work together to provide a supportive environment in which all reach full potential.

However, there are two different viewpoints on career management—the individual perspective and the organizational perspective. Depending on whether the prime emphasis in career planning is on individual needs or organizational needs one of the following career management systems (Figure 9.5) may be chosen:

- Individual-centred system
- Organization-centred system

Individual-Centred Career Management System

When the career management system is oriented towards individual career perspective, the individual's goals and aspirations are the most important. The focus is on the individual's career rather than on organizational needs. Efforts are directed towards

- identifying the individual's career goals;
- assessing the individual's personal abilities and interests;
- planning the individual's life and work goals;
- assessing alternative career paths inside and outside the organization;
- drawing a career path for the individual; and
- noting changes in interests and goals as career and life stages change.

The individual-centred system considers situations both within and outside the organization. Career paths encompass opportunities outside the organization if individual goals cannot be fulfilled within it. For example, a medical representative of a pharmaceutical firm may aspire to rise to the position of Vice President (Sales). However, if it becomes apparent that his/her career aspirations can be best achieved outside the employing organization, the

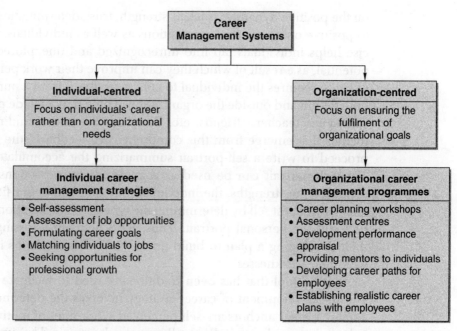

Figure 9.5: Viewpoints in Career Management

employee may decide to leave it after reaching the maximum possible point in the career path.

Individual Strategies for Career Management

According to Gordon (1986), individuals can use the career management strategies explained in this section.

Self-assessment Through self-assessment, individuals can take stock of their own skills, personal characteristics, goals, and aspirations. An evaluation of personal strengths and weaknesses is basic to career planning since it provides a platform for determining which job to select from among alternative offers, the sequence of jobs that will lead to desired career goals, the jobs to seek or avoid, and the strategy to be followed to secure a particular job.

Individuals have a number of options for collecting and analysing data about themselves. For instance, they may complete a series of exercises like writing an autobiography, listing significant experiences, and reconstructing their own career progress.

One of the tools that can be used by managers to understand and leverage their talents is the *Reflected Best Self* (RBS) exercise. This tool has been developed by Roberts et al. (2005) as a core part of 'The Positive Organization' (POS) mission to help organizations improve their practices. The positive organization is an area of research in organizational behaviour that focusses on the positive dynamics (such as strength, trust, determination, etc.) that lead to positive outcomes for organizations as well as individuals. The RBS exercise helps individuals tap into unrecognized and unexplored areas of their potential, as a result of which they can improve their work performance. This exercise requires the individual to collect feedback from a number of people, both within and outside the organization. These may include past and present colleagues, teachers, friends, etc. Based on the understanding gained from themes that emerge from this comprehensive feedback, the individual may proceed to write a self-portrait summarizing the accumulated information. This self-portrait can be used as a guide for future actions. Thus, having identified the strengths, the individual may obtain a better fit between work and his/her best self by determining the type of job description that is likely to best suit the personal portrait. Thus, RBS helps in assessing strengths and then developing a plan to build upon them and also helps individuals deal with their weaknesses.

Another tool that has been traditionally used to facilitate self-assessment and the development of career strategy involves the determination of *career anchors*. Career anchors are self-perceived syndromes of motives, talents, and values that guide an individual's career decisions. The concept of career anchors was developed by Edgar Schein (1978) based on a twelve year study of MBA graduates from the Massachusetts Institute of Technology (MIT). From extensive interviews with the graduates, Schein developed five career anchors. A detailed description of these career anchors is provided in Exhibit 9.3. The career anchor model is designed to guide individuals in contemplating their career movements as well as to assist organizations in helping their employees with career planning.

Assessment of job opportunities Individual career management also requires employees to regularly monitor the job opportunities available within and outside the firm. Thus, an individualized career management requires the employee to consider exiting the organization if the present employer is unlikely to offer opportunities that will utilize the employee's potential. Employees, therefore, must pay attention to company bulletins, recruiting literature, newspaper articles, trade journals, etc. that describe the jobs available. Other sources of job information include friends and family, members of alumni associations, professional societies, etc.

Formulating career goals Once individuals have gathered self-assessment information, as well as information about job opportunities, they should formulate specific career goals for themselves. In determining career goals, individuals should clarify the following:

- Work-related activities they are looking for
- Demands the position will place on personal and family time

Exhibit 9.3

Career Anchors

The five career anchors identified by Schein are:

- *Technical/functional competence* : Individuals high on this career anchor prefer to specialize in a particular functional area such as finance or marketing. They are not interested in general management.
- *Managerial competence* : These individuals prefer to supervise and guide others. Hence they like to assume the general management responsibility.
- *Autonomy and independence* : These individuals place a high premium on autonomy. They are not comfortable working in large organizations. These individuals may be found in positions such as writers, professors, consultants, etc.
- *Creativity*: Individuals with the creative career

anchor, that is, a need to create something new, are often entrepreneurs.

- *Security/stability*: Individuals who prefer long-term career stability fit with this career anchor. Jobs such as permanent government jobs provide such long-term security.

Career anchors form over time. An individual's specific work and life experiences may modify the career anchors. Knowledge about their career anchors can help individuals find a job that fits with these. For instance, individuals with creativity as a career anchor may feel claustrophobic in bureaucratic organizations. A lack of fit between the anchor and the job can cause individuals to leave the organization. Therefore, organizations should also identify their employees' career anchors.

Source: Schein 1978

- Limitations they have with respect to location of the job and mobility if the spouse is working
- What sequence of positions they need to go through to perform effectively on the target position

Matching individuals to jobs Individuals should look for job opportunities that fit with personal goals and aspirations. It is also important for the individual to continuously monitor his/her own career movement over time to ensure that the career is on track. Further, career strategy should be flexible enough to allow individuals to adjust their career direction as their career goals evolve or shift.

The People Action Plan of HSS that focusses on the career aspirations of employees and develops plans to provide opportunities is one example of individual-centred career management. At FedEx Corporation, the company ranked number one by *Business World* in its 2004 survey, employees have the opportunity to rise from the ranks. Managers discuss career paths and interests with their employees. The right type of training need is then identified that will help employees progress through their career paths. The manager then also works with the in-house training department to identify the right opportunities for the employees. SAP Labs projects career development as the responsibility of the individual employee. The firm caters to varying career aspirations of employees while employees are able to steer their own career path at their own speed. At Intel Technologies India, a lot of emphasis is given on the personal growth of employees. Each Intel employee has a development plan on which the employee charts out his/her career. The employee and the manager discuss about the former's career goals and Intel invests on the training that the employee requires to achieve the goal.

Organization-Centred Career Management System

The main purpose of the organization-centred system is to fulfil the goals of the organization. It is concerned with jobs in the organization and on constructing career paths that provide logical progression of people between jobs within the organization. Efforts in the organization-centred system are directed towards

- identifying organizational objectives;
- determining future manpower staffing needs of the firm;
- identifying available career paths within the firm;
- communicating with employees about opportunities;
- assessing employees' potential as well as training needs; and
- matching organizational needs with individual abilities.

In a dynamic business environment, organization-centred career planning and development ensures that capable employees are available to meet the organization's needs at all times.

Infowavz International, an ITeS company, follows an organization-centred career management system. The company communicates the career path to the employee along with the job description and key result areas (KRAs) right at the recruitment stage itself. The career planning form of the firm outlines the organizational structure and the skill sets required for various functions and at different levels in the firm. Infowavz International also evaluates each individual's competencies, strengths, and areas of improvement under a comprehensive 'training needs analysis' (TNA) programme, for current and future roles. Personal counselling and psychometric profiling form part of the process. Based on this, the firm is able to clearly chart out and communicate specific career options to its employees. The firm is also able to help them build skill sets and bridge gaps that would facilitate the employees in developing their careers effectively. This process is repeated at regular intervals including at the time of performance appraisals.

Thus, the organization-centred system looks at individuals filling the needs of the organization, whereas the individual-centred system addresses each individual's personal career goals and development issues. However, the two systems are not separate and distinct. They are complementary and interact with each other. By integrating the needs of the organization and goals of the employees, both the perspectives may be brought together. Individuals whose career goals cannot be fulfilled within an organization are likely to leave the organization sooner or later. If opportunities are not available to the individuals outside the firm, thus making it imperative to continue membership with the organization, they may respond by reduced productivity. Under both the circumstances, it is the performance of the organization that gets affected. Therefore, it is in the interest of organizations to assist employees in career planning so that both the individual and the organizational goals are fulfilled.

Indian Shaving Products Limited (ISPL), a subsidiary of Gillette, believes that it must be an equal partner with each of its employees in planning their careers. Employee goals should fit with the organization's goals and should be complemented with institutional support in facilitating the career choice. At ISPL, the career planning process begins with the employee's self-assessment. The firm uses a competency model known as the Behaviour Event Interview (BEI) to draft career paths for its managers. This model is applied with the help of human resource development consultants, allows each manager to be assessed on 60 competencies, and throws up a career path for the manager. The assessment is followed by a validation of the evaluation by the employee's superior. Differences in perception are ironed out before the career plan is finalized. The company matches the individual employee's competencies against the competencies that possible future jobs will require and then decides whether to let the employee follow that career path or not.

Organizations may undertake various combinations of career management programmes for meeting their career management objectives. Career management programmes include counselling employees to help in their individual career planning, offering career planning workshops, using assessment centres, conducting developmental performance appraisals, providing mentors to individuals, and developing career paths for employees. Examples of comprehensive career planning and development programmes of some organizations are presented in Exhibit 9.4.

Exhibit 9.4

Examples of career planning and development
programmes of some organizations

Zensar Technologies Limited is a leading software solution provider headquartered in Pune (India). All HR processes in Zensar are based on the competency framework. A competency model consisting of 19 behavioural competencies has been developed with the help of reputed consultants. The objective of career planning at Zensar is to chart formal career paths across the

Contd

Exhibit 9.4 Contd

organization and help employees build their careers within the organization. Each path in the firm is a series of positions and for each position, competencies have been identified. Employees, depending upon their career aspirations, can move along a path or even across paths. If there are gaps in the competencies required for the new position, these are bridged through training and inputs given on self-development. Career progression forms containing inputs from performance appraisal, 360 degree feedback wherever applicable, and development centres are prepared to help the employee and his/her mentor arrive at career-related decisions. The development centre is a sophisticated rating device that is conducted at the campus to assess the potential of the middle level managers and help them to enhance the competencies required in their job roles as well as to assume larger roles in the future.

Fannie May Confections Inc., a wholly owned subsidiary of Alpine Confections Inc., is based in Chicago. The Fannie May brand stands for premium quality chocolate and is committed to support the professional development of every member of the work force and offers a variety of career development programmes. The career development programmes play an integral part in increasing opportunities for growth and advancement of all employees. The career development programmes at Fannie May include the following:

- Financial assistance for college education to help employees who seek to enhance their careers through an undergraduate or graduate degree programme
- Career development training for career development opportunities
- Skill development training for enhancing specific professional skills
- Job rotation programmes
- Consultation among employees and managers where, through one-on-one sessions,

employees discuss tailored development strategies
- Lunch and learn sessions which are targeted at employees with an interest in developing goals, writing personal career development plans tied to business objectives, and identifying learning opportunities tailored to meet employees' needs. For managers, these sessions explore career coaching for employees, how to develop mutually beneficial goals tied to organizational objectives, and establishing learning objectives for employees
- Assessment tools to help employees define and clarify their interests, values, and skills while targeting specific organizational learning opportunities
- A variety of courses to enhance employee knowledge or skills related to managing their careers, including managing personal growth and career coaching for managers
- Numerous training programmes for technology and other business disciplines

American Express views career development as a process of giving employees knowledge, skills, and competencies to prepare them for future jobs and responsibilities. The company's employees can choose their own target jobs at the same level in a different function or even at a higher level in a different function. American Express then helps the employees to qualify for that job using a two-pronged tool:

- Professional development process (PDP)
- Performance management process (PMP)

Both PDP and PMP work together to guide the company employees through an entire chain:

- Specific goals are set for the employee, covering business targets and other objectives.
- To help the employee achieve these goals, development planning is provided after assessing the gaps in technical and motivational skills.

Contd

Exhibit 9.4 Contd

- This is followed by coaching, feedback, and performance and potential appraisal. Within this broad framework, American Express enables its employees to plan their careers using a customized development grid. For example, after an employee identifies the target job, assessment reveals where he/she stands on the competency scales required for a particular job. The skills and knowledge required to perform the job, and the soft skills, personality type, strengths, and weaknesses are assessed. The latter constitutes competency assessment. This helps determine how well the individual is suited for that role by determining the gaps between the individual's personality and the desired profile for the job. This gap helps to identify the development plan for the employee, that is, the kind of training or participation in a cross-functional project that the employee may be provided with.
- If more number of employees target a job, the person with the highest competency ratings for that particular job will ultimately get that job.

SAP Labs India is a product development organization having its own definition of success and progress. Growth in the company is not associated with notional promotions. Rather, it means adding more value, migrating to new roles, new areas of work, and increased responsibilities. The firm offers four career paths—technical, people management, quality, and product. Employees are coached to follow the one that would be most interesting to them and the most mutually beneficial to the individual and the organization. A career in R&D at SAP requires an employee to work on one product for years, refining it with newer applications, versions, and upgradations. SAP Labs believes that the more time an employee spends on one product, the more value he/she adds to the firm. Therefore, SAP employees in R&D do not jump from project to project. With six to seven labs worldwide, there are ample opportunities for employees. Human resource managers from all global locations meet once a year to decide on transfer guidelines for the employees to provide them opportunities to shift paths. Career development and training at SAP Labs is viewed primarily as the responsibility of the individual employee. To provide greater opportunities to professionals, the firm has a Global Mobility Programme. There are a number of career paths worldwide and employees can steer their own path at their own speed. The firm caters to varying career aspirations of the employees, be it the desire to work in a cross-cultural environment or the need to explore diverse interests such as product development and consulting.

A variety of approaches are used by organizations to help employees plan their careers. Design and implementation of individual career planning programmes constitute one such approach. Through these programmes, individuals are helped in self-assessment, exploring job opportunities, and matching available jobs with their capabilities.

Organizations may also introduce programmes that respond to varying issues individuals face at different career stages. For example, during the establishment stage, the career management programmes may include

- providing the employee with a mentor;
- regular scheduling of appraisal discussions;
- providing job challenge through job rotations;

- periodic career counselling; and
- helping develop clear career paths.

On the other hand, in the advancement stage, the organization should provide opportunities for independent contributions by employees. During the maintenance stage, employees may experience content plateaus when the content of their job remains the same for too long, or they may experience structural plateau when there is no room for advancement up the hierarchy. *Content plateaus* may be managed by providing job rotation. *Structural plateaus* may be reduced by introducing alternative career paths or reducing external hiring. To deal with mid-career crisis, organizations can provide their employees with educational opportunities to facilitate their shift to a career path that is valued by the organization.

An effective organization-centred career management strategy provides flexible career options for employees and specific and clear career directions for organizational members.

Organizations also help individuals in career management by helping them determine avenues for career advancement. They can accomplish this by objective identification of job progression paths for their employees. These career paths take into account individual career goals. Therefore, fast trackers are provided avenues for speedy movement to the target job. On the other hand, those who prefer a slower career growth can be provided with lateral moves. Exhibit 9.5 presents the highlights of individual and organizational career management strategies.

Exhibit 9.5

Individual and Organizational Career Management Strategies

Individual Strategies

- Self assessment of interests and talents
- Identifying jobs that fit their skills as well as interests
- Continuously seek opportunities for professional growth through training and taking on new and challenging assignments

Organizational Strategies

- Disseminate complete and accurate information about career opportunities in the firm

- Establish realistic career plans in participation with employees and review progress towards career goals
- Provide opportunities for continuous improvement of employee skills through training programmes, assessment centres, in-house or outsourced educational programmes
- Provide career counselling, career development workshops, and self-reading materials

Source: Kossek and Block 2000

DESIGN AND IMPLEMENTATION OF CAREER MANAGEMENT SYSTEMS

Career management systems draw information from both corporate human resource needs and employee career needs. These systems are also tied to other HR subsystems such as goal-setting, performance appraisal, training and development, etc. However, career management systems are frequently designed and operated without having any connection with human resource planning. Moreover, much of the career development activity takes place in isolation in the classroom and consists of exotic exercises that have little connection with employees' careers within the organization.

There is no one way to implement career management programmes. However, Walker (1980) suggested that if certain guidelines are followed, it is likely to increase implementation success.

Identify career planning needs and develop a strategy The first step in the implementation of a career management system involves the identification of career planning needs and developing a strategy based on these. Career needs can be identified through interview data gathered from managers, HR specialists, and other staff specialists. If employees within the firm express the need for career-planning assistance, they are also likely to suggest the type of practices that would best serve these needs. Developing a career management system with employee participation ensures greater commitment to the programme.

Develop necessary resources Career planning resources, such as career planning workbooks containing exercises on self-assessment, videos, and other such material needs to be developed. Related information such as a firm's personnel policies and realistic information on career opportunities available in the firm also need to be provided along with the career planning information. As mentioned earlier, other HR systems, such as performance appraisal, training and development, recruitment, manpower planning, etc. need to be integrated with each other and the career management system. For instance, a firm may modify its performance appraisal system to be more development oriented, or it may develop a detailed profile of all employees to enable an easier identification of potentials for various job vacancies. This is important in order to ensure that the HR systems support the career management programme. Career development programmes in some firms, for example, American Express, SAP Labs, LG Electronics, ICICI, Aviva Life Insurance, and Godrej Consumer Products Ltd (GCPL) are linked with performance evaluation systems.

Introduction of a pilot programme Before introducing the full programme, it is preferable to examine the resources and materials developed to assess their effectiveness and to bring about modifications if needed. A pilot programme may initially be introduced either in one location of the firm or limited to one department. Feedback from the employees regarding the effectiveness of the programme in helping them gain information and skills for developing their career plans may be obtained through questionnaires. Based on the feedback, necessary modifications may be made at this stage.

Introduction of the full programme Finally, the career management programme can be implemented throughout the organization. Before implementation, employees should be provided information about the programme, what it entails, how to be involved in it, and how to use it. Organizations may also set up a career centre that supports implementation by way of providing material, counselling, and workshops. Other factors that contribute to the effectiveness of career management systems are described below.

Involvement of HR and line managers A comprehensive career management system has implications for human resource professionals as well as for managers. Human resource professionals can be involved in the design and implementation of a career management system in various ways. Some of the activities that may be undertaken by them include career counselling, conducting career workshops, providing career paths in the organization, and training organizational members in the development and implementation of appropriate career strategies. Managers can involve themselves by facilitating the ongoing career development of their subordinates. This they can accomplish by assisting in self-assessment, identifying appropriate and realistic career paths for them, serving as mentors for junior employees, creating advancement opportunities that fit with career stage needs of each employee, and otherwise help them in preparing for future goals. For example, at ICICI the immediate supervisor discusses career options with the employee. A manager's main job at Intel Technologies India is to take care of his/her employees' career development. Senior managers at Intel personally train employees. At Sapient Corporation too, the manager helps map out the career of the employees and provides immediate feedback on their performance.

Top management support For the career management system to be effective, it should be driven from the top. Senior management should be involved in the strategic decisions related to the career planning programme, like any other corporate plan. Career planning should fit the nature of the business, resources available to the firm, company philosophy, attitude toward its employees (paternalistic, democratic, etc.), organizational structure, its employment practices and other human resource practices, and the employees for whom it is planned. Data obtained from career management should be used for other HR systems. For instance, if career discussions suggest training needs related to both the individual and organizations goals, the information should be provided to the training department so that appropriate follow-up may be undertaken. Career management systems, therefore, cannot be effective if they have no linkage with other practices.

There is no one right career management system that can be universally implemented. Moreover, the career system should fit the personality of the firm. In simply-structured informal organizations, very formal and complex career systems may not be effective. The HR personnel should work with the senior management in the design and implementation of the career planning system. Finally, it is important for a firm to consider the results that other firms in the competitive environment have been able to accomplish through their career programmes. Since organizations seek to attract, develop, and retain the best people through their career programmes, they should understand how other firms have accomplished these outcomes through their career management systems. The various aspects of a comprehensive career management system are illustrated in Figure 9.6.

Alignment with culture While implementing career planning and development systems, an organization must consider its basic values and beliefs. Organizations must ensure that the career planning and development system reflects the culture of the organization. For example, if an organization believes in providing opportunities for personal growth to its employees, then it is likely to encourage employees to attend career management seminars. Sapient Corporation is one such organization where employees' growth and career are part of the organizational culture. When an employee joins the organization, initiation of the employee takes place through a coaching programme. The programme manager helps map out the career for the new employee and spells out what the employee must deliver for the company. The performance of the employee is closely monitored until the employee completes the project. On completion of the project, feedback is provided immediately rather than waiting till the year end. Further growth within the firm is linked to the performance feedback. Sapient takes up only very high-value consulting tasks. To ensure that the firm creates business value for its clients, Sapient makes sure that its team is rigorously trained. Working on projects requires the employees to stretch themselves and this, in turn, sets them up for success. The company has managed the strain that arises from the stretch by building a culture of care and transparency. All members of the project team have access to the financial data of the project.

Career planning and development affect the relationship that the employee has with the culture of the organization. It also affects the way the various HRM systems of the organization fit with individual systems, needs, and goals. Organizations design strategies for the integration of career and organizational needs. This integration is becoming increasingly critical to ensure organizational effectiveness.

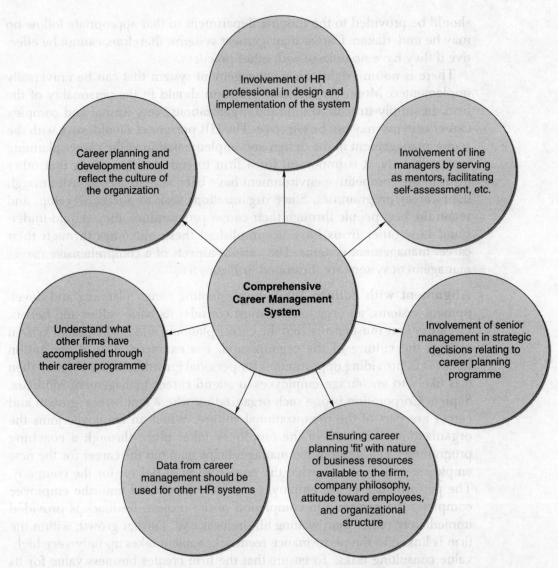

Figure 9.6:   Characteristics of a Comprehensive Career Management System

Culturally, people are attuned to express their identity in terms of the work they do. Therefore, by having a career planning programme in place, individual contribution to the organization can be maximized. Though individuals themselves should be primarily responsible for their own career planning, it is desirable for organizations to provide career planning programmes to facilitate the individual's achievement of personal objectives. This is likely to lead to higher commitment from the individual and a more productive individual–organization relationship.

However, career management programmes are often neither properly planned nor managed. Firms have been viewing career planning programmes as something they implement for the benefit of the employees and that, in the long run, would benefit the firm through improved employee motivation and loyalty. Hence, they have been considered a staff function. Not many firms have formal career programmes such as career counselling and career pathing. Many of the career programmes have traditionally run informally in the organizations. However, recent experiences of organizations have led them to acknowledge that career planning and development is not just something to be done for the employees, but something that should be done for the benefit of the organization too. A properly planned and managed career programme can be a significant HRM tool resulting in cost savings, reduced employee turnover, and increased productivity. Some reflections on how to implement a state-of-the art and successful career management system are summarized in Exhibit 9.6.

Exhibit 9.6

Essentials of a Successful Career Management System

- Top management support to establish a climate conducive for career development
- Responsibility for career development should be shared between the organization, the supervisor, the individual, and the HR personnel
- Training supervisors and managers to facilitate the implementation of organization's career planning
- Integration with other human resource activities such as training, performance evaluation, etc.
- Career-programme objectives should be viewed in terms of organizational performance and effectiveness, even though individual's needs and aspirations are incorporated
- Career systems should be flexible and grow gradually. Firms should avoid having an ambitious career programme just for the sake of having it in place
- Equal access to career planning programmes for all employees

- The immediate supervisor of the individual should serve as the career development agent for the individual. For example, in one of the major IT firms in India, a supervisor cannot be promoted until he/she demonstrates that at least one subordinate is ready for promotion
- Employees should be provided with realistic information about the opportunities available within the firm
- Provide realistic feedback to employees about their success
- The career system should, as emphasized throughout the chapter, provide for the individual's different needs in different career stages
- Climate setting for career development
- Implementation of new career planning programmes should begin with small pilot programmes
- Periodic assessment of employee skills and career management programmes

Adapted from: Morgan, Hall, and Martier1980; Gordon 1986

Following these pre-requisites is likely to result in a successful career management system.

Till now we have emphasized the benefits that accrue to the individual and the organization as a result of a well-designed and implemented career management system. However, a *risk* inherent in implementing career planning programmes is that career planning and development programmes may raise employee expectations by putting additional strains on personnel systems such as training, development support, educational assistance, career development resources, counselling, etc. Raised employee expectations may increase employee anxiety turnover and can be beneficial if this enhances employee motivation. However, if left unfulfilled, it may result in reduced commitment and diminished performance. The solution lies in developing realistic, not raised, career expectations. In a hierarchical organization avenues for promotion are usually limited. In such an organization, realistic career planning should focus on personal development, job importance, and work content rather than on promotability and career ladders. For example, pay-scale promotions and responsibility promotions are delinked in the Centre for Development of Telematics (C-DOT) and the company provides several opportunities for career growth. This allows employees to take higher responsibilities even when they initially join the company at a low pay scale. C-DOT provides career paths for professionals by allowing them to take managerial roles or become experts in their respective technical areas. ITC also offers two broad streams of career, the generalists and specialists, to its employees. The company designs careers without offering vertical movement as the only growth option, thus consciously creating a culture that respects specialization. The focus is on moving people to increasingly higher levels of responsibility or specialization, without it being reflected in their position in the hierarchy. Realistic career expectations minimize dissatisfaction, and enhance employee performance and retention.

ORGANIZATIONAL CAREER MANAGEMENT: A TYPOLOGY

Earlier in the chapter, a list of organizational career management (OCM) practices was identified. Baruch and Peiperl classified OCM into five categories based on factor analysis. The five types of OCM practices are presented in Table 9.4.

Baruch and Peiperl also proposed that there is an association between the types of OCM practices and the features of the organization. The combination of OCM practices that an organization is likely to adopt depends on certain characteristics of the organization. With respect to the above five categories of OCM, the next section discusses the types of organizations that are likely to use each of these (Figure 9.7).

Table 9.4: Categories of Organizational Career Management Practices

Categories of OCM	OCM Practices
Basic	Job postings, formal education as part of career development, pre-retirement programmes, and lateral moves to create cross-functional experience
Active Planning	Performance appraisal as a basis for career planning, career counselling by the direct supervisor, career counselling by the HR department, and succession planning
Active Management	Assessment centres, formal mentoring, and career workshops
Formal	Written personal career planning for employees, dual career ladder, and books and/or pamphlets on career issues
Multi-directional	Peer appraisal, upward (subordinate) appraisal, and common career paths

Adapted from: Baruch and Peiperl 2000

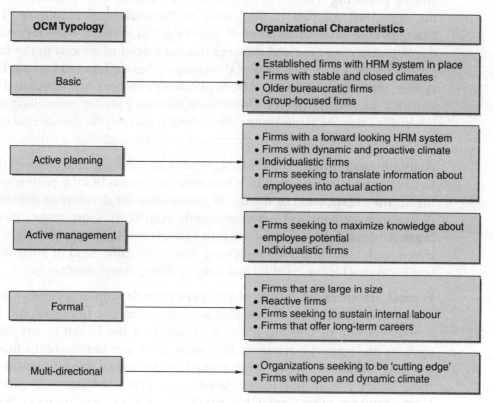

OCM Typology

Basic
Organizational Characteristics
- Established firms with HRM system in place
- Firms with stable and closed climates
- Older bureaucratic firms
- Group-focused firms

Active planning
- Firms with a forward looking HRM system
- Firms with dynamic and proactive climate
- Individualistic firms
- Firms seeking to translate information about employees into actual action

Active management
- Firms seeking to maximize knowledge about employee potential
- Individualistic firms

Formal
- Firms that are large in size
- Reactive firms
- Firms seeking to sustain internal labour
- Firms that offer long-term careers

Multi-directional
- Organizations seeking to be 'cutting edge'
- Firms with open and dynamic climate

Figure 9.7: Fit between OCM and Organizational Characteristics

OCM and Type of Organizations

The categories of OCM and the types of organizations that use these OCM practices are explained in this section.

Basic The practices of this category are elementary and applied in most organizations that have HRM systems in place. Although these practices are widespread, they best fit the older bureaucratic model rather than the new emerging organization. For example, pre-retirement programmes are not very relevant to new firms where most members are not expected to stay till their retirement. These organizations are also so dynamic that job postings become obsolete very fast. New firms are also likely to be reluctant to invest in employee 'education'. They prefer to 'buy' fully qualified personnel due to the cost factor, high employee turnover, and fluctuating skill requirements that render long-term planning impossible. Basic OCM activities have been found to be associated with group-oriented and proactive climates and have always existed in those organizations that took upon themselves the responsibility to facilitate the career progress of all employees at a fundamental level.

Active planning These OCM practices demand an active involvement on the organization's part in the career of the individual employee. These practices also have an element of planning that considers the individual's development over time and the organization's need to fill jobs in the future. Firms that use OCM practices of this category have a forward looking HRM system that takes initiative. Active planning practices are associated with dynamic, proactive climates. Openness is necessary for the counselling activities in this category. Firms using these activities also rely on the internal labour market that reflects the use of career and succession planning within it.

Active management These practices have an informational element that is bi-directional in nature, that is, it involves the process of information gathering for the organization or the use of information for developing individuals. Active management was not significantly related with any measure of the organizational climate. Size of the firm and internal labour market were associated, with these practices, indicating that a particular kind of environment was necessary for the creation and success of the assessment centre.

Formal activities These OCM practices provide employees with a formal system of information and presentation of opportunities. Information is transferred from top to bottom. These activities were not linked to any climate measure and were also relatively little used. However, the size of the firm and the internal labour market were related to the use of these practices even more strongly than they were related to the active management practices. Larger firms are more formal than smaller ones and hence, are more likely to use these practices.

Multi-directional These practices were related to open climates since the success of peer and upward appraisal needs such a climate for feedback. These practices were positively associated with internal labour markets since the latter trust the capabilities and opinions of its employees.

Career Systems and Organizational Characteristics

It is important for HR managers or anyone entrusted with the task of designing a career management system, to recognize that career systems should be developed as actual 'systems' and these should be seen as sets of practices which fit together with the organizational characteristics such as the stage of development, industry, etc.

Established firms that seek to implement a career system should first consider the elements of the 'basic OCM' cluster. Since most firms have these practices, employees would naturally expect their own firm to have these in place. Therefore, not having practices such as job posting, pre-retirement programmes, and lateral moves may be a disadvantage for a firm. Several firms offer lateral moves, for example, Marico, Prudential Process Management Services (PPMS), and Hewlett Packard. Bharat Heavy Electricals Ltd offers pre-retirement material and workshops to its employees. Hewlett Packard, HSS, and Spectramind have internal job posting programmes to help employees in choosing their own career. Firms seeking to sustain internal labour markets and offer long-term careers may go in for the 'formal' category of OCM practices, such as written career planning, dual career ladders, and books/pamphlets on career issues. Dual career ladders in particular were developed in the 1960s and 1970s in large firms such as IBM. These helped scientists and other non-managers to continue to advance their careers without having to enter the management ranks and yet making long-term career development possible. Many public sector firms such as C-Dot follow these practices. The company permits employees to choose from two career paths available—responsibility promotions and technical promotions. Wipro also offers a technical career path along with the management career path.

Firms seeking to maximize knowledge about employee potential, both for the sake of the individual and the organization, may prefer to use active management OCM practices, such as assessment centres, formal mentoring relationships, and career workshops. Xerox has formal mentoring programmes for entry level managers. At LG Electronics too, buddies or peers are nominated to help new hires. Eli Lilly, the pharmaceutical company, assigns a mentor to employees who choose a career path in sales training, marketing, or human resources. KPMG, the global advisory firm, runs a career-ownership workshop directed towards individuals who had undergone their professional training within the firm, particularly those in tax and audit. Firms that seek to translate information about employees into actual action by making specific career plans for individuals and succession plans for firms may best use active planning practices. These include career counselling by the HR department and direct supervisor and performance appraisal as a basis for career planning and succession planning for the firm. Eicher Goodearth Ltd and NIIT use practices from the active planning category. Godrej Consumer Products Ltd, SAS, ICICI, and IOC are some other firms that link performance appraisals with career planning and growth. Modi Xerox, GCPL, GE, and Monsanto India have succession planning programmes within their organizations.

Organizations that seek to be 'cutting edge' may attempt to use multi-directional OCM practices. Procter and Gamble has a 360 degree appraisal system. Managers are accountable for the growth of their direct subordinates and are assessed on this parameter. However, peer and upward appraisals require a lot of organizational support. These practices cannot be implemented in companies which are small, unionized, or have a closed culture. Procter and Gamble functions on the premise that the interests of its employees are inseparable from the interests of the company. The firm also ensures enough career growth for individuals within the firm and views each new employee as someone who will spend his/her entire career in P&G.

Career Systems and Organizational Culture

In designing a career system, an organization is faced with a number of choices. The earlier mentioned typology of OCM and their association with firm characteristics provide an understanding of how organizations can develop their career systems in accordance with their existing culture, an issue emphasized earlier in the chapter. This information can be used by HR managers in setting up their OCM programmes.

When applying OCM practices, it is important for managers to consider the climate of the organization, as has been pointed out earlier. Managers must apply the OCM practices in accordance with the existing climate of the firm. They need to focus on not only what is desirable, but also what is possible, in order to set realistic goals.

Baruch and Peiperl proposed that the climate of the firm may be defined along two dimensions—dynamic and open. Organizations characterized by more stable (less dynamic) and more closed (less open) climates may be best served by the basic and formal OCM categories, since these practices do not demand continual change. On the other hand, more dynamic (less stable) and more open (less closed) firms are likely to benefit more from active planning and multi-directional practices. These require a more direct involvement in employees' career management on a regular basis.

Another aspect of the organizational climate that needs to be considered in adopting OCM practices is the degree to which the firm is individualistic or group focussed. *Individualistic firms* should focus on active planning and active management categories which permit attention to be paid to individual careers. On the other hand, group focussed firms may focus on basic and multi-directional activities. *Reactive organizations* do not have time for new initiatives. Hence, these firms may be able to use only formal OCM practices. Conversely, *proactive firms* benefit from basic OCM practices initially and from active planning and active management practices later.

HSBC has long relied on basic and active planning OCM practices such as job postings, formal training, pre-retirement counselling, lateral movement, and succession planning. More recently, the bank is also moving towards the active management OCM cluster, such as assessment centres, thereby suggesting a more innovative approach to OCM. Unilever has long relied on the active planning and formal OCM practices. The company has career counselling, written career plans, and performance appraisal process linked to career planning. Unilever also has annual succession planning for all senior management roles. Elements of basic OCM are also found at Unilever. For instance, formal education is provided mainly internally and this, along with lateral moves, are provided primarily to the identified high-potential group, which is about ten to fifteen per cent of its managers globally. Electronic Data Systems, one of the world's largest IT firms, believes that individuals are primarily responsible for their own career management. Hence, there are very few OCM practices in evidence in the company. However, more recently, the firm has introduced the 360 degree feedback system to ensure continued employee skill development and is also developing a succession planning system. Therefore, the firm has also begun its OCM with the multi-directional and active planning categories of career practices.

CAREER MANAGEMENT FOR SPECIFIC HR ISSUES: HRD APPROACH

The current business environment has challenged the human resource function to provide competitive advantage to organizations. Career planning and development can be a powerful means of dealing with some of the issues related to managing a stable or shrinking organization in a stagnant economy. Various HR issues have emerged which demand attention. Some of these are, ensuring the continuance of newly hired employees; development and retention of high potential employees; providing growth opportunities in a stable organization; rewarding and retaining technical and professional employees; and motivating plateaued employees. Hall and Hall (1980) suggested some creative techniques for career management that help in coping with these HR problems. We will now briefly discuss some career management techniques for specific HR issues (Figure 9.8).

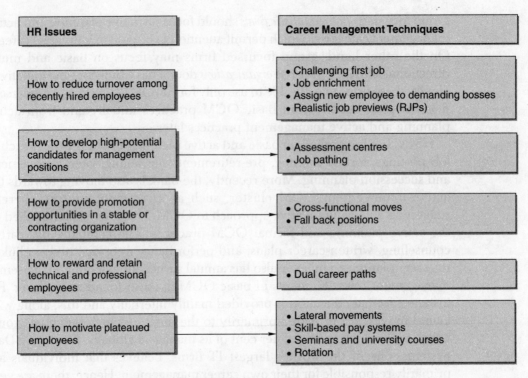

HR Issues		Career Management Techniques	
How to reduce turnover among recently hired employees	→	• Challenging first job • Job enrichment • Assign new employee to demanding bosses • Realistic job previews (RJPs)	
How to develop high-potential candidates for management positions	→	• Assessment centres • Job pathing	
How to provide promotion opportunities in a stable or contracting organization	→	• Cross-functional moves • Fall back positions	
How to reward and retain technical and professional employees	→	• Dual career paths	
How to motivate plateaued employees	→	• Lateral movements • Skill-based pay systems • Seminars and university courses • Rotation	

Figure 9.8: Career Management Techniques for Specific HR Issues

Reducing Turnover among Recently Hired Employees

The cost of employee turnover can be very high, especially in the case of professional and managerial employees. Some companies lose as many as 50% of their employees in the first two years of employment. An organization can save a lot of money by careful management of the entry and first year of new employees who are in the establishment phase of their careers. Companies like AT&T and GE have found that making initial jobs more challenging and stretching decreases turnover and also improves long-term career performance. To reduce turnover, firms can adopt certain measures.

(i) Select a challenging first job for new employees, thus ensuring that new employees experience a feeling of psychological success, that is, accomplishment on a job with a reasonable probability of failure.

(ii) Provide job enrichment by giving the new employees authority and responsibility. This again contributes to stretching initial jobs.

(iii) Assign new employees to demanding bosses—when a boss expects better performance from an employee by setting high performance standards, the subordinate performs better.

(iv) Give realistic job previews by providing new employees with realistic expectations during the recruitment process in the form of company visits, booklets, or talks conveying the demands of the job. These practices can reduce dissatisfaction and turnover among employees when they actually join the firm.

Developing High-potential Candidates for Management Positions

An organization can identify high-performers through assessment centres and other such methods. The real problem, however, is to train and develop these promising candidates once they are identified.

Assessment centres for development As discussed earlier in the chapter, assessment centres were earlier developed for selection purposes and to identify high performers for promotion. More recently, they are being used for employee development too. The use of assessment centres for developmental purposes focusses on providing feedback to the employees. After the employee evaluates and accepts the feedback, the discussion shifts to counselling and identifying the training requirements and developmental assignments that the employee would require for the target job. Used in this manner, assessment centres provide the individual with a specific career plan. The organization, therefore, becomes a partner rather than an adversary in career planning.

Job pathing It involves moving employees through logically sequenced job assignments to help them reach a certain target job faster than the normal course. For example, an organization may stipulate that an individual would take about 15 years to grow to the position of general manager. However, by careful plotting of jobs that provide structured experience to the employees, the position could be reached in about seven years. Hence, job pathing can be used for developmental purposes.

Providing Promotion Opportunities in a Stable or Contracting Organization

When new management positions are available in an organization, career opportunities become abundant. However, during economic downturn or corporate slowdown, careful planning is required for providing career advancement. Some of the ways in which an organization can do so are as follows:

Cross-functional moves Lateral or cross-functional transfers are used to provide opportunities for development, usually at the beginning of an individual's career. Cross-functional transfers throughout the career keep employees updated, open to new learning, and provide them with a broader perspective of the organization. For example, in the early 1970s, three executive vice presidents of Union Carbide traded jobs. The purpose was to give each one of them a better 'big picture' of the total organization and prepare them for presidency. Lateral moves provide opportunities for development and also makes it possible for each individual to take on a more demanding position.

Fallback positions Cross-functional transfers or promotions carry with them a risk, especially when they take place at senior positions. The risk is that the individual may fail in a new job because it is too demanding and beyond his/her level of competence. One way this risk may be minimized is by identifying a fallback position into which the individual can move if he/she is not successful after a promotion or a transfer. When a firm establishes fallback positions, it communicates to the employees that the promotion or transfer involves some risk. The firm accepts some of the responsibility for it and sends a message that moving into a fallback position does not constitute failure and is quite acceptable.

Rewarding and Retaining Technical and Professional Employees

In today's high-tech world, specialized knowledge is as important as managerial skill. Technical and professional employees, such as engineers, information technology experts, scientists, etc., present a special challenge for organizations. Most technical and professional employees would like to have more responsibility that is associated with advancement. However, they prefer to stay in their technical and highly specialized areas rather than move into management as part of the normal upward mobility in an organization. This trend is most common in technology-driven industries, such as pharmaceuticals, chemicals, computers, and electronics. In response to this trend, organizations have started offering dual career paths or ladders. The dual career path is a method of recognizing and rewarding technical specialists and professionals who prefer to contribute their expertise to a firm without having to become managers. This allows technical and professional employees to increase their specialized knowledge, make contributions to their firms, and be rewarded without entering management. On each side, that is, management and technical, the compensation is comparable and at par.

Dual career paths are becoming increasingly popular. An individual may advance up the management ladder or on a corresponding technical or professional ladder. Union Carbide, IBM, and AT&T have used dual career paths for years. Several other firms, such as C-DOT, Ericsson, GCPL, and Eli Lilly encourage their employees to follow a managerial career path or a specialist/technical one. A dual career path permits organizations to retain both highly skilled managers and highly skilled technical specialists. Eli Lilly, the Rs 160 crore pharmaceutical company, for example, has created new career paths to stem attrition. The employees can move into related functions like sales force training, marketing, HR, or clinical trials. For clinical trials, which is a technical function, the company trains the employees to prepare for it. Alternatively, employees can specialize in any one of Lilly verticals, such as cancer, sepsis, cardiology, or diabetes. In this case, the employees are put through a very structured training programme.

Motivating Plateaued Employees

Almost all individuals experience career plateau at least once in their career. It occurs when an employee's work content and job functions continue to remain the same because of lack of promotional opportunities in the organization. Employees find themselves stuck at the same career level. Ference et al. (1977) defined *career plateau* as the point in a career where the likelihood of additional hierarchical promotions or further upward mobility is very low. Career plateau has become more common in contemporary times. As more organizations opt for downsizing, moving to flatter organizational structures, and eliminating middle management layers, more number of employees are forced to remain at the same level for longer periods. Career plateau is also a natural result of a hierarchical organizational structure in which the number of positions is far less at higher levels in the hierarchy.

The term career plateau is viewed as negative and is seen as suggesting failure. This is because success is commonly defined in terms of upward mobility. However, reaching a plateau is not a negative career state. When a person reaches the career plateau, it merely indicates an individual's current career status in an organization. A conceptual model of the career plateau phenomenon as presented by Ference et al. is described in Exhibit 9.7.

Career plateau presents new challenges for the HR function with respect to organizational career planning and development. To deal with the problem of career plateau, several HR approaches can be used:

Lateral movements Individuals may be moved laterally within the organization. Though the status and pay remain unchanged, the employees have the opportunity to learn new skills that increase their marketability. In lateral movements, the firm may use any one of the following two approaches:

- Skill-based pay system: Rewarding employees for the type and the number of skills they have.
- Job enrichment: Rewarding (without promoting) an employee by increasing job challenge, responsibility, autonomy, task variety, etc.

Seminars and university courses By taking these courses, plateaued employees find new opportunities.

Rotation to other departments A formal programme of rotating managers at mid-career stage to other departments may be adopted by firms.

Exhibit 9.7

A Conceptual Model of Career Plateau

This model was based on exploratory interviews conducted with 55 senior executives in nine major organizations. The model presents a method of viewing the career plateau in the context of the entire organizational career. In this model, managerial states are classified based on two parameters:

(i) *Likelihood of future promotions*: This is the organization's estimate of the individual's chances of receiving a hierarchical promotion in the firm.

(ii) *Performance in the present position*: This is the organization's perception of how well the individual is doing in his/her present job.

Individuals can be classified as 'high' or 'low' on these two parameters. The two parameters result in the following classification of managerial career states:

Current Performance	Likelihood of future promotion	
	Low	**High**
High	Solid Citizens (effective plateaus) *Organizationally plateaued*	Stars *Personally plateaued*
Low	Deadwood (ineffective plateaus)	Learners (comers)

The four main career states in this model are:

1. *Learners or Comers*: These are the employees who have high potential for advancement but their present performance is inadequate. For example, trainees are 'learners' since they learn on their jobs. This category may also include longer service managers who have been recently promoted to new positions

which they have not yet mastered. Organizations typically provide assessment and training for learners.

2. *Stars*: Employees whose current performance is outstanding and who have high potential for advancement. They are on the 'high potential' or 'fast track' career paths. This category of employees receives maximum attention in the organization's development programmes. Aviva Life Insurance, LG Electronics, Polaris software Labs, and HLL are some firms that identify the star performers.

3. *Solid Citizens*: This is the largest group in the organization and performs the bulk of organizational work. These employees have low chances of advancement but their current performance is very good.

4. *Deadwood*: These employees present a problem for the organization. These employees neither perform well on their current jobs nor do they have any chance of upward mobility. They receive attention from the organization mostly for dismissal purposes.

Both solid citizens and deadwood are plateaued managers. However, solid citizens are 'effective' plateaus while deadwood represents the 'ineffective' plateau. The challenge that organizations confront is to prevent solid citizens from slipping into the deadwood category.

Within the solid citizen category, there are two types of employees:

1. *Organizationally plateaued employees*: These are employees who have the ability to perform well in higher level jobs but are plateaued because of lack of suitable openings in the firm.

2. *Personally plateaued employees*: These are employees who are plateaued because they are seen either as lacking the ability for

Contd

Exhibit 9.7 Contd

higher level jobs or not ambitious enough for a higher level job. This group of employees is unlikely to be promoted to a higher position even if the firm has suitable openings.

There are no easy answers to know how to:

- bring the ineffective plateaus (deadwood) to an effective level (solid citizens); or
- motivate organizationally plateaued employees who are frustrated by the absence of advancement opportunities.

Adapted from: Ference, Stoner, and Warren 1977

For employees who have reached ineffective plateaus, organizations may restore their performance through the following measures:

- Educational programmes to upgrade employees' technical skills, allowing them to keep pace with the changing job
- Job rotation

For a frustrated manager who has been organizationally plateaued, the potential of job enrichment is very high.

CAREER MANAGEMENT: AN SHRM APPROACH

Business planning, which was traditionally concerned with marketing and finance, has now expanded to include human resources to meet business objectives. Integration of human resource planning (HRP) with business objectives has led to the inclusion of HR managers on corporate business planning teams. All corporate plans are interpreted for their human resource implication. Human resource planning may be appropriately viewed as a macro HR system that provides guidance for the optimum use of the organization's human resources. Human resource planning systems must also incorporate those HRM subsystems that ensure growth and development of potential of all the employees in the organization. It must also determine linkages between individual growth and maximum utilization of human resources and the interaction between these two aspects.

Human resource planning complements individual career planning. Career planning practices help individuals set career goals. Human resource planning, on the other hand, is aimed at creating and maintaining an effective work force to meet the business goals of the organization. It involves strategies for attracting, selecting, and orienting new employees to the firm. It also formulates approaches for matching individual needs with job opportunities, methods for helping employees develop and perform effectively, and ways to smoothen the separation of employees through retirement. By integrating career planning with HRP, employees' needs can be merged with those of the organization. Long-term goals and objectives of the firm are analysed in terms of their implications for manpower requirements—both qualitative (type of skills, such as technical skills, interpersonal skills, etc.) and quantitative (the number of people required)—for the organization to achieve those objectives. By linking employees' career plans with the firm's human resource needs and business objectives, career plans become more realistic and improve the organization's human resource plans. For example, setting up of individual career objectives should be aligned with the organization's business plans. An individual's concern for performance feedback and development planning may be complemented by organizational activities for helping employees to develop and perform effectively.

Career development helps individuals achieve career objectives. Like career planning, career development also requires integration between the corporate business plans and employee career needs. Career development can also be integrated with the company's business goals through HRP. When HRP is included in corporate business plans, career development practices reflect the company's objectives. It is aimed at ensuring the availability of the right number and type of workforce to ensure the achievement of business objectives. Human resource planning includes career development practices aimed at matching individuals to jobs, helping them perform and develop, etc.

Career management activities and programmes of an organization are integrally aligned and consistent with strategic human resource planning. Career management is the next logical phase in HRP. Hence, career management helps align the individual employee's aspirations and needs with those of the organization. This increases the probability that an organization will be able to meet its changing staffing requirements on an ongoing basis.

Today, an increasingly growing number of people seek jobs that offer challenge, responsibility, opportunities for advancement, and quality of work life. Employees prefer to work for organizations who demonstrate concern for their employees' future. Therefore, career planning and development is a rising concern for employees. A firm that has a formalized career management programme is also likely to to attract good quality employees. When firms institutionalize career development plans, they become more successful in recruitment and retention of high talent employees. For years individuals and organizations operated in a relatively ad hoc manner with regard to career development. However, managers, employees, HR professionals, researchers, and consultants believe that only active career management leads to individual and organizational success. Career planning and development not only improves individual performance, but also develops an interface between the individual and the HR system. Career management helps to identify those HR programmes which deal with the issue of individual growth and productivity within the organizational environment.

Since careers are made up of exchanges between individuals and organizations, these exchanges inherently incorporate the idea of reciprocity. The notion of reciprocity between the individual and the organization has been derived from the inducement-contribution model of Bernard and Simon. According to March and Simon (1958), the contributions individuals make to organizations and the inducements organizations provide to individuals should be satisfactory for an effective association to continue. From an individual's perspective, one inducement that an organization can provide is 'challenging work'. If the organization reduces the autonomy the individual has over his/ her work, the individual may perceive the job as no longer offering enough challenge. This may ultimately result in an individual's exit from the organization. From the organization's point of view, the individual contributes 'quality performance' to the organization. If an individual's performance falls below the accepted standards of quality the organization may view the individual as stagnating. The organization may ultimately choose to replace the individual with a better performer.

Individual–organization reciprocity is important to career management and it is a joint responsibility of individuals and organizations. Both the individual and the organization can take specific actions to contribute to successful career management and lead to positive results for each other. These have been discussed in the section on organization-centred and individual-centred career management.

Theoretical career models are very few, and these relate to the individual perspective. For organizational career management, the existing theoretical base is very thin. Schein's model of career development is perhaps the only one that reflects both the individual and organizational perspective. This model is based on the concept of fit between the goals of the organization and the goals of the individual. The model demonstrates that the goals of each party change over time as an individual's career evolves. An organization's goals consist of a series of plans for managing human resources. The organization must continually plan for hiring, developing, retiring, and replacing individuals. The organization can match these activities with the career stages of individuals. An individual's career stages should ideally parallel the organization's planning process. For example, the organization's plan for staffing can mesh with the individual's plan for career choice through recruitment, selection, placement, and training activities. Similarly, the organization's plan for growth and development of individuals can mesh with the individual's early career stage issues, such as how to establish an area of contribution in the firm through job rotation, performance appraisal, and developmental training. Both the organization's planning phases and the individual's career stages follow a cycle or series of stages. When these two cycles are matched with each other, it ensures reciprocity.

Similar to HRP, organizational careers can also be seen at two levels— macro and micro. At the micro level, the focus is on facilitating the careers of individual employees through various activities, such as counselling, career pathing, etc. At the macro level, manpower planners develop organizational charts to track the movement of large number of people through various positions in the organization, identify fast tracks, future staffing gaps, etc. Most organizations rarely attempt to integrate these two types of career planning. More often, organizations use only one of these approaches. For instance, a company may focus only on individuals. Such a firm may do well in developing employees but its overall corporate manpower needs may get ignored. On the other hand, an organization may focus only on corporate manpower plans and pay no attention to training and development of its employees to ensure their movement through various positions. Such a firm ends up merely monitoring career plans and not managing them. It is obvious that both the macro and the micro facets of career management need to be integrated. This can be facilitated by ensuring that manpower planning and career counselling are placed in the same department. Usually, the backgrounds of personnel in these two functions differ, with counsellors usually being from psychology and manpower planners from economics or management. Organizations need to have as much coordination as possible between corporate planning, human resources planning, and individual career planning. However, these three kinds of planning operate in isolation. For instance, an individual may chalk out a career in computer hardware sales at a time when the firm may plan to phase out of hardware business. Similarly, an organization may plan a large expansion of its software business, but it may lack qualified software engineers within the organization and in the external labour market.

Human resource planning clearly forms the base for successful organizational career planning. Only by forecasting the demand for people needed in various future jobs and assessing the current internal supply of people and their potential, can analysts put together a career system for the organization. By careful matching of organizational needs and employees' goals, HRP covers both the individual and the organizational perspectives of career management. A match between individual and organizational career plans determines employee satisfaction and how long employees are likely to stay with the organization. Unfortunately, many organizations prepare career ladders and career paths without considering how current employees fit into those plans. More important than having a career assistance programme in an organization is having a proper match between the organization's strategic needs and the individual's career needs.

Summary

Work today is seen as more than just a means of livelihood. Work and career are seen as expressions of self and values and as aspects of life that should fit harmoniously with other priorities such as family, health, etc. Traditional notions about career, career success, and career management have been radically redefined due to several factors. Business decisions such as mergers, acquisitions, lay-offs and restructuring, changing workforce expectations and career aspirations, altered psychological contract between the employer and employee, and a volatile environment have all contributed to this redefinition. As a result, individuals and organizations both view careers with a whole new perspective. Though the individual and the organizational perspective on careers is very different, both stand to benefit from a well thought out career management strategy.

This chapter discussed career planning, career development, and career management. Four career stages, viz. establishment, advancement, maintenance, and withdrawal, spanning an individual's work life were discussed. Major issues and concerns of each career stage were also identified. The chapter specified the career planning practices and career development interventions that may be used by organizations to help employees attain their career objectives as well as to serve the long-term interests of the organization. Two career management systems, viz., individual-centred and

organization-centred systems, were discussed along with the individual and organizational career management strategies. Guidelines for the design and implementation of an effective career management system were also presented. It was further suggested that organizations must ensure that the career planning and development system reflects the culture of the organization. An organization is faced with a number of choices and alternatives when designing a career system. The chapter presented a useful typology of organizational career management (OCM) practices. The typology included five categories of OCM practices—basic, active planning, active management, formal, and multi-directional. The association of these categories of OCM with firm characteristics was also examined to provide an understanding of how organizations can develop their career systems in accordance with their existing cultures. Human resource development approaches for dealing with some current HR problems such as retention of new entrants and high potential employees were discussed. The chapter ends with a detailed discussion about adopting a strategic approach to career management.

Keywords

Career refers to a series of work related positions occupied by an individual throughout work life and the associated activities, behaviours, attitudes, values, and aspirations. A career involves a long term view of work experiences and a related sequence of jobs that an employee performs during the span of work life, not necessarily with the same company.

Job refers to the grouping of tasks, duties, and responsibilities assigned to an individual as part of work at a point of time. The grouping of tasks, duties, and responsibilities may change over time and hence jobs assigned to individuals may also change.

Career Planning is a personalized ongoing process whereby an individual establishes career goals and identifies the means for achieving these goals. Career planning is concerned with individuals choosing occupations, organizations, and jobs.

Career Development consists of those activities and processes which are undertaken by organizations to help individuals attain their career objectives. It is the process by which career plans are accomplished.

Career Management is a life-long ongoing process that involves setting personal career goals, developing strategies for achieving the goals, and revising the goals based on work and life experiences. Career management programmes include counselling employees in their individual career planning, offering career planning workshops, assessment centres, developmental performance appraisals, providing mentors to individuals, and developing career paths for employees.

Career Stages are those periods at different points in the individual's career span in which his/her work life is characterized by distinctive needs, concerns, tasks, and activities.

Career Path consists of a logical sequence of job progression through which an individual moves during employment with an organization.

Dual Career Paths refer to the method of recognizing and rewarding technical specialists and professionals and allow them to increase their specialized knowledge, make contributions to their firms, and be rewarded without entering management.

Job Pathing consists of a planned movement of an individual through a carefully developed sequence of job assignments to develop the employee's skills, knowledge, and competencies. Job pathing allows for gradual stretching of employees' talents by moving them through selected jobs of increasing challenge and responsibility.

Mentoring refers to the establishment of a close relationship between a subordinate and a superior who takes personal interest in the employee.

Individual-Centred Career Management System is oriented towards the individual's career perspective. The focus is on the individual's career rather than on organizational needs.

Career Anchors are self-perceived syndromes of motives, talents, and values that guide an individual's career decisions.

Organization-Centred Career Management System is concerned with jobs in the organization and on constructing career paths that provide logical progression of people between jobs within the organization. The main purpose of the organization-centered system is to fulfil the goals of the organization.

Concept Review Questions

1. Define the term career. Distinguish between the terms career planning and career development.

2. In recent years, what forces in the contemporary business environment have changed the way that employees' careers have been managed by organizations and by the employees themselves?

3. Describe the four-stage career model. What major issues are confronted by employees in each stage?

4. Discuss the career development needs associated with each career stage. What career development interventions may be adopted by the

organizations to facilitate career development?

5. Suggest a strategy for the design and implementation of career management system by an organization.

6. 'Career management is best viewed as a partnership between the individual and the organization and is therefore a shared responsibility'. In the context of this statement, present the individual and organizational perspectives on career management.

7. Do you agree that career management activities and programmes are integrally aligned and consistent with strategic human resource planning? Elucidate.

Critical Thinking Questions [1]

1. What are your personal career goals/objectives? Where would you like to reach before you retire from work-life? Based on your self-assessment and evaluation of available career

opportunities, do you think your career objectives are realistic? Identify your dream organization where you would like to work. Develop a career path to reach your career goals in this

[1] Adapted from Gordon 1986

organization. Suggest a career management strategy for achieving these career goals. The suggested strategy should have elements of both the individual-centred and the organization-centred career strategies. Make suitable assumptions.

2. Think of two individuals you know who work for organizations and try to fit them into the appropriate career stage.

   (i) Can they be accurately placed? Why or why not?

   (ii) Identify their career concerns and major career planning issues.

   (iii) Which career stage is most stressful in your opinion? Why?

   (iv) Which career planning practices can be used by organizations to help them plan their careers?

   (v) Suggest a career development strategy for them based on their current career development needs.

3. Read the section on the typology of OCM. Which category of OCM seems to be more commonly used and adopted by organizations? Give examples of firms you know of that use one or more of these categories of OCM practices. Examine how the combination of OCM practices that an organization adopts is dependent on its characteristics.

4. Read the incident given below and discuss the following questions.

   Anjana is working as a compensation analyst with Biomed Equipments Inc., a high technology firm, which manufactures state-of-the-art biomedical equipment. She joined the company upon graduation at the age of 21 years. She has been working in the company since the past six years. During the first two years of her employment, she quickly advanced up the organizational hierarchy in the human resources department, moving into the positions of personnel assistant, personnel professional, and finally into her present position of compensation analyst. She had agreed to move into the highly specialized position of compensation analyst on the advice of the Director of HR. According to the Director, this sequence of jobs would prepare her well for higher-level managerial responsibilities.

   Anjana has been a compensation analyst for the last two years. Since last year, she has complained frequently about the lack of challenge on the job. She also feels that now she is ready to assume significant managerial responsibilities. As far as Anjana's performance appraisals are concerned, they have always been positive. She has been promised a promotion for over a year. Now she assumes that she has not yet received a promotion because no position has been available. Anjana has informed her supervisor that she is willing to transfer out of compensation or even out of the human resources department to secure a managerial position. Recently, however, her supervisor implied that Anjana's lack of a professional degree is hindering her advancement.

   - Diagnose Anjana's current career stage and the problem with her career.

   - Identify the major concerns Anjana is confronted with in her present career.

   - What can Anjana do to manage this problem?

   - What types of assistance and services can Anjana's organization provide to correct this problem? Why?

   - Would you advise Anjana to look for a career path outside of Biomed Equipments Inc.? Give your comments based on Anjana's education, experience, performance, and the available opportunities within the firm.

Simulation and Role Play

1. Amar is currently a student at the Management School (MS) of a premier University in Delhi, India, where he is pursuing a full-time MBA programme. He is specializing in the area of

banking and finance. Amar will complete the MBA programme in about five months. Prior to joining the course, Amar has completed his undergraduate studies in commerce from another smaller college of the university. Simultaneously, Amar also completed the cost and works accounting course from Institute of Cost and Works Accountancy (ICWA). Initially, Amar had planned to start working as an accountant upon the completion of his graduation and ICWA course. However, he changed his plans after talking to some friends about the duties of a cost accountant. The long working hours and the amount of travel usually required of a cost accountant led him to question his decision about a career in accounting. Hence, he enrolled for MBA programme at the university in order to diversify his business skills and knowledge. Amar is applying to companies through the placement service of MS. The jobs on offer are in the fields of both accounting and financial management. Now Amar is unsure and confused about the type of career which would be more rewarding. He decided to talk to one of his professors, Prof. Khanna.

Two students should volunteer for this role play. One student will assume the role of Amar and the other student will assume the role of Prof. Khanna.

Brief for Amar. He has to approach Prof. Khanna and state that he needs advice on his career. Amar should provide a background to his dilemma.

Brief for Prof. Khanna. The professor should first inquire about the goals Amar has set for himself. Since Amar has not thought of his career goals, Prof. Khanna should proceed to emphasize the importance of such goals for a rewarding career. The professor can then help Amar clarify his goals by helping him identify the factors which are important in determining these goals. He should also help Amar analyse the possible approaches that could be used in attaining these goals. For instance, he could discuss the concept career mobility that allows Amar to start his career in accounting and then switch to financial management or vice versa.

The role play should end with a clear statement of Amar's career goals, what factors were considered, and why. The role play should also result in the preparation of a formal long-term and rewarding career plan for Amar that would help him achieve his career goals. This career plan should emerge after considering various possible approaches. Specifically, the career plan will lay down the initiatives that Amar should take to facilitate the achievement of his career goals.

2. Assume you are the Executive Director (HR) of a large software firm that encourages employees to develop their knowledge and skill base. For this purpose, your firm has a well-equipped library that subscribes to the latest journals and magazines on related subjects. In addition, your firm also encourages employees to enroll for part-time educational programmes, both in-house and in those provided by institutes. The firm reimburses the course fee. However, the latest employee survey revealed that employees believe that the firm has not taken adequate initiatives in providing career development opportunities to them. Further, you find that employees rarely use the library and the education facilities. As the Executive Director, discuss these findings with the General Manager (software operations) in order to

- identify employee expectations about the initiatives they would like the firm to take;

- suggest ways the firm could encourage employees to use self-development opportunities provided by the firm; and

- devise an organizational career development strategy that will help individuals achieve their career goals.

Classroom Projects [1]

1. While you pursue your present academic course, you are probably simultaneously preparing for entry into an organization that will signal the beginning of your work life. Formulate two goals for yourself that you would like to achieve during the establishment stage of your career. Now form groups of five students. Share your goals with your group members and identify the similarities and differences between your goals. Discuss with your group members the steps each of you will personally take to achieve your goals. In addition, identify what you would expect your organization to do for you to help you achieve these goals. Summarize your discussion and prepare a written report.

2. Form groups of five to six members and discuss the forces that have led to a transformation in how individuals and organizations view careers and career management. Identify the benefits of formalized career management programmes for individual employees and for the organization. What productivity-related costs can be faced by organizations if they do not have career assistance programmes for employees? Report your discussion to the class.

3. Ask students to volunteer to be members of groups of two or three students each to debate for and against the topic, 'Career planning is the sole responsibility of the individual employee. Organizations should not offer career management programmes'. Each group may take about 15 minutes to present their arguments. An open discussion with the class follows highlighting the pros and cons of individual–organization partnership in career management.

4. This exercise needs some out-of-class preparation. As the first part of the project, students are asked to read the description of career anchors from the chapter. They must individually write down the career anchor that best describes each one of them. Students have to submit this report to the class instructor prior to the class. In the second part, the instructor assigns students into small groups based on their primary career anchor. One group should consist of students who have the same primary career anchor. Each group identifies within the general vocational area career paths that are both most consistent and inconsistent with this career anchor. They also discuss whether a combination of career anchors describes one career path better than a single career anchor. Class presentations follow along with discussions of the importance of matching self-assessment with an individual's career and job choice.

Note: The instructor may also use the career anchor questionnaire available in organizational behaviour books to help students identify their career anchors. Feedback may be provided in the event of a mismatch between what the student thinks his/her primary career anchor is and what emerges from the questionnaire.

[1] *Adapted from:* Mainiero, L.A., and C.L. Tromley 1994, *Developing Managerial Skills in Organizational Behaviour*, 2nd edition, Prentice Hall, New Jersey.

Field Projects

1. Read the list of OCM practices provided in Exhibit 9.1 of the chapter. In groups of four, personally visit at least two organizations and study and compare their OCM practices. Use the OCM practices list as a checklist. Conduct interviews with HR managers and some other employees of the firms to obtain the following information:

   • Descriptions of the firm's career management practices and programmes

- Benefits that have resulted for the organization from these programmes
- How well the organizations are utilizing these programmes, especially career counselling, dual ladder, reading materials, etc.
- Gaps between the stated career management programmes and their actual implementation
- Employees' satisfaction with the efforts of the organization's efforts towards facilitating their career growth

Place each organization in the appropriate category of OCM (for example, basic, active planning, etc.). Enumerate the firm characteristics that led you to place the organization in a particular category.

Prepare a report for class presentation.

2. Interview HR managers of one organization belonging to each of the following industries— ITeS, automobile, FMCG, and consulting. Compare the career planning and career development methods of these organizations. Obtain information about how the nature of the industry influences the adoption and use of career planning and development practices.

3. From reports in the newspapers and magazines, or from your own information, identify top performers who have switched careers. For example, those high performing individuals who have moved from industry to academics or between industries (for example, from FMCG to IT). Interview at least one such individual who has made a career change and obtain the following information:

- The factors that prompted the switch
- The career stage of the individual when taking the career change
- The implications of this information on organizational career management practices for the relevant career stage

Submit a written report to your instructor.

Case Study[1]

Career Development at Dataware Services and Systems

Dataware Services and Systems (DSS) is one of the largest producers of silicon chips for the computer industry in India. The company has its headquarters in the hi-tech city of Hyderabad. It was founded in 1985 and since then DSS has grown rapidly in terms of sales and profits. As a result, the company's stock price has also shot upwards many times over.

However, human resources have not been on top of the agenda for DSS. Therefore, human resource policies of the firm have failed to keep pace with the company's growth. The emphasis in DSS has been on developing policies to meet the requirements of external organizations such as the government regulations for IT firms.

The company recently hired Arun Baijal as the Director (HR) for the company. Prior to joining

DSS, Baijal was working with a large blue-chip company in Bangalore as an Assistant Personnel Director. His present position offered him a substantial increase in pay, perks, and responsibility. However, that was not the only reason Baijal had joined DSS. He was aware that DSS had never paid much attention to human resources. Therefore, he believed that his position as the Director (HR) would provide him with the challenge to change the mindset of the company—from a 1950s' human resources outlook to one more compatible with the realities of the 21st century.

Baijal has been with the company for the past six months. During this period, he has been assessing the situation to determine the significant human resource problems at DSS. One HR problem

[1] *Adapted from:* Nkomo, S.M., M.D. Fottler, and R.B. McAfee 1992, *Applications in Human Resource Management: Cases, Exercises and Skill Builders*, 2nd edition, PWS-KENT Publishing Company, Boston.

that he believes is significant is the high turnover among software engineers who work in the R&D department. This is the core function of the company and turnover rates have averaged about 30 per cent per year over the past three years.

Baijal set out to systematically assess the cause(s) of the high turnover problem. He checked area wage surveys and found that DSS was paying five to eight per cent above the market for software engineers. Since a formal exit interview system was not in place in the company, he could not check out what other factors or causes could possibly explain the high turnover. Therefore, he engaged in informal conversations with a large number of employees, including the engineers themselves. He was disconcerted to find out that many of the engineers felt 'to have reached a dead end in the technical aspects of engineering'.

The R&D department, in the last three years, had lost some of the younger engineers who had been considered to be on the 'fast track'. Most of these high achievers had joined the competitors in the local area.

One particular R&D engineer who impressed Baijal was Rubina Chatterjee. Rubina was 29 years old and a B.Tech in Electronics Engineering from the Indian Institute of Technology (IIT), Mumbai. Along with the job, Rubina was pursuing her part-time post-graduate studies in management. She had been with DSS for the last seven years. Out of these seven years, Rubina spent the first three years in an entry-level engineering position and the remaining four as the section chief of one of the divisions of R&D. This promotion was the highest position in the department other than the position of Director of R&D.

When Baijal spoke to Rubina, he was amazed at what she had to say about the company. Rubina claimed that 'the company doesn't really care about its good people'. She went on to express her personal view about the present Director of the R&D Department of the company, John D'Souza. According to her, D'Souza did not want his good people to move up in the organization. Instead, he was more interested in keeping them in his own department, thus ensuring that he meets his own goals. At the same time, he did not have to spend time and resources in orienting and training new people. Rubina further informed Baijal that she had been told by both D'Souza and the former Personnel Director that she had a bright future with the company. Her performance appraisals had also been uniformly excellent.

With respect to the appraisal system of the company, Rubina was particularly critical of the appraisal form being used for the purpose. This appraisal form had no section on identifying the future potential or future goals of the employee being appraised. Further, the appraisal also had no rewards for supervisors who develop their subordinates, no human resources planning to identify future job openings, no centralized job information or job positioning system, and no career paths and/or career ladders. To top it all, there were attitudinal barriers against women in management positions.

Baijal checked the information that Rubina had provided him. He found that the information was accurate. He also heard through the 'grapevine' that Rubina had a very good offer for an excellent position with a competitor of DSS.

For Baijal the challenge was clearly even greater than he had anticipated. He realized he had an immediate problem concerning high turnover of high performing employees. In addition, he was also concerned about a series of interconnected problems associated with career development. However, Baijal is not quite sure about the steps to take to solve the problem.

Questions

1. In which career stage do you find Rubina in? What major career issues is she confronted with?

2. If Baijal decides to develop a formalized career development system at DSS, what interventions should be offered? Why?

3. What further information would Baijal need before proceeding towards a solution to this problem? Why?

4. What problems are likely to be encountered by Baijal in the design and implementation of a formalized career development system at

DSS? Discuss with respect to the 1950s' HR outlook of the company and its prevailing culture.

5. Should the career development activities be integrated with other human resource management activities? If yes, which ones? Why?

References

Baruch, Y. and M. Peiperl 2000, 'Career Management Practices: An Empirical Survey and Implications', *Human Resource Management*, vol. 39, no. 4, pp. 347–66.

Baruch, Y. 1996, 'Career Planning and Managing Techniques in Use', *International Journal of Career Management*, vol. 8, no. 1.

Boerlijst, J.G. 1984, 'Career Development and Career Guidance', in P.J. Drenth, H. Thierry, P.J. Willems, and C.J. Wolff (eds.), *Handbook of Work and Organizational Psychology*, John Wiley & Sons, Inc.

Bowen, D. and D.T. Hall 1977, 'Career Planning for Employee Development: a Primer for Managers', *California Management Review*, vol. 20, no. 2, pp. 33–5.

Dalton, G.W., P.H. Thompson, and R.L. Price 1977, 'The Four Stages of Professional Careers: A New Look at Performance by Professionals', *Organizational Dynamics*, vol. 6, pp. 19–42.

DeCenzo, D.A. and S.P. Robbins 1996, *Human Resource Management*, 5th edition, John Wiley & Sons Inc., New York.

Erikson, E.H. 1963, *Childhood and Society*, Norton, New York.

Ference, T.P., J.A.F. Stoner, and E.K. Warren 1977, 'Managing the Career Plateau', *Academy of Management Review*, vol. 2, pp. 602–12.

Gordon, J.R. 1986, *Human Resource Management: A Practical Approach*, Allyn & Bacon, Boston.

Gutteridge, T.G., Z.B. Leibowitz, and J.E. Shore 1993, *Organizational Career Development*, Jossey Bass Publishers, San Francisco.

Hall, D.T. and F.S. Hall 1980, 'What's New in Career Management', in M.A. Morgan, *Managing Career Development*, D. Van Nostrand Co., New York, pp. 257–70.

Hall, D.T. 1976, *Careers in Organizations*, Goodyear, California.

Holbeche, L. 2001, *Aligning Human Resources and Business Strategy*, Butterworth Heinemann, Oxford, UK.

Huse E.F. and T.G. Cummings 1980, *Organization Development and Change*, 3rd edition, West Publishing Company, New York, pp. 301–3, 306–8.

Katz, R. (ed.) 1988, *Managing Professionals in Innovative Organizations: A Collection of Readings*, Ballinger Publishing Company, USA.

Kossek, E.E. and R.N. Block 2000, *Managing Human Resources in the 21st Century: From Core Concepts to Strategic Choice*, South-Western College Publishing, USA, pp. 24.14–24.16

Lancaster, H. 1999, 'Managing Your Career', *The Wall Street Journal*, May 15, p. B1.

Mainiero, L.A. and C.L. Tromley 1994, *Developing Managerial Skills in Organizational Behaviour*, 2nd edition, Prentice Hall, New Jersey.

March, J. G. and H.A. Simon 1958, *Organizations*, Wiley, New York.

Mathis, R.L. and J.H. Jackson 2003, *Human Resource Management*, 10th edition, Thomson, Australia.

Mc Mahon, J.E. and S.K. Merman 1987, 'Career Development', in R.L. Craig (ed.), *Training and Development Handbook: A Guide to the Human Resource Development*, 3rd edition, McGraw-Hill Book Co., New York, pp. 756–70.

Mondy, R.W., R.M. Noe, and S.R. Premeaux 1999, *Human Resource Management*, 7th edition, Prentice Hall International, New Jersey.

Moorhead, G. and R.W. Griffin 1995, Organizational Behaviour: Managing People and Organizations, 4th edition, Houghton Mifflin Co., Toronto, Canada.

Morgan, M.A. 1980, *Managing Career Development*, D. Van Nostrand Co., New York.

Morgan, M.A., D.T. Hall, and A. Martier 1980, 'Career Development Strategies in Industry: Where are we and where should we be?', in M.A. Morgan (ed.), *Managing Career Development*, D. Van Nostrand Co., New York, pp. 243–56.

Nelson, D.L. and J.C. Quick 1994, *Organizational Behaviour: Foundations, Realities and Challenges*, West Publishing, New York.

Nkomo, S.M., M.D. Fottler, and R.B. McAfee 1992, *Applications in Human Resource Management: Cases, Exercises and Skill Builder*, 2nd edition, PWS-KENT Publishing Company, Boston.

Roberts, L.M., G. Spreitzer, R.Q. Dutton, E. Heaphy, and B. Barker 2005, 'How to Play to Your Strengths', *Harvard Business Review*, January, pp. 74–80.

Schein, E. 1975, 'How Career Anchors Hold Executives to their Career Paths', *Personnel*, vol. 52, pp. 11–24.

Schein, E.H. 1978, *Career Dynamics: Matching Individual and Organizational Needs*, Addison-Wesley Publishing Company, Reading.

Walker, J. 1980, *Human Resource Planning*, McGraw-Hill, New York, pp. 339–46.

Walker, J.W. 1980, 'Does Career Planning Rock the Boat?' in M.A. Morgan (ed.), *Managing Career Development*, D. Van Nostrand Co., New York, pp. 279–85.

Walker, J.W. and J.G. Gutteridge 1979, 'Career Planning Practices: An AMA Survey Report', AMACOM, New York.

Notes

Economic Times, New Delhi, Friday, 10 September 2004.

Economic Times, New Delhi, Monday, 14 June 2004.

'Great Places to Work 2004', *Business World*, 6 December 2004.

http://careers.jpmorganchase.com/emp_programs/careermgmt/, accessed on 25 September 2004.

http://www.careerjournal.com/columnists, accessed on 23 September 2004.

http://www.expressitpeople.com/20040126/cover.shtml, accessed on 22 September 2004.

http://www.fanniemae.com/global/pdf/careers/diversity/diversity_workbook.pdf, accessed on 23 September 2004.

http://www.gecareers.com/careersindia/careerdev/careeratge.jsp, accessed on 25 September 2004.

http://www.zensar.com/pdfs/inv-MGMT-ANLY02-03.pdf, accessed on 23 September 2004.

Human Capital, September 2002, pp. 54–7.

'Managing People: The Business Today Experiential Guide to Managing Workforce 2000', *Business Today*, the fourth bt anniversary issue, 21 January 1996.

'The Best Companies to Work for in India', *Business Today*, 21 November, 2004.

'The Best Employers in India 2003', *Business Today*, 14 September 2003.

'The Best Employers in India', the ninth bt anniversary issue, *Business Today*, 21 January 2001.

10 Mentor Relationships

OBJECTIVES

After studying this chapter, you will be able to:

- discuss the importance of workplace mentoring relationships for accomplishing organizational objectives
- define mentoring and understand its career and psychosocial functions
- identify the stages through which mentor-protégé relationships evolve over time
- appreciate that mentoring relationships may result in positive as well as negative experiences for the protégés
- understand the components essential for the design and implementation of a successful formal mentoring programme in an organization
- appreciate the importance of mentoring in an increasingly diverse workforce
- discuss the strategic human resource management aspects of mentoring relationships

INTRODUCTION

Throughout this book we have emphasized that as the business world becomes increasingly competitive, human resource is being viewed as the most valuable asset of a firm. Hence, it is important that human resources are managed with utmost caution, beyond what is extended to the material resources. Mentor-protégé relationships represent one way organizations may enhance the value of its most valuable asset, its employees.

Informal or natural mentoring has existed throughout the ages even though it may not have been recognized as mentoring or known by this term. What is new about mentoring relationships is the value attributed to the process and recognition of the benefits resulting from it. Mentoring is one of the most important ways by which individuals gain new knowledge and skills. Mentoring has always played an important role in human learning. All of us have had a mentor at some point in our lives. Students pursuing the doctoral programme conduct their research under the guidance of a senior professor. Business leaders often mention that there was a particularly influential person in their lives who played a major role in their professional development.

Mentoring serves as an invaluable developmental tool at an informal level. With increasingly complex workplaces and excessive demands on performance and growth, there is growing recognition that formal mentoring programmes in organizations are important to lead individuals towards a successful career. The past decade has seen organizations become increasingly aware of the value of mentoring and its impact on the performance of the firm. Mentoring has been linked with increasing levels of job satisfaction, career satisfaction, salary, organizational commitment, reduced job stress, and low employee turnover. Over the years, the concept of mentoring has achieved the status of a popular management training and career development tool within organizations. The nature and number of activities linked with the mentoring concept seems to be growing everyday. The current interest in mentoring has manifested itself in an increasing number of formal mentoring programmes.

The previous chapter discussed mentoring as a career development tool. This chapter focuses on mentoring relationships at the workplace and their importance. The traditional as well as contemporary perspectives of mentoring are presented. While presenting a comparison of informal and formal mentoring relationships, the chapter goes on to emphasize the importance of incorporating elements of informal mentoring in formal mentoring programmes of the organization. The individual and organizational benefits of mentoring programmes and the stages in the growth of mentoring relationship have been discussed. A perspective on the design and implementation of formal mentoring programmes within an organization is also presented. The chapter also discusses mentoring with respect to an increasingly diverse and global workforce. Specifically, barriers faced by women in the development of workplace mentoring relationships and mentoring employees belonging to a different country or race are discussed. The chapter goes on to offer a strategic view of mentoring relationships and suggests the criteria for successful mentoring programmes.

THE CONCEPT OF MENTORING

Mentoring is not a new phenomenon; the concept of mentoring as well as the origin of the term 'mentor' dates back four thousand years. It was Homer who introduced the concept of mentoring in the epic, *The Odyssey*. The word mentor has its roots in Greek mythology. The story goes that when Odysseus was leaving to fight the Trojan war, he asked his trusted friend Mentor to provide advice and education to his son Telemachus in his absence. Mentor provided Telemachus with an education that covered the physical, moral, spiritual, and intellectual aspects of life. He helped Telemachus to become a competent young man and on one occasion even saved his life. The concept of mentoring, as understood today, is derived from the relationship between Mentor and Telemachus.

According to Reidy-Croft (2005), mentoring refers to the 'information and advice provided by an older, experienced individual to a younger and less experienced individual to help in latter's growth and development'. The concept is close to the *gurukula* tradition that has been a part of Indian culture. In its simplest form, mentoring may be described as an interpersonal relationship.

The dictionary meaning of the term mentor is a close, trusted, and experienced counsellor or guide.

The origin of mentoring as a process of human resource development (HRD) can be traced to the concept of apprenticeship that emerged during the industrial revolution. The apprentice worked under the guidance of a master. The master (mentor) helped the apprentice (protégé) to acquire skills that the master had.

Reduced to the most basic level, mentoring is about teaching and learning. It plays an important role in learning new knowledge and skills for all human beings. This is as true of our learning experiences on a day-to-day basis as it is of workplace learning. Do you remember the time when a teacher, or a peer, or even your parents, provided you with valuable counsel or advice, or when a teacher assigned you the responsibility of organizing a seminar in your college, while sheltering you from criticism from certain quarters? In each of these instances, you were being mentored. Informal mentoring has always existed in organizations; for example, recognition from seniors through assigning a relatively junior person on an important committee. Mentors have been shown to play a very important role in the career advancement of individuals. To communicate how pervasive mentoring is, Dalton, et al. (1977) labelled one of the career stages in their model as the mentor stage. However, the recognition and value attributed to workplace mentoring relationships, the development of formal mentoring programmes, and the organizational benefits that flow from mentoring are more recent.

Organizations have increasingly begun to develop formal mentoring programmes. This has been a result of the importance that managers as well as organizations give to careers and career development processes. The interest in career development was primarily due to the difficulties that organizations were experiencing in various areas, such as developing talented managers to replace those retiring, reducing employee turnover during early career stages, and facilitating high levels of performance on the part of all employees.

Mentoring has been defined in many different ways. Defining mentoring has not been easy because the nature and number of activities linked to the concept and practices of mentoring seem to be growing every day. Collin (1979) defined mentoring as 'a one-to-one relationship between a more experienced person and an inexperienced person, and only until the latter reaches maturity'. According to Bolton (1980), mentoring exists when 'An experienced person provides guidance and support in a variety of way to the developing novice. In addition to being a role model, the experienced person acts as a guide, tutor, coach, and a confidant'.

An all-encompassing definition of mentoring was provided by Levinson, (1980) according to whom 'The mentor relationship is one of the most complex and developmentally important that a man can have in early adulthood. The mentor is ordinarily several years older, a person of greater experience and seniority in the world the young man is entering'. According to Levinson, a person can qualify to be a mentor even though the protégé may have never met the mentor in person. The author of a book, a leader, or a famous public figure may be considered to be a mentor if a person was influenced by him/her. Similarly, a mentor may not necessarily be in the same organization. Thus, a person's neighbour, father, mother, uncle, or aunt might also take on mentor roles. Haines (2003) described mentoring as a symbiotic relationship between two adults who facilitate each other in achieving mutual career objectives in an organization or professional discipline. According to Reidy-Crofts, 'At their very best, mentoring relationships take advantage of the aspects of an organization's culture that have made it successful and without institutionalizing or dehumanizing transmit these qualities to a firm's next generation of leaders.'

Mentoring vis-á-vis Coaching, Training, and Counselling

Mentoring is different from coaching, training, or counselling. Frequently, the terms 'coaching' and 'mentoring' are used together and in the same context. Though coaching and mentoring share some common approaches they are dissimilar in certain ways. *Coaching* is primarily focussed on the development of skills and performance within the current job. *Mentoring*, on the other hand, is directed towards developing potential and is future-oriented. The concept of training is also different from mentoring. *Training* is a formal procedure organized to enhance employees' job-related knowledge and skills so that they perform their jobs efficiently and effectively. Mentoring goes beyond training for specific jobs. Mentoring also includes facilitating the adjustment of the employee to the organization such that the employee internalizes the culture of the organization and its systems. Thus, mentoring involves imparting of organizational philosophies, values, and culture. Mentoring also makes it possible for the mentor and protégé to have one-on-one interaction as well as share and discuss detailed information on specific issues of concern over time as and when they arise. Such an opportunity is not possible in training.

Distinction also needs to be drawn between mentoring and *counselling*. Mentors serve several roles for assisting the protégés in their progress towards growth, improvement, adjustment, and cultural adaptation. However, it is important for them to define their boundaries of interaction. Confusing their mentoring responsibilities with a counselling role may have an adverse impact on the effectiveness of the mentor. The main points of difference between coaching, counselling, and training with mentoring are presented in Exhibit 10.1.

Exhibit 10.1

Mentoring versus Coaching, Training, and Counselling

Mentoring	Coaching
■ Focus on potential ■ Agenda defined by the needs of the protégé ■ Emphasis on feedback and reflection by the protégé ■ Typically a long-term relationship which may continue throughout life ■ Protégé's manager is not formally the mentor ■ Takes place outside the line manager relationship	■ Focus on the skills and performance on current job ■ Agenda defined by the coach ■ Emphasis on feedback for the learner ■ Addresses a short term need ■ Routine function of a manager for all the staff ■ Takes place within confines of formal manager-employee relationship

Mentoring	Training
■ Emphasis is on internalization of organizational culture, philosophies, and values by the protégé ■ One-on-one interaction between mentor and protégé	■ Emphasis on job related knowledge and skills ■ One-on-one interaction not possible

Mentoring	Counselling
■ Mentors may help the protégé in locating appropriate counselling assistance when they become too emotional or personal Mentor helps protégé to deal with problems but does not serve as counsellor for problems of protégés	■ Helping individuals to work through their emotions and personal problems

Adapted from: http://www.fastpath.co.uk/coaching.htm, accessed on 5 February 2005

Mentoring is about support, development, and problem-solving through experience-sharing. It works best when the mentor is not the direct supervisor nor from the same department. Mentoring has assumed great significance in recent times. It helps organizations achieve several objectives such as

- providing a structured way for employees to train and help each other;
- developing young managers and 'high flyers' as well as other employees;
- reducing entry shock for newcomers to the organization by facilitating socialization; and
- providing on-the-job training and coaching to new employees.

Some of the firms that have introduced formal mentoring programmes in India are Modi Xerox, Honeywell, IBM, ABN AMRO, GlaxoSmithKline (formerly Smithkline Beecham), Johnson & Johnson (J&J), Procter and Gamble (P&G), Ashok Leyland, and Eicher.

Mentors and Protégés

Mentors are 'individuals with advanced experience and knowledge who are committed to provide upward mobility and career support to their protégé'. Mentors have excellent interpersonal skills and technical competence. They also have considerable influence and status within an organization and demonstrate willingness to contribute to the growth of others in an organization. Mentors take an active interest in the career of the protégé by acting as the protégé's guide and friend.

Protégés are 'individuals who receive guidance, coaching, and support from the mentor'. Mentors do many things for their protégés to help them in their careers, such as

- providing support to them when they are just beginning their career and are likely to be unsure about their abilities;
- facilitating job success by nominating them for promotions;
- providing them opportunities to demonstrate their competence;
- helping them get noticed by the top management;
- protecting them from serious consequences of their errors; and
- providing them insulation from situations that may prove to be risky for their careers.

Mentors may take on several roles (see Exhibit 10.2).

Exhibit 10.2

Different Roles of Mentors

	Mentor Role	Description
1.	Sponsor	Creates opportunities for their protégés to prove themselves by ■ assigning protégés to a project ■ asking protégés to analyse a problem ■ asking protégés to make presentations to higher management ■ using his/her influence to facilitate the protégé's advancement
2.	Teacher	■ Presents protégés with hypothetical situations and asks them for solutions ■ Explains the written and unwritten rules of the organization to the protégé

Contd

Exhibit 10.2 Contd

	Mentor Role	Description
3.	Devil's Advocate	▪ Challenges and confronts protégés to provide them practice in asserting their ideas and influencing others
4.	Advocate	▪ Intervenes on behalf of the protégé ▪ Arranges the protégé's involvement in highly visible activities within and outside the organization ▪ Represents the concerns of the protégé to higher level managers
5.	Coach	▪ Teaches relevant skills ▪ Reinforces effective on-the-job performance ▪ Suggests improvement in specific behaviours ▪ Serves as a role model and leads by example ▪ Helps the protégé in defining goals
6.	Adviser	▪ Gives suggestions for career advancement strategies ▪ Helps the protégé recognize opportunities for training ▪ Reviews the protégé's development plan regularly ▪ Helps the protégé in understanding realistic opportunities for career progression within the organization ▪ Helps the protégé in identifying career obstacles and planning actions to overcome them
7.	Counsellor	▪ Facilitates the protégé's efforts for developing strategies to achieve agreed upon goals ▪ Works with protégés to identify career related skills and values ▪ Encourages protégés to evaluate career options and their appropriateness ▪ Provides moral support
8.	Broker	▪ Works to expand the professional network of the protégé ▪ Encourages protégés to interact with each other resulting in mutual benefit ▪ Helps the protégé with identification of resources that are required for career advancement

Adapted from: Reece and Brandt 1997

At McKinsey, the mentor takes the roles of a coach and a guide. The mentor also creates opportunities for the protégé, thus serving as a sponsor. At GlaxoSmithKline, the mentors take on the role of a coach, counsellor, teacher, and adviser. Eicher and Cadbury expect the mentors to serve as role models, and mentors at Merrill Lynch serve as counsellors and advisers to protégés.

Functions of Mentoring

The mentoring process serves two main functions. These are:

Career–related or career support functions These functions are largely work-related and enhance 'learning the ropes', career development, and advancement in the organization. The five career functions identified by Kram (1985) are sponsorship, exposure-and-visibility, coaching, protection, and challenging assignments. When a newcomer is given a challenging project to handle early on in his/her career, or an opportunity to make presentations to the top management, then the manager may be performing the career support function for the newcomer. For example, Patni Computer Systems gives a lot of responsibility and exposure on live projects to newcomers. Dell uses mentoring as a developmental tool to provide guidance and support to employees to help improve their performance and capabilities.

Psychosocial or emotional support functions These functions provide emotional support, and enhance the protégé's feelings of competence and identity. Kram proposed four psychosocial functions. Emotional support is evidenced through role modelling, acceptance-and-confirmation, counselling, and friendship. For example, at Mindtree Consulting, when a subordinate inadvertently contradicted his manager in front of a client, it did not result in dire consequences. Rather the manager assured the subordinate that both of them could treat the incident as a learning opportunity. Thus, the manager provided emotional support to the subordinate. At GlaxoSmithKline, a protégé may seek guidance and support even on personal issues and crises.

These functions are presented in Exhibit 10.3.

Exhibit 10.3

Career and Psychosocial Functions of Mentoring

Functions of Mentoring		Description
Career Functions	Sponsorship	Taking an active interest in nominating a junior for promotion and other positions of responsibility
	Exposure and visibility	Providing opportunities and pairing the junior with key executives and assigning him/her to tasks that provide visibility in the organization
	Coaching	Giving advice to protégés on how to achieve their objectives and gain recognition

Contd

Exhibit 10.3 Contd

Functions of Mentoring		Description
	Protection	Extending protection to the protégé from potentially harmful situations and serious consequences when they make an error
	Challenging assignments	Assigning the protégé to challenging jobs and providing feedback to facilitate development of necessary competencies
Psychosocial Functions	Role modelling	Giving the protégé a pattern of behaviour, attitudes, and values to emulate
	Acceptance and confirmation	Encouraging the protégé and providing mutual support
	Counselling	Facilitating the protégé in his/her working to enhance the self image of the protégé
	Friendship	Interacting socially with the protégé to gain mutual satisfaction

Adapted from: Kram 1985, in Kreitner and Kinicki 2001

A study was conducted by Burke (1984) to examine mentoring relationships in organizations as experienced by protégés. Results indicated that the older mentors were less likely to perform psychosocial functions. When mentors provided more psychosocial functions, they had no influence on the career aspirations of the protégés, and when protégés reported greater career success, they also reported that the mentors provided more career development functions. It was also found that the mentors who performed more career development and psychosocial functions had greater personal as well as career influence on the protégé. They were also seen by the protégés as having more influence on their career success. The conceptualization of mentoring has changed in recent times. The contemporary perspective of mentoring is different from the traditional perspective in several ways.

PERSPECTIVES OF MENTORING

This section explores the traditional and the contemporary perspective of mentoring.

Traditional Perspective

Most of the theories on mentoring have focused on a *traditional* perspective of mentoring. According to Ostroff and Kozlowski (1993), a traditional mentoring relationship is one in which a senior person working in the protégé's organization assists with the protégé's professional and personal development.

Mentoring relationships are largely seen as dyadic in nature, that is, at one point of time there are likely to be only two people—the protégé and the mentor. This type of mentoring relationship is referred to as one-on-one mentoring. A peer or a senior can also perform the role of a mentor.

Organizations with a formal mentoring programme usually assign a mentor to a newcomer. Asian Paints, LG, and Hughes Software Systems are among some of the companies that follow this practice. Focus is on a single or primary mentoring relationship or on the total *amount* of mentoring received by a protégé, on an aggregate, through a series of mentoring relationships over his/her entire career. The amount of mentoring received by a protégé taps the sequence of mentoring relationships experienced by the protégé. This does not incorporate the possibility of a 'configuration of mentor-protégé relationships' occurring simultaneously.

Mentor-protégé relationships are seen to provide developmental benefits only to the protégé and not to the mentor. The effectiveness of a mentoring relationship is largely viewed in terms of the *amount* of mentoring provided. The traditional perspective of mentoring has broadened since the 1990s.

Contemporary and Alternative Perspective

More recently, there has been a re-conceptualization of mentoring due to contextual changes such as changes in the business environment, changing nature of employment contracts, technological changes resulting in importance of knowledge workers, changing nature of careers, and an increasingly diverse workforce. These changes have led to a review of mentoring leading to a shift in the sources and the nature of mentoring relationships today.

Mentoring at work is now viewed with a new and different perspective, that is, the *contemporary* perspective. According to the contemporary mentoring perspective, mentoring is not a sequential dyadic relationship; rather, alternative forms or different types of mentoring are present in an individual's life. Individuals may receive mentoring assistance from multiple sources simultaneously at any one point in time, including senior colleagues, peers, family, and community members. Thus, there may be multiple mentoring relationships. Hence, mentoring may be understood as a 'multiple developmental relationship phenomenon'. Higgins and Kram (2001) called this alternative view of mentoring as the 'developmental network perspective'. Kram referred to it as 'relationship constellation'.

Mentoring functions may exist in several relationships. Though the hierarchical mentor relationship may provide the widest range of career and psychosocial functions, a relationship with peers also offers several functions.

An individual's 'developmental network' refers to a set of people who take an active interest in as well as take actions to advance the career of the protégé by providing developmental assistance. Developmental assistance refers to two types of support, that is, career support and psychosocial support, as mentioned earlier. The developmental network does not consist of all inter-personal relationships of an individual. Burt (1992) proposed that an individual's developmental network is a subset of his/her entire social network and consists of those relationships that are important for the protégé's career development at a particular point of time. Further, developmental network refers to simultaneously held relationships, as opposed to a sequence of rela-tionships. Proponents of the developmental network perspective refer to mentors with one term only rather than using multiple terms such as sponsor, coach, peer, adviser, etc. According to them, the person who extends devel-opmental assistance to a protégé is called a *developer.*

Multiple developmental relationships are also characterized by reciprocity, mutuality, and interdependence. The strength of the mentor–protégé rela-tionship may fall along a continuum from weak to strong. A weak develop-mental relationship is one where the protégé derives the benefit, but the developer does not get the opportunity for learning. A strong developmental relationship is characterized by mutuality where both the protégé and the men-tor grow personally and professionally together.

Alternative Mentoring Models

Several variations to the traditional one-on-one mentoring model have emerged in recent times. Figure 10.1 illustrates alternative mentoring models.

Mentoring circles consist of one mentor working with a group of protégés. It is best suited when there are few mentors and several protégés in an organiza-tion. However, these do not permit personal relationship of one-on-one mentoring. Further, scheduling mentor-protégé meetings is difficult. Mentors also need to know group dynamics in order to understand the protégés better.

Peer mentoring/buddy system is one in which peers often provide mentoring to each other. Buddies are peers who have similar day-to-day responsibilities and may be assigned to new employees. The newcomers learn the ropes from these buddies. This one-to-one interaction can supplement formal training and orientation programmes, thus accelerating the newcomers' productivity and fostering a sense of belonging to the organization.

Team mentoring is provided by formal mentoring teams composed of department managers, human resources representatives, and senior employees playing a role in coaching a group of selected candidates. Each mentoring team member specializes in a specific area and provides assistance to the protégés in this area.

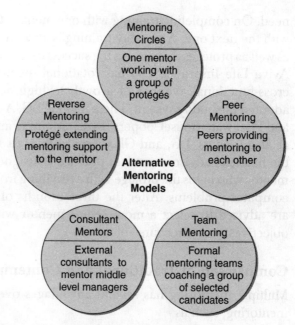

Figure 10.1: Alternative Models of Mentoring

Consultant mentors are external consultants having mentoring qualities engaged by the firm when there is no one in the organization who has the particular skill set or specific experience required. Consultant mentors help prepare middle managers to take on a new or expanded role.

Reverse mentoring occurs when the protégé extends mentoring support to the mentor in certain cases, like the issue of technological change. A protégé who is younger may be better versed with new technology and hence can provide lessons to the mentor.

The concept of *mentoring circle* has been applied by Merrill Lynch & Co., where mentors are higher level managers who volunteer to serve as counsellors or advisers to four individuals during a six-month period. At Intel too, small groups of four or five new employees are sometimes matched with one experienced manager to work on a specific management problem. Eicher follows the *team mentoring* approach through career development groups (CDG). More details about Eicher's CDGs are provided in Exhibit 10.4. The team mentoring approach was also adopted by Winthrop Pharmaceuticals, when faced with a situation where all its top level leaders were to retire within the next four to five years. The HR department of the firm developed what it called 'rotational mentoring' to come up with enough candidates for leadership positions. The corporate team under the rotational mentoring programme identifies each high potential's (protégé's) needs and strengths. Each protégé is matched with a top-level mentor for the amount of time required to meet a particular training need. On completing training with one mentor, the protégé is rotated to work with the next one. A two-day training is also provided initially to the mentors as well as protégés that assures the success of rotational mentoring programmes. Aviva Life Insurance also has rotational mentoring programme to provide cross-functional avenues of growth to high achievers. Several firms have adopted the buddy system. These include LG, Asian Paints, GlaxoSmithKline, and PricewaterhouseCoopers (PwC). Mentors and buddies coach newcomers at Asian Paints, LG, and GlaxoSmithKline. At PwC, each new employee in the financial advisory services practice is assigned for three months to a peer mentor who helps the protégé with everything from locating supplies to solving computer problems. After the three months of peer mentoring, employees are advised to select a more senior mentor with whom to work on career objectives over the course of a year.

Comparison of Traditional and Contemporary Perspectives

Multiple mentoring has several advantages over the traditional one-on-one mentoring, such as

- capitalizing on unique skills of many individuals;
- supporting team building;
- cross training on specific skills; and
- making experienced individuals available to multiple learners at one time.

However, one-on-one mentoring continues to be the most common model adopted by organizations such as HP, Cadbury, Ernst & Young, and Fannie May. A comparison of the traditional and contemporary perspectives of mentoring is presented in Table 10.1.

Table 10.1: Comparison of Traditional and Contemporary Perspectives of Mentoring

Traditional Mentoring	Contemporary Mentoring
One-to-one mentoring	Multiple mentoring
Dyadic in nature	Multiple developmental relationships
Sequential (sequence of mentoring relationships)	Configuration of mentor-protégé relationships existing simultaneously
Senior mentors the junior	Reverse mentoring possible (mentor as the recipient)
Mentors referred to by several terms such as sponsor, coach, or adviser	Mentor referred to as developer

Contd

Table 10.1 Contd

Traditional Mentoring	Contemporary Mentoring
Developmental benefits only to the protégé	Characterized by reciprocity, mutuality, and interdependence
Informal mentoring programmes	Combination of formal and informal mentoring programmes
Available only for few select employees	Available for all who can learn from the experience
Mentor and protégé share common background and personalities	Mentor and protégé often come from dissimilar backgrounds and possess different strengths

Adapted from: http://www.walga.asn.au/projServices/wrts/docs/Reidy Crofts Mentoring Presentation.ppt, accessed on 2 February 2005; Higgins and Kram 2001

Other Classifications of Mentor–Protégé Relationships

Figure 10.2 illustrates the other categories of mentor-protégé relationships apart from the ones discussed earlier. A distinction has been made between *primary* and *secondary* mentoring relationships. The traditional or classical view of the mentoring relationship is characterized by what may be termed as a *primary* mentoring relationship between the mentor and the protégé. Walsh and Borkowski (1999) mention that the primary relationship evolves over a long period of time. This type of mentoring relationship is intense, long-term, and characterized by strong socialization efforts. A *secondary* mentoring relationship, on the other hand, evolves over a shorter period of time and is focussed on acquiring specialized knowledge or skill from a group of influential members of the organization. This form of mentoring is shorter, less intense, and focussed mainly on career related-issues rather than on psychosocial aspects. Secondary mentoring relationships are achieving more significance in organizations and can turn out to be highly effective for enhancing the early career success of new employees.

Mentoring may be training-based or resource-based. *Training-based mentoring* is linked to a training programme such that classroom training is applied to real life experiences with mentors facilitating this linkage. Elements of training based mentoring may be seen at Hughes Software Systems (HSS), GlaxoSmithKline, P&G, Cadbury, Infosys, Tata Administrative Services (TAS), etc. where mentoring is used to orient newcomers and develop high potentials for future leadership roles. In *resource-based mentoring*, a general pool of mentors is available when an employee needs a mentor. Resource-based mentoring is used in combination with other models and is rarely used by itself.

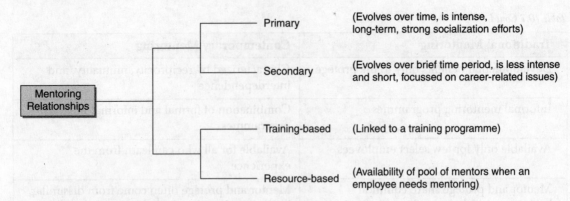

Figure 10.2: Other Classifications of Mentoring Relations

The Mentoring Relationship

Like other human or work relationships, mentoring relationships do not develop and start functioning suddenly or at random but evolve over a period of time.

Phases of the Mentoring Relationship

Mentoring relationships progress through a sequence of stages and develops through four phases (Figure 10.3). Kram (1983) identified four stages of the mentoring process, i.e., initiation, cultivation, separation, and redefinition. The four stages of mentor-protégé relationships and the nature of interaction between the mentor and the protégé during each of these phases in presented in Table 10.2.

Nature of the Relationship

As is evident from the description of the stages of mentoring relationships, each of the stages lasts for a variable, and not a fixed, time period. Typically, mentors are about 15 to 20 years older than the protégé. Age differences much greater or lesser than this have their own drawbacks. Levinson (1980) pointed out that when the mentor is older than the protégé by about twenty years or more, then the relationship may be viewed in parent-child terms by both. This may result in excessive feelings of paternalism on the part of mentor and high dependence on the part of the protégé. The larger the age difference is between the mentor and the protégé, the less likely it is that the mentor would perform psychosocial functions.

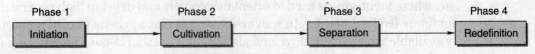

Figure 10.3: Phases of Mentoring Relationship

Table 10.2: Phases of the Mentoring Relationship

Phases	Typical Duration	Characteristics
Initiation	Six months to one year	▪ New employee admires senior manager's competence and recognizes in them the capacity to be a source of guidance and support ▪ Older manager recognizes the younger as having potential and being coachable ▪ Relationship starts and begins to have importance for both individuals ▪ Job expectations become concrete goals ▪ Expectations are met and mutual interests are identified ▪ Interaction and relationship is largely task-centred ▪ Mentor provides visibility, coaching, and challenging work to protégé ▪ Protégés on their part provide assistance and respect and display willingness to be coached
Cultivation	Two years to five years	▪ Strong professional and personal relationship ▪ Number of career and psychosocial functions provided by the mentor increases and reaches peak ▪ Both individuals continue to derive benefits from the relationship ▪ More frequent and meaningful interactions develop ▪ Strengthening of an emotional bond ▪ Mutual growth takes place ▪ Highly productive phase
Separation	Six months to two years	▪ Takes place after a significant change in the structural relationship (transfer or promotion) or in the emotional relationship (feeling of independence, threat, or betrayal) ▪ Protégé desires to work autonomously and no longer wants guidance ▪ Feelings of resentment or hostility on the part of the protégé emerge ▪ Possible conflict and feelings of abandonment by the mentor ▪ Mentor faces midlife crisis and may be psychologically or physically unable to provide career or psychosocial functions ▪ Promotion or job rotation places limits on opportunities for interaction between the mentor and the protégé ▪ Disruption of professional and personal relationship
Redefinition or Retranslation	Indefinite period after the separation phase	▪ End of the mentor relationship ▪ Translating the relationship into a peer like friendship ▪ Stresses of separation, resentment, and anger diminish ▪ Mutual sense of gratitude and appreciation increase

Contd

Table 10.2 Contd

Phases	Typical Duration	Characteristics
		▪ Mentor recognizes that the protégé no longer needs protection and nurturing like in the early years ▪ Mentor continues to support the protégé and takes pride in the latter's accomplishments ▪ Protégé responds with gratitude for the mentor's support during early years but is no longer dependent on him/her ▪ Protégé may develop a relationship with a new mentor

Adapted From: Haines 2003; Kreitner and Kinicki 2001; Kram 1983

GlaxoSmithKline encountered the problem of communication and culture gap between the mentor and protégé from different generations. It was observed that the seniority of the mentor sometimes acted as an inhibiting factor for interaction on personal issues such as dress codes or on issues relating to behaviour of peers or immediate superiors. The problem arose due to the age gap. Hence, GlaxoSmithKline added buddies to their mentoring programme. Buddies were colleagues who were slightly senior to the protégés, but yet close enough to them in age and seniority to understand their problems. Buddies also helped the protégés communicate with their mentors. The buddy is seen as helping the newcomer at GlaxoSmithKline with issues such as peer politics, perceived discrimination, and about purely personal and other issues the protégés could not discuss with their mentors.

When the age difference is lesser, the two may become good friends but the mentoring aspects may be missing. However, exceptions may always be found in the form of effective and fruitful mentor–protégé relationships with the age difference exceeding twenty years or being less than five years.

The mentoring relationship may be initiated by either the mentor or the protégé. Often, the protégé attracts the attention of a mentor because of similar interests, hobbies, or excellent job performance. The mentor believes that the protégé is someone with potential. For example, when a new employee is seen as performing well or having potential, a senior person in the organization may take the newcomer under his/her wing and promote the interests of the junior employee. This usually happens in firms that have informal mentoring programmes. In most organizations that have a formal mentoring programme, mentors and protégés are assigned to each other. Hewlett-Packard, GlaxoSmithKline, and Cadbury all carefully match mentors and protégés after checking for compatibility. On the other hand, the protégé may initiate the relationship by seeking out a more experienced member of the organization in order to understand the formal and informal norms of the organization. McKinsey expects the newcomers to take initiative and seek out their own mentors. At some Intel locations, the protégé chooses one mentor from a list of available mentors in the firm. The online mentor and protégé profiles also allow protégés to choose from a list of mentors recommended as suitable for the protégé.

Some experienced mentors may provide guidance to more than one protégé at the same time. At GlaxoSmithKline, a mentor may sometimes have two protégés. However, most mentor-protégé relationships are exclusive during the cultivation phase of the relationship. This is especially true for informal mentoring relationships which are more intense in nature. Over the course of his/her career, a protégé may have multiple mentors. A protégé may also have several mentors at the same time, with each mentor fulfilling specific needs of the protégé, as discussed earlier in alternative mentoring models. The mentors, too, form mentoring relationships with several protégés during their career span.

Mentor relationships do not continue indefinitely and reach the point of termination at some stage. At HP, mentoring is a time-bound process that ranges from nine months to one year. At Cadbury too, mentoring is finite and concludes with the ending of the formal one year training programme. However, informal mentoring may continue. There are divergent views about the manner in which mentor relationships end. Levinson et al. (1978) proposed that most mentor relationships ended with ill will, hard feelings, and conflict on both sides. The primary reason for the conflict and tensions is the result of the protégés' desire to be independent and stand on their own feet. The mentor, on his part, is unwilling to grant this freedom and independence to the protégé. As a result, the protégé begins to view the mentor, whom he/she once admired and looked up to, as too demanding and critical. The mentor, on the other hand, finds that the young protégé, whom the mentor nurtured, has turned rebellious and ungrateful. Such feelings on both the sides result in considerable negativity. The intensity of the conflict that arises is a function of the intensity of the mentor-protégé relationship.

Mentoring relationships may end on a positive note as well. In these instances, the mentor-protégé relationships are less emotionally intense and also of shorter duration. Moreover, these relationships usually end with one or the other individual moving to another position, inside or outside the organization.

It would be fair to conclude that mentor relationships may end differently and with a variety of outcomes. Whatever be the nature of the ending, it appears that most of the benefits of mentoring relationship are realized after the relationship is terminated. Following the end of the mentor-protégé relationship, the protégé may internalize the admired qualities of the mentor more completely. This internalization later becomes a major source of development for the protégé. Not all mentoring relationships are formally assigned in an organization. A large number of mentoring relationships run informally, as discussed next.

Formal and Informal Mentoring Relationships

A majority of mentor-protégé relationships in organizations are *informal.* That is, two persons establish a relationship when the mentor takes the protégé under his/her wing. Informal or natural mentoring is derived spontaneously and has existed through all ages and at all times. In earlier times, Lord Krishna assumed several mentor roles for Arjuna. However, many organizations, such as, IBM, Modi Xerox, GlaxoSmithKline, Citibank, Motorola, ABN Amro Bank, Eicher Limited, Infosys, TAS, Cadbury, HP, etc. have created formal mentoring programmes. In *formal* mentoring relationships, the organization assigns or matches mentors and protégés, which results in the mentors and protégés being brought together systematically. Hewlett-Packard matches mentors and protégés after checking for compatibility. Both the mentor and the protégé have to undergo a half-day role clarity programme to foster the mentorship process. At Cadbury also, the mentors are screened carefully to serve as role models in terms of both career success and personality attributes. GlaxoSmithKline allots mentors to protégés based on personality profiling for effective behaviour modelling. Thus, formal mentoring relationships develop with organizational intervention. Though formal mentoring has emerged as a trend in this century, organizations have seen a growth in both informal as well as formal mentoring programmes.

Formal and informal mentoring relationships differ on a number of other dimensions. These differences are highlighted in Table 10.3.

Table 10.3:   Formal and Informal Mentoring Relationships

Dimensions of Mentoring Relationships	Informal Mentoring Relationships	Formal Mentoring Relationships
Initiation of the relationship	Develop spontaneously	Develop with organizational intervention (third party) either as voluntary assignment or matching of mentor and protégé
	Initiated when two employees are brought together perceived similarities	Externally directed by a programme coordinator who determines the match between the mentor and the protégé
Basis of the mentor–protégé match	Relationship develops based on mutual identification by the mentor and the protégé (mutual attraction)	Assignment of mentors and protégés to the relationship by a third party; mentor and protégé often have never even met each other before the mentor–protégé match

Contd

Table 10.3 Contd

Dimensions of Mentoring Relationships	Informal Mentoring Relationships	Formal Mentoring Relationships
	High level of identification and interpersonal comfort level with each other	Mentor and protégé may not have high comfort level with each other
Purpose of the relationship	Driven by developmental needs, for example, managers in mid-career getting a sense of contribution to future generations by meeting the protégés' early career needs by guidance and support	Mentors enter into the relationship to meet organizational expectations to be good organizational citizens
	To help the protégés achieve long-term career goals	Often contracted to focus on career goals that are short term and applicable only to the protégé's current position
	Organization benefits indirectly	Organization benefits directly
Phases of evolution	Evolve through four distinct phases: initiation, cultivation, separation, and redefinition	Initiation and separation phases are identified but no empirical documentation of the evolution of formal relationship between these two phases
Motivation to be a mentor	Intrinsically motivated and more personally interested in the protégés' development	More motivated by external factors and likely to be less involved with the protégé
Type of recognition for mentors	More intrinsic rewards and less chances of formal explicit recognition	More explicit organizational recognition
Structure of the relationship	Unstructured	Structured
	Meetings between mentor and protégé are held whenever desired with no set schedule	Mode, frequency, and location of mentor-protégé meetings may be predetermined in a relationship contract signed by both parties
	Goals are unspecified and evolve over time	Goals are set at the beginning of the relationship
	Access to mentoring is limited and may exclude some employees	Access open to all who qualify
	There is no training support	Training and support provided

Contd

Table 10.3 Contd

Dimensions of Mentoring Relationships	Informal Mentoring Relationships	Formal Mentoring Relationships
Length of the programme	Lasts from three to five years	Contracted for a specific amount of time (generally a year)
Interpersonal processes	Mentors more likely to take the role of a developmental supporter of their protégés	Mentors more likely to take the role of a good organizational citizen
	Mentors more likely to actively further the career of their protégés	Mentors more visible and hence less likely to intervene on behalf of the protégé

Adapted from: Blake-Beard 2001; Ragins, Cotton, and Miller 2000

It is evident that there are several points of difference between formal and informal mentoring relationships. While informal mentors enter the relationship by mutual identification and development needs, formal mentors are more likely to enter mentor relationships to meet organizational expectations or to be good organizational citizens. Formal mentoring relationships are public relationships that are monitored by programme coordinators and hence are also sensitive to charges of favouritism. Therefore, formal mentors are less likely to actively promote or undertake career development activities for the protégé. Some formal mentoring programmes are not focussed on career goals of the protégés. Rather, they are often directed towards orienting new employees or providing on-the-job training.

As mentioned earlier, orientating, training new employees, and preparing high potentials for future leadership roles are the major objectives of mentoring in firms such as Infosys, HP, Intel, Microsoft, Cadbury, Modi Xerox, etc. Hence, they may be confused with coaching relationships. Several organizations with formal mentoring programmes reward or recognize managers who serve as mentors in order to encourage them to take the mentoring role. Honeywell and HSS are among those organizations that have 'best mentor' awards.

Examples of formal mentoring programmes followed by some organizations are presented in Exhibit 10.4.

OUTCOMES OF MENTORING PROGRAMMES

The presence (or absence) of mentoring may impact several functions of the organization. The presence of mentoring results in positive organizational

Exhibit 10.4

Formal Mentoring Programmes; Some Examples

Fannie May Confections Inc. A wholly owned subsidiary of Alpine Confections Inc., it is based in Chicago. Fannie May has a Corporate Mentor Programme through which the firm works to

- encourage the advancement of all highly qualified personnel;
- help employees enhance their relationship-building skills;
- enhance personal growth; and
- set and achieve professional development goals.

The mentor programme at Fannie May has three components: the mentor speaker series, the mentor–protégé pairing programme, and the peer mentor programme.

The Mentor Speaker Series Speakers are successful employees from Fannie May and from other private and public sector organizations who serve as role models. The speaker series offers interested employees exposure to these speakers. Speakers discuss their professional experiences and provide motivation and inspiration to participating employees.

The Mentor–Protégé Pairing Programme Consists of formal and informal one-on-one relationships between mentors and protégés that help enhance professional and personal growth, improve skills, and increase networking opportunities. These alliances encourage the transfer of knowledge and experiences of successful employees to the new workforce.

The Peer Mentor Programme A current employee is assigned a newly-hired employee on a short-term basis to help the newcomer become familiar with Fannie May, its people, business, culture, facilities, and activities. The programme also fosters new and valuable working relationships.

GlaxoSmithKline Though mentoring was being practiced informally at GlaxoSmithKline, it became part of the official indoctrination training only in 1996. The objectives were to complement formal training and ensure a smoother cultural transition for the new employees. The mentoring process at GlaxoSmithKline starts with the allotment of mentors to protégés on the same day on which the new entrants (trainees) are indoctrinated in the company's philosophy, vision, and culture. A one-day personality workshop profiles the protégés based on which an appropriate mentor–protégé match is determined. During the next five days of the indoctrination programme for newcomers, the trainees are given a quick rundown on the different aspects of the company's operations. A role-clarity workshop for the mentors is also held soon after. Over the next nine months, as the trainees go through their formal training programme and are rotated through different departments, regular interaction between the mentor and the protégé gets under way. Frequent meetings are ensured, with the mentor and protégé meeting each other once a week during the first month. During the next two months, the mentor–protégé meetings are scheduled once a fortnight. However, the protégé can meet the mentor whenever the protégé feels the need for any help. The mentor goes on to build close ties with the protégé. The protégé may even discuss personal problems with the mentor and also receive guidance and solutions on these matters.

After one month, the mentoring programme for the newcomers is extended to the peer-level through the assignment of 'buddies'. Buddies at GlaxoSmithKline are colleagues drawn from peer groups who are slightly senior to the protégés, but closer in age and seniority to the protégés.

Contd

Exhibit 10.4 Contd

Buddies understand the problems of protégés and help them communicate with their mentors, thus serving as a communication bridge between the mentor and the protégé.

Gradually the meetings between the mentor and protégé become need-based, supplemented by phone calls and e-mail. The mentor and the protégé subsequently review the mentoring process to generate feedback and develop corrective actions.

In India, GlaxoSmithKline has customized the mentoring model to the unique sociocultural context of the country. In order to make the protégés comfortable with the ideas provided by their mentors, the firm draws on classics from India, such as writings from it and the discourses of Sri Aurobindo and Ramakrishna Paramhansa.

Eicher Group The mentoring programme at Eicher is the cornerstone of the leadership development process wherein the superiors are expected to act as role models to subordinates and groom the protégés for leadership roles in the future. The mentoring techniques are labelled career development groups (CDG) that are used to map the career path of all the employees, not just of newcomers. The CDG for each employee (protégé) comprises of the immediate superior, the superior's superior, and a senior professional from a different division. This ensures that the employee gets a cross-functional perspective, and also provides the employee with both functional and behavioural role models. The process forms the basis of the formal appraisal process. The

CDG is responsible for appraising, monitoring, and planning each individual's career and development path. There is close interaction between the mentors and the protégé. The main objective of this mentor programme is to draw out the inherent qualities of leadership in the protégé rather than facilitate the initiation of the newcomer. Career development groups identify the skills that each protégé needs to develop and then creates situations over the next year which tests those skills. Therefore, in the process, the protégé has no choice but to learn the skills and develop leadership qualities.

McKinsey & Co. Mentoring is not a formally integrated programme in McKinsey & Co. and hence is an on going process. The newcomers to the organization are expected to seek out their own mentors. Senior consultants in the firm are aware that they will have to play the role of a mentor. Mentoring, though unstructured, is loosely based on apprenticeship-based learning where the mentor is expected to take the role of a coach and a guide. The mentor is expected to provide perspective in times of crises, clarify choices, and create opportunities for the protégé within the organization. The relationship focusses on the protégés specific needs and continues for a long time. Mentor-protégé relationships at McKinsey span geographical and functional boundaries. Mentors are recognized and appreciated for carrying out the role well. The organization considers competence in being a mentor as an important attribute for leadership.

Adapted from: *Business Today* 1998;
http://www.fanniemae.com/global/pdf/careers/diversity/diversity_workbook.pdf, accessed on 28 January 2005

---

outcomes. Lack of mentoring, however, results in negative outcomes. A discussion of both the positive and negative outcomes of mentoring follows next.

Job performance New employees who have had a mentor perform better on the job and may be more successful in their careers. Senior employees who serve as mentors continue to make a positive contribution to the organization throughout their work-life. Ashok Leyland places about eight to ten junior managers under a middle level manager for mentoring, thus involving middle managers in the in-house training programme of the organization. At Crompton Greaves, it is believed that the additional responsibility of serving as a mentor to a newcomer improves the performance levels of the managers serving as mentors.

Socialization Individuals who have had a mentor during the early years of their career are likely to

- understand and adapt better to the intricacies of the work environment and the culture of the organization;
- stay with the organization much longer; and
- find a better fit with the organization.

Cadbury, Crompton Greaves, BPL, GlaxoSmithKline, Fannie May, HP, LG, Asian Paints, and Modi Xerox are among the companies that have integrated formal mentoring programmes with the induction training of management trainees.

Human resource and succession planning Mentoring helps to groom high potential individuals for

- succession into senior jobs, and
- advancing them through the organizational structure.

Hewlett-Packard, Infosys, and TAS use mentoring to groom high potential managers for future leadership. Intel, India emphasizes that a manager's main role is to take care of the career development of his/her people. Winthrop Pharmaceuticals has developed a rotational mentorship programme to facilitate succession planning.

Leadership development Those employees who serve as mentors get an opportunity to practise leadership behaviour and develop relevant skills. At companies such as GlaxoSmithKline and Fannie May, managers who serve as mentors build upon their relationship-building, coaching, and leadership skills.

Cultural diversity Mentoring programmes help support and promote cultural diversity within the organization. CitiGroup, GlaxoSmithKline, ABN AMRO, Fannie May, Lucent Technologies, and Abbott Laboratories have incorporated diversity initiatives into their mentoring programmes.

Political sponsorship Those who have a mentor find it easier to navigate through the unknown realms of a new organization or position. Mentors are already a part of a power group within the organization and can therefore provide expert advice to the protégé on how to manoeuvre through the different situations that may arise in the workplace. Protégés can build a power base in an organization with the help of the mentor. Mentors facilitate the entry of the protégés into organizational and professional networks and help in increasing the visibility of the protégé within the organization.

Positive Outcomes of Mentoring

Mentoring relationships result in benefits for the individual as well as the organization. The individual benefits encompass both the mentor as well as the protégé. Table 10.4 outlines the individual and organizational benefits of mentoring programmes.

Table 10.4: Individual and Organizational Benefits of Mentoring Programmes

Individual Benefits		Organizational Benefits
Benefits for the Mentor	**Benefits for the Protégé**	
Sense of satisfaction and personal fulfillment from nurturing the professional and personal development of a protégé	Increased self-confidence	Development and retention of high performers and reduced employee turnover
Revitalization of interest in work	Ease of transition into the profession or organization	Increased organizational productivity
Improved job performance of mentors due to fresh perspectives brought about by protégés	More career mobility	More effective organizational communication
Increased peer and organizational recognition for helping nurture young talent	Receives more promotions	Provides a mechanism for modifying or reinforcing (managing) organizational culture
Develops loyal base of support through their protégés	Higher job and career satisfaction	Facilitate organizational learning and preserve organizational legacy
Increased sense of parental pride	Higher income/salaries at an earlier age	Improved morale and motivation
Psychological benefits derived from being seeked and needed during the mid-career stage	Positive career and job attitudes	Enhanced team spirit
Bask in the reflected glory of success achieved by protégés	Career and psychosocial support	Greater job and career satisfaction

Contd

Table 10.4 Contd

Individual Benefits		Organizational Benefits
Benefits for the Mentor	**Benefits for the Protégé**	
Enhanced self-esteem	Faster adjustment and understanding of professional and organizational culture	Easier recruitment, induction, and retention
Fulfill own developmental needs	Increased likelihood of success	Increased organizational commitment
Increased job satisfaction	Likely to sponsor protégés in future	Development of employee skills and knowledge
Enhanced quality of life through establishment of close personal relationships		Foster leadership development and develop successors
Leave a legacy through protégés after they leave the profession or the organization		Foster collaboration

Adapted from: Haines 2003; Blake-Beard 2001; Burke and McKeen 1990; Kreitner and Kinicki 2001

According to GlaxoSmithKline, its mentoring programme has been very successful in retaining management trainees. Moreover, mentoring has also helped employees in combating stress, improved their emotional intelligence, and fostered a culture of empowerment. Winthrop Pharmaceuticals successfully developed sufficient number of employees for leadership positions using its rotational mentoring programme. At Merrill Lynch, the mentoring programme helps protégés learn about the firm's culture and career opportunities. Intel Technologies uses mentoring for the career development of protégés. Hughes Software Systems, Fannie May, and GlaxoSmithKline view mentoring relationships as benefiting the mentor as well by providing mentors with learning opportunities and developing their coaching and leadership skills. At Citicorp, the Citi Cards mentoring programme has been a great success. Launched in 2001 in the US, the objectives of the programme include creating an environment in which employees are empowered and motivated to develop and grow professionally, that in turn improves both the innovation and productivity of business. The *type* of mentoring relationship is likely to determine the benefits accruing from the mentoring relationship. Studies have investigated the effects of being involved in a formal mentoring relationship in comparison to the involvement in an informal relationship and found that informal mentoring relationships provided greater beneficial outcomes for the protégés than formal relationships. For example, informal mentors provided greater career development and psychosocial support functions for the protégés when compared to formal mentors. Several organizations have had informal or spontaneous mentoring programmes before adopting a formal mentoring programme. GlaxoSmithKline and Cadbury both had informal mentoring programmes and instituted formal mentoring from 1996.

The *type* of mentoring relationship is likely to determine the benefits accruing from the mentoring relationships. Research studies suggest that individuals in informal mentoring relationships report greater career satisfaction, organizational commitment, and more positive job attitudes as compared to non-mentored individuals. The benefits of informal mentoring relationships have actually prompted organizations to institute formal mentoring programmes. However, assigned mentoring relationships, that is, formal mentoring, have not been found to be as beneficial as those that develop informally. In informal mentoring, the mentors provided more psychosocial functions for protégés compared to mentors in formal relationships. However formally mentored employees have been found to report greater job satisfaction as compared to non-mentored employees. The non-mentored and the formally mentored employees did not differ on organizational commitment, work role stress, or self-esteem at work.

Negative Mentoring Experiences

The idea that mentoring experiences are always positive has been questioned. The level of satisfaction obtained from mentoring relationships may vary along a continuum. Contemporary mentorship theory supports the idea of a continuum of mentoring relationships as well as the construct of 'marginal mentoring'. Eby, et al. (2000) referred to this continuum as the *quality* of mentoring relationships. Like any other relationship at work, both formal and informal mentoring relationships may be highly satisfying, marginally satisfying, dissatisfying, or even dysfunctional (see Figure 10.4).

The positive aspects of mentoring are sponsorship, coaching, protection, and acceptance, as discussed earlier. Eby et al. proposed that mentoring relationships may also result in a wide range of negative experiences for the protégés. The negative aspects of mentoring include mentor-protégé mismatch, manipulative mentor behaviour, and lack of expertise on the part of the mentor. Evidently, the positive and negative aspects of mentoring are conceptually distinct. Feldman (1999) defined 'dysfunctional or negative mentoring' as a situation where the relationship does not meet the needs of one or both partners and the costs of the relationship are much higher than the benefits.

Negative mentoring experiences do not indicate the absence of positive mentoring. It is possible for the protégé to have both positive and negative

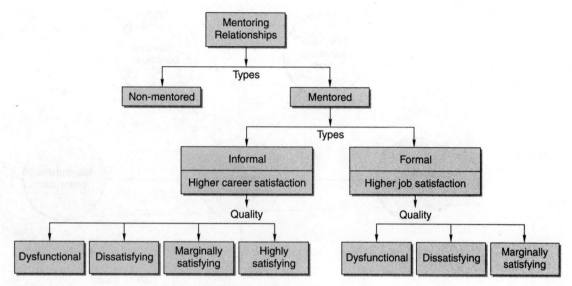

Figure 10.4:   Types and Quality of Mentoring Relationships

experiences with the same mentor. For example, a mentor may provide exposure and visibility to the protégé (positive) but at the same time, also engage in manipulative behaviour toward the protégé by taking credit for the accomplishments of the protégé (negative). It is also possible that some mentoring relationships may start out with positive experiences but over time may become frustrating and destructive. For instance, a newcomer may receive lot of coaching and exposure from a senior experienced person initially. However, the mentor may withdraw active support to the protégé after a few months to encourage the protégé to take initiative. This may, however, be seen by the protégé as neglect or exclusion by the mentor.

Negative experiences vary in severity. For example, mentors feeling threatened by their protégé, mentor and protégé not liking each other and feeling forced into the relationship, negative behaviour targeted towards a particular protégé, such as neglecting the protégé are part of negative experiences. Informal mentoring is often preferred by protégés over formal mentoring because of these negative experiences.

Five major themes, or broad types of negative mentoring experiences were reported by Eby et al. (Figure 10.5). These include the following.

Mismatch within the dyad Perceived mismatches between the mentor and the protégé in terms of values, work styles, and, personality

Distancing behaviour This occurs when mentors do not have time for the protégés and are self absorbed. This also refers to mentors who neglect their protégés or intentionally keep them out of important meetings.

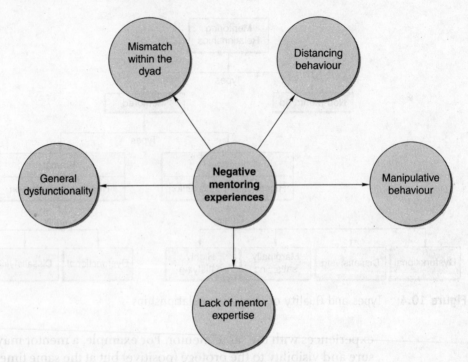

Figure 10.5: Types of Negative Mentoring Experiences

Manipulative behaviour This includes the theme of 'position power', where the mentor uses his/her power in a manipulative manner and when the mentor delegates too much or too little work to the protégé. Another theme within this broad category of 'manipulative behaviour' is that of politicking. This refers to mentor deceit, mentor sabotage, taking credit for a protégé's hard work, and engaging in political behaviour to serve his/her own end.

Lack of mentor expertise This refers to lack of interpersonal and technical expertise on part of the mentor

General dysfunctionality This occurs when the mentors shows negative attitude towards their work, the organization, or have some personal problem, such as drinking, etc., that interferes with their ability to mentor.

Though some relationships may result in purely positive or negative experiences, some other mentoring relationships may be primarily positive, primarily negative, or neutral.

Primarily positive The protégé receives high levels of career-related and psychosocial support and experiences few relational problems. For example, there may be a lack of mentor expertise as the mentor may not be technically adept but due to his/her political connections within the organization, may be able to provide positive mentoring in the form of career-related support (exposure, sponsorships, and protection from risks) and psychosocial support (serve as confidant and counsellor).

Primarily negative Characterized by recurring problems and few positive experiences. In such a case, the mentor and the protégé may not get along interpersonally (mismatch). The mentor may provide career support in the form of coaching to the protégé but may not provide career support functions such as visibility, challenging assignments, sponsorship, and protection. There may also be an absence of psychosocial support functions such as, counselling, acceptance, confirmation, and friendship. These types of mentor-protégé relationships have more problems than benefits and hence are most likely to terminate.

Neutral The relationship may not provide many benefits but is also not necessarily harmful to the protégé. The mentor may provide coaching (career support) and acceptance and friendship (psychosocial support) to the protégé but may not provide other career related support such as protection, visibility, and sponsorship. This type of mentorship has been referred to as 'marginal mentorship'.

Levinson et al. (1978) made a distinction between the types of mentors also. They classified mentors as 'good mentors', 'bad mentors', and 'good enough mentors'. Good enough mentors labelled 'marginal mentors'. These mentors have only limited value to offer. Marginal mentors fall mid-way on a continuum anchored with highly satisfying relationships on one end and highly dissatisfying relationships on the other. Since it is possible to terminate destructive relationships, a large number of mentors may simply be 'marginal'. The mentoring functions that the marginal mentors provide are limited either in scope or degree. Hence, it is likely that the marginal mentors may not meet some or most of the protégé's developmental needs.

Costs Associated with Mentoring Relationships

While discussing the outcomes of mentoring relationships, we focussed on the benefits resulting from mentoring programmes and relationships. However, mentor-protégé relationships may also carry with them potential costs and risks. When mentoring relationships, whether formal or informal, are dissatisfying for the protégé, they may result in unfavourable outcomes. Ragins, et al. (1994) stated that more than the *type* of mentoring relationship, it was the *quality* of the mentoring relationship that may determine the outcomes of mentoring. Thus, protégés in highly satisfying relationships will have a more positive attitude towards work than non-mentored employees. In some cases, non-mentored individuals may express more positive attitudes than protégés in a dissatisfying mentor-protégé relationship. The costs associated with mentor-protégé relationships are presented in Table 10.5.

Table 10.5: Costs Risks Associated with Mentor–Protégé Relationships

Costs/Risks to the Mentor	Costs/Risks to the Protégé
▪ Time and effort involved in developing mentoring relationship ▪ A poorly performing protégé may reflect poorly on the mentor's competency and judgment in the choice of a protégé ▪ Risk of being displaced or 'backstabbed' by ambitious or disloyal protégés ▪ Risk of being seen as playing favourites with their protégés ▪ Protégés may lack the talent to perform at a high level ▪ Protégés may not take feedback seriously ▪ Protégés may play the mentor against supervisors or associates thus harming the mentor's reputation ▪ Protégés may become highly dependent on their mentors ▪ Protégé may become resentful	▪ Protégé may develop unrealistic expectations regarding career advancement or promotion ▪ Protégés may become targets of jealousy and gossip ▪ Protégés' success gets linked to the success of the mentor ▪ Protégés may live in the shadow of the mentor; this may undermine their own feelings of self-worth and independence ▪ Protégés may get sucked into the political dynamics of the organization by getting associated with a mentor ▪ When mentor loses in a major power struggle, the protégé may lose out too ▪ Protégés may work under heightened scrutiny ▪ The mentor may always take credit for the protégé's work ▪ The mentor may not keep commitments ▪ The mentor expects too much from the protégé by way of gratitude ▪ The mentor may not be willing to 'let go' when protégés are ready for independence

Adapted from: Burke and McKeen 1990; Murray 2001; Ragins and Scandura 1994

It is obvious that while the mentor-protégé relationships are mutually beneficial for the mentor and the protégé, they may also be potentially destructive or costly.

As mentioned earlier, historically, mentoring relationships in organizations have largely been informal. To replicate the benefits derived from informal mentoring relationships, many organizations have begun to develop formal mentoring programmes. The development of formal mentoring systems in organizations needs to carefully consider several aspects related to the design of the mentor programme.

DESIGN AND IMPLEMENTATION OF FORMAL MENTORING PROGRAMMES

Several organizations such as Xerox, ITC, Coca Cola, ABN AMRO Bank, Procter and Gamble, Eicher, Intel, Microsoft, etc. have developed formal mentoring programmes to promote mentoring relationships as part of their

HRD strategy. These programmes are usually established in the hope that they will lead to the same outcomes as that of informal mentoring. To increase the likelihood of success of formal mentoring programmes, it is important to give careful attention to the design and implementation phases of these programmes.

A formally introduced mentoring programme in an organization has several components. The different aspects of mentoring programme design should be integrated in order to make the programme successful. Price, et al. (1997) suggested that in designing a successful formal mentoring programme, the HR manager needs to make decisions about several design features (Figure 10.6). The characteristics of a formal mentoring plan are as follows:

1. Defining the programme purpose, i.e., goals and objectives
2. Outlining the programme structure by matching process, length of the programme, and frequency of scheduled meetings
3. Identifying mentors and protégés and develop training modules for mentors
4. Defining mentor and protégé responsibilities
5. Evaluating the mentorship programme

Defining the Programme Purpose

The first step in the design of a formal mentoring programme in an organization involves establishing the goals and objectives of the programme. Organizations must clearly determine what purpose(s) the mentoring programme is intended to serve. Goals and objectives of the mentoring programme may be intended to

- acquaint new employees to the organization and adjust to workplace culture;
- help new employees successfully start and advance in their careers;
- be an integral part of the overall employee development process;
- reduce employee turnover;
- improve recruiting efforts; and/or
- groom an employee for management (succession planning).

Goals may also include increasing productivity, building relationship networks, and building career management skills. Mentoring goals should be integrated with the goals of the organization and based on the current or long term needs of the organization. Mentoring programmes may be directed towards the new employees as well as the current employees of the organization. The new employees are both the young, inexperienced individuals just starting out on their careers as well as those employees who have changed jobs. Most organizations, as discussed earlier in the chapter, use mentoring programmes for orientation of new employees, career development of high

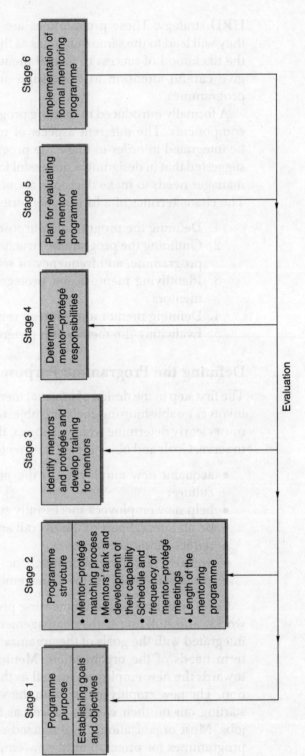

Figure 10.6: Stages in the Design and Implementation of a Formal Mentoring Programme

potentials, and to develop leaders for future. At Infosys, mentoring is used as part of succession planning. Intel's mentoring programme started as a way to train new managers quickly in an industry that changes with high speed. Intel's initiative has nothing to do with career advancement of the employee; rather, what matters most is the employees' ability to do the right things right away in a competitive environment, and to learn from someone they have probably never met. Therefore, Intel does not limit the programme to newcomers alone. Rather, the voluntary programme is open to everyone; from workers on the factory floor to senior level engineers.

In order to achieve the primary goals and objectives, mentoring programmes must accomplish the following.

- Successfully orient the protégé to the job as well as the workplace
- Provide role models for the protégé to ensure that employees are successfully integrated into the organizational culture

The design and implementation of the formal mentoring initiative of Microsoft is presented in Exhibit 10.5.

Exhibit 10.5

Design and Implementation of a Formal Mentoring Programme

Microsoft is a large firm with more than 50,000 employees who are technology savvy. The mentor programme was launched in the US in 2002 and expanded internationally in 2003.

Key components of implementing this large-scale initiative were:
- Developing Strategy/Planning
- Communicating/Recruiting
- Matching
- Training
- Providing ongoing support
- Evaluating

Developing Strategy/Planning The mentor programme ownership was within the HR department's employee and management development group. There were two full time experts prospective as well as HR and IT support for the programme. The firm introduced three pilot mentoring programmes in 2001 before formally launching the initiaitve.

The main Objectives or Goals of the Mentor Programme were to

- create career development and professional growth opportunities;
- facilitate employees developing each other;
- create connections throughout Microsoft;
- share knowledge and resources;
- enhance the work environment; and
- improve employee retention.

Communicating/Recruiting Senior level support was enlisted for the initiative. The firm started a company-wide awareness drive, presentations were made to groups of employees, booths were set up at conferences and the cafeteria. The programme was marketed through posters, T-shirts, pens, etc., and the initiative was linked to performance reviews.

In order to recruit mentors, recruitment e-mails were sent, and the 'Recommend-a-Mentor'

Contd

Exhibit 10.5 Contd

programme was launched. A mentor programme website was also launched. The web components included programme information, mentor programme resources available, MyMentoring, online training, and FAQs.

Matching The mentor programme website was used for matching mentors and protégés. Mentor and protégé profiles are on the website and contain information related to their work history, experience, education, mentoring goals, preferences, and Microsoft competencies. Mentors must have two years of Microsoft experience, while protégés must have at least one year of Microsoft experience. All regular employees are eligible to participate. Contractors and interns are not eligible. The approach to matching participants is based on programme goals, that is, job function, skills, language, gender preferences, diversity goals, etc. The protégé picks from among the recommended mentors by viewing the profiles online. Programme administrators apply complex algorithm and business rules automation for matching mentor and protégé. They may use manual matching as well. In Microsoft's US office, the mentor-protégé communication process goes on weekly. At international locations, the mentor programme is for key people/high performers.

Source: Phillips-Jones, Scovil, and Conrad 2003

Training Half-day in-class workshops are conducted for mentors as well as protégés. On-line training option is also available. For p eer mentoring also there are workshops and on-line training. In addition, quarterly events are scheduled, participant panels are held, guest speakers are invited, and advanced training topics are covered.

Evaluating Progress The firm conducts on-line surveys three, six, and twelve months into partnerships. Feedback about mentor-protégé behaviour and skills, satisfaction with the programme, and progress toward reaching mentoring goals is obtained. Periodic focus group discussions, interviews, critical incidents, and unobtrusive measures are also used for evaluating. The evaluation data is stored and reported.

In 2003, there were more than 2,000 mentor-protégé pairs, and more than 5,000 participants in the first year. Approximately 5,888 employees were trained with more than 50% choosing the on-line training option. The biggest challenges for Microsoft's mentor programme were recruiting mentors and ensuring that protégés take responsibility for driving and managing partnerships. The employees of the organization have reported high satisfaction with training and the overall mentor programme.

Determining the Programme Structure

Once the goals and objectives of the formal mentoring programme have been clarified, the programme design must concentrate on determining the structure of the programme. Decisions about the following aspects of mentoring programme structure need to be made.

- The mentor–protégé matching process
- Mentor's rank and department
- Frequency of scheduled meetings between mentor and protégé
- Length of the mentoring programme

The Mentor–protégé Matching Process

In formal mentoring programmes, the mentor–protégé matching (pairing) process plays an important role in the development of the mentoring relationships. Hewlett-Packard, GlaxoSmithKline, and Cadbury match mentors and protégés very carefully to ensure compatibility. At Infosys, a new three tier model of leadership has been implemented. Tier 1 leaders consist of business leaders including business units heads, Tier 2 and Tier 3 leaders consist of high potential candidates who may become Tier 1 or Tier 2 leaders in the next few years. Each Tier 1 leader is mentored by one of the members of the Board of Directors. In turn, each Tier 2 or Tier 3 leader is mentored by a member in a tier above them.

The initiation of the mentoring relationship, that is, who initiates the relationship, is an important determinant of how the mentoring relationships develop. The mentor, the protégé, or the organization may initiate the mentoring relationship. In most organizations, formal mentoring relationships develop with organizational intervention, either as careful matching of mentor-protégé or as voluntary assignment of mentor to protégés. A formal mentor programme may incorporate either the one of the following two mentor-protégé matching process: *voluntary participation* or *mandatory assignment* to the programme.

Voluntary programme In a voluntary mentor programme, both the mentor and the protégé have the freedom to decide whether they want to be a part of the programme. At GlaxoSmithKline, serving as a mentor is a matter of choice, but being offered the mentoring role is seen as an achievement on the career graph of the mentor. Employees who volunteer to be mentors become a part of the mentor pool of the organization. Zensar Technologies has a structured mentoring programme where the pool of mentors is drawn from experienced line managers.

Voluntary mentoring programmes allow members a choice in the matching process as well, that is, the mentors may choose their protégés and vice versa. Intel allows protégés to choose a mentor from a list of mentors. Alternatively, Intel also has an employee database that has created an intranet-based questionnaire that could match protégés with the right mentor. The potential mentors at Intel list their top skills on Intel's internal employee site. Protégés click on topics that they want to master, such as leadership, Intel culture, or networking. Then an algorithm computes all the variables and the database lists all the possible mentor–protégé matches.

Mandatory programme On the other hand, some organizations may make it obligatory for employees to take the role of mentors. In these organizations, protégés may be assigned to a mentor rather than mentors and protégés choosing each other. These are *mandatory* mentor programmes with third party matching.

Assigned or mandatory mentor relationships may result in poor mentor-protégé matches leading to negative outcomes. Though harder to create and set up, voluntary programmes are preferable. Voluntary programmes provide both career and psychosocial support leading to career development. Mandated relationships, on the other hand, may result in only career support limited to general job orientation. Therefore, the most beneficial method of pairing may be when mentors and protégés select each other.

The choice of the mentor–protégé matching process may be influenced by the prevailing culture of the firm. An organization that has had a culture of informal mentoring is more likely to adopt the voluntary approach. For example, Honeywell leaves the mentor–protégé linkage to chance, but recognizes and publicly rewards mentors.

Mentor's Rank and Department

Another structural concern relates to the appropriate number of organizational levels between a formal mentor and a protégé. This was referred to as 'mentor rank' by Ragins, et al. (2000). Usually, firms assign a senior manager as a mentor to a newcomer. This is the case at Infosys, Merrill Lynch, Phillips Software Centre, Cadbury, etc. There is, however, a growing trend towards buddy partnerships. When an individual joins Tata Teleservices Ltd (TTSL), the new employee is assigned to a friend or buddy for a month's time. The buddy takes care of the new entrant, guiding and helping the newcomer to adjust.

In recent years, the traditional notion of a mentoring relationship between an older more experienced employee and a younger less experienced employee has broadened to include different kinds of mentoring. Apart from the classic relationship of the protégé with a mentor who is at least two steps above the protégé in the organizational hierarchy, mentoring relationship with the direct supervisor is also seen as a real possibility. Kale Consultants has a 'buddy' programme where an immediate senior is assigned to help the newcomer to settle faster and avoid mistakes. More recently, peers, groups, and even subordinates have been suggested as sources of mentoring. In keeping with the developmental network perspective, it is quite possible for an individual to be mentored by the direct supervisor, a higher ranking manager from another department, a peer, or by all of them simultaneously. The CDG at Eicher is an example where an individual is simultaneously mentored by the immediate superior, superior's superior, and a senior professional from a different division.

Another aspect related to mentoring programme structure concerns whether the mentor should be from the same department as the protégé or from a different department. Typically, informal mentors are often in a department other than that of the protégé, though they may be from the same department as well. Hewlett-Packard and Cadbury both draw mentors from functions other than the protégé's own function. When mentors are from the same functional area, they are in a better position to intervene on behalf of the protégé.

Frequency of Scheduled Meetings

Mentor programmes may also differ with respect to whether they offer guidelines for the frequency of scheduled meetings between the mentor and the protégé. Programmes that specify the schedule and frequency of mentor–protégé meetings may be more effective than programmes that did not have any such guideline. The frequency of interaction between the mentor and the protégé was found to be important for the development of a successful mentoring relationship as well as protégé satisfaction with the relationship in a study by Cornelius (2001). Face-to-face meetings are important for the success of the mentoring relationship especially in the beginning of the relationship when both the mentor and the protégé are still in the process of developing rapport and trust with each other. GlaxoSmithKline specifies the frequency of meetings between the mentor and the protégé during the period of the formal mentoring programme. At Merrill Lynch, mentors meet protégés once a month. Since each mentor has four protégés in this firm, they may meet the protégés either collectively or individually.

It is also important that the scheduled meetings between the mentor and the protégé have an agenda. This ensures that the discussion stays focussed. However, the degree to which these meetings are structured should be limited. If not, then these meetings may end up being too formal. The mentor-protégé meetings must retain spontaneity in order to retain the characteristics of informal mentoring relationships. At Intel, the mentor and protégé, and not the people who run the programme, define the limits of what may and may not be discussed in the scheduled meetings. Similarly, at GlaxoSmithKline, protégés go beyond work-related topics and may also discuss and seek guidance and support of the mentor on personal issues.

Length of the Mentoring Programme

Various contextual factors, such as the complexity of the job, the position of the protégé in the organizational hierarchical structure, and the work experience of the mentor, all will determine how long the formal mentor–protégé relationship will continue. Price, Graham, and Hobbs (1997) suggest that the maximum time for formal mentoring programmes varies. However, they added that new employees, especially the young and inexperienced ones, require between three to six months of formal mentoring, with six months being the longest in most cases. At HP, mentoring is a time-bound process, ranging from nine to twelve months. At GlaxoSmithKline, the formal process is of nine months duration, while at Merrill Lynch, formal mentoring lasts for a six month period.

Identifying Mentors and Protégés

Identifying mentors is the most important aspect of a formal mentoring programme. The success of the mentorship programme rests to a large extent on the *skills* of the mentor. An employee who is mentored by a competent mentor will not only be an asset to the organization but is also likely to become a mentor for future employees. According to Price, Graham, and Hobbs, some of the characteristics of a competent mentor include.

- commitment to the mentoring activities and willingness to make a time commitment;
- familiarity with the job of the protégé;
- understanding of the organization's structure and culture;
- good interpersonal and communication skills; and
- skills to serve as a guide, counsellor, and adviser to the protégé.

Providing mentoring support for protégés is time-consuming for mentors. Therefore, mentors who are high performers do not have the time or interest to engage in the emotional aspects of mentoring relationship. Hence, they are less likely to provide psychosocial functions. Therefore, mentors need not necessarily be the highest performers. However, they should definitely have good job skills. Intel firmly believes in this and proposes that the high potential employee, the rising star, or a fast track executive of the organization is an unlikely mentor. At Intel, the mentor is an average performer, who may not be at the top management level, but is someone who understands and can tap into the informal people network of the firm, and knows the Intel culture. Cadbury usually selects a senior manager who has spent more than five years in the company to serve as a mentor. GlaxoSmithKline also assigns the mentor role to a manager who has spent at least five years with the organization, ideally in a line function.

Experienced employees who volunteer or are assigned to the role of a mentor should be trained before they begin to serve as mentors to new employees. Though people may have the right work experience to be able to coach the less experienced, they may lack the interpersonal skills needed for mentoring others. The chances of successful mentoring can be substantially increased by training mentors in effective training techniques and how and when to apply different skills like coaching. Zensar Technologies provides training to its line managers to function as mentors. *Mentor training* may include

- formal written guidelines for mentors about the various roles they would be required to play;

- a discussion of mentoring and the concerns the mentor(s) might have;
- development of mentor–protégé meeting schedules;
- development of challenging and visible assignments for the protégé;
- information and practice in how to prepare for mentoring sessions, demonstrate a skill or a procedure, and coach an employee; and
- evaluation of the protégé's performance.

In addition to carefully selecting and training the employees who may serve as mentors, it is also important to identify potential protégés for the formal mentor–protégé relationship. The *skills* that the protégés should demonstrate include an acceptance of challenges, openness to receiving feedback, and motivation to grow and improve. At HP and GlaxoSmithKline, both the mentor and the protégé undergo training. At HP training involves a half-day role clarity programme for mentor and protégé to foster the mentoring process. At GlaxoSmithKline too, a role clarity workshop is held after assigning the protégé to the mentor.

A sketch of the mentor and protégé skills and qualities is presented in Exhibit 10.6. It is only when both the mentor and the protégé demonstrate an open and a positive attitude towards mentoring that the programme is likely to succeed.

Exhibit 10.6

Skills and Qualities of Mentors and Protégés

Mentors
- Willingness to help others and share knowledge
- Willingness to take responsibility for someone else's growth and development
- Positive attitude and sensitivity to the feelings of others
- Knowledge of the organization and its people as well as the ability to be effective and credible as a mentor
- Mentor's rank, status, and prestige within the organization
- Technical competence and good job skills
- Interpersonal skills and competence
- Respect from peers in the organization

- Knowledge of the use of power
- Patience to train less experienced employees and ability to share credit
- Skills in giving feedback and evaluating
- Upward mobility of the mentor

Protégés
- Self-perceived need for growth
- Receptivity to feedback and coaching
- Motivation to seek and accept challenging assignments
- Ability to perform in more than one area
- Willingness to assume responsibility for own growth and development

Adapted from: Burke and McKeen 1990; Haines 2003

Defining Mentor and Protégé Responsibilities

In a successful mentor-protégé relationship, both the mentor and the protégé have certain responsibilities. A formal mentor programme design clearly determines the responsibilities of the mentor and the protégé. Price, Graham, and Hobbs (1997) have identified these responsibilities.

Mentor Responsibilities of Mentors

The mentor responsibilities include orienting the protégé towards his/her job, development of a personal relationship with the protégé, and evaluating the protégé.

Orientation of the protégé The mentor has to orient the protégé on the physical and human resources aspects of the organization.

Physical organization of the firm The mentor should provide the protégé with an understanding of the physical plant, the resources available to employees such as type of computer and software used, working knowledge of organizational structure, issues regarding parking, safety, and security. The protégé should be introduced to personnel responsible for benefits information and plant maintenance. The mentor must also train the protégé in the use of company resources to answer common questions related to company practices.

Human resources of the firm It is the mentor's responsibility to foster team interaction and communication, acquaint newcomers with colleagues and peers, and communicate to them the team goals related to the company's mission.

Developing a personal relationship with the protégé The mentor has to develop a communication style with the protégé that is comfortable for both of them. Mentors have to schedule formal and informal meetings to build a relationship and create a professional development plan for the protégé to accomplish the goals of the mentor programme.

Evaluating the protégé The mentor should observe the protégé at work both formally and informally. He/she should advise the protégé on performance expectations, assess the job performance of the protégé, and observe how the protégé relates with others. The protégé should learn team-building skills and and solve problems. The mentor should guide the protégé on developing objectives that builds strengths and overcomes obstacles.

Responsibilities of Protégés

For the mentoring relationship to successfully accomplish its goals, the protégé also needs to demonstrate commitment to the mentoring process. The protégé should be willing to invest time to gain knowledge of the company and its products by reading company literature, such as annual reports, employee handbook, etc. The protégés should ask questions and engage in problem solving as and when necessary to complete the task and demonstrate competence in performing the job.

It should be the endeavour of the protégé to perform the job to meet or even exceed expected performance standards, consider the advice and guidance provided by the mentor, and follow the mentor's suggestions for performance improvement. The various aspects of the organizational culture such as whether to address supervisors by first name or last name, what is the appropriate dress code expected of employees, etc. should be observed by the protégés. They should try to internalize and assimilate appropriate social and business behaviour.

Evaluating the Mentor Programme

The evaluation of the formal mentoring programme, just like any other HR programme, is essential in order to determine how successful the programme has been. This helps in identifying and introducing appropriate modifications and changes to the programme. Evaluation will incorporate separate and periodic assessments of all aspects of the programme, such as the programme structure, long term results of the mentoring programme, the mentor, and the protégé, to determine their effectiveness. At GlaxoSmithKline, though the quality of mentoring is not linked directly to the performance evaluation of the mentors, feedback is obtained from the protégé and is filed for reference. At Tata Teleservices Ltd, a new employee assesses the buddy under certain specified parameters. Evaluation of formal mentoring programmes may focus on aspects such as how much learning has taken place, psychosocial and career benefits, costs associated with the mentorship programme, and contribution of the programme in the accomplishment of broader organizational objectives.

It is important to plan how the formal mentoring programme will be evaluated and to ensure that the evaluative tools are in place prior to the implementation of the programme. To obtain an accurate picture of how successful the mentoring programme has been, it is important to continue evaluation even after the formal programme closes. Evaluation will involve comparing the formally mentored employees with a control group of employees who do not have formally assigned mentors in the organization but are at a similar stage of development on criteria such as the performance, promotions, compensation, and turnover. This comparison will help in understanding the degree to which the formal mentoring programme has been successful. Evaluation should also lead to a follow-up action plan to introduce necessary modifications to the existing programme.

Implementation of the Formal Mentoring Programme

The implementation of the mentoring programme requires the development and implementation of a formal plan for integrating the major design components of the programmes, such as programme objectives, structure, mentors, protégés, and evaluation. The successful implementation of a formal mentoring programme in an organization requires *leadership support* as well as a champion of the programme within the organization. The champion is usually someone at a senior level in the organization. Programme implementation requires establishment of some specific business objectives for the programme which can be used to measure the effectiveness of the programme. The champion establishes these objectives along with other members of the organization. In some companies such as Intel, there is a mentor champion.

Implementation of mentoring requires that the mentor assesses the level of employees' knowledge and skill in a particular task. The mentoring activities chosen by the mentor should be appropriate to the protégé's knowledge and experience of the task. For example, if the protégé neither has the knowledge nor experience, then the mentor may have to provide training, coaching, and also monitor the performance of the task by the protégé. If the protégé has substantial knowledge as well as experience of a particular task, then the mentor needs to monitor the former only periodically and no training may be required. During the implementation phase it is important to ensure that the *resources* needed by the mentors and the protégés are available, for instance, training time as well as opportunity to meet face-to-face regularly.

Ongoing support to the participants should be provided throughout the programme. The ongoing support includes planning activities for the monthly meetings between the mentor and the protégé, for example, providing discussion topics and bringing together all the protégés after the initial training. When protégés meet, it facilitates the sharing of best practices and also provides support to other programme participants. Ensuring regular interaction between the mentors and the protégés and following up on mentoring sessions is also crucial to successful implementation of the mentoring programmes. Mentor-protégé interaction enhances satisfaction with the relationship, besides ensuring that the mentor is readily available to the protégé.

To encourage mentors to be willing to accept formal mentoring roles, firms may institute rewards for best mentors. Honeywell has created the Lund Award (named after a now-retired executive who coached several of Honeywell's key executives during his career) to encourage managers to serve as mentors. The award is given to one manager from each division and includes US$3000 and an invitation to attend a three-day discussion with executives to share ideas. Hughes Software Systems has several awards for its employees under the popular awards category, one of them being the 'great mentor' award. This award provides peer recognition to the employee. The winner of the award is then assigned a special role, for example, the winner of the 'best mentor' award leads the implementation of the mentoring programme. McKinsey gives special recognition to those employees who excel as mentors.

To ensure implementation success, it is advisable for firms to start with the introduction of a pilot mentorship programme. Creating a successful pilot programme involves determining a strategic purpose, getting a champion for the programme from the highest level, determining length of the programme, frequency of mentor-protégé meetings, choosing appropriate mentoring models, and matching participants and providing orientation to them. The participants meet regularly and finally the relationship comes to an end. The pilot programme is then evaluated for its success. The results of evaluation lead to programme changes and expansion.

BARRIERS TO MENTORING

In spite of careful attention being given to details of programme design and implementation, formal mentoring programmes and relationships may sometimes fail. The failure may be the result of barriers such as personal barriers on the part of both the mentor and the protégé or organizational barriers. Clutterbuck (2005) identified three categories of problems due to which formal mentorships in an organization may fail (Figure 10.7). These are discussed in this section.

Contextual Problems

These problems arise due to organizational barriers and relate to issues of clarity of purpose or to the degree of support provided by the organization for the programme and the mentor-protégé relationship. For example, a newcomer may be assigned to a mentor by the organization without giving any orientation to the mentor or the protégé about what their mutual responsibilities are, how often they need to meet, and what purpose the relationship should serve. It is unlikely that such a relationship will be effective. Another contextual problem may arise when the organization penalizes both the mentor and the protégé for taking time out of their work for their meetings. Cultural differences should also be taken into account in determining programme purpose, as it may otherwise be met with resistance. More on this aspect is discussed later under the section on 'race and mentoring'.

Interpersonal Problems

The reactions of people who are not included in the mentor-protégé relationships may result in interpersonal problems with mentoring programmes. For example, the protégé's direct supervisor may feel threatened by the proximity of the protégé to a senior manager. Hence, line managers should be included in the overall design and management of the programme. Incompatibility of personality and personal values between the mentor and the protégé may

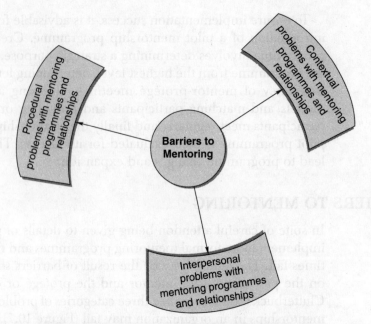

Figure 10.7:   Reasons for Failure of Formal Mentoring Programmes

also lead to interpersonal problems creating attitudinal barriers to the success of the relationship.

Procedural Problems

These problems relate to the manner in which the implementation of the programme is managed. For instance, the mentor and the protégé may be given very specific instructions about the content of discussion in their scheduled meetings, or, at the relationship level, mentors may become overly directive and critical of protégé efforts, or they may not provide any advice or guidance to the protégé. These problems also arise when mentors lack the necessary skills for effective mentoring discussed earlier in the chapter.

Therefore, it is important for organizations to carefully design and implement mentoring programmes to ensure their success. For mentor programmes to effectively accomplish their goals it is essential to develop a holistic approach. When an organization has made a decision about starting a formalized mentoring programme, it is advisable for the organization to carefully plan and approach the implementation in stages. The success of a mentoring programme is not ensured by just having a formal mentoring programme in place. Several factors play an important role in its success. These issues are addressed in the section on strategic approach to mentoring relationships.

MENTORING RELATIONSHIP: A STRATEGIC HRM APPROACH

An organization should develop a mentoring programme when there are clear business or strategic reasons, such as sharing of organizational knowledge or accelerating the development of future leaders. It is also important to ensure that the goals of the mentoring programme are integrated with the goals of the organization. One of the goals that all organizations, irrespective of industry, type, and size, seek to accomplish through mentoring is to attract and retain high performing top talent by demonstrating the organization's commitment to developing employees through mentoring.

Retaining employees is a key challenge, since cost of a replacement employee (new employee acquired to replace the employee who quit) is much higher than the cost of retaining a high performing employee. Other business objectives that mentoring helps to achieve include career development of the protégé as well as the mentor, development of high potential employees, succession planning, visibility for women employees, overcoming the 'glass ceiling' for women, and supporting diversity goals.

To be effective it is important that the mentoring programme supports the informal mentoring relationships that already exist. Hence, informal and formal mentoring relationships should run concurrently. For protégés to get the maximum benefit out of a formal programme, it is important for the formal programme to incorporate the dynamics of informal mentoring.

Mentoring should also support company values and help in the perpetuation of organizational culture by making the protégé aware about its culture and structure. Mentoring serves the purpose of creating and promoting a high performance culture for three reasons—it creates a sense of belonging by promoting the acceptance of the organization's core values throughout the organization; it promotes socialization and therefore also promotes a sense of belonging and membership; and it leads to interpersonal exchanges among the employees of the organization.

The firm should facilitate conditions conducive to the formation of developmental networks rather than the formation of formal mentoring dyads. This is especially important since in a dyadic relationship the protégé may become dependent on the mentor for his/her career development. In a developmental network, employees get to form networks with higher level managers, peers, subordinates, as well as outsiders leading to informal mentoring relationships. An organization can encourage the formation of developmental networks by providing opportunities for cross-departmental interaction, implementing reward systems to reinforce the development of peers and subordinates, developing cross functional teams, having fast track individuals on teams, and providing training on how to build relationships and achieve goals.

Since mentors have a profound influence on the protégés, it is important to train senior managers to enhance their leadership. However, not all senior managers become mentors, though organizations may create a culture that will facilitate the process where each supervisor serves mentoring functions. For mentoring programmes to be successful, it is important to ensure that there is a willingness to devote time, effort, and a sense of commitment to the mentor–protégé relationship.

Zey (1985) suggested a strategic approach to enhance the likelihood of successful mentoring relationships (Figure 10.8).

- *Communicate mentoring goals* to all persons involved clearly explaining the role and function of mentoring relationships. This also involves managing unrealistic expectations about the role of mentor and protégés by providing an opportunity to both to clarify their expectations at the very beginning of the relationship. Further, the mentor as well as the protégé should check with each other that their goals are being met during the course of the relationship.
- *Ensure co-operation* from the entire organization for mentoring to be successful by clearly explaining the rationale, mechanics of mentoring, and programme benefits to peers, managers and supervisors, through materials, group/peer discussion, and organization wide meetings. Suggestions regarding the operation of the mentoring programme as well as about potential problems should be sought on a regular basis.
- *Involve the direct supervisor* in the formal mentoring programme. Since the direct supervisor rarely assumes the role of formally assigned mentor for the protégé, the supervisor may have apprehensions that the protégé may have access to information and resources from the mentor that are not available to the supervisor. By including the direct supervisor in the advisory group established to define programme expectations and to monitor the impact of the formal programme, the supervisor may be brought into the information loop. This will ensure that their concerns are addressed, and also help them understand how their roles differ from that of the assigned mentor.
- *Ensure autonomy* of the mentor–protégé selection process.
- *Manage the resentment of non-participating peers*, that is, those who are not selected for the formal mentoring programme. Those not selected may feel that they are being deprived of an opportunity for visibility and career advancement within the organization. They may also believe that those who are selected for the programme are receiving preferential treatment. Strained relationships between peers have a negative impact on productivity. The strategies to manage this challenge may include sharing information with peers or providing opportunities to all employees to participate in some form of developmental activity.
- *Ensure commitment* of the mentor to the programme by clearly demonstrating to them the job and career benefits that they will receive as a

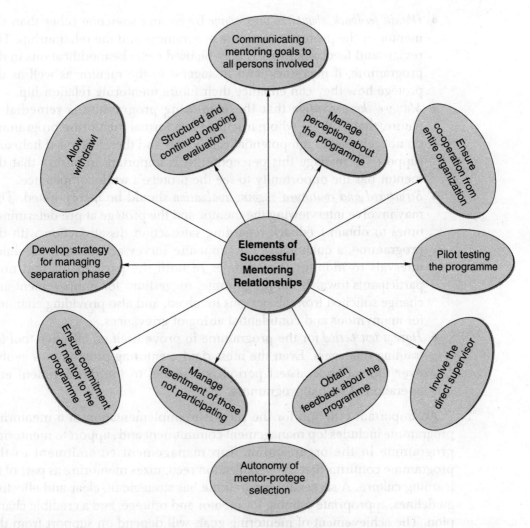

Figure 10.8: Key Elements of Successful Mentoring Relationship

result of mentoring the protégé. It is important to foster reciprocity, that is, determine how, along with the protégé, the mentor also benefits from the relationship. A senior manager should not be forced into participating in the programme.

- *Develop a strategy for managing the separation phase* of the mentoring relationship. At the end of the formal mentor programme, the effectiveness of the programme and future viability of the relationship should be assessed by the mentor and protégé.
- *Allow withdrawal* from the mentoring relationship to the mentor as well the protégé, if either of them feels that the relationship is of no benefit.

- *Obtain feedback about the programme* by having someone other than the mentor or the protégé review the programme and the relationship. The review and feedback process may be used to make modifications in the programme, if necessary, and to suggest to the mentor as well as the protégé how they can enhance their future mentoring relationship.
- *Manage the perception* that the mentoring programme is remedial in nature, that is, those who participate in a formal mentoring programme do not represent high potential candidates and therefore need help and support. To manage this perception, it is important to ensure that the mentor has the opportunity to see the protégé's work competence.
- *Structured and continued ongoing evaluation* should be incorporated. This may involve interviewing the mentor and the protégé at pre-determined times to obtain feedback regarding satisfaction/dissatisfaction with the programme, a quantitative questionnaire survey at regularly scheduled intervals to monitor the attitudes of both the participants and non-participants towards the programme, suggestions for improvement and change solicited from all persons involved, and also providing channels for anonymous and confidential airing of grievances.
- *Have a test period* for the programme to prove itself an effective tool for training managers. Even the most rigid mentoring programmes evolve over time. Hence, a test period is essential to the development and operation of such a programme.

An important criterion for the successful implementation of a mentoring programme includes top management commitment and support to mentoring programme in the organization. Top management commitment to the programme confirms that the organization recognizes mentoring as part of its learning culture. A successful programme has strategic fit, clear and effective guidelines, appropriate training for mentor and protégé, and a credible champion. The achievement of mentoring goals will depend on support from the top management, an advisory team with diverse members, training the mentoring partners, and benchmarking the practices of other successful programmes.

The components of an HR strategy for successful mentoring programmes in organizations are presented in Exhibit 10.7.

By following the recommendations given in Exhibit 10.7, mentoring programme may be designed and implemented in ways that best facilitate the development of effective mentoring relationships and, at the same time also facilitate organizational goal attainment.

Mentoring programmes are integrally linked to other subsystems of HRM such as management development, performance and potential appraisal, career development, succession planning, orienting and socializing new

Exhibit 10.7

Components of HR Strategy for Successful Mentoring Programmes

- Visible support from the top management
- Clearly stated goals of the programme
- Healthy organizational climate (organization should not be laying off employees)
- Some informal mentoring already exists in the organization
- Involving employees in the development of the programme by obtaining their opinions about the structure, the operation of the programme, and the criteria for assessing the success or failure of a particular relationship
- Training senior managers to mentor (in the process also enhancing their leadership abilities)
- Public commitment on the part of the mentors
- Obtaining both mentor and protégé input in the design of the programme
- Set short term goals for the programme such as increasing productivity, building relationship networks, and building career management skills
- Organize a trial period for each party to get to know each other and determine their compatibility
- Providing extensive orientation training to both

- the mentor and the protégé to define their roles (role assignment) and to give guidance on how to develop the relationship
- Clearly stated responsibilities for each participant
- Emphasize realistic expectations concerning the relationship for each participant
- Create a structure that ensures one-on-one meetings between the mentor and protégé on a regular basis to set goals and objectives for the relationship
- Prefer voluntary relationships to mandated partnerships by trying to allow each party to select the other
- Ensure that the mentor is outside the formal chain of command of the protégé
- Formally recognize mentors for their involvement in order to encourage participation in the programme
- Protégé involvement in mentor selection
- Established duration and contact between the mentor and protege
- Have the protégé to ultimately take responsibility for the relationship
- Elicit feedback from all participants
- Promote a long-term association

Sources: Lindenberger and Zachary 1999; Cunningham 1993; Phillips-Jones http://www.mentoringgroup.com/08-98-PG/ideas.htm, accessed on 13 February 2005

employees, and succession planning. Mentoring can work in most firms, regardless of size, culture, or sector. More than any training programme, mentoring can communicate to employees the complexity of procedures and the unique nature of the company. Mentoring needs to be viewed as a flexible exercise that reflects the unique culture and objectives of a firm. Hence, no two mentoring programmes are the same, and imitating mentoring processes of another organization will not be as effective. For mentoring to be successful, the programme must be adapted to the needs of a unit, department, or division within an organization. More than the formal mentoring programme per se, the success of the programme may be dependent on strengthening the linkage of the mentor programme with other HR mechanisms and on matching the programme goals with the strategic needs of the organization as well as prevailing cultural values. Formal programmes will be most effective when there exists a need for mentorship, and this need is recognized and accepted by all the parties involved in the formal programme. Firms with formal, long-standing mentoring programmes claim demonstrable increases in productivity and efficiency.

Earlier in the chapter we discussed that an effective mentoring programme benefits the mentor, the protégé, and the organization. Within this context, Burke and McKeen (1990) discussed the implications of the mentoring process for the organizations. They proposed that if mentoring relationships are important for meeting organizational needs and if people who are mentored are more likely to take the role of a mentor, it is potentially beneficial for organizations to facilitate and encourage mentor-protégé relationships. This may be achieved by ensuring the following.

- Every manager should be given an opportunity to mentor.
- Mentoring programmes should be linked with the performance appraisal process. Performance appraisals should have a section to evaluate the effectiveness of each manager's mentoring ability.
- Every mentor should be trained to identify potential protégés.
- Mentors should learn the importance of modelling behaviour as well as how to systematically coach others.
- Managers should provide experiences to their subordinates to help them understand and imbibe the culture of the organization.
- Managers should also help protégés decipher the political codes of the organization as well as help them understand how those who have influence on their careers view them.
- Mentoring should be used by organization for succession planning. An important aspect of mentoring is that the mentor learns the process of teaching others.

There are some mentoring relationships that pose special challenges for design and successful implementation. These include mentoring women employees, mentoring employees from different nationalities or regions, and mentoring employees geographically distant from mentors. These issues are discussed in the next section.

SPECIAL ISSUES IN MENTORING

With an increasingly diverse workforce in this era of globalization, mentoring relationships confront special challenges. These refer to issues related to women in workforce, racial diversity in multinational organizations, and e-mentoring (Figure 10.9).

Women and Mentoring

Traditionally, mentoring has been associated with the career advancement of men. The role of mentoring in the career advancement of women has not been defined. Women working in organizations with predominantly men employees often do not have a peer group to rely on for psychosocial support. A good example is that of Mrs Kiran Bedi, the country's first woman IPS officer. She had to face several stereotypes and, in the face of uncertainty about her potential, had to repeatedly prove her merit and competence. Mentoring reduce helps the job stress experienced by women employees of such men dominated organizations. Reinforcement and feedback provided to protégés during mentorship are important for women employees and help them to develop their feelings of self efficacy.

A longitudinal study conducted by McIlhone (1984) among women managers working in AT&T found that women employees who had mentors advanced more rapidly in the organization than those who lacked mentors. Mentoring may increase the probability of success for women employees in the organization. Research studies have compared women in mentoring relationships with those who did not have a mentor and found that these women protégés in companies report higher job satisfaction, are more successful in their jobs, demonstrate greater self-confidence, and utilize their skills in an optimum manner.

Women managers confront greater organizational, interpersonal, and individual barriers to advancement in the organization. Therefore, this group of

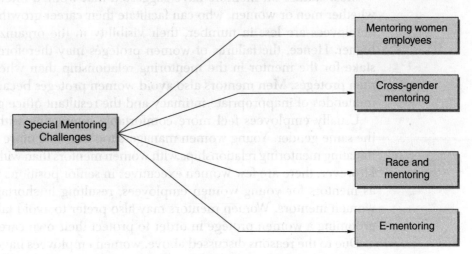

Figure 10.9: Special Mentoring Challenges

employees also face a lack of upward mobility in the organization, the prover-
bial 'glass ceiling'. Women employees who have mentors benefit in several
ways. For instance, mentors may

- help women advance in organizations by building their self-confidence;
- provide them career guidance;
- familiarize them with the political dynamics of the organizations by
  direct training or by using role models;
- provide them an insight into corporate politics; and
- help women employees overcome gender-related barriers to advancement in organizations.

Several organizations have started diversity initiatives which also focus on
women employees. ABN AMRO, Citibank, PricewaterhouseCoopers, and
GlaxoSmithKline are some firms that have mentoring initiatives for women
employees and minorities. Procter and Gamble provides women employees
with ample opportunities for advancement and has several women oriented
mentoring programmes, such as 'Mentor Up' and 'Women Supporting Women
Workshop'. Approximately 20% of the women employees in P&G have
reached the level of director in the organizational hierarchy. Over 40% of new
hires at management level in the company over the past 15 years have been
women. Abbott Laboratories has institutionalized a mentoring programme
with full support from the top management. The programme is designed to
help women enter the company, develop, and stay in the company. Mentoring
programmes at Abbott are largely responsible for creating the environment
that has led to retention of its women employees and for its comparatively
low employee turnover rate.

Most studies on mentors have suggested that women often lack mentors,
whether men or women, who can facilitate their career growth. Since women
employees are less in number, their visibility in the organization becomes
higher. Hence, the failures of women protégés may therefore have more at
stake for the mentor in the mentoring relationship than when they mentor
men protégés. Men mentors also avoid women protégés because of potential
innuendos of inappropriate intimacy and the resultant office gossip.

Usually employees feel more comfortable interacting with colleagues of
the same gender. Young women managers too may feel more comfortable in
initiating mentoring relationships with women mentors than with men mentors.
However, there are few women executives in senior positions who may serve
as mentors for young women employees, resulting in shortage of available
women mentors. Women mentors may also prefer to avoid taking the risk of
grooming a women protégé in order to protect their own career interests.

Due to the reasons discussed above, women employees have relatively few
mentorship opportunities. Within the limited mentoring scope available for

women protégés, it is more likely that they are matched with men mentors in an organization. The pairing of a women protégé with a men mentor constitutes a cross-gender mentoring relationship, which has its own unique problems, as discussed in the next section.

Cross-gender Mentoring Relationships

Cross-gender mentoring relationships are those in which mentors and protégés belong to opposite genders. There may be two types of cross-gender mentorships: men mentor–women protégé and women mentor–men protégé. However, a women mentor paired with men protégé is rarely seen, primarily because relatively few women hold senior management positions.

The past decade has witnessed demographic shifts in the workplace. More specifically, there has been a change in the gender composition, with more women joining the workforce. However, the number of men employees in organizations is still greater than that of women. Women, therefore, are less likely to have the opportunity for forming natural mentoring relationships at workplace. To provide opportunities for professional and career development to women executives, it is important for firms to develop planned or formal mentoring programmes.

In spite of the benefits of mentoring relationships in general, cross-gender mentoring relationships result in certain complexities and unique difficulties. The issues raised in cross-gender relationships are typical and not found in men–men or women–women relationships. For example, the potential for intimacy in cross-gender relationships is a source of anxiety that can be threatening for men and women who work together. This problem is more likely when a man serves as a mentor to a woman since women protégés frequently get paired with men mentors. A major challenge concerns managing the degree of mentor–protégé intimacy. Men and women in cross-gender mentoring relationships have greater visibility and hence are likely to be subject to public scrutiny. Rumours, if they develop, can have a negative impact on the professional and personal life of one or both of the individuals. Public scrutiny, therefore, places limits on the performance of quality career and psychosocial functions. Some cross-gender dyads opt to take on a father-daughter form of relationship. Sometimes, men may avoid mentoring women protégés to avoid destructive office gossip. Often men mentors bring in too much distance between themselves and their protégé to deal with unwanted remarks from other colleagues. Too much distance may marginalize the benefits of mentoring relationships. Women who have a men mentor in an organization also experience peer resentment. Due to intense peer-group competition for advancement, the women stands out as someone who receives special attention if she receives regular coaching from a men mentor.

Each of the above complexities of cross-gender mentoring relationships has the potential for adverse outcomes for both mentors and protégés. These problems can, however, be pre-empted by adhering to certain characteristics for successful mentoring relationships, such as, communication of mentoring goals to all participants, mentor's commitment to the programme, and so on.

In order to enhance the effectiveness of cross-gender formal mentoring relationships, organizations should hold open discussions about the new workplace dynamics, for example, about more women in the workplace. More women should be introduced at higher levels of the organization in order to facilitate the creation of new modes of interaction and new corporate values. Women entering the organization must be taught the teaching and coaching process so that they become effective mentors for younger women employees. Organizations may reward mentoring relationships and include cross-gender mentorship as an important part of this reward programme. Such steps are likely to increase the access of women to successful mentoring relationships and, hence, enhance their organizations success.

Workplace Diversity and Mentoring

Changes in the composition of the workforce are also characterized by more individuals entering the world of work at a younger age. A large number of women are entering the world of work and individuals are starting to work at a younger age. Diversity of the workforce, however, goes beyond demographic changes. Organizations today have employees from different nationalities and different cultural and religious backgrounds. Individuals coming from different backgrounds bring different attitudes toward the job and the organization, as well as different needs and values. In addition, organizations have the challenge of developing a culture in which employees from different nationalities or races work together in harmony. Diversity is viewed as a matter of ethics that focusses on respecting all individuals and providing them with equal opportunities.

In India, diversity has been a concern even before economic liberalization brought in the era of multinational corporations. Different states in India have their unique sociocultural backgrounds. Each state in India may be viewed as a sub-culture within the Indian culture. Regional differences have often played an important role in promotions, transfers, career opportunities, defining the 'in-group' and 'out-group' members, and in the formal and informal power dynamics in organizations in both the public and private sector and in government departments. There have been instances where the informal culture has resulted in the majority of all recruits hailing from a particular state or region of the country. This often resulted in discouraging Indians from other parts of the country from accepting an employment in those organizations. Stereotypes about individuals from different states and regions have further resulted in magnifying regional differences. Liberalization has opened up boundaries not only at the global level but across the country as well. Employees are now more open to mobility across the country.

Establishing a mentoring program is an effective way to approach diversity in the workplace. It can be used to train and motivate employees, develop skills and leadership, and mark the organization as an employer of choice. Informal mentoring often develops between mentors and protégés because they share similar backgrounds, attitudes, and interests. Therefore, employees from a particular state or region in India or from a different country may seek support and establish informal mentoring relationships with older employees belonging to their own state, region, or country. Hence, it is obvious that when employees come from different nationalities, there are certain problems in establishing formal mentor–protégé relationships. Different cultures need different mentoring approaches. For example, one culture may focus on mentoring primarily as a one-way learning experience where only the protégé gains benefits of mentoring, with an emphasis mainly on career–support functions. Another culture may consider mentoring to be a two-way learning process that requires the protégé to take responsibility for his/her own learning.

However, companies often assume that mentoring relationships are similar across all countries or cultures. When multinational corporations introduce a mentoring programme in another country without taking into account the differences in mentoring style, the mentoring programmes will most likely meet with resistance. It is important that firms understand that the concepts of mentoring and the responsibilities of mentors are likely to differ across different countries. A European company introducing a mentoring programme in its US subsidiary may face programme failure if they fail to appreciate these differences. The vice versa is also true.

DuPont has had a formal mentoring programme since 1985 for employees from different races. Since 1985, the number of employees from minority communities in top management has risen by about 20%, even though the total number of managerial positions has dropped in absolute terms. Mentoring thus helps manage prejudices and discriminatory behaviour towards minority groups.

Several organizations are adopting diversity initiatives, which go beyond mentoring for women. Aviva Life Insurance, ABN AMRO Bank, Intel, Hewlett-Packard, Procter and Gamble, GlaxoSmithKline, Lucent Technologies, Citibank, and Johnson & Johnson are some examples of such companies. GlaxoSmithKline has an internal development programme for both women and minorities. This allows minority scientists to leave their present jobs and work at another position within the company. If possible, they may stay on in their new positions as permanent replacements or may return to their previous jobs. There is a diversity council within the R&D department of the company.

This council pays the rather high bill for a temporary replacement while the scientist explores the new position. The firm also has an outreach programme with colleges and universities and provides mentoring to students, who are its potential employees. These programmes require the GlaxoSmithKline scientists to go to campuses and discuss their work with students. Summer internships give prospective scientists (students) a taste of the work-life.

E-mentoring

Mentoring relationships are sensitive to time and space constraints. Mentoring interactions between mentor and protégé may be hampered by a variety of factors. For example, location of the office (spatial factors) may prevent people who might excel as mentors from serving in this capacity or mentoring activities may be hampered by daily schedules and organizational surroundings.

With technology reaching high levels of sophistication and the advent of the information technology (IT) revolution, the internet has become an integral part of day-to-day existence. People use the internet to communicate and to develop friendship. Members of under-represented populations, such as minorities in a country, can use the internet to be in touch with people from their own community. The internet can be useful for mentoring relationships because it expands the number and variety of mentoring relationships that can be facilitated at a given time. It also expands the time and space available for mentoring relationships. The internet can also be used to support the design and implementation of the mentor programme. For example, it facilitates the on-line matching of mentor and protégé based on employee databases. The internet can also be used to communicate and disburse information about the features of the mentoring programme, present material on-line, and also to provide on-line training for mentors. Microsoft and Intel are good examples of firms that have e-mentoring programmes.

Mentoring through the internet or e-mentoring or tele-mentoring, as it is often called, has the advantage of an expanded time continuum by allowing for mentoring on the mentor's schedule and convenience. The mentor is no longer constrained by meeting times, lunches, and appointments in scheduling meetings with the protégé. The mentor can log on at will to help the protégé. Moreover, when mentors are in characteristically short supply, the internet expands the number of potential mentors in an organization beyond the constraints of a group, organization, or region.

As organizations increasingly become multi-locational, resulting in employee transfers across locations and frequent travel, e-mentoring may become an important developmental tool.

====== Summary ======

In today's knowledge-based economy, people are the key to competitive advantage. However, corporate leaders have yet to discover satisfactory answers to address 'people issues'. Globalization, mergers and acquisitions, restructuring, changing workforce demographics, and expectations have all contributed to an increasingly complex workplace and placed excessive demands on performance and growth. Consequently, organizations are looking for ways to ensure that new employees understand the organization and reach performance standards faster. Organizations are also concerned about developing leaders, retaining high performers, and building a learning culture. Mentoring is being adopted by organizations as a tool for career development, socialization, succession planning, leadership development, managing cultural diversity, job performance, and employee retention. The success of informal mentoring in the past has encouraged firms to institute formal mentoring programmes.

This chapter discussed the concept of mentoring, its origin, and roles and functions of mentors. The traditional as well as contemporary perspectives of mentoring were presented. The four stages of a mentoring relationship—initiation, cultivation, separation, and redefinition—along with the characteristics of each stage were discussed. Highlighting the differences between formal and informal mentoring, this chapter reiterated the importance of building elements of informal mentoring into the design of a formal mentoring programme. Individual and organizational benefits of mentoring programmes and the costs associated with mentoring relationships have been outlined. It was emphasized that mentoring relationships exist on a continuum and may result in positive, as well as negative, experiences for the protégé. Guidelines for the design and implementation of a successful formal mentoring programme were also presented. The chapter presented a discussion about adopting a strategic approach to workplace mentoring relationships, suggested the criteria of successful mentoring programmes, and emphasized the need to integrate mentoring programme with other subsystems of HRD. The chapter ended with a brief discussion of workforce diversity and resultant challenges for workplace mentoring such as cross-gender mentoring relationships, workplace diversity, and e-mentoring.

====== Keywords ======

Buddies are peers who have day-to-day responsibilities similar to that of protégés and may be assigned to new hires to ease their transition to work life. Buddy–peer relationships are typically one-to-one.

Career Support Functions are mentoring functions that are work-related and enhance learning the ropes, career development, and advancement in organization.

Consultant Mentors are consultants engaged by the organization to mentor employees when there is no one in the organization who has the skill set or specific experience required for mentoring.

Contemporary Mentoring Relationship occurs when individuals receive mentoring assistance from multiple sources simultaneously or at any one point in time, including senior colleagues, peers, family, and community members.

Cross-gender Mentoring Relationships occur between mentors and protégés belonging to opposite genders, that is, men mentor–women protégé and women mentor–men protégé.

Dysfunctional or Negative Mentoring leads to a situation where the relationship does not meet the needs of one or both partners, and the costs of the relationship are much higher than the benefits.

E-mentoring is the use of the internet for mentor–protégé matching, communicating about the programme, and training and evaluating the mentor programme.

Formal Mentoring is the process of systematically bringing together mentors and protégés through third-party intervention, that is, the process of the organization as assigning or matching mentors and protégés.

Informal Mentoring is the act of natural and sponteneous mentoring.

Mandatory Mentor Programmes make it obligatory for employees to take the role of mentors. Protégés may be assigned to a mentor rather than having mentors and protégés choose each other.

Marginal Mentors have expertise and knowledge, but are of limited value. Marginal mentors fall mid-way on a continuum anchored with highly satisfying relationships at one end and highly dissatisfying relationships on the other.

Mentoring Circles refers to mentoring programmes where one mentor works with a group of protégés.

Mentoring is a process where an experienced person serves as a role model, tutor, coach, confidant, and provides guidance and support in a variety of ways to the new employees in an organization.

Mentors are individuals with advanced experience and knowledge who are committed to provide upward mobility and career support to their protégés. Mentors have excellent interpersonal skills and technical competence as well as considerable influence and status within an organization.

Multiple Developmental Network consists of a set of people who take an active interest in as well as take actions to advance the career of the protégé by providing developmental assistance.

Primary Mentoring Relationship is an intense long-term relationship that is characterized by strong socialization efforts and evolves over a period of time.

Protégé is an individual who receives guidance, coaching, and support from a mentor.

Psychosocial Support Function are mentoring functions that provide emotional support and enhance protégés feelings' of competence and identity.

Quality of Mentoring Relationships refers to the possibility that the level of satisfaction obtained from mentoring relationships may vary along a continuum.

Race Mentoring refers to the mentoring process where the mentor and protégé belong to different racial groups, nationalities, or regions.

Reverse Mentoring occurs when the protégé extends mentoring support to the mentor on issues such as new technology.

Secondary Mentoring Relationship is one focussed on acquiring specialized knowledge or skills from a number of employees who hold considerable influence in the organization. This form of mentoring is shorter, less intense, and focussed mainly on career-related issues rather than on psychosocial aspects. It also evolves over a brief period of time.

Team Mentoring consists of formal mentoring teams composed of department managers, human resource representatives, and senior partners, each of whom specializes in a specific area and provides assistance to the protégés in this area.

Traditional Mentoring Relationship refers to a single or a primary mentoring relationship in which a senior person assists with the protégé's personal and professional development. These are dyadic in nature.

Voluntary Mentor Programme refers to the process that lets both the mentor and the protégé have the freedom to decide whether they want to be a part of the formal mentoring programme or not.

Concept Review Questions

1. What do you understand by the term 'mentoring'? How is mentoring different from coaching, training, and counselling?

2. Who is a mentor? What different types of roles do mentors perform when mentoring a protégé?

3. How does the relationship between the mentor and the protégé change over time? Discuss with reference to the four stages of the mentor–protégé relationship.

4. Discuss the individual and organizational benefits of mentoring programmes. What potential risks are associated with mentor–protégé relationships?

5. Describe the important issues that should be addressed in the design and implementation of a successful formal mentoring programme by an organization.

6. Deliberate on the strategic HRM issues that need to be addressed by organizations in order to ensure the success of mentor programmes.

7. What are the special challenges faced by workplace mentoring relationships in the contemporary business environment?

Critical Thinking Questions

1. Think of three or four organizations that you are familiar with. Do these firms have a formal mentoring programme? Discuss the main features of the mentoring programmes of these firms. In your opinion, what perspective of mentoring—traditional or contemporary does each of these organizations follow? What advantage does the contemporary perspective have over the traditional view of mentoring with respect to the effectiveness of workplace mentoring relationships?

2. Experience suggests that an individual's aunt, uncle, a teacher in school or college, or even a friend from one's peer group, may serve as a mentor for an 4individual. Each one of us has had a mentor or mentors at some point in our lives. Have you ever had a mentor in your life? Recall your interactions and relationship with the chosen mentor. Trace the initiation and growth of the relationship with your mentor. Describe how the characteristics of your relationship with the mentor evolved over time. What qualities did the mentor have that you admired and how long did the relationship last? What psychosocial functions were performed by your mentor and what benefits did you receive from this mentoring relationship? Evaluate whether the relationship came to an end on a positive note or with conflict.

3. Examine the differences between 'informal' and 'formal' mentoring relationships along various dimensions. Why is it important to build in characteristics of informal mentoring into the formal mentoring programme of the organization? Substantiate with illustrative examples from industry. What are your proposals regarding the design and implementation of a formal programme that has elements of mentoring relationships that develop informally?

4. Read the incident given below and discuss the questions that follow.

Madhu joined as a lecturer in the department of civil engineering of an engineering college of repute in Mumbai. Until this time, this department had no women faculty member. Madhu came to the department as its first woman lecturer. She was a shy and reserved person whose style was very different from other faculty members. Since all other faculty members were men, and also senior to her in the field, Madhu found it difficult to interact with her colleagues. She nevertheless took the initiative to interact with them. In her several attempts to get to know more than a dozen members of the senior faculty, she felt rebuffed. On certain occasions, she even felt that the behaviour of her colleagues was offending. Her colleagues did not believe that she was a lecturer; one of them thought she was a new technician; another presumed she was the spouse of a colleague; another did not want to talk about any serious subject with her, etc. The situation was compounded because she was not formally introduced to other faculty members.

In short, none of her colleagues made an attempt to initiate conversation with her and were rather uninterested in getting to know Madhu. On her part, Madhu soon found it difficult to trust any senior person in the department. She discussed her situation with a woman friend and decided to build mentoring relationships with senior people away from this university. She began systematically to correspond with senior faculty at four other universities in two other countries.

She was soon invited to give a paper at one of these places, and during the subsequent trips, she got to know several other senior colleagues from around the world. One of these scientists later spoke very positively of Madhu's work in a discussion with a senior colleague in her own department. Thereafter, Madhu was slowly able to develop the professional relationships at the college as she had wanted. As an important side benefit, when Madhu came up for her first promotion, her letters of

recommendation were very impressive, as they came from professors in several different countries.

1. Why do you think it was important for Madhu to have a mentor?

2. Examine Madhu's mentoring relationship with respect to the initiation and cultivation phases of a mentoring relationship.

3. Evaluate the type and quality of mentoring relationships experienced by Madhu.

4. Would you say that Madhu's mentoring experiences in the department of civil engineering were negative? Why?

5. What role can Madhu play in providing mentoring opportunities and mentoring relationships to women faculty who may subsequently join the college?

Adapted from: http://onlineethics.org/div/cases/vignettes.html, accessed on 14 February 2005

Simulation and Role Play

1. Prakash is an engineer who graduated very recently from a premier engineering college in India. He has joined M/s XYZ Locomotives as a graduate engineer trainee (GET), approximately three months back. Prakash had been a meritorious student and always performed well in his studies. XYZ Locomotives has a formal mentoring programme for GETs. Mr Satpathy has been assigned as mentor to Prakash. Mr Satpathy is vice president (works) and very well respected in the firm. Mr Satpathy and Prakash first met during the formal introduction as part of the 15-day orientation programme for GETs. A formal meeting between the mentor and protégé has been scheduled over lunch next Saturday.

Two students should volunteer for this role play. One student will assume the role of Prakash and the other student will assume the role of Mr Satpathy.

Brief for Mr Satpathy He should make Prakash feel comfortable by asking him about his experiences until now and his expectations about

work and career in the organization. Satpathy should assume the role of a guide, encourage Prakash to ask questions about various aspects, and provide information to Prakash to address some of his protégé's concerns.

Brief for Prakash In the role of a protégé, the student should try to obtain information about day-to-day work, expectations of the organization, expected performance levels, and other professional advice about internal working such as internal organizational dynamics from the mentor.

At the end of the role play, Prakash should get a better perspective about the aspects that he was unsure about. The meeting should result in drawing up an agenda for future mentor–protégé meetings, and also clarify the expectations of the mentor as well as the protégé from the relationship. The role play should end on a positive note with the participants getting to know more about mutual interests. Mr Satpathy should reassure Prakash of his support and assign him to an important project.

2. Amit is a bright young engineer who graduated with honours from a top engineering college of the country. He joined Supreme Disk Technology as a design engineer. This firm is located in south India and 90% of its employees, including most middle and all top level managers belong to that part of India. Amit is from the northern part of India and therefore has few colleagues from a similar regional background. The first project he was assigned was to reduce the cost of Supreme's popular but mature product, the re-writable CD. Amit has been a quick learner and made several suggestions that were later implemented and benefited the firm. A year later, the project had its objective of 20% cost reduction largely because of the ideas given by Amit. However, Amit's supervisor credited others more than Amit. His subsequent assignments also showed the same pattern.

After three years with the firm, Amit started feeling increasingly dissatisfied due to lack of recognition or promotion. Many of the people who had started with Amit at the company were moving into managerial positions. Amit was doing an excellent job and was disgruntled with the lack of opportunity to move up. Amit realized that his others colleagues were networking with seniors in the firm since they belonged to similar regional backgrounds. Their children played together and they met socially on various occasions. Amit felt that his being from a different culture was the reason for his lack of upward mobility. Amit approached the general manager of the firm to discuss his concerns.

Two students should volunteer for this role play. One student will assume the role of Amit and the other student will assume the role of general manager.

Brief for Amit The student should express Amit's anguish at not getting recognition for his performance. He should also communicate Amit's feeling that his being from a different region was stalling his career growth. The student should also communicate Amit's expectations from the firm.

Brief for General Manager The general manager should give a patient ear to Amit and ask questions about Amit's experiences in the firm during the last three years and seek Amit's suggestions on the actions management can take to manage these perceptions, and also to be fair.

At the end of the role play, the general manager should be able to appreciate the concerns of employees coming from different regional backgrounds. The role play participants should come up with a draft of a diversity mentoring programme. Suggestions about incorporating diversity training to sensitize senior managers of the firm to the needs of employees coming from different regions should also be generated.

Adapted from: http://onlineethics.org/div/cases/asian.html, accessed on 14 February 2005

3. You are a keen young executive and you have been assigned a mentor who is usually inaccessible. You find it difficult to arrange any meeting, as your mentor always seems to be in meetings or is travelling and does not manage to attend the planned meetings. Your mentor think that giving you feedback on your performance, giving advice, or protection from adverse situations is important. However, you want real help with feedback, assignment on challenging tasks that provide visibility, and being nominated for positions of responsibility.

- What will you do?
- What general recommendations about the design and implementation of a mentoring scheme would prevent or minimize such problems?

A role play may also be designed around this situation. The protégé will persuade the mentor of the importance of providing mentoring support.

4. Assume you are the senior manager in the HR department of a fast growing IT firm. The firm is only four years old, but it has already positioned itself as a major competitor to the best IT firms in the country. Given this scenario, the firm offers tremendous opportunities for career advancement for the high performers. As the HR manager, you would like to introduce a formal mentoring programme in the firm to further the career goals of the employees and also to further the achievement of organizational goals. Since top management support is essential for the successful implementation of a mentoring programme, you plan to discuss this issue with the managing director (MD) of your firm.

Prepare a proposal for the MD clearly outlining the purpose, structure, mentor–protégé responsibilities, and programme implementation strategy. Make suitable assumptions about the size, structure, workforce manpower strength, and other such aspects as may be essential in developing your proposal.

Classroom Projects

1. Form groups of three or four students each. Ask each group to take a position for or against the topic, 'All famous people who are successful in their careers have had mentors'. Ask the members of each group to develop arguments in support of their chosen position on the topic. Allow fifteen minutes before the group discussion after which each group presents its arguments. Give ten minutes time for presentation by each group. An open discussion with the class follows highlighting the benefits as well as pitfalls of mentoring relationships for the individual in the relationship. Alternatively, you may also discuss the following debate topic, 'Workplace mentoring is important because it helps individuals as well as the organizations achieve several objectives'. Let the class debate the pros and cons of workplace mentoring relationships.

2. This class exercise has two objectives: to identify the qualities of an effective mentor and to explore the various roles that mentors can play.

Each student is to think of an earlier time in their lives and identify one person who was a mentor to them. Each student is allowed ten minutes to deliberate on the following aspects.

- The reason this mentor was important
- The qualities of the mentor that were considered valuable
- The roles that the mentor played in their lives, for example, a philosopher, guide, counsellor, etc.

Students should form groups of four or five and share the information with group members. Group members need to list the mentor qualities as well as mentor roles that were identified by each member of the group. Te frequency of citation of each of the mentor qualities and mentor roles were cited by group members is determined. Two summary tables (samples provided below), one for mentor qualities and another for roles played by mentors may be used for tabulating frequencies.

Summary Table for Mentor Qualities

Mentor Qualities	Group Member 1	Group Member 2	Group Member 3	Group Member 4

Summary Table for Mentor Roles

Mentor Roles	Group Member 1	Group Member 2	Group Member 3	Group Member 4

Each group prepares and presents a report discussing the mentor qualities and mentor roles that were considered important by the majority of group members. These are the mentor qualities that protégés of this age group most commonly look for. The group presentations should be followed by a general class discussion about what protégés seek in the mentor and reasons thereof.

3. The students may be asked to think of the first job they are likely to have upon graduation from this course. Ask the students to list down the concerns they would have when they join a new organization. They may identify issues such as concern about their job performance, being accepted by organization members, career advancement, learning and growth, and so on. The students may be further asked to list the qualities they would like their mentors to have and the expectations they would have from their assigned mentors in the organization.

Is there a difference in the qualities and the roles expected by the students between the mentors they had in the past and the mentors they would like to have when they begin their work life in the future? What factors may have contributed to this difference?

Field Projects

1. Visit two organizations that have a formal mentoring programme. Interview the HR managers to obtain information on the various aspects of the formal mentoring programmes of these organizations. You may also interview four or five line managers in each of these organizations to understand their perception of and satisfaction with the mentoring programme. Compare the mentor programmes of these two firms with respect to the

   - objectives of the programme;
   - length of the mentor programme;
   - the mentor-protégé matching process;
   - type of mentoring relationship (dyadic or multiple);
   - frequency of scheduled meetings between mentor and protégé;
   - functions served by the mentors; and

   - employee satisfaction with the mentoring programme,

   On the basis of the above features of the mentor programme, present a critical appraisal of the mentor programmes of both the organizations. What modifications would you suggest to improve the effectiveness of each of these mentor programmes?

   Given below is the 'Mentoring Functions Questionnaire' by Scandura and Viator (1994). Visit two organizations that have a mentor programme and request at least ten managers from the line function of each organization to complete this questionnaire. These managers may be having a mentor assigned to them by the organization or may be in a voluntary mentoring relationship with another member of the organization. Each manager should respond to the questionnaire with reference to his/her own mentor within the firm. The questionnaire also asks the managers to report the kind of mentoring relationship—mandated or voluntary—that they are in.

The responses to each statement of the questionnaire are obtained on a five-point scale ranging from 'strongly agree' to 'strongly disagree', where

5 = strongly agree (SA), 4 = agree (A), 3 = not sure (NS), 2 = disagree (D), and 1 = strongly disagree (SD).

Mentoring Functions Questionnaire

1. Do you have a mentor in this organization?
   Yes   No

2. Has the mentor been assigned to you formally by your organization or you do have a voluntary mentoring relationship with your mentor?
   Assigned mentor   Voluntary mentor

3. Is your mentoring relationship with your mentor voluntary or mandated by your organization?
   Voluntary   Mandated

Scoring

The statements related to career development functions are 1, 2, 3, 4, 6 and 14.

The statements related to social support functions are 5, 7, 10, 12 and 15.

The statements related to role modelling functions are 8, 9, 11 and 13.

S. No.	Mentorship items	SA	A	NS	D	SD
1.	Mentor takes a personal interest in my career					
2.	Mentor has placed me in important assignments					
3.	Mentor gives me special coaching on the job					
4.	Mentor advises me about promotional opportunities					
5.	I share personal problems with my mentor					
6.	Mentor helps me co-ordinate professional goals					
7.	I socialize with my mentor after work					
8.	I try to model my behaviour on my mentor's					
9.	I admire my mentor's ability to motivate others					
10.	I exchange confidences with my mentor					
11.	I respect my mentor's knowledge of the profession					
12.	I consider my mentor to be my friend					
13.	I respect my mentor's ability to teach others					
14.	My mentor has devoted special time and consideration to my career					
15.	I often go to lunch with my mentor					

Source: Scandura, T.A. and R. Viator 1994, 'Mentoring in Public Accounting Firms: An Analysis of Mentor–Protégé Relationships, Mentorship Functions and Protégé Turnover Intentions', *Accounting, Organisations & Society*, vol. 19, no. 8, pp. 717–34.

Total the score of items for each mentor function separately. Higher score for a function indicates that the protégé believes that the mentor performs that function to a higher degree

Based on the scores, prepare a report about the main functions performed by mentors in these organizations. Did one category of functions dominate? Did you find differences in the mentoring functions performed when the mentor was assigned (mandated) compared to when the protégé was in a voluntary relationship with the mentor? What inferences would you draw about the mentoring relationships in each of these organizations? Suggest recommendations for improving the quality of the mentoring relationships.

Submit a written report to your instructor.

2. Identify one organization that has a formal mentoring programme and another organization that has no formal or informal mentoring programme. You may identify the organizations based on information from business magazines and/or by contacting firms directly.

From each of the two organizations identified by you, interview two or three managers about their mentoring experiences (or lack of mentoring).

1. Compare the experiences of mentored individuals with those of non-mentored managers.

2. Did the mentored managers demonstrate an advantage over non-mentored managers?

3. Did you find a difference in the mentoring experiences of managers who were at different phases of the mentoring relationship?

4. Were the mentoring experiences of the mentored managers always positive?

5. Identify the types of negative experiences cited by the managers. Which types of negative experiences (as per the types discussed in the chapter) were expressed by the managers interviewed?

6. Prepare a report based on your analysis of the interview data for submission to your instructor. Also prepare a class presentation.

Case Study[1]

Mentoring at Coca-Cola Foods

Mentorship is considered an important training and development tool in academic literature and is present as a formal programme in many companies. It has recently been prominent in popular literature as well. Having a mentor has been linked to mobility and career advancement and may be even more important for women and minorities. Additionally, mentoring has been distinguished as different from typical superior–subordinate relationships and as being composed of a number of different career–enhancing functions such as

coachng, sponsorship, facilitating exposure, and offering protection.

Many companies have developed formal programmes designed to promote mentoring relationships as part of their human resource development strategy. The Coca-Cola Company is one such organization.

The Coca-Cola Company is the global soft-drink industry leader with its headquarters in Atlanta, Georgia. Coca-Cola is the company's flagship

[1] *Adapted from*: Veale, D.J. and J.M. Wachtel, 'Mentoring and Coaching as part of a Human Resource Development Strategy: An Example at Coca-Cola Foods', *Management Development Review*, vol. 9, no. 6, pp. 19–24, used with permission

Other Sources: http://www.cokecce.com/srclib/1.1html, accessed on 27 February 2005; http://www.knet.co.za/cocacola/history.html, accessed on 27 February 2005; http://www.cocacola.com, accessed on 27 February 2005

brand, but there are 160 other soft-drink brands that are manufactured and sold by The Coca-Cola Company and its subsidiaries in nearly 200 companies around the world. Approximately 70% of the sales volume and 80% of the company profits come from outside the US. The brands of The Coca-Cola Company represent some of the most popular beverage brands in the world. The company is in the non-alcoholic beverage business with its product line extending beyond traditional carbonated soft drink categories to beverages such as still and sparkling waters, juices, isotonic drinks, fruit punches, coffee-based drinks, and tea.

The Coca-Cola Company traces its beginning to 1886, when an Atlanta pharmacist, Dr John Pemberton, began to produce Coca-Cola syrup for sale in fountain drinks. Coca-Cola was registered in the US patent office in January 1893. The company began to diversify after 1955 by producing new products, acquiring new businesses, and entering new international markets. In 1960, The Coca-Cola Company purchased the Minute Maid Corporation, a producer of fruit juices.

The company acquired the Duncan Foods Corporation in 1964. The Coca-Cola Foods division (later Coca-Cola Foods) came into existence in 1967 from the merger of its Duncan and Minute Maid operations.

In 1986, the Coca-Cola Company consolidated all of its non-franchised US bottling operations as Coca-Cola Enterprises Inc. (CCE). Coca-Cola Enterprises initially offered its stock to the public on 21 November 1986 and is listed on the New York Stock Exchange under the symbol 'CCE'. By 1988, Coca-Cola Enterprises grew into the world's largest marketer, producer, and distributor of products of the company. While CCE distributes over half of all Coca-Cola products in the US, small franchise businesses continue to bottle, can, and distribute the company's drinks worldwide.

Today, Coca-Cola is the world's most recognizable trademark, recognized by 94% of the population. Coca-Cola trucks travel over 1,000,000 miles a day to supply consumers with soft drinks. The company sells approximately 4.3 billion unit cases of its products each year. Coca-Cola Enterprises employs approximately 74,000 people who operate 454 facilities, 55,000 vehicles, and 2.5 million vending machines, beverage dispensers, and coolers. The company aims to create a workplace of fairness, equality, and opportunity for each of the employees.

Coca-Cola Foods believes that human resource development (HRD) is a key to building competitive advantage through people and to the creation of a high-performing organization. The struggle at Coca-Cola Foods has been to maximize and/or optimize human resource department's contribution to business success. The approach at Coca-Cola Foods has been

- to strengthen the link between business strategy and developmental focus;
- to involve leadership of the organization in all aspects of development; and
- to use a variety of developmental tools to match personal and organizational needs better.

The mentoring process which Coca-Cola Foods uses to develop their people is clearly a developmental tool that involves leaders in the organization. This helps considerably to strengthen the link between development and business strategy.

Coca-Cola Foods views mentoring as a process that achieves its purposes primarily through building a relationship. The mentor is usually someone higher up in the organization, someone who has experience and knowledge about the culture and dynamics of the organization. It is a formal relationship structured around the developmental needs of the protégé. In most cases, the mentor and protégé are from different departments so that there are no direct reporting relationships involved. On the other hand, Coca-Cola views coaching as an interaction that enhances performance. By providing goals, techniques, opportunities to practice and feedback, the coach helps the person increase competence and the probability of success. Coaching can occur down the hierarchy, up it, or laterally. In coaching, the relationship is not of utmost importance; rather the agreement that the coaching is valuable is the critical element.

Mentoring at Coca-Cola Foods is the creation of a formal relationship between two people of different departments and status in the organization. The goals of the mentoring relationship are to help protégés understand the organization and their role in it better. With the help of someone more experienced in the organization, the protégé learns more about the culture, mission, and context of how things get done. Additionally, the protégé gains a confidant (i.e., a neutral coach and observer), who can help him/her plan a career within the organization. Since much is built on the one-on-one relationship, the selection of people who are to be the mentors and protégés is critical.

Coca-Cola Foods makes sure that those selected as mentors are who have been successful, enjoy working for the organization, are wise in the ways of the organization, and can get things done. Additionally, Coca-Cola Foods ensures that the mentor is comfortable with being a listener, with being asked questions, and with being a teller of advice and perspective. Protégés, on the other hand, need to be ready for a relationship in which they understand the fact that they do not know a lot of things and hence need to learn. The protégés need to be comfortable asking questions and revealing concerns. Coca-Cola Foods uses a ten-part mentoring process. Most facilitated mentoring programmes have a formal process that defines each step of the programme and audits its progress. Although the process depends on the needs of the sponsoring organization, most programmes follow the ten-step process listed below.

1. Protégé identified
2. Identifying developmental needs
3. Identifying potential mentors
4. Mentor/protégé matched
5. Orientation for mentors and protégés
6. Contracting
7. Periodic meetings to execute the plan
8. Periodic reports

9. Conclusion
10. Evaluation and follow-up

Each step is explained below.

1. *Protégés identified* In this step, Coca-Cola Foods identifies the group of people who are eligible for the mentoring programme. This can be done in a variety of ways—looking at certain job levels, departments, employee characteristics, etc. Once the target group is identified, specific protégés can be identified by having them volunteer, nominated by a boss or other sponsor, or compete for selection through application and testing.

2. *Identify developmental needs* In this step the developmental needs are determined and an individual development plan is prepared. This can be done by having the protégés disclose what they think their developmental needs are, having bosses determine these needs, and/or having skill deficiencies revealed through assessment.

3. *Identify potential mentors* This step produces a pool of individuals who can serve as mentors. They may volunteer for the role, may be chosen by a protégé, or may be recruited by senior managers. Prior to selection, a mentor's general ability and willingness to handle the role should be assessed.

4. *Mentor–protégé matching* A mentor is selected for a specific protégé after considering the skills and knowledge needed by the protégé and the ability of the mentor to provide practice or guidance in those areas. It is critical that their personalities and styles of work are compatible.

5. *Mentor and protégé orientation* Before the start of the mentoring relationship, an orientation is held for both mentors and protégés. For mentors, this orientation covers time commitments, types of activities, time and budget support, the relationship with the natural boss, reporting requirements, and the protégé's responsibility for the development. For protégés, orientation covers introduction to the mentor,

the range of functions performed by the mentor, schedule of meetings, etc.

6. *Contracting* A clear agreement is an essential foundation for a good mentoring relationship. The key points of the agreement are a development plan, confidentiality requirement, the duration of the relationship, frequency of the meetings, time to be invested in mentoring activities by each party, and the role of the mentor.

7. *Periodic meetings* Most mentors and protégés meet for performance planning, coaching, and feedback sessions. The frequency can be determined by the nature of the relationship and by geographical proximity. At these meetings, both parties are candid about progress of the process.

8. *Periodic reports* It is easy to evaluate the success of the mentoring programme if periodic status reports are submitted by both the mentor and protégé. Depending on the level of formality in the programme, this step may or may not occur.

9. *Conclusion* A mentoring relationship concludes when the items delineated in the initial agreement have been accomplished or when time or business or budget constraints prevent the relationships from continuing. It may also be concluded when one of the pair believes it is no longer productive for them to work together.

10. *Evaluation and follow-up* After the relationship concludes, both the mentor and protégé are questioned via interviews or other assessment instruments about the value of the process, timing, logistics, time constraints, and any other valid concerns that could affect the mentoring process.

Conditions for Success of Mentoring Programmes

Successful mentoring programmes generally need voluntary participation from both mentor and protégé outside the normal hierarchy relationships;

one-on-one relationships; integration with other developmental efforts; commitment to the programme by the protégé's boss, and the creation and communication of policies and procedures. The policies and procedures should include a format for contracting, a requirement of confidentiality, meeting and feedback guidelines, and a duration limit for the formal programme.

Some of the advantages of mentoring programmes are that the protégé adopts the work culture of the organization better, improves his/her performance, has increased commitment to the organization, and experiences increased job satisfaction. Mentor programmes are low-cost and provide highly relevant learning and better cross-functional knowledge. In addition, such a programme can be used as a selling point for potential employees.

Some Caveats

Some concerns are that there is a potential for the protégé to play the mentor against the boss and that the relationship can lead to breaches of confidentiality that may hurt the parties involved; protégés can be the focus of gossip and jealousy and may develop unrealistic expectations about their potential; and that the protégé may not take responsibility for his/her own development.

Conclusion

Coaching is a relationship activity designed to improve performance. Generally, coaching is informal and occurs between the boss and the employee(s). Mentoring is a more formal process, based on a one-on-one relationship with someone distant in the organization. A mentor's purpose is broader in scope than that of a coach. Coca-Cola Foods believes that both processes are an important part of its human resource development effort and that it is a key to building competitive advantage and to the creation of a high-performing organization.

As stated previously, the struggle at Coca-Cola Foods has been to maximize and/or optimize the human resource department's contribution to business success. Since there is a great deal of evidence regarding the important contributions that mentors make to career success, and because Coca-Cola Foods has tied mentor programme to business goals, it would seem that the company's approach is in line with both the scientific evidence and with recent ideas of achieving competitive advantage through people.

Questions

1. Discuss the differences between mentoring and coaching based on the information in the case.
2. What goals does the mentoring programme of Coca-Cola Foods help the protégé achieve?
3. Evaluate the ten part mentoring process used by Coca-Cola Foods.
4. Demonstrate how Coca-Cola Foods has forged a link between mentoring and business strategy.
5. What conditions are important for the success of mentoring programme?

References

Barker, P., K. Monks, and F. Buckley, *The Role of Mentoring in the Career Progression of Chartered Accountants*, ISSN 1393–290X, DCUBS Research Papers, 1996–97, no 16. http://www.dcu.ie/dcubs/research_papers/no16.htm, accessed on 3 February 2005.

Blake-Beard, S.D. 2001, 'Taking a Hard Look at Formal Mentoring Programmes: A Consideration of Potential Challenges Facing Women', *The Journal of Management Development*, vol. 20, no. 4, pp. 331–45.

Bolton, E.B. 1980, 'A Conceptual Analysis of the Mentor Relationship in Career Development of Women', *Adult Education*, vol. 30, pp. 195–207.

Burke, R.J. 1984, 'Mentors in Organizations', *Group & Organization Studies*, (pre-1986), vol. 9, no. 3, pp. 353–72.

Burke, R.J. and C.A. McKeen 1990, 'Mentoring in Organizations: Implications for Women', *Journal of Business Ethics*, vol. 9, nos 4, 5, pp. 317–32.

Burt, R.S. 1992, *Structural Holes: The Social Structure of Competition*, Harvard University Press, Cambridge, Massachusetts.

Collin, A. 1979, 'Notes on Some Typologies of Management Development and the Role of Mentors in the Process of Adaptation of the Individual in the Organization', *Personnel Review*, vol. 8, pp. 10–14.

Cornelius, V. 2001, *Factors that Contribute to the Satisfaction of Mentors and Protégés Taking Part in a Formal Mentoring Program*, ISSN 1038-7448, No. WP 2001/09, RMIT Business Working Paper Series, RMIT School of Business.

Cunningham, J.B. 1993, 'Facilitating a Mentorship programme', *Leadership and Organization Development Journal*, vol. 14, pp. 15–20.

Dalton, G.W., P.H. Thompson, and R.L. Price 1977, 'The Four Stages of Professional Careers: A New Look at Performance by Professionals', *Organizational Dynamics*, vol. 6, no. 1, pp. 19–42.

Eby, L.T. 1997, 'Alternative forms of Mentoring in Changing Organizational Environments: A Conceptual Extension of the Mentoring Literature', *Journal of Vocational Behaviour*, vol. 51, pp. 125–44.

Eby, L.T., S. McMamus, S.A. Simon, J.E.A Russell 2000, 'The Protégé's Perspective Regarding Negative Mentoring Experiences: The Development of a Taxonomy', *Journal of Vocational Behaviour*, vol. 57, pp. 1–21.

Eby, L., M. Butts, A. Lockwood, and S. Simon 2004, 'Proteges Negative Mentoring Experiences: Construct Development and Nomological Validation', *Personnel Psychology*, vol. 57, no. 2, pp. 411–47.

Feldman, D.C. 1999, 'Toxic Mentors or Toxic Protégés? A Critical Re-examination of Dysfunctional Mentoring', *Human Resource Management Review*, vol. 9, pp. 247–78.

Greenberg, J. and R.A. Baron 1995, *Behaviour in Organizations*, 5th edn, Prentice Hall of India Ltd, New Delhi.

Haines, S.T. 2003, 'The Mentor–Protégé Relationship', *American Journal of Pharmaceutical Education*, vol. 67, no. 3, pp. 1–7.

Higgins, M.C. and K.E. Kram 2001, 'Reconceptualizing Mentoring at Work: A Developmental Network Perspective', *Academy of Management Review*, vol. 26, no. 2, pp. 264–88.

Homer 1969, *The Odyssey*, Simon and Schuster, New York.

Kram, K.E. 1986, 'Mentoring in the Workplace', in D. T. Hall et al. (eds.), *Career Development in Organizations*, Jossey-Bass, San Francisco.

Kram, K.E. 1983, 'Phases of the Mentor Relationship', *Academy of Management Journal*, vol. 26, pp. 608–25.

Kram, K.E. 1985, Mentoring at Work: Developmental Relationships in Organizational Life. Glenview, IL: Scott, Foresman.

Kreitner, R. and A. Kinicki 2001, *Organizational Behaviour*, 5th edn, Irwin McGraw Hill, Boston.

Levinson, D.J., C. Darrow, E. Klein, M. Levinson, and B. McKee 1978, *Seasons of a Man's Life*, Alfred A. Knopf Inc., New York.

Levinson, D.J. 1980, 'The Mentor Relationship', in M.A. Morgan, *Managing Career Development*, D. Van Nostrand Co., New York, p. 117.

Lindenberger, J.G. and L.J. Zachary 1999, 'Play 20 Questions to Develop a Successful Mentoring Programme', *Training and Development*, vol. 53, pp. 12–14.

McIlhone, M. 1984, 'Barriers to advancement: The Obstacle Course', in R. Ritchie (Chair), The successful woman manager: How did she get there? Symposium conducted at 92nd Annual Meeting of the American Psychological Association, Toronto, Canada.

Murray, M. 2001, *Beyond the Myths and Magic of Mentoring: How to Facilitate an Effective Mentoring Process*. San Francisco: Jossey-Bass, pp. 47–70.

Ostroff, C. and S.W. Kozlowski 1993, 'The Role of Mentoring in the Information Gathering Processes of Newcomers During early Organizational Socialization', *Journal of Vocational Behaviour*, vol. 42, pp. 170–83.

Phillips–Jones, L., J. Scovil, and S. Conrad 2003, 'Best Practices in Mentoring: Making Resources Count', paper presented at 2003 ASTD International Conference Session #W201, http://www.1.astd.org/astdInterim0304/pdf/handouts/W201.pdf, accessed on 2 March 2005.

Price, C., C. Graham, and J. Hobbs 1997, 'Workplace Mentoring: Considerations and Exemplary Practices', *New Directions for Community Colleges*, vol. 97, pp. 49–59.

Ragins, B. R. and T.A. Scandura 1994, 'Gender Differences in Expected Outcomes of Mentoring Relationships', *Academy of Management Journal*, vol. 37, no. 4, pp. 957–71.

Ragins, B.R., J.L. Cotton, and J.S. Miller 2000, 'Marginal Mentoring: The Effects of Type of Mentor, Quality of Relationship, and Programme Design on Work and Career Attitudes', *Academy of Management Journal*, vol. 43, no. 6, pp. 1177–94.

Reece, B.L. and R. Brandt 1997, *Effective Human Relations in Organizations*, 6th edn, All India Publishers and Distributors, Chennai.

Scandura, T.A. and R. Viator 1994, 'Mentoring in Public Accounting Firms: An Analysis of Mentor–Protégé Relationships, Mentorship Functions and Protégé Turnover Intentions', *Accounting, Organisations & Society*, vol. 19, no. 8, pp. 717–34.

Scandura, T.A. and E.A Williams 1998, *Initiating Mentoring: Contrasting the Reports of Protégés in Assigned and Informal Relationships*, Proceedings of the Southern Management Association Meeting, New Orleans, Los Angeles.

Scandura, T.A. and E.A. Williams 2002, 'Formal Mentoring: The Promise and the Precipice', in C.L. Cooper and R.J. Burke (eds), *The New World of Work: Challenges and Opportunities*, Blackwell

& Publishers Ltd, United Kingdom, pp. 241–57.

Walsh, A.M. and S.C. Borkowski 1999, 'Cross-Gender Mentoring and Career Development in the Health Care Industry', *Health Care Management Review*, vol. 24, no. 3, p. 717.

Veale, D.J. and J.M Wachtel, 'Mentoring and Coaching as Part of a Human Resource Development Strategy: An Example at Coca-Cola Foods',

Management Development Review, vol. 9, no. 6, pp. 19–24.

Zey, M.G. 1984, *The Mentor Connection*, Dow Jones-Irwin, Homewood, Illinois.

Zey, M.G. 1985, 'Mentor Programmes: Making the Right Moves', *Personnel Journal*, vol. 64, pp. 53–57.

Notes

Business Today, Managing People: The Business Today Experiential Guide to Managing Workforce, 2000.

Business Today, 21 January 2001.

Business Today, 21 November 2004, 'The Best Companies to Work for in India'.

Business Today, 14 September 2003, 'The Best Employers in India 2003'.

Business World, 6 December 2004, 'Great Places to Work 2004'.

Choudhury, P.R., 'Are You Mentoring Your Managers', *Business Today*, 22 June 1998, pp. 73–77.

Clutterbuck, D., 'Why Mentoring Programmes and Relationships Fail', http://www.workinfo.com/free/Downloads/100.htm, accessed on 2 February 2005.

'How Productive are New Hires', http://www.expressitpeople.com/20030714/cover.shtml, accessed on 3 June 2005.

http://managementmentors.cycloneinteractive.net/why_mentoring/best_practices.shtml##, accessed on 2 February 2005.

http://www.aicpa.org/pubs/jofa/nov1999/gregg.html, accessed on 13 February 2005.

http://www.ajpe.org/aj6703/aj670382/aj670382.pdf, accessed on 2 February 2005.

http://www.expressitpeople.com/20031208/management1.shtml, accessed on 6 March 2005.

http://www.fastpath.co.uk/coaching.htm, accessed on 5 February 2005.

http://www.walga.asn.au/projServices/wrts/docs/Reidy Crofts Mentoring Presentation.ppt, accessed on 2 February 2005.

http://www.www2wk.com/evidence/evidence2.asp, accessed on 2 February 2005.

Warner, F. 2002, 'Inside Intel's Mentoring Movement', Fast Company, 57 (April), in, http://pf.fastcompany.com/magazine/57/chalktalk.html, accessed on 6 March 2005.

http://www.fanniemae.com/global/pdf/careers/diversity/diversity_workbook.pdf, accessed on 28 January 2005.

Phillips-Jones, L., '*The Mentoring Group*', http://www.mentoringgroup.com/08-98-PG/ideas.htm, accessed on 13 February 2005.

11

Work–Life Integration

OBJECTIVES

After studying this chapter, you
will be able to:

- discuss the emergence of work–
  life issues since the 1970s
- the environmental trends that
  have impacted work–life issues
- understand the terms 'work–
  family conflict', 'work–life
  balance', and 'work–life
  integration'
- identify the main types of formal
  work–life initiatives
- detail the benefits of work–life
  initiatives
- explain the importance of
  family-friendly workplace
- understand the significance of
  adopting a strategic approach to
  work–life integration

INTRODUCTION

Until not very long ago, organizations looked at 'work' and 'life' as independent domains. The conflicting demands of work and personal life have always existed in the lives of employees. However, there was an unwritten rule that employees were not to let their personal life interfere with their work–life as these were two compartmentalized spheres. Employees were expected to place the organization's interests ahead of their own. Work versus personal life was seen as a zero sum game.

While organizations accepted responsibility for providing employees with a conducive and pleasant atmosphere at work, what happened to the employee outside the work domain was not the concern of the employer. In the past, personal needs were usually met with indifference reflected in reactions such as, 'What happens to you outside the office is your own business; What you do in the office is our business'.

With changing times, attitudes have changed. Globalization, technological advancements, changing work arrangements, organizational flexibility, changing family structures, and competition for quality talent are trends that have forced organizations to view employees as 'whole persons'. A growing number of organizations are now adopting programmes that help employees balance the conflicting demands arising out of their multiple roles. From viewing the employees' work–life/work–family programmes as primarily social welfare measures, organizations have advanced to integrating them as part of the overall HR strategy of the firm.

The present chapter presents various concepts such as work–family conflict, work–life balance, and approaches towards work–life integration. Emphasizing the need to view work–life integration initiatives as an integral part of HR strategy, the chapter discusses various factors for emergence of work–life balance as a critical management challenge and the types of work–life initiatives offered by organizations. Issues such as the process of development of formal work–life initiatives and the role of work–family culture in the utilization of work–life benefits are also discussed.

CHANGING NOTIONS OF THE WORK–FAMILY RELATIONSHIP

Work is defined as membership in a market or employing organization that compensates the worker for his/her contributions. The primary goal of work is to provide extrinsic rewards to the employee. These include bonuses, paid holidays, profit-sharing, etc. However, work may also provide intrinsic rewards, such as increased responsibility and freedom on the job, opportunities for growth, more challenging work, etc.

Family, like work, is a social organization that demands certain contributions from its members. These contributions are required for the maintenance and well-being of the family.

These descriptions of work and family are broad enough to encompass not only nuclear families (in which one parent works or both parents work) but also working teenagers; single working adults with siblings, parents, or other relations; and individuals who work and have immediate or extended families.

Traditionally, work and personal (family) life have been seen as competing priorities; a gain in one domain would be perceived as a loss in the other domain. For long, organizations have expected their employees not to allow their personal lives to intersect and interfere with their work lives. Traditionally, there has also been a gendering of work–family conflict. Work–family conflict has been viewed primarily as an experience confronted mainly by 'married working women'.

This may be traced back to the cultural stereotypes that have persisted for years. Even when married women shared the bread-winner role with men, they were still supposed to fulfill all their household responsibilities. Married men largely could simply choose not to do housework. In addition, most married working women usually have the responsibility for caring for their husbands, children, and elderly parents or in-laws.

Though organizations offered some degree of support through work–life programmes such as maternity leave, crèche facilities, etc., these programmes, were largely the outcome of statutory requirements or part of welfare measures within the purview of the organization's social responsibility.

Several business and societal trends have brought about a radical transformation in the traditional notions of work, family, and their relationships. Organizations today understand that professional and personal life cannot be

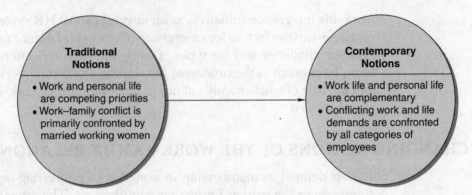

Figure 11.1: Changing Notions of Work and Personal Life

strictly compartmentalized. It is accepted that pressures from work and family can interfere with each other to a large extent (Figure 11.1)

Organizations and managers today have come to accept the impact that work–life has on personal life and vice-versa. Recent years have seen a growing number of managers operate under the assumption that personal life and work life are complementary to each other and not competing priorities.

This assumption is based on a win–win approach for both the organization and the employees. It helps employees balance their work lives with their personal lives and leads to positive outcomes for the employee and the organization. No longer do managers believe that every time an employee's personal interest 'wins', the organization 'loses' by paying the price at its bottomline. Therefore, a growing number of organizations have begun to adopt 'work–family programmes' or 'family-friendly' practices. Hughes Software, NIIT, SmithKlineBeecham, Infosys, and Indian Oil Corporation (IOC) are some of the firms that have introduced work–life human resource (HR) initiatives. These initiatives are no longer gender-centric, it is now increasingly being accepted that all categories of the workforce are likely to be confronted with family or life demands at all stages of their careers.

Dual-career couples, single parents, working single men and women, and couples as well as single men and women with care-giving responsibilities with care-giving responsibilities all confront varying degrees of conflicting demands from their work and non-work roles. Organizations recognize this by attending to work–life issues in order to reduce employee burnout and enhance productivity.

WORK–LIFE ISSUES

Work–life issues or concerns refer to those aspects of an employee's work or family life that may have an influence on one another. For example, a working mother with care-giving responsibilities may find it difficult to accept a promotion that entails a transfer.

Initial interest in work–family issues was the result of two developments that occurred during the 1970s. These developments included an increase in the number of women entering the workforce and the growth of dual-career families where both the spouses were working. This trend resulted in organizations being urged to acknowledge employees' family and other personal commitments. Work–family issues, however, were regarded as a women's issue and was primarily a social rather than a business concern.

The focus on work–life concerns is more recent. It is a broader concept than work–family issues. *Work–life issues/concerns* encompass all non-work related demands and hence are not restricted to only family demands. The time that an employee may want to devote to his/her hobbies, such as participating in theatre groups or going for mountaineering, etc., are examples of how demands from non-work activities may be at odds with work-related demands.

Both women and men face conflicts between work and family demands as well as the resultant stress. Stress levels resulting from work demands as well as those from family have increased over the years. This has made it difficult for organizations to ignore the significance of employees' non-work demands on their performance, commitment, and job satisfaction. Equations both at the workplace and at home have changed in the networked era. While in the machine age, work and family were seen as two independent domains, in the networked age there is a complete overlap between the two domains. These shifts are summarized in the Table 11.1.

Table 11.1: Shifts in Equations from Machine Age to Networked Age

	The Machine Age	The Industrial Age	The Networked Age
Work–life Issues	Work and family were two independent domains	Work started spilling into family time and was often carried home	Workdays span 24 hours with brief time intervals for non-work activities
Home Issues	Traditional roles with men working and women taking care of household chores	Dual career couples with both men and women working but women still tending the household chores	Dual career couples with both men and women working as well as attending to home issues
Support	None	Availability of help like baby sitters, crèches, old-age homes, and maids	Hands-free executive support firms that provide services as diverse as managing the laundry and the kid's homework

Adapted from: Business Today, 21 January 2001

Work–Life Issues: Changing HRM Perspectives

There has been a change over time in the way work–life issues have been viewed by organizations. Organizations' perception of work–life issues has determined the nature of their HRM practices of helping employees manage their work–life issues. Human resource professionals started addressing work–family issues as late as in the 1980s. From viewing work–family HR practices as a *benefit* provided to employees, organizations changed to developing family-friendly practices to retain skilled employees. Recently, organizations have come to realize that employees' work–life and personal life are inter-dependent. The following section traces the evolution of the HRM perspective on work–family issues from being within the purview of *employee benefits* to a necessity of providing *work–family balance* to enabling *work–life integration*.

Employee Benefits

Historically, work-family policies have been thought of as a *benefit* directed towards helping employees in managing short-term or occasional family demands (for example, childbirth or illness). The underlying assumption was that work should be the primary priority in a person's life. Originally, *work–family policies* were designed to minimize family intrusions on work that compete for an employee's time and energy, such as caring for a sick member of the family. Therefore, work-family policies were developed by organizations in a *reactive* way to ensure that family demands were not interfering with an individuals' performance on the job. Work–family policies were developed in response to employee requests for organizational support for family/life needs or when a family demand became urgent. In due course, these demands took the shape of a 'policy' of the organization. Eicher Goodearth Ltd. started in-house services for their employees when they realized that employees found it difficult to get certain household chores done due to work demands. Employees can just log in their complaints, for example, about a music system that needs repair, at a centralized complaint centre in the office. The firm then takes care of the repairs.

Progressive organizations today have moved beyond focussing on child-related or spouse healthcare related family-friendly practices to include elder care and support for various household demands such as payment of bills, taking care of repairs of electronic goods, and so on. Hughes Software, GE, and Hewlett-Packard have made arrangements with a third-party concierge services company to help employees in chore management. PricewaterhouseCoopers emphasizes care for older family members of employees. Similarly, NIIT gives an off to every NIITian on the 1st of January to celebrate 'Granny Gratitude Day' and spend time with senior family members.

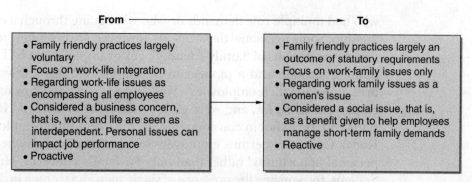

Figure 11.2:   Changing Emphasis in Family Friendly HR Practices

Work–Family Balance

In the context of skill shortages, work–family issues came to be viewed primarily as a *recruitment and retention matter.* This formed the basis of the business argument for the development of 'family friendly employment policies'. *Family-friendly practices* refer to those HR programmes and practices of an organization that are designed to help employees balance their work and family roles. Examples of family-friendly practices include dependent care support, health management programmes, medical leave, family vacations, etc. The last two decades of the twentieth century saw growth in family-friendly policies in both range and specification. Practices such as crèche facilities, family leave, part-time work, various forms of flexi-time and such measures emerged to enable those with family commitment to work more flexibly. Firms such as NIIT, IOC, Hughes Software Systems, Tata Steel, and Infosys have been pioneers in offering family friendly HR practices. A more detailed account of the business benefits of family-friendly practices is given later on in this chapter.

The development of formal family-friendly practices has been uneven. These practices appear to be more prevalent in the public sector and in large private sector organizations than in smaller firms, and more likely to be available to skilled workers than to non-skilled workers. Moreover, family friendly practices are often developed for a core workforce. 'Core workforce' refers to the high performers in the firm whom the organization wishes to attract, motivate and retain, but who are aware that there are no guarantees about the security of their jobs.

Work–Life Integration

Work–family programmes earlier tended to be directed at employees with the most visible kinds of work and personal life conflict. For example, while organizations devised programmes to allow a working mother to take care of a newborn, they did not formalize initiatives to support single men and women who had multiple role demands or who were going through a crumbling relationship. Some personnel departments, however, are beginning to think beyond traditional notions of 'family-friendly'. For example, when NIIT, a leading IT training institute and a pioneer in developing employee-friendly HR practices, provided their employees a wedding anniversary allowance, their single employees asked for, and were given, a dating allowance. At Infosys, the day starts with breakfast in consideration for the many single employees. Eastman Kodak Company permits employees to take a leave of absence for a 'unique personal opportunity' rather than only for family concerns. Hughes Software Systems, recognizing the presence of single men and women in their workforce, provide breakfast and dinner at the company cafeteria, a well-equipped gym, a library, and sports facilities. Bank of America is another company that provides benefits to single employees such as time off for pursuing personal interests. Today, organizations recognize an increasing diversity of lifestyles and work styles and, therefore, the need to accommodate many different types of work and personal life interactions (see Exhibit 11.1).

Exhibit 11.1

Singles Friendly Workplace

Overwork and exhaustion are felt by single people as well and they too have legitimate needs outside work just like those with families. Still, they are usually left out when employers develop benefits for employees with family demands. The American Association for Single People (AASP) was formed in late 1998 to look into the welfare of single employees and to ensure the beginning of what may be termed as a 'singles friendly workplace'. Recognizing that single/unmarried employees may be experiencing inadvertent workplace discrimination, the AASP conducted a survey of Fortune 500 companies in the year 2000 to identify firms that considered the unique needs of this group of employees. The AASP instituted a Singles-Friendly Workplace Corporate Leadership Award for the Fortune 500 companies based on the survey to honour companies for having policies and practices that respect the needs of single and unmarried adults. New York City-based Cendant, which provides travel and

residential real estate services, was one of only six Fortune 500 companies to receive the award. However, AASP cited 20 major corporations, including Xerox, Nationwide Insurance, Delta Air Lines, and Viacom as having singles friendly practices, who are beginning to think beyond traditional notions of 'family-friendly' practices. Xerox Corporation offers full-time employees with at least five years of service $2,000 or 2 per cent of the purchase price, whichever is less, toward first-time home purchases.

Dr Mary Young, a work–family expert in Boston, Massachusetts USA, studied the conflicts felt by single employees when trying to balance their personal life and work life. Many of the singles that Young studied experienced high stress due to their single status. According to Young, the key to supporting singles in managing their conflicting role demands was to offer enough flexibility to workers so that individual needs could be met wihtout any judgement from others.

Contd

Exhibit 11.1 Contd

Young suggested some singles friendly practices that may be adopted by firms. These are as follows:

Need-blind This means that organizations offer workers a set amount of time off to use as they want. This time does not have to be used strictly for family responsibilities, which makes it more equitable for singles who want to just hang out with friends.

Time banks Under this plan, an employee can 'buy' or 'sell' time off. Employees can buy 40, 80, or 120 hours a year from the employer or simply sell back to the company any unused time off at the end of the year.

Sabbaticals This gives all employees the chance to recharge themselves; it usually constitutes unpaid leave.

Flexible work arrangements Many employees express the desire to work where they want, when they want, as they can easily use a computer to work from home and complete their assigned tasks.

Life cycle benefits Often referred to as cafeteria benefits, it allows employees to choose what benefits they want, at what time in their life. This allows employers to contain costs while meeting individual needs.

On-site services It is becoming more common for companies to offer such services as dry-cleaning, take-home meals, health clubs, or even car maintenance so that workers can devote more personal time to enjoyable pursuits.

Every organization must evaluate its benefits programme to detect any inequities and ensure that singles in the workforce have the same access to flexible scheduling or leave as employees with families. Firms might also consider implementing work–life benefits such as mortgage assistance, wellness programmes, or financial planning services that will appeal to employees regardless of family status. It is important that HR professionals keep in mind these and other changes in family demographics since these might affect the workplace over the next decade.

Adapted from: http://www.unmarriedamerica.org/workplace, accessed on 3 February 2004

The emphasis of family friendly HR practices has moved from framing work and nonwork related issues as involving "work-family" only, towards a broader concept of *"work–life integration"*. For companies, there is obviously a realization that work and personal life of employees are interdependent and that, personal issues can impact job performance.

Thus, family-friendly HR practices initially related to childbearing and were benefit-oriented. Over time, however, organizations have recognized the strategic importance of family-friendly practices. This is evident in firms' increasing emphasis on becoming and being 'employee-friendly' or 'employer of choice'.

Environmental Trends Impacting Work–Life Issues

It is important to understand the range of business and environmental trends as well as socio-economic and demographic forces that have led to the strategic importance of work–life issues. In an environment characterized by corporate downsizing, mergers and acquisitions, globalization, multinational alliances, and global staffing, human resources have the potential to create value for the firm that cannot be imitated by competitors. This recognition on the part of organizations has led to an increasing competition for attracting and retaining quality employees. Today, competition is not limited to competitors within the region or country. Rather, organizations are confronted with global competition for quality human resources. Terms such as 'lifelong employment' and 'loyalty' no longer seem to be relevant.

With increased global competition, organizations are also faced with the need to improve productivity, efficiency, performance, quality, and profit margins. Organizations are responding to these pressures by reducing the workforce, which results in lower loyalty. At the same time, organizations are faced with an unprecedented need for committed employees in order to stay ahead of competitors.

Employees too are likely to change jobs more often to advance their careers. Aspirations of employees and their expectations of employers have increased. Employer concern for personal needs, both on and off the job, is likely to be increasingly important to the growing number of employees. When employees are helped to balance their work lives with the rest of their lives, they feel a stronger sense of commitment to the organization. This sense of commitment causes improvement in their performance on the job. Improved employee performance on the job leads to a winning organization.

In such an environment, organizations have recognized that employees are their biggest assets and they must be cultivated and kept happy for the company to deliver and grow. Management is confronted with challenges such as attracting, motivating, and retaining high performers and therefore, is experimenting with alternative ways of doing so. By offering work–life programmes as one of the alternative options, organizations are looking to become a 'great place to work in'.

Lobel, Googins, and Blankert (1999) identified some of the trends that have encouraged organizations to offer a wide array of family supportive services to meet the needs of individuals with diverse work and personal lifestyles (Figure 11.3). We will now briefly discuss these trends in this section.

Globalization Many firms headquartered in one country have a large proportion of their workforce located all over the world. Organizations are witnessing greater cross-cultural management and interaction. Multinational alliances between companies present a complex set of challenges that derive from merging organizational cultures and practices, which may vary widely around the work–life domain.

Hence, management is confronted with an increased need for understanding a complex array of work–life issues around the world. Globalization has brought

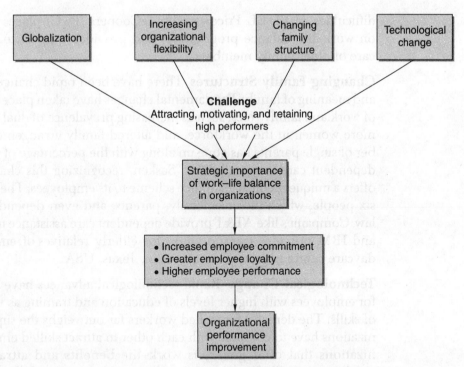

Figure 11.3: Environmental Trends Impacting Work–Life Issues in Organizations

in its wake expansion of business activity to a calendar of 24-hour-days, 365 days a year. Work–life programmes such as part-time work, flexible scheduling, and other forms of non-traditional work scheduling can become important business initiatives that meet service demands as well as strategic considerations. Sasken, Hewlett-Packard (HP), GlaxoSmithKline (GSK), C-DOT, and KPMG are some firms that offer flexible work arrangements for their employees.

Increasing Organizational Flexibility Many organizations are developing new organizational structures such as teams and cross-organizational alliances as well as new job designs. Innovative job designs include flexible work arrangements, such as telecommuting, job sharing, time off for dependent care, or sabbaticals. New corporate structures and job designs need to be linked to work–life issues since it is important to define what kind of workplace supports diverse individual lifestyles as well as business goals. At Sasken, on completion of two years of service, employees become eligible for a sabbatical of one year, during which the organization commits to pay 50% of the employee's current salary. Since the office works round the clock at Sasken, the mess/cafeteria also functions 24 hours and all snacks provided after 11.00 p.m. are at the company's expense. Complete medical coverage is provided for employees, as well as for employees' children with learning difficulties, in BHEL. PricewaterhouseCoopers (PwC) places high emphasis on work–life balance programmes and provides support to employees for care of older family members.

Changing Family Structures There have been rapid changes in the nature and meaning of family. Fundamental changes have taken place in the structure of work and family roles, such as increasing prevalence of dual career couples, more women in the workforce, and altered family arrangements. The number of single parents has gone up along with the percentage of workforce with dependent care responsibilities. Sasken, recognizing this change in society, offers a unique medical insurance scheme to its employees. The scheme covers six people, which includes family, parents, and even dependent parents-in-law. Companies like AT&T provide dependent care assistance to its employees and IBM provides transportation for elderly relatives of employees and a daycare centre near its plant at Austin, Texas, USA.

Technological Change Rapid technological advances have created a need for employees with higher levels of education and training as well as new sets of skills. The demand for skilled workers far outweighs the supply, and organizations have to compete with each other to attract skilled employees. Organizations that offer generous work–life benefits and attractive working conditions are likely to have an edge in recruiting and retaining desirable employees. Technological changes also have implications for flexible work arrangements leading companies like AT&T and IBM to provide flexible work schedules to their employees. GlaxoSmithKline also offers compressed work-weeks and flexi-time. It provides all area sales managers with a laptop to enable them to work from home. With increasing competition for attracting and retaining valued employees, the ability of an organization to address personal and family needs becomes critical. Hindustan Lever Limited (HLL) allots houses nearer to the office to women employees with children. The accounting firm KPMG offers on-site child care in evenings and Saturdays during tax time and often reimburses overtime childcare costs from January to April. At NIIT, in addition to maternity leave, a parent can choose to work half-days on half-pay till the child turns one. In some cases telecommuting is also encouraged. Maruti Udyog Limited (MUL) is another firm that provides paid maternity leave for 36 additional weeks beyond the statutory provision, if required. Firms that acknowledge and respond to the radically different family forms and values will create a competitive strategy for the future.

Links between environmental trends and work/life issues can be advantageously utilized by managers to demonstrate that work–life initiatives significantly add value to the business. There are many more trends and different set of people like CEOs, line managers, etc. will identify different trends. These four trends are broad enough in scope to be meaningful in most settings.

Work–Family Relationships: Some Related Terms

Edwards and Rothbard (2000) explained some other terms commonly used in work–family literature. These terms must also be understood to fully appreciate the concept of work family balance or integration discussed in this chapter.

Spillover The term refers to the influence of work on family and vice versa. Spillover could be in both directions—work to family as well as—family to work and the outcome could be either negative or positive. Spillover may take place for moods, values, skills, and behaviour. Positive spillover takes place when the energy, happiness, and satisfaction at work spills over into positive feelings and energy at home. An employee who is praised by his/her superior at work feels so good that he/she takes the family out for dinner experiences positive spillover. Similarly, the happiness of an employee whose child has won admission to an engineering college of repute may spill over to work in the form of higher performance and positive interactions with colleagues. Negative spillover from work to family is demonstrated when the problems or conflicts at work make it difficult for the individual to participate in family life effectively and positively. When an individual is bypassed for promotion, it may result in irritable behaviour at home, or when family problems are weighing, down the individual it may be difficult to display full participation at work. Other terms that capture the essence of spillover are extension, generalization, familiarity, and similarity.

Compensation This represents the efforts to offset dissatisfaction in one domain by seeking satisfaction in another domain. This is also referred to as complementarity, competition, or contrast. Compensation occurs when an employee decreases involvement in the dissatisfying domain and increases involvement in a potentially satisfying domain. Such an employee may, therefore, reallocate importance, time, or attention from a dissatisfying domain to a potentially satisfying domain. Compensation is intentional as it represents active attempts by the employee to reallocate involvement or seek alternative rewards. For example, when an employee is not satisfied at work, perhaps due to decreased rewards at work, the person may intentionally devote less time, attention, or importance to work and more towards family or to other personal activities in order to yield desired rewards in that domain.

Segmentation This refers to the separation of work and family, such that the two domains do not affect one another. Segmentation was earlier viewed as a natural division of work and family since the two domains were separated in time and space and were thought to inherently serve different functions. However, more recently work and family have been demonstrated as closely related domains. Therefore, segmentation is now viewed as an active process whereby people maintain a boundary between work and family. For example, when a person intentionally suppresses the negative work feelings at home, the person is trying to separate the two domains. In such a situation, the person will not let negative work mood to affect his/her mood and behaviour with family members or friends. Other terms used in a similar context are compartmentalization, separateness, and independence.

Resource drain This involves the transfer of finite personal resources, such as time, attention, and energy, from one domain to another. However, it is not the same as compensation. Compensation is an active response to dissatisfaction in one domain, whereas resource drain refers to the transfer of resources between domains, regardless of the impetus for the transfer. In response to increased demands of time at work, a person may spend less time sleeping or pursuing a hobby in order to ensure that family time is intact. This is an example of resource drain. The transfer of resources is not due to dissatisfaction in one domain, but rather directed towards fulfilling the demands of one or more domains.

Congruence The term 'congruence' refers to the similarity between work and family, owing to a third variable that acts as a common cause. These common causes may include personality traits, general behavioural styles, and socio-cultural forces. For example, an individual may be predisposed to satisfaction, which may influence both work satisfaction and family satisfaction. This may result in a positive relationship between the two forms of satisfaction. However, it is different from spillover. Spillover attributes these similarities to the *effect* of one domain on another. Yet, congruence attributes this similarity to a third variable that affects both domains. For instance, general intelligence and aptitude of an individual may contribute to skills that may be of use to an individual at work as well as with the family. In this case, general intelligence and aptitude becomes the third variable.

Work–Family Conflict

The demands and pressures of work and family may give rise to work–family conflict in an individual.

Greenhaus and Beutell (1985) defined work–family conflict as 'a form of inter-role conflict in which the role pressures from the two domains, that is, work and family, are mutually non-compatible so that meeting demands in one domain makes it difficult to meet demands in the other'. That is, participation in the work role is made more difficult by virtue of participation in the family and vice versa. The major concern in this most widely used definition of work–family conflict is that role conflicts cause problems of role participation. Hence, differences in values, social relationships, and requirements between work and family do not constitute conflict per se.

An employee may be faced with work–family conflict, for example, when he/she has to attend the parent–Teacher meeting in the child's school or when he/she has a doctor's appointment for an ageing parent. The demands and pressures of work make it difficult for the employee to stretch time for such activities.

Work–Family Conflict

Three major types of work-family conflicts have been identified in work–family literature (Figure 11.4).

Time-based Conflicts

These arise when time spent on role performance in one domain precludes time spent in the other domain because of depletion of energy or stress. An employee finding it hard to take time off from work to go for a family picnic experiences time-based conflict.

Strain-based Conflicts

These arise when strain in one role affects an employee's performance in another role. This type of conflict does not connote conflicting demands. Rather, it occurs when the demands from one domain cause tension, anxiety, fatigue, or dissatisfaction for the employee thereby reducing his/her personal resources of energy and physical or mental capacity. When an employee is tending to a terminally sick spouse or parent, the mental and physical strain resulting from the experience may hamper the employee's performance at work.

Behaviour-based Conflicts

These occur when there is incompatibility between the behaviour patterns that are desirable in the two domains and the employee is unable to adjust behaviour when moving from one domain to another. Behaviour-based conflict, too, need not involve conflicting demands. It occurs when a behaviour

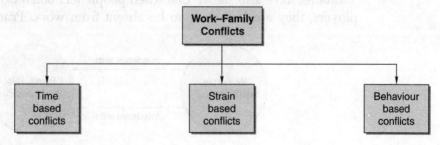

Figure 11.4:   Types of Work–Family Conflicts

developed in one domain interferes with the role performance in another domain. This may often be true for those in the teaching profession. Teachers, by virtue of their jobs, may be more assertive and dominating in interpersonal relations. If they inappropriately apply the same behaviour patterns with family members, it may inhibit their performance in the family domain.

Conflict between these two roles, that is, work role and family role, may arise in two situations (Figure 11.5): when demands of work role interfere with family role performance, and when demands of family role interfere with work role performance.

Generally, conflict between work and family (life) is viewed in terms of the interference of the demands from family role on the performance of an individual's work role. For example, family demands such as childcare, elder care, spending time with family, and repairs of household items are potential situations which may interfere with an individual's performance on the job. Therefore, most firms developed HR practices that would provide the employee with time off for fulfilling family demands. However, the converse is as true. Work demands are also equally likely to interfere with an individual's capacity to fulfill family (life) demands. For example, when an individual postpones his own or family members' health check-up due to lack of time off from work or when the individual has no leisure time for himself/herself or for the family, the situation has the potential for causing stress resulting from interference of work demands on family role performance.

A lot of research has been conducted linking work–family conflict and family–work conflict to possible outcomes in the home and workplace. Most researchers have indicated, directly or indirectly, that work–family conflict results in decrease in individual performance at home or at the workplace as well as lack of performance improvements for the individual, the group, or the organization. Various researchers have consistently shown work–family demands to influence key work and personal outcomes ranging from job, life and family satisfaction, performance, and turnover. Research suggests that family problems can have major financial costs for employers in terms of high health insurance claims, lost work-days, and reduced productivity.

Studies have also shown that when people feel taken care of by their employers, they are less likely to be absent from work. Prudential Insurance

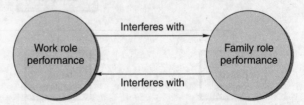

Figure 11.5: Directionality of Work–Family Conflict

Company reported that a back-up childcare centre the company opened near its New Jersey office in 1997 resulted in an estimated savings of $800,000 a year in costs associated with employee retention and absenteeism. It may not be difficult to see that the employees of firms that provide work–life programmes are more likely to 'go the extra mile' to ensure that the company succeeds. When the organization takes interest in the employee's personal life, the employee feels more committed and obliged to return the favour.

WORK–LIFE BALANCE

Work–life balance is the term used to describe those practices at workplace that acknowledge and aim to support the needs of employees in achieving a balance between the demands of their family (life) and work lives. The Work Foundation, earlier known as The Industrial Society, believes that 'Work–life balance is about people having a measure of control over when, where and how they work. It is achieved when an individual's right to a fulfilled life inside and outside paid work is accepted and respected as the norm, to the mutual benefit of the individual, business and society'.

The concept of work–family (life) balance has emerged from the acknowledgement that an individual's work–life and personal/family life may exert conflicting demands on each other. Conflict is a normal part of life and is a natural result of the conflicting demands arising from multiple roles, such as that of a mother, daughter, daughter-in-law, wife, friend, and employee. Various examples of conflicts have been discussed earlier in the chapter. Advantages will be discussed later in this section along with examples to learn how firms encourage work–life balance.

Work–family literature has moved beyond 'family' to incorporate the complete personal life of an individual. Hence, the concept is about work–life balance, not just work–family balance. In order to manage the negative spillover of conflict, it is important to balance the demands from both the domains. Work–life balance is about adjusting work patterns to achieve overall fulfillment. A good work–life balance enables the business to thrive and at the same time enables the employees to easily combine work with other aspirations and responsibilities.

Work–life balance should not be understood as suggesting an equal balance or scheduling equal number of hours for each of one's work and personal activities. A positive work–life balance involves achievement and enjoyment. A good working definition of work–life balance may be meaningful daily achievement and enjoyment in each of the four quadrants of life—work, family, friends, and self.

The best work–life balance varies for an individual over time. At different stages of career and age, different factors become important for an individual.

The right balance for an individual today will probably be different tomorrow. For instance, the right balance for an individual when he/she is single will be different from when he/she gets married or when he/she is nearing retirement. The right balance is also different for different individuals. There is no one work–life balance that fits all because all of us have different priorities and different styles of life. However, it is not just balance that an individual desires, since the term 'balance' connotes choosing from the two options— work and life. What one actually seeks is work–life integration (WLI).

Work–Life Integration

It is important to understand that work and family are not two 'separate spheres', but interdependent domains with permeable boundaries. Work–life integration is the combination of two or more roles/domains. Individuals may move from one role to another several times a day. These role transitions involve crossing role boundaries, switching back and forth among one's currently held roles. For example, on work days, employees may play the role of a parent and spouse at home, transitioning to employee after reaching the workplace, and transitioning back to the role of spouse and parent on reaching home after work. Telecommuting employees may need to switch roles more frequently.

Work–life integration can be understood in terms of two mechanisms, i.e., flexibility and permeability. *Flexibility* is the ability of the boundary between two or more roles/domains to expand or contract to accommodate the demands of one domain or another. For instance, a female telecommuter may be called upon to play the role of a mother at any time of the day. Hence, she would require flexibility in her work roles. *Permeability* refers to the extent to which a boundary allows psychological or behavioural aspects of one role/ domain to enter and overlap one another. A call centre operator who is not allowed to receive visitors or accept personal calls at work has an impermeable work role boundary.

When two or more roles, for example, that of an employee and mother, are both flexible and permeable, then they are said to be integrated, leading to work–family (life) integration. Some organizations recognize this linkage and adopt initiatives that allow working families to integrate these domains. Other organizations, on the other hand, express concern over the blurring of boundary between work and family that employees may experience when there is too much of work–family integration. Such organizations believe that this might lead to lower outputs from the employee. For example, this kind of blurring of boundaries may occur when an employee is at his/her workplace but he/ she is involved in household decisions due to technological advances.

On the other hand, when boundaries of two or more roles are highly segmented, they became impermeable due to distinct schedules, behaviours and people in each domain, so that transitions between domains require more effort.

When the two domains of work and family are separated, boundaries are clearer and more easily maintained. When role sets are highly integrated, role transitions become less difficult, but they can also confound the demands of these roles, increasing the chance of role blurring. *Work–family blurring* or work–family boundary ambiguity can be defined as the experience of confusion or difficulty in distinguishing one's work from one's family roles in a given setting in which these roles are seen as highly integrated, such as doing paid work at home. The integration-segmentation distinction should not be viewed as a dichotomy but as a continuum.

Work–family programmes should be offered by organizations in ways that allow employees to have control in managing their work family boundaries. This holds especially true for telecommuters and other employees who bring some of their work home. Research suggests that integrative work family arrangement can help employees balance work and family life (for example, by scheduling work around family demands, spending more time with family, etc.). However, if work and family life become so highly integrated that the work family boundary is blurred, it may result in negative outcomes such as, stress, work family conflict, and dissatisfaction with both work and family life.

To reduce the chances of this work family blurring, organizations must respect the schedules that employees set for telecommuting or flexitime work. These must also be supportive of employees in terms of shifting schedules to accommodate family needs. Employees who work from home can minimize this blurring by boundary work activities like discouraging family members and visitors from interrupting one's work, working only in a particular room of the home, and so on. Those with flexible work hours may need to maintain a fairly consistent schedule that allows for specific blocks of 'family time'.

WORK–LIFE INITIATIVES

Work–life initiatives may simply be defined as any programme designed to alleviate individual conflict between work and family. Work–life programmes may range from one-time personnel changes such as a maternity leave to transformation of the corporate culture such as a balanced work–life environment. They may also range from informal to formal work–life programmes designed to help employees achieve a better work–life balance. Formal programmes then become part of the firm's HR policy. The 'wedding scheme' of NIIT that entitles all employees getting married a one-time allowance of Rs 5000 and an interest-free loan of up to Rs 10,000 is a formal initiative (policy) of the firm. On the other hand, an organization may respond positively to an employee's requests for support as and when required without having a formal programme. For instance, an organization may sponsor an employee for a formal course of study and reimburse the fees, even though there may not be a formal policy in place regarding this.

Formal WLI of organizations can be categorized into the following four main types of employer support:

- Time and place flexibility
- Information
- Financial
- Direct

The focus of each type of employer support is given in Table 11.2.

The range of organizational practices relating to work–life relationship may fall along a continuum. The continuum reflects the differences between organizations and managers on how they view the relationship between work and personal life (Figure 11.6). This continuum may extend from the trade-off approach at one end, to the leveraged approach at the other. When organizations take the *trade-off* approach, they believe in the zero-sum principle, that

Table 11.2: Types of Formal Work–life Initiatives (Employer Support)

S.No.	Type of Employer Support	Focus
1.	Time and Place Flexibility	Part time work, flexible scheduling like flexitime and telecommuting, job sharing, leaves of absence, family leave like maternity/paternity leave, and any paid/unpaid family leave.
2.	Information	Resource and referral programmes for providing information about dependent care, giving options like child and elder care provider, support groups, pre-retirement planning, and supervisor training on how to effectively manage subordinates work–family integration needs.
3.	Financial	Flexible spending accounts in which employees set aside pre-tax money each year into an account from which they get reimbursed, stipend vouchers for care giving expenses, tuition reimbursements, health benefits for dependents, long term care insurance.
4.	Direct	On or near site company sponsored day care centres, sick care, dependent care, concierge services to run errands for busy employees such as dry cleaning, grocery shopping, etc., It also includes family counselling, personal financial planning, and holiday and vacation care.

Adapted from: Kossek and Block 2000

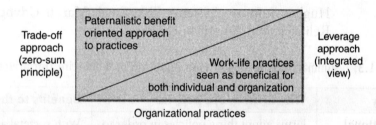

Figure 11.6:   Continuum of Organizational Practices Relating to Work–Life Relationships

is, either the business wins or the personal life, but not both. Such firms are more likely to adopt a paternalistic and benefit-oriented approach when they offer any family-supportive practices such as on-site crèches.

However, an increasing number of organizations today adopt 'life friendly' or 'family friendly' policies to attract and retain talented workforce. Such organizations take an *integrated approach* to work–family relationship. In this approach, employees and managers work together to find ways to meet the needs of both the organization and the employee. Agilent Technologies, for example, tracks employee satisfaction through Pulse, the company's online survey. Immediate action plans are formulated to address areas of employee concern.

When the approach of organizations and managers reflects the view that work–life balance practices help employees achieve more satisfying personal lives and also adds value to business, they are following the *leveraged approach*. Business benefits of work–life initiatives are discussed later in this chapter.

Work–Life Initiative Theories

Organizations may adopt WLI for a variety of reasons. Firm adoption of work–life programmes has been examined within four theoretical frameworks:

- Institutional theory (DiMaggio and Powell 1983)
- Resource Dependence Theory (Pfeffer and Salancik 1978)
- Managerial Interpretation (Milliken et al. 1998)
- Organizational Adaptation (Daft and Weick 1984)

The rationale for firm adoption of WLI and the benefits of WLI adoption for the firms varies by theory. Table 11.3 provides a comparison of these theories. Exhibit 11.2 presents work–life initiatives of some firms. In the 'Best Employers in India 2002' study by Hewitt Associates, the 25 best employers that emerged were found to share between themselves 'sensitivity towards a balance for work and personal life'. Some of the firms that encouraged work–life balance in the study were Polaris Software Lab, Hewlett Packard,

Hughes Software Systems, Tata Steel, Maruti Udyog Ltd, LG Electronics, Reliance, and American Express.

Table 11.3: Summary of theories of Firm Adoption of Work–Life Initiatives

Theory	Why firms adopt policies	Benefits to the Firm
Institutional	Firms adopt these policies in order to gain legitimate acceptance within the society and its environment. It is a reactive theory which assumes that firms react to pressures.	With societal acceptance of the firm, more people will be to invest in the organization and more people will be interested to apply for employment with the organization.
Resource Dependence	Firms implement work–life initiatives in order to acquire human resources. It is a proactive theory which presupposes that firms offer enticements recognizing their dependence on qualified human resources.	Work–life initiatives serve as enticements for employees and potential employees of the firm. Hence, such firms attract a larger applicant pool (more women and parents) and are thus able to secure the necessary human resources.
Managerial Interpretation	Adoption of work–life initiatives occurs when key management persons interpret work–life policies as important for the firm	Importance of work–life policies may be firm specific, thus programmes are only offered if management deems them as relevant.
Organizational Adaptation	Firms adopt work–life initiatives in an attempt to align themselves with the changing business environment.	Firms continually recognize and interpret changes in the environment in order to remain competitive in their industry.

Adapted from: Cook 2004

Exhibit 11.2

Work–Life Initiatives of Some Firms

Company	Family-friendly Practices
NIIT	<ul><li>Employee gets the day off on his/her birthday</li><li>On marriage, the employee gets interest free loan in addition to a wedding allowance. Company provides car to the couple to reach the venue on the wedding day</li><li>In addition to maternity leave, a parent can choose to work half day with half pay till the child turns one year. Telecommuting is also allowed in some cases</li></ul>

Contd

Exhibit 11.2 Contd

Name of the	Family-friendly Practices
Sasken	▪ Flexi-time, no attendance logging mechanism, casual dress code except for corporate client meetings ▪ Since the office works round the clock, the cafeteria also functions 24 hours to keep the employee energized. All snacks provided after 11.00 p.m. are free ▪ Unique medical insurance scheme that covers six people, which includes family, parents, and even dependent parents-in-law ▪ After four years at Sasken, an employee is eligible for hibernation leave of six weeks Employees are encouraged to take leave and time off to spend with their families, as well as in recognition of the fact that this break from work would forestall burnout
KPMG	▪ Flextime, job sharing, compressed work week, and telecommuting ▪ During 'tax time', KPMG offers on-site child care on evenings and Saturdays at many offices
PwC	▪ Places important emphasis on employee use of the life-balance programme ▪ No cost immediate telephone access to professional advice on how to plan and prepare for the family, find and choose child care, care for older family members, understand teenage children, and manage other major life changes ▪ Alternative work arrangements
SmithKline Beecham	▪ Child care and other family initiatives like children's Fridays and bring your child to work day ▪ Commuting alternatives ▪ On-site health clinic, fitness centres, wellness seminars, and fitness programmes once every quarter
Merrill Lynch	▪ Childcare centres, summer camps, resources and referrals for childcare, tuition, back-up childcare, family childcare homes, before- and after-school programmes ▪ Adoption reimbursement and parenting education ▪ Flexible work arrangements ▪ Help with dependents ▪ Family leave ▪ Wellness programmes ▪ Campaigns for women's achievement
Prudential	▪ Flexible programmes ▪ Family illness days ▪ College scholarships and preparation, summer camp ▪ Dependent care grants ▪ Parenting seminars and materials, adoption assistance ▪ Employee recreation events and discounts, resource and referral

Benefits of Work–Life Initiatives

With human resources being viewed as a source of competitive advantage in the new economic era, the issue of work–life integration becomes crucial for sustaining a happy, healthy, and committed workforce. The pressures emerging from work–life conflicts experienced by employees may affect the ability of organizations to realize the full potential of their workforce. Organizations recognize that personal issues can impact job performance and work–life balance is an important issue for attracting, retaining, and getting the best out of their employees. Providing employees with work–life programmes can result in benefits for the organization in terms of reduced recruiting and training costs. Happy workers work well together and are less likely to leave the organization. When organizations take initiatives to organize leisure for its employees (for example, an evening at a pub once a month concept at Ericsson) or when it helps the employees in meeting with household chores (for instance, concierge services at GE and Hewlett-Packard) it promotes an image of a 'caring' employer.

When dependent care or other non-work problems are taken care of, employees may respond by improved performance and productivity. Whenever, HCL Comnet sends one of its employees to client sites abroad, it distributes free telephone coupons to their family members to help them keep in touch. Measures such as these on the part of the organization ensure that the employees can focus on performing their jobs well. Many organizations implement family-friendly policies such as flexi-time because it helps them recruit better talent, increase productivity, and reduce absenteeism.

It is important for firms to demonstrate how work–life policies translate into benefits for organizations by being able to attract and retain satisfied and happy workforce who are able to perform to the best of their abilities. Exhibit 11.3 illustrates the organizational and employee benefits of work–life initiatives.

However, not all organizations take the 'employee friendly practices' route. Organizational characteristics have been found to influence the adoption of work–life initiatives. Large-sized organizations, organizations faced with higher competition, those having more women in their workforce, and where managers perceive the linkage between work–life issues and firm productivity are more likely to adopt work–life initiatives.

Current research has addressed organizational benefits that may accrue as a result of adoption of work–life initiatives. Evidence suggests a relationship between work–life policies and perceived firm performance. Investor's response to work–life programme announcements has been found to be positive, thus increasing the company's stock price. Researchers have also concluded that rather than a single work–life practice, grouping of work–life policies may be a source of sustainable competitive advantage. Human resource

---

Exhibit 11.3

Organizational and Employee Benefits of Work–life Initiatives

An organization strives to recruit and retain talented employees to achieve positive business outcomes, such as high performance, productivity, lower employee turnover, and absenteeism. Employees needs relate to superior quality of life, enjoyable and satisfied work–life, good salary, and sufficient leisure time. Though, the needs of business and that of the employees differ, it is possible to balance work and life to achieve synergy through a good work–life strategy by an organization. The following matrix presents the case for adopting work–life initiatives from the perspective of both the firm and the employee.

What organizations want:

- Increased employee productivity
- Reduced absenteeism
- To attract and retain talent
- To become world-class employers
- To improve employee health

Organizations benefit from work–life strategy through:

- Financial savings

- Increased productivity
- Lower absenteeism
- Improved customer service
- A more motivated and satisfied workforce

What employees want:

- A good quality of life
- An enjoyable work life and career progression
- Training and development
- Good health
- Affordable childcare and elder care
- Further education
- Leisure time with family, friends, and for travel and hobbies
- More money

Employers benefit from supporting employees want because employees become:

- More motivated
- More satisfied at work
- More productive
- More co-operative
- Better at managing their time

Source: http://www.employersforwork–lifebalance.org.uk, accessed on 15 February 2004

---

policies of organizations that are designed to help employees balance their work and family lives can have an effect on employee turnover, absenteeism, and organizational commitment.

Family problems may also lead to major financial costs for employers since an employee with family/life problems is unlikely to work to his/her full potential. Good work–life balance policies and practices are good for business and some benefits can be directly measured financially such as, financial savings, productivity, absenteeism, etc. A 1997 survey of more than 150 executives conducted by the Whirlpool Foundation found a link between work–life practices such as flexible work arrangements, childcare, elder care, financial assistance, etc. and business results including improved productivity, reduced absenteeism and turnover, enhanced employee satisfaction and morale, and decreased health care costs. One year after opening its on-site child-care centre at its New Jersey headquarters, Allied Signal Inc. found that parents who were using the centre were more focused and productive at work. 'Lost worktime' for these parents also decreased by 89%.

Technology firms seem to be going out of their way to make working 'fun' where employees can find the right balance between work and life. HCL Perot Systems at Noida provides its employees with trekking breaks and Art of Living courses. Teams at Chennai based Polaris, occasionally break-out into impromptu get togethers dubbed as JLT (just like that) parties where activities include balloon busting, races, eating competitions, painting competitions, and dumb charades.

Similarly at TCS, at least one fun event is scheduled every month and there is an annual Family Day in June. Most of these companies use these practices for achieving a range of benefits, the foremost being controlling attrition. The belief is that firms with better work environment lose less people and have higher productivity and profits.

The quality of work–life that an organization provides is often the determining factor in an individual's decision in joining an organization. Organizations, therefore, are also emphasizing on various work–life practices to build a reputation of being an 'employer of choice'. When Hewitt Associates conducted a study on Best Employers in India in 2002, an individual's talent clearly emerged as a critical success factor in hiring decisions. Since talent is also the most difficult to attract, motivate, and retain, the study found that the best organizations attempted to differentiate themselves as employers of choice to ensure that they have an edge in the talent market. Among the factors consistent across all best employers were a high degree of employee satisfaction, commitment, and morale; unique HR practices; effectiveness of HR practices in meeting employee needs; alignment of HR practices to business context, and a sensitivity towards a balance for work and personal life.

HR News reported in 1997 that with changes in social and cultural values, large number of students on the threshold of entering the labour market have no inhibition or guilt in openly admitting that an attractive job is one that provides them the opportunity to balance their work and a rewarding life outside work.

Despite the increasing evidence for work–life interdependence and an ever-growing number of work–life programmes, advocates for work–life initiatives have faced considerable difficulties convincing the business world that the initiatives do add-value to the organization. This is mainly because senior managers often view work–life programmes with a narrow perspective.

According to the survey by Centre for Work and Family in 1995, senior managers believe that work–life issues were the responsibility of benefits department and they were entirely unrelated to pressing business issues. The advocates of family-friendly policies need to link work–life initiatives to overall business objectives. However, the scenario shows signs of looking up. Vijay Thadani, co-promoter of NIIT has re-designated himself as Chief Fun Officer (CFO). Thadani had this to say, 'there is a new intruder into our lives. It is causing terror in NIIT. As the CFO I declare a prolonged war against that intruder-seriousness'. Similar philosophy is cited by the co-founder of HCL Perot Systems.

FAMILY-FRIENDLY WORKPLACE

The terms 'family-friendly workplace' or 'family-friendly company' refer to a workplace that, to some extent, acknowledges and responds to the work and personal/family responsibilities assumed by employees. A family-friendly workplace develops and implements policies that allow employees to simultaneously fulfill work and family responsibilities.

Organizations differing in the extent of adoption of work–life initiatives may also differ in the extent to which they are family-friendly. However, the concept of a family-friendly workplace is not an either/or concept. Rather, it is a continuum. In order to create a family-friendly workplace an organization must design and implement benefits, practices, and policies to help employees balance their work and non-work lives by providing provisions for flexible work schedules, dependent care supports, etc. These constitute the '*benefits approach to work–life*'. Apart from these, organizations must create workplace cultures and climates that reflect concern for employees' lives outside of work. LG Electronics ensures this by not only bringing the families right to the firm's doorstep, but by going to their doorstep. Representatives from the company visit employees' homes and tell them what employees do at work. They also welcome families to the office premises to get a feel of where their loved ones work. Sasken has an active sports club and also conducts workshops for yoga and stress management. At GlaxoSmithKline, TGIF (Thank God it is Friday) is celebrated once every quarter and on that day employees leave office one and half-hours earlier than the scheduled time. The company also holds annual picnics for employees and their families. Maruti Udyog has a Golden Week, which is a shut down for two weeks in June and December to match the holidays of children. It is also important for organizations to periodically review current work processes and practices to determine which ones lead to work inefficiencies and employee stress. For instance, Infosys found that due to peak-time traffic its employees were finding it difficult to reach office in time or they had to start from home very early. Infosys responded by changing its office timings so that its employees could avoid the rush hour and hence be fresh and energetic to take on office work. The company also provided company transport to its employees to facilitate commuting.

Although organizations have become quite vocal about the importance of being 'family friendly', many of them still have a long way to go in implementing family-friendly practices. Most of them have not yet determined how to move beyond formal policy adoption. Employers are struggling to understand how to best implement work–life balance programmes and policies to really make them work well so as to meet their dual agenda of employee well-being and benefits for the company. Moreover, there will always be employees who are willing to put their career before their family and personal needs—this set of employees are likely to be most promotable, since they will be willing to do whatever the company needs without letting family demands come in the way.

Organizations still do not consider the satisfaction of employees' personal needs as similar to meeting customers' needs as employees are internal customers of the organization. Rather, organizations have a paternalistic approach to the adoption of work–life initiatives. Largely, the use of work–life integration policies is seen as benefiting the individual employee far more than the firm. While the benefits component is viewed as the most visible indicator of a family-friendly workplace, implementation of supportive work policies is considered as the most important component.

Progressive organizations realize that adopting all the family-friendly policies in the world will not help employees achieve desirable work–life balance if they are afraid to utilize these programmes because the general culture does not support their use. For instance, a firm may introduce flexitime to enable employees some control over their work schedule. Yet the organizational culture may be quite different with managers demanding that employees work long hours. In such a culture, an employee may not prefer to use flexitime option and would stay late in office more for the sake of appearing to work than for productive work. By doing this, the employee tends to extend the temporal boundaries of work cutting into family time resulting in conflict.

Some organizations have cultures which encourage employees to utilize the benefits of work–life balance initiatives. Employees at Morgan Stanley, the investment bank headquartered at UK, are cared for with benefits that include two on-site restaurants, two health clubs, a medical clinic, dry cleaner, and back-up child care services as part of one of the many initiatives set up to promote better work–life balance. What really keeps employees here is the sense among them that they are all seen as people first, not just employees. Phrases such as 'we hire nice people', and 'talent is more important than specific skill' indicate that managers at Morgan Stanley are willing to invest in people to help them to learn, grow, and advance in their careers. Thus organizational culture and HRM practices can facilitate or impede work–life balance. This concept is explained in detail in the next section.

WORK–FAMILY CULTURE

It is not enough for organizations to implement family-friendly practices such as flexitime and extended parental leave, to reduce employees' work–life conflicts. It is more important for the firm to have a supportive culture that encourages employee utilization of work–life benefits.

Work–life (family) culture may be defined as shared assumptions, beliefs, and values regarding the extent to which an organization supports and values the integration of employees' work and family lives. A family-supportive organizational culture refers to the global perceptions that employees have regarding the extent to which the organization is family-supportive.

Similar to organizational culture and climate, work–family culture focuses on employees' perceptions of the informal and intangible aspects of work–family culture. However, formal benefits offered by the organization influence this culture. For instance, a firm may have a benefit policy that allows women employees to extend maternity leave beyond what is legally stipulated. However, if the employee runs the risk of being termed unprofessional if she extends her maternity leave, she may be reluctant to utilize the stated 'family-friendly' benefit.

Thompson et al. (1999) suggested that there are three components of a supportive work–family culture (see Figure 11.7). These are discussed below.

Components of Work–Family Culture

Organizational Time Demands

The extent to which there are expectations for long hours of work and for prioritizing work over family. Certain professions like corporate law and investment banking are known to have excessive time demands.

Perceived Career Consequences

Refers to the degree to which employees perceive positive or negative career consequences of using work–family benefits. For instance, employees may

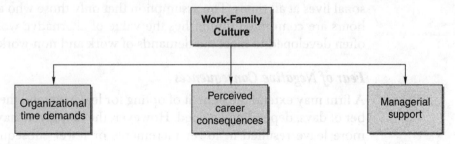

Figure 11.7: Components of Work-Family Culture

believe that utilization of flexitime may damage their career progress because of norms for 'face time'.

Managerial Support

The extent to which individual managers are sensitive to and accommodating of employees' family needs. For instance, at American Express, the company places high emphasis on maintenance of a healthy balance between employees' work and personal lives. Sitting late in office and working on weekends is strictly discouraged. It is the managers' responsibility to ensure that employees complete their leave entitlements of 12 optional holidays for the year.

Utilization of work–family programmes by employees is influenced by contextual variables, especially in the use of flexible policies. Research has shown that employees' perceptions regarding the degree to which their organization has a supportive work culture is linked to the degree to which they utilize work–family benefits. Often, organizations spend time, money, and energy developing and implementing work–life benefits that remain unutilized by employees because of an unsupportive work–family culture. Consequently, neither the organization nor the employees benefit from these programmes. There is a big difference between offering work–life programmes and ensuring that they are effectively used and valued by employees.

Employees are often reluctant to take advantage of work–life programmes. There are two main reason for this reluctance.

Organizational Culture

Where there has been a tradition of 'face time' and 'workaholic hours'. For example, in some organizations there is an unwritten rule that an employee cannot leave office before the boss. In such organizations an employee who leaves office right in time meets with disapproval. The impact of workplace culture in undermining formal family-friendly policies is particularly evident in relation to the pervasive long hours culture, especially in white-collar, professional, and managerial jobs. In firms with long hours culture, employees are expected to demonstrate commitment by putting work before their personal lives at all times. The assumption that only those who are working long hours are committed diminishes the value of alternative work arrangements often developed to meet the demands of work and non-work responsibilities.

Fear of Negative Consequences

A firm may extend the benefit of opting for leave beyond the stipulated number of days, depending on need. However, the employee may find that taking more leave resulted in lower increments or fewer subsequent promotions. Some organizations offer formal programmes to women employees that permit them to work reduced hours or extend leave because of child care demands. However, these women employees are likely to still lose out on promotions due to the long hours culture that undervalues employees who use work–life programmes to make more time for their families. This may be seen often in government jobs, such as university positions. If a lady faculty member extends her leave due to child-care demands, she may have to take earned leave and when that gets exhausted, she would be required to go on unpaid leave. This period of unpaid leave will then not count towards her service tenure resulting in adverse effect on her chances for promotions.

Organizations may have a climate for boundary separation between work and family. Some organizations have loose work–life boundaries and allow employees to bring children to work and some have tight boundaries where even receiving personal calls while at work is prohibited. While employees have preferences for the degree of integration and separation between work and family, the culture of the organization dictates the degree of permeability between the family and work roles. For instance, norms at workplace may dictate that family pictures on one's desk are acceptable (integration) or that socializing with co-workers outside of work is not acceptable (separation).

By implementing work–life practices, an organization communicates to its employees that their non-work life is important and valued. Respect for an employee's non-work life is an important component of a family-supportive organization. Work–life balance is a clear theme at Hewlett-Packard. Besides providing flexible work arrangements, the firm also provides for additional ten days leave for an employee's marriage, ten days for preparing for higher education, eight days for legally adopting a child, and five days for bereavement in the family. If required, the employee can take leave beyond the stated time, depending on the need.

Outcomes of Work–Family Culture

Employees' perception of a supportive work family culture or climate has been associated with important work outcomes and employee attitudes. Sasken, a leading provider of telecommunications software services and solutions to network equipment manufacturers, offers a number of family-friendly practices to its employees. Sasken's efforts in this area demonstrate that an environment of belonging and trust go a long way in not only retaining employees but also unleashing their full technological potential and excellence. The company screened all the World Cup matches for the employees at its auditorium, thus creating a fun element within the organization. The company has a firm belief that 'sports are a great way of getting together', which will ultimately foster team feeling and further organizational interests.

The organizational culture has also been found to be related to employee health and well being and organizational productivity through its relationship

---

Exhibit 11.4

Special Case of Knowledge Workers

In the contemporary environment characterized by transition to knowledge economy and the 'new' workforce, the knowledge worker's discussions about family friendly or flexible working practices have become less relevant. The very notion of work–family or work–life boundaries have been challenged since knowledge workers have highly permeable work–life boundaries, as technology enables them to work round the clock. Knowledge workers are most likely to have access to formal or informal support programmes, flexibility, and support.

They have control over their own working hours and can be flexible to fit in family or personal demands. Yet, paradoxically, they are the most likely to be under pressure to work long hours. These longer working hours are then constructed as a choice and pressure is intensified.

The reason that increased autonomy and flexibility fails to empower many knowledge workers to manage work–life boundaries is because family friendly policies help those such as factory workers, who have rigid working hours, where control of hours at the workplace is by the clock rather than the nature or amount of work done.

For knowledge workers, on the other hand, the temporal boundaries between work and non-work are controlled instead by organizational culture. Subtle pressures, such as expectations of high commitment and involvement, lead workers to put in long hours or taking work home. As the nature of the work performed by this new workforce is more open-ended, creative, and more complex, the boundaries between work and non-work time has become increasingly blurred.

---

with work–family conflict, turnover intentions, stress, absenteeism, and organizational commitment. Exhibit 11.4 discusses the relevance of work–family or work–life boundaries with respect to knowledge workers.

The majority of research on work–family culture has focussed on the positive or negative impact it has on employees, thereby, making a strong business case for work–life supportive organizations. However, it is important to acknowledge other reasons, largely societal and legal in nature that exists for the presence of work–family practices in organizations.

HRD APPROACHES TO WORK–LIFE INTEGRATION

The primary purpose of organizations is business. Hence, there may be a fundamental conflict between the efficiency and productivity oriented values of an organization on one hand and the work–life needs of employees, on the other. Since organizations have to jointly manage these competing values, employees may often receive mixed-messages related to work–life balance. Kossek and Block (2000) proposed two perspectives of HRD that may be adopted by organizations for managing these competing values (Figure 11.8).

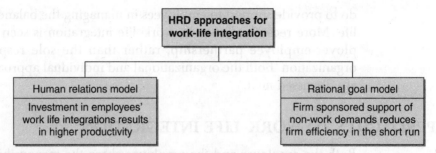

Figure 11.8:   HRD Perspectives on Work–Life Integration

Perspectives of HRD

Long-term View or the Human Relations Model

This view sees investment in employees' work–life integration needs as a means for promoting productivity through caring about workers. This perspective assumes that when employees are provided with support in dealing with personal needs, organizational productivity will be maximized in the long run due to higher employee morale and commitment.

Short-term View or Rational Goal Model

The major concern here shifts to quarterly maximization of output and shorter timeliness. According to this perspective, employee needs for firm sponsored support of non-work demands may negatively influence firm efficiency over the short run. For example, if an employee takes leave of absence to complete some personal work, efficiency is hurt over the short run since the employee is not productive during the leave period.

Organizations must learn to simultaneously manage these competing values if they have to be effective. Organizational need for efficiency and profits must be managed concurrently with employee needs for organizational support to personal off-the-job demands. Failing to jointly implement both imperatives may lead to greater organizational efficiency and effectiveness in the short run. But in the long run, the organization may suffer due to the presence of burnout, stress, and an unhappy work force. For instance, an organization may not offer additional leave to employees to take care of some of their non-work demands, such as leave for preparing for higher education, marriage, or caring for an elderly relative. Though in the short run, the organization may ensure work performance leading to organizational benefits, but in the long run, the strains of conflicting time and role demands may stress out the employee. This may ultimately have an adverse effect on organizational productivity.

As debate surrounding the importance of facilitating work–life integration has gained intensity, emphasis has largely been on what the organizations can do to provide support to employees in managing the balance between work–life. More recently, however, work–life integration is seen as involving employer-employee partnership, rather than the sole responsibility of the organization. Both the organizational and individual approaches to work–life are discussed next.

APPROACHES TO WORK–LIFE INTEGRATION

Both the employer and the employee share the responsibility for work–life balance integration.

Organizational Approaches

In selecting the approaches towards work–life integration, organizations must consider the extent of corporate involvement in employees' personal lives. This approach must fit with the organizational mission, culture, values, company's way of doing business, and the needs of the workforce. As described by Kossek and Block, three organizational approaches to work–life balancing are possible (see Figure 11.9).

Social Arbiter Approach

Firms that reflect this philosophy emphasize a separation between work and family. According to this approach, the employer should get involved only if the employees request help or if the organization feels that non-work issues are getting in the way of performance. Hence, this approach is reactive. The organization does not get involved in the non-work lives of their employees

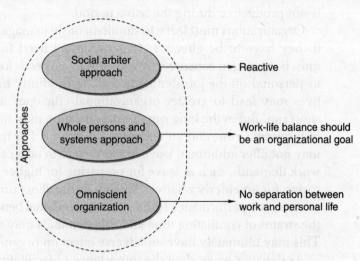

Figure 11.9: Organizational Approaches to Work–Life Integration

until there is a performance problem. Providing concierge services, on-site crèche, or ATM services are examples of this approach.

Whole Persons and Systems Approach

According to this approach, work–life balance should be an organizational goal. The organizations should view employees as internal customers and demonstrate more sensitivity to their needs. This perspective reflects the human relations approach to management and promotes 'whole systems' and 'whole persons' approach to employment. By implementing holistic work–life programmes, organizations will have employees who will be more loyal and committed. The range of family friendly practices at Sasken, Hewlett-Packard, Hughes Software Systems, American Express, Reliance, LG, Tata Steel, NIIT, Infosys, Eicher and so many other organizations are based on belief that an environment of belonging and trust goes a long way in retaining employees and maximizing their full potential.

Omniscient Organization

In this approach, the organization attempts to make workplace a home to employees. Hence, there is virtually no separation between work and personal life. Therefore, recognizing that people spend most of their waking hours in office, Infosys, provides dormitories for employees who may want to sleep over and a gymnasium for breaks during the day. With workplace developments such as telecommuting and flexible workplace options, there is a blurring of boundaries between the work and personal domains. Employees working from home may have greater flexibility, as discussed earlier. However, they often face the dilemma of defining what a work–day is. The omniscient approach places the onus of separating the two domains on the employer. However, the omniscient organization faces HR issues such as how to measure performance appraisal when the boss rarely sees the telecommuter face-to-face and what constitutes absenteeism for a telecommuter.

Each of these approaches has its pros and cons. There is no one best way to manage the increasing work and family demands of employees. Organizations and their employees must enter into a dialogue over the fundamental conflict that exists and what appears to be the best approach for meeting organizational and individual needs.

Contemporary thinking on work–life balance largely advocates that it is the responsibility of the firm to design formal HR programmes to facilitate employees in meeting work and family demands. However, for true work–life balance to occur, employees need to be responsible for bringing about a balance between work and other parts of their life.

Individual/Employee Approaches

Facilitating work–life integration is not the sole responsibility of the firm. Rather, the main responsibility for managing a career, reducing negative spillover, and achieving a good work–life balance lies with the individual employee. Consciously or unconsciously, most employees let their work–life spill over into their personal life to the extent of overpowering the latter by working late hours or by getting official work home. When managers say that 'I have no time for myself or family', they have often chosen it to be like this. This is because they feel more valued and want to receive more recognition at work than they do for being a good parent or elder care giver. Employees need to self-reflect on their own value for managing the integration of work and personal life.

Employees may use several mechanisms to cope with rising family and personal demands they face off the job. *One* coping mechanism is to psychologically minimize the attention that the families actually need. They may, for instance, start believing that children have grown up and are independent and therefore, do not need so much of the parents' time. A *second* coping mechanism is to rely on paid help for meeting many of the off-work demands. A *third* mechanism is when employees dream that someday they will take the time to have a rich and rewarding family life. Hence they may resolve the current conflicting demands by giving more attention to work issues.

Organizations with a long term strategic view of work–life balance provide employees with training to help them address personal issues that prevent them from achieving this balance. However, even if the organization puts work–life programmes in place and also trains employees to address their skills in work–life balancing, long term work–life balance may still remain elusive.

True work–life balance can be achieved only when both organizational approaches as well as employee approaches are complementary. The paternalistic view in which the organization 'takes care of' employees and their families is no longer acceptable. Contemporary thinking places greater emphasis on employee empowerment and employer-employee partnership for facilitating work and personal life effectiveness.

Work–life balance programmes offered by an organization may therefore, be best represented as a ladder. The individual employee and the organization are the two legs of the ladder. It is only when both the legs are in place that company initiatives transform into a complete ongoing corporate work–life strategy. When both the company and the employee accept their responsibility in supporting the work–life ladder, employees respond by improved performance through increased commitment. For a long term positive outcome from work–life programmes, however, it is important that the culture of the organization is supportive of such programmes.

DEVELOPMENT OF WORK–LIFE INITIATIVES

We have seen that balancing work demands with life demands is a shared responsibility between the employer and employee. It is the employer, however, who must design and implement formal work–life balance programmes in the organization. The organization should also encourage employees to utilize these programmes by providing supportive culture.

Formal adoption of work–life initiatives by organizations progresses through a sequence of stages. According to the Families and Work Institute Model, there are three basic stages associated with the development of family friendly initiatives (Figure 11.10).

In *stage one* the organization adopts separate initiatives in a piecemeal manner that does not challenge existing work norms about the primacy of the work role over the family role. Policies are mainly viewed as benefits for the employees. This stage is that of 'developing a programmatic response'. When an organization ties up with a bank to set up an ATM facility in its premises or providing concierge services to employees is an example of stage one.

In *stage two*, the firm develops an integrated approach and establishes a number of work family programmes in place. The top management begins to champion these programmes. When Vijay Thadani at NIIT redesignated himself the CFO, he was exemplifying top management commitment to making the company a great place to work in where employees have 366 days of fun. The work–life programmes are seen as comprising the core of HRM policy. Hence, all HRM practices are evaluated for their impact on work–family issues. Company productivity and bottom-line impact of work–life practices are beginning to be measured.

When the organization reaches the *third stage* of changing the culture, it believes that by having a culture supportive of employees' work–family needs, the firm will be able to attract high performers. Work–family practices are integrated with other HRM practices of the organization. Company mission statements may be changed to reflect values supporting personal employee needs. Performance evaluations of managers may also reflect how well work–family needs of subordinates were handled. For example, when the vision

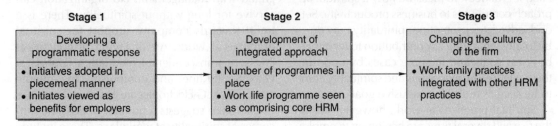

Figure 11.10:   Stages in Development of Family-Friendly Initiatives in Organizations

statement of a company says that the goal of the organization is to become 'employer of choice', the firm has moved towards the third stage.

Exhibit 11.5 discusses the issue of 'quality of life', which emphasizes the need for a holistic approach to work–life integration.

Exhibit 11.5

Holistic Approach to Work–Life Integration: Quality of Life

Workplace stress and pressures confronted by an employee due to conflicting role demands and their desire to lead a fulfilling life have brought to the fore the issue of 'quality of life'. Feelings of alienation and striving for meaning of life have also created a desire for the search of larger purpose of life among employees. Employees are no longer content with a challenging job, fast promotions, material attainments, and social status. There is a yearning for a more holistic approach to life. While spirituality is a personal journey for most individuals, there is a growing acceptance of accommodating spirituality at workplace. Feelings of 'wholeness' and 'being complete' are integral to spiritual growth as well as to the concept of work–life integration.

Traditionally, businesses have focused on productivity, market share, earnings, and profits. Spiritual approaches to business are viewed as expressing non-material values such as meaningfulness, job satisfaction, creativity, dignity, and empowerment to name a few. To the extent that these values have inspired business practices, business may be seen as having become progressively spiritual. Talk about spirituality at workplace, however, creates atleast two problems. First, it is difficult to measure how a spiritual approach contributes to business productivity. Second, advocates promoting spirituality may do so by totally separating its contribution to legitimate business goals and in some cases by opposing them. Hence, business goals and spirituality come to be seen as mutually exclusive goals.

Spiritual practices at work, however, are on the rise and several firms are beginning to employ spiritual practices. *Business Week*, in 1995, detailed spirituality as a management tool that could potentially impact the bottom-line. It cited spiritual practices at firms such as AT&T, Boeing, and Lotus Development. AT&T hired a values coach to help its leaders define their personal values more clearly. Boeing had managers listen to poet David White thrice a month for a year to help them think differently about their company and their lives. Closer home, NTPC conducts morning yoga and meditation sessions for its employees and Samtel required all of its managers and executives to go through the sensitivity training programme.

Does spirituality help a company become more profitable? Spirituality is not separate from business, but one of its components. They are like a computer's hardware and software—both are important. The material dimension of business includes products, assets, cash flow, market share, profits, etc. The spiritual dimension involves ones relationship to these material factors—one's openness and responsiveness to them and whether one uses them appropriately to achieve business goals. Taking this perspective, it becomes easier to see how spirituality is integrated with management. No organization can survive for long without spirituality. There is a trend towards company support for spiritual practices at work. Art of Living discourses at Ericsson, transcendental meditation courses at GlaxoSmithKline, and compulsory five-minute exercises at LG Electronics are just a few examples.

Literature suggests a number of possible outcomes of spirituality at workplace. These include

Contd

Exhibit 11.5 Contd

greater motivation, self-fulfillment, a caring and humanistic organizational culture, better teamwork, creativity, deep personal fulfillment, honest communication, and increased ethical behaviour. Though specific outcomes of spirituality at work have not been quantitatively demonstrated, it can be predicted that higher spirituality makes employees happier, more balanced, and compassionate. These may then affect the variables listed above through reduced stress and better decision making.

The fear is that adopting the spiritual route may turn out to be a management fad as several others before it. However, even a fad is useful if it helps to advance the bottom-line results. Spirituality in the workplace seems to be a good fit for the future of organizations looking for high involvement strategies. In a high-tech economy, technology keeps changing everyday and people are the cutting edge assets of organizations. Spirituality may not provide all the answers but it is definitely an avenue for exploration.

Adapted from: Phillips 2000; Schourberg 2001

In moving from stage one of adoption of work–life initiatives, that is, simple programmes to the third stage of organizational culture change, it is essential that work–life programmes are linked to an organization's strategy, so that work–life balance is considered essential to business success.

STRATEGIC APPROACH TO WORK–LIFE INTEGRATION

As seen earlier in the chapter, firms today are moving from single-issue programmes and policies to meet the needs of employees with young children towards a more strategic and comprehensive approach. Moreover, work–life practices should also be linked to various individual employee attitude and organizational outcomes.

Two aspects important to adopting a strategic approach to work–life integration practices are discussed below. These are:

- linkage of work–life integration practices with strategic HRM
- culture change supportive of work–life integration practices

Linkage of Work–Life Integration Practices with Strategic HRM

Strategic HRM literature suggests that HRM is a means for achieving competitive advantage for an organization. How the employees are managed and their resultant attitudes influence their commitment to the organization. This ultimately determines their performance and hence that of the organization.

Consistent with this perspective, the relationship of a variety of human resource practices with firm performance measures, such as earnings per share, firm profits, productivity, etc., has been studied by researchers such as Delaney and Huselid (1996), Macduffie (1995), and Arthur (1994). Though individual

HR practices that are included as part of strategic HRM by different researchers vary to some extent, work–family practices have been noticeably excluded by all. Work–life practices are referred to in literature as 'progressive' or 'innovative' but they have been rarely considered as 'strategic'. There has been very little research investigating their linkage with organizational or business level benefits.

Most management studies still do not view employer responsiveness to personal needs as an integral part of HR strategy or the design of high-performance work systems. Rather, work–life practices are seen as benefits provided by the organization to employees and with no tangible benefits for the organization. Yet, as we have seen earlier in the chapter, bundles of inter-related work–family practices may be an HR approach related to competitive advantage resulting from financial cost savings, higher productivity, reduced absenteeism, and increased employee commitment, among others.

The resource-based view of the firm suggests that an internal organizational resource can provide sustained competitive advantage when the strategic advantage is not easily imitated. A firm may imitate a work–life practice of another firm, such as, tying up with a hospital to provide free check-ups and on-site health camps. However, what cannot be imitated is the employee's sense of belonging and the broader corporate philosophy of the organization. The likelihood of imitation of work–family bundles is reduced because of non-economic barriers that are likely to interfere with their adoption, even if they have firm level benefits. Non-economic barriers to the adoption of work–family bundles include the management's belief system and attitudes about managing employees.

Adoption of work–life practices also requires the management to demonstrate high levels of trust and at the same time to relinquish control. In adopting these practices management may be shaky about employing workers who are currently on 'family track' and therefore may have less stable employment patterns and thus less organizational commitment. Hence, it requires an organization to make major changes to move from a situation of 'no work–family policies' to providing a comprehensive work–family bundle.

The adoption and imitation of comprehensive set of work–family policies is not likely to be easy. It is this lack of imitation that provides the firm with a competitive advantage. The famous family friendly practices of NIIT, such as, birthday allowance, dating allowance, granny day, marriage anniversary allowance, etc. or that of Infosys that provides on-site gym facilities are not easily imitable. Though the practice per se may be replicated by other firms, what cannot be replicated is management attitude, beliefs, and trust communicated to the employees.

Most research focusing on work–life policies has been largely programmatic, that is, it studies the firm-level effects of single work–family policies in isolation and lacks integration to HR policy relationships. Strategic HR has proposed a 'bundle' approach, rather than focusing on single HR practices. The idea of bundles in strategic HRM reflects the belief that groups of HR practices have congruence and when adopted as bundles, send a coherent HRM message to employees. The bundle approach focuses on the extent to which different HR practices are related and interactive in a way that suggests an organization level approach or philosophy. In accordance with the bundles approach, a work–family bundle can be defined as a group of complementary highly related and, in some cases, overlapping human resource policies that may help employees manage non-work roles.

Dependent care services, flexible scheduling programmes (including family leave), information and referral services, concierge services, educational assistance, and sabbaticals, etc are the types of individual work–family practices that may be part of a work–family bundle.

The bundle approach is less focused on specific practices and more focused on the relationship and interaction between several practices to suggest an organizational level approach. As a result, an HR bundle is more appropriate for investigating firm-level effects than the individual practices. However, neither researchers nor managers have tried to link work–life practices with bundles of other HR practices, such as performance appraisal, training, selection, career development, etc.

If work–life balance practices are adopted as part of a package (bundle) of other HR practices that invest in attracting and retaining the high performers, then employees will not only feel valued, they will also be motivated to stay with the employer for a longer duration. This results in benefits for the employer because the top talent is less likely to leave. By permitting its women employees to telecommute if they do not want to return immediately to work on completion of maternity leave, NIIT ensures that it retains its high performers. When, in addition, the firm ensures that such an employee's upward mobility is not compromised due to her opting for telecommuting, it is a good example of integrating work–life practices with other HR practices. Similar outcomes accrue to HLL which not only allocates houses nearer the office to women employees with children, but in some cases, also gives them the option to work from home. Ericsson arranged a leadership training programme in the Kumaon hills and ensured that not only do employees enhance their skills but, at the same time, can also unwind from the daily work routine. The organization also arranged a talk by Chinmaya Mission on the 'Art of Living and Motivation' for its employees thus bringing together personal development programme and work–life integration. Polaris Software builds camaraderie among employees and breaks down hierarchy through its monthly 'Bonzertm' programme, where, among other things, seniors and juniors alike dunk their heads into tubs full of water trying to grab floating apples with their teeth, with hands tied behind their back. The company philosophy is that 'happy people work better together'.

There is increasing evidence that suggests that family issues and personal life have critical implications for the workplace, in terms of business benefits discussed earlier. However, relatively little attention has been directed to demonstrating firm level linkage of work–life practices. This is partly because *how* work–family bundles add value to the firm is not very clear. This is true of other HR practices too since demonstrating a direct relationship between HR practices and organizational performance is difficult.

Thus, an organization may provide time-off to employees from work to study further and also reimburse their tuition allowance as part of their work–life balance initiative. However, it is difficult for the firm to demonstrate a simple direct relationship between the work–life practice and employee productivity or organizational performance. Intervening variables, such as enhanced employee skills and commitment are more likely to be the direct result of such a programme.

When organizations offer bundles of work–family policies, they communicate signals to the current as well as potential employees that lead them to draw conclusions about the values and philosophies of an organization. Since work–family programmes offer relief for non-work concerns, employees may feel that they are receiving special treatment. Work–family policies are perceived as symbolic of organizational concern for employee well being and as representing the value system of the firm resulting in intangible benefits to organizations. In the work context, employees are likely to reciprocate by contributing extra effort, developing a concern for the overall success of the organization, and by embracing its goals These intervening outcomes then lead to firm-level outcomes. Consequently, enhanced organizational performance is likely to emerge.

According to traditional organizational behaviour theories, work–family benefits should not affect the performance of employees. According to the two-factor theory of motivation by Herzberg (1968), benefits are not likely to promote job performance since they are extrinsic job characteristics. Developments in *Social Exchange Theory*, on the other hand, support the possibility that workers may feel obligated to exert extra effort in return for additional benefits in the form of work–family benefits. This is the norm of reciprocity. Although the norm of reciprocity is universal, it is not unconditional, however, according to more recent researchers on social exchange theory.

An action on the part of one party may elicit different obligations depending on the extent to which the individual targeted by the action values it. Thus, the same work–family benefits may be differently valued by different employees, subsequently incurring different obligations to the organization. While one employee may feel obligated by the organization's policy of compulsory health check-up for its employees at company cost, another employee may view it as a right. The more useful the additional benefits are perceived to be by the employees, the more they are likely to want to give something extra back to the organization.

Culture Change Supportive of Work–Life Integration Practices

Progressive organizations are now recognizing the need to move beyond implementing work family policies towards achieving more fundamental culture change, with work–life balance as a strategic business issue. Companies such as Infosys, PricewaterhouseCoopers, NIIT, American Express, HSS, Hewlett Packard, and Eicher Goodearth Ltd fall in this class of organizations. Work place norms and culture, as pointed out earlier can have major consequences for employees, their families, and employers. Therefore, organizations now look at the employees as individuals and family people too.

For an organization to be supportive of work–life integration and to achieve strategic linkage, it should recognize the role of *workplace culture* in creating pressure and a commitment to achieving culture change in the desired direction. For any culture change to take place top management support is crucial. Top management must embrace and communicate a vision that supports work–life balance through company's mission statement, intranet, e-mail, and newsletters. Intranet may be used to remind an employee about his health check-up date or to communicate various family friendly practices of the firm. Further, top and middle level managers must model new behaviour such as take leaving on their child's birthday in the middle of the week there by communicating that some family events have priority over work. Companies may also set up task forces and committees to help resolve work–life issues. It may also be of advantage to provide managers with the training that is needed to create a supportive culture. Training is needed to ensure that employees are aware of how to make these programmes useful and to communicate that supervisors support their implementation. Organizations must also educate managers on the value of workplace flexibility and its compatibility with superior business results. Managers may also be held accountable for a family-friendly culture in their performance reviews, by instituting rewards for managers for being supportive of their subordinates' efforts to combine work and family. For instance, if a manager's subordinate does not avail his/her entire quota of stipulated leave, then the manager's score on performance appraisal may reflect this. A step in this direction has been taken by American Express, as mentioned earlier in the chapter. The company strictly discourages sitting late in office and working on weekends. This initiative is led by the leadership who 'walk the talk'. Managers in American Express have to ensure that employees avail their leave entitlements for the year. At the heart of work–life approaches is a respect for employee's choices. The focus of work–life initiatives should be on the entire workforce, rather than specific groups of employees.

Organizations must recognize the importance of a supportive workplace culture for effective implementation of innovative work–life policies. Cultural change is more about changing practice rather than policy and the deeper assumptions, beliefs, and values underlying these practices. It also involves strategic initiatives to examine all organizational systems, not just HR systems.

Ford foundation studies (Bailyn et al. 1996) researched the culture change approach in a number of organizations, including Xerox. Work–life concerns of the workforce in these organizations were reframed as organizational issues. For example, if long working hours made it difficult for workers to

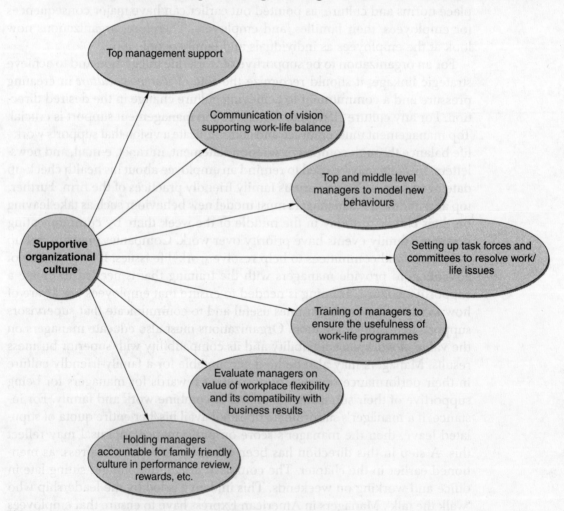

Figure 11.11:   Key Characteristics for Achieving Organization Culture Supportive of Work–Life Integration

manage their family demands, then these workers with family demands were not regarded as the problem. Rather, the organizational system which created the problems was focused upon. The researchers engaged the work teams to examine ways in which work could be redesigned so that the needs of both the worker and the business could be met. Though the process involved having to surface and deal with resistance among managers, all the solutions that emerged from the process had demonstrable bottom-line benefits. While the process is generalizable to different contexts, the solution is not.

Action research does not provide generalizable solutions. Specific interventions that lead to culture change are workplace specific. Important details about the *process of change* may be generalized. The main process to emerge from Ford Foundation studies (Bailyn et al. 1996) suggests the importance of the following main themes of the change process:

1. framing work–life as a strategic business issue,
2. communicating the business case of work–life policies throughout the organization,
3. confronting resistance in managers and challenging assumptions,
4. involving and consulting with all employees,
5. supporting managers,
6. addressing all systems, not just HR policies,
7. development of a full range of measurable outcomes, and
8. continual cycle of implementation, measurement, evaluation, feedback, identifying barriers, seeking new solutions, and sustaining momentum.

Work–life balance can be integrated with company philosophy and mission statement. For example, Benesse, an educational publishing company in Japan, states that its company philosophy is 'to provide support for people at all life stages'. It is also important to ensure that employees recognize the link between the various work–life initiatives the organizations adopts and the improvements in benefits that accrue to everyone in the firm. These initiatives make the organization an 'attractive employer' ensuring that the company attracts high-quality employees, which ultimately boosts the profitability of the organization. Therefore, organization-wide communication of business benefits is important. It is also important to pay attention to developing a higher level of acceptance about work–life conflicts. Often, employees do not utilize work–life initiatives because they do not want to let others know that they have problems outside work. Resistance to work–life practices should be confronted. For example, resistance to the use of flexi-time may be managed by helping employees understand that flexi-time helps them to make time up rather than lose pay for absence. Top management can also help in dealing with resistance by serving as role models, that is, if they utilize flexi-time, other employees will be encouraged to do so. The implementation of any new work–life (or any HR) practices should follow an employee involvement exercise. When employees' views are sought on the design and implementation of practices, they acknowledge these and also facilitate the introduction and implementation of the change process. The implementation of work–life initiatives should not be isolated from other HR practices. There should be integration between all the HR practices of the firm and the evaluation criteria. Factors such as, turnover, absenteeism, performance appraisals, etc. should be measured in order to evaluate the success of these initiatives. These criteria should be continuously monitored and the report shared with management. This process reflects that employers and employees are 'in partnership' together to manage work and family responsibilities in a way that leads to productive work places and a dynamic society.

Summary

Conflicting demands and pressures from work and life (family) can interfere with each other since the two domains are complementary, not conflicting priorities. Acceptance of this reality by the organizations and new business and societal trends, have seen the growth of family-friendly practices at workplace. Adopting a win-win approach, growing number of organizations believe that helping employees balance and integrate their work lives with the rest of their lives leads to positive outcomes for both the employee and the employer. Work–family practices should be viewed as part of overall HR and business strategy that is related to a firm's competitive advantage.

This chapter discussed work–family conflict, balance, and work–life integration. Three types of work–family conflicts were identified: time based, strain-based, and behaviour based. The chapter discussed the importance of balancing the conflicting work and life demands. It further highlighted the importance of not only achieving a balance but 'integrating' the work and life spheres. Formal work–life initiatives were identified under four categories of employer support, viz, time and place flexibility, information, financial, and direct. The importance of a supportive culture in developing a family-friendly workplace was also discussed. A family-friendly workplace facilitates the implementation of work–life initiatives. However, the culture of the organization plays an important role in the utilization of work–life programmes. Human resource development approaches for work–life integration were discussed. The chapter ends with a detailed discussion about adopting a strategic approach to work–life integration.

Keywords

Work–Life Issues refer to those aspects of an individual's work or family life that may have an influence on one another.

Work–Family Conflict is a form of inter-role conflict in which the role pressures from the two domains, that is, work and family, are mutually non-compatible so that meeting demands in one domain makes it difficult to meet demands in the other.

Work–Life Balance Individuals having a measure of control over when, where and how they work. It is achieved when an individual's right to a fulfilled life inside and outside paid work is accepted and respected as the norm, to the mutual benefit of the individual, business, and society.

Work–Life Integration involves integration between two or more roles/domains. When two or more roles, for example, that of an employee and mother, are both flexible and permeable, then they are said to be integrated leading to work–family (life) integration.

Work–Life Initiatives are programmes designed to alleviate individual conflict between work and family to help employees achieve a better work–life balance. These may range from informal to formal programmes.

Family-Friendly Workplace refers to a place of work that, to some extent, acknowledges and responds to the work and personal or family responsibilities assumed by employees such that employees can simultaneously fulfill work and family responsibilities.

Work–Life (Family) Culture is a set of shared assumptions, beliefs, values, and global perceptions held by employees regarding the extent to which an organization supports and values the integration of employees' work and family lives. Similar to organization culture and climate, work–family culture focuses on employees' perceptions of the informal, intangible aspects of work–family culture.

Organizational Approaches to Work–Life Integration are measures or initiatives that are taken by the organization towards work–life integration to support employees in meeting their competing demands from work and family.

Individual Approaches to Work–Life Integration refers to mechanisms that employees use to cope with rising family and personal demands they face off the job. For example, psychologically minimizing the attention that the families actually need.

Work–Family Bundle consists of a group of complementary highly related and, in some cases, overlapping human resource policies that may help employees manage non-work roles.

Concept Review Questions

1. Define and compare the terms work–family conflict, work–family balance, and work–life integration. Do you think work and family are two compartmentalized spheres?

2. Why is it important to link work–life initiatives with the overall HR and business strategy of the firm? How do work–life initiatives benefit the organization as well as the individual employee? Give examples.

3. Discuss the main types of formal work–life initiatives that organizations can provide to their employees. Describe work–life initiatives of some organizations that you are familiar with.

4. Describe the different possible organizational and individual approaches to work–life integration.

5. What is a family-friendly workplace?

6. Identify the dimensions of a supportive work–family culture. Discuss how workplace culture may undermine the utilization of formal family-friendly policies.

7. Discuss the major aspects that are important for adopting a strategic approach to work–life integration.

Critical Thinking Questions

1. Read the section on stages in the development of work–life initiatives. Do you think all firms should strive to be stage three companies as described in the model? Explain your rationale and give examples of firms you know of that are at each of these three stages of development of work–life programmes.

2. Read the case given below and discuss the issues raised[1].

   Rita is a 45 year old married women with two kids aged 12 and 16. Her husband works full-time as a high powered lawyer in Delhi city. Rita has always given up career growth

[1] *Adapted from*: Schutte, K. '*The Usability of Work/Life Policies and Programs*', University of Saint Mary, Kansas City, Kansas.

to help her family have a more balanced life and to be there for her kids. Rita works for Encore Limited as a sales representative. Encore is widely known for their long hours and unwillingness to work with employees on issues of work–life balance. Rita's daughter is scheduled to undergo surgery on her knee and will need a few weeks of rehabilitation. Rita and her husband are debating who will take time off to be with their daughter.

- What type(s) of work–family conflict is Rita confronted with?

- What factors (related to herself, her family, and her work group) will impact Rita's decision for taking time off?

- How will she determine if the company policies that allow for flexible hours or part-time positions are 'usable'?

3. Do you know any individual who is confronting severe work–life (family) conflict? Which of the three types of conflicts is he/she facing at work? Assuming the organization is not family-friendly, what strategies will you suggest the individual should adopt to bringing about a balance in the two domains?

4. Give examples of various work–life conflicts that students like you are likely to face. For example, conflicts between the demands of the course you are pursuing, your leisure time activities, or family expectations. How do you attempt to ensure work–life integration?

Simulation and Role Play

1. Axis Entertainment is a small size firm in the entertainment business. There are 150 employees in the organization out of which, only 30 are women. Of these 30 women, only six are single. The firm does not have formal work–life initiatives beyond what is stipulated by law, such as maternity leave, etc. Shalini is an employee with elder care responsibilities. In recent times, she has had to devote a lot of time and energy towards her responsibilities caring for her parents. As a result she has taken excess leave of absence from the company. This has now reflected poorly in her performance appraisal. Her immediate boss, Mr Sharma, has called her for her performance discussion.

   Two students should volunteer for this role play. One student will assume the role of Mr Sharma and the other student will assume the role of Shalini. Shalini should convince

Mr Sharma of the necessity of her taking leave. She should also convince Mr Sharma that the firm should adopt flexible work scheduling and a more liberal leave policy. After initial resistance, Mr Sharma is able to empathize with her situation. The role play should end with a draft preparation of a formal work–life initiative proposal to be placed before HR department for approval.

2. Assume you are the Vice President (HRD) of a firm that has some family-friendly practices. However, you find that the employees are reluctant to utilize work–life benefits. In consultation with the General Manager (HRD):

   - Identify the reasons for non-utilization of work–life benefits by the employees.

   - Suggest a strategy for making the culture of the firm family-friendly for the employees that supports utilization of the benefits.

Classroom Projects [1]

1. The purpose of this activity is to discuss the linkages between work and family. The class

may divide into three groups. Two groups (group A and B) each having about eight to

---

[1] Some of the classroom and field projects have been adapted from Sloan Work and Family Research Network, Boston College website http://www.bc.edu/bc_org/avp/wfnetwork/rft/classact/actorg.html, accessed on 15 February 2004.

ten members, defend one of the following statements in a ten minute presentation to the class:

Group A: An individual's work and family lives are more likely to *interfere* with one another than strengthen one another.

Group B: An individual's work and family lives are more likely to *strengthen* one another than interfere with one another.

Group C: This group serves as the judges for the debate.

Groups A and B may take 30 minutes to prepare their ten minute presentation. Group C is given 30 minutes to establish the *criteria* it will use to judge the debate. Group A makes its presentation followed immediately by Group B. Group C announces the 'winner' and explains the basis for its judgement. The instructor should facilitate a discussion on when work and family interfere with one another and when they strengthen each other.

2. Ask volunteer groups of two or three members each to debate for and against the topic, 'work and family- the twain shall never meet'. Each group may take about 15 minutes to present their arguments. An open discussion with the class follows highlighting the pros and cons of integrating the two domains.

3. Form groups of five to six members and discuss the productivity related implications of offering work–life programmes (for example, on retention, absenteeism, productivity, commitment, etc.). Can you think of any productivity-related costs of not offering work–life programmes? Report your discussion to the class.

Field Projects

1. Obtain brochures from several companies representing different sectors (e.g. insurance, medical, software, manufacturing, etc.). Examine these brochures and identify the companies that have some form of family-friendly programmes. In groups of four members personally visit at least two of these organizations to study and compare their work–life balance practices. Conduct interviews with HR managers and some other employees of the firms to obtain the following information:

   - Description and listing of the firms' work–life programmes
   - The reasons for adoption of the work–life programmes
   - How well these programmes are being utilized in each of these firms
   - Did you notice a gap between the design of work–life programmes in these organizations, their actual implementation, and utilization?
   - Are the employees satisfied with organizational support for their personal needs?

   Prepare a report for class presentation.

2. Interview two managers to assess the stage of development of work–life initiatives that their organization has reached.

3. Contact one male and one female employee working in the same organization. Interview them about their work–life issues and what support the organization provides to them for balancing their work life and family life? On the basis of their responses, can you say that work–life programmes have a gender bias in favour of female employees? Or do you think that practices of the firm place women employees at a disadvantage, that is, they are not gender sensitive?

Case Study

Narmada Bank International[1]

The origins of Narmada Bank International (NBI) can be traced back to early twentieth century, when it was set up as a private bank by two partners. Over the years, NBI expanded through a series of mergers. By 1970, NBI had made some twenty takeovers and had also expanded overseas. By the early 1990s, NBI had offices in 30 countries.

The organization's interest in work–life balance dates back to the late 1980s when the organization noticed that it was losing disproportionate numbers of senior women employees. Research revealed a number of reasons for the trend but the overriding issue was their lack of control and flexibility in how and when to do their work. When these findings were shared company-wide, Anita Puri, head of benefits division of HR, was amazed to receive a more powerful response from senior men in the firm. She explained that it was as if men were saying that, 'we also have the same sort of issues but we don't feel we can raise them as legitimate issues because we are men and it won't do our careers any good.'

Being a major retail bank, the employees of NBI have played a vital role in its success. From the mid 1990s, NBI conducted research and feasibility studies with the help of experts in the work–life balance area. One of the key findings showed that for both men and women, finding the right balance between work and home was the most critical factor in deciding whether or not to move to a different organization. Since competition in the banking sector has increased manifold, if employers want to attract and retain their staff, they have to offer something extra to be attractive. Work–life balance policies can often be that extra policy detail that appeals to staff looking to strike more of a balance in their lives. Top management at NBI realized that to be an employer of choice, NBI needed to be progressive, and so the bank introduced a formal flexible working scheme, *Work Options*, in early 1999. *Work Options* is one of the policies aimed at creating a better work–life balance for employees. Other schemes on offer cover career breaks, job sharing, leave (encompassing compassionate, emergency and parental), and many other areas.

Nobel David is the head of a team of 12 people, split between two locations—Mumbai and Delhi. Together, they make up the bank's group manpower planning and information team. Every month they have to work around the bank's reporting cycles and working to time scales that are very tight. These time scales can not be moved because the clients in the organization rely on them.

A lot of the work for David's team comes in at a moment's notice and can involve senior members of the team dropping everything to work on it. For instance, if Pratyush Verma, the group HR Business Director, is meeting the bank's chief executive and he needs something urgently, David's team just does not have the luxury to postpone it.

The team has the responsibility to meet the information needs of the company's HR function. It can tell how many employees are on sick leave, how many are leaving, how many are joining, how many are going through disciplinary and grievance procedures, and how many are coming up to 25 years service. In 2004, the team gave monthly updates to around 50 business units or customers. However, an imminent restructuring will see this figure rise to nearer 300.

Nobel David maintains that in his team, the effort is to create a work environment where there is cooperation and everyone looks out for each other to get the work done because the pressures are very demanding. This tough world of numbers, facts, and figures seems to be an unlikely

[1] Adapted from CIPD, the online magazine of the Chartered Institute of Personnel and Development, http://www.peoplemanagement.co.uk, accessed on 15 February 2004.

environment for the 'soft' concept of work–life balance to thrive in. Yet, David's team has been successful in warding off any negative consequences such work pressure might have had.

When the bank introduced *Work Options*, some members of David's team had expressed an interest in joining. In particular, they wanted to take advantage of the option to work a compressed week. Initially, David wasn't convinced by its business sense. He was concerned that the morale of team members would be hit if members who weren't working on a flexi-time basis found themselves covering for colleagues who were. However, having seen colleagues in other departments opt for the scheme, David decided to take a closer look at how it might benefit his own staff. He came up with a team approach that would allow everyone to work a compressed fortnight, that is, nine days out of every ten. The time off would be scheduled for the days when the team wasn't working at its peak.

David took the proposal to the members of his team. He went well-prepared by arming himself with a ten page question and answer booklet that he hoped would anticipate everything the team members might ask him. The booklet proved to be a master move. With most of their questions answered quickly, his team was happy to support the idea mooted by David of a compressed fortnight. He had designed the scheme to ensure that there were no gaps at any time in the service the team offered to the organization. It also ensured that every member had a valid role to play. As far as David is aware, this team approach to flexible working is still unique within the bank.

At NBI, by the end of the year 2003, less than 3,600 employees of the total workforce of 50,000 at the bank worked flexibly as a direct result of *Work Options*. Of these, 16% were men and 18% were managers. Anita Puri believes that traditionally, work–life balance and, in particular, flexible-working policies have been seen to be to do with women only. Hence, Puri felt quite pleased with the data that show that the flexible plan was being used by men and managers. This was encouraging since the whole basis of *Work Options* at NBI was

to give the policy as well as the bank's approach to work–life balance, a broad appeal.

Any employee at NBI who wants to join the *Work Options* scheme is required to put forward the business case for their participation to their line manager. That starts a process which will end with a solution that works for the employee and the bank. An important part of the programme is its 'reason neutral' approach, that is, the reason for opting for the work option doesn't form part of the decision-making process. Puri said that previously managers were required to make value judgments when an employee put up the case for joining *Work Options*. That didn't happen anymore. Rather, the present decision-making process was about whether extending flexible option is a viable business proposition or not.

Though the company has come a long way since then, there are still people who need to be convinced of the benefits of investing in work–life balance policies. According to Anita Puri, 'NBI has made good progress, but in any large organization, things only work as well as the local line manager allows them to work. *Work Options* has not been embraced as fully as it should have been in all parts of the organization. However, our monitoring system allows us to work with different parts of the business to move things forward.'

The banking union, Banking Employees Association (BEA) represents 10,000 of NBI's 50,000 employees. It believes the company is setting a good example in terms of giving staff the opportunity to participate in work–life balance schemes, but it feels such policies—not surprisingly—can run into implementation problems on the ground. According to BEA's national secretary, B. M. Jha, flexible-working requests from NBI's branch employees are sometimes refused because of pressures to meet work targets at staff branches during peak hours. Jha says that *Work Options* should be treated more sympathetically in terms of individual cases so that certain people did not lose out because of staff shortages.

The union has raised its concerns with the NBI management. The bank, on its part, is keen to ensure that this programme is a success and has agreed to sit down with the union and find a way to resolve these issues. Jha believes that at a more fundamental level, the old culture of the bank—one of long hours and unclaimed overtime pay—doesn't fit very well with the principle of work–life balance. He claims some staff still felt inhibited about requesting flexible working, feeling that it might damage their long-term career prospects and may make them appear disloyal to their colleagues. Moreover, pressure on staff is increased due to job cuts in the competitive environment. This also ensured that making provision for work–life balance was a challenge.

Anita Puri, however, was more positive about the future. She pointed out that NBI was currently engaged in a complete review of the company's entire work–life balance offering. This, according to her, was evidence of the organization's continued and very real commitment to the success of work–life balance programme. In the review, the company was investigating the viability of expanding its provision in various areas on a broader level. Puri said that the war for the right talent was by no means over, so it was crucial that the company remained leading edge in terms of its work–life balance policies.

According to the CEO of NBI, work–life balancing was a strategic responsibility at the top

and there has to be total commitment to achieving it. This comes from effective communication—from a strong, positive message from the top for achieving operational efficiencies at ground level. He further stated that there was still a perception that flexible ways of working can be abused. According to him, if there's a good management system in place to ensure the system is fair and equitable, then it can, and does work.

Meanwhile, back at group manpower planning and information, flexible working has given David's team a new-found confidence and good morale. David said that though it was hard to quantify but it was evident that people were having fun at work. The team was being more proactive in terms of understanding customers' needs, something it used to shy away from in the past for fear of not meeting customer expectations.

David points out the business benefits, 'this means the level of service we are giving HR business partners is better than it's ever been, which means they must be able to work better in their business units, which ultimately must have a good impact on the organization as a whole'.

Perhaps more importantly for David, a keen golfer, flexible working has given him an extra day every fortnight to pursue his hobby without cutting into family time.

Questions

1. Is work–life balance largely an issue involving only women?

2. What employee and organizational benefits did NBI gain as a result of adopting work–life balancing as a strategic responsibility?

3. What is Jha's view about utilization of work–life benefits? Citing instances from the case, discuss how the culture of the firm influences utilization of work–life programmes.

4. Narmada Bank International is lauded for its

approach to work–life balance policies. Yet, Nobel David's team approach to flexible work is considered unique within NBI and highly successful. What characteristics of David's flexible work offering made it so successful? What is the role of managerial attitude in implementation of work–life balance practices?

5. Suggest a plan to NBI to ensure that more employees utilize work–life balance practices.

References

(2000), Harvard Business Review on Work and Life Balance, Boston, USA: Harvard Business School Press

Arthur, J.B. 1994, 'Effects of Human Resource Systems on Manufacturing Performance and Turnover', *Academy of Management Journal*, vol. 37, pp. 670–87.

Arthur, M.M. and A. Cook 2003, 'The Relationship Between Work–Family Human Resource Practices and Firm Profitability: A Multi–theoretical Perspective', *Research in Personnel and Human Resource Management*, vol. 22, pp. 219–52.

Bailyn, L., R. Rapoport, D. Kolb, and J. Fletcher 1996, Relinking Work and Family: A Catalyst for Organizational Change, Ford Foundation, New York.

Becker, B. and B. Gerhart 1996, 'The Impact of Human Resource Management on Organizational Performance: Progress and Prospects', *Academy of Management Journal*, vol. 39, pp. 779–801.

Blau, P. 1964, *Exchange and Power in Social Life*, Wiley, New York.

Business Today 2001, 'The Work–Life Balance', (First BT–Hewitt Associates study on the best employers in India), 9th Business Today Anniversary Issue, 21 January, pp. 101–8.

Business Today 2003, 'Geeks and their Funny Bone', Business Today, July 6, pp. 136–8.

Center for Work and Family 1995, Behind the Scenes: Corporate Environments and Work–family Initiatives, Boston College, US.

Daft, R.L. and K.E. Weick 1984, 'Toward a model of organizations as interpretation systems', *Academy of Management Review*, vol. 9, pp. 284–95.

Data on the Business Benefits of Work–Life Programmes, Compiled by Andrew Wilson, Director, Ashridge Centre for Business and Society, Ashridge, UK.

Delaney, J.T. and M.A. Huselid 1996, 'The Impact of Human Resource Management Policies on Perceptions of Organizational Performance', *Academy of Management Journal*, vol. 39, pp. 949–69.

DiMaggio, P. and W. Powell 1983, 'The iron cage revisited: Institutional isomorphism and collective rationality in organizational fields', *American Sociological Review*, 23, pp. 111–36.

Edwards, J.R. and N.P. Rothbard 2000, 'Mechanisms Linking Work and Family: Clarifying the Relationship Between Work and Family Constructs', *Academy of Management Review*, vol. 25, no. 1, pp. 178–99.

Friedman, S. and E. Galinsky 2001, Survey: Mastering People Management, *Financial Times*, edited by John Laxmi for Wharton School.

Friedman, S. D., P. Christensen, and J. DeGroot 1998, 'Work and Life: The End of the Zero–Sum Game', *Harvard Business Review*, November–December.

Galinsky, E., D. Friedman, and C. Hernandez 1992, 'Stages in the Development of Work–Family Programs', *The Corporate Reference Guide of Work–Family Programs*, New York: Families and Work Institute, pp. 9–15.

Greenhaus, J.H. and N.J. Beutell 1985, 'Sources of Conflict Between Work and Family Roles', *Academy of Management Review*, vol. 10, pp. 76–88.

Herzberg, F. 1968, 'One More Time: How do you Motivate Employees?', *Harvard Business Review*, vol. 90 (no. 1), pp. 53–62.

Kossek, E.E. and R.N. Block 2000, 'Managing Human Resources in the 21st Century: From Core Concepts to Strategic Choice', USA: South-Western College Publishing.

Lambert, S.J. 2000, 'Added Benefits: The Link Between Work–Life Benefits and Organizational Citizenship Behaviour', *Academy of Management Journal*, vol. 43 (no. 5), pp. 801–15.

Lewis, S. and Dyer, J. 2002, 'Towards a Culture for Work–Life Integration?' in C.L. Cooper and R.J. Burke (eds), *The New World of Work: Challenges and Opportunities*, Blackwell Publishers, Oxford, UK, pp. 302–16.

Lobel, S.A., B.K. Googins, and E. Bankert 1999, 'The Future of Work and Family: Critical Trends for Policy, Practice, and Research', *Human Resource Management*, vol. 38 (no. 3), pp. 243–54.

MacDuffie, J.P. 1995, 'Human Resource Bundles and Manufacturing Performance: Organizational Logic and Flexible Production Systems in the World Auto Industry', *Industrial and Labor Relations Review*, vol. 48, pp. 197–221.

Madsen, Susan R. 2001, 'Work and Family Conflict: A Review of the Theory and Literature', Paper presented at the International Conference of AHRD held at Tulsa, Oklahoma, USA.

Milliken, F.J., L.L. Martins, and H. Morgan 1998, 'Explaining organizational responsiveness to work–family issues: The role of human resource executives as issue interpreters', *Academy of Management Journal*, vol. 41, pp. 580–92.

Perry-Smith, J.E. and T.C. Blum 2000, 'Work-Family Human Resource Bundles and Perceived Organizational Performance', *Academy of Management Journal*, vol. 43 (no. 6), pp. 1107–17.

Pfeffer, J. and G.R. Salancik 1978, *The External Control of Organizations*, Harper and Row, New York.

Phillips, S.L. 2000, 'Spirituality in the Workplace: Ten Things the HR Professional Needs to Know', in Pfeiffer and Jones (eds), The 2000 Annual vol. 2, Consulting, Jossey Bass, pp. 153–66.

Schourberg, G. 2001, 'Spirituality and Business: Where's the Beef?', in Pfeiffer and Jones (eds), The 2002 Annual: vol. 2, Consulting, John Wiley & Sons, Inc., pp. 261–75.

Strachan, G., and J. Burgess 1998, 'The "family-friendly" workplace: Origins, meaning and application at Australian workplaces', *International Journal of Manpower*, vol. 19, no. 4, pp. 250–65.

Thompson, C., L. Beauvais, and K. Lyness 1999, 'When work–family benefits are not enough: The influence of work–family culture on benefit utilization, organizational attachment, and work–family conflict', *Journal of Vocational Behavior*, vol. 54, pp. 392–415.

Notes

Business Today, January 21, 2001 issue, p. 102.

http://www.employersandwork-lifebalance.org.uk/work/definition.htm, accessed on 15 February 2004.

http://www.employersforwork-lifebalance.org.uk, accessed on 15 February 2004.

http://www.hewittasia.com/hewitt/ap/india, accessed on 18 February 2004.

http://www.unmarriedamerica.org/workplace, accessed on 3 February 2004.

Cook, A. 2004, *Corporate Decision-Making Process: How Organizations Decide to Adopt Work/Life Initiatives*,

a Sloan Work and Family Encyclopedia Entry, Boston College, http://wfnetwork.bc.edu/encyclopedia_entry.php?, accessed on 15 February 2004.

Pfeiffer and Jones, The 2000 Annual: Vol. 2, Consulting, Jossey Bass.

Pfeiffer and Jones, The 2002 Annual: Vol. 2, Consulting, John Wiley & Sons, Inc.

Sloan Work and Family Encyclopedia (http://www.bc.edu./bc_org/avp/wfnetwork/rft/wfpedia/, accessed on 15 February 2004.

12 International Human Resource Management

After studying this chapter, you
will be able to:

- classify international business
  operations into its four types:
  international, multinational,
  global, and transnational

- define 'international human
  resource management' and
  understand how it differs from
  domestic human resource
  management

- appreciate the reasons for the
  increasing importance of
  international human resource
  management

- gain an overview of the external
  environmental factors that have
  a significant impact on
  international business operations

- understand the importance of
  managing cultural differences for
  the success of international
  business operations

- discuss three approaches—
  ethnocentric, polycentric, and
  geocentric—to managing and
  staffing subsidiaries of
  multinational organizations

- acquire an understanding of
  international HR practices

INTRODUCTION

Throughout the book, we have emphasized the trend
towards globalization of business and its impact on HRM.
As increasingly larger numbers of organizations conduct
business beyond national boundaries, they confront the
challenge of managing their global human resources.
Global competition and differences in organizational
environment across nations have encouraged global organizations to develop international HR strategies. International HR strategies for hiring, developing, compensating,
and appraising human resources are important for successful
utilization of people to secure competitive advantage for
global organizations.

The present chapter begins with emphasizing that globalization has resulted in internationalization of business. A brief
overview of the types of international business operations is
presented. The chapter defines international human resource
management (IHRM) and describes the reasons for the
increase in its importance. The differences between IHRM
and domestic HRM are discussed. The impact of external
environmental factors—economic, market, social, political,
and cultural—on international business operations is highlighted. The significance of managing cultural differences
between the country in which the subsidiary is located and
the country in which the organization is headquartered for
an organization to be successful in international business is
emphasized. International HR practices—international staffing, pre-departure training for international assignments,
repatriation, performance management in international
assignments, and compensation issues in international assignments—are also discussed.

TYPES OF INTERNATIONAL ORGANIZATIONS

A major consequence of globalization has been the internationalization of business. However, organizations differ in the degree of internationalization of business. Several firms that claim to be international are actually national companies that export overseas. Executives of these organizations are of national origin. In such an organization, opportunities for an international career are limited. Some other organizations may be more international in their operation, for example, an organization that is owned by the parent organization whose nationality differs from the countries in which this organization has operations. A company may be based in Europe or Asia where there is a clear market for its product, but its parent could be American. Executives in this type of organizations belong to the country in which these organizations have operations. However, the parent organization exercises strict control over working practices and managerial styles of its subsidiaries located in other countries. Organizations having international business operations can be classified into four types: (1) international; (2) multinational; (3) global; and (4) transnational (see Figure 12.1).

International Corporation

An international corporation is a domestic firm that builds on its existing capabilities to penetrate overseas markets. Honda, General Electric, and P&G are examples of firms that used this approach to enter European markets. These firms adapt their products to overseas markets but do not make changes in their normal operations.

Multinational Corporation (MNC)

An MNC has operating units (subsidiaries) located in foreign countries. Often, these subsidiaries function as autonomous units. Each subsidiary provides its

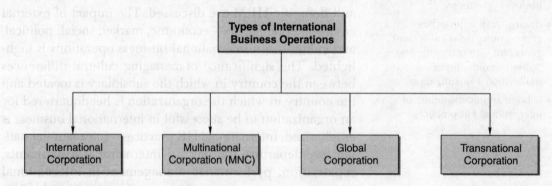

Figure 12.1: Types of International Business Operations

goods and services for the geographical region surrounding the country of operation of the subsidiary. Shell, Philips, and Xerox are examples of MNCs.

Global Corporation

It is a type of MNC that maintains control over its worldwide operations (subsidiaries) through a centralized home office. These firms treat the entire world as a single market and try to maximize efficiency on a global scale. Japanese company Matsushita is an example of a global corporation.

Transnational Corporation

This type of organization provides autonomy to independent country operations but brings these separate operations together into an integrated whole through a networked structure. A transnational corporation combines the local responsiveness of an MNC and the efficiency of a global corporation. A transnational corporation is an ideal type and is rarely seen to exist in reality. However, companies like Ford and Unilever have restructured themselves to function as a transnational corporation (see Exhibit 12.1).

Though international business may take various forms, as outlined above, any organization that conducts business outside its home country may be referred to as an international business. As organizations develop strategies to expand internationally, they face several complex issues in their quest to gain competitive advantage. Organizations send large numbers of their employees abroad to manage their international operations. For example, HLL appointed

---

Exhibit 12.1

Restructuring Unilever

Unilever has formed a regional resource pool for the Asia-Pacific region consisting of managers drawn from the ranks of Unilever companies. This global resource pool is staffed largely by managers based in India, China, Japan, and Thailand. These managers will report to the regional Unilever head but will continue to be on the payroll of the local company. Unilever will pay a fee to the local company for using these managerial resources, and other local companies that use the regional resource pool will pay Unilever in turn. Responsibilities have been differentiated. For any particular category, for example soaps, the regional resource pool managers will be responsible for brand building and development and will report to the regional head. The local company will be responsible for functions such as sales, brand promotion, and other sales-related activities. It is likely that categories such as soaps, detergents, and beverages will be managed by the India operation, toothpastes will be handled by either Indonesia or India, and that hair care will be Japan's responsibility. In the new structure, the region will have a keen interest in ensuring that the Indian business does well too, but will focus on what the parent company wants and how the local company's strategy fits in.

an expatriate as its CEO. There is also trend toward employing foreign-born managers at the headquarters. There are several foreign-born CEOs in the US in companies such as Kellogg's, McDonald's, GlaxoSmithkline, and Coca-Cola.

A major challenge for organizations operating internationally is to locate and nurture human resources required for implementing a global strategy. The process of internationalization of business has several implications for HRM practices. Human resource management is critical to the success of any international business. Earlier in the book, we emphasized that HR strategy should be derived from corporate business strategy and that organizational success or failure depends on the quality of its human resources. It follows that HRM should be a strategic partner in the international operations of a firm. The rapid pace of globalization and internationalization has conferred a strategic role for HRM.

INTERNATIONAL HUMAN RESOURCE MANAGEMENT

All the HRM practices discussed throughout this book are equally applicable to international business. A major difference is the setting—international human resource management (IHRM) involves the application of HRM practices to an international setting. Hence, a simple definition of IHRM is 'the process of managing people in international settings'. Scyllion (1995) defined IHRM as 'the HRM issues and problems arising from the internationalization of business, and the HRM strategies, policies, and practices which firms pursue in response to the internationalization process'. International human resource management is the management of human resources in business operations in at least two nations. Thus, IHRM focusses on employees who are on an international posting or on an international assignment. Though IHRM involves the same HR activities as domestic HRM (staffing, performance management, development, compensation, etc.), the two differ in certain ways.

Differences between IHRM and Domestic HRM

International HRM differs from domestic HRM in a number of ways (see Table 12.1). One difference is that IHRM has to manage the complexities of operating in, and employing people from, different countries and cultures. A major reason for the failure of an international venture is the lack of understanding of the differences between managing employees in the domestic environment and in a foreign one. A management style successful in the domestic environment often fails if applied to a foreign environment without the appropriate modifications. The reasons that IHRM is more complex than domestic HRM are described below (Dowling 1988).

- International HRM addresses a broader range of activities than domestic HRM does. These include international taxation, coordinating foreign currencies and exchange rates, international relocation, international orientation for the employee posted abroad, etc.
- Human resource managers working in an international environment face the problem of addressing HR issues of employees belonging to more than one nationality. Hence, these HR managers need to set up different HRM systems for different locations. Human resource managers in a domestic environment administer HR programmes to employees belonging to a single nationality.
- International HRM requires greater involvement in the personal life of employees. The HR manager of an MNC must ensure that an executive posted to a foreign country understands all aspects of the compensation package provided in the foreign assignment, such as cost of living, taxes, etc. The HR manager needs to assess the readiness of the employee's family to relocate, support the family in adjusting to a foreign culture through cross-cultural training, and to help in admitting the children in schools. The HR department may also need to take responsibility for children left behind in boarding schools in the home country by the employees on foreign postings. In the domestic environment, the involvement of the HR manager or department with an employee's family is limited to providing family insurance programmes or providing transport facilities in case of a domestic transfer.

Table 12.1:   Differences between IHRM and Domestic HRM

International Human Resource Management	Domestic HRM
■ Addresses a broad range of HRM activities	■ Addresses a narrow range of HRM activities
■ HR issues relate to employees belonging to more than one nationality	■ HR issues relate to employees belonging to single nationality
■ Greater involvement of HR manager in the personal life of employees	■ Limited involvement of HR manager in the personal life of employees
■ Greater exposure to risks in international assignments; human and financial consequences of mistakes in IHRM (such as wrong selection of manager to be posted abroad) are very severe	■ Limited risks in domestic assignments
■ Has to manage several external factors such as government regulations of foreign country	■ Limited external factors to deal with

- There is heightened exposure to risks in international assignments. These risks include the health and safety of the employee and family. A major aspect of risk relevant to IHRM today is possible terrorism. Several MNCs must now consider this factor when deciding on international assignments for their employees. Moreover, human and financial consequences of mistakes in IHRM are much more severe than in domestic business. For example, if an executive posted abroad returns prematurely (before the expiry of his tenure of posting), it results in high direct costs (such as cost of pre-departure training, relocation cost, travel expenses, etc.) as well as indirect costs (damage to company reputation and international customer relationships.
- International HRM has to deal with more external factors than domestic HRM. For example, government regulations about staffing practices in foreign locations, local codes of conduct (like acceptability of giving gifts), influence of local religious groups, etc. If an American organization is sanctioned license by the Indian government to set up its subsidiary in India, the American company is under legal obligation to provide employment to local residents.

There has been a growth in the interest in IHRM over time. Some of the reasons for this increasing recognition of IHRM are presented in Exhibit 12.2. In recognition of the importance of IHRM, many organizations have full-time HR managers who are assigned with the responsibility for assisting globalization of the organization. McDonald's, Coca-Cola, TCS, etc. are

Exhibit 12.2

Reasons for the Increasing Importance of IHRM

- Increase in the number and significance of global organizations with the rapid growth of internationalization and global competition.
- Recognition that the success of global business depends on the quality of the human resources of the global firm and how effectively these resources are managed and utilized.
- Costs of poor performance or failure in international assignments are very high, such as loss of market share, loss of reputation of the firm, etc.

- International managers are in short supply; this places constraints on the successful implementation of global strategies.
- For organizations that are new to international operations, business failures are often linked to poor management of human resources. Performance of managers on international assignments needs careful management.
- Success of any global organization is based less on structural innovations and more on the development of a different organizational culture. Hence, HR strategy plays a more important role in the international firm.

Source: Storey 2001

examples of such organizations. Coca-Cola organizes a two-week HR orientation programme twice a year for its international HR staff. Through this programme, international HR managers of Coca-Cola get an opportunity to share information about HR practices and programmes established in any subsidiary of Coca-Cola in the world that can be successfully adopted by others.

EXTERNAL ENVIRONMENT AND IHRM

Environmental factors significantly influence international business operations. Economic (for example, creation of free trade zones), market, social, and political factors play an important role in influencing the level of involvement an organization might choose in its international operations. The *political environment* of the country of operations is an important factor that a company has to deal with when setting operations abroad. For example, Tata Chemicals acquired the Kenyan operations of a firm that was located in the Masai tribal areas. In order to run the operations of the firm successfully in this region, it was important for the local management of Tata Chemicals to cultivate good relations with the chiefs of the tribe. The case of TCS in China is similar. The biggest problem of Indians posted there was that of finding vegetarian food. The mayor of the town set up a vegetarian restaurant for the TCS employees. Apart from these factors, the *cultural environment* of a country has an important influence on decisions in international business. Countries differ from each other with respect to their cultures. The culture of the country in which business is proposed and how it compares with the culture of the country in which the organization is headquartered affects the decision to extend operations to that country. Culture is the way of life of a group of people. The operations of global corporations extend to at least two countries. Therefore, cultural diversity is inherent in global organizations. In international business, ignorance of cultural differences can lead to unfortunate consequences. Many international ventures fail because of lack of understanding or appreciation of cultural differences. For example, cultural differences may exist with respect to how people prefer to take decisions, the appropriate physical distance between two people engaged in conversation, and the extent to which people tend to follow schedules or be on time for an appointment. An example of cultural differences between countries with respect to the tradition of giving gifts is presented in Exhibit 12.3.

The success of an organization in international business is to a large extent influenced by its success in managing cultural differences as well as the development of a business strategy and an HR strategy consistent with the culture of the host country (country in which the subsidiary is located). Just as societies have cultures, all organizations also have cultures. Apart from the national

Cultural Differences in Giving Gifts

When presenting a gift to a person belonging to a different culture, several issues have to be kept in mind. These include the choice of gift, how it is presented, when it is given, etc. A wrong gift can create a bad impression and sour a relationship forever. The custom of gifting varies from culture to culture, place to place, person to person, and even from time to time. Some societies consider gifts a form of bribery, whereas in some societies it is an essential part of social interaction.

The **Chinese** perceive gifts as bribes. When giving a gift to a Chinese person, it is important to point out that the gift is on behalf of the giver's company and is being given to the person's company. Customarily, the Chinese decline a gift three times before finally accepting it. They expect others also to do the same when they give a gift. This custom prevents the recipient of the gift from appearing greedy. When the Chinese person accepts the gift, the giver must express his pleasure.

The **Japanese** expect a gift the first time someone meets them. For the Japanese, gift giving is an art form. It carries the message of friendship, respect, and gratitude. The Japanese custom is to reciprocate the gift with a gift that is of half the first gift's value. For them, how the gift has been wrapped is more important than the gift itself. The exchange of gifts continues throughout the course of business. The Japanese refuse the gift once or twice but then accept it with both hands. With the Japanese, it is important to downplay the gift and convey that the relationship is far more important.

In the **Middle East**, alcohol or alcohol-based items, clothes, or food items should not be gifted. Perfumes should not be alcohol-based. Green is a good colour in Islam. Wood or handicrafts made of wood are considered low-value items, and are best avoided.

In **Latin America**, gifts help build strong and lasting friendships and make a good first impression. Latin American people treat business and personal issues alike. Therefore, it is important for the giver to find out the lifestyle, likes, and dislikes of a person and select a gift that conveys how important the person is to the giver. Wrapping is considered important since it conveys the value of the friendship. When wrapping the gift, it is inappropriate to use black or purple paper or yellow, white, or red flowers as they symbolize death.

People in **Europe**, the **US**, and **Canada** do not have much protocol about gift-giving except the usual avoidance of colours that symbolize death, funeral, or romance. In France, music and books are good choices for gifts. When visiting a German household, a good choice for a gift is a bouquet of unwrapped flowers.

Source: *The Economic Times*, 16 June 2006

cultures, it is also important to examine the fit between organizational culture and the culture of the host country. These two types of culture fits, that is, between cultures of two countries and between culture of an organization and that of the host country, influence the nature of HRM practices. For example, an American firm may administer a ban on smoking while at work, but the organization will have to think before it considers extending the ban to its offices located in another country. Different HRM approaches and practices are appropriate in different cultural environments. Management styles successful in one cultural setting may lead to failure in another cultural setting. Managers at Coca-Cola are extremely sensitive to cultural differences that exist between more than 200 countries where the company has operations.

It is important for IHRM strategies and practices to acknowledge cultural differences between countries. If HRM must take on a strategic significance in international business, culture should be accepted as integral to managing human resources across national boundaries. The purpose of IHRM is the allocation of human resources to the operating unit in a foreign country in order to ensure effective organizational performance. We will now discuss a few IHRM practices.

IHRM PRACTICES

As mentioned earlier, strategic IHRM involves an extensive selection system, training for international assignments, strategies for repatriation programme, etc. This section discusses five IHRM practices.

1. International staffing
2. Pre-departure training for international assignments
3. Repatriation
4. Performance management in international assignments
5. Compensation issues in international assignments

Before selecting an employee for an international posting or assignment, an organization must establish the specific purpose for the assignment. Is it to set up a new business or to develop a new market? Is the purpose to transfer technology? Is it to manage an independent subsidiary or to prepare an individual for a top management position, or is it a temporary assignment to a vacant position? In the last couple of years, several expatriates have assumed key positions in various organizations in India in sectors spanning IT, aviation, banking, consumer goods, and durables. An *expatriate* is a manager who is posted to a country other than the country of his or her birth. Expatriate CEOs are taking control of organizations in India for different reasons. Some of them are: to put them back on track (for example, HLL and Coca Cola Bottling); to teach them how to run an entirely new business (such as running a low-cost airline); or to ensure that the current capabilities of Indian business are taken to the next level of development (for example, at Intel). Leading Indian organizations—such as Wipro, Ranbaxy, the A V Birla Group, and even L&T—are expanding overseas and transforming themselves into global corporations. Having worked for long in protected markets, these firms do not have the exposure or the large talent pool to execute their global agenda. These organizations are hiring expatriates or non-resident Indian CEOs because they bring with them knowledge of and experience in global practices. A successful global manager also serves as an attraction for competent people to accept job offers in these firms. These global managers on their part also get the opportunity to build a global organization from scratch.

After the purpose of the international assignment has been specified, the organization can initiate the process of selecting the most appropriate employee for the assignment.

International Staffing

This refers to the process of selecting employees for staffing international operations of an MNC. Multinational organizations (the headquarters as well as the foreign subsidiary) can be staffed using three different sources (see Table 12.2 and Figure 12.2).

Home Country or Parent Country National (PCN)

They are the citizens of the country in which the headquarters of the MNC is located. They are not the citizens of the country in which they are working and where the business is located. For example, an American citizen who is posted to an overseas subsidiary, say in India, of an organization that is headquartered in the US is a PCN. Parent country nationals are also called expatriates. They are generally managers, technicians, subsidiary heads, and experts. There are about 25 Koreans in the Indian subsidiary of Samsung, while LG has close to 30 Koreans. Maruti has 15 Japanese heading the key functions in India, such as marketing, finance, and production, but only at the top level. Nokia, the Finnish telecom major, has about 100 Finns at key positions in the Indian operations of the firm.

Host Country Nationals (HCN)

They are those employees of an organization who are the citizens of the country in which the foreign subsidiary is located. For example, an Indian manager working in Indian subsidiary of a US company is an HCN. IBM and Unilever are examples of firms that hire HCNs. Home country nationals are generally used for staffing middle and lower management levels. Tata Motors' Daewoo venture in Korea employs HCNs (locals) to do most of the work. Tata Consultancy Services has recruited a senior management team in Latin America made up mostly of HCNs though the top management is Indian. Satyam has hired local talent (HCNs) for its operations in Malaysia and Hungary.

Third Country Nationals (TCN)

These are the citizens of a country other than the country where the organization is headquartered and the country that is hosting the subsidiary. A British

Table 12.2:   Three Sources of International Staffing

	Parent Country Nationals (PCN)/Expatriates	Host Country Nationals (HCN)	Third Country Nationals (TCN)
Advantages	■ Ensure proper linkage between foreign subsidiary and the headquarters ■ Knowledgeable about how the parent company operates ■ Use of PCN helps develop global capabilities in the organization	■ Are familiar with the local norms and culture ■ Not Expensive like PCN ■ Well-versed with local language	■ Are less costly than PCNs ■ Have substantial international experience
Disadvantages	■ Expensive, since organizations are responsible for costs related to relocation, cost-of-living, special schooling, family benefit packages, etc. ■ Lack of awareness about the culture of the country may lead to loss of contracts, or premature recall of expatriate ■ Expatriate failure can be very expensive	■ May not Appreciate the needs of the headquarters ■ May have a local view rather than a global view about the operation of the subsidiary	■ Are in high demand, but short supply ■ TCNs pose greater HR challenges in terms of cross-cultural diversity management
Most Suitable	■ When MNC is in the start-up phase ■ To ensure that foreign subsidiary complies with policies of headquarters ■ When host country lacks technical expertise	■ When the subsidiary is well-established ■ To establish networks locally for market and business expansion ■ Technical expertise is available	■ Have proven technical expertise

citizen who works in the Indian subsidiary of an organization headquartered in the US is a TCN. A TCN is usually posted as the head of the subsidiary located in a foreign country. Nokia relocated its India chief to Singapore as the marketing head of the Asia-Pacific region. Cadbury's India CEO, an Indian, moved to the Asia-Pacific region headquarters in Singapore as commercial strategic director.

Usually, when an organization is in its initial stage of international expansion, it relies on PCNs or expatriates to set up operations and to establish activities

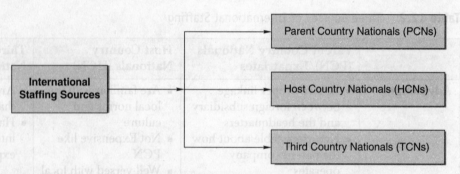

Figure 12.2: Sources of Staffing International Business Operations

in the foreign country. This is especially true when the subsidiary is being set up in a less-developed country. Gradually, the organization moves towards hiring HCNs.

Earlier, MNCs used to staff top-level management positions of the foreign subsidiary with expatriates or PCNs only. However, there is a trend towards greater internationalization of staffing. Organizations such as IBM, ABB, and PepsiCo are hiring TCNs to head their foreign subsidiaries. Since 2005, several Indian managers have been posted to assume key global positions in the most developed markets such as the UK and the rest of Europe. Software firms such as Intel, IBM, and HP have a number of Indians in their regional offices in other countries such as Hong Kong and Singapore. Government restrictions on the employment of foreign nationals imposed by the host country government restrict the number of PCNs that an MNC can employ in its foreign subsidiary. Generally, the host country government gives license to the MNC for setting up its subsidiary in that country on the condition that it will generate employment for host country citizens.

Approaches to Staffing Subsidiaries

International staffing practices of MNCs are also influenced by the attitudes that the top management executives at headquarters hold towards employment of foreign executives in headquarters and the subsidiaries. Three primary attitudes towards building MNCs have been identified: ethnocentric, polycentric, and geocentric. These three attitudes describe the MNC approaches to managing and staffing their subsidiaries (see Figure 12.3). Each approach has important implications for international recruitment and selection practices (see Table 12.3).

Ethnocentric The foreign subsidiary has little autonomy. All strategic decisions are made at the headquarters. Expatriates, that is, the PCNs, staff key positions at headquarters as well as at the foreign subsidiary. Korean firms in India such as LG, Samsung, and Hyundai are still headed by Koreans. The

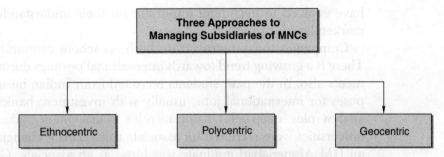

Figure 12.3: Approaches to Managing and Staffing Subsidiaries of MNCs

top management team is generally Korean. Koreans also control critical areas of operation such as finance, production, quality, and purchase. There is a dual structure at each functional level with one Korean manager and one Indian manager for each function. The dual structure is justified as the Korean managers bring international expertise, and because they interface with the parent company. However, this means that mid-level Indian managers rarely get exposure at strategy meets and hence cannot further their careers in the global set-up. Almost all personal interactions with the global bosses are conducted with Korean managers. Indians do not interact with the global bosses when they come visiting. Korean companies have very few or almost no Indians in their global operations yet.

Polycentric The MNC treats each foreign subsidiary as a distinct entity. The subsidiary has some autonomy in making decisions. Managers following this approach staff foreign subsidiaries of their firm with HCNs. The staff at headquarters consist exclusively of PCNs. Host country nationals are rarely, if ever, promoted to positions at headquarters. Parent country nationals are also never posted to the foreign subsidiary.

Geocentric This approach focusses on an integrated global philosophy. Managers at all levels at both headquarters and the subsidiary may be PCNs, HCNs, or TCNs. Ability, and not nationality, is the key to staffing. Hence, search for managerial positions takes place on a global basis.

As more professionals become mobile, the recruitment pool for organizations has transcended national boundaries. Companies look at the global pool of managers when hiring at the top. Managers who have had experience in multiple locations, be it in the Asia-Pacific region, Helsinki, or Washington, are better placed today to handle global operations. Organizations today need people with diversified global experience; therefore, it is important to have expatriates heading operations of organizations. Companies are keen to tap the global talent pool and seek professionals who have considerable global exposure. From being mere ambassadors of organizations, expatriate managers have evolved to becoming important for their understanding of the global marketplace for products and services.

Companies today recruit from business school campuses internationally. There is a growing trend towards international postings during summer placements also. In the past, students recruited from Indian business school campuses for international jobs, usually with investment banks, were hired for analyst roles, a step below associate roles. Management graduates from western universities were recruited for associate roles. This is changing now. In 2005, an IIM Ahmedabad graduate was hired as an associate. Global companies hiring from Indian campuses are now placing these students on an equal footing with recruits from other international business schools. There is truly an emerging geocentric attitude to international staffing. With organizations working across geographies, local expertise is taking a back seat to global orientation and mobility as firms strive to create a management cadre for the future. Moreover, companies recruiting for international positions have access to a larger pool of experienced candidates since most business schools have developed separate lateral placement programmes in which students with work experience can seek jobs above the entry level.

Though the top management of MNCs may in general adopt any one of the above attitudes, the organization may be forced to adopt a dominant attitude on implementation. For example, an organization may have a dominant ethnocentric approach to staffing its foreign subsidiaries. However, regulations of the government of a particular host country may stipulate the appointment of HCNs to key positions in the subsidiary. For this particular subsidiary, the firm may follow a polycentric approach.

Table 12.3 describes the advantages and disadvantages of the three approaches to staffing foreign subsidiaries of MNCs.

Table 12.3: Three Approaches to Staffing Foreign Subsidiaries of MNCs

Staffing Approach	Advantages	Disadvantages
Ethnocentric	<ul><li>It helps when there is a lack of qualified HCNs</li><li>Facilitate coordination between the subsidiary and the headquarters</li></ul>	<ul><li>Reduces promotion opportunities for HCNs</li><li>PCNs take time to adapt to the culture of the country where the subsidiary is located and may make mistakes during this time</li><li>Compensation of PCNs is higher than that of HCNs and therefore causes inequity</li></ul>

Contd

Table 12.3 Contd

Staffing Approach	Advantages	Disadvantages
Polycentric	▪ Employing HCNs avoids the cultural adjustment problems of expatriate managers and their families ▪ Employment of HCNs is less expensive ▪ Avoids the turnover of key managers in the foreign subsidiary, which is inevitable in ethnocentric approach	▪ Results in a gap between PCNs at headquarters and HCNs at subsidiaries ▪ HCNs have limited career growth opportunities—they cannot progress beyond senior management positions in the subsidiary ▪ PCNs also do not get exposure to other cultures ▪ Over time, decision-making may become limited since neither HCNs nor PCNs get cross-cultural exposure
Geocentric	▪ Focusses on competence and ability rather than nationality ▪ Develops international executive team having cross-cultural skills	▪ Host government may impose immigration controls to ensure higher levels of HCNs employment ▪ It is accompanied by high training and relocation costs ▪ Requires greater control and centralization of staffing process

It is extremely important to give careful attention to the selection of a manager for an international assignment. There is no certainty that a manager who has been successful in one country will be so in another country as well. There are several reasons that a manager may fail in an international assignment. These include the inability to adapt to a different environment, personality problems, emotional immaturity, family-related problems, inability to cope with the greater responsibilities of overseas work, limited employment opportunities abroad for the spouse, lack of technical competence, and lack of motivation. Among the primary causes of expatriate failure in a foreign assignment is bad selection (see Exhibit 12.4).

Exhibit 12.4

Causes of Failure of Expatriate Managers

▪ Bad selection
▪ Cultural maladjustment
▪ Lack of understanding of the work practices of the foreign country

▪ Failure of family to adjust to the foreign country
▪ Poor performance
▪ Repatriation issues

In order to maximize the likelihood that the expatriate manager will be successful and will readily adapt to the demands of the foreign assignment, it is important to determine appropriate selection criteria. Selection of PCNs and TCNs requires consideration of many more factors than selection of HCNs. In addition to technical and administrative skills, the ability to adapt to the cultural environment and lifestyle changes are critical to successful performance in a foreign posting. If an executive is not willing to be posted abroad for reasons such as unwillingness of the family to go abroad or because of the 'toughness' of culture of that particular country, then these issues also have to be taken into account during the process of selection of a manager for international posting. The selection process should provide a realistic picture of the culture the employee will live and work in and the life and job he will have. Selection for international postings is a two-way process between the individual and the organization. On the one hand, HR managers draw up a comprehensive description and specification of the job in question and assess the employees to determine the extent to which they have the skills and competencies relative to the needs of the foreign assignment. On the other hand, a prospective candidate may also refuse to accept the offer of a global posting due to reasons such as family considerations and reluctance to move to another country.

Many skills are required for a manager to be successful in a foreign environment. Though the performance of a manager depends on several combinations of factors, the lack of certain key characteristics increases the chance of failure. The key considerations for selecting managers for global postings and the key requirements for success in global assignments are presented in Figure 12.4 and described briefly in Table 12.4.

Companies such as Colgate Palmolive and Whirlpool have identified a set of skills that they view as critical for success in global assignments. Many organizations have begun to use personality tests and other means of assessment in order to determine the suitability of the employee for a global assignment. For example, Motorola uses personality tests, intelligence tests, assessment centres, and role play exercises to assess potential candidates for international postings. Apart from tests, an important input for assessing the suitability of an employee for global assignments is his/her past performance record. If the employee has not performed well at home, he/she is unlikely to be successful abroad.

Another source of information for the selection of a manager for a global assignment is the interview method. Extensive in-depth interviews of candidates and their spouses by senior executives of the organization provide insight into the reasons that the employee wants to be considered for a foreign posting, the readiness of the family to move abroad, and other such factors. Both the candidate and the family members are screened for their adaptability to a

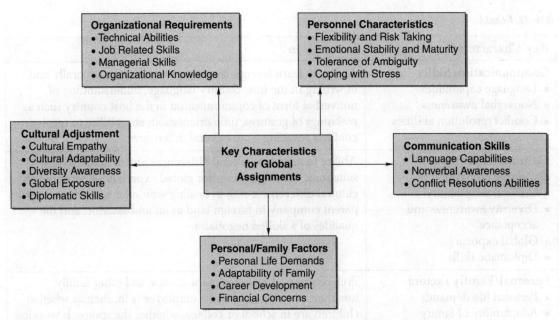

Figure 12.4: Key Characteristics Required for Success in Global Assignments

foreign country. A candidate and his or her family may be very keen and willing to take a foreign posting. However, if they are not adaptable, culturally sensitive, or emotionally mature, they are unlikely to be able to complete the duration of their posting. Through adaptability screening, the family is made aware of the types of stresses and personal issues that may arise during the period of the transfer abroad. The family thus has a chance to refuse the transfer rather than risk a costly failure and relocation.

Table 12.4: Key Characteristics for Selection

Key Characteristics	Description
Organizational Requirements ■ Technical abilities ■ Job-related skills ■ Managerial skills ■ Organizational knowledge	Knowledge of the organization and how it operates, knowledge of the firm's products, services, etc. to successfully represent the firm in a foreign country, needed technical skills and job related KSAs, and management skills
Personal Characteristics ■ Flexibility and risk-taking ■ Emotional stability and maturity ■ Tolerance of ambiguity ■ Coping with stress	Ability to withstand the stress related to living and working in a foreign county, emotional stability, flexibility, ability to withstand physical demands of travel, time zone changes, etc. Personal characteristics play an important role in the successful completion of a global assignment.

Contd

Table 12.4 Contd

Key Characteristics	Description
Communication Skills ▪ Language capabilities ▪ Nonverbal awareness ▪ Conflict resolution abilities	Ability to learn foreign language, to communicate orally and in writing in the host-country language, understanding of nonverbal form of communication in the host country such as meanings of gestures, time orientation, etc., ability to resolve conflicts resulting from cultural differences.
Cultural Adjustment ▪ Cultural empathy ▪ Cultural adaptability ▪ Diversity awareness and acceptance ▪ Global exposure ▪ Diplomatic skills	Ability to adjust to cultural differences and to adapt to new situations, experience in prior global experiences, sensitivity to cultural differences, skill in dealing with others, representing the parent company in foreign land as an ambassador, and the qualities of a skilled negotiator.
Personal/Family Factors ▪ Personal life demands ▪ Adaptability of family ▪ Career development ▪ Financial concerns	Preferences and attitudes of the spouse and other family members, the stage of life the employee is in, such as whether children are in school or college, whether the spouse is working or not, impact on future career, as well as financial implications of foreign posting

Source: Bohlander

Pre-departure Training for International Assignments

A foreign posting means much more than moving luggage and changing time zones; it means starting a whole new life—new home, new school, new friends, new neighborhood, and new culture and traditions. There is no culture uniform to the world. The culture in western Europe is different from the culture in the US, eastern Europe, or in the Far East. American society does not believe in rituals, ceremonies, or formality. Hence, Americans prefer to come to the point directly in any business meeting. However, in Saudi Arabia, it is customary to make formal small talk on matters unrelated to business before coming to the main meeting agenda. An American dealing with a Saudi Arabian will need to be cautious. Coming straight to the point will make the Saudi Arabian very uncomfortable, which may result in failure of talks. When going to work in a different country, a manager should gain an understanding of such cultural differences.

After selecting the must *suitable* and *willing* manager for an international assignment, organizations must necessarily provide training to the selected candidates. The training should focus on global skills that are important for success abroad, such as appreciation of cultural differences, understanding of the socio-political atmosphere of the country of posting, etc. One of the main reasons for the failure of an expatriate is the low cross-cultural quotient. Unfortunately, many organizations do not make a systematic effort toward training their executives in these respects. Executives posted in a foreign country are often left to fend for themselves without any support from the organization. Very often, these expatriates learn the culture of the country of their posting through informal advice received from other expatriates. The initial months of the foreign posting therefore turn out to be very painful. It is at this stage that the failure rate can be high resulting in premature return of the manager.

Therefore, cross-cultural training and relocation services have become very important today. Most Indian firms do not provide orientation sessions to employees prior to their departure for international assignments. Multinational corporations have a more focussed approach towards pre-departure training. Top and middle level managers of MNCs are extended cross-cultural training, and their families also are given culture familiarization sessions. Organizations like Coca-Cola, Texas Instruments, Procter & Gamble provide intensive training to employees to prepare them for international assignments. Organizations usually extend the initial culture orientation for employees at the home country. The training sessions are conducted mostly in the country of posting. The executives usually arrive at the host country much before their training starts in order to get a feel of the place. There are two broad dimensions that a global executive needs to work on: (1) the personal conduct; and (2) the business code of conduct. While it is easier to adjust to the business code of conduct, the challenges at the personal level are quite formidable.

In addition to the employees, their families also need to be prepared to handle the foreign assignment as effectively as possible. For successful relocation of an employee to the country of posting, the organization must take into consideration the employee's family, lifestyle, children, preferences, etc. Both the employee and his/her family attend a pre-departure training programme. The pre-departure is also called *expatriation*, which is 'the process of preparing and sending employees to their foreign assignments'. The pre-departure orientation and training provided to the expatriates and their families significantly affects the success of the expatriate. The objectives of the pre-departure training programme are to make it easier for the manager to assume job responsibilities and be effective on the job in the foreign country as soon as possible and to facilitate the cultural adaptation of the manager and his/her family as quickly and as effectively as possible.

Expatriate training and development programmes incorporate three elements: (1) language training; (2) cultural training; and (3) managing personal and family life (see Figure 12.5).

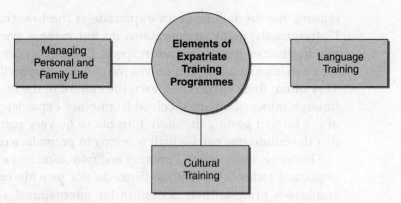

Figure 12.5: Elements of Expatriate Training Programmes

Language Training

This involves learning the language of the foreign country. Café Coffee Day provides cross-cultural counselling and language assistance to its employees. Tata Consultancy Services also imparts language skills to its managers being posted abroad. Mahindra & Mahindra provided their executives with Chinese language training courses and sessions in Chinese culture and customs when the firm set up a joint venture in China. Similarly, Chinese employees too were given English language training.

However, learning the language is only one aspect of language training. Managers on international assignments should also understand how the usage of the same word differs across countries. For example, the phrase 'to table the report' means 'to discuss the issue now' in the UK, whereas in the US it suggests that 'the discussion of the issue should be postponed for now'.

In India, saying that the consignment will be dispatched in one month really means 'We will try to dispatch in one month'. Hence, a delay of about a week is expected and not taken very seriously. However, in the West, not meeting the committed deadline is not taken kindly, and results in penalty or even cancelled orders. A commitment to a deadline is valued very highly by Western managers. Managers should also learn the meaning of certain gestures and non-verbal communication. Certain gestures that are acceptable in one culture may be offensive in another. The notions of acceptable physical distance in business interactions, eye contact, punctuality, and time orientation are interpreted differently in different cultures. For example, in India, a senior manager is not expected to be punctual. Coming late for a meeting communicates the status and importance of the person. In Western cultures, severe penalties are there for not meeting deadlines. In Arab countries, it is considered rude to set deadlines.

Cultural Training

Managerial attitudes and behaviour are culturally conditioned and are different in different cultures. For example, in India it is considered a sign of friendship to drop in casually at one's colleague next door, but is absolutely unacceptable in Europe. While one culture may reinforce participative management, another may prefer a more directive management style. It is important for a manager to understand how things are normally done in a particular culture. Training on cultural differences helps managers understand work attitudes and motivation in other cultures. For example, in the US, people are more individualistic, whereas in eastern countries, people emphasize cooperation. Similarly, in Japan there is higher loyalty to the organization. In Latin America, on the other hand, employees are loyal to individual managers. Japanese managers use a participative style of management while managers in European countries are more autocratic. To help Indian managers imbibe Korean cultural values, Korean companies employing Indian managers inculcate in them Korean values that emphasize team cohesion and loyalty. Initial orientation sessions for fresh recruits in Korean firms involve learning the organization's songs, protocols, and values. At Satyam, there is a specific India-oriented diversity programme called 'Crossover' that comprises a team of more than one hundred associates from thirty-two countries. At 24/7 Customer, a BPO firm, the process of 'culture sensitization' of the employees takes place in two phases. In the first phase, the inductees are introduced to the linguistic, economic, and social conditions of the country of posting. In the second phase, in-depth knowledge about values, appropriate gestures, habits, and consumer behaviour are imparted.

Managing Personal and Family Life

Training also seeks to minimize the risk of culture shock. One of the reasons for failure in foreign postings is personal and family stress. This stress may be caused due to several day-to-day issues; for example, inability to read road signs, ignorance about where to shop for groceries, currency conversion, etc. Stress may also be because the spouse of the candidate may be working (employed) and unable to move with the employee to another country. Some firms are attempting to assist dual-career couples in finding suitable employment in the same location. At Café Coffee Day, relocation of employees is a regular feature. In the case of married employees, Café Coffee Day provides spouse job search assistance if the employee requests it.

Pre-departure training programmes generally have two phases (see Exhibit 12.5).

Large consulting organizations have well-designed programmes for preparing their employees for cross-border assignments. For example, Boston

Exhibit 12.5

Two Phases of Pre-departure Training Programme

Phases of the Training Programme	Content of the Programme Phase
1. For the manager	■ Job description ■ Objectives and goals of the manager ■ Relationship between the subsidiary and the parent company and with other subsidiaries ■ Management practices of the host country ■ Political, legal, and economic environments of the host country
2. For the manager and his/her family	■ Language training ■ Area study (host country's culture, climate, geography, currency, etc.) ■ Cross-cultural training

Source: Guy and Mattock 1991

Consulting Group (BCG) has three mechanisms in place by which its employees (consultants) get exposed to international operations.

1. There are cross-country project teams for specific assignments. These teams together deliver the client's requirements.
2. There are regular practice area meetings in which all the consultants of a particular area across countries meet periodically to exchange notes on new developments.
3. Consultants are sent abroad on 'ambassador' programmes under which they work typically for a period of one to two years in another country.

These mechanisms provide a platform on which individual consultants can learn on their own initiative how business is conducted in other parts of the world. For individual coaching, BCG provides a two-layer system in which each consultant is assigned a mentor and a 'buddy' on one's arrival in a new country. The buddy is generally at a comparable level as the consultant's, and guides the latter through the social milieu as well as provides practical advice and help on the personal front. For example, New Zealanders find it offensive if they are asked to rush through their tea break because of a lot of pending work. A buddy helps the consultant understand these cultural differences. The mentor, on the other hand, is a comparatively senior person who guides the consultant by providing functional and organization support to the consultant and thus helps him to deliver better.

The role of an organization in facilitating the adjustment of expatriates in foreign country extends beyond pre-departure training. The manager should be helped with relocation to the foreign country, transport of possessions, finding housing in foreign country, admissions of children in school/college or arranging boarding school for children if they are not accompanying parents, and obtaining a driving license. The organization thus helps the employee with settling in the foreign country. Organizations are taking proactive steps to make relocation easier for their employees. Patni has an intranet site that answers relocation queries of transferees in order to make relocation easier. Patni also conducts regular briefing sessions and orientation seminars for the employees. It also provides information about local resources and community networks for employees and their families. It is important that the organization provides continuing support and maintains regular contact with the manager.

A major apprehension that managers have in accepting a foreign posting is the loss of contact with the headquarters and the resultant isolation. Managers on global assignments also experience anxiety over their future career growth and prospects within the organization. The parent company should address such concerns and anxieties by taking initiatives such as

- maintaining regular contact with the manager posted overseas through phone and e-mail;
- keeping the manager informed of important company developments and changes; and
- ensuring regular interaction of the manager with other managers and professionals at the headquarters, which may be achieved by
  - organizing development programmes for expatriates at the headquarters on a regular basis; and
  - assigning a mentor to the expatriate—the mentor should be a senior executive in the headquarters and should ensure that the manager's career interests at headquarters are protected.

A major concern for both the manager posted abroad and the organization is the re-entry of managers into the parent company, that is, at the headquarters, after a stint abroad. This is called repatriation.

Repatriation

Repatriation is the process of bringing an expatriate home after he/she has completed the international assignment. For the expatriate, the return to the headquarters of the organization or its subsidiaries within the parent country is accompanied with certain fears and anxieties. It is important that the organization takes appropriate initiatives to manage these anxieties and to ease the re-entry of expatriate managers into the parent company. Table 12.5

Table 12.5:   Repatriation—Expatriate Fears and Organizational Practices

Fears and Concerns of Expatriates	Organizational Practices for Repatriation
■ Organization may not have planned adequately for the manager's return back home. The manager may be left without a portfolio for a few days. ■ An extended overseas stint may result in loss of visibility for the manger in the parent company. This may adversely affect the manager's career prospects. ■ Loss of contact with and understanding of the informal power structure at the headquarters. ■ Fear that their peers may be promoted ahead of them. ■ Fear that if they fail in their foreign posting, the failure may adversely affect their once-promising career. This fear is augmented by the fact their failure abroad may be due to political upheavals or diplomatic fiascos in the foreign country and not due to lack of ability. ■ Loss of special compensation packages that they have in their foreign assignments, resulting in net decrease in their total income. ■ A sense of loss of social status. In a foreign country, the individual enjoys important social status and is a special guest in several functions. In the parent company, the person loses such privileges.	■ Organization can enter into a repatriation agreement with the manager that specifies the maximum tenure of the foreign posting, the nature of position he or she will be given upon return, as well as the salary to be expected upon return. ■ A senior manager at headquarters may be assigned as a mentor to the expatriate. The mentor will protect the expatriate's career interests at headquarters and serve as his/her advocate. ■ A senior manager may serve as a sponsor for the expatriate. The sponsor will monitor the performance, compensation, and career path of the expatriate manager and plan for their return. The sponsor begins to scout for a suitable position for the expatriate 6 months to 1 year prior to his/her return. ■ To ensure the expatriate's familiarity with the informal power structure at headquarters, home leave of the expatriate may be combined with extended stay at the head-quarters to work on a specific time-bound project.

Source: Guy and Mattock 1991

presents some of the fears and anxieties of the expatriate managers and also the organizational practices that can help alleviate these concerns.

Organizations that manage their expatriates successfully follow three practices; they (1) create knowledge and develop global leadership skills, (2) ensure that candidates have cross-cultural skills to match their technical abilities, and (3) prepare people to make the transition back to their home offices. These three practices make international assignments successful.

Performance Management in International Assignments

Assignment to a foreign posting helps a manager acquire invaluable experience. Performance is the result of a combination of several factors such as motivation, ability, working conditions, and the like. When assessing expatriate performance, it is important to consider the variables that influence success or failure in a foreign assignment: the compensation package; the task assigned to the expatriate; the headquarters' support; the environment in which the performance occurs; and the cultural adjustment of the individual and the accompanying family members.

Compensation Package

The financial benefits expected along with the career progression potential associated with the international posting are often important determinants for accepting the posting. If these expectations are not realized, motivation may be lost and, thus, performance may be affected.

Task Assigned to the Expatriate

The organization should clearly communicate the task assigned to as well as the role expectation from the expatriate while on the foreign posting. This involves imparting cross-cultural training along with technical skills. When the expatriate fails to understand cultural differences in behaviour and ways of working, it will adversely affect his/her behaviour.

Headquarters' Support

The level of support provided by the headquarters to the expatriate and his/her family is an important performance variable and goes beyond monetary compensation. This strongly affects the psychological adjustment of the expatriate and, hence, his/her performance. The manner in which the expatriate and his/her family is received at the foreign subsidiary also plays an important role.

Environment

The environment in which the performance occurs, that is, at the subsidiary or foreign facility, with its societal, legal, economic, technical, and physical demands, significantly influences expatriate performance.

Cultural Adjustment

Cultural adjustment of the expatriate and of the accompanying family members affects performance as well.

Evaluating the performance of a manager on a foreign assignment is difficult and poses unique challenges. Difficulty in evaluating expatriate performance is an important factor contributing to the career uncertainty of the expatriate within the organization at the end of the foreign posting. A major problem with expatriate performance evaluation emerges due to the dual allegiance of the expatriate manager—to the host country and to the parent country (domestic). Superiors in the two locations use different criteria to evaluate performance of the expatriate and have different notions of what constitutes 'good performance'.

A major difficulty with the performance evaluation of the expatriate by superiors at the home country (domestic) arises due to lack of regular communication between the two. Domestic managers are often unaware or unable to understand and appreciate the experiences of the expatriate. It is also difficult to assess the contribution of the expatriate to the organization. A senior manager in the host country is in a better position to observe an expatriate manager's performance on a regular basis. However, the host country manager's notions of what constitutes good or bad performance are culturally influenced, and culturally-influenced perceptions may not be truly reflective of the actual level of performance of the expatriate.

Both home country and host country evaluation sources should be used in appraising expatriate manager's performance. Decisions about the manager's promotions, rewards, pay increases, and other administrative decisions are handled at the home country office of the organization. However, the host country evaluation provides an important input for making these decisions.

Compensating Managers in International Assignments

One of the most complex aspects of IHRM relates to expatriate compensation. Different countries have different norms for employee compensation. Organizations also have to adhere to compensation laws of the country in which they have operating units. Apart from legal issues related to international compensation, the dominant values of each culture determine the relative significance of different components of the compensation package. For example, Americans who come from a highly individualistic culture, may value performance-linked pay plans since money remains the most important motivator. On the other hand, in cultures such as India, Japan, which are less individualistic, pay plans may emphasize equity and personal needs, with non-financial incentives (such as prestige and influence) playing an important role as motivators.

When designing a compensation plan for an expatriate manager, it is important to ensure that compensation is strategically aligned, yet flexible enough to accommodate particular needs of employees posted in specific locations. It is important to remember that different employees have different financial needs. Employers generally make a generic estimate of the cost of an employee's living expenses. They should instead develop an actual-cost budget and review it even before they offer relocation. Expatriate compensation must be competitive, fair, and consistent with international compensation norms. While designing compensation packages for expatriates, organizations must consider the host country's compensation laws, cost of living, tax policies, value of currency, conversion rate, etc. An example of the influence of income tax laws of the foreign country of operation is that non-resident Indians (NRI) deputed to India have to pay tax in India on their salary even if their salary is paid abroad by the foreign parent company. Highly skilled employees are often deputed by the parent company to India for carrying out work in India for their subsidiaries or affiliated companies. Most often, the foreign parent company continues to pay the salary of the deputed employee in his/her own home country. Salary income of the non-resident technician posted in India that relates to work carried out in India is taxable in India. However, if the stay of such a person comes under the short-stay exemption (less than 183 days in a fiscal year), such an employee will not be taxable in India. This person then would be taxable in the US (assuming that the parent company is based in the US) even with respect to the salary relating to work carried out in India. The Indian company to which these employees have been deputed pays a smaller sum to them for meeting their day-to-day expenses. This is called the living allowance. This living allowance is exempted from income tax in India.

Health benefits are popular as part of expatriate pay. Most MNCs offer their expatriate managers worldwide medical insurance. Frequently, employers provide free cover to the manager but require him/her to pay, at least in part, the premiums for the inclusion of family members in the company medical plan. Expatriates are also compensated for cost of housing, schooling of children, and for an annual vacation to the home country along with the family. Thus, typically, the expatriate compensation includes several components. (see Figure 12.6)

A global manager costs more to the organization in India than a home country national. The expatriate CEO in a low-cost airline takes home between US$150,000 and US$250,000 per month. In addition, the CEO has

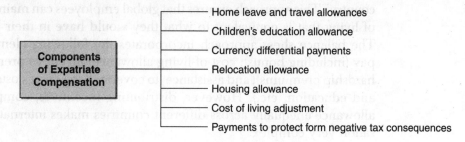

Figure 12.6: Components of Expatriate Compensation

Source: Mathis and Jackson 2003

performance bonuses and stock options. Citibank has a local resource pool and a global resource pool. The talent pool consists of those managers who the bank grooms to take up positions anywhere in the world. The global resource is 100% more expensive than the local pool. Chief executive officers with global experience in firms such as GE, Citibank, and Unilever are used to getting huge performance bonuses linked to delivery of targets. This often runs into several millions and is often several times higher than the salary. Korean companies have a different way of awarding bonuses. Hyundai, Samsung, LG, and even smaller Korean firms guarantee an annual bonus to their employees and pay the basis on a quarterly basis. The bonus usually equals a few months' salary of the employees. These benefits are provided to all employees everywhere in the world. Individual performance in Korean firms is linked more to profit sharing. Salary hikes are linked to growth in productivity and not simply to more experience or age.

For software firms, salary increases along with innovatively designed flexible-benefit packages are considered part of a global package. Software houses have identified benchmark positions. These benchmark positions could be high-end technocrats or business leaders with designations such as vice president, project director, project manager, etc. These benchmark positions are paid at par with global compensation levels irrespective of the size of the software firm. For example, a project manager working in India is paid Rs 2–2.5 million per annum in India. The same project manager, when deputed for an international assignment, would be paid US$65,000–75,000 (Rs 3.25–3.75 million) annually. After tax and expenses, the manager would be able to save about US$1,000–1,200 (Rs 50,000–60,000) per month. In the Indian context, the corresponding salary will also result in similar savings. Thus, the international compensation levels are similar to Indian ones. The benchmarked positions are paid at par with their global counterparts.

Most MNCs use the *balance sheet approach* to compensate employees. The balance sheet approach seeks 'to equalize the purchasing power of employees at comparable positions in international assignments and those in the home country'. This approach ensures that global employees can maintain a standard of living that is equivalent to what they would have in their home country. The balance sheet approach incorporates the following elements: the base pay (including bonus); cost-of-living allowance; incentive premiums (such as hardship premiums); and assistance (to cover moving costs, costs of automobile and education, etc.). However, distributing incentives, compensation, and allowance unequally across different countries makes international compensation very complex.

Recently, organizations have been moving towards a *global market approach* for compensating global mangers. This approach follows the geocentric management philosophy. It provides certain core components to all managers irrespective of their country of posting. These components include insurance benefits, relocation expenses, etc. Many organizations are trying to incorporate lump-sum allowances to the expatriate manager as a financial perquisite. Lump-sum allowances are paid directly to the relocating employees to cover their relocation expenses. This approach renders greater uniformity to international compensation though it also requires greater administrative effort.

Summary

As organizations have gone global in their operations, the impact of cultural differences as well as workforce issues regarding staffing, motivating, and developing global managers have caught the attention of HR managers. As the world becomes boundary-less, the ability to work in a cross-cultural environment becomes a valuable asset for any executive. Understanding, managing, and even exploiting these cultural differences could well spell the difference between success and failure in several business situations. The chapter provided a brief insight into international business. The term 'international human resource management' was defined and the reasons for the increasing significance of IHRM were outlined. The differences between IHRM and domestic HRM were examined. The chapter also emphasized the importance of external environmental factors, particularly the significance of cultural differences between the countries of operation, in determining the successful performance of an organization in international business. It discussed the key skills and characteristics required by a manager to be successful in a foreign environment; the process of selecting employees for staffing the international operations of an MNC; and the three sources of staffing international operations—parent country nationals, host country nationals, and third country nationals. The chapter discussed three approaches to managing and staffing international operations—ethnocentric, polycentric, and geocentric. It emphasized the importance of a pre-departure training programme as well as managing relocation issues for the employee and for the family to ensure that the expatriate manager completes the international assignment successfully. The fears and anxieties of the expatriates and the initiatives that an organization can take for managing these concerns and for successful repatriation were also discussed. The variables that influence success or failure in a foreign assignment and the unique challenges of evaluating the performance of a manager on a foreign assignment were also examined. The chapter ended with a brief discussion of the issues related to expatriate compensation.

Keywords

Ethnocentric Approach provides very little autonomy to the foreign subsidiary. All strategic decisions are made at the headquarters. All key positions at headquarters as well as at the foreign subsidiary are staffed by expatriates or parent country nationals.

Expatriates are managers who are posted to a country other than the country of their birth.

Expatriation is the process of preparing employees for foreign assignments and sending them to foreign locations.

Geocentric Approach focusses on an integrated global philosophy and takes a global approach to organizational operations. Both the headquarters and the subsidiary may be staffed with either PCNs, HCNs, or TCNs. Ability, and not nationality, is the key to staffing.

Global Corporations are a type of MNC that maintains control over its subsidiaries across the world through a centralized home office. These firms treat the entire world as a single market.

Home Country or Parent Country Nationals (PCN) are citizens of the country in which the headquarters of the MNC is located. They are not the citizens of the country in which they are working and where the business is located.

Host Country Nationals (HCN) are those employees who are the citizens of the country in which the organization's foreign subsidiary is located.

International Corporation is a domestic firm that builds on its existing capabilities to penetrate overseas markets.

International Human Resource Management (IHRM) is the process of managing people in international settings and involves activities in at least two nations. It refers to the HRM issues and problems arising from the internationalization of business and the HRM strategies, policies, and practices that firms pursue in response to the internationalization process.

International Staffing is the process of selecting employees for staffing the international operations of an MNC.

Multinational Corporations (MNC) have operating units (subsidiaries) located in foreign countries. Each subsidiary functions as an autonomous unit and provides its goods and services for the geographical region surrounding the country of operation of the subsidiary.

Polycentric Approach treats each foreign subsidiary as a distinct entity. The subsidiary has some autonomy in making decisions. Foreign subsidiaries are staffed by HCNs while the headquarters is staffed exclusively by PCNs.

Pre-departure Training Programme seeks to prepare an expatriate manager for working in an organization located in a foreign culture. Pre-departure is also called expatriation.

Repatriation is the process of bringing expatriates home after they have completed the international assignment.

Repatriation is the process of bringing expatriates home after they have completed a foreign assignment.

Third Country Nationals (TCN) are the citizens of a country other than the country where the organization is headquartered and the country that is hosting the subsidiary.

Transnational Corporations provide autonomy to independent country operations but brings these separate operations together into an integrated whole through a network structure.

Concept Review Questions

1. Define IHRM. Analyse the reasons for the rise in the importance of IHRM.

2. How does IHRM differ from domestic HRM?

3. Identify the major environmental factors that an organization must consider when setting up business operations in a foreign country.

4. Who is an expatriate? What are the advantages and disadvantages of using expatriate managers instead of host country nationals?

5. What are the major factors of success and failure in a foreign assignment? Why does the performance evaluation of a manager on a foreign assignment pose unique challenges?

6. Why is it important to provide a comprehensive pre-departure training to an employee who is going abroad on a foreign posting and to his/her family? Identify the major components of a pre-departure training programme.

7. What are the major components of expatriate compensation? What factors have to be considered in designing an international compensation package?

1. What are the advantages and disadvantages of the three primary approaches towards managing and staffing subsidiaries of MNCs? Do you think that recent times have seen a movement towards the geocentric approach? Why? Cite examples of some organizations that follow a geocentric approach as well as of those organizations that follow an ethnocentric approach.

2. What do you understand by the term 'repatriation'? What are the major concerns and anxieties of managers who are on international assignments? What initiatives can the organization take to address these concerns and to facilitate repatriation of the manager posted abroad?

━━━━━━━━━━━━━ **Simulation and Role Play** ━━━━━━━━━━━━━

1. Assume you are the HR manager of the Indian subsidiary of a large MNC headquartered in the US. The organization has recently set up a subsidiary in China. You have been assigned the responsibility of selecting the director of sales and marketing for the Chinese subsidiary. What criteria will you use to select the person? Which of the three staffing sources will you prefer to staff this position—PCN, HCN, or TCN? Why?

2. XYZ is a leading Indian pharmaceutical firm that is expanding overseas and transforming itself into a global corporation. The firm has functioned in a protected market for very long and hence does not have the exposure or the large talent pool to execute its global agenda. Mr Shivkumar is the director (HR) of the India headquarters as well as for the global operations of the firm. He has earlier worked with reputed MNCs and joined XYZ for the challenge it provided in setting up its global operations. Also, Shivkumar wanted to return to India after having worked for about 15 years in the US in two or three reputed MNCs. XYZ has recently set up its operations in western Europe. The CEO, Mr Satyajit, is the owner of the organization. XYZ has to select a manager to head its operations in western Europe. Satyajit thinks that a PCN will be the best choice for this position. Shivkumar, on the other hand, believes that a geocentric approach to staffing should be followed. The executive search firm hired by XYZ forwarded resumés of two managers to the organization. Mr Nath, one of the candidates shortlisted by the search firm, has extensive global experience and has worked in two or three countries. Mr Ghosh, the second candidate, on the other hand, has had a successful and stable career in India. Mr Ghosh is very well acknowledged for his technical skills in professional circles. Shivkumar and Satyajit have reached a deadlock over the selection of the head of the firm's operations in western Europe.

   • One student should assume the role of Shivkumar and another student should assume the role of Satyajit.

   • The student who has assumed the role of Shivkumar should argue in favour of selecting Nath. The student who has assumed the role of Satyajit should support the selection of Ghosh.

   • The two actors in this role-play should put forth arguments to support their choice of candidate. The role-play should end with the two actors reaching a decision on which candidate to hire for the foreign posting.

   After the role-play is over, the instructor invites observations and questions from the class. The instructor leads the discussion on the relative importance of technical skills versus cultural adaptability in selecting candidates for global operations, the importance of adopting a geocentric approach to expatriate selection, the unique challenges of an international assignment, and the various factors that deter-

mine success and failure in international assignments.

Classroom Projects

1. Form groups of four or five students. Each group should

   - list the range of information that should be provided to an expatriate to help him/her get ready for the international assignment as well as for returning from a posting abroad;

   - make a rough draft of how this information should be incorporated into the company website;

   - generate a list of FAQs that most managers leaving for a foreign posting would have and would appreciate answers to;

   - generate a list of FAQs for expatriates in foreign postings who are concerned about their move back into the location of the parent organization; and

   - suggest how an organization can increase the interactive value of the company intranet to address the concerns of managers being posted abroad as well as managers due to return after completing an assignment in a foreign country.

   Each team prepares a report for presentation and discussion in the class. The instructor facilitates the discussion and emphasizes the importance of communication in managing employee concerns regarding expatriation and repatriation. The instructor also helps students understand the role that an interactive company website can play in alleviating stress for expatriating and repatriating employees.

2. The objective of this exercise is to help students gain an understanding of the importance

of providing training to the manager who is going abroad on an international assignment. For this classroom project, the students should be asked to do some prior reading and reference. A week before this project is taken up for classroom discussion, the instructor forms the students into groups of four or five. Each group is asked to identify a country it would like to study. Each group gathers information about the various environmental factors of the selected country through resources in the library and through information available on the internet. Each group brings this information to the classroom when the exercise is to be conducted and designs a pre-departure training programme for a manager (and his/her family) who is being posted to the country that it chose. Each group prepares a report for presentation and class discussion. The instructor guides the discussion towards the importance of developing cultural sensitivity in managers and their families who are proceeding for an assignment abroad and the content, duration, and location of the pre-departure training programme. The instructor also helps the students understand the economic, political, social, and cultural differences between countries and how these differences influence the design of the pre-departure training programme. The discussion should end by highlighting the fact that most expatriate failures are due to cultural maladjustment of the manager and/or his/her family rather than lack of any technical skill.

Field Projects

1. Each student is asked to speak with a foreign student who is on campus to find out the latter's first experience of Indian culture.

   - Which aspects of Indian culture did they already know about?

   - What were the sources of this knowledge?

– Which cultural aspects of India were they ignorant about and that caused culture shock?

– How did they familiarize themselves with various customs and traditions of India once they had arrived?

– Who helped them?

– Did the university have a formal orientation programme for foreign students to facilitate their cultural adjustment in the country as well as in the university?

Design an orientation programme for foreign students of your university once they have arrived in the country. What information will you include in the orientation programme? What will be the duration of the programme? What initiatives will you suggest the university to adopt to take care of the recurrent concerns of foreign students during their stay in India? What insights do you gain from your study with respect to the cultural preparation of executives posted abroad?

Prepare a report for submission to the instructor and for class presentation.

2. The objective of this field project is to help the students gain an understanding of the HRM issues related to expatriate managers. The instructor should divide the class into groups of five. Each group is asked to visit one organization belonging to one of the following industries—IT, aviation, banking, consumer goods, and durables. Group members conduct interviews with HR managers as well as few middle-level managers of the firms to obtain the following information.

• In which country is this firm headquartered?

• What staffing sources is this organization using in its subsidiary in India at various hierarchical levels?

• What is the number of PCNs and TCNs in the organization in India?

• What kind of training were the PCNs and TCNs provided prior to their arrival in India?

• What initiatives are in place to ensure that PCNs and TCNs continue to have visibility at the headquarters?

• How is the performance of these executives evaluated?

• What specific compensation issues regarding tax are faced by the organization with respect to these employees?

• What are the various elements of the compensation package for these employees?

• Is the design of the compensation package of the PCNs and TCNs different from the HCNs?

Each group prepares a report for class presentation as well as a written report for submission to the instructor. The groups make presentations in the class highlighting the various HR practices followed by MNCs when sending employees on international assignments. When all groups have made their presentations, the instructor should engage the entire class in a discussion about the significance and complexity of IHRM. The instructor should also help the students identify the similarities, differences, and trends in various international HRM practices across different industries the student groups visited.

Case Study

Natural Pharmaceuticals Ltd

Natural Pharmaceuticals Ltd (NPL) was established in 1988 as a private limited company. The headquarters of the firm is at Gurgaon, near Delhi. With liberalization and changes in the business environment, NPL has transformed into an MNC. Today, it is a truly global firm with 30 manufacturing facilities in 15 countries and 10,000 employees worldwide. The company markets its products in more than 50 countries and nearly 75% of its sales come from outside India. Its corporate goals are (1) to be a global major in the pharmaceutical industry; (2) to consistently meet or exceed financial goals; (3) to be known worldwide for product quality; and (4) to have high-performing and trained human resources.

At NPL, some basic HR programmes and practices are standard and consistently followed at each of its entities in every country it operates in. For example, there is a standardized employee manual with policies and practices for orientation of new employees, a consistent grading system for salary administration, written job descriptions, and schedule of performance appraisals. All manuals and materials have been translated into the languages of the countries in which NPL has its operations. Though standard HR programmes are administered consistently at each of NPL's global locations, each entity of NPL is also free to add to the standard HR programmes. However, certain HR standards have to be adhered to by each business operation in each country. The HR function is given high importance in the organization. There are sixty HR staff members in the fifteen countries where NPL operates. Every employee of the company has an HR-related criterion tied to his or her performance goals.

The company seeks to ensure that corporate goals are met and cultural values of the company are maintained across its operations worldwide. One way NPL maintains the culture of the firm is by conducting bi-monthly communication meetings in each operating unit. These meetings are top-down communication exercises that seek to update all employees of a particular unit on its activities. NPL also holds annual communication meetings that are attended by the general manager, the chairman of the company, the chief operating officer, the executive vice president, and the corporate vice president of human resources in addition to other senior executives of the local entity and the region. The entire group spends one day at each location. During this tour, they observe the factory, the new equipment, and facilities and meet the employees. The annual communication meetings are intended to ensure that employees feel part of the larger entity. Employees of NPL working in different parts of the world are in frequent contact with each other. This and the common HR practices help NPL maintain its culture and also strengthen the global team of the company.

Each unit of NPL has certain unique needs. The company, therefore, follows the philosophy of hiring experienced HR professionals who belong to the country in which NPL has operations. The company believes that hiring host country nationals (HCNs) as HR managers has certain advantages since HCNs know the local language, have credibility, know the law, and know how to recruit. The values of the company emphasize respect for individual cultures of each country while maintaining the unique global culture of NPL at the same time.

The company moves its employees around its locations worldwide so that they may learn from each other. Thus, it makes considerable investment in expatriates. This brings with it the need to address the challenges of people working abroad for extended periods, typically three to four years. The company is addressing the issue of employee mobility by a two-pronged strategy. On one hand, HCNs are used wherever it makes business sense, for example where expatriates are less acceptable. On the other hand, the company is becoming increasingly selective about who goes on an overseas assignment. It chooses people who are independent, self-starters, technically knowledgeable, and culturally sensitive. Finding the right people for overseas posting has been difficult. The HR department identifies employees whose skill profiles match requirements and explores their willingness for an international career. Very few organizations use a specific list of competencies to select people for international roles; however, NPL has identified a list of six key characteristics: (1) conflict resolution skills; (2) leadership; (3) social orientation; (4) effective communication; (5) ability to cope with stress; and (6) flexibility.

Recently, NPL has started recruiting global managers who it considers core managers for international postings. These managers are internationally mobile, speak a minimum of three languages, and demonstrate high potential. The company has built a core of 30 such managers.

In global business, international exposure is seen as an essential part of preparation for senior management positions. Typically, employees progress from heading an international team to running a large business with profit-and-loss responsibility. The development of global managers at NPL is through assignments or postings abroad.

Posting to a foreign country often leads to considerable disruption for employees with families creating barriers to readiness on the part of a manager to relocate. To eliminate barriers to successful expatriation, NPL has devised a 'partner assistance' policy. This policy seeks to alleviate the financial hardship experienced by an expatriate manager when the accompanying spouse has to give up his/her job. The spouse is provided support in finding work in the country of the expatriate manager's location. If finding a job for the spouse is not possible, then NPL helps these spouses remain current in their own career field. It does this by providing relevant literature, sponsoring a distance learning course, or by helping the spouse attend a professional conference. Vocational and educational training is provided locally; childcare is provided as well. Before leaving for the foreign assignment, the manager receives a mini-severance payment to compensate to some extent the loss of spousal income. To prepare the manager and his family for foreign posting, NPL provides career counselling, language lessons, and training related to the culture of the destination country for both partners.

For people who are on a foreign posting, the challenge of repatriation is managed by ensuring information flow from the parent company. Typically, while on assignment, employees receive all local press releases and highlights of the home business so that they are up to date with key issues. The company intranet helps in maintaining contact. Expatriate managers are encouraged to maintain regular contact with the parent company.

Various initiatives at NPL for managing global HR issues have ensured that the company is held together by an underlying common set of values, thus maximizing the motivation of employees across all operations of the company.

Questions

1. What initiatives has NPL taken to ensure that company values are maintained across its operations worldwide? In what ways do these initiatives help manage the anxieties of the expatriate manager?

2. In your opinion, is it a good strategy to standardize certain HR practices and programmes at all organizational locations in the world? Explain.

3. Why do you think it is important to customize HR activities to the culture of the host country?

4. There is a scarcity of managers who have the mix of skills required for global assignments. How will the development of core managers for international postings help NPL manage shortage of global skills?

5. Examine the content of the expatriate training programme of NPL. What other measures can NPL adopt to make the programme more effective?

6. What practices does NPL have to facilitate repatriation of employees on foreign postings?

References

Bohlander, G., S. Snell, and A. Sherman 2002, *Managing Human Resources*, 12th edn, Thomson South-Western, Singapore.

Dowling, P.J., D.E. Welch, and R.S. Schuler 2004, *International Human Resource Management: Managing People in a Multinational Context*, 3rd edn,

Thomson South-Western, Singapore.

Dowling, P.J. 1988, 'International and Domestic Personnel/Human Resource Management: Similarities and Differences', in R.S. Schuler, S.A. Youngblood, and V.L. Huber (eds), *Readings in Personnel and Human Resource Management*, 3rd edn, West publishing, St. Paul, MN.

Guy, V. and J. Mattock 1991, *The New International Manager: Action Guide for Cross-Cultural Business*, Kogan Page, London.

Holbeche, L. 2002, *Aligning Human Resources and Business Strategy*, Butterworth Heinemann, Delhi.

Mathis, R.L. and J.H. Jackson 2003, *Human Resource Management*, 10th edition, Thomson South-Western, Singapore.

Scullion, H. 1995, 'International Human Resource Management', in J. Storey (ed.), *Human Resource Management: A Critical Text*, Routledge, London, pp. 352–82.

Stewart Black, J. and H.B. Gregersen 1999, 'The Right Way to Manage Expats', *Harvard Business Review*, March–April, pp. 52–62.

Storey, J. 2001 (ed.), *Human Resource Management: A Critical Text*, Thomson Learning Singapore.

Notes

The Economic Times, 25 September 2006, 'Get Rich Culturally', New Delhi, p. 6.

The Economic Times, 31 July 2006, 'MNCs Trust Own Men More', New Delhi, p. 7.

The Economic Times, 29 June 2006, 'Cracking the Culture Code', *Times Ascent*, New Delhi, p. 22.

The Economic Times, 16 January 2006, 'Have Wings, Now Fly', New Delhi, p. 17.

The Economic Times, 19 December 2005, 'How India Inc. Integrates with the World', New Delhi, pp. 1, 6.

The Economic Times, 13 December 2005, 'Inwha's the Best Korean Envoy', New Delhi, pp. 1, 19.

The Economic Times, 1 December 2005, 'Competitiveness Conundrum', New Delhi, p. 15.

The Economic Times, 21 February 2005, 'Unilever Puts Talents on Hire for Group Cos', New Delhi, pp. 1, 8.

The Economic Times, 30 December 2004, 'Foreign Employees Deputed to India Liable to Pay Income Tax', New Delhi, p. 6.

The Economic Times, 27 December 2004, 'Not Such a Small World After All', New Delhi, p. 5.

The Times of India, 31 May 2006, 'When Hari Met Sally', *Times Ascent*, New Delhi, p. 1.

The Times of India, 15 March 2006, 'A Moving Story', *Times Ascent*, New Delhi, p. 1.

Index

A

Alternative HR strategies   36
   contract companies   37
   examples   36
   healthcare organizations   39
   manufacturing   37
   retail banking   40
Approaches to SHRM   20
   best fit approach   20
   best practice approach   26
   'HR bundles' approach   25
   Indian context   33
Approaches to HR evaluation   144
   balanced scorecard   149
   benchmarking   161
   business consulting approach   147
   business excellence model   165
   HR scorecard approach   154
   stakeholder approach   145
   utility or analytical approach   146
Appraisal   482
   360 degree   482

B

Best fit approach   20
   drawbacks   24
Best practice approach   26
   drawbacks   26
Business environment trends   52
   downsizing   56
   globalization of business   53
   mergers and acquisitions   55
Business strategy and training   369
   linkage   369

C

Career   575
   contemporary notions   575
   development   590
   stages   581

Career management   578, 617
   an SHRM approach   623
   HRD approach   617
   systems   598
Career management systems   598
   design and implementation of   607
   individual-centred   598
   organization-centred   602
Career planning   577, 584
   methods/practices   585
Changing nature of employment relationship   79
Changing nature of work   60
   flexible work arrangements   65
   industry and occupational shifts   60
   outsourcing   65
   technological advancements   63
Clusters of HR measures   142
   external strategic measures   143
   internal operational measures   143
   internal strategic measures   143
Career systems   615
   and organizational characteristics   615
   and organizational culture   616
Career development   578, 590
   interventions   590
Compensation   512
   business strategy and   547
   financial   512
   non-financial   522
   types of   512
Compensation and rewards   511
   approaches   530
   determinants   525
   new developments   538
   total strategy   560

D

Demographic, societal, and workforce trends   66
   ageing population and ageing workforce   71

changing family structures 76
contingent workforce and workforce
    feasibility 78
educated knowledge workforce 74
global workforce 77
shortage of skilled talent 70
women in workforce 75
workforce diversity 67
Distinctive HR practices 27

E
Employee selection 287
    competency based 297
    methods 287
    new approaches to 295
Executive compensation 543
    trends 543
Environmental trends affecting HRM 52
    business environment 52
    changing nature of work 60
    demographic, societal, and workforce 66
    employment relationship 79

F
Family-friendly workplace 733
Formal mentoring programmes 666
    design 666
    implementation 677
Forecasting 220
    human resource demand 220
    human resource supply 228
    matching demand and supply 237

H
Hiring 323
    a diverse workforce 323
    alternatives to 327
    in BPO firms 334
HR bundles approach 25
Human resources 5
    and competitive advantage 7
    and resource-based view (RBV) 7
    and VRIO framework 7
    as assets 5
    investment perspective of 9
    role of 2

HR strategy 17
    and business strategy 17
    Beaumont's classification of 20
    Schuler and Jackson's classification 22
Human capital 5
Human resource management 14, 126
    a changing function 83
    a changing function 83
    and change 99
    and environmental trends 52
    and firm performance 126
    evaluation 122
    from personnel management to 14
    in knowledge economy 80
    role in managing culture change 104
    roles associated with 83
    technology and 94
    to SHRM 14
HR practices 27
    distinctive 27
Human resource environment 51
    overview 51
HR outsourcing 89
    benefits and pitfalls 90, 91
    decision of 92
    uniqueness of HR activities 91
    value of HR activities 90
HR evaluation 123
    approaches to 144
    criteria 125
    definition and overview 123
    focus 124
    level of analysis 125
    rationale 132
    scope of 124
    strategic linkage 125
HR–firm performance linkage 126
    measurement problems 130, 131
HRM performance 133
    measures of 133
Human resource acquisition 261
    an overview 261
HR evaluation 122
    a background 122
    definition and overview 123
    outcomes 125

processes   125
rationale for   132
Human resource planning   181
an overview   181
and outsourcing   242
business strategy and   182
horizons   212
objectives of   193
perspectives of   191
process   214
significance of   186
Human resource demand forecasting   220
qualitative methods   224
quantitative methods   225
Human resource supply forecasting   228
methods of forecasting external
supply   229
methods of forecasting internal
supply   230
HR and line managers   89
partnership of   89

I

Investment in human resources   10
factors determining   11
risks involved   10
Indian SHRM approaches   33
HRD as an approach   35
HRD framework   35
integrated systems model   33
vis-à-vis the western approach   36
International human resource management
764
and domestic HRM   764
external environment and   767
practices   769
International organizations   762
types of   762

J

Job analysis   195
and SHRM   206
competency-based   210
components of   198
information obtained from   197

methods of collecting information   199
process   203

M

Management development   414
competency based   414
Management of HR   83
partnership of HR and line managers   84
roles associated with   83
Managing HR shortages   240
Managing HR surpluses   239
Measures of HRM performance   133
external strategic measures   143
internal operational measures   143
internal strategic measures   143
Mentor–protégé relationships   649
classifications of   649
Mentoring   637
barriers to   679
coaching, training, and counselling   639
e-mentoring   692
functions of   643
mentors and protégés   641
outcomes of   656
perspectives of   644
special issues in   686
the concept of   637
women and   687
workplace diversity and   690
Mentoring relationship   650
costs associated with   665
cross-gender   689
formal and informal   654
nature of   650
phases of   650
strategic HRM approach   681
Multisource feedback   482

O

Organizational career management   612
a typology   612
Organizational strategy   23
Miles and Snow's classification   23
Outsourcing   286
recruitment 286

P

Performance management   434
   competency-based   487
   developmental functions   440
   developments in   469
   evaluative functions   440
   from performance appraisal to   435
   methods of   454
   objectives of   437
   problems in   464
   strategic linkage of   496
   technology and   492
Performance management systems   443
   developing   443
   effective   467
Pay and reward programmes   534, 538
   competency based   534, 538

R

Recruitment   268
   internal versus external   268
   methods of   269
   new approaches to   280
   sources   268
   strategic   317

S

Strategic human resource management
  (SHRM)   3
   and HR strategies   16
   approaches to   20
   definition and concepts   3
   difference from traditional HRM   15
   evolution of   13
   four components of   3
   Indian context   33
   meanings of   15
   objectives   15
   shift in focus   14
   theoretical perspectives   29
Strategic fit   18
   conceptual framework   18
   types of   19
SHRM approaches   33
   HRD as an approach   35

HRD framework   35
   integrated systems model   33
Staffing   265
   effectiveness   320
   external influences on   265
   internal influences on   267
   process   302
Strategic recruitment and selection   317

T

360 degree appraisal   482
   factors impacting   485
Technology and HRM   94
   operational aspects of HR   98
   relational aspects of HR   98
   transformational role of HR   99
Theoretical perspectives on SHRM   29
   economic perspective   31
   fit perspective   29
   functional perspective   30
   typological perspective   31
Total compensation and rewards   560
   strategy   560
Training and development   356
   basic concepts   357
   HRM approaches to   368
   methods of   383
   new developments in   408
   process of   373
   purposes of   361
   significance of   364
   special forms of   397
   the need for   356
Trends in business environment   52
   downsizing   56
   globalization of Business   53
   mergers and Acquisitions   55
Types of equity   537
   external   537
   individual   538
   internal   537

W

Work–family culture   735
   components of   735
   outcomes of   737

Work-family conflict 720
Work-family relationships 709
  changing notions of 709
  some related terms 719
  types of 721
Work-life 723
  balance 723
  initiatives 725
  integration 724
Work-life initiative 727
  benefits of 730
  development of 743
  theories 727
Work-life integration 738
  culture supportive of 749
  HRD approaches to 738
    individual/employee approaches 742
    organizational approaches 740
    strategic approach to 745
Work-life issues 710
  changing HRM perspectives 712
  environmental trends impacting 715